THE STATISTICAL ACCOUNT OF SCOTLAND

General Editors: Donald J. Withrington and Ian R. Grant

VOLUME IX

DUNBARTONSHIRE, STIRLINGSHIRE & CLACKMANNANSHIRE

THE
STATISTICAL ACCOUNT OF SCOTLAND

GENERAL EDITORS' INTRODUCTION

The *Statistical Account of Scotland* has been used by generation after generation of social historians enquiring into the local or national affairs of Scotland in the later 18th century. It is an unrivalled source, and historians of other countries, as well as their sociologists, geographers and natural scientists, have long regretted having no similar body of evidence available to them. Sir John Sinclair, determinedly cajoling the parish ministers of the Established Church to respond to his long list of over 160 queries, intended his statistical enquiry to enable the country, and its government, not only to assess its current state but to prepare better for a better future—"ascertaining the quantum of happiness enjoyed by its inhabitants and the means of its future improvement", moral as well as economic or political. The quality of the returns he received was generally good and was often excellent, and the parochial reports provided the Scots of the 1790s with a uniquely valuable analysis of their own times: the same reports provide us today with an incomparable view of Scotland two centuries ago, through the sharp eyes and the often sharp words of men who knew their localities very well indeed.

However, the original *Account*, printed in twenty-one volumes in the course of the 1790s, is difficult and often exasperating to use. Sinclair published the parish returns just as they came in to him; therefore the reports for one county or for part of one county may be scattered throughout a dozen volumes or more. Readers of the original printing must have the index in volume xx in order to search out easily the particular returns they want, and even then they may overlook the supplementary replies eventually published in volume xxi. Furthermore, Sinclair's indexes of subjects and persons in volume xxi are woefully inadequate.

In this new edition we have brought together the parish returns in groupings by county and have printed them in alphabetical order, thus avoiding a major difficulty in using the earlier compilation. This new arrangement will not only assist those who wish to use the *Account* as a whole, it will also be especially useful to local historians and to others engaged in local or regional researches with an historical basis: and the new format makes much easier a direct comparison of the Sinclair *Account* with the *New Statistical Account*, published by counties in 1845. So large is the volume of material for Aberdeenshire and Perthshire, however, that these counties have required two volumes each in this reissue. And we have decided to gather together in one volume all the returns from western island parishes, in the Inner and Outer Hebrides and in Bute, rather than leave them scattered among the returns from mainland Ross-shire, Inverness-shire and Argyll: these have a coherence in themselves which would be lost if placed with their respective counties.

Each of the twenty volumes in this reissue is being edited by a scholar who contributes an introduction showing the significance of the *Statistical Account* reports for the region and assessing their importance for modern historical and other social studies. Each volume will also contain an index (of the more important topics discussed in the returns, but not of persons or places) which will make the *Account* more accessible to and more immediately useful to all students, not least to pupils in schools where Scottish local studies are being introduced or extended. We are grateful to James Hamilton for his help in preparing the indexes.

We believe that the significantly improved format of this reissue will make more widely useful, and more widely used, an already acknowledged vital work of standard reference.

Ian R. Grant   Donald J. Withrington

THE

STATISTICAL ACCOUNT

OF

SCOTLAND
1791–1799
EDITED BY SIR JOHN SINCLAIR

VOLUME IX

DUNBARTONSHIRE, STIRLINGSHIRE & CLACKMANNANSHIRE

With a new introduction by
I. M. M. MACPHAIL

EP Publishing Limited
1978

This is volume IX of a reissue in twenty volumes of *The
Statistical Account of Scotland*, originally published between
1791 and 1799. In this reissue all the parish accounts for
individual counties are printed together for the first time,
with a new introduction and index in each volume.

Volume I of this reissue carries a general
introduction by Donald J. Withrington.

ISBN 0 7158 1000 6 (set)
0 7158 1009 X (vol. IX)

Printed in Great Britain by
The Scolar Press, Ilkley, Yorkshire

CONTENTS

1. These pages are misnumbered and actually run on, consecutively, from 296.

INTRODUCTION

THE counties of Dunbarton, Stirling and Clackmannan extend from west to east across mid-Scotland, the southern portions of the three counties forming what is known as the Central Belt or the Midland Plain of Scotland. Each county however contains extensive tracts of hilly country: in the neighbourhood of Loch Lomond in the west, the mountains are rugged in the extreme, while the Kilpatrick Hills, the Campsie Fells and the Ochils, although mainly under 2,000 feet, are for the most part uninhabitable moorland and rough grazing. There is thus a variety of geographical features which is reflected in the accounts of the parishes contained in this volume.

The boundaries of the three shires have been altered in certain respects since the time of the *Statistical Account*. For example, about one third of the parish of Kippen was part of Perthshire up until 1890. A much older redistribution explains the peculiar detached portion of Dunbartonshire—the parishes of Kirkintilloch and Cumbernauld. At one time part of Stirlingshire, they formed the medieval barony of the Flemings of Kirkintilloch, one of whom, as sheriff of Dumbarton in the fourteenth century, found it convenient to make an exchange with the sheriff of Stirling whereby six parishes—Fintry, Campsie, Balfron, Drymen, Buchanan and Strathblane—became part of the sheriffdom of Stirling and in return the lands of the Fleming barony became part of the sheriffdom of Dumbarton.[1]

The accounts of the various parishes published in this volume were intended to be written, and generally were written, by the parish ministers, most of whom submitted their accounts within the first two years after being requested by Sir John Sinclair to do so. Other ministers, for one reason or another, were a long time in completing the

---

1.   Sir William Fraser, *The Lennox* (1874), I, 26–31.

task. Pressure of various kinds was put upon the dilatory ministers. In 1793, the General Assembly of the Church of Scotland urged them to fulfil the duties imposed upon them, and Sinclair himself kept up a constant stream of letters to the recalcitrants.[1] The accounts of parishes in the three counties which appeared in the earlier volumes of the *Statistical Account* tended to be brief, some of them particularly so—for example, Muiravonside, Logie, Denny, Cumbernauld, each of which consisted of only two pages. On the other hand, the later volumes contained some lengthy accounts, those of Clackmannan, Kippen and Falkirk running to over forty pages each, that of Campsie to seventy-three pages and that of Kilsyth to over a hundred. The length of the later accounts may have been due partly to a spirit of emulation but in the case of the parish minister of Bothkennar, whose account appeared in Sinclair's seventeenth volume, he actually shortened his description of agricultural conditions by referring the reader to the already published accounts of the neighbouring parishes of Polmont and Airth.[2]

Not all the returns came from the pens of the respective parish ministers. Gavin Gibb, who was translated from Fintry to Strathblane in 1791, wrote the statistical accounts of both parishes, while the account of Killearn parish, where the minister, James Graham, was either unable or unwilling to accomplish the task, was compiled by David Ure, at that time a minister without a charge and employed by Sir John Sinclair in various duties involved in the preparation of the *Statistical Account.*

Some of the ministers achieved distinction or notoriety in spheres outwith the church. Duncan MacFarlane was only twenty years old when he was presented in 1792 to the parish of Drymen, where his father had been minister for almost half a century. He was renowned for his scholarship and in 1823 was appointed principal of Glasgow University[3]. John Stuart of Luss was a scholar also but in a different field

1.   Rosalind Mitchison, *Agricultural Sir John* (1962), 153.
2.   Bothkennar, 184.
3.   J. Guthrie Smith, *Strathendrick* (1896), 93.

from MacFarlane. His father, Rev. James Stuart, had been minister of Killin (where he was succeeded in 1789 by another son, Patrick) and with the assistance of Dugald Buchanan, schoolmaster, catechist and poet in Rannoch, had translated the New Testament into Gaelic. John Stuart was inducted into Luss in 1777 and followed in his father's footsteps by taking the main part in the production of a Gaelic translation of the Old Testament, which was published in four sections between 1783 and 1801. One of Stuart's collaborators was the minister of Cardross in Dunbartonshire, John Macaulay, grandfather of the historian, Lord Macaulay, Stuart also produced a revised edition of the New Testament in 1796. He was the last minister to preach in Gaelic at Luss[1].

The two longest and most detailed accounts in this volume were written by the ministers of neighbouring parishes in Stirlingshire, Campsie and Kilsyth. The minister of Campsie, James Lapslie, achieved notoriety by his efforts to bring Thomas Muir to trial in 1793. A staunch Tory, Lapslie took it upon himself to inform the authorities of Muir's political activities, even although he was on terms of intimacy with Muir's family and was said to have enjoyed their hospitality for weeks at a time. He travelled through to Edinburgh in order to give evidence at Muir's trial at the High Court but, although he attended daily, he was not called as a witness. His appointment to the chaplaincy of the Blue Gown Beggars in Stirling, a sinecure worth £50 a year (his only duty being to preach a sermon annually) was universally regarded as recognition by the authorities of services rendered and inspired one of the most effective of Kay's cartoons. Lapslie's unpopularity in the parish dated

1.   T. M. Murchison, "An Seann Tiomnadh" in *Stornoway Gazette*, 3 May 1969. At the beginning of the eighteenth century, all the inhabitants of Luss and Arrochar parishes used Gaelic for ordinary conversation. By the time of the *Statistical Account* it was still the language most prevalent and best understood, particularly by old people north of Luss. On the opposite side of Loch Lomond, in Buchanan parish, the indigenous population spoke both Gaelic and English; but when the Wordsworths visited Inversnaid in 1803 they found some difficulty in obtaining answers in English (Arrochar, 7; Luss, 111; *Macfarlane's Geographical Collections* (1906), i, 354–355; Dorothy Wordsworth, *Recollections of a Tour Made in Scotland, A.D. 1803* (1904), 108).

back to his presentation in 1783 against the wishes of the congregation, most of whom, including all the elders, seceded. In 1797, Lapslie's support for the unpopular Militia Act roused so much hostility in the parish that the out-buildings of the manse were set on fire during the absence of the minister and his wife[1]. In his account of the parish of Campsie, he showed himself a keen observer of nature and an informed commentator on the agriculture of the district, as befitted one whose father was a farmer in the parish. Among the many topics covered in his lengthy contribution, his description of funeral customs and his comparison of conditions in the parish in 1714, 1744, 1759 and 1794 are worthy of special notice. It is not surprising that he records at length and with a feeling of indignation what he considered the seditious activities of the Society of the Friends of the People. According to Lapslie, the members of the society were mainly young lads and a few half-educated people whose vanity induced them to mislead their more ignorant companions[2].

Rev. Robert Rennie of Kilsyth was, like Lapslie, son of a farmer in the parish of which he was the minister and claimed to have over five hundred relatives in the parish[3]. Rennie and Lapslie were related by marriage, both having taken brides from the family of the Stirlings of Glorat. Rennie was one of the many agriculturalists of the period who examined the possible utilization of peat soil and its conversion into arable land, and his researches on the subject earned for him a reputation outside Scotland. He was actually invited by Tsar Alexander of Russia to be professor of agriculture in St Petersburg University. The Tsar already had a Scotsman, Barclay de Tolly, as one of his leading generals but Rennie, to whom the Tsar presented a gold ring and other gifts, declined the invitation. As might be expected, his account of the parish of Kilsyth is particularly valuable for his observations on agricultural conditions[4].

1.   Hew Scott, *Fasti Ecclesiae Scoticanae* (1920), iii, 377; J. Cameron, *The Parish of Campsie* (1890), 2–19; J. Kay, *Portraits* (1877), iii, 112.
2.   Campsie, 262, 270–271, 272–275.
3.   Kilsyth, 508.
4.   *Fasti*, iii, 480.

The minister of Kirkintilloch, adjacent to Campsie and Kilsyth, William Dunn, had the unique distinction for a Scottish minister of his time of having spent three months a prisoner in the tolbooth of Edinburgh. Unlike Lapslie of Campsie, Dunn was sympathetic to the cause of political reform, as were most of his parishioners, and a sermon which he delivered before the synod of Glasgow and Ayr was later published as a pamphlet, dedicated to "the Friends of the Constitution in Church and State and to the People". The local branch of the Society of the Friends of the People passed a motion of appreciation of the sermon and when sheriff's officers, investigating the activities of Thomas Muir, confronted Dunn with the society's minute book, the minister tore out the relevant pages, an offence for which he was sentenced to three months' imprisonment[1].

Rev. David Ure, author of the parochial account of Killearn, was not the parish minister, nor even at the time of writing the account a minister in Scotland. He had, after some years as a schoolmaster, become assistant to the minister of East Kilbride but on the death of the latter failed to secure presentation by the patron and betook himself to Newcastle. His history of Rutherglen and East Kilbride, published in 1793, brought him to the notice of Sir John Sinclair, who employed him in various tasks in connection with the *Statistical Account*—the parochial accounts of Killearn, Rutherglen and East Kilbride, the "General Views" of the agriculture of the counties of Dunbarton, Roxburgh and Kinross, and the editing of several of the last volumes, including the general indexes, of the *Statistical Account*. He was an enthusiastic student of geology, and on his journeying throughout Scotland, he invariably travelled on foot, braving all weathers. His survey of the agriculture of Dunbartonshire, which was published in 1794, is a remarkable achievement for one not personally connected with the county and is a valuable supplement to the parochial accounts. Ure at last secured, probably through the influence of Sir John Sinclair, presentation to the parish of Uphall in 1796 but lived for only two years thereafter[2].

1. *Ibid.*, iii, 483; T. Johnston, *Old Kirkintilloch* (1937), 24–26.
2. *Chambers's Biographical Dictionary of Eminent Scotsmen*, ed. T. Thomson (1875), III, 474–475.

Ure's survey of the agriculture of Dunbartonshire was one of a set of surveys covering the whole of Scotland, commissioned by Sir John Sinclair for the newly-formed Board of Agriculture, of which he was first president. He himself was responsible for the survey of the northern counties. These "General Views", as they were designated, were originally intended as draft reports and were printed with wide margins for comments and recommendations to be submitted to the Board of Agriculture. Because of the deficiencies in the first "General Views", the Board of Agriculture decided to commission new reports, which were much fuller surveys, covering manufactures and communications as well as agriculture, and appeared about fifteen years after the first reports. Both sets of "General Views" are valuable sources of information, which help to round off the picture presented in the *Statistical Account*[1].

The eighteenth century saw considerable changes in the Scottish rural scene, involving a new agrarian system, new crops, new rotations of crops, new methods of cultivation, new machines and new breeds of livestock. Before the eighteenth century, Scottish farming had changed little, if at all, since the Middle Ages and was characterized by inefficiency at all stages of cultivation and by pitifully poor yields. Generally, if the oats or barley seed produced a four-fold yield, it was reckoned a "noble return"[2]; but a three-fold yield was then more common, whereas a twelve-fold yield would be considered average today. The changes which have been called the "agricultural revolution" had begun in the early part of the eighteenth century in East Lothian but it was not until the second half of the century that they were adopted in the three counties described in this volume. The initiative in introducing new ideas and new methods came from a few great proprietors, who after the Union of Parliaments in 1707 became more interested in the

1. The "General Views of Agriculture" of Dunbartonshire were written by Rev. David Ure in 1794 and by Rev. Andrew Whyte and Dr. Duncan MacFarlan in 1811, of Stirlingshire by R. Belsches in 1796 and Rev. Patrick Graham in 1812, and of Clackmannanshire by John F. Erskine of Mar in 1797 and Rev. Patrick Graham (along with that of Kinrossshire) in 1814.
2. D. Ure, *General View . . . of Dumbartonshire* (1794), 45; H. Hamilton, *Economic History of Scotland in the Eighteenth Century* (1963), 38.

social life of Edinburgh and London and on their travels to
and from these cities learned of the improvements carried
out in other districts[1]. In Dunbartonshire, Stirlingshire and
Clackmannanshire, there was a noticeable lack of wealthy
proprietors, which helps to explain the slow advance of
agricultural improvements.

The majority of landholders were feuars, who held their
lands by a charter from their superiors in return for a small
rent fixed in perpetuity. Sometimes the land consisted of
only a few acres, as a result of subdivision among heirs-
portioners, but a feuar, no matter how small his property,
still considered himself to have the standing of a laird.
Certain parishes in Clackmannanshire contained a high
proportion of these "bonnet lairds". In the parish of Dollar,
where the Argyll family had feued out their lands to their
kindly tenants, the holdings varied from 10 to 200. Scots
acres, and in the neighbouring parish of Tillicoultry, where
the first Lord Colville had feued out four-fifths of his land,
the average size of the holdings was 30 Scots acres[2].
Stirlingshire and Dunbartonshire also had many small
lairds. The lands of the barony of Mugdock had been feued
out by the Earls of Montrose in the middle of the seventeenth
century and likewise the lands of Strathblane nearby[3]. The
sixth Earl of Wigton, who was of the opinion that the
Union of Parliaments was destined to ruin Scotland, feued
out his estates to his tenants in the parishes of Kirkintilloch,
Cumbernauld and Denny. There was thus a high proportion
of small properties in these parishes, as also in the parishes of
Airth, Campsie, St Ninians and Slamannan[4]. In Kilmaronock, where William Cochrane, brother of the Earl of
Dundonald, had feued out the lands of Aber on Lochlomondside, there were about eighty small proprietors in the
latter half of the eighteen century; and "nothing can be
conceived more wretched than the state of cultivation" on
the Aber lands[5]. The small laird had "no stimulus to the

1.   R. H. Campbell, *Scotland since 1707* (1962), 6.
2.   R. Forsyth, *Beauties of Scotland* (1806), iii, 543. Four Scots acres were equal
     to five English acres.
3.   J. Guthrie Smith, *Strathblane* (1886), 34.
4.   Airth, 134; Alva, 146; P. Graham, *General View ... of Stirlingshire* (1812), 68.
5.   A. Whyte and D. MacFarlan, *General View ... of Dumbartonshire* (1811), 20.

improvement of his property. He is perfectly contented to live as his forefathers had done. He leaves his property as he found it"[1]. Some feus had been subdivided to such an extent that the property could not afford to keep a horse, and in such cases the land was overcropped—"scourged to the last extremity"—to provide meat for the family and fodder for a cow or two[2]. The standard of cultivation might well be described as wretched on smaller properties but the bonnet laird, although at times overburdened with debts incurred by providing "tochers" (dowries) for his daughters, was inured to the prospects of poor harvests and accepted them as part of his lot. Ramsay of Ochtertyre, writing of Kilpatrick lairds at the beginning of the eighteenth century, remarked that a number of families of moderate fortune lived together there in great cordiality[3].

There were few signs of agricultural improvement in the three counties until the second half of the century. John Erskine, Earl of Mar, "Bobbing John", before he left Scotland on the collapse of the "Fifteen" rebellion, was "at great pains in embellishing his seat in Alloa" but was considered a "great promoter of ornamental planting" rather than an agriculturalist. A namesake of Mar, John Erskine of Carnock, about the same time planted trees enclosed with hedgerows at Tulliallan near Alloa. About 1730 George Abercromby, father of the famous general, Sir Ralph Abercromby, enclosed a plantation of Scots firs which were cut down after 1760 and the enclosure replanted[4]. By the end of the century, the Duke of Montrose, Sir James Colquhoun of Luss and the last MacFarlane of Arrochar were planting large areas on

1. Graham, *Stirlingshire*, 69.
2. Ure, *Dumbartonshire*, 14.
3. J. Ramsay, *Scotland and Scotsmen in the Eighteenth Century* (1888), ii, 339. According to Ramsay, "the bottle was their bond of union". The phrase "as gash as Garscadden" derives from a story told by the New Kilpatrick parish minister in 1839 of a social meeting of Kilpatrick lairds, one of whom asked, "Is na Garscadden looking unco gash?" To which his host replied, "And so he may for he has been with his Maker this half-hour but I didna like to disturb the conviviality of the company by saying onything about it" (*New Statistical Account, Dumbartonshire*, 46). A fuller account appeared in J. Strang, *Glasgow and its Clubs* (1857), 104. John Galt recounted the story with different names in *The Last of the Lairds* (1826).
4. J. F. Erskine of Mar, *General View . . . of Clackmannanshire* (1797), 56–59.

Lochlomondside with trees to be cut down in due course for timber. Except on the Duke of Argyll's estate of Rosneath and the Erskine estates in Clackmannanshire, there were however few plantations in the lowland districts of the three counties until much later in the century. When Pennant visited Stirling Castle in 1769, he proclaimed the view from the top of the castle as the finest in Scotland—to the east a vast plain rich in corn, adorned with woods; but, according to the minister of Kilsyth in 1796, there was not a strip of planting in the parish and trees were so scarce "a child might number them"[1].

By 1770, what Ramsay of Ochtertyre caustically described as "the fever of improvements, so common and malignant", was spreading through mid-Scotland[2]. In Dunbartonshire, the Argyll family was granting to tenants in the parishes of Rosneath and Rhu (Row) leases enforcing certain conditions of cultivation, and similarly Hamilton of Barns of Clyde, two of whose tenants, John Paterson and William Brock, started operations in 1761 on rich, clayey loam, worn out by the old system, and were highly commended by Andrew Wight on his tour of the county in 1777. Lord Stonefield, on his estate of Levenside (now Strathleven), was in 1774 giving premiums of a guinea to tenants for each acre of potatoes, turnips or cabbages; and Sir Archibald Edmonstone was providing new houses for his tenants in Cardross parish and encouraged them in draining their lands[3]. In Stirlingshire, some tenants of the Duke of Montrose in Buchanan parish were showing laudable initiative although one of them still retained the old distinction between outfield and infield in 1777; Sir James Montgomery, on his wife's estate of Killearn, was

1. Buchanan, 195; Luss, 89; Arrochar, 2; Kilsyth, 409; Graham, *Stirlingshire*, 213; J. MacFarlane, *History of Clan MacFarlane* (1922), 146; Thomas Pennant, *A Tour in Scotland, 1769* (1771), 209.
2. Barbara L. Horn, *Letters of John Ramsay of Ochtertyre, 1799–1812* (1966), 121; R. Belsches, *General View . . . of Stirlingshire* (1796), 29. A. Brown described 1763 as "the great era of planting and enclosing" by which the arable land near Glasgow had "entirely changed its face" (*History of Glasgow* (1795, 1797), ii, 194.
3. Cardross, 23, 24; Ure, *Dumbartonshire*, 46, 47; A. Wight, *Present State of Husbandry in Scotland* (1778, 1784), iii, 307; Levenside Rentall Book, 1774–1779 (in possession of Mrs. M. Calderwood, Rosneath).

giving "an example of the most perfect husbandry" to his neighbours; and James Erskine, Lord Alva, abolished tenants' "servitudes", encouraged them in new methods of cultivation and built new streets of houses in the village of Alva[1]. In Clackmannanshire, cultivation was "going briskly" by 1775, although farmers with sheep on the Ochils, "the finest sheep pasture in Scotland", were prevented from making improvements as much of the pasture remained a commonty[2].

Where were the motives which induced landlords to become "improvers"? The example of other landlords in England and East Lothian has already been mentioned. The economic motive was not so strong as might at first appear; at any rate, some of the best-known improvers, Cockburn of Ormiston and Sir John Sinclair himself, found themselves in grave financial difficulties—not, it might be added, entirely due to unremunerative farming improvements[3]. Capital laid out on tree-planting was as safe an investment as a landlord could hope for but it was very much a long-term investment. Many of the early improvers were tree-planters and the profitable enterprise in afforestation on Lochlomondside later in the century has been mentioned above[4]. But improving landlords were actuated by a variety of motives, not least the desire to follow the current

1. Alva, 146–148; *New Statistical Account, Stirlingshire*, 182; Wight, *Husbandry in Scotland*, iii, 335, 340, 344. Sir James Montgomery owned the estate of Stanhope in Peebles-shire, where he introduced the cultivation of turnips and improved the breed of horses. As Lord Advocate, he was responsible for the Entail Act of 1770, which dispensed with some of the restrictions on owners of entailed estates (one third of Scotland was entailed) and enabled them to grant long leases, provided the tenants enclosed their farms, and to incur expenditure on improvements which could be paid off in part by their successors. (R. H. Campbell, *Scotland since 1707*, 28; W. Ferguson, *Scotland: 1688 to the Present* (1968), 170; J. E. Handley, *Agricultural Revolution in Scotland* (1963), 37.)
2. Wight, *Husbandry in Scotland*, 104–123. The commonty of the Hills of Tillicoultry was divided in 1775 (Ian H. Adams, *Directory of Former Scottish Commonties* [1971], 65).
3. Campbell, *Scotland since 1707*, 29.
4. Campbell, *An Economic History of Scotland in the Eighteenth Century* (1963), 65–66. Sir Walter Scott in *Heart of Midlothian* had the laird of Dumbiedykes in 1736 on his deathbed advising his son, "Jock, when ye hae naething else to do, ye may be aye sticking in a tree; it will be growing, Jock, when ye are sleeping".

fashion, to keep up with the Campbells and Edmonstones. Improvements which involved considerable expenditure and a scientific knowledge of agriculture became socially prestigious and enabled a proprietor to gain social and political advantages[1]. There was also a certain degree of paternalism so far as some landowners were concerned, most notably in the case of the Argyll family with its tradition of chieftainship of clan Campbell and particularly in that of the fifth duke who, although mainly non-resident, maintained a regular correspondence with his chamberlains on estate management, "meticulously controlling the life of the inhabitants of his estates"[2].

Some of the more sweeping changes carried out in the name of improvement in the last quarter of the eighteenth century were on properties recently acquired as speculative purchases. Two estates in Stirlingshire, which had been forfeited by their Jacobite owners after the "Fifteen" rebellion and purchased by the York Buildings Company of London, changed hands about the same time[3]. Kilsyth, formerly the property of the Livingstones, Viscounts Kilsyth, was bought in 1782 by Campbell of Shawfield, who had held a long lease of the estate, and it was sold shortly afterwards for £41,000 to Sir Archibald Edmonstone of Duntreath. Edmonstone, who had sold his Irish possessions in county Antrim to raise the money for the purchase, was interested in the exploitation of the "almost inexhaustible" reserves of coal in Kilsyth but started on a policy of agricultural improvements as well. His first success was achieved by straightening and deepening the course of the river Kelvin[4]. Another of the forfeited estates sold by the York Buildings Company at this time was Callendar, once the possession of the Livingstones, Earls of Callendar. The

1. Hamilton, *Economic History*, 55–56; S. G. E. Lythe and J. Butt, *Economic History of Scotland, 1100–1939* (1975), 118.
2. Eric R. Cregeen, *Argyll Estate Instructions, 1771–1805* (1964), p. ix.
3. Falkirk, 297. The York Buildings Company, which had spent over £300,000 in the purchase of forfeited estates in Scotland in 1719 and 1720, was forced to sell these estates for the benefit of their creditors in 1783 (Hamilton, *Economic History*, 65).
4. Kilsyth, 413–416, 432; Graham, *Stirlingshire*, 78, 93; W. Nimmo, *History of Stirlingshire* (3rd ed., 1880), ii, 201; P. Anton, *Kilsyth: A Parish History* (1893), 169 *et seq*.

purchaser was a member of an Aberdeenshire family, William Forbes, who had made a fortune in England and who "outstripped all others in the extent and rapidity of his improvements"[1]. Two other Stirlingshire improvers of the last quarter of the century were Robert Dunmore and Peter Speirs, sons of Glasgow merchants who had amassed fortunes in the American trade. Robert Dunmore, who married into one of the old families of Stirlingshire, the Napiers of Ballikinrain, made a number of speculative purchases of coal-bearing land at a time of rising coal prices and controlled a vast complex of enterprises—coalmines, cotton-mills, printfields. He founded a village for his employees at Balfron and encouraged his farming tenants in new methods so that the Endrick valley, which had formerly "almost the appearance of a wilderness, smiled with cultivation"[2]. Peter Speirs was the son of Alexander Speirs of Elderslie, who purchased the estate of Culcreuch in the parish of Fintry from another branch of the Napier family and in 1780 conveyed the property to his son. Like Dunmore, Speirs of Culcreuch started cotton manufactures and built a village, Newtown of Fintry; but he also introduced agricultural improvements and induced his tenants to make changes[3]. With all these proprietors, improvements were made possible by the possession of adequate financial resources, and their activities were by no means confined to estate management and farming but included commercial, industrial and manufacturing interests.

1. Falkirk, 297–299; Belsches, *Stirlingshire*, 22; Graham, *Stirlingshire*, 67. Forbes bought up stocks of copper at the time when the Admiralty decided on a policy of copper-sheathing the hulls of ships in the Royal Navy. He incurred some unpopularity through his evictions of small tenants, and during the unrest of 1797 fled from his home for fear of the mob. In his panic-stricken flight he mistook the blaze of the Carron Ironworks for his own house on fire and carried on post-haste to Edinburgh where he asked for a troop of cavalry to restore order (H. M. Cadell, *The Story of the Forth* [1913], 182).

2. Baldernock, 172; Balfron, 177, 178; Campsie, 221; Killearn, 380, 393–394; Kilsyth, 432; T. M. Devine, "Glasgow Colonial Merchants and Land, 1770–1815", in J. T. Ward and R. G. Wilson, *Land and Industry* (1971), 208, 212, 225; Belsches, *Stirlingshire*, 56; Smith, *Strathendrick*, 204.

3. Fintry, 332, 333, 336, 338; Devine, "Glasgow Colonial Merchants", 209–210; Smith, *Strathendrick*, 260. Speirs also married a daughter of one of the old landed families, the Grahams of Gartmore (Nimmo, *Stirlingshire*, ii, 131).

Enclosing of the open fields with hedges or dykes was still going on apace in the three counties at the time of the *Statistical Account*[1]. Strips of land held "runrig" by different individuals were re-allocated in compact blocks, ridges were levelled, and baulks between the ridges brought into cultivation. New crops were sown and with new rotations helped to produce better yields for the staple crops of oats and barley. The cultivation of potatoes (and later turnips) was beneficial in clearing the ground of weeds; and clover and rye-grass improved the fertility of the soil by storing nitrogen in their roots. In the last decade of the eighteenth century, turnip cultivation was still in its infancy in many parts of the three counties. In Stirlingshire it was increasing in the stock-raising districts, but in the neighbourhood of towns was greatly discouraged by the depredations of poor people and children[2]. Potato cultivation was by that time universal in Dunbartonshire and to a slightly lesser extent in the other two counties. "Not a family almost but has a piece of ground cultivated with this valuable exotic", wrote Ure about Dunbartonshire. In Clackmannanshire, potatoes were "much cultivated" and mechanics in towns and villages were willing to rent a ridge or two of potato ground at a good price[3]. In the parish of Buchanan in west Stirlingshire, potatoes were the staple diet for the "common people" for half of the year. By 1811, it was claimed that potatoes formed "the chief sustenance of the labouring classes in Dunbartonshire generally, and that from the health and strength of those who lived on them appear to afford a wholesome and nourishing diet"[4].

1. "Not a year passes but several thousand acres are surrounded with fences", wrote Ure in 1794 in his *General View of the Agriculture of Dumbartonshire*. It should be noted that the fences of the eighteenth century were either dykes or hedges. Wire fences were not introduced until after the middle of the nineteenth century and it is said that horses turned out to grass often ran into them at first (R. B. Cunninghame Graham, *Notes on the District of Menteith* [1907], 84).
2. Cardross, 22; Kippen, 538; Ure, *Dumbartonshire*, 57; Erskine, *Clackmannanshire*, 41; Belsches, *Stirlingshire*, 33.
3. Ure, *Dumbartonshire*, 52; Erskine, *Clackmannanshire*, 41.
4. Buchanan, 190; Whyte and MacFarlan, *General View . . . of Dumbartonshire* (1811), 131; Sir John Sinclair, *An Account of the System of Husbandry adopted in the most improved Districts of Scotland* (1812), ii, 132.

Potatoes had been cultivated in gentlemen's gardens in Scotland from the seventeenth century but they were first grown as a field crop in the second quarter of the eighteenth century in the parish of Kilsyth in Stirlingshire. Rev. Robert Rennie, minister of Kilsyth, narrated with pride in the *Statistical Account* the successful career of Robert Graham of Tamrawer from his first experiment on a small patch of half an acre in 1739 to his wonderful season of 1762, when from one peck of seed potatoes, planted with the dibble and hand-hoed, he obtained a crop of 264 pecks. Graham became the first potato merchant to supply the Glasgow market. "If the name of any man", wrote the Kilsyth minister, "deserves to be handed down to succeeding ages with honour and gratitude, it is that of Robert Graham, Esq., of Tamrawer"[1]. But in the *General View of the Agriculture of Stirlingshire*, which was published in the same year as Rennie's account, there appeared another version of the origin of field cultivation of the potato, giving the honour to Thomas Prentice, a day labourer in Kilsyth parish. The account of Prentice's "persevering exertions", which began about 1728, was based on a memoir submitted to the Board of Agriculture by William Wright, M.D., F.R.S., and included a reference to Robert Graham's later success. There is some doubt, however, about Dr Wright's claim for Prentice. It is surprising, to say the least, that Rennie, who was a native of the parish of which he was minister, should not have given credit to Prentice, if Wright's story was correct, as well as to Graham[2].

Some parochial accounts contain details of the various rotations of crops practised at the end of the century. In Slamannan, the farmers generally kept one half of the ground in cultivation with crops of oats, barley and flax and one half in grass. In Drymen, the people had no idea of resting the infield but ploughed it without intermission, raising crops of oats and barley. Both old and new methods

1. Kilsyth, 475–478; 105 pecks of potatoes were raised from one peck planted in the garden of a Mr. Barclay in Tillicoultry (Tillicoultry, 772).

2. Belsches, *Stirlingshire*, 31–32. It has been suggested that there may have been confusion with Henry Prentice, who is credited with having introduced field cultivation of the potato into the Lothians in 1746 (R. N. Salaman, *History of the Social Influence of the Potato* [1949], 390).

were to be found in the parishes of Kippen and Fintry, some of the farmers following the example of the improving laird, Speirs of Culcreuch, who first cleared the ground with a crop of turnips or potatoes, sowed barley with grass seeds the second year, raised hay for two years, pastured his livestock for one or two years, and then again sowed turnips or potatoes. In Kippen parish, the farmers in the carse followed the old system of infield—kept in a constant rotation of barley, oats and beans—and outfield sown with three successive crops of oats and then pastured, but were beginning to introduce summer fallowing and sowing of grasses. In Dunbartonshire, one fourth of the farmers still practised the "murdering system" of infield and outfield, strenuously defending their practice with the rhyme:

"If land is three years out and three years in,
'Twill keep in good heart till the de'il grows blin'"

But in most of the low-lying areas of the three counties farmers had established rotations beneficial to their soil and to their mode of farming. In the carse land of St Ninians parish, where, according to the minister, there existed "the highest degree of modern cultivation", there was a six-year rotation—fallow, wheat, beans, barley with sown grasses, grass, oats—lime being applied in the fallow year and dung before sowing the barley[1].

Dunbartonshire and Stirlingshire were fortunate in having very rich and fairly accessible deposits of limestone, often in conjunction with coal; but many farmers had to wait for cheap transport of the lime until nearly the end of the century, when the Forth and Clyde Canal and turnpike roads made it available. In Baldernock, Campsie, Cumbernauld, Kilsyth, Kirkintilloch and New Kilpatrick parishes there were abundant reserves of limestone beside the coal necessary for burning the limestone. In Buchanan, Drymen, Kilmaronock, Killearn and Dumbarton parishes, where limestone was to be found either in outcrops on the moors

---

1. Alloa, 670–671; Baldernock, 169–170; Clackmannan, 721; Drymen, 282; Falkirk, 297; Fintry, 332–333; Gargunnock, 257; Kippen, 540; St Ninians, 574; Slamannan, 601. Examples of the new rotations are to be found in the *General Views*—Ure, *Dumbartonshire*, 45–48; Belsches, *Stirlingshire*, 29–30; Erskine, *Clackmannanshire*, 48–50.

or interbedded with shale in the glens, peat was used as fuel. In east Stirlingshire and Clackmannanshire, lime was obtained from Lord Cathcart's estate of Sauchie near Stirling and Lord Elgin's limeworks at Charlestown on the Forth, from where it was transported to Alloa Shore. Slamannan farmers were doubly unfortunate as the nearest supply of lime was six miles distant and was accessible only by poor roads[1]. As for dung, which had been in use to restore the fertility of the soil from time immemorial, farmers were generally keen to obtain additional supplies, but when Gavin Gibb was inducted to the parish of Strathblane in 1791, the local farmers so little appreciated the value of dung as a fertiliser that he was offered dung for his glebe on condition only that he paid for the carriage. Elsewhere, in west Stirlingshire and Dunbartonshire, copious supplies could be obtained from populous towns like Glasgow and Greenock; as transport was by water, the farmers with land near the Clyde benefited most[2].

The eighteenth century also saw the introduction of new machines which helped to relieve the drudgery of the farmer's life. The old Scots plough, heavy and clumsy, drawn by four horses and requiring as many men to work it, was replaced by the lighter and more efficient chain-plough, invented by James Small of Blackaddermount in Berwickshire in 1765, and the chain-plough was in turn replaced by Small's swing-plough[3]. By the end of the century, the old Scots plough was still common in west and

1. Alloa, 676; Baldernock, 172; Buchanan, 197; Campsie, 217, 225–226; Cardross, 23; Clackmannan, 729; Drymen, 282; Killearn, 389; Kilmaronock, 46; Kilsyth, 425–427; Kippen, 543; Kirkintilloch, 75; New Kilpatrick, 56; Old Kilpatrick, 64; Ure, *Dumbartonshire*, 34–35.

2. J. Guthrie Smith, *Strathblane*, 222. The dung from Greenock and Port Glasgow was reckoned superior to that from other towns. The explanation offered by the authors of the second *General View . . . of Dumbartonshire* omitted any consideration of the diet or habits of the people of these towns. They suggested that the dung also contained the sweepings of herring-curing yards (refuse salt, putrid fish, blood, etc.) "calculated to promote a powerful and rapid agitation". When the herring fishing was in decline, the dung was not considered so effective (Ure, *Dumbartonshire*, 32; Whyte and MacFarlan, *Dumbartonshire*, 198).

3. J. E. Handley, *Agricultural Revolution in Scotland* (1963), 46, 49; T. B. Franklin, *History of Scottish Farming* (1952), 124 *et seq.*

north Stirlingshire, in Buchanan, Gargunnock, Killearn and Kippen parishes, but the swing-plough was almost universal in other parishes. In Clackmannanshire interest in the new plough was created and maintained by ploughing matches, which were introduced into the county by an East Lothian farmer, Hugh Reoch of Hilltown of Alloa. All of the forty ploughmen who competed in a ploughing-match at Clackmannan in 1791 used Small's plough and the winner, Alexander Virtue, was invited to Windsor to demonstrate his technique on the royal farm[1]. Another Scottish invention of the period was that of Andrew Meikle's threshing-machine, first introduced into common use in Clackmannan parish in 1787. It replaced the traditional method of threshing by flail, the most arduous work of the farming year; and the minister of Gargunnock was not alone in considering the threshing-mill as "one of the most useful instruments of husbandry ever invented"[2]. The use of new methods and new machines among tenant farmers was promoted by farmers' clubs and among landlords by the Highland and Agricultural Society, which was founded in 1784 and within a few years devoted its attention solely to agricultural matters[3]. The Board of Agriculture, set up in 1793 at the instigation of Sir John Sinclair, also gave an impetus to the development of modern farming, and the county surveys (the so-called *General Views* mentioned earlier) must have moved some old-fashioned landlords and tenants to change their ideas.

Most of the agricultural improvements noted above were carried out on arable farms in the lowland districts of the three counties. The highland region was traditionally dependent on stockraising. Cattle were reared in the glens and straths, and at the end of the summer, when they were in prime condition, they were brought down by drovers to the markets at Crieff, Doune or Falkirk. The markets at or near Falkirk were held continuously from the early years of

1. Alloa, 669; Buchanan, 197; Clackmannan, 721; Gargunnock, 360; Killearn, 391; Kippen, 540, 542; New Kilpatrick, 54.
2. Alloa, 669; Gargunnock, 360; Hamilton, *Economic History*, 80–81.
3. Handley, *Agricultural Revolution*, 77; Hamilton, *Economic History*, 68; W. Chrystal, *The Kingdom of Kippen* (1903), 54.

the eighteenth century but increased in scale and importance after the collapse of the "Forty-five". The market (or tryst, as it was called) was at first held on a commonty at Reddingrig and, after the commonty was divided about 1773, was moved to Rough Castle, west of Falkirk. When the Forth and Clyde Canal was under construction, it was decided to find another site as the canal would interfere with access from the north; and in 1785 Falkirk Tryst was fixed at Stenhousemuir near Larbert, where it continued to be held until just before 1900. At the time of the *Statistical Account*, there were three trysts annually, on the second Tuesdays of August, September and October; and at the October trysts between 20,000 and 30,000 head of cattle were sold[1]. The vast expansion of the cattle trade brought financial benefit to Falkirk and its environs and encouraged farmers in Stirlingshire to become graziers. According to the Kilsyth minister, the strath between Kilsyth and Strathblane was "the best in Scotland for grazing"[2]. Dunbartonshire farmers also made the most of their proximity to the area where the cattle were bred. It was estimated that in 1793 there were as many as 13,000 black cattle imported from the highlands in summer to the county and sold the following year to English graziers at the Falkirk Tryst[3].

A different kind of cattle-farming was practised in Clackmannanshire. Before the discriminatory act of 1788 which forced James and John Stein to close their distilleries at Kilbagie and Kennetpans near Alloa, the "draff" from the whisky-distilling at Kilbagie was used to feed about 7,000 cattle and about 2,000 pigs. The cattle were sold to butchers

1. A. R. B. Haldane, *The Drove Roads of Scotland* (1952), 138–140.
2. Fintry, 333–335; Kilsyth, 470–472; Strathblane, 637–640. Earlier in the eighteenth century (and also in the seventeenth century) farmers in the parishes of west and north Stirlingshire paid blackmail to the MacGregors of Glengyle for the protection of their cattle (Campsie, 269; Killearn, 401–406; Strathblane, 625–626).
3. There was also a cattle fair on Dumbarton Muir, where over 8,000 head of Highland cattle was sold annually (Ure, *Dumbartonshire*, 60, 97).

for the Glasgow and Edinburgh markets and the pigs were killed and cured as bacon and pork for England[1].

In the hillier parts of the three counties, the whole basis of farming was transformed in the eighteenth century by the introduction of the blackface breed of sheep. The old highland sheep was a small, white-faced, long-legged animal with very fine wool. The blackface sheep (in the eighteenth century generally called the Linton breed) was a native of the southern uplands, hardier and more coarse-woolled than the old highland breed but reckoned to provide three times as much mutton and four times as much wool[2]. It was able to find nourishment on the roughest grazing and to survive all but the severest winters. It was first introduced into the Highlands by a Galloway farmer, John Campbell of Lagwine near Carsphairn, who was tenant of Glenmallochan near Luss about the middle of the century, and his example was soon followed in other districts bordering on the lowlands[3]. On the Lochlomond-side hills the sheep-farmers, generally south-country men, kept their sheep for breeding, selling off the lambs to the lowland farmers for fattening, as is the practice also today. The Luss parochial account contains many interesting

1. Clackmannan, 726–729; Hamilton, *Economic History*, 107–108. The number of pigs in Clackmannanshire was in marked contrast to the numbers in the west of Scotland. In Dunbartonshire, as also in the Highlands generally, there was said to exist a prejudice against pork, and the number in the whole county was so small that they "hardly deserve to be mentioned"; a similar prejudice was recorded in Stirlingshire but by 1812 it was "wearing out" (Ure, *Dumbartonshire*, 68; Graham, *Stirlingshire*, 302, 394). It has been suggested that it was the lack of food for the pigs that prevented the farmers or cottars from keeping them. The feeding habits of pigs tended to be destructive of unenclosed land. When potatoes became plentiful and enclosures common, the number of pigs increased (David Murray, *Old Cardross* (1880), 52–53; Handley, *Agricultural Revolution*, 148).

2. Campsie, 236–237; Malcolm Gray, *The Highland Economy, 1750–1850* (1957), 90; Ure, *Dumbartonshire*. 63 *et seq.*, The Linton breed was so-called from the market at West Linton where breeders from the southern uplands sold their sheep. Another notable market for blackface sheep in the period before the farmers in the highlands started sheep-breeding was at East Kilbride, near Glasgow, in early June, 50,000 to 60,000 sheep being sold annually according to one estimate (*ibid.*, 65).

3. *Ibid.*, 63. The credit for the introduction of black face sheep to the highlands is sometimes attributed to an Alloa sheep farmer, James Yule, who wintered twenty score of hogs in 1759 at Cambusmore near Callander (Alex. Campbell, *Journey from Edinburgh through parts of North Britain* [1810], ii, 375).

details of sheep-farming of the period. including a statement of expenditure and income in managing a stock of 500 breeding ewes[1]. By the time of the *Statistical Account,* it was estimated that there were in Luss parish 7,500 sheep, in Arrochar parish about 10,600, and in the whole of Dunbartonshire about 26,000. Sheep-farming proved lucrative for landlord as well as tenant: a farm in Arrochar which had been rented in 1745 for £8 a year was leased forty years later to a tenant paying £80[2]. On the parapet of a stone bridge in Glen Luss near Glenmallochan is carved, with a ram's head, an appropriate symbol of the importance of sheep-farming in the parish[3].

The blackface sheep were not confined to the mountains of Lochlomondside but were to be found on the Campsie Fells and the Ochils. In Campsie parish there were at the time of the *Statistical Account* about 1,600 "muir ewes", including what the parish minister, Lapslie, called "the best blackfaced ewes in Scotland", the flock of David Dun who also rented a sheep-grazing in Fintry parish. Dun, who was designated by Lapslie "the Scotch Bakewell", was interested in rearing black cattle as well as sheep[4]. Farmers on the Ochils did not keep flocks of breeding ewes but bought their blackface sheep each year at West Linton or at other markets, as it was thought that the lambs were not able to survive a severe winter. For the famous Tillicoultry serges (which by the end of the eighteenth century were woven in Alloa) English wool was used[5].

Sheepfarming on a large scale such as was practised in the highland parts of Dunbartonshire and Stirlingshire involved the displacement of the small tenants (Glen Finlas in Luss parish, which had at least forty-five tenants in 1602, had only three by the end of the nineteenth century) but, as in other districts on the borders of the lowlands, those evicted

1. Luss, 104–107.
2. Arrochar, 2; Luss, 104; Ure, *Dumbartonshire,* 63.
3. Archibald Edmonstone of Spittal of Ballewan in Strathblane parish was so proud of his blackface sheep that he had a snuff-mill made in the shape of a ram's head (Smith, *Strathblane,* 100).
4. Campsie, 236–239; Fintry, 333–334.
5. Alva, 149–150; Tillicoultry, 771.

drifted into the towns—in the case of the Lochlomondside cottars into the Vale of Leven where they could procure work in the printfields and bleachfields.

The eighteenth century, which saw the transformation of agriculture, was also the period of the first industrial revolution in Scotland, the change-over in the textile industry from a domestic to a factory system of manufacture, the large-scale development of the coal and iron industries, the beginnings of the chemical and engineering industries. The parish ministers, who could write most knowledgeably about farming, were less well fitted to describe the conditions in industry or to discuss the factors which brought about changes in industry. Even where the parish accounts are extensive, they often fail to mention the name of an owner, as for instance in the accounts of Bonhill and Old Kilpatrick; and in other cases, for example that of Cumbernauld, they are so abbreviated as to provide very little information at all. The modern view of the Scottish industrial revolution favours the hypothesis that the last two decades of the eighteenth century, to which the *Statistical Account* relates, were the period of "take-off" in the Scottish economy[1]. But the ministers, when they treat of industry, tend to furnish details of technological changes and of the establishment of new enterprises rather than to attempt an analysis of underlying factors—the accumulation of capital with the gowth of the cattle trade, the linen industry and the American trade, the widening of horizons generally, the forging of links with England with its more advanced technology, and the development of entrepreneurship[2]. This is understandable, of course, but the result is that the changes in industry as reflected in these accounts require to be supplemented from other sources in order to obtain a due appreciation of the industrial revolution at the end of the eighteenth century.

1. R. H. Campbell, "The Industrial Revolution: a revision article" in *Scottish Historical Review*,xlvi (1967), 37–38; T. C. Smout, *A History of the Scottish People*, 1560–1830 (1969), 240, 248.
2. *Ibid.*, 249.

The extent of the contribution of Glasgow merchants to these industrial developments has been a matter of controversy in recent years[1]. It is true that, on the whole, merchants did not become industrialists but merchants' sons, like Robert Dunmore of Ballindalloch and Peter Speirs of Culcreuch, did involve themselves in industry, as the accounts of Balfron and Fintry testify? There are a number of similar examples in other parish accounts, although identification of the merchants concerned is not to be obtained from the *Statistical Account* alone. James Dunlop of Garnkirk, son of a Virginia merchant and himself active for years as a merchant in America, was one of those responsible for founding in 1776 the Dumbarton Glasswork Company (about which the parish minister wrote only three lines) and also had extensive coal-mining interests[3]. Robert Dunmore was involved in two concerns mentioned in the Old Kilpatrick accounts, the Dalnotter Ironworks and the Duntocher Wool Company, in which James Dunlop was also a partner[4]. The large printfield at Cordale mentioned in the Bonhill parish account was laid out by William Stirling, whose father, a Virginia merchant, was one of the "founders of the mercantile greatness of Glasgow"[5]. The lack of names of persons and placed in the accounts makes it all the more necessary to investigate other sources of the economic history of the period.

Coal-mining had been an established industry in Scotland from medieval times and in the first half of the eighteenth century was still being run on traditional lines. The parochial accounts of Alloa, Campsie and Kilsyth contain detailed descriptions of working methods in Clackmannanshire and Stirlingshire. Dunbartonshire was not without

1.   R. H. Campbell, *Scotland since 1707* (1965), 46–47.
2.   See p. xx notes 2 and 3.
3.   J. C. Logan, 'The Dumbarton Glass Work Company' (unpublished M. Litt. thesis, Strathclyde University, 1969), 6; S. G. E. Lythe and J. Butt, *Economic History*, 166. Andrew Houston, one of Dunlop's partners in the Dumbarton Glasswork Company, was also the son of a West India merchant.
4.   George Thomson, "The Dalnotter Iron Company", in *Scottish Historical Review*, xxxv (1956), 14, 19.
5.   J. O. Mitchell, *Old Glasgow Essays* (1905), 4–6; *Old Country Houses of the Old Glasgow Gentry* (1878), 85; A. Brown, *History of Glasgow* (1797, 1799), ii, 214.

its coal-mines but the accounts of Kirkintilloch and Cumbernauld parishes are disappointingly slight and only that of New Kilpatrick contains significant details[1]. It was in Clackmannanshire and Stirlingshire that innovations in the industry first occurred. From the middle of the century some mine-owners were beginning to make use of Newcomen's steam engine to pump water out of flooded workings and thus make possible the opening of new seams[2]. One of the many difficulties experienced in the coal industry was that of surface transport and for this reason the more prosperous mines in earlier times were located near the firths of Forth and Clyde or on the rivers leading into the firths. Roads were unsuitable for heavy traffic until nearly the end of the century and instead of relying on road transport a number of collieries constructed waggon-ways —the forerunners of the modern railways. Before the proprietors of the Alloa pits built waggon-ways to the shore, the small tenants were obliged to transport the coal in their carts, inefficient and expensive as that was. With the construction of waggon-ways at the two main pits at Alloa in 1768 and 1774, the sales of coal were increased fifty per cent[3]. The increasing demand for coal from the towns, particularly Glasgow, and the requirements of the expanding iron industry pushed up the price of coal. This had been steady for a century up until 1770, according to the Kilsyth minister, but thereafter it doubled in the next twenty years. It might have increased much more were it not for the

1. Alloa, 665–667, 679–682; Campsie, 220–226; Kilsyth, 432–435; New Kilpatrick, 55–56. The accounts of Airth, Alva and Clackmannan also include details of coal-mining in these parishes (Airth, 136; Alva, 160–161; Clackmannan, 724–725). In Cumbernauld parish, where coal was "in abundance", there was no colliery working at the time of the account, and in Kirkintilloch parish, where it was in "great abundance", there is no reference in the account to any coal being extracted (Cumbernauld, 37; Kirkintilloch, 75).

2. There was a steam engine in use at the Elphinstone colliery in the parish of Airth before 1750 and another at Carron Hall by 1760. The engine installed at the Colleyland pit in Alloa parish in 1764 was considered to be "one of the best of the old construction" (*New Statistical Account, Stirlingshire*, 345; Airth, 134; Alloa, 667).

3. Alloa, 682. A waggon-way also led from the coal-pit to the glassworks in Alloa (Alloa, 661; Erskine, *Clackmannanshire*, 62–64). The coal for Dumbarton glassworks was brought from Knightswood (now part of Glasgow) at first by river and later by the Forth and Clyde Canal (Logan, 'Dumbarton Glass Work Company', 11).

construction of two canals, the Forth and Clyde Canal and the Monkland Canal, which brought the rich inland coal-fields within easy reach of the towns on the east and west coasts and proved of immense value to the Scottish economy[1].

One aspect of coal-mining which is referred to in only one of the parish accounts is the employment of collier serfs. Since the seventeenth century, when a series of acts of parliament had made it possible for mine-owners to apprehend vagrants and to receive convicted criminals for work in the coal-mines, colliers had been treated as serfs[2]. Although the child of a collier was legally free, in practice he was regarded as bound to work in the mine through the laird's custom of making a gift to the parents at the time of the christening. This gift was considered as "arles" (earnest money), binding the parents to bring up the child as a collier. Invariably the father did so, for in Scotland the winning of coal was a family business[3]. Prisoners might have their sentences commuted to life service as colliers and were then forced to wear an iron collar for the rest of their lives. (The full story of the sentence passed on Alexander Stewart, the collier serf whose collar was dragged up out of the Forth about 1790, is related in the parochial account of Alloa[4].) The emancipation of collier serfs was brought about by acts of parliament in 1775 and 1799 and the pressure of economic forces. None of the parish accounts except that of Alloa makes any reference to the act of 1775 which, according to its writers, had not been very effective either in improving the lot of the colliers or in securing for the mine-owners a more plentiful supply of labour[5]. The act of 1799, which gave the colliers full emancipation, led to an exodus from the mines and a shortage of man-power in the coal industry which was not to be overcome for a generation. The collier's work was filthy and dangerous;

1. Hamilton, *Economic History*, 234–240; R. H. Campbell, *Scotland since 1707*, 88–89. The Monkland Canal was first proposed in 1769 in order to break the monopoly of the Glasgow merchants.
2. W. Croft Dickinson and G. Donaldson, *A Source Book of Scottish History* (1954), iii, 386–388.
3. W. Ferguson, *Scotland: 1689 to the Present* (1968), 187–188.
4. Alloa, 664–665, 679–681; *New Statistical Account, Stirlingshire*, 184.
5. Alloa, 679, 681; Ferguson, *Scotland: 1689 to the present*, 189.

and his wife and daughters, who were employed as coal-bearers, were destined also to lead a life of hardship and drudgery. Working conditions in the mines were not to be improved until well on into the nineteenth century.

Before the Carron ironworks was founded in 1759, Scotland did not possess a native iron industry. The charcoal furnaces in the Highlands at Invergarry, Abernethy, Bonawe and Furnace, were owned by English companies, using English ore (apart from a short time at Abernethy) and employing mainly English or Irish labour. Only the charcoal, which was made from the timber growing in the Highland glens, was Scottish[1]. But Abraham Darby's new method of smelting the iron ore with coke as fuel instead of charcoal opened up the possibility of blast burnaces in the coalfields of mid-Scotland. The establishment of the Carron ironworks near Falkirk, using Scottish iron ore and Scottish coal, was an achievement accomplished despite many difficulties. Its claims to be considered "the outstanding economic enterprise in Scotland for some time" rests not merely on the fact that it was the first modern Scottish ironworks but on the scale and the range of the company's activities. It was to rely for some time on English technology and on English workmen and was also faced with recurrent financial crises[2]. Within a few years, however, Carron pots and pans were being sold throughout Europe, and Glasgow merchants were obtaining from Carron machines for West Indian sugar-mills and hoes, shovels, anvils, pipes, stoves and grates for the home market. By the time of the *Statistical Account,* the Carron Company was established as foremost in Europe in many respects; and the company's short, wide-calibre gun, the carronade, was being used by French as well as British men-o'-war[3].

A full description of the Carron ironworks is contained in the account of the Falkirk parish minister, who estimated that the number of employees was then about 2,000. The

1.   Hamilton, *Economic History*, 189–193; A. and N. L. Clow, *The Chemical Revolution* (1952), 320; R. H. Campbell, *Scotland since 1707*, 64–65.
2.   *Ibid.*, 67; Cadell, *Story of the Forth*, 156, 163; R. H. Campbell, *Carron Company* (1961), 10.
3.   *Ibid.*, 72, 105, 108.

blast furnaces belching forth fire and smoke at night, "frightful to behold" (as the Slammanan minister wrote in 1777) were regarded with mingled admiration and awe by the local people; and the Falkirk minister himself, heedless of the effects of atmospheric pollution, wrote that "in the darkness of night the flashes of light from the iron-works at Carron appear in awful and sublime majesty"[1]. They proved an irresistible attraction for the tourists. One of these was Robert Burns, whose failure to gain admission on the Sabbath despite his using a fictitious name, elicited from him the verse quoted in the Falkirk parish account. To this a response was given in a verse, which does not quite match the poet's, by an employee called Benson, the father-in-law of the engineer, William Symington:[2]

> If you came here to see our works,
> You should have been more civil
> Than to give a fictitious name
> In hopes to cheat the Devil.
> Six days a week to you and all,
> We think it very well;
> The other, if you go to church,
> May keep you out of hell.

There were two other ironworks in the area described in this volume—one at Sauchie in Clackmannan parish and the other at Dalnotter in Old Kilpatrick parish. The Sauchie ironworks was started in 1792 by a firm called the Devon Company with the intention of exploiting the extensive seams of coal and limestone on the estate of Sauchie, which belonged to Lord Cathcart. The two furnaces were situated only three miles from the port of Alloa, through which the firm was able to import iron ore and to export manufactured articles[3]. The Dalnotter Iron Company was founded by Glasgow colonial merchants in 1769. The ironworks, which started operations soon afterwards, did not engage in the smelting of iron ore or in iron-founding, its slit-mill and forges using mainly bar iron imported from Russia. When Pennant made his tour of Scotland in 1772, 'all sorts of

---

1. Falkirk, 290, 312; Nimmo, *Stirlingshire* (1777), 463'
2. Campbell, *Carron Company*, 39; Cadell, *Story of the Forth*, 185.
3. Clackmannan, 729–731.

husbandry tools" were being manufactured at Dalnotter. Hoes, axes, nails, hinges and tools were being exported; saws, cutlasses, spades, shovels, harness chains and parts of ploughs were turned out for the home market. The number employed in the various works at Dalnotter at the time of the *Statistical Account* was nearly 300, this being the only information given by the parish minister about the ironworks. As early as 1786, the company was advertising in the *Glasgow Mercury* for a schoolteacher to teach the employees' children. (The Dalnotter ironworks had a fairly brief history as the site was acquired in 1813 and a cotton-mill erected; but a small spade forge which continued in operation until the 1880s was probably part of the original works[1].)

In the last two decades of the eighteenth century, cotton-mills seemed to be sprouting besides the rivers and waters of the Central Lowlands, using water-power to drive the spinning-machines. Many of the parish accounts in this volume make reference to the recent establishment of such mills. The cotton industry grew out of the older linen industry, which was mainly a cottage industry, the spinning and weaving being carried out by the women (the spinsters) and men (the weavers) respectively. There were other processes in the manufacture of linen cloth which lent themselves to large-scale production, as, for example, the dressing of the flax or lint, as it was usually called, by heckling and scutching in mills operated by water-power, and the processes of bleaching, dyeing and printing[2].

In west Dunbartonshire, the valley of the River Leven, which joins Loch Lomond and the River Clyde, was one of the first districts in Scotland to have the process of bleaching performed on a large scale. In 1728 a bleachfield of twelve acres was laid out at Dalquhurn near the modern village of Renton and another of nine acres near Loch Lomond. In those days bleaching was a protracted affair: the linen was laid on fields and regularly watered, the watering and the

1. G. Thomson, "The Dalnotter Iron Company" in *Scottish Historical Review*, xxxv (1956), 12, 14, 17; *New Statistical Account, Dumbartonshire*, 26, 29.
2. In 1772 there were 252 lint-mills in Scotland, including 28 in Stirlingshire and 16 in Dunbartonshire (Hamilton, *Economic History*, 136).

heat of the sun whitening the cloth. In time. bleaching by chemical processes (sulphuric acid and chloride of lime) was introduced[1]. It was in 1786 that a firm of Glasgow merchants, John Todd and Company, started calico (cotton) printing on one bank of the River Leven with a bleachfield on the opposite bank; and in 1770 William Stirling, who had been engaged in printing cotton handkerchiefs at Dalsholm on the River Kelvin near Glasgow, moved down to Cordale near Dalquhurn on the Leven to take advantage of an abundant supply of pure water. In 1791, Stirling's sons acquired the original bleachfield of Dalquhurn, which had belonged at one time to their great-uncle, Dr William Stirling[2]. By the time of the *Statistical Account*, the Vale of Leven had four bleachfields and three printfields, those of the Stirling family being the most extensive in Scotland; and it was claimed that the calico (for variety and fineness of colour) was the first in Britain, with the possible exception of those near London[3]. The Vale of Leven was not the only district with a plentiful supply of water suitable for bleaching and printing linen and cotton. In 1796, it was said that there were thirty large printfields in the vicinity of Glasgow. In addition to those in the Vale of Leven, the authors of the parochial accounts mention printfields or bleachfields in Campsie (2), Strathblane (3), New Kilpatrick (6) and Old Kilpatrick (4)[4].

1. *Ibid.*, 138–141; Clow, *Chemical Revolution*, 133.
2. J. Neill, *Records and Reminiscences of the Parish of Bonhill* (1912), 14, 15; "William Stirling and Sons" in *Glasgow Herald*, 2 Feb. 1880.
3. Bonhill, 12; Cardross, 26–28. The northern part of the Vale of Leven was included in Bonhill parish and the southern part in Cardross parish. Tobias Smollett, the novelist, was born at Dalquhurn and a monument to him (the Latin inscription is given in full in the Cardross account) still stands in the middle of the village of Renton, which was founded in 1782 for the accommodation of the printfield and bleachfield workers and named after Cecilia Renton, wife of Alexander Smollet of Bonhill (Joseph Irving, *History of Dumbartonshire* [1860], 355).
4. Campsie, 244–245; Strathblane, 442; New Kilpatrick, 55; Old Kilpatrick, 66; A. Brown, *History of Glasgow*, ii, 212–217. For a detailed description of the processes of bleaching and printing at Milton and Littlemill in Old Kilpatrick parish, see I. Lettice, *Letters on a Tour through various Parts of Scotland in the year 1792* (1794), 189–197. It was at Milton printfield that Cartwright's power-loom was first used on a large scale in Scotland. In 1794, when there was a shortage of calico for printing, 40 looms were fitted up; and it was from Milton that John Mitchell in 1801 obtained a pair of looms which he increased to 200 in his mill at Pollokshaws in the next two years (*New Statistical Account, Lanarkshire*, 152).

The first cotton-mills in Scotland were built at Penicuik in 1778 and at Rothesay in 1779, but the great proliferation of cotton-mills came after the introduction of Crompton's mule, which made it possible to produce a strong, fine cotton yarn and which required water-power to drive it. Some of the mills mentioned in the *Statistical Account* were small, like the mill at Luss which employed only 30 or 40 hands, or the mill at Kilsyth where an adventurer from London had installed ten or twelve spinning jennies and, when he found himself in financial straits, absconded and left a trail of debts behind him. Others were considerably larger, although none matched the scale of David Dale's establishment at New Lanark. The cotton-mill erected at Fintry by Peter Speirs of Culcreuch was intended to employ a thousand hands and, at the Ballikinrain cotton-mill of Robert Dunmore at Balfron, nearly four hundred hands were employed. In both Fintry and Balfron the mill-owners built villages for their employees[1].

In contrast to the expansion of the linen and cotton industries of Scotland in the eighteenth century, the woollen industry, adversely affected by the Union of Parliaments, which brought it into competition with the highly successful English woollen industry, took a long time to recover and existed mainly as a cottage industry[2]. In Stirlingshire and Clackmannanshire, however, coarse woollen cloth was woven for sale throughout the kingdom, Stirling and Bannockburn being noted for tartan manufacture. The "abolition and prescription of the Highland dress' in 1747 crippled the industry in Stirling, where the weavers turned to carpet manufacture after 1760. By the last decade of the century there were 30 carpet looms in Stirling belonging to three companies, and the colours of Stirling carpets were "allowed to be very fine". Tartan manufacture was still thriving in the nearby village of Bannockburn, where almost all the cloth required for the soldiers of the highland regiments was woven. The wool was brought mainly from Peebles-shire and Roxburghshire and spun and dyed in the

1.   Balfron, 178; Fintry, 336; Kilsyth, 503; Kippen, 536; Luss, 109; Stirling, 619.
2.   Hamilton, *Economic History*, 134, 156–157.

town of Stirling[1]. Only a few miles away, Tillicoultry and Alva weavers had been making woollen cloth for many years, and Tillicoultry serges were held in high regard all over the south of Scotland. By the end of the century the industry had declined in Tillicoultry; but in Alva it was still in a flourishing condition, 47 weavers being employed in the production of Scots blankets and serges, still called Tillicoultry serges. The wool used by the Alva weavers came from England, that of the Ochil sheep being kept for cloth for local people. Both Alva and Tillicoultry were to continue in woollen manufacture for many years afterwards[2].

The location of bleachfields, cotton mills and ironworks was determined by the availability of natural resources and led to the growth of new towns and villages, but the creation of new villages in some cases reflected rather the paternalism of the Scottish landlord[3]. Mention has already been made of the villages of Renton, Balfron and Fintry which were founded to provide accommodation for workers in printfields and mills. Other factory villages were founded or grew up by 1800 at Killearn, Milton in Old Kilpatrick and Milngavie (spelt "Millguy" by the parish minister) in New Kilpatrick. Grangemouth was "conceived" by Sir Laurence Dundas of Kerse, who cut the first sod for the Forth and Clyde Canal in 1768; and it was his successor, Sir Thomas (later Lord) Dundas who gave it the present name. Its situation near the terminus of the canal and its proximity to the Carron ironworks vastly increased its potential as a seaport[4]: Grangemouth has expanded steadily over the last two centuries, but in many instances the industries which brought about the creation of the factory

1.   Stirling, 619; St Ninians, 579; Belsches, *Stirlingshire*, 55. John Lane Buchanan described the kilts worn by the men in the Western Isles about 1790 as of tartan or "fine Stirling plaids if their money can afford them" (*Travels in the Western Hebrides from 1782 to 1790* [1793], 85).
2.   Alva, 151; Tillicoultry, 784; *New Statistical Account, Stirlingshire*, 187; *Third Statistical Account of Stirlingshire and Clackmannanshire* (1966), 552.
3.   T. C. Smout, "The Landowner and the Planned Village in Scotland, 1730–1830" in N. T. Phillipson and Rosalind Mitchison, *Scotland in the Age of Improvement* (1970), 85, 97.
4.   Falkirk, 308; Graham, *Stirlingshire*, 352; Robert Porteous, *Grangemouth's Modern History* (1970), 1, 2, 15.

villages collapsed and the villages today provide homes for commuters from and to the cities and large towns. Helensburgh on the Firth of Clyde had its beginnings in 1776 when Sir James Colquhoun of Luss advertised, in the *Glasgow Journal,* land to feu for building and added that "bonnetmakers, stocking, linen and woollen weavers will meet with proper encouragement". But the village was of slow growth and is not even mentioned in the parish minister's account published in 1792. By the end of the century, however, it had become "a place much frequented in the summer season for bathing quarters"[1].

The Forth and Clyde Canal, which runs for almost its entire length through Stirlingshire and Dunbartonshire, was constructed in the decades immediately preceeding the publication of the *Statistical Account.* The parish minister of Falkirk, who regarded it as the principal factor in bringing about the "astonishing improvements" of recent years, gave a detailed description of the canal, the construction of which started in 1768 but was thereafter delayed time and again. It was finally opened for through traffic in July, 1790 when "amidst the shouts and approbation of an astonished multitude" a hogshead full of water from the Firth of Forth was poured into the Clyde to symbolise the establishment of communication between the eastern and western seas. But it was not as a short-cut between the east and west coasts that the canal was important so much as being a water-way for the transport of heavy goods—coal, iron ore, iron manufactures, limestone. The freestone from the quarries in Kilsyth, which provided the material for the building of the bridges in the "New Town" of Glasgow, was brought by canal. Not only industry but agriculture also benefited for, with the opening of the canal, inland farmers who were remote from the sources of supply were able to utilise lime which would otherwise be unobtainable[2].

1.   W. C. Maughan, *Annals of Garelochside* (1896), 114–118; T. Richardson, *Guide to Loch Lomond, Loch Long, Loch Fine and Inveraray* (2nd ed., 1799), 100.
2.   Falkirk, 304–308; Kilsyth, 429–430; Campbell, *Carron Company,* 117–122, 211. It was on the Forth and Clyde Canal that the engineer, William Symington, carried out his second steamboat experiment in October, 1789, and his third experiment (with the *Charlotte Dundas*) in March, 1802 (D. D. Napier, *David Napier, Engineer* [1917], 95, 96).

Until near the end of the eighteenth century, most roads in central Scotland were in permanent need of repair. Even the military roads from Dumbarton to Stirling and from the Fruin Bridge to Ardlui, "the first well-made highways", were fit only for marching soldiers. In some places so little attention had been paid to the gradient—for example, at Firkin Point on Lochlomondside—that it was "inconvenient to travellers and oppressive to horses". The road from Campsie to Fintry went over a hill described by the former minister of Fintry as "almost perpendicular"; a horse could scarcely crawl up it with only half a load and it was impassable in winter. The main road from Stirling to Dunfermline was "remarkably bad" and sometimes made almost impassable by heavy vehicles using it. As late as 1768 there were no passable roads in the parish of Old Kilpatrick for lack of bridges across streams which in flood became unfordable[1]. The old system of statute labour whereby all tenants, cottars and servants were obliged to give six days' service on roadmaking and repair was quite inadequate. The compulsory work on the "parish road days" was grudgingly given; and in many parishes it was being commuted to a money payment. But it was not until the setting up of turnpike trusts that worthwhile improvements were effected—trustees being empowered by act of parliament to repair existing roads and construct new roads, the expenditure being recouped by charging tolls at toll-houses and turnpike gates and by an assessment imposed in lieu of the former obligation to perform statute labour. The improvements made by the turnpike trusts were carried out in many parishes in the last two decades of the century and were "very generally praised" by the writers of the parochial accounts[2]. Benefits accrued to travellers and farmers and

1. Arrochar, 6; Fintry, 338; Kippen, 521, 544; Old Kilpatrick, 66; Slamannan, 602; Erskine, *Clackmannanshire*, 76. The first bridge over the River Leven at Dumbarton was built only in 1765 and the bridges on the Forth near Cardross and at Frew in 1772 and 1783 respectively.
2. Gargunnock, 355, 370; Kippen, 544; Strathblane, 644; Erskine, *Clackmannanshire*, 76; Hamilton, *Economic History*, 225. The ministers of Kippen and Gargunnock, writing before the military road was made a turnpike road, were destined to be disappointed as the road was re-routed and their villages by-passed. The old road by Touch, Gargunnock House, Leckie and Boquhan to Kippen can still be traced (*New Statistical Account, Stirlingshire*, 59; *Stirlingshire: An Inventory of the Ancient Monuments* (1963), ii, 423).

to industry. In the parish of Campsie, where there had been no cart or chaise in 1714 and only a few carts and no chaise in 1744, there were in 1794 as many as 200 carts, 4 post chaises, 3 coaches and one two-wheeled chaise[1].

The changes in the Scottish economy in the late eighteenth century were not without effect on the lives of the people. In the towns and industrial villages wages were high enough to enable the workers to enjoy a much higher standard of living[2]. In comparison with the basic wage for a labourer of a shilling a day those in industry were well paid—a linen printer in the Vale of Leven earning 21 shillings a week, a glass-worker in Dumbarton 25 shillings a week, while children in the printfields under eight years of age could earn from 4 to 8 pence a day. In Old Kilpatrick parish where there was "not an idle person to be seen", all the young persons dressed well, the men wearing hats and coats of English cloth and the women silk and calico gowns with black hats and cloaks. Their chief amusement when they met was dancing; and, upon such occasions according to the minister, there was a "pleasant cheerfulness and innocence among them". The Kirkintilloch minister praised "the industry, sobriety, frugality and charity" of the people but expressed his concern about the tendency of young children, "able to subsist by the profits of their own labour", to become independent of parental control and acquire "habits of extravagance"[3]. In a lengthy disquisition on the changing times, the minister of Kippen contrasted the different ways of life before and after the coming of industry to a rural parish: although the necessaries and conveniences of life were procured with facility, the "disproportioned rewards of labour generally tend to enervate the sinews of industry, foster idleness, introduce a total relaxation of morals, and consequently lead to poverty and wretchedness"[4].

1. Campsie, 272–274.
2. The improvements in diet, dress, etc. are mentioned in detail in some of the accounts—Campsie, 272–274; Falkirk, 301–303; Kilsyth, 500–501.
3. Dumbarton, 43; Kirkintilloch, 80, 82; Old Kilpatrick, 71. The inhabitants of Kirkintilloch were in general healthy and vigorous with the exception of young women spinners, for whose tendency to hysterics the minister gives an interesting explanation (Kirkintilloch, 80–81).
4. Kippen, 546–550.

Most of the parish ministers who commented on the manners and morals of their parishioners praised them for being sober and industrious. Such was the case in the parishes of Arrochar, Kirkintilloch and Luss in Dunbartonshire, Airth, Baldernock, Killearn and St Ninians in Stirlingshire, and Clackmannan, Dollar, and Tillicoultry in Clackmannanshire. In Killearn, the five public houses were frequented mainly by travellers, and among the local people there was "little time wasted in idleness, intemperance or political cabals". In Clackmannan, although the people were in general sober and industrious, men of the lower classes were much addicted to the drinking of whisky, which was not surprising considering the proximity of the distilleries of Kilbagie and Kennetpans and the practice by farmers of giving women reapers a mid-morning dram of whisky as part of their wages. Tillicoultry people were also sober and industrious but the minister there related how a collier who had been confined to bed for eighteen months with rheumatism or gout was cured of his trouble by drinking freely of new ale on Handsel Monday and had not suffered a relapse. Whisky drinking was all too common in some parishes—Bonhill, Dumbarton, Rosneath and Rhu in Dunbartonshire, Gargunnock, Larbert and Stirling in Stirlingshire. In Gargunnock "everything is bought and sold over a bottle"; even at tea-drinking, which had become universal, the last cup was "qualified" with whisky "to correct all the bad effects of the tea". The Larbert minister complained that while whisky was to be had "in abundance" yet "a drink of good ale cannot be got", a criticism echoed by the Stirling minister who described the local beer as "thin, vapid, sour stuff". Even in the sober and industrious parishes there may have been less knowledgeable ministers who were unaware of the extent of whisky drinking in their parishes—for which, in the *New Statistical Account* published about fifty years later, there was plenty of denunciation by ministers of excessive tippling by their parishioners.[1]

1. Airth, 140; Arrochar, 8; Baldernock, 168; Balfron, 182; Bonhill, 16; Buchanan, 201; Clackmannan, 746; Dollar, 767; Dumbarton, 44; Gargunnock, 373; Killearn, 397; Kirkintilloch, 80; Larbert and Dunipace, 558; Luss, 111; Rosneath, 122; Rhu, 127; St Ninians, 583; Stirling, 628; Tillicoultry, 794.

The problem of the relief of the poor was to give consider-able trouble to the authorities, both local and national, in the nineteenth century, and there is evidence in this volume of early manifestations of the difficulties which lay ahead. While in Dollar parish there had been no beggars "in the memory of man", the people in Gargunnock were harassed by vagrants "from other places". In Fintry "a plague of mendicants from other places" made "nightly depreda-tions" and the parish of Kilsyth was "infested by a crowd of sturdy beggars at all times, especially at harvest when all the males are at work in the fields". In Baldernock and Strath-blane the mendicants were also said to be "from other places", in the case of Baldernock from the "manufacturing villages". As the accounts of these parishes were published in 1795 or later, it may be that the sturdy beggars had found themselves unemployed when some mills, printfields and bleachfields closed down as a result of the financial crisis of 1793, which brought about a stagnation of trade much lamented in the Killearn account. But although Robert Dunmore, proprietor of a mill and bleachfield, was himself declared bankrupt, his works in Killearn and Balfron con-tinued to function, and Balfron was the only parish in west Stirlingshire where the minister could claim that there were no vagrant poor. Some of the vagrants may originally have come from the Highlands: the minister of Buchanan parish, extending as far as the north end of Loch Lomond, complained about the number of people who had been displaced by the creation of large farms which were let to tenants living outside the parish and contributing nothing to the relief of the poor. In the burgh of Stirling, according to the minister, nearly all those on the poor roll bore highland names and had left, or been forced to leave, their highland homes. They had sought shelter in Stirling, which was well endowed in charitable bequests and which was obliged, after the incomers had been resident for three years, to rank them among the "necessitous poor"[1].

1. Baldernock, 171; Balfron, 181; Buchanan, 200; Dollar, 761; Fintry, 337; Gargunnock, 366; Killearn, 393; Kilsyth, 507; Stirling, 623; Strathblane, 644. The Stirling minister also ascribed the great number of paupers in the burgh to the presence of the castle garrison. Generally, the garrison consisted of old soldiers, "ignorant, vicious and debauched", some of whom married women like themselves and, worn out with intemperance, left behind after death families "beggared, unprincipled and debauched" (Stirling, 626).

The Scottish system of poor relief depended mainly on church collections, charitable bequests, payments for the use of the mortcloth at funerals and, in some places, fines for immorality, and was usually administered by the kirk sessions. The workhouse, common in England, was hardly known in Scotland in the eighteenth century, those which had been set up lapsing after a few years. Where the ordinary sources of the poor's fund proved insufficient, it was competent for the heritors of a parish to raise an assessment or poor rate as in England, and the first assessments in Scotland were imposed in 1740, "a year of scarcity", in a few parishes in the south of Scotland in order to compel non-resident heritors to contribute their quota to the relief of the poor. By 1790 there were assessments for poor relief in 92 parishes, chiefly in the towns of parishes near the English border, but in only five of the parishes described in this volume—Airth, Clackmannan, Falkirk, Logie and St Ninians[1].

In some parish accounts, mention is made of friendly societies—a form of mutual aid and insurance against illness, accident and death. In Kilsyth a weavers' society was started as early as 1760; in time it attracted "multitudes" who had no connection with weaving, so that in 1795 there were more than 350 members. Both Kilsyth and Campsie had masonic societies and in the latter parish there was a benevolent society, founded in 1786 and possessing a capital fund of £110 by 1794. The Carron Company workers had a number of friendly societies in the parishes of Falkirk and Larbert. In addition to those mentioned in this volume, we learn from the later *New Statistical Account* that there were also in existence in the last decade of the eighteenth century friendly societies in Airth, Alloa and Baldernock. These mutual benefit organisations were to be "a blessing to

---

1. Airth, 138; Clackmannan, 690; Falkirk, 295; Logie, 561; St Ninians, 585; Erskine, *Clackmannanshire*, 92–95; Thomas Ferguson, *Dawn of Scottish Social Welfare* (1948), 173–185; Stewart Mechie, *The Church and Scottish Social Development, 1780–1874* (1960), 64–67. There is a detailed description of the arrangements for poor relief in the Slamannan account. In Campsie parish, the fine paid by a fornicator, in addition to appearing for public rebuke on two Sabbaths, was a crown, which went to the poor's fund (Campsie, 259).

many" in the days long before the welfare state was conceived[1].

Very few ministers fail to refer to the schools and schoolmasters in their parishes. In rural parishes generally, the schoolmaster's lot was one verging on poverty, although there was none in the three counties so impoverished as the septuagenarian schoolmaster in Heriot, Midlothian, who was also session clerk, precentor, beadle, gravedigger, yet his total income did not exceed £8 per annum[2]. The schoolmaster in a rural parish usually had a salary of £100 Scots or £8. 6s. 8d. sterling, but the scholars' fees might amount to as much again and, in addition, he might have extra emoluments as session-clerk (for the registration of baptisms and the proclamations of marriages). In Gargunnock, the total income was scarcely £16 per annum: "common sense," the minister commented, "must revolt at the idea of his being in a worse plight than a day-labourer". In Bothkennar, where the schoolmaster had a house and garden and his total emoluments "scarcely exceeded" £20 per annum, the minister expressed the hope that "in this age of liberality and improvement" something would be done for the encouragement of schoolmasters, so often "straitened to obtain the necessaries of life". The Kilsyth minister, in a stirring plea for an adequate salary, made a practical suggestion that the parish schoolmaster be appointed to another office in addition to his own—that of postmaster if he lived in a post town or that of land surveyor if he lived in a country parish. Only in the Campsie parish account is there any detailed information about the syllabus or the methods of teaching. The insistence on the daily study of the Bible and on the repetition of parts of the Shorter Catechism was in accordance with the church's control over the schools in the rural parishes, and the regular inspection of schools by ministers ensured the

---

1. Campsie, 253; Falkirk, 296; Kilsyth, 452; Larbert and Dunipace, 557; *New Statistical Account, Stirlingshire*, 160, 174, 386; *New Statistical Account, Clackmannanshire*, 35.
2. *Statistical Account of Scotland* (Withrington and Grant), ii: Lothians, 272–273.

schoolmaster's attention to religious instruction as of paramount importance[1].

In burgh schools, the schoolmaster was much better
remunerated and enjoyed a higher status in the community.
In Clackmannan, the parish schoolmaster received a salary
of £40 per annum and, in addition, a house and garden and
scholars' fees, while the master of one of the other five
schools in the town had an income of £50 a year. In the
burgh of Stirling, the rector of the grammar school received
a salary of £40 a year together with a house and, in addition,
the fees of some seventy scholars. His assistant teacher, who
was in the parish account called an usher (an English term
introduced in the late eighteenth century in Scottish
grammar schools to replace the more dignified but mis-
leading title of "doctor") received from 1796 onwards
1s. 6d. and the rector 2s. per quarter from each of the
scholars[2]. The Dumbarton minister's account contains no
reference to the grammar school except to remark on low
fees that were charged there. But in 1794, the three masters
then appointed to the grammar school were expected by the
town council to earn, in salaries and fees, the sums of £70,
£65 and £60 respectively, and in addition whatever was
received in Candlemas gifts and private teaching. The
Candlemas gifts of money (which lasted in Dumbarton and
other burgh schools until 1832) were generally in keeping
with the parents' circumstances; and as the scholar who
brought in the largest sum was named "king of the school",

1. Bonhill, 18; Bothkennar, 188; Campsie, 260–262; Gargunnock, 367;
    Killearn, 398; Kilmaronock, 48; Kilsyth, 446; Rosneath, 121; Rhu, 126;
    St Ninians, 589. The Society for Propagating Christian Knowledge, which
    brought some form of education to remote parts of the Highlands and
    Islands, was responsible for a school in both Luss and Buchanan parishes.
    In Buchanan (and probably in Luss) the schoolmaster acted also as catechist,
    his total salary for both duties being £10 a year with about £4 in scholars'
    fees (Buchanan, 199; Luss, 111).
2. Alloa, 701; Clackmannan, 734; Falkirk, 294; Stirling, 616. James Clark, the
    doctor in Stirling Grammar School, was granted a pension of £15 for life on
    his retirement in 1778, but it was to be paid out of the salary of his successor.
    Clark's salary had been £20 and his successor was paid £15 and the doctor's
    share of the fees (A. F. Hutchison, *The High School of Stirling* [1904], 108).

the emulation of fathers aspiring to a higher social position could produce a considerable amount[1].

In contrast to the parish dominies and their penurious lot, most of the ministers generally enjoyed a comfortable living. The stipends of the Stirlingshire ministers were estimated in 1812 to average £264, including the value of a glebe. But at the time of the *Statistical Account* the ministers of Balfron, Fintry and Polmont received less than £100, and those of Alva, Bothkennar and Rosneath were little better off[2]. The stipend usually consisted of money and victual (oatmeal and barley) and, in some parishes, additional payments such as 16 stones of cheese in Kilsyth, 6 stones of salmon in Dumbarton, and cartloads of coal in Alloa and Falkirk[3]. It was to the advantage of the minister to have most, if not all, of his stipend payable in victual in times of rising prices. The Strathblane minister in 1793 successfully applied to the teinds court for a decree fixing the whole payment in grain: with the augmentation, the value of the living was estimated at only £130 a year. The writers of the Alloa account, where a similar conversion was made in 1793, commented that it "gave security for the stipend's rising with the other necessaries of life"[4]. The manses were in general substantial buildings, although the Gargunnock minister considered his manse "too small for the accommodation of a family". Those of Balfron, Gargunnock, Larbert, Polmont and St Ninians have survived, in one form or another, to modern times. While the ministers of Alva, Clackmannan, Kilsyth and Old

1.   Dumbarton Town Council Minutes, 4 July 1794. The Candlemas gifts in Dumbarton Grammar School in 1705 amounted to over £13 sterling for the schoolmaster and £1. 10s. for the doctor (A. W. Anderson, *Papers of the Rev. John Anderson* [1914], 93). On at least one occasion in Stirling, the highest contribution was a sovereign (Andrew Bain, *Education in Stirlingshire from the Reformation to the Act of 1872* [1965], 257).
2.   Graham, *Stirlingshire*, 390; Alloa, 699; Balfron, 181; Bothkennar, 187; Fintry, 367; Rosneath, 125. In the parish of Alloa, where the minister received the equivalent of just over £100, with a manse and a glebe of 14 acres of "fertile ground" and two cartloads of coal a week, there was also an assistant minister with a stipend of £70, provided out of a bequest from Lady Charlotte Erskine.
3.   Alloa, 699; Dumbarton, 41; Falkirk, 292; Kilsyth, 445.
4.   Strathblane, 645; Alloa, 700.

Kilpatrick commented favourably on their commodious and pleasant residences, the ministers of Arrochar, Denny, Dollar and Luss took advantage of the occasion to draw attention to the need for repairs[1]. The glebes varied in extent and quality from parish to parish. Some parish accounts are lacking in detailed information about the glebes but we are told that in Airth, Alva, Baldernock, Balfron, Kilsyth, Slamannan and Tillicoultry they extended to 10 acres or more, the largest mentioned being that of Balfron with 18 acres[2].

Not so comfortably settled were the ministers of the dissenting congregations, those who had seceded from the Established Church of Scotland. The minister of the Secession Church at Buchlyvie received £50 a year as stipend (provided from the income obtained by charging seat rents) and also a house and garden, while the minister of the Relief Church in St Ninians, attended by a large number of former adherents of the Established Church, had as much as £100 a year and a large house. From other sources we learn that the dissenting ministers at Balfron and Kilsyth in the 1790s received £70 and £83 respectively[3]. Details of the dissenting ministers and their congregations were grudgingly given by some parish ministers and in a few cases there is no information at all, e.g., in Campsie parish, where the settlement of the minister had provoked the secession of the majority of the congregation of the Established Church[4].

Although there are many gaps in the information provided by the parish ministers about the dissenting congregations, the reader of the *Statistical Account* can hardly fail to be impressed and perhaps perplexed by the number and variety of the Protestant sects existing in Scotland at the

1. Alva, 155; Arrochar, 5; Clackmannan, 737; Denny, 278; Dollar, 761; Gargunnock, 367; Kilsyth, 445; Luss, 110; Old Kilpatrick, 67; *Stirlingshire: An Inventory of the Ancient Monuments* (1963), ii, 314, 319, 320, 364, 376.
2. Airth, 138; Alloa, 700; Baldernock, 171; Balfron, 181; Kilsyth, 445; Slamannan, 605; Tillicoultry, 787.
3. Kippen, 531; St Ninians, 587; Robert Small, *History of the Congregations of the the United Presbyterian Church* (1904), i, 214.
4. J. Cameron, *The Parish of Campsie* (1892), 5–6.

end of the eighteenth century. (The Roman Catholic church, which in modern times bulks so largely in part of the three counties, is conspicuous by its absence from nearly all the parochial accounts.) The divisiveness of Scottish presbyterianism, which itself originated in a schism based on an appeal to the authority of the Bible, had already been manifest in the seventeenth century; but without doubt the most significant factor in producing secessions in the eighteenth century was the right of patrons to select the minister of a parish, a right removed from them by the Scottish parliament in 1690 but restored by the British parliament in 1712. Time after time a disputed settlement led to the secession of members and adherents of the parish church and the setting up of another, separate, presbyterian church.

The oldest sect of dissenters, however, was composed of those who did not accept the state establishment of 1690. They were known as Covenanters, Cameronians or Macmillanites (so-called after one of their early ministers, John Macmillan of Balmaghie) and later, after 1743, as the Reformed Presbyterian Church. They were to be found in small numbers in a few Stirlingshire parishes, and in Stirling itself had a church with as many as 120 adherents. In the parish of Rosneath there were 14 Cameronians. According to the parish minister who wrote in the *New Account*, they belonged to families descended from fugitive Covenanters who had settled there in the seventeenth century, seeking the protection of the Earl of Argyll[1] The first or original secession from the Established Church took place in 1733 in a protest against patronage, led by Ebenezer Erskine, minister of the third charge in Stirling. He and three colleagues formed themselves into a separate presbytery, calling it the Associate Presbytery, and by 1742 there were 20 ministers and 36 congregations adhering to it. Two years later, a split occurred in their ranks over the question of the burgess oath, which the more extreme ministers regarded as implying approval of the established religion

1.   Falkirk, 291–292; Rosneath, 119; Stirling, 617; Ferguson, *Scotland: 1689 to the present*, 112; *New Statistical Account, Dumbartonshire*, 115.

and a full account of the controversy over the burgess oath is contained in the parochial account of Stirling. By the beginning of the nineteenth century it was estimated that there were 135 Anti-burgher congregations and 127 Burgher congregations in Scotlands, both sects being strongly represented in Stirling, Falkirk, Alloa, Balfron, Kilmaronock and Renton (in Cardross parish)[1].

The other large dissenting body, the Relief Church, also originated as a protest against patronage, in order to provide for "the relief of Christians oppressed in their Christian privileges". From 1762, when two ministers, Thomas Gillespie and Thomas Collier, formed the Presbytery of Relief, disputed settlements produced more and more support for the new church, but it was not so strongly represented in our three counties as the churches of the earlier secession. In the parish of St Ninians, which was in turmoil for eight years before 1773 over the patron's right to appoint a minister, the majority of the Established Church seceded but after some years those who remained purchased the right of patronage and formulated rules for the process of calling a minister[2].

Some smaller sects mentioned in the *Statistical Account* owed their existence primarily to ministers who gained a devoted following by their inspired preaching. A sect which is represented in this volume by a single adherent (in Kilsyth parish) was that of the Glasites[3]. In Stirling there were 33 Bereans, "disciples of Mr Barclay", who held the Bible to be "the only certain rule of faith and manners".

1. Stirling, 615; Ferguson, *Scotland: 1689 to the present*, 123–125; R. Forsyth, *Beauties of Scotland*, iii, 428.
2. St Ninians, 587–588; Ferguson, *Scotland: 1689 to the present*, 126.
3. John Glas, minister of Tealing near Dundee, was able to hold a congregation enthralled with sermons lasting two to three hours; and, being deposed in 1728 for refusing to accept certain passages in the Confession of Faith, he moved to Dundee, where he gathered about him the first independent congregation in Scotland. His followers, the Glasites or Sandemanians (so-called after his son-in-law) were known in north-east Scotland as the "Kailites" from their practice of sitting down after the morning service on the Sabbath to a common meal which invariably started with kail broth: *Scottish National Dictionary*, s.v. "Broth-kirk"; *Chambers's Biographical Dictionary of Eminent Scotsmen* (1875), iii, 115–116.

Introduction

Rev. John Barclay had been assistant minister of Fetter-cairn, where he attracted a great number of hearers from other parishes and in 1772 was prohibited from preaching by jealous colleagues in the presbytery of Fordoun. Apart from the Stirling congregation, the only Bereans mentioned in this volume were a family in Baldernock[1].

Most of the longer accounts contain references to the antiquities and history of the parishes. The remains of the Antonine Wall, which ran across Scotland from the Forth to the Clyde, would certainly have been more evident in the eighteenth century than today but there is little information in the ministers' returns which is not more fully detailed in the descriptions of eighteenth-century antiquaries such as Gordon and Horsley. The Stirling minister refrained from dealing with the subject of antiquities. To do so, "however desirable, would only be to wander into a labyrinth of conjecture". The Kilsyth minister simply referred the reader to Horsley's *Britannia Romana* and Henry's *History of Great Britain,* while the Falkirk minister quoted at length from the latter. The minister of Kirkintilloch recorded the find of a stone with a legible inscription, which a German archaeologist, Hübner, has described as an impossible reading. The Old Kilpatrick minister mentioned the discovery of a bath-house near the Roman fort at Duntocher in 1775, but it is from another source that we learn of the finds made there in that year[2]. As for antiquities other than Roman, the ministers provided little information of value to the archaeologist of today. The medieval motte at Balcastle in the parish of Kilsyth was described as "perhaps the most beautiful, regular and entire of any Pictish fort in Scotland". The eighteenth century was the heyday of the romantically inclined antiquaries, and it is not surprising that the minister of Baldernock stated categorically that the group of rocks called the Auld Wives' Lifts

1. *Ibid.,* i, 84–87. The early Christians of Berea were commended for searching the scriptures to see if the things spoken by Paul were true (*Acts,* xvii, 11). The teachings of the Bereans are detailed by the minister of Crieff in the *Statistical Account* (Withrington and Grant), xii: N. & W. Perthshire, 295.
2. Falkirk, 325–327; Kilsyth, 485; Kirkintilloch, 74; Old Kilpatrick, 70; Sir George MacDonald, *The Roman Wall in Scotland* (1934), 294, 330.

was one of those "structures erected by the Druids in their sacred groves." Most fanciful of all are some of the suggested derivations of place-names; the Alva minister, however, wisely thought it better "to acknowledge ignorance than to offer what can neither amuse or inform"[1].

It is obvious from this survey of the parish accounts in this volume that they are not in all respects reliable sources of information; but almost every account contains references to curiosities not otherwise recorded. It is from the *Statistical Account* that we know that the water in Loch Lomond rose several feet and was "uncommonly agitated" at the time of the Lisbon earthquake in 1755; that the largest salmon taken in the River Leven weighed 45 pounds; that the island of Inchmurrin was used as a retreat for insane persons and pregnant ladies; that in an ash tree, 33 feet in circumference, the proprietor of Bonhill had constructed a round room over 8 feet in diameter; that rats could not live in the soil of Rosneath parish; that stilts were used by people in the parish of Dollar for crossing the River Devon; that during the construction of the Forth and Clyde Canal there was a plague of toads from Dullatur bog[2]. It is indeed possible to claim that this volume, although it requires to be supplemented in various respects, offers not only to the student of social and economic history but also to the general reader a uniquely rich fund of information about eighteenth century Scotland.

I. M. M. MACPHAIL

---

1.   Kilsyth, 484; Baldernock, 174; Alva, 141.
2.   Luss, 88; Bonhill, 10, 17, 20; Rosneath, 122; Dollar, 752; Kilsyth, 498.

APPENDIX I

liii

CLACKMANNANSHIRE

1791	Alloa	5816	4802[9]	5214	−17	−10
1791	Clackmannan	1913	2528	2961	+32	+55
1792	Dollar	517	510	693	−1	+34
1792	Tillicoultry	757	853[10]	916	+13	+21
		9003	8693	9784	−3	+9

SUMMARY TABLE

Dunbartonshire	13857	18728	20707	+35	+49
Stirlingshire	40798	48928	50769	+19	+24
Clackmannanshire	9003	8693	9784	−3	+9
	63658	75849	81260	+19	+28

†   The dates given in this first column indicate, as nearly as possible, the actual year in which the count of population was made. The parish account itself often gives this information; failing that, the date is either that indicated by Sinclair at the start of each volume of the published *Account* or is the date of publication of the appropriate volume in the 1790s. A figure with quotation marks in the listed populations for the 1790s indicates that the minister estimated rather than made a particular count of the number of inhabitants in his parish.

1.   The minister reported about 2000 examinables above 6 years old (that is, at an age capable of being examined on the Catechism): using Webster's formula for estimating the total population, we get 2323.

2.   The minister states that, by an exact list taken in 1788, the population was then 1664.

3.   An enumeration in December 1792 gave 1381 inhabitants: by Whitsunday 1793 a new printfield and bleachfield had brought in 200 more.

4.   In 1783 'the number of souls was then about 730'.

5.   In December 1783 the population was reported as 1627.

6.   The minister reports a population of 3000 above 12 years of age, "consequently about 4000 in all". Using Webster's formula (as in the case of examinables), the estimated total would be 4065 and this figure has been preferred.

7.   "About 30 years ago . . . it was reckoned that the souls contained in each of the three counties" in which the parish lies (Stirlingshire, Perthshire and Clackmannanshire) "amounted to about 500, making in all 1500".

8.   In 1790 the population amounted to 4483.

9.   In 1784 the number of inhabitants was reported to be 5025; in 1788 it was given as 5166.

10.   There had been 903 inhabitants in 1789.

APPENDIX II

DUMBARTON—DUNBARTONSHIRE

The spelling of the names, Dumbarton for the burgh and Dunbartonshire for the county, has been a subject of controversy for many years. In this volume both the burgh and county names appear almost invariably with the first syllable as "Dum", one of the few exceptions being in the account by Rev. James Oliphant, minister of Dumbarton, who spelt the first syllable as "Dun". Of the other eleven ministers in the county, all but one used the prefix "Dum" for both names.

The earliest forms of the name in medieval charters, "Dunbritan" and "Dunbretane", represent a phonetic rendering of the Gaelic *Dun Breatann*, "fortress of the Britons". Before the end of the thirteenth century, the first syllable had already changed to "Dum", and although the name is found also with the prefix "Dun" thereafter, by the beginning of the seventeenth century forms with "Dum" had become standard in all state documents referring to the burgh or the shire—acts of parliament, the register of the privy council, the register of the Great Seal; and it is "Dumbartane" which appears in the royal charter of confirmation of 1609. From the middle of the seventeenth century until 1716, the town clerks of Dumbarton actually wrote the name as "Dunbritan", presumably basing their spelling on that of the early charters, which were frequently consulted in connection with the protracted disputes with Glasgow over trading privileges.

Standardisation of spelling was not regarded as important until comparatively recent times but by the middle of the eighteenth century "Dumbarton" and "Dumbartonshire" had become standard in each of their official applications, although at times there appeared variants such as "Dunbritton" and "Dunbarton". Such variants were used by some of the county gentry, who presumably prided themselves on knowing the derivation of the name. They made no distinction however between the burgh and the shire names; and, indeed, as there was only an inchoate county administration, the form "Dunbarton" appears mainly in reference to the town or castle in the eighteenth century. From the county gentry were appointed the commissioners of supply, who in their infrequent deliberations began to use the "Dun-" spelling, and also the turnpike trustees who set up milestones still to be seen, with "Dunbarton Cross" on them. The spelling used by Rev. James Oliphant for the town, shire and presbytery was therefore not in ordinary use at the time but its appearance in the *Statistical Account* conferred a semi-official cachet upon it. On the other hand, in the *General Views of the Agriculture* of the county, produced for the Board of Agriculture, the "Dum-" spelling was used for both town and county, and in the *New Statistical Account* of 1845 the "Dum-" spelling was invariably used for both names.

By the middle of the nineteenth century the "Dum-" form was standard for both town and shire names—in acts of parliament, parliamentary elections, law courts, registration of births, etc., atlases, the press— but the commissioners of supply still clung to what they (wrongly) regarded as the old spelling. The county council, which was authorised by act of parliament in 1889 for "Dumbartonshire", inherited not only some of the responsibilities of the commissioners of supply but also their spelling. After a few years, however, they illogically restricted the "Dun-" spelling to the county name and accepted the "Dum-" spelling for the burgh's name. In the 1930s, the county council managed to persuade the Director General of the Ordnance Survey to change the spelling on O.S. maps to "Dunbartonshire". After representation by the town clerk of Dumbarton, the Director General admitted that a mistake had been made and agreed to restore the old spelling but later decided to defer a change until agreement had been reached between the parties concerned. The Ordnance Survey spelling is universally regarded as authoritative and as a result the "Dun-" spelling has now become almost standard, although it was not until the 1960s that Glasgow and Dumbarton newspapers changed to the new form. For the sheriffdom and the register of sasines, the old "Dum-" spelling is still used in referring to the shire.

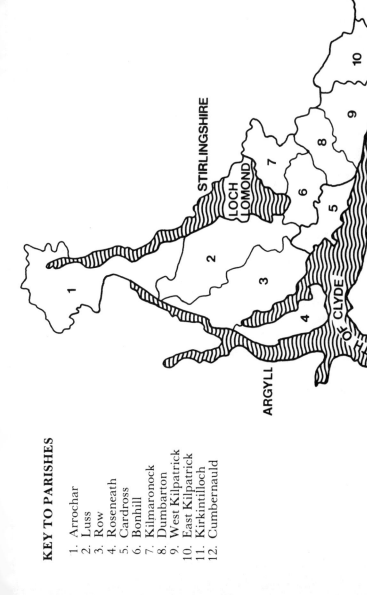

DUNBARTONSHIRE

STIRLINGSHIRE

LANARKSHIRE

RENFREWSHIRE

ARGYLL

LOCH LOMOND

FRITH OF CLYDE

KEY TO PARISHES

1. Arrochar
2. Luss
3. Row
4. Roseneath
5. Cardross
6. Bonhill
7. Kilmaronock
8. Dumbarton
9. West Kilpatrick
10. East Kilpatrick
11. Kirkintilloch
12. Cumbernauld

PARISH OF ARROQUHAR.

(County of Dumbarton.)

By the Rev. Mr JOHN GILLESPIE, *Minifter of that Parifh.*

Name, Situation, and Extent.

ARROQUHAR is a Celtic word, which fignifies a high or hilly country. It is generally pronounced, in the Gaelic language, *Arrar*, which is a contraction of *Ardthir*, *ard* fignifying high, and *thir* a country. The name is very defcriptive of the place, which is high and mountainous, having very little flat or arable ground in it. The extent of the parifh is near 14 miles long, exclufive of 4 farms, which lie on the eaft fide of Lochlomond, near the north end of it. The mean breadth may be computed at 3 miles. It is fitu- ated in the county and prefbytery of Dumbarton, and in the fynod of Glafgow and Ayr.

Soil, Climate, and Difeafes.—The furface of fome of the farms is fmooth, and clothed with a beautiful verdure, inter- mixed with heath and bent ; of others rocky, but the inter- mediate fpaces afford excellent pafture for fheep When the pafturing of black cattle prevailed here, the furface was moft- ly covered with heath, and had a difmal appearance ; but fince the introduction of fheep, the country has affumed a different afpect. The climate is very temperate in this place,

it

it being fcreened by the mountains from the northerly and eafterly winds, the cold in winter is not fo intenfe as in the low country ; but there are frequent and heavy falls of rain fiom the fouth and fouth-weft, accompanied with high winds. There are no local diftempers prevalent here, except fevers, to which the poorer people are fubject at the latter end of winter and beginning of fpring. With refpect to the fmall-pox, the people begin now to fee the advantages of inoculation, and to be more reconciled to it, though it is not yet much practifed among the lower clafs.

Sheep, Horfes, &c.—The number of fheep in the parifh amounts to about 10,600 ; horfes, 60 ; black cattle, 460. The fheep, in general, are black faced, and of the Linton kind. The white wool has fold here, thefe two years paft, at about 7 s. *per* ftone of 24 lib. Englifh weight, and the laid at 5 s. On an average, 8 or 9 fleeces of the white, and 5 or 6 of the laid wool go to the ftone. If a premium were given annually for the beft tups, there would be a competition, and confequently a confiderable improvement made both on the fheep and wool. It is expected, that the Hon. Board of Truftees in Edinburgh, will give the fame encouragement to this diftrict of the county of Dumbarton, for the improvement of the breed of fheep, that they give to fome other counties in the Highlands of Scotland.

Trees.—There is a confiderable deal of oak growing in this parifh, on the banks of Lochlomond. But as the woods are generally cut about 20 or 24 years of age, there is no great timber in them, except fome ftandards left at laft cutting.

Population.

Population.—In the month of March 1791, there were living in the pariſh of Arroquhar 379 perſons, of whom there were,

Under 10 years of age, -	105
Above 10, - - -	274
Total,	379

Abſtract of Births and Marriages for the laſt ſix Years, as entered in the Pariſh Regiſter.

	Births.	Marriages.
1785	11	8
1786	10	6
1787	11	5
1788	19	4
1789	9	4
1790	18	3
	78	30

From the above it appears, that there are, upon an average, 13 baptiſms, and 5 marriages annually. From the year 1769, to 1775, the average of baptiſms is nearly 12; but the marriages do not amount to 1 yearly. Hence it appears, that the population of this pariſh, ſince 1769, has increaſed, which is owing, probably, to the high price of labour, and the encouragement given to tradeſmen and day labourers to reſide in it. There has been, however, a decreaſe of 87 upon the whole, within theſe 40 years, as the return to Dr Webſter, in 1755, was 466. There is no regiſter of burials kept in the pariſh.

Heritors,

Heritors, Rent, &c.—There are only two heritors, one of whom is proprietor of nearly the whole parifh, but does not refide in it. The rent, after Whitfunday next, will be near 1200 l. Sterling. The farms, which were let in leafe about 7 years ago, and, fince that time, pay, on an average, double the former rent, and are ftill increafing in value. After the introduction of fheep into this country, the proprietors found it their intereft, to let as much ground to one man as he could ftock, fo that the principal farms in this parifh and neighbourhood are in the hands of a few. One man pof-feffes now what was formerly thought fufficient for 5 or 6 tenants, and yet the condition of the lower clafs is not ren-dered worfe. About 40 years ago, fome of the tenants could afford to pay very little more than the public burdens for thefe farms, which now pay a high rent to the proprietor. Formerly, every tackfman was bound to perform work with men and horfes, a certain number of days yearly, or to pay fo much in lieu thereof, in the option of the mafter ; but in moft of the leafes, which have been granted of late, thefe perfonal fervices, and the other cafualties payable by the te-nants, are converted into cafh, and included in the rent.

Occupations.—The fmall tenants and cottagers find employ-ment, either in repairing the high roads along with the mili-tary, building dykes, manufacturing timber and barks in woods, or at the herring fifhing, which they generally at-tend, from the beginning of harveft till New Year's day.

Prices of Labour.—On an average, the wages of a man fer-vant are 1 s. a day, from the beginning of February till the beginning of November, without victuals. The day's wages of a wright are 1 s. ; of a taylor 8 d.; of a carpenter 1 s. 6 d. ; of a fhoemaker 8 d. ; and of a mower of hay 1 s. befides

ſides their maintenance. The wages of women ſervants, in general, .re 3 d. a day; but in harveſt 6 d. excluſive of their victuals. When they eat in their maſter's houſe, they receive, on an average 3 l. a year, and the men ſervants, about 6 l. In this pariſh they all eat in the houſe, except ſhepherds, who live at a diſtant corner of the farm. Theſe have a benefit from the maſter, that is to ſay, a houſe, 52 ſtones of meal, 2 cows grafs, ground for potatoes, and grafs for 60 ſheep in the hill, which may amount in all to 14 l. or 15 l. Sterling *per annum.*

Church.—The pariſh of Arroquhar was originally an appendage of the pariſh of Lufs, and was disjoined from it in the year 1658. The ſtipend, including the glebe, is below the *minimum.* The manſe, which is in bad repair, was built in the year 1754. Sir James Colquhoun of Lufs, Bart. is patron.

Poor.—The number of poor, upon the roll at preſent, is 9. The weekly collections amount to about 7 l. Sterling a year, which are diſtributed, together with the intereſt of 50 l. Sterling, left to the poor of the pariſh, by the late Robert Carmichael of Broomly, and the intereſt of another ſmall ſum appropriated for their benefit.

Fiſh.—The fiſh, which frequent Lochlong, are cod, haddocks, ſeath, lythe, whitings, flounders, mackarel, trouts, and herrings. Nobody in this place, a few individuals excepted, give themſelves the trouble of fiſhing any of theſe ſpecies, but the latter, which are ſometimes got in abundance. For theſe two ſeaſons paſt, each man employed in the herring fiſhing, has cleared 8 l. on an average, between the middle of harveſt and the 1ſt of January.

Fuel.—The common fuel is peats, which are got in abundance in the hills. But it fometimes happens, that after all the expence and trouble of cafting and fitting them up, the feafon may be fo wet as to put it out of the power of the tenants to get them home. The better fort of farmers, who live near Lochlong, make ufe of coals, which coft about 5 s. 6 d. the Glafgow cart, including freight, &c. It is believed, upon the whole, every thing being confidered, that they are cheaper than peats.

Prices of Provifions.—The average price of oat meal may be eftimated at 1 s. *per* peck. Sometimes Irifh meal is imported into Lochlong, and fold under that price; but meal manufactured in the country is often above it. The average price of butter is 9 d. *per* lib.; of common cheefe, 5 s. the ftone tron weight; of a hen 1 s.; and of eggs, 3 d. the dozen. The price of beef is regulated by the Glafgow and Dumbarton markets.

Roads and Bridges.—The principal roads and bridges in this parifh are kept in repair at the expence of government. The line of road, which leads to Inverary, being the moft public, is kept in good order; but the line from Tarbert, leading to Tyndrum, is much neglected. In feveral places, particularly at the point of *Farkin,* and at *Craig-an-aren,* the road has been ill planned. Inftead of bringing it up a fteep hill, it fhould have been brought, at both places, round the point along the fide of the loch, which would not have been much longer, and might have been executed at nearly as little expence as the prefent line. It is much wifhed, that the roads in thefe places may be foon altered, and the pulls taken off, which are fo inconvenient for travellers, and fo oppreffive to horfes. The other roads are kept in repair at the expence

pence of the tenants and cottagers. Laſt year the former were affeſſed at the rate of 11 s. for every 30 l. of real rent. This affeſſment varies according to circumſtances. The *ul-timatum* is 12 s. for every ploughgate, or 30 l. Sterling of rent, which the commiſſioners of ſupply cannot exceed. The latter pay from 1 s. 6 d. to 2 s. 6 d. according to their abilities. The bye-roads in Arroquhar might be kept in good repair with the one half of the money levied in it, or perhaps with leſs; notwithſtanding, the affeſſment is as high as it is in theſe pariſhes within the diſtrict, where the roads are bad, (the truſtees having it in their power, to appropriate the ſurplus money to any other part of the diſtrict, where they think it neceſſary), which is conſidered as a grievance.

Poſts.—Every night, about 8 o'clock, (Wedneſday excepted), a poſt arrives from Inverary, and another, at the ſame time, from Dumbarton. Theſe are ſucceeded by other two, who wait their arrival, and ſet out ſoon after with the mails. They meet near the head of Lochlong, where they are all ſtationed, (which is half way between the poſt towns, or 22 miles diſtant from each), and ſucceed one another alternately. There being no allowance made for horſes, they are obliged to travel on foot, which is a laborious taſk in winter. It very rarely happens, however, that the ſnow is ſo deep on the road as to ſtop travellers. In March 1782, the communication between Dumbarton and Inverary was interrupted for a few days; but ſuch a fall of ſnow, ſo uncommon at that ſeaſon, may not happen again in a century.

Language.—Both the Gaelic and Engliſh languages are ſpoken here. The former is moſt prevalent, and is beſt underſtood, particularly by the old people. The names of places are Gaelic, and deſcriptive of their local ſituation.

General

General Character.—The greater part of the people in the
parifh are *Macfarlanes,* who have always had, till of late, a
ftrong attachment to the laird, as their chief; and while this
fubfifted, mifanthropy and ferocity of manners were prominent features in their character. Several circumftances, however have occurred, to deftroy the influence of the feudal
fyftem in this place. The military roads, which were made
after the year 1745, opened a free communication with other
parts of the kingdom, and an intercourfe with ftrangers.
The confequence of this was, that the mind expanded by
degrees, to embrace, within its grafp, people of other denominations, and to weaken that prejudice which it conceived
in favour of an individual, and a particular clan. The fet-
tlement of fome graziers here, from the low country, contributed likewife to produce thofe happy effects. They were
at firft confidered by the natives as aliens, and invaders of
property, to which they had no natural right, being neither
lineal defcendents, nor collateral branches of the Macfarlane
race. Such was their antipathy to their new neighbours,
that they made feveral abortive attempts to extirpate them.
This, however, gradually fubfided, and they lived together
afterwards in habits of friendfhip. The fale of the eftate
of Arroquhar, which happened fome years ago, contributed
alfo not a little to extinguifh the remains of that fyftem of
barbarity, which fo long retarded the progrefs of civilization
in Europe. In proportion as it loft its influence, the manners
of the people changed to the better. They are now civil,
well bred, honeft, induftrious, and not addicted to an immo-
derate ufe of fpirituous liquors.

PARISH OF BONHIL.

(*County of Dumbarton.*)

By the Rev. Mr GORDON STEWART, *Miniſter of that Pariſh.*

Name, Situation, Extent, &c.

THE pariſh of Bonhil is ſituated in the county and preſbytery of Dumbarton. It is 4 and one half miles in length, and about 4 miles in breadth, forming nearly a ſquare. The ancient mode of ſpelling the name of the pariſh was *Buneil*, which, in the opinion of ſome judges of the Gaelic language, means a *bottom* or *hollow*. Others imagine, that it ſignifies the *ſurgeon's reſidence*, as the antient family of Lennox had a manſion houſe in the pariſh, and ſeveral places derive their names from their ſervants and dependants. Bonhil was erected into a pariſh by that family *. The original diſtrict was very ſmall, and, about the middle of the laſt century, lands were disjoined from the pariſhes of Luſs and Kilmarnock, and annexed to that of Bonhil.

The

* The time of its erection is mentioned either in Keith's Hiſtory of the Biſhops, or in Duncan Stewart's Hiſtory of the Stewarts, vol. 2d. The three Tullicheum, Stockragent, Cameron, and Auchindinnans, were disjoined from the pariſh of Luſs ; the lands of Balloch, Ledreſtbeg, Bellagan, and Blurhich, were disjoined from the pariſh of Kilmarnock.

The fouth end of Loch-Lomond is furrounded by part of it; but a defcription of that lake will more properly belong to another parifh. This part of the lake, with the Leven which iffues from it, divide the parifh nearly into two equal parts.

River.—The Leven, though not fo large as the Tweed or the Tay, may be reckoned amongft the large rivers in Scotland. It is remarkable for the foftnefs of its water, and the clearnefs of its ftream. Thofe who are judges of the Gaelic language, derive its name from the words *Le,* which fignifies *fmooth* or *foft*, and *Avon*, a *river.* It iffues from Loch-Lomond at Balloch, and falls into the Frith of Clyde at Dumbarton Caftle. In a ftreight line from the lake to the Clyde, it will meafure about 5 miles; but the courfe of the Leven, owing to its windings, will be more than 9 miles. The fall from the lake to the Clyde is 22 feet. The river is notwithftanding navigable for one half of the year. The tide comes up the river more than a third of its length; and where the tide fails, the veffels are drawn up the river with horfes. Thefe veffels are conftructed long and narrow, on purpofe for the navigation of the Leven, in order to draw little water. They are chiefly employed in bringing coals and lime, and other heavy articles, to the manufacturers, and to the gentlemen who refide upon the banks of the Leven and of the lake; and in carrying down the wood and barks that grow upon the banks, with flates from the flate quarries in the parifh of Lufs.

Fifh.—The Leven produces falmon, parr, and a variety of trout, and other fmall fifh. The falmon it produces are reckoned among the beft in Scotland. Whether this is owing to the fhortnefs of the run from the fea, or their coming

ing into the river early in the ſeaſon, is uncertain. When
the ſeaſon is mild, there are ſalmon in the river in the end
of December. The greateſt number is taken in the months
of March and April. The largeſt ſalmon ever taken in the
Leven weighed 45 lib. troy weight. The ſalmon fiſhing in
that part of the Leven which lies in the pariſh of Bonhil,
rented, about 50 years ago, at 300 merks. The laſt leaſe was at
the rate of 150 l. Sterling. This riſe of rent has not been owing to the increaſe of ſalmon in the river; but has principally
ariſen from two cauſes, the great riſe in the price of ſalmon,
and the greater attention that has been paid to the fiſhery,
with the improved methods which have been adopted. The
price of ſalmon here depends upon the Edinburgh and Glaſgow markets. In the beginning of the ſeaſon, or before the
firſt of May, a conſiderable quantity are ſent over land to
Perth, and from thence to London.

There is at preſent ·a law ſuit depending about the right to
the trout fiſhings in the Leven. The queſtion is, whether a
charter from the Crown, granting the ſalmon and *other* fiſhings
in the Leven, gives an excluſive right to the trout fiſhings ? Or
whether trouts are to be reckoned among the *res nullius,* or
to be conſidered as annexed to land, and that every proprietor has a right to the trout fiſhing oppoſite to his property ?

Population.—The return to Dr Webſter, in 1755, was 901
ſouls. From a liſt of the inhabitants, taken in January 1791,
it appears that they amounted to 2310 in all. Of that number there were 562 under 10 years of age. In the year 1790,
there were 82 births, 47 burials, and 21 marriages, whereof
there were only 9 inſtances, in which both parties belonged
to the pariſh. There is an imperfect record of births, as far
back as the year 1677, from which it appears, that there
were

were 38 births that year. The population of the parish has been since decreasing, until 1768, when the first printfield was erected. There were only 27 births that year, and, by a list of the inhabitants, taken in 1769, the population was about 640 above 6 years of age. It has varied since 1768, according to the briskness or dulness of manufactures; and therefore, if the list of the inhabitants had been taken during the summer, the population would have been about 100 souls more than are above stated.

Professions.—Of the above number there are 993 employed by the three printfields, whereof 507 are women; besides 67 boys and girls under 10 years of age. It is not easy to state the number employed at the bleachfields, as it varies so much at different seasons of the year. Besides these, there are 7 smiths, 15 shoemakers, 12 taylors, 21 wrights, and 6 millers of different kinds; 2 distillers, 4 excise officers, 8 shopkeepers, and 14 keepers of alehouses.

Manufactures.—Some peculiar excellencies in the water of Leven, have encouraged several manufacturers to settle in this parish. The Leven is remarkable for the softness of its water, which fits it, in a peculiar manner, for the purposes of bleaching. It is seldom or never muddy, as the rivers and burns, from the Highland hills, fall first into Loch-Lomond, where the mud they carry along with them subsides. It is not, therefore, subject to the sudden risings and fallings which most other rivers are liable to. By gradually rising and falling, it is fitted for the different kinds of machinery, which are so convenient and necessary for carrying on the manufactures. There are at present 3 printfields, and 4 bleachfields in the parish. The duties paid to government from them for one year, ending 5th July 1790, amounted to

8971 l.

8971 l. 9 s.; thofe of this laft year, ending 5th July 1791, to 13,296 l. 8 s. 4 d.; from which it is evident, that the trade has increafed rapidly. From thefe duties, a calculation may be made of the value of the goods manufactured. By a ftatement laid before the Houfe of Commons, a few years ago, the duties upon printed linens and muflins were fuppofed to be equal to 10 *per cent.* of the whole value. There can be no calculation made of the value of the goods bleached on the banks of the river.

The firft printfield on the Leven was begun about the year 1768; the other two were erected a few years ago. At firft, the printing bufinefs was almoft wholly confined to handkerchiefs, and in thefe no great variety of colours was attempted; it was all done by what is called block printing. They afterwards erected copperplate preffes. Thefe preffes were at firft driven by the hand; but as they required great force, the man who drove the prefs was obliged to reft frequently: This kept the other 2 idle, for there were 3 men employed about every prefs. To remedy this, they have conftructed fome preffes to be driven by water, one of which, driven by 2 men, can print from 20 to 30 dozen of handkerchiefs in one hour. Thefe preffes, at firft, were almoft wholly employed in printing handkerchiefs; but of late they have improved them, fo as to print two or more colours upon their fineft linens and muflins, leaving the fprigs and flowers to be put on afterwards by the block printers. At the printfields upon the Leven, they have contrived, of late, to do a great deal of work by machinery driven by water, which formerly was done by the hand, and at great expence. Their calicoes, for variety and finenefs of colour, are reckoned the firft in Britain; the neighbourhood of London itfelf can fcarcely be excepted.

Wages.

Wages.—For fome years after the firft printfield was erected, the bufinefs was conducted upon a fmall fcale, and that
part of it, which is properly called the printing, was almoft
wholly done by apprentices, bound for the term of 7 years,
at the rate of 3 s. *per* week for the firft 3 years, and 4 s. for
the laft 4 years. The common labourers had, in general,
10 d. *per* day. Some years ago, feveral new printfields were
erected in Scotland, and the trade came to be greatly extended and improved by the old ones, which occafioning a great
demand for journeymen, their wages rofe amazingly. For
fome years paft, the wages of a journeyman may be ftated at
18 s. *per* week ; and thofe of a common labourer at the printfields, may be reckoned at 6 s. *per* week. Thofe who have
acquired any degree of fkill in bleaching or dying, may get
about 7 s. weekly.

Of the hands employed at the printfields, there is nearly
an equal number of both fexes. The wages given to
the women, at firft, were generally at the rate of 3 s. *per*
week. They are now in general paid by the piece, and they
may be faid to earn 14 s. *per* month, at an average. The
greater part of the women are employed in pencilling. A
great variety of colours cannot be put upon the printed cloth
without the affiftance of the pencil. The boys and girls
have, in general, 6 s. 8 d. *per* month ; a very few of them
have 8 s.

Formerly, the operative manufacturers were employed by
their mafters at day's wages ; but the mafters, for fome time
paft, have found it their intereft to give fo much money for
the piece of work, and to leave it to the operative hands to
do much or little as they choofe. As foon as the trade came
to be put upon this footing, fome of the operative people
difcovered

difcovered amazing induftry, and made very great wages; al-though the mafters had the fame quantity of work done for lefs money, than formerly when the men were at days wages. For thefe two years paft, however, there have been violent difputes between the mafters and fervants, about the prices for the different pieces of work; the mafters, on the one hand endeavouring to reduce the prices, and to lower the wages, to what they thought the trade could bear; and the fervants, on the other, endeavouring to keep up the prices, and entering into thofe illegal combinations, that are now be-come fo common among the manufacturers of this country. Among other manoeuvres, they appointed a committee of their number, from the different printfields in the weft of Scot-land, to meet and to regulate the prices, which they were to o-blige their mafters to give for the different pieces of work. They were to allow no perfons to be employed, but fuch as came under certain regulations which they had framed; and, that the number of hands might not increafe too faft, the mafters were not to be allowed to take in more apprentices, than the operative fervants thought proper. Thefe meafures obliged the mafters to commence profecutions, and to imprifon fome of their hands laft fummer, and a kind of compromife has been made between the mafters and fervants for a time; but it will be eafily forefeen, that one of the parties muft be in complete fubjection to the other, before the trade can be up-on a proper or fure footing. The apprentices to the print-ing bufinefs are, after the firft or fecond year, generally em-ployed at piece work; and, from the prices that are allowed them, they can make from 8 s. to 10 s. *per* week.

Manners.—From this change in the wages of the manu-facturers upon the banks of the Leven, it will be eafily fup-pofed, that their manners and mode of living has undergone
fome

fome change. At firft they were remarkable for fobriety : Their principal food was porridge and potatoes; even milk and bread was confidered as a luxury. They difplayed their zeal and their learning in declaiming againft patronage and Arminian preaching; and the man who was able to fpare fome money to fupport a diffenting clergyman, came to confider himfelf as a man of confequence. In procefs of time religious difputes came in fome meafure to be neglected or forgotten; and then, like moft other manufacturers, they came to be extravagant in the articles of drefs, tea, and fpiritous liquors, &c. They are only beginning, however, to ufe butcher meat. It may appear paradoxical, but it is a fact, that among the common labourers, who receive moderate wages, there are many who fave a little money ; whereas, among thofe who receive great wages, fuch inftances are more rare.

Villages.—There are two villages built in the parifh, befides feveral houfes built upon feus, or long leafes, by the manufacturers adjoining the printfields. In one of the villages, the houfes are built upon feus, at the rate of 8 l. *per* acre ; in the other, upon a leafe of 99 years, at the rate of 6 l. *per* acre. The grounds occupied by the printfields and bleachfields, are feued at the rate of 2 l. 10 s. *per* acre. Some of the ground, adjacent to the villages and printfields, is rented at 2 l. *per* acre.

Rent.—The valued rent of the parifh is 2180 l. 9 s. 2 d. Scotch. It is impoffible to fay exactly what the real rent may be, as a great deal of the land is in the proprietor's own hands ; but it is fuppofed to be about 2500 l. Sterling.

Soil and Produce.—The parifh is all inclofed and fubdivided. The foil, as in moft others, is various. The low ground,

upon

upon the banks of the Leven and the lake, is partly a rich loam, and partly a light gravel. The rising ground is more wet, and tilly, and some part of it covered with heath. The produce of the ground is barley or bear, oats, pease, potatoes, and turnips, with a small quantity of wheat and flax; but the greater part of the land is either under hay, or in pasture.

Wood.—There are about 250 acres planted with Scotch firs and larix. A cutting of the natural wood, at 20 years of age, is worth about 2350 l. Sterling. The ash tree, in the church yard of Bonhill, deferves a particular description, being no less remarkable for its uncommon fize, than for its extensive spreading, and the regularity of its branches. The trunk is 9 feet in length, the girth, immediately above the furface of the ground, is 25 feet; about 3 feet above the surface it measures 19½ feet; and, at the narrowest part, 18 feet. It divides into 3 great branches; the girth of the largest is 11 feet; of the second, 10; and of the third, 9 feet 2 inches. The branches hang down to within a few feet of the ground, and, from the extremity of the branches on the one fide, to that of those on the other, it measures no less than 94 feet. There is another large ash tree in the parifh, though it is greatly decayed, only the trunk, and part of fome of the branches remaining. The trunk is about 11 feet in length; the girth, immediately above the furface of the ground, is 33 feet; at the narroweft part it meafures 19 feet 10 inches. The proprietor has lately fitted up a room in the infide of it, with benches around, and 3 glass windows. The diameter of the room is 8 feet 5 inches, and from 10 to 11 feet high.

Mills.

Mills.—There are 3 corn mills in the parish; at one of which they have erected machinery for making pearl barley, and for grinding wheat and madder. There is likewise a mill for dreffing flax, and they are erecting machinery for grinding logwood.

Cattle.—There are about 160 horfes, and about 100 fheep in the parish; but it is impoffible to fay any thing with certainty refpecting the number of black cattle, as it varies fo much at the different feafons of the year, many being brought from the Highlands in the beginning of fummer, and flaughtered in the end of the feafon.

Ecclefiaftical State and School.—The ftipend is 82½ bolls of victual, and about 27 l. in money, paid by a decreet in the year 1654. The kirk was built in the year 1747, and the manfe in the 1758. The Duke of Montrofe is patron The fchoolmafter's falary is 200 merks. There is no diffenting meeting houfe in the parish; but there is a kirk of relief in the neighbouring parish of Kilmarnock, which is attended by 210 perfons, above 6 years of age, from this parish. There is alfo a Burgher Seceding meeting houfe in the parish of Cardrofs, which is frequented by 180 perfons from that of Bonhill. There are likewife a few Antiburgher Seceders, and 6 or 7 Covenanters.

Heritors.—The number of heritors is 27, the greater part of whom have but fmall properties; the reft being divided among 9 or 10, who generally refide, the greater part of the year, in the parish.

Poor.—The number of poor is from 30 to 35. The funds for fupporting them are, a capital of fomething above 300 l.
Sterling,

Sterling, which is lent out at intereſt; and the ordinary collections in church, with the mort-cloth dues, and the fines
for fornication, which amount in all to 40 l. or 50 l. Sterling
a year.

Fuel.—The companies get their coals by water. A cart,
weighing 12 cwt. coſts 5 s. Sterling. The operatives, who
get them in ſmall quantities, and by land, from Dumbarton,
pay 6 s. *per* cart. The farmers carry their coals in carts about
13 or 14 miles, and pay 2 s. 6 d. at the pit. Coals are alſo
got ſome miles nearer, but of an inferior quality, at 18 d. *per*
cart at the pit.

Antiquities.—The antient family of Lennox had a manſion
houſe at the ſouth end of Loch-Lomond; but nothing remains at preſent but the foſſé, which is ſtill entire. The tradition is, that the materials of the manſion were carried from
this place to one of the iſlands of the lake, to build a caſtle
there, as a place of greater ſafety, and where a conſiderable
part of the building ſtill remains, though in ruins. They
had another houſe in the pariſh, which is entire, and is at
preſent poſſeſſed by Mr Yule of Darleith. From its ſituation, and from the ſmallneſs of its ſize, it is ſuppoſed to have
been kept as a hunting ſeat. There is no inſcription to aſcertain the date; but it is believed to have been built by the
antient family of Lennox, before the eſtate came into the
poſſeſſion of the Stewarts. The whole lands in the pariſh
formerly belonged to the family of Lennox; but in the 15th
century, the Darnly family, by marriage, got one half of the
eſtate, and the titles. The other half went to the Ruſky
family. This laſt half was afterwards divided between the
families of Napier and Gleneagles. The Darnly family got
the greateſt part of this pariſh. That of Gleneagles got
fome

fome farms, whereof they are ftill in poffeffion of the fuperiority, along with confiderable feu duties.

Mifcellaneous Obfervations.—The oldeft inhabitant at prefent in this parifh, is a man of 87 years of age.—There are two licenced diftillers in it.—The woods are famous for the number of woodcocks that frequent them during winter; and the river and lake for a great variety of fea fowl. In fevere feafons fwans frequent the lake.—Inchmarin, one of the iflands in Lochlomond, is at an equal diftance from the parifhes of Bonhill, Lufs, Kilmarnock, and Buchanan. Some parts of Lennoxfhire, now Dumbartonfhire, were formerly annexed to Stirlingfhire. From this circumftance, it is not determined to what county it belongs; and as it pays no ftipend, it is equally undetermined to what parifh. It is the largeft ifland in the lake; is about 2 miles long, and from half a mile to one mile broad. It is beautiful, and finely wooded. The Montrofe family ufe it as a deer park, where they keep about 200 fallow deer. The ruins of the caftle, formerly belonging to the Lennox family, are ftill upon this Ifland The perfon, who has the charge of the woods and the deer, refides with his family upon it. Some years ago, many perfons difordered in their fenfes, were fent to it as to a place of confinement; and thofe of the fair fex, who were fo unfortunate as to give *pregnant* proofs of their frailty, were fent here to avoid the reproach of the world. At that time the neighbouring clergyman, who happened to be a ftrict difciplinarian, and very zealous againft fornicators, claimed Inchmarin as belonging to his charge: But owing to complaints of abufe, the proprietor, for fome time paft, has not allowed his forrefter to take lodgers.

PARISH OF CARDROSS.

(COUNTY AND PRESBYTERY OF DUMBARTON—SYNOD
OF GLASGOW AND AYR.)

By the Rev. Mr ALEXANDER M'AULAY, *Minifter.*

Situation, Extent, Rivers, Surface, and Soil.

CARDROSS is wafhed on the eaft border by the river Leven, and on the fouth by the Frith of Clyde. Its
length, from Dumbarton Bridge to its boundary with the parifh of Row, is about 7 miles; its breadth, from the conflux
of the Leven and Clyde to its junction with the parifh of
Bonhill, is 3 miles. The fituation of the parifh is peculiarly
beautiful: The Clyde runs for 7 miles along its coaft, and,
being partly oppofite to the flourifhing towns of Port-Glafgow and Greenock, it commands a profpect of the whole
fhipping, that great fource of induftry and wealth to the
weftern part of Scotland. The ground along the Frith has a
gradual afcent from the fhore, for upwards of two miles, till
it terminates in a ridge of hills, which feparate it from the
lands in the neighbourhood of Leven and Loch-Lomond. The
foil contiguous to the fhore is of a light gravelly nature; but,
at a fhort diftance, it contains a confiderable mixture of clay.
The lands adjacent to the Leven partake fomething of the
nature of carfe.

Agriculture.

Agriculture.—Farming has not yet made that progreſs, which, from the advantageous ſituation of the pariſh, might have been expected. It has, however, for theſe 10 years paſt, been making rapid advances. In order to promote this, the proprietors have contributed much. Beſides their own example, which ſeldom fails to produce in the end the beſt effects, they have incloſed almoſt the whole grounds, and laid them out, in many places, in ſuch diviſions and ſubdiviſions, as are beſt ſuited to their reſpective farms. Farmers, and, indeed, men of every deſcription, overcome with difficulty prejudices which they have early imbibed. Theſe prejudices operate as a ſecond nature, and, for a long time, bid defiance to the ſoundeſt arguments. It is a practice in this pariſh with many, of never beginning to plough till the 10th day of March. However inviting the ſeaſon may be prior to this period, it matters nothing ; they adhere to the cuſtom of their fathers. To begin ſooner, it is thought, would prove detrimental to the ſoil, and injurious to the enſuing crop. This late plowing occaſions a late ſeed-time, and of courſe a late harveſt, a circumſtance which is, for the moſt part, accompanied with many diſadvantages This prejudice, however, is beginning gradually to loſe its influence, and in a ſhort time, it is hoped, it will be effectually removed.

Produce.—The common produce of the pariſh is oats and bear ; and, of late, where the ſoil is of a ſtronger quality, conſiderable crops of wheat, peaſe, and beans are raiſed. Potatoes are every where cultivated. The farmers, within theſe few years, have begun to ſee the advantage of green crops ; accordingly a number of fields are laid down in clover and rye-graſs, but the culture of turnips is only in its infancy.

Manure.

Manure.—There is plenty of lime-ftone on the lands of Camis-Eſkan, the property of the family of Colgrain : Large quantities are regularly burnt, with which the neighbourhood is ſupplied. The expence of burning is confiderable, as the coal is brought by water from Glaſgow, at the rate of between 5 s. and 6 s. the 12 cwt. On the ſhore there is a good deal of ſea ware driven in, during the winter and ſpring, which is carefully collected, and when laid upon lee ground proves an excellent manure. Befides this, which is called *blown ware*, large quantities of it are cut every third year. This, adhering to the ſtones and rocks within water-mark, grows in three years to a confiderable length, and contains a greater abundance of thoſe ſalts and juices which promote vegetation. As Cardrofs lies oppofite to Port-Glaſgow and Greenock, and as the Frith is only from 2 to 4 miles in breadth, there is an eaſy acceſs by water to theſe towns. In confequence of this, it has become an object of great importance to the farmer to import from them ſtreet dung; and, although this is done at great expence, each full cart, including every charge, amounting at leaſt to 2 s. Sterling, yet the returns amply compenfate the whole trouble and outlay.

Draining, &c.—Few of the farmers in this parifh are poffeffed of a capital, ſufficient for carrying on extenfive improvements. They with difficulty ſtock their farms, which are rented in general from 20 l. to 50 l. Sterling. They embrace the readieft methods in their power, of raiſing articles to pay their rents, and cannot afford to wait thoſe diftant, though ſure returns, with which the improving farmer muft lay his account. Before this parifh can be improved, a large capital muft be employed in draining. The climate, like that of every other parifh near the mouth of the Clyde, is wet. In confequence of the heavy, and almoft inceffant rains,
which

which fall in the harveſt and winter months, the lands are
for a long time drenched in water, and, of courſe, rendered
much leſs valuable both to the proprietor and tenant. Nothing but draining can remove this inconvenience, and facilitate improvement; and as the proprietors are chiefly intereſted in this, their exertions, it is hoped, will every day be
more and more employed to promote ſo important an end.

Cattle.—Formerly almoſt every farmer kept a few ſheep;
but now, excepting on three farms, this practice is entirely
given over. Too little attention, in general, is given to the
breed of milk cows. It is alſo a practice too much followed, to overſtock the ground; in conſequence of which, the
growth of the cows is injured, and the produce of the dairy
diminiſhed. The breed of horſes is greatly improved. Their
price, in the Glaſgow market, is from 15 l. to 30 l. Sterling.

Farm Houſes.—It muſt afford great pleaſure to the traveller
to obſerve the neat farm houſes, which are interſperſed
through this country. In this pariſh they are every year increaſing in number, a circumſtance which does no ſmall credit to the proprietors. Sir ARCHIBALD EDMONSTON of
Duntreath, Bart. member of Parliament for Dunbarton.ſhire,
in this, and, indeed, in every other pariſh where his extenſive property lies, has furniſhed an example, which, it is hoped, will ſoon be generally followed. His tenants are all well
lodged, and, comparatively ſpeaking, elegantly. Inſtead of
the old low-built and confined houſes, which their fathers inhabited, Sir Archibald has given them houſes and offices
ſuited to their reſpective farms, upon a plan, which conveys
an idea of neatneſs and improvement that is highly pleaſing.

Woods

Woods and Fuel.—The natural wood is confiderable; it will bring, at a cutting, betwixt 2000 l. and 3000 l. Sterling. Befides this, there are nearly 200 acres planted with Scotch firs, larixes, &c. Thefe plantations are all fucceeding well, and being laid out with judgment and tafte, give an appearance of improvement to the country, which cannot fail to pleafe. Coal is the principal fuel, 12 cwt. of which, brought by water, cofts in the Cardrofs Bay, where it is unloaded, 5 s. Sterling. Many of the farmers bring their coals from Kilpatrick, and pay at the pit 2 s. per cart. Attempts have been made to find coal in this parifh, but as yet they have proved unfuccefsful.

Rents, Proprietors, &c.—The valued rent is 3000 l. Scotch. It is difficult to fay what the real rent amounts to, as many of the proprietors retain confiderable farms in their own hands. The value of land, however, muft be on the rife. The great influx of ftrangers, in confequence of the manufactures upon the Leven, occafions an increafing demand for whatever the parifh produces. Thus the farmers find a ready and convenient market at home, a circumftance which cannot fail to accelerate the improvement of the country, and increafe the real rent of the proprietors. In the neighbourhood of the Leven, many inclofures are let upon leafes, for between 2 l. and 4 l. Sterling per acre. There are 13 heritors, 3 of whom poffefs more than two thirds of the whole.

Roads.—The two great roads through the parifh, the one leading to Loch-Lomond, the other running along the Clyde, are kept in the beft poffible repair. To thefe the ftatute labour, now commuted, is annually applied. Great praife, however, cannot be beftowed on the crofs or parifh roads. But as the commiffioners muft be fenfible of the neceffity of

crofs

crofs roads for the improvement of the country, no exertion, we are convinced, will be wanting on their part to promote fo laudable an end.

Population.—The population has of late greatly increafed. From a lift taken in November 1793, it appears there were no fewer than - - - - 2194 fouls.
The return to Dr Webfter, in 1755, was only 795

Increafe within thefe 38 years 1399

Of the above number there are
Children under 10 years of age - - 614
Ditto above that age - - - - 482
Heads of families, including both hufbands and
wives - - - - 847
Hired fervants - - - - 251

2194

In the village of Renton, about - - 1200
In the reft of the parifh - - - 994

2194

	Births *.	Marriages.
Regiftered in 1791	75	17
—————— in 1792	60	21

Print-fields.—The print-fields of *Dalquburn* † and *Cordale* are by far the moft confiderable and extenfive of any in Scotland.

---

* It is difficult accurately to afcertain the number of children that are annually born, as many, who are not of the eftablifhment, neglect their regiftration. There is no regifter of deaths.

† The ground, now occupied by the former, was early in this century fet apart chiefly for a bleach-field. A few coarfe handkerchiefs,

land. Meffrs Stirlings, who purchafed this field from the
original proprietors, are well known. At firft they had a
field at Dafholm, in the neighbourhood of Glafgow, where
they carried on the bufinefs of printing to a confiderable extent. Upwards of 20 years ago, they removed from that fituation to the river Leven in this parifh. To this they
might have been led by a variety of circumftances, but by
nothing more than by the foftnefs and tranfparency of the
water of the Leven, fo peculiarly fitted for the purpofe of
bleaching. A neck of land, in the form of a peninfula, occafioned, it would appear, by the river forfaking its former
channel, was the place marked out as the moft proper to anfwer the end which they propofed. Accordingly, in 1772,
a purchafe was made of this fpot, called *Cordale*, and upon
it houfes have been built, and machinery conftructed, to an
extent, and upon a plan, which muft have coft the company
an amazing fum.—At thefe fields, the property of this company, there were employed, in fummer 1792, 876 perfons.
Of thefe 300 were girls (*pincellers*), and about 130 were
boys, from 8 to 15 years of age. It may be proper to obferve, that the boys are in general healthy, active, and ly,
having nothing of that pale and fickly look, which common
marks thofe boys who are employed in the cotton fpinning.
The wages for one month, July 1792, amounted to within a
trifle of 1000 l. Sterling. It would be to no purpofe to enter here into a minute detail ; the Statiftical Account of the
parifh

kerchiefs, it is true, were then printed ; but nothing fine or valuable in the printing line was carried on, till about 20 years
ago, when it was purchafed by a company in Glafgow, under
the firm of M‘Alpine, Fleeming, and Co. Buildings were raifed, and machinery conftructed, by this company, at great expence ; an extenfive capital was employed, and every appearance
promifed fuccefs. This flattering profpect, however, was foon
clouded. Difputes arifing among the partners produced a fale
of the property, and a diffolution of the company.

pariſh of Bonhill, already publiſhed, contains all the neceſſary information: To it the reader is referred . Suffice it to
obſerve, that every diviſion of labour takes place at theſe two
fields, which is known to facilitate the work, and to carry
the art to a high degree of perfection. The goods manufactured are ſaid to rival, in the London market, to which
moſt of them are ſent, even thoſe of the fineſt quality that
are the manufacture of the firſt print-fields in England.

Villages.—In the year 1782, the hands employed at the
above fields had become ſo numerous, that it was extremely
difficult to accommodate them, in houſes and lodging in the
neighbourhood. Mrs SMOLLETT of Bonhill, whoſe lands
lay moſt contiguous, readily embraced this opportunity of
improving her family eſtate, and of accommodating the public. Accordingly, a village was planned by the advice, and
under the direction of her ſon, now her ſucceſſor. No ſooner
was this plan adjuſted, and the terms of building fixed upon,
which are from 9 d. to 14 d. the fall, upon transferable leaſes
of 99 years, than a great number of ſteadings were purchaſed, and houſes immediately built. The firſt ſtone was laid
in 1782, and the village was called *Rentoun* by the feuers, in
compliment to the preſent Mrs Smollet, who had been active
in encouraging an undertaking of ſuch importance, both to
her family and to the public. Since the above period, the
village has rapidly increaſed. It conſiſts of three principal
ſtreets, which run in a direction from north to ſouth, parallel to one another. Theſe again are interſected by a number
of other ſtreets, all laid off at regular diſtances. The demand for houſes, every where upon the Leven, has, within
theſe few years paſt, been very great. In conſequence of
this, beſides the village of Rentoun, a number of houſes have
been

been built in this parifh, op ofite to Dumbarton, upon feus from Mr Dennilton of Colgrain; and a village is juft now begun upon the property of Mr Graham of Grmore, which it is probable, when the prefent ftagnation of bufinefs is over, will faft increafe in population.

Diftillery, Mills, Ferries, &c.—There is one diftillery, which confumes of the produce of the parifh about 500 bolls of bear and barley. The number of public houfes, or rather whifky fhops, has of late been greatly diminifhed. The Juftices have for this year given licence to only two in the village of Rentoun, to fell fpirits of home produce. There are three corn mills, at two of which the multure on the aftrieted lands, is nearly in the proportion of one peck and an half the boil, confifting of 8 ftones. This proves a great difcouragement to improvement. There are 4 different ferries, two of thefe are of great antiquity, as appears from the charters of the proprietors. The prices of labour, victuals, &c. are nearly the fame as in Glafgow and its neighbourhood.

Fifheries.—The *Zair* or *Yair Fifhings*, fo productive in this parifh, feem to be almoft peculiar to it. A yare is built of ftones gathered from the tide water mark, about 4 feet in height, and of confiderable length, and ftretces out into the river in the form of a crefcent, or of three fides of a fquare; but to give it a probability of fucceeding, it muft proceed from a point of land, fo as to inclofe a bay. The diftance which it is extended from the fhore is fuch, as to make it appear, or to *crown*, as the fifhers term it, about two hours before low water. Were it placed farther into the fea, or built higher, the furf would be continually beating it down. In fpring tides, the water retiring quickly, great quantities of fifh, particularly herrings, are occafionally taken within
thefe

these inclosures ; and salmon, in small quantities, during the spring and summer months. Along the Cardross shore there are many such inclosures, but those most happily situated are the properties of Mr Denniftoun of Colgrain, and Mr Noble of Noble-Farm. The rights to these yare fishings prove them to be of very high antiquity, being granted by crown charters above 500 years ago, and confirmed by all subsequent charters. By these, the proprietors of the soil have the right of exercising yare fishings upon the shore to low water-mark. Some of these rights extend as far as a man can ride beyond low water, and from that throw a twelve-feet spear. This extent of shore, during the herring season, is attentively guarded, that the fish which may entrap themselves in these yares, may neither be alarmed by, nor taken in the nets of the boat-fishers.—It is remarked, from the earliest accounts of this kind of fishing, that the herrings visit the river Clyde, at nearly 3 equal periods in 100 years, each period consisting of several years fishing. The mode of securing what fish may be in the yares, is with a hand-net. By ancient custom, two thirds belong to the yare proprietor, and one third to the fisher, if a tenant upon the adjoining lands. But when strangers are permitted to fish, they have only one fourth part of their success allowed them.

Church, &c.—The church of Cardross originally stood in the eastern extremity of the parish, opposite to Dumbarton, and separated from it by the river Leven. This situation must have been very inconvenient to the parish, and therefore, in 1643, a new church was built in the place where it now stands, the most centrical, indeed, that could have been chosen, and the most convenient to the parish at large. The church is a neat building, well lighted and well seated. It underwent a complete repair in 1775, and, by the care and attention

attention of the heritors, it is kept in the beft poffible order. The manfe was built about 60 years ago; fince that period it has undergone frequent repairs. Upon the fucceffion of the prefent incumbent, in 1791, the heritors, with the greateft franknefs, laid out 200 l. Sterling in repairing of the manfe and offices. The crown is patron, and the minifter titular. Cardrofs is one of the few parifhes in Scotland, where the right of titular is vefted in the incumbent. From a late inveftigation, in afcertaining the right of patronage, it appears, that it was neither a menial church, nor ever annexed to any religious houfe, and therefore, as the Crown is patron, it continues at this day precifely in the fame ftate as before the Reformation; with this difference only, that there has been a dilapidation of 11 bolls of meal. Befide the parifh church, there are other two houfes for public worfhip; the one of the Burgher perfuafion in the village of Rentoun; the other of the Relief, lately built in the neighbourhood of Dumbarton. Thefe diffenters confift chiefly of people connected with the printfields. The farmers, in general, are attached to the eftablifhment.

School.—The fchoolmafter draws no falary from the heritors. The emoluments of his office arife from his fchool, which, at an average, may be frequented by 40 or 50 fcholars, and from a donation of the family of Kilmahew. This donation confifts in the yearly payment of 5 l. being the intereft of 100 l Sterling funk for the behoof of the fchoolmafter, and placed under the management of the heritors. Befides this fum, which was bequeathed for the above purpofe by a younger branch of the family, the proprietor himfelf executed a deed, difponing to the public teacher a right to an acre of land, a cow's pafture upon a fpecified farm, and 5 bolls 1 firlot of bear, payable from certain other farms upon

on the eſtate of Kilmahew.   Over and above the fees for
teaching, and the ſaid donation, the perquiſites of ſeſſion-
clerk may be equal, *communibus annis*, to 5 l. Sterling.

Poor.—The poor are ſupplied from two ſources—from the
weekly colʼeĉtion, which, with the proclamation money, may
amount annually to upwards of 30 l. Sterling; and from a
legacy bequeathed a few years after the Revolution, by a Mrs
Muir, a native of this pariſh, and originally of the name of
Watſon.   This legacy conſiſted of 500 l. Sterling, to be applied under the direĉtion of the uſual managers of the poor,
for the behoof of the indigent living within a certain diſtriĉt
of the pariſh, ſpecially named in the deed of mortification.
The above ſum was, early in this century, laid out in the purchaſe of land, which by the laſt let, produces a revenue upwards
of 70 l. Sterling *per annum*.   There are no begging poor, and
the heritors have never as yet been ſubjĉted to any aſſeſſment.   The number upon the ſeſſion roll varies, but, in general, there are a dozen and upwards, who receive quarterly
a ſmall contribution.   The number entitled to the benefit of
Mrs Muir's mortification alſo varies according to circumſtances.

Eminent Men.—Contiguous to the village of Rentoun, in
the old houſe of Dalquhurn, was born the celebrated Dr
Tobias Smollett.   He was the grandſon of Sir James
Smollett of Bonhill, Bart. a gentleman of conſiderable property in this county, a member of the laſt Scotch Parliament, and a commiſſioner in framing the Union.   The father of Tobias being a younger ſon, received, according to
the cuſtom of his country, only a ſmall ſhare of Sir James's
fortune, and, dying at an early period of life, left his family,
conſiſting of two ſons and a daughter, in circumſtances not
the

the moft affluent. The two brothers received the rudiments
of their education in the fchool of Dumbarton. The elder,
whofe name was James, was bred a foldier, and amongft his
acquaintance was diftinguifhed for his addrefs, and thofe talents of wit and humour, which afterwards charaCterifed
Tobias. A premature death, (he having perifhed at fea off
the coaft of America), robbed the world of thofe talents,
which, if ripened by time and ftudy, might have fhone forth
with diftinguifhed luftre. Tobias, the younger, was educated
in the medical line, ferved an apprenticefhip to a furgeon in
Glafgow, and foon after aCted as mate aboard a man of war.
In this capacity he was prefent at the fiege of Carthagena,
the particulars of which he defcribes in *Roderick Random*
with fo much life. Tobias could not long continue in this
fituation. His afpiring genius difdained the drudgery to
which his profeffional line expofed him. He was a man of
the moft polifhed manners, and fineft addrefs, talents which
feldom fail to recommend the phyfician. But with thefe he
poffeffed a pride which counteraCted their influence. He
could not ftoop to that infinuating flattery fo prevalent in
the world, of which even the wife and knowing have often
become the dupes. His mind was chiefly turned to the ftudy
of life and manners, in delineating which he is perhaps furpaffed by few. In this particular, as a painter of life and
character, he has refleCted the higheft honour upon the place
of his nativity, and muft ever be confidered by his country
among the firft of her fons in literary reputation. As a hiftorian, he may be inferior to Hume and Robertfon in refinement of thought, and political obfervation; but when the
fubjeCt leads to defcription, or to the delineation of character,
his powers appear unrivalled. To the greateft genius, he
joined the moft unremitting application. One proof of this
cannot fail to be noticed, which is, that in lefs than 14 months
he

he collected materials, compoſed, and prepared for the preſs, his whole Hiſtory of England : An effort to which his narrow and ſtraitened circumſtances might have directed him, but to which nothing but the moſt diſtinguiſhed abilities, and the moſt vigorous application, could have been equal. He married a Jamaica lady, and by her had an only daughter, who was cut off in the bloom of youth. After a life chequered by a variety of incidents, he died at Leghorn, whither he had gone for the recovery of his health, in 1771, in the 51ſt year of his age. Adjacent to the place of his nativity, a column was lately raiſed to his memory by his couſin, with the following inſcription :

Siſte viator !
Si lepores, ingeniique venam benignam ;
Si morum calidiſſimum pictorem,
Unquam es miratus,
Immorare paululum memoriae
Toʙiæ Smollett, M. D.
Viri virtutibus hiſce
Quas in homine et cive,
Et laudes et imiteris,
Haud mediocriter ornati ;
Qui in literis variis verſatus,
Poſtquam, felicitate ſibi propria,
Seſe poſteris commendaverat,
Morte acerba raptus,
Anno aetatis 51.
Eheu ! quam procul a patria,
Prope liburni portem in Italia,
Jacet ſepultus:
Tali tantoque viro, patrueli ſuo,
Cui, in decurſu, Lampada

Se

Se potius tradidiffe decuit,
Hanc columnam.
Amoris eheu! mane monumentum,
In ipfis Leviniae ripis
Quas, verficuiis, fub exitu vitae, illuftratas,
Primis, infans, vagitibus perfonuit,
Ponendam curavit
JACOBUS SMOLLETT de Bonhill.

Antiquities.—A little weft of the Leven, upon a fmall eminence called *Caftle hill*, ftood, it is faid, a caftle, at times the
refidence of King Robert Bruce. In this caftle, of which
no veftige is now difcernible, that favourite prince, as hiftory
and tradition informs us, breathed his laft. A farm in the
neighbourhood ftill pays to the fuperior a feu-duty called
dog-meal. This tax is fuppofed to have been originally impofed for the maintenance of his Majefty's hounds.

Character.—The people in general are fober and induftrious. The introduction of manufactures has, no doubt,
produced fome change in their habits and manners; and
whether this change may operate more in the end to their
advantage or hurt, time alone can determine.

PARISH OF CUMBERNAULD.

(PRESBYTERY OF GLASGOW, SYNOD OF GLASGOW
AND AIR, COUNTY OF DUMBARTON.)

By the Rev. MR. WILLIAM STUART.

Name, Extent, &c.

CUMBERNAULD is of Celtic derivation ; *cumar an alt* in that language fignifying a meeting of ftreams ; and there is a remarkable collection of fprings and ftreams, flowing in all directions, part running into the Forth and part into the Clyde, within the bounds of this pariſh, which extends 7 miles in length, and 4 in breadth. The furface has a romantic appearance, being beautifully variegated by fmall hills and dales. The higheft part of the pariſh is Fanny-fide-muir, a very deep mofs, bearing nothing but heath, well ſtocked with muir-fowl. On the fouth fide are two lochs, about a mile long, and a quarter of a mile broad. The remainder of the pariſh is moſtly arable ground, chiefly a heavy clay, though fome farms are of a light early foil ; the climate is ſharp and cold in the winter feafon, but in fummer it is generally tolerably

ably

ably agreeable, efpecially about the village of Cumbernauld, which lies in a hollow, almoft furrounded with the policy or pleafure ground belonging to Cumbernauld houfe, a fine feat of Lord Elphinftone.—This parifh and that of Kirkintilloch formerly conftituted one parifh, called Lenzie.

Natural Productions.—There is abundance of coal in the north part of the parifh, but none of it is wrought at prefent: there is alfo a good deal of peats. Seven lime quarries are wrought in different parts of the parifh : Much of the lime is carried by the great canal to Glafgow and other places; and there is abundance of whin, moor, and free ftone. The chief vegetable productions are oats, a confiderable quantity of bear, a few peafe and beans, a good deal of flax and potatoes, a fmall quantity of wheat, and a few turnips.

Population, Ecclefiaftical State, &c.—According to Dr. Webfter, the total number of inhabitants in this parifh in 1755 amounted to 2303, at prefent the number is reduced to about 1600. There are about 56 births and 14 marriages in the year. The church was built in 1659, Lord Elphinftone is patron. In the parifh are two meeting houfes, one of that fect of Seceders called Burghers, the other of the Antiburghers. There is a fchool-houfe and garden in Cumbernauld village, where above 80 fcholars are annually educated. The funds for the maintenance of the poor arife chiefly from weekly collections at the church doors.

Mifcellaneous Obfervations. —The roads are kept in repair by affeffment. A new turnpike road from Edinburgh to Glafgow was lately carried through this parifh, paffing by the village of Cumbernauld, near which a large commodious inn

was

was erected at the expence of L. 1000. Confiderable remains of the celebrated Roman wall, called Graham's Dyke, are to be feen in the north part of the parifh, as alfo veftiges of the military road running parallel to it. Many curious antiquities have been found near them, particularly at Caftlecary; and on the rock at Croyhill, the marks of fire are ftill vifible, faid to have been applied by the Romans for the purpofe of foftening the ftone, which is exceffively hard. The great canal betwixt the Forth and Clyde paffes through the north part of the parifh, near the dyke. In the neighbourhood of Caftlecary is a pretty high water fall.

PARISH OF DUNBARTON.

(COUNTY OF DUNBARTON.)

By the Rev. Mr JAMES OLIPHANT.

Name, Situation, Soil, &c.

THE ancient name of the parish was *Dun britton*, a Gaelic compound, fignifying " the fortification of the Bri-" tons;" whence it appears that the caftle has given name to the parifh. This caftle, fituated on a moft remarkable bitopped infulated rocky hill, at the junction of the Clyde and Leven, is too well known to be particularly mentioned here. The parifh lies in the county of Dunbarton, is the feat of a prefbytery, and belongs to the Synod of Glafgow and Ayr. The form is nearly circular, extending in length from 2 to 3 miles, and in breadth from 1 to 2. Great part of the parifh is flat, the remainder afcends gradually to the neighbouring hills, with a fouthern expofure. The parifh is bounded by the frith of Clyde on the fouth, the water of Leven and parifh of Cardrofs on the weft, the parifh of Bonhill on the north, and that of Weft Kilpatrick on the eaft.

Soil, &c.—The foil is fertile, but rather fhallow. The air falubrious, excepting at times when a heavy fog rifes from and hovers over the Clyde and Leven. Fevers prevail very much. Many die of confumptions, and the natural fmall pox is very mortal. The fpreading and mortality of thefe

difeafes

difeafes are to be attributed to ill-aired and crowded low houfes, and to an over anxiety for conftant prayers over the difeafed.

Rivers and fiſh.—The Leven is navigable by coafting vef-fels above the town of Dunbarton ; fo far up the tides rife. Salmon and trout are taken in large quantities. The former frequently fells fo high as 1 s. 6 d. *per* lb. tron, on the fpot, feldom falls below 6 d, and never below 4 d. Through the whole fpring feafon, the Leven falmon is excellent, but the Clyde is not fiſhed before Whitfunday. Trout generally fells at 4 d. *per* pound. Very large eels, and a large fpe-cies of flounder, are often caught by the falmon-fiſhers. A fpecies of fea animals, moſt deſtructive of the fal-mon, are almoſt every fummer feafon found in num-bers, playing in the Clyde off the caſtle ; they go up fome-times two miles higher, but generally keep lower down. Thefe are called buckers, pellocks, or porpoifes. The fal-mon fiſhery employs 16 men.

Population.—According to the returns made from hence to Dr Webſter about 1750, this pariſh then contained 1427 fouls. In 1790, the number of examinable perfons above fix years of age was found to amount to about 2000 (103 above 70 years of age, and two near 100,) of whom 1850 refided in the town of Dunbarton, and 153 in the country part of the pariſh. In that year 86 were baptifed, 58 were buried, and 30 couples married. From the regi-fters, it appears, that in 1644, 44 died ; in 1654, 33, in 1664, 42 : In 1690, 73 were baptifed, 50 died, and 12 couples were married. The increafe of population is to be attributed to the eftabliſhment of glafs-works in the town, and of printfields in the neighbourhood. Almoſt the whole

of

of the inhabitants are of the eftablifhed church, there not being above half a dozen feeders in the parifh.

Manufactures.—The minifter's daughters manufacture nuns thread to a great extent. There is in the town a confiderable crown and bottle glafs manufactory, which employs 130 hands, and pays L. 3,800 *per annum*, of duties to Government. The extenfive printfields in the neighbouring parifhes employ about 86 inhabitants of the town of Dunbarton.

Town of Dunbarton.—This town was erected into a royal burgh by King Alexander the II. in 1221 ; it lies on the eaft bank of the Leven, has a good harbour, where large brigs lie fafe in all weathers. About 2000 tons of fhipping belong to this place, which employ 70 feamen. The town is entirely free of all impofts or borough taxes ; but is by no means in a flourifhing or increafing ftate, owing to the letters of deaconry preventing ftrangers from working at their trades, without coftly entries. Several families have removed from Dunbarton to Renton, Bonhill, and other new villages, to be nearer the printfields where they are employed. There are about 130 handy-craftfmen, freemen of the burgh, befides the mafters of the tailor, hammerman, fhoemaker, weaver, and cooper trades.

Heritors, &c.—There are in the parifh 52 heritors, about 40 of whom refide ; 21 farmers, befides feveral fmall portioners, 130 handicraftfmen, 78 apprentices and journeymen, 2 ftudents of divinity, 1 minifter, 7 attornies, and 3 furgeons.

Productions, &c.—The productions of this parifh are wheat, oats, barley, and a little flax ; perhaps one third of

the

the ground may be in fown grafs and pafture, about 100
acres in growing woods and planting, and there may be
200 acres of commonty belonging to the town, to which
the burgeffes may fend their cows or horfes for about 7 s.
a year. The parifh does not fupply the tenth part of the
provifions confumed in it. Great quantities of corn, meal
and butter, are imported from Ireland, and of cheefe from
Ayrfhire. Eggs are generally fold at 4 d. the dozen, butter
9 d. the pound, beef 6 d. mutton 6 d. hens 1 s. each.

Wheat is fown in October, November, December, or
even January, and reaped generally in Auguft. Oats are
fown from the end of March, to the middle of April, and
reaped the end of Auguft, September, fometimes not till the
beginning of October. Barley is fown the end of May, or
beginning of June, and reaped in Auguft or September.

Rent.—Houfe rent is not low. The town's fifhing on
the Leven yields at prefent a rent of L. 55, and on the
Clyde, of L. 23 yearly The laft fet yielded L. 140 a
year, and thefe fifhings were once let fo high as L. 300
a-year. Small parcels of land are often transferred. A
piece of ground of four acres, lately fold here, brought a
price of L. 472; but that was a fingular cafe.

Fuel.—The fuel generally ufed is coal, brought from
Glafgow or Knightswood, four miles below that town:
A cart of coals, containing 12 cwt. cofts 3 s. 6 d. ready
money at Glafgow, pays 1 s. $1\frac{3}{4}$ d. of freight and dues, for
deepening the Clyde, and $1\frac{1}{2}$ d. cartage from the quay, total
4 s. $9\frac{1}{4}$ d. Peats are dear, 2 s. the fmall cart, and only ufed
for kindling the fire.

Stipend, &c.—The right of patronage to the church lies
in the magiftrates and town-council; the ftipend is, 100
bolls

bolls of meal, 20 bolls of barley, 6 ftone of falmon, and L. 27 in money, with L. 7 in lieu of a glebe. There never was a legal manfe here. Mr William Blair, who was minifter here in 1620, bequeathed a houfe for the refidence of his fucceffors in office in all time coming, on condition of the town-council's upholding the fame. This houfe was after-wards exchanged for a better, and the laft for one ftill more fo, above L. 150 having been given by the town for the excambions. The council alfo pay for communion-ele-ments, and for the whole reparations of the minifter's houfe, and of the fchool. The church and church-yard walls are kept in repair by the kirk-feffion.

Poor.—The number of poor receiving alms is about 70 ; the annual amount of contributions at the church-doors, for their fupport, is L. 53 or L. 54 ; the hire of the mort-cloths produces L. 7 or L. 8 ; about L. 6, 6s. are received by the publication of banns, and about L. 9 from the rent of feats in the church. Befides thefe, a large fum was bequeathed in 1660, by Sir John Buchanan of that ilk, to the poor of the parifh : Several loffes from the principal have been fuf-tained, but there ftill remains L. 851, the intereft of which (excepting L. 10, paid to two public fchoolmafters,) is re-ligioufly applied to the relief of the poor. Sir James Smol-let of Bonhill in 1732, mortified 50 merks a-year, to be diftributed immediately after the facrament, to fuch of the poor as were communicants. The whole annual diftribu-tions amount to above L. 110.

Prices of Labour.—Common labourers receive 1 s. a-day ; carpenters 1 s. 8 d. ; mafons fometimes 2 s. ; joiners 1 s. 6 d. ; tailors 8 d. and victuals ; linen-printers common-ly earn 21 s. a-week, not including extra work ; many of the glafs-houfe men 25 s. a-week ; girls flowering muflin can

make

make 1 s. a-day and upwards. Male-ſervants wages in general are high ; female-ſervants receive generally 30 s. the
half year, and ſome of them more. Common labourers
may bring up their familiesc omfortably, if they are induſtrious and temperate.

Advantages and Diſadvantages.—It is very advantageous
to the heritors and their tenants, that being ſo near a ſea-
port town, they have high prices, in ready money, for e-
very thing they raiſe, and are employed with their horſes,
almoſt as often as they chuſe, or can be ſpared from huſbandry. There are excellent roads through all the pariſh
made by the military, and no turnpikes, except one on
the way to Glaſgow. School fees are very low, ſo that almoſt
every perſon has an opportunity of following any branch
of learning. Packets ſail every day to Greenock and Port
Glaſgow ; and a ſtage-coach ſets out three times a-week to
Glaſgow. The chief diſadvantage is the high price of
fuel.

Miſcellaneous Obſervations.—The people are very fond of
a ſea-faring life ; many enliſt in the army, chiefly in the
artillery, and in the highland regiments. The advantages
of ſociety are enjoyed ; but here, as in many other places, a murmuring ſpirit often appears, and a diſpoſition
to cenſure public meaſures. Many of the people are
expenſive, eſpecially in the article of whiſky. There
are three fairs held in this pariſh, at which there uſed to be
expoſed great quantities of linen-yarn ; numbers of ſheep,
cows, horſes, and great herds of highland cattle are ſtill ſold.
There is plenty of free ſtone, both of a white and red colour. The ſhore is flat and ſandy, not a ſtone to be ſeen a-
long it, except ſuch as have fallen from the caſtle-hill. The
common ſea-weed is often uſed for manure, by the farmers
neareſt to the coaſt.

PARISH OF KILMARONOCK.

*(County and Preſbytery of Dumbarton—Synod of Glaſgow
and Ayr.*

By the Rev. Mr. ANDREW WHITE, *Miniſter.*

Name, Erection, and Extent.

KILMARONOCK ſignifies the cell, chapel, or burying-
place of St. Maronoch, or St. Marnoch. About the
middle of laſt century, a conſiderable part of the pariſh was
disjoined from Kilmaronock, and annexed to Bonhill. Its preſent extent is about 5 miles in length, and from 2 to 4 miles
in breadth. From the Dumbarton moors, the ground has in
general a gentle declivity towards the north.

River, Lake, Hills, and Soil.—The windings of he river
Endrick, through a plain of more than 3000 acres, the Houſe
of Buchanan ſituated in the middle of the plain, with the extenſive lawns and foreſts belonging to the Duke of Montroſe,
preſent to the traveller through this pariſh a moſt beautiful
landſcape. Lochlomond, with its numerous iſlands and variegated banks, the ſurrounding hills, and towering moun-
ns,

tains, with the cloud-capt Benlomond, combine to render the fcenery very picturefque.—On the banks of the Endrick, the foil is a deep rich loam, very favourable for pafturage or tillage ; on the rifing ground above the plain, the foil is in general a cold wet till ; and, towards the moors, of a moffy quality.

Agriculture.—That there are feldom inftances of good hufbandry on fmall farms, except on foils of the greateft fertility, or where there is a command of manure, is a maxim which is verified in this parifh. Many of the farms are fo fmall, as to yield but a fcanty fubfiftence to the farmer ; and as no lime or ftimulating manures can be got but at a high price, little attention is paid to the melioration of foil, or rotation of crops. From the price of labour and manure, compared with the benefit of rearing and fattening cattle, fome of the moft judicious farmers, in this parifh and neighbourhood, find their intereft in having their grounds in pafture rather than tillage. But as agriculture is acknowledged to be the moft permanent bafis of the wealth of a country, it would certainly redound to the honour and intereft of gentlemen, who are poffeffed of large eftates, to exhibit a pattern of improvement ; or, if this is not found convenient, judicious and experienced farmers might be more encouraged, by letting leafes on one or more lives. Such a practice, it is evident, would be attended with the moft beneficial confequences ; at leaft, it would certainly be preferable to the cuftom, of granting leafes of arable farms for nine, or even nineteen years ; where the farmer no fooner begins to improve, than he purfues an oppofite fyftem, of exhaufting his farm by too frequent cropping, from the idea that he may be turned out at the expiration of the leafe, and a ftranger who offers more rent preferred.

Mill.

Mills and Multures.—There are three corn-mills in the parish ; the greateſt part of the lands are thirled, or aſtricted to one or other of theſe mills. The multure, in general, after a deduction of feed and horſe-corn, amounts to about a twelfth part of the crop ; a ſervitude not only highly oppreſſive to the farmer, but which has a tendency to prevent emulation among the millers, in the execution of their buſineſs.

Fiſheries.—The Endrick abounds, at certain feaſons, with ſalmons, pikes, trouts, perches, pars, &c. There is an excellent ſalmon fiſhery in Lochlomond, near the place where the Endrick diſcharges into the lake. As the ſalmon are not now interrupted in their courſe up the Leven, as formerly, the fiſheries, on the banks of the lake, are likely to turn out very profitable to the different proprietors.

Population.—The population of this pariſh is on the decline, chiefly owing to the increaſe of trade and manufactures at Bonhill and Balfron, where many of the people have ſettled. The return to Dr. Webſter, in 1755, was - 1193
From an enumeration in 1792, there were found to be only - - - - - - - - 820

Decreaſe, - - - - 373

Of theſe there were, below 10 years of age, - 210
The number of families was - - - - 175

No authentic account can be given of the births, as many of the people, and particularly the Diſſenters, decline to have them inſerted in the pariſh regiſter.

Heritors and Rent.—The number of heritors is 54. The greateſt part of them have but ſmall properties : 32 are reſident,

dent, and 22 non-refident. The valued rent is 3329l. 16s. 6d. Scotch : The real rent cannot be eafily afcertained, as a great part of the lands are in the hands of the proprietors.

Church and Schools.—The church has much the appearance of antiquity. The manfe was built in 1751, and fince that time it has been enlarged and repaired. The ftipend, by a late augmentation, befides the glebe, is 6 chalders of meal, 1 chalder of bear, and 40l. 5s. Sterling in money, including communion elements. Lord Stonefield is patron.—The parochial fchoolmafter has 100 merks falary. The number of fcholars is ufually about 40. His living is only about 15l. per annum. Befides the parochial fchool, there are generally other two. The fchoolmafter of one of them has 50 merks falary, befides fchool fees. If fome fuitable encouragement is not foon given to fchoolmafters, it is apprehended, that, in many places, the education of children will be totally neglected.

Prices of Labour, Fuel &c.—The wages of a good ploughman, for the year, befides board and lodging, are from 8l. to 12l. Sterling. Thofe of a woman fervant, for the year, befides board, are from 3l. to 4l. Sterling. The prices of provifions are nearly the fame with the Glafgow and Dumbarton markets.—Peats are the common fuel. Coals are brought from Kilpatrick, a diftance of 12 or 14 miles.

Roads.—The military road from Stirling to Dumbarton, after croffing the Endrick, by an excellent modern bridge, paffes, from E. to W., through the parifh. There is alfo an excellent turnpike road, which is now nearly completed, leading from this place by Eafter Kilpatrick to Glafgow.

Springs,

Springs, Woods, and Game.—Every field almoſt abounds with perennial ſprings, oozing from rocks of free-ſtone. Of theſe *St. Maronoch's Well* is the moſt famous. From the ſprings collected, ſmall rivulets run, interſecting the grounds, and render them very convenient for paſturage.—There are ſeveral woods in the pariſh, the value of which has conſiderably increaſed within theſe few years. The woods on the banks of Lochlomond, belonging to Miſs Buchanan of Drumkill, and John Buchanan, Eſq. of Ardoch, abound with woodcocks, in the beginning of winter.—The moors, on the confines of the pariſh, are much reſorted to by the ſportſmen, in the hunting ſeaſon. There is a general complaint, that the birds are much ſcarcer within theſe few years. This may be partly accounted for from the increaſe of the ſtock of ſheep, and the ſmall inducement the ſhepherds have to preſerve the game.

Antiquities.— There are the remains of 2 Romiſh chapels. At *Catter*, now the property of the Duke of MONTROSE, there is a large artificial mound of earth, where, in ancient times, courts were held; near to which the Duke of Lennox had a place of reſidence. There is not now the ſmalleſt veſtige of the building. The caſtles of Kilmaronock* and Batturret †, now in ruins, appear to have been formerly very magnificent edifices.

Miſcellaneous Obſervations.—There are no towns nor villages in the pariſh, nor any manufactures carried on. The

men

* The property of Robert M'Goune, Eſq. of Mains.
† The property of George Haldane, Eſq. of Gleneagles.

men are, in general, employed in hufbandry ; but, as the
farms are fmall, they are not oppreffed with hard labour.
The women are engaged in fpinning flax, or in work they
receive from manufacturers. The people are grave and fober;
but fome of them are rather difpofed to be litigious*.

* About the beginning of the prefent century, the parifh was much expofed
to the depredation of certain freebooters, who carried off the cattle, fo that the
farmers, for their protection engaged to pay them, or others, a certain tax, named
black meal, which was regularly exacted until 1745, when a better police was
eftablifhed.

PARISH OF NEW OR EAST KILPATRICK.

(Counties of Dunbarton and Stirling.—Prefbytery of Dunbarton.—Synod of Glafgow and Ayr.)

By the Reverend Mr GEORGE SYM.

Origin of the Name.

THIS parifh is called New, or Eaft Kilpatrick, relatively to Old, or Weft Kilpatrick, with which it formed one parifh till the year 1649, when a divifion and new erection took place. The name Kilpatrick, *Cella Patricii,* common to both, is derived from Patrick, the tutelary faint of Ireland, whom legends and tradition make a native of Kilpatrick. A writer quoted in *Britan. Eccles. Primordia,* fays, " Natale patricii folum inter caftrum Dunbritannicum et civitatem Glafcuenfem pofitum; accepto ab ipfo nomine Kirkpatrick vel Kilpatrick;" adding, that his father was a prefbyter, and grandfather a deacon, and that he was carried captive with his two fifters into Ireland, and fold to one of the petty princes of that country, who employed him as a fwine herd. But a local tradition informs us, that he was compelled to leave his native country by the malice and refentment of the Devil, who, provoked at his fanctity and fuccefs in preaching the gofpel, fent a band of witches againft him; that the weird-fifters fell upon him fo furioufly, that he was forced to feek fafety by flight; that finding a little

boat

boat near the mouth of the Clyde, he went into it and
ſet off for Ireland ; that they ſeeing it impoſſible to pur-
ſue him, for it ſeems they were not of that claſs of witches
who can ſkim along the waters in an egg ſhell, or ride
through the air on a broom ſtick, tore a huge piece of a rock
from a neighbouring hill, and hurled it, with deadly purpoſe,
after him ; but that, miſſing their aim, the ponderous maſs
fell harmleſs, and afterwards, with a little addition from art,
formed the Caſtle of Dunbarton. This ſurely is ſufficient
proof, that Kilpatrick both derives its name from, and gave
birth to, the celebrated ſaint of Ireland.

Number and Rent of Farms.—There are two large graſs
farms, which pay about 200 l. of rent each. Of corn farms
there are 6, at 100 l. or a little above—about 50 between
30 l. and 100 l.—and above 40 below 30 l. ; but among the
laſt are included a few cottage lands, each ſufficient only to
maintain a cow. Almoſt all thoſe above 30 l. and ſome alſo
of thoſe below it, employ a plough and 3 or 4 horſes ; and
two of the largeſt employ two ploughs each. All theſe are
excluſive of the lands occupied by the greater proprietors
themſelves, and by the tackſmen of bleachfields and mills.
Leaſes are commonly for 19 years. The average rent of arable land is about 15 s. *per* acre ; there is ſome at 30 s. and a
good deal below 12 s. Every new leaſe brings an addition of
rent to the landlord ; and hitherto few of the tenants have
reaſon to complain. In general they live much more comfortably, are better fed, better clothed, and better lodged,
than when they paid but the half of their preſent rent. The
raiſing of the rent has ſtimulated their induſtry, and their
induſtry is repaid in the enjoyment of more of the comforts
of life. And the generous landlord, it is to be hoped, will
never rapaciouſly extort from the huſbandman all that is not
neceſſary

neceffary to a bare fubfiftence. The farmers form the moft induftrious, fober, and ufeful clafs of men, and deferve more than any other liberal encouragement.

Mode of Farming, &c.—Though the farmers in this parifh have, of late years, made confiderable improvement in the knowledge and practice of agriculture, they ftill adhere pret-ty much to the old method ; the ftubborn nature of the foil, they fay, and probably with truth, does not wholly admit of the new.

The crops are wheat, oats, barley, peafe, beans, potatoes, turnip, flax, and clover and rye-grafs. Of wheat, very little is now fown, a fucceffion of unfavourable feafons having dif-couraged the culture of it. Peafe, beans, flax, and turnip, are alfo fown in but fmall quantities. The principal crops are oats, barley, potatoes, and clover and rye-grafs.

Till lately, very little land, except for fallow, was plowed before the month of January. It is a general opinion among the farmers here, that, unlefs the foil be dry, and free from tough-rooted weeds, winter plowing is prejudicial to the crop, wet clay land being apt to cake even after froft, and tough or dry-rooted weeds, which are not eafily deftroyed by froft, fprouting before the corn is fown, and therefore cho-king it the more readily after it is come up. They begin now, however, to give lefs weight to thefe objections.

The greater part of the farmers plow with three horfes, fome with four, and but very few with two only.

The ufual time of fowing wheat is October ; oats, peafe, and beans, from the beginning of March to the end of April ; and barley, clover, and rye-grafs, from the beginning to the middle of May. Potatoes are planted about the middle of April ; in large fields with the plough, in fmall plots with the dibble.

Hay

Hay harveſt begins about the middle of June; and corn harveſt ſometimes about the middle of Auguſt, though commonly later, and continues often till the beginning of November. From 200 to 300 ſtone *per* acre is reckoned a good crop of hay, and of oats and barley 7 or 8 bolls.

A few years ago, a club was formed by the farmers in this and other pariſhes in the neighbourhood of Glaſgow, for the purpoſe of promoting and diffuſing the knowledge of agriculture, which has probably had a very conſiderable effect: And, with a view of exciting emulation among their plowmen, they have begun to have annual plowing matches, at which premiums are given to thoſe that excel.

Number of Horſes, &c.—There are about 360 horſes, 1450 black cattle, and 150 ſheep. Of the black cattle, a conſiderable number are bought lean, in the Highlands, and fattened for the butchers. The price, when bought, from 2 l. 10 s. to 5 l.; when ſold, after being fed about a year, from 4 l. 10 s. to 8 l.

Air, Diſeaſes, &c.—The air is reckoned very wholeſome. There are no diſeaſes peculiar to the pariſh. Beſides the ſmall pox and chincough, the moſt common are fevers, conſumptions, hyſterics, and diarrhoeas, which, however, are not frequent. The ſmall-pox is leſs deſtructive now than formerly, from the more common practice of inoculation. The prejudices againſt that moſt ſucceſsful improvement in the medical art, though ſtill very prevalent, begin to wear off.

There are many inſtances of longevity. Within the laſt year, there died one man in his 95th year, who was able, within a few days of his death, to walk in a forenoon above a mile to a neighbouring farm, and return; another man in his 89th year; and a woman in her 91ſt: And there is now
living

living a man near 93, who reaps and threſhes his own corn, thatches his own houſe, and walks to Glaſgow, 5½ miles diſtant, and returns the ſame day.

Villages.—The only conſiderable village is Millguy, which contains about 200 inhabitants, who are moſtly employed as bleachers, printers, and pencillers of cloth.

Bleachfields.—There are ſix bleachfields, of which two are for printed cloths only, and one partly. All theſe together employ about 220 people.

Mills.—There are four oat mills, two barley mills, one ſnuff mill, and one paper mill. The paper mill employs three vats, and about 25 workmen. The kinds of paper made are poſt, foolſcap, pot, and lappings ; and the quantity about 2500 l. worth *per annum.*

Coal and Lime Works.—There are two colleries in the pariſh, one at Knightſwood, and the other at Culloch, which have both been wrought beyond the memory of any perſon alive.—The coal at Knightſwood is light and friable, very little ſulphureous, does not cake, burns quickly, and leaves a ſmall quantity of white aſhes. In digging for this coal, the ſtrata met with are, blue clay ; blaize ; hard white free-ſtone ; blaize, mixed with what the workmen call grey-plies, probably a ſpecies of *ſchiſtus cinereus ;* ſpungy white free-ſtone ; iron-ſtone three inches thick ; blaize, and grey-plies ; then the coal three feet four inches thick, with ſix inches of ſtone in the middle. Beſides the main coal, there are two thinner ſeams in the ſtrata of blaize above, not worth working. The main coal lies at various depths, from 18 to 50 fathoms, according to the height of the ground, the dip of the coal, and

the

the interruption of troubles.—The dip is from north-weſt to ſouth-eaſt. The price of a cart of coals of 12 cwt. at this work is 2 s. 6 d.; and about 26,000 carts are ſold annually. The coal is nearly exhauſted in Knightſwood lands, but it extends through thoſe in the neighbourhood. This colliery employs about 60 men and boys, and 20 horſes.

At Culloch the coal is more heavy, leſs inflammable, and conſiderably ſulphureous. The ſmall coal cakes ſtrongly; the great leaves a ſlag, with a great deal of brown aſhes. It is, however, a good ſtrong coal, and, mixed with that of Knightſwood, makes an excellent fire. The ſtrata here are clay; blaize, with ſeveral ſeams of ironſtone through it, ſome 4 inches thick; limeſtone, from 3 to 4½ feet thick; then the coal, from 4½ to 5 feet thick. The price of the cart of 12 cwt. is 2 s.; and about 13,000 carts are put out in a year, a great part of which is uſed in burning the limeſtone. The depth of the coal is from 13 to 36 fathoms, and the dip from north-weſt to ſouth-eaſt.

At Culloch is alſo the only limework in the pariſh. The limeſtone is wrought after the coal has been taken out from below it. It is burnt in draw-kilns, of which two, capable of burning each 20 chalders a-day have been lately erected. The lime is of an excellent quality, and is ſold at 10 s. *per* chalder of 32 wheat buſhels. About 3000 chalders are made annually. At this place the lime and coal works together employ about 70 men and 20 horſes, and they are both on the increaſe.

Heritors, Valuation, and Rental —The pariſh is divided a-mong nine greater, and eight ſmaller proprietors. Of the former, five reſide conſtantly or occaſionally; all the latter conſtantly. The valued rent of the whole is 5311 l. 16 s. 2 d. Scots, and the real rent may be about 5000 l. Sterling.

Church,

Church, &c.—The Duke of Montrofe is patron of the pa-rifh. The minifter's ftipend confifts of 70 bolls 3 ⁹₂ pecks of meal, 10 bolls of bear, 45 l. 16 s. 8 d. Sterling money, a manfe, and a glebe of 4 acres.

Schools.—There is a parifh fchool, with a falary of 100 l. Scots. The fees are, for Englifh, 1 s. 6 d.; for writing, 2 s.; and for arithmetic, 3 s. *per* quarter. Poor fcholars are paid for by the feffion out of the poor's funds. The number of fcholars is, at an average, about 40. Befides this there is another, attended by an equal number of fcholars, but with-out a falary, at the village of Millguy; and a houfe is now building for a third in the north part of the parifh. There is alfo one in the borders of Old Kilpatrick for the accom-modation of the eaft part of that, and the weft part of this parifh, to the fupport of which the feffions of both parifhes contribute a fmall fum annually.

Price of Labour, &c.—The wages of fervants living in their mafter's family are, a good plowman, 12 l.; a common farm-fervant, 9 l. or 10 l.; and a maid-fervant, 3 l. or 4 l. a-year. Thofe of day-labourers employed conftantly, 10 d. but more generally 1 s.; of day-labourers employed occafionally, 14 d. in winter, and 18 d. in fummer; of mafons, from 20 d. to 2 s.; and of wrights, 18 d. to 20 d. The price of labour has rifen greatly within thefe four or five years, from the great demand for the public works and manufactures carry-ing on in this part of the country.

The price of all kinds of provifions is nearly the fame as in Glafgow.

Poor.—The number of poor on the parifh-roll at the laft general diftribution in December 1791 was 19. Of thefe,

5

5 receive ſupply regularly, from 3 s. to 5 s. each a month; and, beſides this, 5 s. 10 s. or 15 s. at each of two half year-ly diſtributions; the reſt at theſe general diſtributions only, or as occaſion requires.

The funds are, the collections at the church on Sundays, and other days of public worſhip, the intereſt of 115 l. in bank, and the intereſt of 40 l. part of a late donation, on bond to the ſeſſion. Theſe funds have been hitherto ſuffi-cient to ſupport all the poor of the pariſh in a very compe-tent manner, and none of them are allowed to beg.

There is no way of ſupporting the poor ſo eaſy, and ſo little expenſive, as from the collections at church. Aſ-ſeſſments are attended with more trouble, and are conſider-ably more expenſive; for many claim to be admitted on the poor's roll when the poor are ſupported in this way, who, in the ſame circumſtances, would make greater exertions to ſupport themſelves before they applied for ſupply out of the funds provided in the other way. Aſſeſſments, however, are certainly the moſt equitable method of ſupporting the poor. When heritors, either from non-reſidence or unfre-quent attendance upon public worſhip, contribute nothing, or do not contribute their juſt proportion; and when, from a ſpirit of ſectarianiſm, many others withdraw from the eſta-bliſhed Church, and alſo contribute nothing, it is often im-poſſible, and always unfair and unreaſonable, that thoſe only who do attend the church ſhould bear the whole burden of the poor.

Population.—The population by Dr Webſter's table in 1755 was 1390. The number of inhabitants, young and old, in the year 1788, when an exact liſt was taken, was 1664; to which, from the erection of two of the bleachfields ſince that time, and other cauſes of increaſe, as many may perhaps be be now added as will make the number 1700. From the regifter of baptifms about the time of the Revolution, fuppofing the proportion between the baptifms and population the fame then as at prefent, the number of inhabitants appears to have been at that time 1460; fo that, in the fpace of a hundred years, the population has increafed about 240, that is, by about the number of perfons employed at the bleachfields and paper mill. That it has not increafed more is owing to the conjunction of fmall farms, and the deftruction of cottages. The number of males is to that of females nearly as 10 to 9. The average number of marriages for the laft 10 years is 16, of baptifms for the fame time 57, and of burials for the laft 9 years 28. The rule given for finding the population of a diftrict, by multiplying the births by 26, or the deaths by 36, feems not to be well founded.

Canal, &c.—The great canal between Forth and Clyde paffes through the fouth part of the parifh. It is carried over the river Kelvin by a ftately aqueduct bridge, planned by Mr Whitworth, and executed by Mr Gibb. The foundation of the bridge was laid June 15. 1787, and it was finifhed in June 1790. The length is 350 feet, the breadth 57, of which the canal occupies 27½, and the height, from the furface of the river to the top of the parapet wall, 57. It ftands upon 4 arches, each 50 feet wide, and 37 high.

Advantages and Difadvantages.—From the preceding account, it appears that this parifh enjoys confiderable advantages: Abundance of coal and lime within itfelf, and to be had eafily from other places too, by means of the canal; its vicinity to Glafgow, diftant only about fix miles from the middle of the parifh, where there is a ready market for all kinds of product; plenty of ftone for building; and rivers
proper

proper for mills and bleachfields. The principal difadvantages are, the ftubborn nature of a great part of the foil, and the want of good roads. The latter difadvantage, however, will foon be in a great meafure removed, two lines of turnpike road being now carrying through the parifh, leading from Glafgow, the one to Drymen, and the other to Balfron. If to thefe were added a good crofs road from eaft to weft, there would remain little caufe of complaint on this account. The difficulty of procuring dung in fufficient quantity for the land, is alfo no fmall difadvantage. The farmers in the fouth part of the parifh, indeed, carry it, but at a very great expence, from Glafgow, Port-Glafgow, and Greenock; but it will not bear the expence of carriage, added to its price, from thefe places to the north part; fo that the farmers there are confined to the quantity made on their farms, which is commonly far from fufficient.

OLD KILPATRICK,

(COUNTY OF DUMBARTON.)

By the Rev. Mr JOHN DAVIDSON,
Minister of the Parish.

Origin of the Name.

KIRK or KIL-PATRICK takes its name from St Patrick, the tutelar faint of Ireland, who, tradition fays, was a native of the parifh. There are many circumftances favouring this tradition ; though Mr O'Halloran, an Irifh writer, fuppofes that he was rather a native of Wales. In a burying place in the church yard, there is a ftone of great antiquity, with a figure faid to be that of St Patrick upon it ; and fome go fo far as to affert, that he was buried under it. In the river Clyde, oppofite to the church, there is a large ftone or rock, vifible at low water, called St Patrick's ftone ; and Pennant fays, " Ireland will fcarce " forgive me if I am filent about the birth-place of its tu- " telar faint. He firft drew breath at Kirkpatrick, and " derived his name from his father, a noble Roman, (a " Patrician), who fled hither in the time of perfecution *."

Situation,

* Pennant's Tour, Vol. II. p. 160. 5th edit.

Situation, Extent, Soil, &c.—The pariſh is beautifully
fituated upon the river Clyde, in the Preſbytery of Dumbarton, and Synod of Glaſgow and Ayr. The church ſtands
near the turnpike road, 10 miles below Glaſgow. Before
the disjunction of New Kilpatrick, the pariſh was of great
extent. It is ſtill, however, larger than the ordinary ſize
of pariſhes in this part of the country, being about 8 miles
long, and, in ſome places, from 3 to 4 miles broad. The
foil of the arable part of the pariſh is generally thin, ſandy, or gravelliſh ; but it is in ſome places clay, and in o-
thers clay with a till bottom. The furface of the low
part of the diſtrict, towards Clyde, is rather plain and level ; the north part is hilly and mountainous, and in many
places covered with heath and wood.

Rivers, Hills and Proſpects.—The principal river is the
Clyde, and it is the boundary of the pariſh upon the ſouth.
It abounds with falmon, ſmelts and trouts, which are
caught in great plenty ; and herrings have been taken, as
high up the river as Lord Sempill's houſe, about a mile
above the church. There are ſeveral ſmaller rivulets,
which, as will be afterwards ſhown, have added very
much, by the number of works erected upon them, both
to the wealth and population of the pariſh. From the
hills above the church, which are continuations of the
Grampians, and from one in particular, called Dumbucks,
there are excellent diſtant views, terminated on the one
hand by the lofty mountains of Arran, with their heads
ſometimes above the clouds, and on the other, by the
foaring top of Benlomond. From the Chapel hill, the
property of the family of Blantyre, and from Dalnotter
hill, the property of the Lord Preſident, both fituated upon the turnpike road from Glaſgow to Dumbarton, within half a mile of the church, the obſerver is delighted
with the variety of the ſcenery, and richneſs of the proſpect.

fpect. The banks of fo fine a river as the Clyde, the ftriking figure of Dumbarton caftle, the wonderful divifion in the ridge of mountains above Bouling Bay, and the numerous woods,—all unite in rendering this profpect perhaps one of the beft in Scotland. Mr Farrington, Royal Academician of London, fome years ago was employed to take different views upon the rivers Forth and Clyde. He is a man of eminence in his profeffion, and the view from Dalnotter hill is fuppofed by many to be the beft of the collection.

Climate and Difeafes.—The climate is mild and temperate, though, as is the cafe upon all the weft coaft of Scotland, very rainy at fome feafons of the year. No epidemical difeafe, however, prevails among the inhabitants. They are generally healthy, and though inftances of extreme longevity cannot be produced, yet a man of the name of Daniel Montgomery, belonging to the parifh, died within thefe 2 years at the well authenticated age of 93 ; and during the incumbency of the prefent minifter, he has known many perfons of both fexes live to the age of 85.

Proprietors and Rents.—There are about 33 heritors, great and fmall, in the parifh, the principal of whom are Lord Blantyre, the Lord Prefident, Sir Archibald Edmonftone, Mr Hamilton of Barns, Mr Buchanan of Auchintorly, Mr Stirling of Law, Mifs Buchanan of Auchintofhan, and Mr Dreghorn of Ruchill. The valued rent of the parifh is L. 4441 : 13 : 8 Scotch. The real rent is about L. 5000 Sterling. Almoft all the arable lands in the parifh are inclofed and fubdivided. The average rent of arable land, in the low part of the parifh, is from 20 s. to 30 s. *per* acre.

Cultivation.

Cultivation.—When the prefent incumbent became minifter of the parifh in the 1745, the ftate of agriculture was
moft wretched. The rent of arable land, even in the low
part of the parifh, at an average, did not exceed from 2 s.
6 d. to 7 s. 6 d. an acre. The diftinction of outfield and
infield, or croft land, univerfally prevailed. There
were few or no inclofures, and the tenants were miferably
accommodated with houfes. The croft land, though every
year ploughed, produced little crop. There were no carts in
the parifh. The difference is now wonderful. In few
parts of the country are the farmers in a more profperous
fituation, the rents better paid, or the beft mode of cultivating the foil better underftood. In general, the tenants obferve ftrictly the following method : They never have above
a third of their farm in tillage at a time. They take but
two crops of grain and one of hay from that third, and it is
never broke up again till it remains in pafture grafs 3 or 4
years. To this is to be afcribed the flourifhing ftate of the
tenants *. Their grounds being thus treated, and well
dunged

---

* This change took place about 20 years ago. The example was fet
by fome of the principal heritors, who were at great pains and expence to
introduce it, and it is now becoming general over the parifh. The method
purfued with fo much effect by the heritors, was either to fummer-fallow
and improve their eftates themfelves, and then let them out in leafe ; or,
where they were fo large as not to admit of this, to let out the parts
which they had not fummer-fallowed, allowing the tenant a deduction of
a year's rent for each inclofure he fhould fummer-fallow, till the whole
farm was once gone over, at the average rent of the farm *per* acre, provided he gave the inclofure 4 ploughings, and as many harrowings, laid on
a certain quantity of manure, and made and formed new ftreight ridges
of a proper breadth. By thefe means, the tenants were induced to alter
their former fyftem of cultivation, and they continue in the new courfe,
the beneficial confequences of which are abundantly felt. They bring
dung from Port-Glafgow and Greenock by water carriage, and they cart
their lime from a lime-work near the eaft boundary of the parifh. They
generally ufe two horfe ploughs, though, in fome places, where the foil
is

dunged and limed, produce excellent crops, and their pafture grafs is remarkably rich and nourifhing. The diftinction of outfield and infield is totally fuppreffed. Carts
are univerfally ufed. Convenient and centrical farm houfes are built upon almoft every farm, many of them flated.

Produce and Cattle.—The crops raifed are corn, bear,
barley, wheat, peafe and potatoes; and there are ready markets for all thefe, either at the different villages and works
in the parifh, or at Glafgow. The horfes and black cattle
in this diftrict are of the beft kinds. Several of the tenants
rear them. On the grounds of the upper part of the parifh,
great numbers of cattle and fheep are paftured. The hills
of Cockney always produce remarkably fat cattle and fheep.
Better feldom appear in the Glafgow or Paifley markets.

Manufactures.—This parifh, from its local advantages, (having a great many falls of water, iffuing from the high
grounds,) from its good roads, and its vicinity to Glafgow,
is full of different manufactories, all of which are in a thriving fituation, and employ at high wages a very great
number of people *. To give the reader an idea of the number

is clay, 3 and 4 horfes are thought neceffary. As all perfonal fervices are
juftly confidered as deftructive, they have been neceffarily abolifhed in a
part of the country where agriculture has arrived to fo high a pitch of
perfection. Thirlage, however, and mill fervices, ftill remain. But
thefe. it is hoped, will foon alfo be fuppreffed. Even ftatute-labour,
known in almoft every county in Scotland, is here converted into money.

* The prices of labour and provifions, in this and in all the parifhes adjoining to Glafgow, are regulated in a great meafure by Glafgow. As
thefe have been detailed by fome of the clergy in the neighbourhood, it
is thought unneceffary to repeat the particulars here. In general, it may
only be obferved, that they bear a proportion to one another, and that all
ranks and degrees of perfons in the parifh are now much more wealthy,
and in a much more profperous fituation, in every refpect, than their anceftors.

ber and the kind of manufactories, a liſt of them is ſubjoined.

Two printfields of great extent, having 595 perſons belonging to the works; but as 280 of theſe do not reſide in the pariſh, they are not comprehended in the number of inhabitants after mentioned:

Number of perſons employed,	595
One bleachfield, which employs	50
One paper manufactory employs,	84
One ſmith and iron manufactory employs	273
One woollen manufactory, (and which was the firſt of the kind in Scotland,) employs	321
Total number of perſons employed,	1323
Deduct for non-reſidenters,	280
Total reſidenters employed,	1043

One of the printfields pays a weekly duty of near L. 200 Sterling to Government, and is ſuppoſed to be the fourth or fifth largeſt in Scotland. The works and machinery of the wool mill are complete for making and finiſhing 1000 yards of cloth a-day, which requires 1200 lb. of wool.

Roads and Bridges.—Thirty years ago there were no paſſable roads for carriages in the pariſh, owing to the want of bridges, for, in floods, the rivulets were unfordable. Even the great road from Glaſgow to Dumbarton, which communicates with the Weſt Highlands, was at times in the like ſituation. About 20 years ago, the Duke of Argyle, Lord Frederick Campbell, and Sir Archibald Edmonſtone, in the moſt patriotic manner, undertook to make the part of the high road, from the Eaſt confines of the pariſh, to the town of Dumbarton, a ſtretch of 8 miles, and to take their chance of the tolls for indemnification, which, at the time, was a

very

very uncertain fecurity. The road was accordingly foon made in the completeft manner; and thefe gentlemen have now the fatisfaction of having conferred a lafting advantage on the country; while, from the increafe of the manu- factures of Glafgow, and the number of travellers, the turn- pike duties have repaid their advance of money. As thefe du- ties are now perfectly fufficient to fupport the road, independ- ent of the ftatute money, the latter is applied to the other roads in the parifh, which, owing to the good management of a refiding heritor, who takes charge of the application, are all likewife in good order. The ftatute money of the parifh amounts to L. 63 : 6 : 8 Sterling yearly, and is upon the increafe. It is raifed by an affeffment of 18 s. Sterling upon each L. 100 Scotch of valued rent, and of 2 s. Sterling upon each houfeholder. Good roads fhould be the firft ob- ject of improvement in every country. It is to their being fo good in this parifh, that a great part of its profperity may be afcribed.

Ferry.—The ferry of Erfkine, almoft oppofite to the church, is the communication for foot paffengers, horfes, and carriages, acrofs the river in this part of the country. The quays have lately been removed to more proper fitua- tions, and it is now a very convenient and ufeful ferry.

Church.—The church is a very ancient building, and was formerly a branch of the abbacy of Paifley. The ftipend is 89 bolls 2 firlots 1 peck 2 lippies of meal, and L. 45, 13 s. 4 d. Sterling of money, including L. 4 : 3 : 4 Sterling for furnifhing communion elements. The manfe is plea- fant and commodious; and, fince an exchange with the fa- mily of Blantyre, who very liberally made a confiderable addition to the glebe, it is now a very good one, confifting

of

of 9 acres of excellent arable land. Lord Blantyre is patron.

Population.—From an accurate account taken in ſummer
1792, the number of ſouls, including thoſe employed at the
public works, but excluſive of the 280 non-reſident perſons,
are,

Males above 8 years of age,	- -	961
Males below 8 years of age,	- -	265
Females above 8 years of age,	-	933
Females below 8 years of age,	-	293

In whole, 2452

In Dr Webſter's report in 1755, this pariſh is
ſaid to have contained 1281 ſouls, - 1281

Increaſe, 1171

This important increaſe of inhabitants is, in a great meaſure to be attributed to the number of works carried on
in the pariſh, and the great influx of people which they heve
occaſioned ; for the number of inhabitants, independent of
the works, has not increaſed in a great degree, the number
now being only 1409 ſouls, whereas, in 1755, there were
1281 ; an increaſe of only 128.

Poor.—The poor in the pariſh are few, conſidering the
number of inhabitants, and even theſe conſiſt of old or diſeaſed people who are unable to work ; for it has been obſerved, that none but the truly neceſſitous ever deſire to receive public charity. In this part of the country, the people have a proper pride, and are naturally averſe at *coming*
(as they call it) *upon the poor's box.* There have never,
therefore. been any aſſeſſments for the poor. They are
ſupplied out of the collections at the church door, and from
the

the ftock of the poor's fund; but, owing to the few refiding heritors in the parifh, and a degree of fanaticifm among fome of the lower fort of people, which takes them to other meetings than the Eftablifhed Church, the collection at the church door is lefs now than formerly, and it is to be feared that an affeffment may foon be neceffary, which, wherever it takes place, is attended with many pernicious confequences *.

Minerals.—In feveral parts of the parifh, there are coal and lime pits which have been wrought, and at prefent there is one coal-work going. Freeftone in great quantities is to be found in many places, fome of it of an excellent quality for building. The ftones ufed in building the fea-locks at Bowling Bay, and many of the bridges upon the weft end of the canal, were taken from the eftate of Mifs Buchanan of Auchintofhan, and are confidered to be of the beft kind of freeftone.

Antiquities.—The Roman wall, (or, as it is commonly called, *Graham's dike*, from a tradition, that a Scottifh warrior of that name firft broke over it,) between the Forth and Clyde, which was firft marked out by Agricola, and completed by Antoninus Pius, and which terminated

at

---

* Under this article, the minifter is happy in having an opportunity of doing juftice to the proprietors of the numerous works. While they have added, in a great degree, to the wealth and population of the parifh, he can fafely fay, that in no inftance have they increafed the number of poor. Their poor are uniformly fupported from funds eftablifhed among themfelves. At feveral of the works, weekly collections are made by the workmen, which are accumulated into a capital, and, by the judicious management of the proprietors, they are thereby enabled, not only to maintain their poor, but alfo to employ furgeons and fchoolmafters for the benefit of the workmen and their families;—a line of conduct highly proper, and meritorious, and well worthy the imitation of every mafter manufacturer.

at Dunglaſs *, is ſtill diſcernible in many parts of the pariſh ; as are alſo ſeveral Roman camps in the neighbourhood
of it, particularly one upon a hill at Duntocher †.—At
Sandyford, near the village of Kilpatrick, before the road
was repaired, and before a bridge for horſes and carriages
was built over the burn there, a large ſtone, ſuppoſed to have
been an obeliſk, intended to commemorate ſome remarkable
event, had been taken from near the Roman wall, where,
it is ſaid, it had ſtood, and was uſed by the country people
as a bridge for foot paſſengers. It is now in the poſſeſſion
of

* Dunglaſs was once a ſite of the Romans, and, in Oliver Cromwell's
time, a caſtle and a place of ſome ſtrength, but was blown up by the treachery of an Engliſh boy. The ruins of ſome of the buildings are ſtill to
be ſeen. It was formerly the property of the Colquhouns of Luſs, who
likewiſe enjoyed the whole tract of country from that to Dumbarton, and
it at preſent retains their name, being called the Barony of Colquhoun.
This caſtle, however, and the barony have, for many years, been in the
poſſeſſion of Sir Archibald Edmonſtone's family, and his vaſſals. But
though the family of Luſs have now no property in the pariſh, they have
ſtill very large eſtates in the county. The maſſacre of the Colquhouns by
the Macgregors in 1602, is an inſtance, among many, of the barbarous ſtate
of this country at that time, and occaſioned acts of Parliament prohibiting
any perſon from uſing the name of Macgregor. Theſe acts are now very
properly repealed.

† In 1775, a country man in digging a trench upon the declivity of
this hill, turned up ſeveral very uncommon tyles. The tyles are of 7 different ſizes, the ſmalleſt being 7 inches, and the largeſt 21 inches ſquare.
They are from 2 to 3 inches in thickneſs, of a reddiſh colour, and in a condition perfectly found. The leſſer ones compoſed ſeveral rows of pillars,
which formed a labyrinth of paſſages of about 18 inches ſquare, and the
larger tyles being laid over the whole, formed a floor ; above which, when
it was diſcovered, there lay about two feet deep of earth. The building
was ſurrounded by a wall of hewn ſtone. Various conjectures have been
made with regard to the nature of theſe remains of antiquity. The moſt
probable is, that it was uſed as a *ſudorium*, or hot bath, for the uſe of the
neighbouring garriſon.——Near this, there is a Roman bridge, over the
Duntocher burn ; which, though it has been often repaired, ſtill retains
ſtrong marks of antiquity.

of Mr Donald of Mountblow, and refembles the ancient obelifks near Brechin, called the Danifh ftones of Aberlemno.

Charaƈter.—The people of this parifh may be faid to anfwer the general charaƈter of the Scotch, for they are fober, honeft, and induftrious. The demand for workmen and artificers is fo great, that there is not an idle perfon to be feen. At the wool mill and printfields, great numbers of young perfons are conftantly employed, many of them below 8 years of age, who earn from 4 d. to 8 d. a-day. And, as there are fchoolmafters in the vicinity of all thefe works, the youth, when not engaged at their employments, go to fchool. In this way their bufinefs and education are united, while their morals are not endangered by idlenefs. —All the young people of the parifh drefs well. The men wear hats and coats of Englifh cloth. The young women put on filk and calico gowns, and black caps and cloaks. They meet together occafionally, and make merry. Their chief amufement is dancing, and upon thefe occafions there is a pleafing cheerfulnefs and innocence among them.

Mifcellaneous Obfervations.—Inoculation is now generally praƈtifed in the parifh, which is a happy circumftance, both on account of the population, and the difference it occafions in the look of the people. The practice is not, however, of above 30 years ftanding. The minifter was among the firft who began it. He tried it with fuccefs in his own family about the year 1761-2, fince which the cuftom has gradually crept in, and is now univerfal. An inftance of the proper and rational conduƈt of a tenant in the parifh, towards his family, may be here mentioned. He has had 12 children, and he inoculated every one of them. The extenfion of the great canal to Bowling Bay, where it joins

the

the Clyde, muſt be attended with very advantageous conſequences to the nation. The number of veſſels that ſail
upon it, loaded with all kinds of merchandiſe, and ſome of
them from ſea to ſea, is daily increaſing.—The hiſtory of
the Bargarran witches, in the neighbouring pariſh of Erſkine, is well known to the curious. That this pariſh, in the
dark ages, partook of the ſame frenzy, and that innocent perſons were ſacrificed at the ſhrine of cruelty, bigotry, and
ſuperſtition, cannot be concealed. As late as the end of the
laſt century, a woman was burnt for witchcraft at Sandyford, near the village, and the bones of the unfortunate victim were lately found at the place. While we review
with pity and regret, the deplorable ſituation of human nature at that time, we feel a ſenſible pleaſure in contempla-
ting the change that has already taken place, which is indeed highly increaſed, by indulging the fond hope, that the
period is faſt approaching, when all kinds of ſuperſtition and
bigotry, will for ever be baniſhed, from the face of the earth.

PARISH OF KIRKINTILLOCH.

(COUNTY OF DUMBARTON.)

By the Rev. MR. WILLIAM DUNN.

Extent, Situation, Surface, &c.

THE diſtrict, which now conſtitutes the pariſh of Kirkin-tilloch, made, in the time of the Romans, a part of the northern boundary of the province of Valentia. When, at an after period, the country was divided into pariſhes, it acquired the name of Weſter Leinzie. Under that denomination, it was given, by Robert I. of Scotland, to Sir Robert de Fleming, in conſideration of the eminent ſervices, he had performed, in the courſe of the long and bloody conteſt, which that monarch carried on with the Engliſh, for the poſſeſſion of the Scottiſh throne.

The great Roman wall, commonly called Graham's dyke *,

paſſing

---

* *Roman Wall.*—The remains of the Roman wall, and of three large forts, and as many watch-towers built upon it, may ſtill be diſtinctly traced in this pariſh. The wall proceeds through Kirk-intilloch for the ſpace of 5 miles, between eaſt and weſt. The

firſt

paſſing through the whole length of the pariſh, its former
name was probably derived from that circumſtance, ſince
Leinzie, may, by no very fanciful etymology, be conſidered
as a provincial corruption of the Latin term, *Linea*. Its preſent appellation, Kirkintilloch, or rather Caerpentilloch, is
ſaid to ſignify, in the language of the antient inhabitants of
North Britain, " the end of a long tongue or promontary of
" riſing ground," which is exactly deſcriptive of the ſituation
of the town, ſtanding on the extremity of a ridge, advancing
from

firſt of theſe poſts upon the eaſt ſide, ſtands upon the top of the
Barr-hill; a ſituation ſo elevated, as to command a view of almoſt
the whole length of the wall, both eaſt and weſt. The fort is a
ſquare area of 150 yards. Some vaults belonging to it, have lately been diſcovered. Theſe are ſtill entire; and are covered above
with flat bricks, and floored with a mixture of lime and black
and white gravel, reſembling ſand from the ſea-ſhore, very
unlike any that is now to be found in this neighbourhood. The
next of theſe forts, proceeding weſtward, is ſituated three miles
diſtant, at the village of Auchindowie: this appears an oblong
rectangular figure, extending 150 yards one way, and 70 another.
It is now almoſt defaced; one part of the area being now a corn-
field, while another is occupied by the houſes of the village; and
the reſt has been cut away in opening the canal between the Forth
and the Clyde.——Two miles onward, in the ſame direction, is
the fort of Peel; ſituate on a piece of riſing ground, at the weſtern end of the town of Kirkintilloch; oblong and rectangular,
90 yards in length, 80 in breadth; ſingular, in being ſituated on
the north ſide of the wall, whereas the others ſtand upon the
ſouth ſide.——Stones, bearing inſcriptions, have been dug a-
mong the ruins of all theſe forts: But the only words of theſe inſcriptions, that could be read, were, LEGIO SECUNDA AUGUSTA
FECIT.

from the fouth, into a plain on the banks of the Kelvin. From the town, the name came at length to be extended to the whole diftrict.

The parifh is fituated in the fhire of Dumbarton, or Lennox, in the prefbytery of Glafgow, and fynod of Glafgow and Ayr. It is of a triangular figure, no where exceeding 5½ miles in length. Its breadth varies confiderably.—The face of the ground, although diverfified throughout by a fucceffion of waving fwells, is no where broken into abrupt precipices; and, excepting in one place of inconfiderable extent, no where deformed by rugged rocks.———There are no lakes in the diftrict. The Kelvin is the principal river, which, of itfelf, is a confiderable body of water, and, which is joined in its courfe along this parifh, by many fmaller ftreams; in particular, by the Skinna, and the Luggie. The latter paffes through the town of Kirkintilloch.

Soil, Foffils, and Animals.—The hufbandman finds a confiderable diverfity of foils, through the lands in this diftrict. The ground along the fouthern part of the Kelvin, is of a deep, marfhy nature, and is often overflowed by the river. The foil of a fmall tract, towards the north-eaft angle, is of a light reddifh earth, upon a whinftone and gravelly bottom. Around the town of Kirkintilloch, the foil is a light black loam, 16 or 18 inches deep, on a reddifh tilly bottom. A ftrong natural clay prevails through the fouthern, and the eaftern parts of the parifh. Tracts of mofs, affording a black peat earth, are interfperfed here and there, throughout the whole diftrict.———Lime, coal, and freeftone, are found in great abundance.—The ftreams by which the parifh is watered, afford falmon, trout, perch, and pike.——We have the common domeftic animals,—horfes, cows, fwine, and a few fheep.——Our draught-horfes are ftrong, gentle, and handfome ſome. Our milch-cows often yield 8 Engliſh gallons of milk in a day.

Cultivation and Produce of the Lands.——The lands in this pariſh are almoſt entirely arable ;—and we have happily abundance of the beſt manures. Our farmers, accordingly, are chiefly employed in agriculture. Oats, barley, hay from ſown graſſes, flax, peaſe, beans, and a ſmall proportion of wheat, are our chief articles of crop. Turnips begin to be cultivated among us. Dung, lime, a compoſt of earth with other materials, and an addition of ſimple earth, of a different nature from the ſoil of the field upon which it is laid, are the manures principally made uſe of.

A chalder of lime, conſiſting of 16 bolls, each of which contains 3 firlots, wheat meaſure, is, at preſent bought, at any of the lime-works, in the neighbouring pariſh of Campſie, for 6s 8d.

The average produce of oats and barley, through theſe lands, may, in moderately favourable ſeaſons, be about 5 or 6 bolls an acre : And, in years of moderate plenty, their average price in the market, is from 13s to 14s, a boll. The farms are in general ſmall ; conſiſting commonly of about 50 acres each. The farmer is often proprietor, in feu, of his own farm. The lands may be eſtimated as either actually yielding, or, at leaſt, capable of yielding from 15s to 20s an acre, of yearly rent.

Town, and the Employments followed in it.——The town of Kirkintilloch is a very antient burgh of barony. It was erected about 1170, by William, King of Scots, in favour of William Cumin, Baron of Leinzie, and Lord of Cumbernauld ; and ſtill holds of the barony of Cumbernauld, for the payment of 12 merks Scots, of yearly feu-duty. The privileges with which

it

it has been endowed, are very ample. Its burgeſſes elect their own magiſtrates, independently of the lord of the barony. The magiſtrates are two baillies ; and are annually choſen. They are impowered by the charters of the burgh, to hold courts, levy fines, impriſon offenders, or even baniſh them from their liberties ; and in ſhort, to exerciſe every right with which the baron himſelf was veſted, before the erection of the burgh. Theſe rights, the community have continued, ever ſince that period, to enjoy, undiſturbed. They were, in no degree, affected by the act, by which the Britiſh parliament, in 1748, aboliſhed the heritable juriſdictions in Scotland. A large tract of land was alſo annexed to this burgh at its erection ; and is now feued out, from time to time, in moderate parcels, as purchaſers offer. ——Linens and cottons, of different ſorts, are manufactured here.——The weavers are the moſt numerous claſs of mechanics in it. Many of the other mechanical employments, which ſupply the neceſſaries, and the ordinary conveniencies of life, are likewiſe practiſed.—Mr Stirling, younger of Glorat, a gentleman of diſtinguiſhed public ſpirit, lately erected a ſmall cotton-mill. Hand-machines, for ſpinning cotton, were, at the ſame time, introduced. The undertaking is in a very thriving condition. And, as the pariſh affords ſeveral other happy ſituations, it is probable, that theſe may ſoon be occupied by more works of the ſame kind.

Highways, and the Canal.—One of the great roads between Glaſgow and Edinburgh, paſſes through the town of Kirkintilloch ; which is 7 miles diſtant from the former, and 49 from the latter.—None of our rivers are navigable; but the great canal between the Forth and the Clyde, paſſes through the whole length of this pariſh. After having been frequently propoſed, ſince the Union, this canal was at length begun in 1768, and
finiſhed

finifhed in 1790. The trade upon it is already great, and is rapidly increafing. One of its firft effects has been, to equalize, in a great meafure, the price of grain, throughout all the corn-countries in Scotland; to the temporary lofs of the landholders, in the fouthern, and to the gain of thofe in the northern diftricts.

State of the Landed Property.——In the beginning of the 14th century, the whole parifh, excepting the burgh lands of Kirkintilloch, and the fmall barony of Wefter-Gartfhore, (which has, for many generations, been poffeffed by that antient and refpectable family, the Gartfhores of Gartfhore,) were the entire property of the noble family of Fleming. But, in the long feries of years, which has elapfed fince that period, that great eftate has been gradually difmembered, partly in forming eftablifhments for the younger branches or connexions of the family; and partly by fupplying the enlarged expences, required by thofe new modes of life, which have been introduced in the progrefs of fociety. The laft remainder of it was fold off, in 1757 : And nothing now continues in the poffeffion of the former proprietors, but the feu-duties, and fome other cafualities of feudal fuperiority.

The Poor.—The poor of this parifh are not numerous. The weekly collections at the church-doors, have hitherto been found more than fufficient for their fupport. Thefe happy circumftances are to be afcribed chiefly, to the minute fubdivifions of the landed property in the parifh, and to the general manners, and perfonal habits, which ufually attend agricultural induftry. But, it is to be feared, that if a greater proportion of the inhabitants, fhall be induced to apply themfelves to manufactures, one difadvantage which muft neceffarily arife from this increafe of induftry, is fuch a change in the manners

of

of the lower claffes, as may reduce them much oftener to a
ftate of helplefs poverty.

State of Population.—The whole inhabitants of this parifh,
have been found, upon a very accurate furvey, to amount,
at prefent, to the number of 2639.

Of thefe 1536 refide in the town.

Among whom are 185 weavers

11 ftocking-makers

15 fmiths

20 houfe carpenters, and cabinet-makers

10 mafons

10 fhoemakers

4 faddlers

6 coopers

A good many taylors; and a few hairdreffers.

In 1751, the Rev. Dr. Erfkine, at that time minifter of
Kirkintilloch, now of Edinburgh, found the number of the
families in the town, to be 195.

The families in the country 226.

The perfons in the town, from eight years of age, upwards,
575.

Thofe in the country, from 8 years of age, upwards, were
796.

The addition of the Seceders and Quakers, at that time in the
parifh, to thefe numbers, make up 1400 examinable perfons in
the parifh. The return of fouls to Dr Webfter, was 1696.
Hence, it appears, that the increafe of numbers, within thefe
laft 40 years, amounts to 943.

Character and Manners.—The inhabitants of this parifh are,
in general, a virtuous and induftrious people. That pride of

mind

mind, and impatience of contradiction, which the poffeffion of landed property frequently infpires, perhaps may occafion too many law-fuits. The prefent minifter was told, before he came amongft them, that they were often difpofed to treat their clergymen with neglect and unkindnefs; but he has experienced nothing in his miniftry, that could juftify fuch an accufation. The exiftence of Seceders, and of feceding meeting houfes, has perhaps no bad effect upon the manners and fentiments of the people, either here, or any where elfe throughout the kingdom. They are in fome degree fpies and checks upon the members of the eftablifhed church; and the difcourfes of their clergy are often adapted, with fingular felicity, to the capacity and the prejudices of the leaft enlightened claffes in the community.——The fmall number of the poor, dependent upon alms, and the liberal provifion made for them, by voluntary contributions, are facts implying, in fo populous a parifh, no common praife: they befpeak induftry, fobriety, frugality, and charity, to be the leading features in the moral character of thefe people.—— As to their external appearance, they are of a middle ftature; and, being free from hereditary difeafes, while they enjoy the advantages of an open fituation, and a pure, although rather moift air, they are, in general, vigorous and healthy. Some, indeed, particularly the females, are not a little fubject to hyfterics; a difeafe, the prevalence of which in this place, has, with fome fhew of probability, been attributed, partly to the dampnefs of our earthen floors, and partly, to the effects of fpinning, for which, the women in this neighbourhood are defervedly famous [*].

Probable

* The women, when engaged in fpinning, efpecially in winter, fit by the fire-fide, and keeping, as their cuftom is, always the fame ftation, the one fide fide is expofed to the chilling cold of the

Probable Improvements.——It is eafy to fee, that the parifh of Kirkintilloch, fituated as it is, in the vicinity of a great, an opulent, an induftrious, and a commercial city, and in a tract of country, where a paffion for manufactures is fo prevalent, interfected by a canal which joins the two great-eft navigable rivers in the kingdom, and which promifes to fpread cultivation, opulence, and induftry, every where a-long its banks; divided, too, by the great road between the two principal cities in Scotland; poffeffing fuch varieties of excellent foil, and fo plentifully fupplied with fuel, manure, and materials for building:—With fuch advantages, it is eafy to fee, that the population, wealth, and induftry of this parifh, can hardly fail to increafe confiderably, even be-fore the clofe of the prefent century. The value of the lands may yet be greatly raifed, by the introduction of more improve-ed modes of agriculture: and fcarcely any place can enjoy circumftances more favourable to manufacturing induftry. It is, indeed, probable, that either manufactures or agricul-ture, might long fince, have attained a ftate of ftill greater improvement, if they had not mutually checked one another's progrefs. The facility, with which a piece of ground has been hitherto obtained, in feu from the burgh, has generally tempt-ed the trader and the manufacturer, to retire too early to en-

joy

the feafon, and the other is relaxed by the warm influence of the fire. Befides, in turning her lint-wheel, the perfon who fpins, commonly employs but one foot, and ufes chiefly the hand of the fame fide, in making the thread. Thus the labour is very unequal-ly divided, by which the health of the body muft naturally be af-fected. Laftly, the wafte of faliva in wetting the thread, muft deprive the ftomach of a fubftance effential to its operations, whence, all the fatal confequences of crudities, and indigeftion, may be ex-pected.

joy the conſequence, which landed property confers, and to
the pleaſures which imagination fondly, but too often fallaci-
ouſly, aſcribes to a life ſpent in rural employments: Whilſt a-
gain, the profits of ſpinning, and the manufacturing ſpirit of
the country, have commonly induced the farmer to pay only
a partial attention to the cares of huſbandry.

Corruption of Morals likely to attend the increaſe of Induſtry.
——One unhappy circumſtance, that may attend the increaſe
of induſtry, and the introduction of new manufactures among
us, is too important to be overlooked: Children becoming
ſooner able to ſubſiſt by the profits of their own labour, will,
of conſequence, ſooner diſregard the authority of their parents,
acquire earlier habits of expence ; and, being expoſed to the
infection of vice and diſſipation, before the powers of their
minds are in any degree matured, or their characters formed,
—will be much more worthleſs in manhood, and more helpleſs in old age. It would be a happy circumſtance, therefore,
if politicians could contrive ſome means, to preſerve the virtue
and morals of the people, while they are endeavouring to increaſe their numbers, to enliven their induſtry, and to augment their wealth *.

* The advantages reſulting from our late improvements is attended with one circumſtance, of which, we have reaſon to complain, which is this, that the uſe of lime upon our lands, the filth,
which is conveyed into our rivers, from the coal-works in the neighbourhood, and the machinery which have been erected, have already rendered a ſalmon fiſhery, which was conſiderable, very inſig-
nificant ; and, indeed, there is too much reaſon to apprehend, that
the fiſh in our rivers will be almoſt totally exterminated by the joint
effects of theſe different ſources of deſtruction.

PARISH OF LUSS.

(County and Presbytery of Dumbarton.—Synod
of Glasgow and Ayr.)

By the Rev. Mr John Stuart, *Minister.*

—————

Situation, Extent, Erection, and Disjunctions.

THE parish of Luss is situated in the county and prefbytery of Dumbarton, and in the fynod of Glafgow
and Ayr. It is about $8\frac{1}{2}$ Englifh miles long from S. to N.
and from $2\frac{1}{2}$ to 5 miles broad. It is bounded on the fouth
by the parifhes of Bonhill and Cardrofs; on the north by the
parifh of Arrochar; on the eaft by Lochlomond; and on the
weft by the parifh of Row. It was formerly of great extent,
reaching, on the weft fide of Lochlomond, from the one end
of that lake to the other, and comprehending fome of the
lands on its eaft fide, together with moft of its iflands.

By an act of the Privy Council, in the year 1621, the
lands of Buchanan were disjoined from this parifh, and annexed to that of Inchcalloch. About the year 1650, the
lands of Auchindennan, Cameron, Stockrogert, and Tulli-
chewen were disjoined from it, and annexed to the parifh of
Bonhill. In 1658, the lands of Arrochar were disjoined
from it, and formed into a feparate parifh. But the lands

of

of Caldanach, Prefstelloch, and Conglens, belonging once to the parifh of Inchcalloch, are now annexed, *quoad omnia*, and the lands of Bannachrae, belonging properly to the parifh of Row, are confidered as annexed, *quoad facra*, to that of Lufs.

Soil. Surface, Climate, Longevity, and Difeafes.—The foil is in general light and gravelly, but in fome parts there is good loam. The principal level land lies near Lochlomond, and chiefly where the rivers difcharge themfelves into it, formed probably in the courfe of ages, by the fand and foil carried down from the higher grounds by the torrents. Scarcely one twelfth of the furface is arable. The greateft part is hilly and mountainous. The climate is mild and temperate. Snow feldom lies many days on the low grounds. In fevere winters, the degree of cold has been found to be confiderably greater near Glafgow and Edinburgh than in this country. Hollies, and other plants in the hedges and gardens, have there been killed by the froft, when here they remained unhurt. The mountains and woods break the force of the winds in every direction; and the exhalations from that part of the lake which never freezes, may perhaps likewife ferve to temper the atmofphere. The air, though often moift, is remarkably healthful. Many of the people live to a great age. The venerable lift of old perfons, in the little village of Lufs, in 1769, is well known *. A man who refided in it

many

* Rev. Mr James Robertfon, minifter, aged   90
  Mrs Robertfon, his wife   — —   86
  Ann Sharp, their fervant   — — 94
  Niel M'Naughtan, kirk-officer   — — 86
  Chriftian Gay, his wife   — — — 94
  Walter Maclellan   — — — 90

Pennant's Tour in 1769, *4to. p.* 225.

many years, died in February 1790, aged 96. In 1793, the
following were living in it:

Hector Maclean, aged	—	—	—	91
Mary Macfarlane	—	—	—	88
Janet Walker	—	—	—	84
Elizabeth Macwattie	—	—	—	81
Margaret Macgregor	—	—	—	80
Duncan Gray	—	—	—	78
There is one woman in the parish aged			—	97

Some families in it ſeem to have a hereditary right to long
life. There are two brothers and two ſiſters german in it,
whoſe father was 96, and their mother 82 years old at their
death, and whoſe ages, in 1793, when added together, made
310 years. The eldeſt of the brothers is ſtill in good health,
and has at preſent alive 3 ſons and 4 daughters, 54 grand-
children, and 10 great-grand-children. In 1793, there were
likewiſe 4 ſiſters german living in the pariſh, whoſe ages together made 312 years. The people are ſubject to few diſeaſes. Fevers and conſumptions are the moſt common. The
former of theſe are generally imported from other parts, and
ſpread by infection.

Lake and Proſpects.—Lochlomond, either for extent, or
variety and magnificence of ſcenery, is not perhaps to be
equalled by any lake in Great Britain. Its beauties are ſo
well known, and have already been ſo well deſcribed by
others, as to make any new deſcription of them unneceſſary *.
There are ſeveral fine views of them to be ſeen from the
high road on each ſide of it, and from the adjacent heights,
each of which has its admirers. Thoſe which are commonly reckoned beſt, are from the top of the higheſt hills in
the

* *See* Pennant's Tours in 1769 and 1772, &c.

the iflands of Inchtavanach and Inchmurren, the Strone-hill near Lufs, and the point of Farkin; but, in order to have this laft view in the greateft perfection, it is neceffary to a- fcend confiderably higher than the line of the road. Loch- lomond is about 24 Englifh miles long, in fome parts above 7 miles broad, and contains above 20,000 acres of water. Its depth fouth from Lufs feldom exceeds 20 fathoms, or 120 feet. North from that it is much greater. Oppofite to the point of Farkin it is 66, and a little farther north 80 fa- thoms. For about a mile fouth from Tarbet it is, with little difference, 86 fathoms; but about two miles north from it, oppofite to Alt-garv, it is 100 fathoms, which is probably the greateft depth of the lake. Beyond that its depth gradually diminifhes to its north end. The north and deeper part of Lochlomond is never covered with ice; but fouth from Lufs, in fevere frofts, its furface has been fo completely frozen, as to render it fafe for men, and even for horfes and loaded fleds, to go from each fide to the different iflands. It is re- markable, however, that part of the narrow found between the iflands of Inchtavanach and Inchconagan, the average depth of which no where exceeds two fathoms and a half, and where there is no perceptible current, yet was never known to freeze, not even in the year 1740. This, perhaps, may be owing to fome fprings rifing there, fed by the adja- cent high grounds. After great floods in winter, the fur- face of Lochlomond has been known to rife about 6 feet higher than it is after much drought in fummer. Its average height above the level of the fea is 22 feet; but that it is now confiderably higher than it once was, and is therefore gaining upon the ground, there is clear evidence. Acrofs the channel of the river Falloch, at the north end of the lake, there are ftones fixed at regular diftances, once evidently in- tended for enabling paffengers to ftep from one fide to the

other,

other, but now never covered with leſs than 4 or 5 feet depth
of water. Near the middle of the Bay of Camſtraddan,
when the water is low, there is a heap of ſtones to be ſeen,
where the Colquhoun's of Camſtraddan are ſaid to have once
had their family reſidence. Cambden, in his *Atlas Britannica*, deſcribes an iſland as exiſting there in his day, in which
there was *a houſe and an orchard**. About 5 miles farther
ſouth, at a diſtance from the ſhore, there is another heap of
ſtones, ſaid to be the ruins of a church. A field oppoſite to
it is ſtill called *Ach-na-heaglais*, or the church-field. This
riſe of the ſurface of the lake, is probably owing to the ſand
and mud ſubſiding near the mouth of the Leven, and dam-
ming up the water.

Iſlands.—There are at preſent about 30 iſlands in Lochlomond, ſmall and great. Moſt of them are finely wooded.
Some of them are inhabited, and prove, at times, commodious aſylums to the diſordered in mind. Ten of them are
conſiderable in ſize; four of theſe belong to the pariſh of
Luſs: 1ſt, *Inchtavanach*, above three quarters of an Engliſh
mile long, and about two furlongs and a half broad, contains
135 Scotch acres, of which 127 are under a good oak wood,
which is moderately valued at 1000 l. each cutting, once in
20 years. The remaining acres are outfield, and carry at
times a good crop. The iſland is not at preſent inhabited.
A monk is ſaid, at a remote period, to have fixed his reſidence there, from whom it derives its name of *Inch-ta-vanach,*
i. e. the iſland of the monk's houſe. A ſweeter retirement,
or more adapted for contemplation, he could not perhaps
have choſen. 2*dly*, *Inchconagan*, ſituated on the eaſt ſide of
Inchtavanach, and ſeparated from it only by a narrow ſound,

above

---

* *See* Pennant's Tour in 1772, 4to, p. 155.

above half a mile long, and about two furlongs and a half broad, contains 94 acres, which are all under a natural oak and fir wood. 3*dly,* *Inchmoan, i. e. the mofs ifle,* lying a little to the fouth of Inchconagan, about three quarters of a mile long and a quarter broad, contains 99 acres, moftly of mofs, from which the village of Lufs and the neighbourhood are fupplied with peats. 4*thly, Inchlonaig,* near a mile long, and above a quarter of a mile broad, contains 145 acres, 66 of which are under a natural wood of old yews. The whole ifland has for many years been kept as a deer park by the family of Lufs.

Phenomena.—Lochlomond has been long famed for three wonders, viz. *fifh without fins, waves without wind,* and *a floating ifland.* Vipers, which abound in the iflands, and are fo far amphibious as to fwim from one to another, are probably the *fifh without fins.* A man of undoubted veracity, who lives in the village of Lufs, affirms that he has feen one of them attempt to get into a boat in which he was, and that it was inftantly killed. A fwelling *wave without* any *wind* perceptible at the time, is not peculiar to this lake. It may be obferved, wherever there is a great extent of water, if a calm immediately fucceeds a ftorm. But independent of any commotion in the atmofphere, at the time of the remarkable earthquake at Lifbon, in 1755, the water of Loch-lomond rofe fuddenly fome feet above its former level, and was otherwife uncommonly agitated; and fome phenomena of this kind, obferved at a remote period, may have been the *wonder* alluded to. A fmall ifland lying near the weft fhore of Inchconagan, is called *the Floating Ifland.* It is now, at leaft, fixed there; but that it may have once floated is credible. In that cafe, it muft probably have been a moffy fragment, detached by the waves from the neighbouring ifle of

Inch-

Inchmoan, and kept together by the matted roots of coarse grasses, gales, or Dutch myrtles, willows, &c. In a small lake in the Highlands of Perthshire, a *floating island* of this kind actually exists *.

Rivers.—There are 4 rivers in the parish, all of which discharge themselves into Lochlomond, but none of them are remarkable for size; 1*st*, The river *Froon*, which rises in Glenfroon, and enters into the lake near the south end of the parish. 2*dly*, The river of *Finlass*. 3*dly*, That of *Luss*. And, 4*thly*, That of *Douglass*, which forms a great part of the boundary between the parishes of Luss and Arrochar.

Woods, &*c.*—There are 880 acres under natural wood. Of these there are about 700 almost entirely under oak woods, which have been usually cut down once in 20 years, and at last cutting produced about 14000 bolls of bark †. A cutting of the whole oak woods of that age, at an average of prices for 15 years past, may be valued at 7600 l. They are of such extent as to admit of their being properly divided into 20 separate *hags* or parts, one of which may be cut every year. The cutting commences about the beginning of May, or as soon as the bark can be easily peeled, and must be over before the middle of July. Formerly there was little attention paid to the manner in which the work was performed; but now care is taken that the trees shall be all cut down and peeled close to the ground, so as to make the young shoots rise as much as possible directly from the earth, and acquire roots of their own, independent of those of the parent stock. For the same purpose, in rough and high grounds,

---

* *See* Pennant's Tour in 1772, 4to. part II. p. 18.
† The boll of bark contains 10 stones Dutch weight,

grounds, burning the heath, or any brufh-wood which can be collected about the ftocks, is found to have an excellent effect. After the woods are cut, they are, for 5 or 6 years, carefully preferved from cattle. At that period, at 10 or 12, and at 15 or 16 years of age, they are weeded or cleared from broom, briars, or whatever elfe is prejudicial to them, and properly thinned. The firft weeding is much for the benefit of the wood, but makes no immediate returns to the proprietor. The hoops got at the fecond will bear about one fourth of the expence; and at the third, will do fomething more than clear the whole. Trees of every kind thrive in this country amazingly. An oak in the Bandry wood 96 years old, is 7 feet 3 inches in girth two feet above the ground, has in its trunk, which is 21 feet high, 45 folid feet of timber, and is computed to have 4 bolls of bark. Another oak near the houfe of Camftraddan, which is about 80 years old, is 7 feet 2 inches in girth two feet above the ground, has in its trunk 36 feet of folid timber, and is computed to have $2\frac{1}{2}$ bolls of bark. But the trees of the greateft fize in this parifh are at Rofedoe. A yew tree there, at the height of $2\frac{1}{2}$ feet above the ground is $12\frac{1}{2}$ feet, and a fycamore, at the fame height, $13\frac{1}{2}$ feet in girth. Their age is uncertain.

The natural woods of this country confift of oak, afh, yew, holly, mountain afh, birch, hazel, afpen, alder, crab, hawthorn, and willows. Oaks thrive only in dry ground. Afhes abound on the banks of the lake and near rills of water. Yews are rarely found but in the iflands. Hollies are fcattered through the woods, and mountain afhes often grow in elevated fituations. The remaining kinds are lefs valuable, and frequently, therefore, diftinguifhed by the name of *barren timber*. The other indigenous plants are nearly the fame as in other parts of the Highlands, in fimilar foils and fituations.

tions. A few are to be found, which are uſually conſidered as rare ; as, *iſoetes lacuſtris*, or quillwort ; *ſubularia aquatica*, or awlwort ; *aliſma ranunculoides*, or leſſer water plantain ; *oſmunda regalis*, or flowering fern ; *lichen Burgeſii*, or crowned lichen, &c.

Wild Animals.—The following is a liſt of the wild animals, obſerved for ſome years paſt in this part of the country. The names of ſuch as are migratory, are diſtinguiſhed by an aſteriſk (*) before them.

I. QUAD-

I. QUADRUPEDS.

Latin Names.	English.	Scotch.	Gaelic.
Cervus dama. Lin.	Fallow deer	——	Fiadh
Cervus capreolus. Lin.	Roe	——	Earba
Canis vulpes. Lin.	Fox	Tod	Sionnach, balgaire
Catus sylvestris. Klein.	Wild cat	——	Cat fhiadhaich
Ursus meles. Lin.	Badger	Brock	Broc
Martes abietum. Raii.	Pine martin	——	Taghan
Mustela putorius. Lin.	Polecat	Foumart	Fòclan
Mustela vulgaris. Klein.	Common weasel	Whitret	Neas
Mustela erminea. Lin.	Stoat, or ermine	——	——
Mustela lutra. Lin.	Otter	——	Dòran, dòr-chù
Lepus timidus. Lin.	Common hare	Mawkin	Maigheach
Lepus hieme albus. Forst.	Alpine, or white hare	——	Maigheach gheal
Mus rattus. Lin.	Rat	——	Radan
Mus amphibius. Lin.	Water rat	——	Radan uisge
Mus sylvaticus. Lin.	Field mouse	——	——
Mus musculus. Lin.	Common mouse	——	Luch
Mus agrestis. Lin.	Short-tailed mouse	——	——
Sorex araneus. Lin.	Foetid shrew mouse	——	Dallag
Talpa europaeus. Lin.	Mole	Mouldwart	Famh, air-reathabh
Erinaceus, europaeus. Lin.	Urchin	Hedge-hog	Gràineag
Vespertilis murinus. Lin.	Common bat.	——	Ialtag, dialtag.

II. BIRDS.

II. BIRDS.—LAND-BIRDS.

Latin Names.	English.	Scotch.	Gaelic.
Falco fulvus. Lin.	Ringtail eagle	Black eagle	Iolair dhubh
Falco ossifragus. Lin.	Sea eagle		Iolair
Falco Haliaetus. Lin.	Osprey		Iolair uisge
Falco milvus. Lin.	Kite	Glead	Clamhan-gabblach, eroman-lochaidb
Falco buteo. Lin.	Common buzzard		Clamhan
Falco aeruginosus. Lin.	Moor buzzard		
Falco cyaneus. Lin.	Henharrier		An t-eun fionn
Pygargus accipiter. Raii.	Ringtail		Breid-air-tóin
Falco tinnunculus. Lin.	Kestrel		————
Falco subbuteo. Lin.	Hobby		
Falco nisus. Lin.	Sparrow hawk		Speir-sheeg
Strix otus. Lin.	Long-eared owl		
Strix stridula. Lin.	Tawny owl		————
Strix ulula. Lin.	Brown owl	Howlet	
Strix flammea. Lin.	White owl		
Lanius excubitor. Lin.	Great shrike		Cumhachag, cailleach-oidbche
Corvus corax. Lin.	Raven	Corby	Cailleach-oidbche gheal
Corvus frugilegus. Lin.	Rook	Craw	Fitheach
Corvus cornix. Lin.	Hooded crow	Hoody	Creumbach, rócas
Corvus pica. Lin.	Magpie	Piet	Fionnag
Corvus glandarius. Lin.	Jay	Jay-piet	Pioghaid
Corvus monedula. Lin.	Jackdaw	Daw	Scriachag choille
Cuculus canorus	Cuckoo	Gouk	Cathog
			Cuthag, cuach

II. BIRDS.—LAND BIRDS.

Latin Names.	English.	Scotch.	Gaelic.
* Alcedo ifpida. Lin.	Kingfisher		
Certhia familiaris. Lin.	Creeper		
Tetrao tetrix. Lin.	Black Cock		*Coileach dubh*
Lagopus altera. Plinii. Raii. Syn.	Grous	Moor fowl	*Coileach-ruadh*
Tetrao lagopus. Lin.	Ptarmigan		*Tarmachan*
Tetrao perdrix. Lin.	Partridge	Pertrick	*Cearc-thomain*
Columba palumbus. Lin.	Ring dove	Cufhet dow	*Smùdan*
Turdus pilaris. Gefner.	Fieldfare	Feltifare	*Liatruifg*
Turdus mufcus. Lin.	Throstle	Maevis	*Smeòrach*
Turdus iliacus. Lin.	Redwing		
Turdus merula. Lin.	Black bird		*Lon dubh*
Turdus torquatus. Lin.	Ring ouzel		*Dubh-chraige*
* Sturnus cinclus. Lin.	Water ouzel	Water craw	*Gobha-uifge*
Ampelus garrulus. Lin.	Chaterer		
Loxia pyrrhula. Lin.	Bullfinch		*Corcan coille*
Loxia chloris. Lin.	Greenfinch		*Glaifean darach*
Emberiza miliaria. Lin.	Common bunting	Bunting	*Gealag-bhuachair*
Emberiza citrinella. Lin.	Yellow hammer	Yellow yelding	*Buidheag bhealaidh*
Emberiza fchaeniclus. Lin.	Reed sparrow		
* Emberiza nivalis. Lin.	Snow bunting	Snow fleck	*Eun an t-fneachdaidh*
Fringilla carduelis. Lin.	Goldfinch	Gold fpink	
Fringilla caelebs. Lin.	Chaffinch	Green lintwhite	
Fringilla montifringilla. Lin.	Brambling		*Bricean beatha*

II. BIRDS.—LAND-BIRDS.

Latin Names.	English.	Scotch.	Gaelic.
Fringilla domestica. Lin.	Sparrow		Gealbhan
Linaria. Gesner.	Linnet	Lintwhite	Gealan-lin
* Muscicapa grisola. Lin.	Fly catcher		Uiseag
Alauda arvensis. Lin.	Sky lark	Laverock	
Alauda arborea. Lin.	Wood lark		Riabhag choille
Alauda pratensis. Lin.	Tit lark	Titling	Riabhag mhonaidh
Motacilla alba. Lin.	White wagtail		Breac-an t-sil
Motacilla flava. Lin.	Yellow wagtail		
* Motacilla phaenicurus. Lin.	Red start		Ceann-dearg
Motacilla rubecula. Lin.	Red breast		Broin-dearg
Motacilla trochilus. Lin.	Yellow wren		
Motacilla regulus. Lin.	Golden crested wren		
Motacilla troglodytes. Lin.	Wren		Dreathan
* Motacilla Oenanthe. Lin.	Wheat-ear		
* Motacilla rubetra. Lin.	Whin-chat		
* Motacilla rubicula. Lin.	Stone-chatter		Cloichearan
Motacilla sylvia. Lin.	White throat		
Parus major. Gesner.	Great titmouse	Ox-eye	
* Parus caeruleus. Gesner.	Blue titmouse		
Parus ater. Lin.	Colemouse		Caicheag chean-dubh
* Parus caudatus. Gesner.	Longtailed titmouse		
** Hirundo rustica. Lin.	House swallow		Gobhlan-gaoith
* Hirundo riparia. Lin.	Sand martin		Gobhlan-gairebhich

II. BIRDS.—LAND-BIRDS.

Latin Names.	English.	Scotch.	Gaelic.
* Hirundo apus. Lin.	Swift		
* * Caprimulgus Europaeus. Lin.	Goatfucker		

WATER-FOWLS.

Latin Names.	English.	Scotch.	Gaelic.
* Ardea major. Lin.	Heron		Corra riathach
* Scolopax rusticola. Lin.	Woodcock		Coileach coille.
Scolopax gallinago. Lin.	Common snipe		Croman loin.
Scolopax gallinula. Lin.	Jack snipe		
* Tringa vanellus. Lin.	Lapwing	Teuchit, peesweep	Curcag, adharcan-luachrach
* Tringa hypoleucos. Lin.	Common landpiper		
* Charadrius morinellus. Lin.	Dotterel		Amadan mòintich
* Haematopus ostralegus. Lin.	Pied oyster-catcher	Sea-piet	Gille-bride
* Rallus aquaticus. Lin.	Water Rail		
* Colymbus cristatus. Lin.	Great crested grebe		
* Colymbus minor. Brisson.	Dusky grebe		
* Colymbus auritus. Lin.	Little grebe		
* Alca Arctica. Lin.	Puffin	Tom-noddy	Spàg-re-tòin, Fachach
* Colymbus glacialis. Lin.	Northern diver		Bur-bhuachaill
* Colymbus immer. Lin.	Imber		
* * Mergus stellatus. Brunnich.	Speckled diver	Arran-ake	

Colymbus

II. BIRDS.—WATER-FOWLS.

Latin Names.	English.	Scotch.	Gaelic.
* Colymbus septentrionalis. Lin.	Red-throated diver		
Larus canus. Lin.	Common sea mall	Sea-maw	
Larus tridactylus. Lin.	Tarrock		Faoileann
Larus minuta. Lin.	Lesser tern		Steirneal
* Mergus merganser.	Goosander		
* Mergus serrator. Lin.	Red breasted goos-ander		
* Mergus albellus. Lin.	The smew		Sioluiche
* Anas Cygnus ferus. Lin.	Wild swan		Eala
* Anas anser. Lin.	Wild goose		Muir-gheadh
* Anas clangula. Lin.	Golden eye		
* Anas boschas. Lin.	Mallard	Common wild duck	Lacha chinn uaine
* Anas ferina. Lin.	Pochard		
* Anas penelops. Lin.	Wigeon		
Anas crecca. Lin.	Teal		Crann-lacha
Pelecanus Carbo. Lin.	Cormorant		
Pelecanus graculus. Lin.	Shag	Skart	Scarbh

III. REPTILES.

Latin Names.	English.	Scotch.	Gaelic.
Rana temporaria. Lin.	Frog	Puddock	Losgann
Rano bufo. Lin.	Toad	Tead	Losgan dubh
Lacerta agilis. Lin.	Scaly lizard	Ask	Dearc-luachair

Lacertus

III. REPTILES.

Latin Names.	*Engliſh.*	*Scotch.*	*Gaelic.*
Lacertus vulgaris. Lin.	Brown lizard	——	——
Coluber Berus. Lin.	Viper	Adder	Nathair
Anguis fragilis. Lin.	Blind worm	——	——

IV. FISH.

Latin Names.	*Engliſh.*	*Scotch.*	*Gaelic.*
Lampetra. Raii.	Lamprey	Lamper-eel	Deala-thóll
Muraena anguilla. Lin.	Eel	——	Eaſgann
Pleuroneċtes Leviniae	Lochlomond floun-der	Fluke	Leabag
Perca fluviatilis. Lin.	Perch	——	Muc-lochaidh, creagag uiſge
Salmo Salar. Lin.	Salmon	——	Bradan
Salmo trutta. Lin.	Sea-trout	——	Gealag
Salmo Fario. Lin.	Trout	——	Breac
Salmo Alpinus. Lin.	Charr	——	Tarragheal
Salmo Lavaretus. Lin.	Gwiniad †	Powan	Pollag
Salmulus. Raii.	Samlet	Parr	Gobhlachan
Efox Lucius. Lin.	Pike	——	Geat iaſg
Cyprinus Rutilus. Lin.	Roach	Braiſe	——
Cyprinus Phoxinus. Lin.	Minow	——	Mion-iaſg.

† PENNANT.

Population.—According to the returns made to **Dr** Web-ſter in 1755, compared with the population in March 1793, the number of ſouls in this pariſh has decreaſed within theſe 40 years.

STATISTICAL TABLE OF THE PARISH OF LUSS.

SOULS, FAMILIES, SEXES, &c.

Population in 1755	978	Perſons under 8 years of	
———— in 1793	917	age - -	203
	———	——— above that age	714
Decreaſe	61	Married perſons	280
Number of families	112	Widowers - -	15
Males - -	448	Widows - -	36
Females - -	469		

CONDITIONS, PROFESSIONS, &c.

Proprietors reſiding occa-ſionally - -	1	Coopers - -	4
		Corn-millers -	3
Ditto non-reſiding -	2	Lint-millers -	1
Clergymen - -	1	Flax-dreſſers -	1
Members of the Eſtabli-ſhed Church	915	Weavers - -	11
		Taylors - -	3
Seceders - -	2	Shoemakers -	4
Schoolmaſters -	2	Journeymen and appren-	
Scholars - -	120	tices to weavers, tay-	
Farmers - -	76	lors, and ſhoemakers	18
Innkeepers and retailers of ſpirits, ale, &c.	9	Male-ſervants -	38
		Female-ſervants -	47
Exciſe officers -	1	Poor - -	10
Shopkeepers - -	3	Capital of their funds L.	150
Smiths - -	2	Annual income L.	37
Maſons - -	2	Boats - -	21
Carpenters and joiners	7	Wheel-carriages -	2
		Carts	

Carts   -   -   59   Ploughs *   -   -   57

EXTENT AND VALUE OF PROPERTY.

	A.	R.	F.
Number of Scotch acres arable -	1538	0	26.20
———— ———— in meadow -	109	2	39.40
———— ———— under pafture	14,873	3	31
———— ———— woods -	880	1	33
Total acres †	17,402	1	9.60

Length in Englifh miles   -   -   - $8\frac{1}{2}$
Average breadth in ditto   -   -   - $3\frac{1}{2}$
Valued rent in Scotch money   -   L. 1500   0   0
Real rent in 1793, in Sterling ditto   1600   0   0

VALUE OF STOCK.

110 Draught horfes at L. 10 10 0 each L. 1155	0	0
4 Carriage horfes ——— 30 0 0 ——— 120	0	0
6 Saddle horfes ——— 15 0 0 ——— 90	0	0
20 Beft cattle ——— 8 0 0 ——— 160	0	0
514 Inferior ditto ——— 3 10 0 ——— 1799	0	0
1875 Beft fheep ——— 0 14 0 ——— 1312	10	0
5625 Inferior ditto ——— 0 10 6 ——— 2953	2	6
8 Swine ——— 0 15 0 ——— 6	0	0
Total value of ftock L. 7595	12	6

* Though the above number of ploughs is kept for the fake of convenience, a much fmaller number would be fufficient for all the tillage of the parifh.

† The number of acres, excepting in one farm, where they are computed from the produce and ftock, is afcertained by actual furveys made in the years 1770 and 1776.

ANNUAL

ANNUAL PRODUCE.

Crops.	Number of bolls ſown.	Produce per boll. B. F. P.	Total produce. B. F. P.	Price per boll. L. s. d.	Total value. L. s. d.
Oats	625	4 2 0	2812 2 0	0 15 0	2109 7 6
Bear	47	8 0 0	376 0 0	0 18 0	338 8 0
Peaſe	25	5 2 0	137 2 0	0 16 0	110 0 0
Potatoes	87	12 0 0	1044 0 0	0 9 0	469 16 0
Flax	—	—	Stones.	Price per ſtone.	
Meadow hay, or natural graſs	—	—	84	0 14 0	58 16 0
Sown graſs	—	—	1320	0 0 4	220 6 8
			1430	0 0 6	360 15 0
Straw, at 3 s. 6 d. per boll, of corn and bear	—	—	—	—	557 19 9
Paſture, at 2 l. per horſe, 1 l. per cow, and 2 s. per ſheep	—	—	—	—	1524 0 0
Annual produce of woods and plantations	—	—	—	—	400 0 0
—— ſlate quarries	—	—	—	—	500 0 0
Total value of annual produce					L. 6649 8 11

TABLE

TABLE OF MARRIAGES, BAPTISMS, AND BURIALS,

From 1700 *to* 1719.

Years.	Marriag.	Baptisms.		
		Males.	*Fem.*	*Total.*
1700	6	15	12	27
1701	6	15	9	24
1702	8	4	5	9
1703	9	13	4	17
1704	7	8	14	22
1705	9	17	17	34
1706	8	11	13	24
1707	10	9	9	18
1708	15	12	11	23
1709	7	21	16	37
1710	8	20	16	36
1711	12	19	5	24
1712	12	12	15	27
1713	8	16	21	37
1714	10	8	24	32
1715	6	17	18	35
1716	12	17	11	28
1717	7	15	9	24
1718	12	3	9	12
1719	9	13	11	24
Total number for 20 years preceding 1720 —	181	265	249	514
Annual average	$9\frac{1}{20}$	$13\frac{5}{20}$	$12\frac{9}{20}$	$25\frac{7}{20}$

TABLE

TABLE OF MARRIAGES, BAPTISMS, AND BURIALS,

From 1774 *to* 1793.

Years.	Marriag.	Males.	Fem.	Total.	Bur.
		Baptiſms.			
1774	3	24	12	36	11
1775	11	20	14	34	12
1776	9	15	11	26	17
1777	9	17	13	30	10
1778	7	17	15	32	13
1779	10	16	10	26	5
1780	3	16	11	27	17
1781	12	15	14	29	17
1782	13	14	10	24	10
1783	5	14	16	30	10
1784	12	11	14	25	11
1785	11	15	14	29	12
1786	9	13	16	29	12
1787	11	12	9	21	7
1788	10	15	11	26	15
1789	4	14	17	31	11
1790	4	12	12	24	13
1791	4	13	21	34	12
1792	12	7	15	22	17
1793	11	15	13	28	8
Total number for 20 years preceding 1794	170	295	268	563	240
Annual average	$8\frac{5}{10}$	$14\frac{15}{20}$	$13\frac{2}{5}$	$28\frac{3}{20}$	12

From the foregoing table of marriages, baptiſms, and burials, as recorded in the pariſh regiſter, it appears that the
population, for 20 years paſt, is not very different from what
it was at the beginning of this century. About 35 years
ago, upon the introduction of ſouth country ſheep, an union
of farms took place, which, at the time, muſt have diminiſhed

fhed the number a little. But that lofs has fince been more
than compenfated, by the additional hands employed in the
flate-quarries and other works.

Agriculture, Produce, and Imports.—The principal crops are
oats, bear or big, and potatoes. Peafe and flax are likewife
raifed, but in fmaller quantities. Upon fome of the farms,
artificial graffes have of late been cultivated with fuccefs.
Oats, peafe, and flax, are fown from the middle of March
to the end of April, and bear from the end of April to the
beginning of June. Potatoes are planted from the middle
of April to the 10th of May. The crops are commonly
reaped from the beginning of September to the beginning of
October, and all got in before the middle of that month.
But in unfavourable feafons, the harveft is fometimes not
over till the 10th of November. The parifh does not fupply itfelf with meal. About 200 bolls are annually imported.

Horfes and Black Cattle.—Few horfes are bred in the parifh. They are generally bought at the different markets,
for the purpofes of agriculture. Cows are moftly kept for
the convenience of families. Befides maintaining the ftock,
however, a few calves are fattened every year for the butcher,
and fome young cattle are reared for fale.

Sheep.—The higher grounds are now ftocked almoft entirely with fheep, of which there are about 7500. They are
all of the black-faced Linton kind, and kept almoft entirely
for breeding, for which the nature of the pafture is more
adapted than for fattening. A breeding ftock of 600 fheep,
for taking care of which one good herd or fhepherd is reckoned

koned fufficient, commonly confifts, at Whitfunday, of the
following proportions :

Breeding ewes - - - -	500
Year old ewes, for fupplying the place of older ewes	80
Tups - - - - -	20
	600

STATEMENT OF THE YEARLY EXPENCE OF MANAGING A BREEDING STOCK OF 600 SHEEP.

To a herd's wages, paid commonly by the pafture
    of 60 fheep - - L. 7 10 0
To his own and his dog's maintenance 6 10 0
To a grey plaid given him - 0 6 0
    ————— L. 14 6 0
To the expence of fmearing 140 of faid ftock   2 6 0
To ditto of fhearing or *clipping* the whole of
    faid ftock - - - - 0 17 0
To ditto of gathering and bringing to market   1 10 0
To intereft of ftock, at 13 s. per head for the
    breeding ewes and tups, and 9 s. 6 d. for
    the year old ewes, being 376 l. - L. 18 16 0
To rent - - - - - 52 10 0
    ————— L. 90 5 0

AMOUNT OF THE ANNUAL SALES.

By 330 draft lambs, being the ufual number for
    fale, after referving the proportion neceffa-
    ry for maintaining the ftock, loffes, &c.—
    300 of ditto fold at 4 l. 10 s. and 30 of the
    worft, called *fhots*, at 2 l. 5 s. per clad fcore L. 67 10 0
By 54 draft or *flack* ewes, at 6 s. 6 d. - 17 11 0
                          Carried forward L. 85 1 0

Brought forward	L. 85	1	0
By 10 *yeld* ewes, being fuch as either had not lambs, or loft them early, at 11 s.	5	10	0
By 6 old tups, at 12 s.	3	12	0
By 460 fleeces white, 10 to the ftone, 46 ftones, at 7 s.	16	2	0
By 140 fleeces laid, 7 to the ftone, 20 ftones, at 5 s.	5	0	0
	L. 115	5	0
Yearly expence	90	5	0
Neat profit	L. 25	0	0

The profit arifing from fuch a ftock, feems inadequate to the trouble and rifk; but it is to be obferved, that, in moft fheep farms, there are fome low arable and grafs grounds, the produce of which, in eftimating their value, is feldom taken into the account. Much depends upon the times, and much upon management. In the event of a fevere winter or fpring, the number of lambs for fale falls often one third fhort of the foregoing ftatement. The difeafe called *braxy*, is at times very deftructive to them, though not nearly fo much fo of late, as when the grounds were firft laid under fheep. It feldom attacks any but the lambs or *hogs*, i e. yearlings. Wedder lambs are more fubject to it than ewe lambs, and the fatteft and beft frequently fall a facrifice to it, when the lean efcape. It is moft fatal to them on a change of weather from froft to thaw, or thaw to froft, but efpecially during hoar froft. In open winters few fuffer by it. Taking care that the pafture is neither too rich nor too poor, is reckoned the moft effectual way of preventing it, and changing the pafture immediately, the moft effectual way of curing it. With the view of preventing difeafes, deftroying vermin, defending

fending from rain, and preferving the wool, it is ufual, about
the beginning of November, to *lay* the tups and lambs, and
a few of the weakeft ewes, with tar and butter. For the
the fame purpofe, many now *bathe* the reft of their fheep
with a ftrong infufion of tobacco, broom tops, &c.

Farms, Rents, &c.—The fize of the farms is various. In
the lower part of the parifh, where the principal dependence
is upon grain and black cattle, befides the lands poffeffed immediately by the proprietors, there are 10 farms, containing
from 50 to 164 acres, and paying from 20 l. to 80 l. Sterling of rent; and there are 54 fmaller poffeffions, rented
from 2 l. 10 s. to 20 l. There are likewife 12, which may
be properly called *fheep farms*, containing from 222 to 2880
acres, moftly of hill pafture, and paying from 11 l. to 80 l. of
yearly rent. The average rent of a fheep's pafture in the parifh at prefent, (for which an acre and a half of hill ground
is neceffary), is from 1 s. to 1 s. 6 d.; but on any lands which
have been let of late, it is confiderably higher. Upon two
of thefe fheep farms, the fmaller tenants have a common
right of pafture to 6 or 7 horfes; and there is one hill, confifting of 784 acres, which is laid moftly under fheep, and
which is entirely in the hands of 11 of the fmaller tenants,
each of whom is entitled to keep there a certain proportion
of cattle. Befides the faid grain and fheep farms, there are
feveral cottages, to which a garden, and fometimes an acre,
or half an acre of land is annexed. The tenants of the
fmaller farms, as well as the cottagers, depend often more
upon days labour, or fome other employment, than upon the
produce of any land they poffefs.

Wages, Provifions, Fuel, &c.—The common wages of men
fervants are from 7 l. to 9 l. a year, with their maintenance;

of

of maid fervants, from 3 l. to 4 l. The ufual day's wages of
men are from 8 d. to 10 d. with maintenance, and from 1 s.
to 1 s. 3 d. without it; of women, 6 d. with it.—The price
of provifions of every kind is very much regulated by the
prices in Dumbarton and Greenock, which are the neareft
market towns. For thefe 4 years paft, oat meal has fold from
16 s. 6 d. to 20 s. per boll; the beft lambs, weighing from
15 lb. to 18 lb. from 4 s. to 5 s.; a hen, from 10 d. to 1 s.;
a chicken, from 3 d. to 4 d; butter, at 12 s. the ftone; cheefe,
from 4 s. 6 d. to 6 s. the ftone.—Coals, including the freight
from Glafgow or Scotftown, coft from 6 s. 6 d. to 10 s. the
cart, which fhould be 12 cwt. Peats and fticks are the
common fuel, and not much lefs expenfive.

State of Property, &c.—There are 3 heritors, one of whom
refides occafionally. Sir JAMES COLQUHOUN of Lufs, Bart.
is proprietor of far the greateft part of the lands in the parifh. The family refidence is about 3 miles fouth from Lufs,
at *Rofedoe* or *Rofsdow, i. e.* the black promontory or head-
land, a name which is not now very applicable to it, as it is
finely wooded, and the black mofs which once abounded
there is now moftly converted into meadow. There is an
excellent modern houfe there, which commands fome noble
views of the lake. It was built by the late Sir James Colquhoun, who refided in the parifh for many years, the influence of whofe authority and example, in checking all tendency to diforder, and in promoting the interefts of virtue
and religion, is ftill fenfibly felt, and his memory, therefore,
much and juftly refpected.

Minerals.—There are two flate quarries, one upon the
eftate of Camftraddan, and the other upon the eftate of Lufs.
From the former of thefe, for 5 years paft, from 250,000
to

to 360,000 ſlates, and from the latter quarry, from 100,000
to 170,000 ſlates have been annually exported. Some of
them were ſent to Greenock, Glaſgow, and Paiſley, but
the greater part to the banks of the Leven, and acroſs Lochlomond to Stirlingſhire. The ſlates are of an excellent quality, and were ſold at from 1 l. 4 s. to 1 l. 15 s. the thouſand. From 10 to 20 hands have been employed in the
Camſtraddan quarry, and about 10 in the other. Some of
them work upon days wages ; but the greater part by the
piece. They commonly get at the rate of 15 s. per 1000,
and it takes 1 s. 4 d. per 1000 to lead the ſlates from the
quarry to the ſhore. In the ſouth end of the pariſh there
is likewiſe a very good free-ſtone quarry, from which the
ſtones to the houſe of Roſedoe, and the other principal houſes
in the pariſh, have been taken ; but it is only wrought occaſionally.

Manufactures.—In 1790, a cotton-mill was erected near
the village of Luſs. It is of the ſize moſt ſuitable to the
place, ſufficiently large to give bread to ſuch as might otherwiſe be in want of employment, but not to give encouragement to the vices which are ſo apt to abound, wherever a
promiſcuous multitude of people are aſſembled. From 30
to 40 hands, young and old, have been uſually employed in
it. Of late, owing to the general ſtagnation of trade, little
work has been carried on in it. A thread manufacture, upon
a ſmall ſcale, is likewiſe carried on at Dunfin, near the ſouth
end of the pariſh.

Antiquities.—About a mile and a quarter ſouth from Luſs,
there are the remains of a large *cairn,* or heap of ſtones,
called *Carn-ma-cheaſoig,* or, the *Cairn of St. Keſſog,* who is
ſaid, at an early period, to have ſuffered death there, and

to

to have been buried in the church of Lufs. He was long revered, therefore, as the tutelar faint of the parifh *. In the church-yard there are fome ftone coffins of confiderable antiquity. Each of them confifts of one entire ftone, with a cavity cut out of it, fit for holding a dead body at its full length, and a ftone lid for covering it. There is no infcription upon either of them.

Church †, *&c.*—The church is uncommonly good. It was built in 1771, by the late Sir James Colquhoun of Lufs, without laying any part of the burden upon the other heritors. The manfe was built in 1740, is infufficient, and at prefent in need of repair. The living confifts of 72 bolls of oat-meal, at the rate of 8¼ ftones per boll, 6 bolls of bear, 19 l. 12 s. 9¼ d. Sterling in money, and a good glebe. There is a procefs of augmentation at prefent depending. Sir James Colquhoun is patron of the parifh.

Schools

* The high veneration in which the memory of this faint was held in early times, appears from a charter to John, Laird of Lufs, preferved in the chartulary of Lennox, which Robert, King of Scotland, confirms in the 10th year of his reign :

"Omnibus hoc fcriptum vifuris, vel audituris, Malcolmus "Comes de Levenax, falutem in Chrifto. Noveritis nos ob re- "verentiam et honorem fanctiffimi viri filii Kessogi patroni "noftri dediffe, conceffiffe et hac praefente. Charta noftra con- "firmaffe dilecto et fideli Bachulario noftro Domino Joanne de "Lufs, et haeredibus fuis quibufcunque talem libertatem, quod "nos nec haeredes noftri prifas captiones feu carriagia infra "terras fuas de Lufs, quas de nobis tenet haereditarie capiemus. "Conceffimus fimiliter,' &c.

† The church of Lufs was one of the 6 churches within his diocefe, which, in 1429, John Cameron, bifhop of Glafgow, with the confent, and at the defire of their refpective patrons, erected into prebendaries.

Schools and Poor.—There are two schools, for each of which a good house has been lately built. One of these is the parish school, in which the number of scholars is generally from 30 to 50. The salary is 10 l. Sterling. The school fees for reading English are 1 s. 6 d. per quarter; for reading and writing, 2 s.; for arithmetic, 2 s. 6 d.; and for Latin, 5 s. The other school is supported by the Society for propagating Christian Knowledge. The number of scholars who attend it, during the whole or part of the year, is about 80. The emoluments of the schoolmaster consist of 13 l. Sterling of salary, a dwelling house, garden, cow's grass, and some school fees. The children of the poor are taught gratis.

The Society have likewise of late allowed a salary for a sewing school at Luss. The number of poor, at present upon the roll, is 10. Some of these get weekly, and others occasional supplies, according to their necessities. The funds for their support arise from the collections on Sunday, rents of seats in the church, marriage and mort-cloth dues, and the interest of 150 l. Sterling of stock, amounting, at an average, to 37 l. Sterling yearly. L. 50 of the said stock were bequeathed by the late Robert Carmichael, Esq; of Broomley.

Language and Character.—South from Luss, English, and north from it the Gaelic, is the prevailing language. The service in church is performed in each of these.—The people, in general, are sober and industrious, humane and charitable. They are regular in their attendance on the ordinances of religion. The example, in this respect, of the families of chief rank for many years past, has, without doubt, had considerable influence upon those in inferior stations.

Roads, Ale-houfes, &c.—The roads have of late been much attended to, and are at prefent in good repair. In the 1786, an act of Parliament was obtained for converting the ftatute labour of this county into money, which has had good effects.—There are 9 licenfed ale and whifky houfes, and one inn. Four years ago there were 5 licenfed ftills for diftilling whifky; now there is but one of 36 gallons.

Advantages and Difadvantages.—The principal difadvantages, under which this parifh labours, are the great expence of fuel, the fcarcity of natural manures, and the high price of labour, and of every neceffary of life, owing to the neighbourhood of fo many great manufacturing concerns; but that neighbourhood, on the other hand, is a great advantage to fuch as have any articles to difpofe of.

Hints for Improvements.—Woods in general, and oak woods in particular, are now become valuable every where, and efpecially upon the banks of Lochlomond. Whatever, therefore, relates to their improvement, muft be well worthy the attention of every proprietor. An acre of oak wood here, at an average, is worth from 10 s. to 12 s. a year; which is a much greater return than could be had from as much ground of equal quality in any other way whatever.— The firft great object to be attended to, is the inclofing the great body of the wood with a fufficient ftone dyke. The temporary wooden fence, which is commonly raifed round it every time it is cut, feldom lafts above 4 years, and often amounts to one third, fometimes to one half the expence of a ftone wall. The wood thus inclofed fhould, as foon as circumftances will permit, be taken entirely into the proprietor's hands, whofe intereft it will be to encourage the natural growth of oak, afh, holly, and other valuable timber, and

to

to plant all the vacant ſpaces with trees ſuited to the ſoil. Oak woods are never entirely out of the reach of cattle, and they ought never, therefore, to be permitted to enter them. For 4 or 5 years, all agree they muſt be carefully preferved from them; and, after that time, if they are thriving, and the *ſtool* is ſufficiently thick, the paſture in them is no object. As to the age at which an oak wood ſhould be cut, there are different opinions. That there is a period, however, beyond which it ſhould not be permitted to grow, cannot be doubted. After it is cut, the moſt vigorous ſhoots are always obſerved to ſpring from well rooted young ſtocks, from 3 to 6 inches in diameter. Some of theſe will grow the firſt year from 4 even to 7 feet in height, and near the ground will meaſure above half an inch in diameter. In proportion as the parent ſtocks are older and larger, the ſhoots are leſs vigorous, and when the ſtocks are 13 or 14 inches in diameter, there are either no young ſhoots at all, or they are very feeble. If the great object, therefore, be to produce, at ſtated periods, a quantity of bark for the market, it muſt be the ruin of a copſe kept for that purpoſe to allow it all to grow very old. If in this country it exceeds much the uſual period of 20 or 22 years, the bark becomes inferior in quality, and the *ſtool* will ſuffer more by age, than the additional value of the timber and bark can compenſate. In order to make any oak wood, however, fell to advantage, it is neceſſary that there ſhould be a certain proportion of timber of different ſizes, as well as bark. At every cutting, therefore, it is uſual to leave ſo many *ſtandard* trees of different ages, for the benefit of future ſales. Theſe ſhould always be healthy and vigorous, and either in the outer ſkirts of the wood, or in vacant ſpaces, where they are detached from other trees. When left without judgment in the thickeſt part of the wood, being deprived

ved

ved of their former fhelter, they feldom thrive themfelves, and by their drop and fhade hurt all the young growth a-round them. Prunning or lopping off great branches from any of thefe ought carefully to be avoided. Though the fcar may heal outwardly, yet it never fails to introduce rot-tennefs, lefs or more, into the heart, which hurts the timber, and impairs the vigour of the tree.

As to the arable and beft grafs grounds, the inclofing them, as well as the woods, with a fufficient fence, is the firft great improvement of which they are capable. Of what kind the fence fhould be, nature, if attended to, will feldom fail to direct. In high and expofed fituations, hedges will not fucceed; but there ftones commonly abound. In the lower grounds, where ftones are not plentiful, hawthorn hedges may be raifed with advantage. But of all plants for this purpofe, holly promifes to anfwer beft. Holly thrives every where in this country, as in its native foil; and it makes not only the moft ornamental, but likewife the clofeft and the beft of hedges. The time which it takes to raife the-plants from the feed, and the expence of getting them from a nurfery, is the great bar to the general ufe of them. That bar might here be eafily removed; the hollies which grow wild in the woods, naturally lay their own branches, which, as foon as they touch the ground, freely take root. With a little affiftance from art, a fufficient number of well rooted plants could foon be got, which might fafely be tranf-planted at fuch an age as to make almoft an immediate fence.

The having the whole lands of a country engroffed into *a few hands*, is certainly much againft the public intereft. Every man, however, who depends entirely upon the pro-duce of his fields, ought to have, at leaft, as much land as is fufficient for affording himfelf and his family a comfortable
                                                                fubfiftence

ſubſiſtence and conſtant employment ; and if he poſſeſſes any
waſte land, he ought to have ſufficient encouragement from
the proprietor for taking it into tillage, and improving it.
When the caſe is otherwiſe, he is under a temptation of
ruining his ground, by over-cropping it, one of the moſt
prevailing errors in the preſent Highland ſyſtem of farming.
But the man, on the other hand, whoſe chief dependence is
upon days labour, or ſome other employment, ought to have
land ſufficient only for ſupplying his family with milk, potatoes, and other neceſſaries, but not ſo much as to divert his
attention from his proper buſineſs. Grazing farms, and eſpecially ſheep farms, muſt, from their nature, be on a greater
ſcale. In them a great range, and a variety of paſture, are
indiſpenſibly neceſſary. As much as the ſtate of property,
therefore, will permit, their boundaries ought to be the
great boundaries of nature. When the paſture of a hill or
mountain is parcelled out among two or three different tenants, without any inacceſſible *gullies* or rocks to form a line
of ſeparation, the cattle of each will be conſtantly treſpaſſing
ſomewhere, and therefore conſtantly chaced from one part to
another, ſo that neither will receive much benefit from it.
Common paſture, in ſuch a caſe, is ſeldom found to be a remedy for the evil. Whatever wiſe and juſt regulations may
at firſt be laid down for fixing the proportion of cattle to be
kept by each, they are never in fact adhered to ; and the
ground is always overſtocked.

The preſent breed of ſheep in this pariſh may perhaps be
changed with advantage. In every attempt of this kind,
however, great caution is neceſſary. The trial ſhould firſt
be made with ſmall parcels, and rather by the proprietors
than by the tenants. Sheep are delicate animals, ſubject to
many diſeaſes, and when they are taken from one country
to another, or even from one farm to another, it takes

ſome

fome time before they are habituated to their new fituation, and thrive in it. When a man takes a fheep farm, therefore, he endeavours, if poffible, to purchafe from the outgoing tenant the ftock of fheep upon it, which he reckons at the rate of at leaft 2 s. a head more valuable to him than to any other.

Though the tenants are now more comfortably lodged than they once were, there is ftill, in that refpect, room for improvement. In a country which abounds fo much with flates, it may appear furprifing that fo few of the houfes fhould be covered with them, though there can be no doubt, but in the iffue, they would be found lefs expenfive than any thatch which could be ufed. The great obftacle to the ufe of them for that purpofe, at prefent, is the expence of the timber required. That obftacle, it is hoped, will in time be removed. When the extenfive and thriving plantations, in different parts of the country, have grown up, timber will be more eafily got.

All thefe improvements, however, are more wanted in many other parts than here, where fome of them have already taken place. Within thefe 26 years, above 4000 l. Sterling have been laid out upon the eftate of Lufs alone, in inclofing the woods and arable grounds with fufficient ftone dykes and other fences, and in planting; not to fpeak of the fums expended upon other improvements. Within the fame fpace of time, near 100 acres of wafte land have been brought into tillage, and now produce tolerable crops.

PARISH OF ROSENEATH.

(County of Dunbarton.)

By the Rev Mr George Drummond.

Name, Situation, Soil, &c.

THE ancient name of the parish was *Roſſnachoich*, which is a Gaelic word signifying the "Virgin's "Promontory." The parish is situated in the most westerly part of Dunbarton-shire, in the Synod of Glasgow and Air. It is a peninsula, nearly in the form of a parallelogram, being about 7 miles long and 2 broad, and is bounded on the land-side towards the N. by the parish of Row, on the W. by Lochlong, on the S. by the frith of Clyde, and on the E. by Gairloch. It is a continued ridge of rising ground, without any high hill or mountain, although some parts of it are rocky. The higher grounds are covered with heath; but the lands near the shore are green. The soil is various, part of it being fertile, and part barren; part of it deep, and part shallow. The air is naturally dry, but is frequently moistened with showers. It is in general healthy. There are several small rivulets; but, from the situation of the parish, no large rivers. We have a lake of about a mile in circumference, that abounds with perch.

Coaſt,

Coaſt, Fiſheries, &c.—The extent of coaſt is about 13 miles. The ſhore is in ſome places flat and ſandy, but in general rocky and low. The fiſh commonly caught are herring, cod, mackerel, ſkate, flounders and ſalmon. Salmon are ſold from 1 d. to 3 d. a-pound. The other fiſh are ſold by gueſs or number, according to their ſize. The ſalmon and herrings are caught with nets; the other fiſh with lines. Greenock and Glaſgow are the markets in which the fiſh caught here are generally ſold. There is a ſtrong current in the Gairloch, between the pariſhes of Roſeneath and Row, oppoſite to the church of Row, where there is a ferry. There are two bays on the coaſt, one called Callwattie, and the other Campſoil; in which laſt there is good anchorage, and ſafe harbour for ſhips of any burden. In the Duke of Argyle's park there is a remarkable rock, which, though now at a conſiderable diſtance from the ſhore, bears evident marks of having been waſhed by the ſea. Its greateſt perpendicular height is 34 feet. It is called Wallace's Loup, *i. e.* Leap, from a tradition, that the renowned Wallace, being cloſely purſued by a party of his enemies, jumped down this rock on horſeback, and eſcaped unhurt; but his horſe was killed by the fall, and was buried at the foot of the rock, where his grave is ſhewn.

Produce, Rent, &c.—The average produce of an acre is not eaſily eſtimated, both from the farmers being backward in diſcloſing their affairs, and from a want of knowing the number of acres in the pariſh. The pariſh could ſufficiently ſupply its inhabitants with proviſions, if they were not obliged to ſell the produce for ready money, in order to pay their rents: When this is the caſe, they are under the neceſſity of buying proviſions again for their own ſupport; the purchaſe-money for which ariſes from the profits of the herring-fiſhery. The land-rent of the pariſh is about L. 1000

L. 1000 Sterling. The annual rent of a cottage and yard is from 10 s. to 20 s. One falmon-fifhery, with a piece of ground, lets for L. 30 a-year. The Duke of Argyle has difcovered a flate-quarry in this parifh, which at prefent promifes pretty well. Several thoufand flates are already dug out, formed, and fhaped for ufe.

Population.—According to Dr Webfter, the number of the people was 521. At prefent, there are

Under 10 years,	54	Smiths, - -	3
Between 10 & 20,	82	Shoemakers, -	4
—— 20 & 50,	140	Tailors, - -	5
—— 50 & 70,	102	Carpenters and appren-	
Above 70 -	16	tices, -	6
	——	Seamen, -	6
Total,	394	Herring-fifhermen,	96
		Salmon-fifhermen,	2
Males above 10 years,	180	Ferrymen, -	2
Females ditto,	160	Houfehold fervants,	22
Farmers, -	48	Seceders, -	5
Weavers, - -	7	Cameronians, -	14
Mafon, -	1		

TABLE.

T A B L E of Marriages, Births and Deaths, from January 1780, to ditto 1790.

Years.	Marriages.	Births.	Deaths.
1780,	5	16	3
1781,	6	13	4
1782,	5	16	9
1783,	4	14	5
1784,	4	19	4
1785,	5	18	6
1786,	7	12	1
1787,	5	14	4
1788,	6	17	10
1789,	8	14	5
Average,	5¼	15	5

There are 98 houſes in the pariſh, all which are detached, there being no towns nor villages. The proportion of bachelors to married men and widowers, is as 2 to 3. Each marriage produces, at an average, nearly 3 children. The decreaſe in the population, from what it was 40 years ago, is not to be aſcribed to the attraction of neighbouring manufactures, but is owing partly to one proprietor having taken into his own poſſeſſion ſome farms upon which ſeveral families formerly lived, and partly to ſome other farms being let to fewer tenants; yet, even at preſent, we are ſtocked with inhabitants.

Church, School, Poor, &c.—The church was rebuilt in 1780; the manſe in 1770. The ſtipend is moſtly paid in victual; and, at an average, including the glebe, may be eſtimated at L. 110 Sterling. The Duke of Argyle is patron.

tron. The number of heritors is 3; 2 of them reside constantly in the parish; and sometimes the Duke of Argyle, who is the chief proprietor. The schoolmaster's salary is L. 8, 9 s. Sterling; average of fees and perquisites, L. 8, 7 s.; number of scholars in winter, 38; at other times fewer. The quarter-fees for reading are 1 s.; for reading and writing, 1 s 6 d.; for reading, writing, and arithmetic, 2 s.; for Latin, 2 s. 6 d.; but which last has not been taught for several years. The number of poor is 13. The annual amount of contributions for their relief, including the interest of the parochial funds, is L. 18 Sterling.

Price of Provisions and Labour, &c.—The present current prices of beef and veal, are from 5 d. to 7 d. the pound; formerly they were from 2¼ d. to 4 d. the pound; mutton and lamb, at present, from 4 d. to 6 d. a-pound; formerly 2 d. to 3¼ d. the pound. A hen, which now sells at 1 s. sold formerly at 4 d.; a chicken, now 4 d. and 5 d. sold formerly for 2 d.; butter, at present from 9 d. to 1 s. the pound, formerly at 3¼ d. and 4 d.; skimmed-milk cheese, at present 3 d. formerly 1¼ d. the pound. Barley sells now at 15 s. a-boll, Dunbarton-shire, 8 stone the boll, which is a peck and a half larger than Linlithgow measure, formerly it sold at 9 s. or 10 s.; oats, at present 13 s. a-boll, formerly 8 s. A common labourer's wages a-day, without victuals, are from 10 d. to 1 s. and 1 s. 2 d.; a carpenter or wright, 2 s. a-day; a mason, 2 s. a-day; a tailor, 8 d. a-day and his meat. Peats are the common fuel used here; some few families use coals, which are brought by water down theriver Clyde, from the neighbourhood of Glasgow. The price of them at the shore here, including freight, &c. is 5 s. the cart. The cart should be 1200 weight. Peats are sold at 6 d. the creel. The average expence of a common

mon labourer and his wife may be eſtimated at L. 11 Sterling yearly : Many of them have actually brought up
pretty large families upon the wages they receive, and that
without running much in debt.

Miſcellaneous Obſervations.—There are no ale-houſes, but
plenty of whiſky-houſes, here, which are rather unfriendly
to the morals of the people. Twelve new houſes have
been built within theſe 10 years ; for each of theſe, except 3, an old houſe has been pulled down. There are almoſt no cottagers employed in agriculture, unleſs by the
Duke of Argyle. It is difficult to ſay whether it is better
to employ them or hired ſervants. It is believed, that the
cheapeſt and moſt expeditious method of carrying on work
in this part of the country, is letting it by the piece, when
it can be done ſo. For theſe 20 years and upwards, no perſon
whatever, reſiding within this pariſh, has been impriſoned,
except one poor man a ſhort time for a ſmall debt. Here rats
cannot exiſt : Many of theſe have, at different times, been
accidentally imported from veſſels lying upon the ſhore ;
but were never known to live 12 months in the place.
From a prevailing opinion, that the ſoil of this pariſh is
hoſtile to that animal, ſome years ago, a Weſt India planter
actually carried out to Jamaica ſeveral caſks of Roſeneath
earth, with a view to kill the rats that were deſtroying his
ſugar-canes. It is ſaid this had not the deſired effect ; for
we loſt a very valuable export. Had the experiment ſucceeded, this would have been a new and profitable trade
for the proprietors ; but perhaps, by this time, the pariſh of
Roſeneath might have been no more.

PARISH of ROW,

(COUNTY OF DUMBARTON.)

By the Rev. Mr JOHN ALLAN.

Name, Situation, Soil, Fiſh, &c.

THE name *Row* is a Gaelic word, and ſignifies ' a
' point.' Very near the place where the church is
ſituated, there is a pretty long point running out into the
ſea.—The pariſh is ſituated in the preſbytery of Dumbarton, and Synod of Glaſgow and Air. It is between 13
and 14 miles in length, and about 3 in breadth ; bounded
on the E. by the pariſh of Cardrofs; on the N. E. by Lufs;
on the N. W. by Lochlong; on the W. and S. by the Gare-
loch, which ſeparates it from Roſeneath, and the frith of
Clyde, which ſeparates it from Greenock. The E. end of
the pariſh is pretty flat, the greateſt part of it hilly, and towards the N. E. mountainous. The ſoil in general is light,
and where it is properly cultivated, pretty fertile. The
air is ſharp and healthy. Fevers are the prevalent diſtem-
pers. The ſea-coaſt extends about 12 miles, for moſt part
flat and ſandy, but in ſome places high and rocky.—Salmon, haddocks, ſmall cod, whitings, ſmall flounders, and
ſometimes mackerel and herring, are caught in the lochs
before

before mentioned, the quantity not great. Salmon is ſold at
6 d. the pound, tron weight, at an average; mackerel, ¼ d.
a piece; haddocks, &c. 1½ a-pound. The beſt ſeaſon for
ſalmon is from the beginning of April to the end of July;
mackerel, in June and July; haddocks, from December to
March; cod and whitings, in the ſummer months. Salmon, herring, and mackerel are taken with nets; the other
kinds of fiſh with long or hand lines. The town of Greenock is the principal market. A ſpecies of whales, called
Bottle-Noſes, have ſometimes run a-ground during the tide
of ebb, been taken, and oil extracted from them. Porpoiſes and ſeals are likewiſe to be ſeen occaſionally. Sea-
ware is uſed all along the coaſt for manuring land, and
kelp is ſometimes made, but in very ſmall quantities.
Twenty or thirty years ago, all the hills were covered with
heath; but ſince the introduction and increaſe of ſheep,
the heath has gradually leſſened, and the hills begin to have
a green appearance.

Population.—At the time of Dr Webſter's report, the
numbers were 853. About 50 or 60 years ago, it appears the amount of the population was about 1300. The
preſent amount is about 1000. The number of males
486, of females 514. It appears from the regiſter, that
there are more males than females born; but many of the
young men leave the pariſh in queſt of employment, ſome
as ſailors, others as tradeſmen or ſervants. There is one
village in the pariſh, lately built, which contains about
100 ſouls. The annual average of births, from May 1.
1760 to May 1. 1770, is 40; from May 1. 1770 to May 1.
1780, 34; and from May 1. 1780 to May 1. 1790, 33.
There was no diſtinct regiſter of burials prior to 1783,
nor can the number of deaths in it be exactly aſcertained
now that it is kept; becauſe ſome of the people have
                                                    their

their burying places in the neighbouring parishes, and some from other parishes are brought here. The annual average, however, may be about 14. The annual average of marriages from May 1760 to May 1770 is 7; from May 1770 to May 1780, 9; and from May 1780 to May 1790, 10. There are in the parish 65 farmers, their families are about 325 in number. There is only 1 family of Seceders. The population, as hath been already observed, has decreased these last 10 or 20 years, owing to many of the farms being now possessed by 1 tenant, which were formerly occupied by 3, 4, and sometimes more, each of whom accommodated a cottager; besides, some of the farms have of late years been entirely kept under grass, and no tenant upon the grounds. Each marriage, at an average, produces about 6 children.

Agriculture, &c.—There are from 4500 to 5000 sheep; the average price of white wool is 7 s. the stone, and the wool laid with tar 5 s. The parish does more than supply itself with provisions, Greenock is the market for the overplus of grain and potatoes, Glasgow, Paisley, Port-Glasgow, Greenock and Dumbarton, for beef, mutton, &c. Oats and peas are sown from the 20th March to the first week in May; potatoes from the middle of April to the 20th of May; bear from the 10th of May to the 8th or 10th of June. The crops are reaped in general from the beginning of September to the 20th of October.

Stipend, School, Poor, &c.—The value of the living, including the glebe, is about 100 guineas. The Duke of Argyle is patron. The church was rebuilt in the year 1763. The manse in 1737. There are 8 heritors; 1 small proprietor resides constantly, and another occasionally.—There are 2 schools; the salary of the parochial
schoolmaster

ſchoolmaſter amounts to L. 80 Scots; during the winter he generally has from 30 to 40 ſcholars, in ſummer about half that number; his emoluments, including ſeſſion-clerk dues, ſcarce amount to L. 18 Sterling a-year.—About 30 years ago, one of the then heritors of the pariſh, Mr Glen of Portincaple, mortified a piece of land for the ſupport of another ſchoolmaſter; the number of ſcholars taught by him is conſiderably greater, and his emoluments at leaſt equal to the parochial one.—There are at preſent 8 poor who receive regular ſupply, and about the ſame number occaſionally. The funds are the weekly collections at the church-door, amounting to from L. 10 to L. 12 a-year, together with the intereſt of about L. 220 of ſtock, L. 50 of which was lately bequeathed by Robert Carmichael, Eſq; of Broomley, a late proprietor in the pariſh of Bonhill.

Prices, Wages, &c.—The preſent price of beef, veal, and mutton, is 6 d. the pound, tron weight; in harveſt, and beginning of winter conſiderably cheaper; butter, from 9 d. to 10 d. the pound; cheeſe, from 4 s. to 6 s. the ſtone; a hen, from 1 s. to 1 s. 3 d. Theſe articles of proviſions have doubled in price from what they were 40 years ago. Bear ſold, winter and ſpring 1791, at from 16 s. to 18 s. the boll; oats at 16 s. and oat-meal at from 1 s. to 1 s. 1 d. the peck.—The wages for labourers in huſbandry are from 10 d. to 1 s. a day. The uſual wages of men ſervants employed in huſbandry, are from L. 8 to L. 9 a year; females, from L. 3 to L. 4.—The fuel commonly made uſe of by the tenants, is peat or turf, which is cut in the moors of the reſpective farms. Coals are likewiſe brought from the neighbourhood of Glaſgow, the price of which is greatly increaſed of late years.

Miſcellaneous

Mifcellaneous Obfervations.—There are feveral remains of Popifh chapels. Within thefe laft 20 or 30 years, there have been found in different places, 4 ftones fet upon edge, with a large flag covering them, the opening about $4\frac{1}{2}$ feet by $2\frac{1}{4}$, in which human bones were depofited.—The people are fond of a fea-faring life ; during laft war, from 25 to 30 able bodied feamen, from this parifh, were employed in the navy. But they are not fond of a military one.—The people in general are not expenfive, a few individuals are much addicted to dram drinking ; and the young people, efpecially the females, fond of drefs, and more expen-five in that way than their circumftances can well afford.—There are about 11 ale or rather whifky houfes ; one pro-perly called an inn, being one of the ftages on the line of road, lately made by the Duke of Argyle, between Inve-raray and Dumbarton.—Englifh is generally fpoken, but many underftand and frequently converfe in Gaelie.

STIRLINGSHIRE

STIRLINGSHIRE

PERTHSHIRE

CLACKMANNANSHIRE

LINLITHGOWSHIRE

LANARKSHIRE

DUNBARTONSHIRE

FIRTH OF FORTH

LOCH LOMOND

KEY TO PARISHES

1. Buchanan
2. Drymen
3. Killearn
4. Balfron
5. Kippen
6. Gargunnock
7. Fintry
8. Strathblane
9. Baldernock
10. Campsie
11. Kilsyth
12. Denny
13. Dunipace
14. St. Ninians
15. Stirling
16. Lecropt (part)
17. Logie
18. Alva
19. Airth
20. Larbert
21. Bothkennar
22. Falkirk
23. Polmont
24. Muiravonside
25. Slamannan

PARISH OF AIRTH.

(*County of Stirling.*)

By the Rev. Mr ROBERT URE.

Origin of the Name.

THE name *Airth*, is of Gaelic extraction, and is derived from the word *ard* or *ardhé*, which, in that language, ſignifies a high or eminent place. Probably it bears that name, becauſe the hill of Airth, on the ſouth-eaſt corner of which the church and manſion-houſe are built, riſes conſiderably higher than the grounds immediately adjacent. The perpendicular height of this hill is upwards of 70 feet. From the manſion houſe of Airth, and every part of the Hill, there is a delightful and extenſive proſpect, over a country rich, populous, and beautifully diverſified. In this proſpect, part of 10 or 12 counties are to be ſeen.

Situation and Extent.—Airth lies in the county and preſbytery of Stirling, and in the ſynod of Perth and Stirling. The extent of the pariſh, upon the ſide of the river, is about 6 miles, its medium length 5, and its breadth fully 2 miles. The figure is irregular, and approaches neareſt to the parallellogram. The whole pariſh is a plain, the hills of Airth and Dunmore excepted. This laſt hill is termed, by ſome writers, *Airth-beg*, or Little Airth.

Soil.—The foil is, in general, a ftrong deep clay, but the Hill of Airth is a very rich mould. It is believed, a great part of the low ground, near the river, once made part of its bed, as many fea fhells are mingled with the earth; and a few years ago, an anchor was found upon Dunmore hill, by the Earl of Dunmore, about half a mile from the prefent courfe of the river, when digging a few feet below the furface. At a fmall diftance from the fame place, there is a large ftone, called *Carling Stone*, to which the cables of fhips are fuppofed to have been faftened, and of which there are ftill evident marks. On the weft fide of the parifh, there are part of two moffes, called the Moffes of Dunmore and Letham. Within thefe 25 years, 100 acres of ground have been gained from that part of the Mofs of Dunmore which belongs to the Earl, and added to the arable land. Here are fettled 30 families, called *Mofs Lairds*, as the ground is given them for a certain number of years, at a very low rent, in recompence for their labour in clearing away the mofs. The fettlers are induftrious and healthy. The mofs is from 5 to 10 feet deep, and when removed, the foil under it is not inferior to that of the neighbouring Carfe.

Climate, &c.—The air is pretty dry, and free from fogs; and, though mifts are frequently feen on the diftant hills and high grounds, yet they are feldom experienced here. The people, in general, are healthy and laborious. The fea breezes, doubtlefs, contribute to the health of the inhabitants on the river fide. Though the people in the Carfe are faid to be much fubject to the ague, of late years inftances of that difeafe have been few.

Rivers and Fifh.—There is a fmall river, which runs through the parifh, from weft to eaft; it takes its rife in St.
Ninian's

Ninian's pariſh, and diſcharges itſelf into the Forth, at *Higgin's Neuck.* Stream tides flow in this rivulet a mile or more from its mouth. In time of great rains, it overflows its banks ; if theſe fall in harveſt, it is hurtful to the farmers in its immediate neighbourhood. This ſmall river is between 20 and 30 feet in breadth in many places, and has 5 ſtone bridges over it. One of theſe is on the public road, leading from the villages of Dunmore and Airth, to Carron and Falkirk. It is called the Abbey-town Bridge, which name corroborates an opinion many have entertained, of there having been formerly an abbacy at Airth, belonging to the Abbey of Holyroodhouſe ; and that this bridge had that name, from its being the direct road to the abbey town. It alſo appears, from ſeveral old writs, that the pariſh of Airth belonged to the Biſhop of Edinburgh, during the times of Epiſcopacy. The fiſh caught in the river Forth are ſalmon, herrings, flounders, and trouts. Cod and turbot are alſo ſometimes taken. Salmon are chiefly caught in July and Auguſt, with ſtaff-nets, at the time of low water, and are all conſumed by the pariſhioners. Within theſe 25 years, 300 acres have been gained from the river Forth, and made good arable ground. It is defended from the river by a ſtrong dike of ſods.

Hills, Coal, &c.—The hills of Airth and Dunmore abound with free-ſtone, and the rock, in many places, is within a few feet of the ſurface. The ſtones are uſed for building walls and houſes. There is a fine coal under the rock in both hills, and in the flat fields around. The greateſt part of the level free coal of the former was wrought ſome time ago ; at preſent there is no work carrying on, although there is a great deal of coal ſtill in the ground, which might be wrought to advantage. The latter, viz. Dunmore, has been

wrought

wrought, to confiderable extent, for many years paft, and the work is ftill carrying on. This coal confifts of 3 or 4 feams ; a great deal of the parifh, and adjacent places, are fupplied from it, and a confiderable quantity is exported. The fire engine at thefe coal works, is the fecond that was built in Scotland.

Ferries.—There are two well known and much frequented ferries in the parifh, viz. the ferries of Kerfie and Higgin's Neuck. The former is about half a mile in breadth. The proprietor, John Francis Erfkine, Efq; of Mar, lately built a pier upon each fide of the river, which renders it commodious for paffengers, and all kinds of carriages, with or without horfes, either at high or low water. The latter, viz. Higgin's Neuck, is about a mile in breadth. There is a paffage boat once a day, from Airth and Dunmore to Alva, and the places oppofite ; its time of departure varies according to the tide. There are three harbours, viz. Airth, Dunmore, and Newmiln, all of which are within the precincts of the cuftomhoufe at Alloa. At each of them veffels are occafionally built.

Wood.—There is a wood of confiderable extent upon the Hill of Dunmore, which confifts of birch, oak, afh, elm, beech, and fir. On the fide of the hill, contiguous to the mofs, upwards of 40 acres have lately been planted with oaks and firs, moft of which are at prefent in a very thriving condition. There are a great number of fallow trees planted about many farmers houfes, and interfperfed through the fields, which add greatly to the beauty of the country.

Orchards.

Orchards.—There are 9 in the pariſh, which let annually at from 10 l. to 20 l. each. The fruits which they produce are, apples, pears, cherries, and plumbs.

Rent.—The rents are paid chiefly in meal and barley, at the rate of 10 firlots *per* acre ; which, when converted, are, at an average, for the laſt 20 years, from 1 l. 14 s. to 1 l. 18 s. *per* acre, and upwards. When the rent is paid all in money, it is from 1 l. 14 s. to 2 l. 2 s. according to the quality of the ſoil. The valued rent of the pariſh is 8638 l. 16 s. Scotch.

Farms.—The farms are moſtly ſmall ; few exceed 50 or 60 acres, and the greateſt number are from 20 to 30. The farmers generally put 3 horſes into their ploughs ; but of late, the mode of uſing only 2 horſes, which are driven by the ploughman, has taken place, and, it is hoped, will ſoon univerſally prevail throughout the pariſh.

Produce.—The crops are wheat, barley, oats, beans, peaſe, and p⟩tatoes. The wheat is ſown after fallow or potatoes. Thoſe who ſow no wheat, divide their farms nearly into 3 parts, one of which is ſown with barley, another with oats, and a third with peaſe and beans. Of theſe the barley crop is by far the moſt expenſive, as it requires moſt manure and labour. There is more grain produced in the pariſh than is ſufficient to maintain its inhabitants. Many bolls of beans and peaſe are ſent to Falkirk every Thurſday, and ſold there. Barley is ſold to diſtillers and brewers in the neighbourhood ; but moſt of the oatmeal is conſumed in the pariſh.

Mode of Agriculture, and Expence of Labour.—The barley fields muſt be three times plowed. The firſt plowing is in November,

November, the fecond in March, and the laft in the end of April or beginning of May. Previous to the laft, a quantity of lime and dung is fpread upon the fields. The effects of the lime are particularly beneficial; in hard clay ground, it feparates the ftiff particles from each other; and, if the foil is foft and wet, it fucks up the exuberant moifture. The farmer fhould be very attentive, as to the time and manner of putting lime on his barley fields. Perhaps the beft time is the beginning of November, when the ground fhould be plowed with a very thin and flight furrow, as the lime natu-rally finks into it. By its being put on at this feafon, the fa-line particles, and hot burning quality of the lime, are ab-forbed by the earth, and incorporated with it through the winter; whereas, if it be deferred till after the fecond or third plowing, little advantage is derived from it that feafon; and in cafe of much drought, it is often found to be hurtful. There is a prejudice entertained by many farmers, that lime is not beneficial to light fandy ground. This opinion may be prefumed to proceed from the want of a fair trial; for it is well known, that lime incorporates with fand, and tends to confolidate its fmall particles, and to give the ground a pecu-liar ftrength and firmnefs. The farmers often roll their bar-ley fields with a heavy wooden or ftone roller: This, in a dry feafon, is of great ufe, as it tends to preferve the moif-ture in the ground, and hinders the drought from penetrat-ing into it; but if heavy rains fall foon after the rolling, it is neceffary to open the furface with the harrow. It may be obferved, that the barley fown in April is the ftrongeft grain; but that fown in the middle of May is the moft prolific. Beans and peafe are fown in the beginning of March, the oats immediately after. Ploughmen's wages, at prefent, are from 8 l. to 10 l. *per annum.* Thofe of fervant maids,

from

from 2 l. 10 s. to 3 l. About 20 years ago, the former had from 5 l. to 6 l. ; and the latter, from 30 s. to 40 s.

Population.—The number of inhabitants, in 1755, was 2316. The population has not since decreased. The families in the parish are 508 ; these families, by the nearest computation, exceed $4\frac{1}{4}$ in each family at an average; and the whole population may be stated at about 2350. The villagers are about 1200; tradesmen and seamen about 140. The annual average of births, for the last 10 years, is 66 ; of deaths, 54 ; and of marriages, 20.

Decline of Trade.—The trade in Airth, prior to the year 1745, was very considerable, but has since been on the decline, owing to a number of vessels being burnt at that period. The occasion of this was, that the rebels, having seized a small vessel at a narrow part of the river, called Fallin, by means of it transported a number of small brass cannon to the harbours of Airth and Dunmore, near each of which they erected batteries, and placed their cannon. Upon the King's vessels coming from Leith to dislodge them, a reciprocal firing took place. The commanders of the King's vessels, finding their efforts ineffectual, sailed down the river with the tide, and gave orders to burn all the vessels lying on the river side, to prevent them falling into the hands of the rebels, who might have used them as transports, and harrassed the people on both sides of the river. The loss of these vessels were severely felt by the trading people in Airth, and trade has since removed to Carronshore and Grangemouth.

Shipping.

Shipping.—There are at prefent 8 veffels belonging to the parifh. Some of thefe are employed in the Baltic, others in the coal and lime trade.

Church and Schools.—The ftipend is 69 bolls of meal and barley, and about 1000 merks of money, with a manfe, and glebe of 10 acres of good arable ground. The patron of the parifh is James Graham, Efq; of Airth.—There is an efta-blifhed fchool in it, and a fchoolmafter, who has a dwelling houfe and legal falary allowed him by the heritors. The number of fcholars, taught in it, is between 70 and 80. There are fome other fchools of leffer note; but the mafters of thefe have no allowance, except what is given them by the parents of thofe children whom they inftruct.

Heritors.—There are 5 heritors, who refide conftantly or occafionally in the parifh, and 6 who do not refide in it. Befides thefe, there are feveral leffer heritors and feuers.

Poor.—The number of poor fupplied weekly is 30; and of occafional poor, there are about 12. They are fupplied by an annual affeffment, which the heritors voluntarily impofe upon themfelves, the one half of which is paid by them, and the other by their tenants. By the intereft of money, the affeff-ment, and the weekly collections, the fum given annually to the poor is between 80 l. and 90 l. Sterling.

Antiquities.—There are 3 antient towers in the parifh, one at Airth, another at Dunmore, and a third at Powfouls. The tower at Airth was built before Sir William Wallace's time, who lived at the beginning of the 14th century. If credit can be given to Blind Harry's poetical hiftory of that hero, he fays, that Wallace came privily into this tower, flew the
captain

captain and 100 men, and relieved his uncle, who was a prifoner in it. This tower is in good repair ; it makes part of the
houfe of Airth, and bears the name of *Wallace's Tower*.
The antiquity of the other two is not accurately afcertained.
In one of the aifles of Airth church, belonging to the family
of Airth, there is a black marble ftone built in the wall, with
the *Bruce's* arms elegantly engraved above it, bearing the
following infcription in very neat legible characters.

M. S.

ALEXANDRO BRUSSIO,
EX ROBERTI BRUSSII SCOTORUM REGIS
FILIO NATU SECUNDO, PROGENITO,
BARONI AIRTHENSI.
PRIMUM IN BELGIO PER ANNOS XLII.
DEIN IN ANGLIA PRO TRIBUNO REGIO.
Viro cum ftrenvo tum pientiffimo,
Ætatis, anno LVI. vitaque fimvl defvncto,
A. D. XVII. Kal. Oct. CIƆ DC XLII.
G. LAUDERUS AFFINIS, M. P.

BRUSSIUS hic fitvs eft ; pietate an clarior armis,
Incertum eft; certum regibus ortus avis.

Heer lyes a branche of Bruffe's noble ftemm,
Airth's Baron, whofe high worth did fvte that name,
Holland his courage, honovred Spain did feare,
The Sweeds in Fvnen bought the trial deare.
At laft his Prince's fervice called him home,
To die on Thames his bank, and leave this tombe,
To bear his name unto pofteritie,
And make all braue men loue his memorie.

Mineral

Mineral Springs.—There is a well, near Abbeytown Bridge, called *Lady-Well*, which is thought to be medicinal. Numbers have ufed it, and ftill ufe it, as fuch. It is fuppofed to have obtained that name, from the holy water, in the time of Popery, being taken from it, to fupply the abbacy, or Catholic chapel, then at Airth.

General Character of the People.—The morals of the people are, in general, good; and moft of them are fober, induftrious, and attentive to their refpective employments. They are particularly regular in attending Divine worfhip every Sunday, at the parochial church, and are, upon the whole, a well-behaved and refpectable fet of people.

PARISH OF ALVA.

(COUNTY OF STIRLING.)

By the Rev. Mr JOHN DUNCAN.

———————

Name.

IN the writings of the laſt century, and before that time, the name of this pariſh was generally written Alvath, or Alveth; but that mode of ſpelling has been difuſed almoſt a complete century. Whether the preſent name, Alva, be of Gaelic origin, is not altogether certain. Fanciful etymologies can never yield ſatisfaction to the judicious antiquary; and therefore when nothing rational can be offered, it ſeems better to acknowledge ignorance, than to offer what can neither amuſe nor inform.

Situation.—This pariſh and barony is a part of the county of Stirling, although it happens to be totally disjoined from every part of it. No certain account can now be given, how this has happened. It is ſurrounded by the ſhire of Clackmannan on the eaſt, ſouth, and weſt, and on the north, it is bounded by a part of the county of Perth. It extends in length, from eaſt to weſt, ſomewhat more than two miles

and

and a half; and from fouth to north, rather more than four miles. Tillicoultry, is the adjacent parifh on the eaft. The river Devon, which has its fource in the barony of Alva, after a long courfe, at firft almoft due eaft; and then fouthward through Glen-devon, makes a fudden turn weftward, near the church of Fofloway, and paffing through the parifhes of Muckhart, Dollar, and Tillicoultry, gently glides along the fouth boundary of this parifh, and divides it from the parifhes of Alloa and Clackmannan, which are fituated on the fouth *. The parifh of Logie is next adjacent on the weft.

Extent, &c.—The lands of Alva extend over a very confiderable portion of that long range of hills, diftinguifhed by the name of Ochills; the remaining grounds are extended over part of that valley, which lies between the foot of thefe hills, and the river Devon. The mean breadth, from the banks of the river to the bottom of the hill, may be about three fifth parts of a mile.

That portion of the Ochills now under review, when feen from the fouth at the diftance of a mile or two, appear to be one continued range, with little variation in height; but as the mountain flopes towards the fouth, it is interfected by exceedingly deep and narrow glens, through each of which, ftreams of water run, that difcharge themfelves into the Devon.

---

* It is impoffible to view this little river of clear water, without admiring its beauty, in its wonderful paffage through the rock, at the Rumbling Bridge, and Caldron Lin; and its numberlefs meandrings, after it defcends into the valley, eaft of Dollar; whence it glides generally in a deep bed with little fall, till it reaches the Frith of Forth, at the Cambas miln, directly oppofite to where its fource began. When fwelled by heavy rains, or the melting fnow, it overflows its banks, and covers the greateft part of the low grounds.

von. By means of thefe, the fore ground of this part of the
Ochills, is divided into three feparate hills, diftinguifhed by
the names of Wood-hill, Middle-hill, and Weft-hill of Alva.
On the brow of this laft hill, is a very high perpendicular
rock, which, for what reafon is not known, has obtained the
name of Craig Leith. It has been long beyond memory, remarkable for the refidence of that fpecies of hawks, the falcon,
which is ufed for the diverfion of hunting. One pair, and only
one pair, it is affirmed by the inhabitants of the place, build a
neft on the front of this tremendous rock. Thefe are faid to
hatch their young annually ; and, when their progeny are of
a proper age, the parents force them to feek a new habitation,
till at laft, however long they may be fuppofed to live, the
parents themfelves muft yield their refidence to their furvi-
vors. In former times, when that fport was in fafhion, a
hawk of this breed was thought a valuable acquifition. They
are ftill in great requeft among our own nobility, who love
that fport ; and very lately, an Englifh gentleman noted for
his fkill in that diverfion, fent his fervant all the way from
Yorkfhire, to procure fome of this breed. In order to come
at the neft, he was let down by a rope faftened round his
waift, while the end of it was held faft by'ten or twelve people, who ftood at a convenient diftance from the edge of the
precipice ; and he was obferved fcrambling on the face of the
rock, exploring the neft of the bird.

The houfe of Alva ftands on an eminence, projecting
from the bafe of the Wood-hill, and near the eaft end
of the parifh. The height of this projected part of the
hill, is about 220 feet above the water of Devon, which runs
in the valley below. The hill rifes immediately behind the
houfe, to the height of 1400 feet, making the whole height

1620 feet *. From the ſummit of this hill, there is a very extenſive proſpect to the north eaſt, the ſouth, and ſouth weſt. The view to the north weſt, is a little interrupted by the hill of Dalmiot, a part of the Ochills, lying in the pariſh of Logie. From the top of the Wood-hill, however, the mouth of the Frith of Forth, the Baſs, North Berwick Law, with the windings of the Forth, can eaſily be deſcried, together with the coaſts of Fife and eaſt Lothian, &c.

The village of Alva is ſituated at a ſmall diſtance from the bottom of the Weſt hill. A ſmall rivulet, which iſſues from the glen which ſeparates the Weſt from the Middle hill, runs along the eaſt ſide of the village ; and not only affords a conſtant and plentiful ſupply of water, but adds very much to the beauty of the village. This receives a farther addition, from a thriving plantation of foreſt trees growing on a ſteep bank on the eaſt ſide of the rivulet, and affording a comfortable ſhelter from the north eaſt winds, which, of all others, are the moſt violent in this diſtrict. It is not certainly known, when this village began to be built. There is undoubted evidence, however, of Alva being a pariſh above 500 years ago †; and it is probable that a village, very inconſiderable perhaps, may then have exiſted. Even at preſent the village is not extenſive, and does not contain much above 130 families, including a few ſingle perſons each of whom occupy a part of a houſe. About the end of the laſt, and beginning of this

---

* The hill continues to riſe gradually for about two miles farther north, untill it reaches the top of Ben-Cloch, which is the higheſt point of the Alva hills, and the ſummit of all the Ochills ; and according to the obſervation taken by Mr Udney, land ſurveyor, is about 2420 feet above the level of the Devon. The view from the top of Ben-Cloch is the moſt extenſive and beautiful any where to be found, and is viſited by all travellers of curioſity who delight in fine proſpects.

† Vide Chartulary of Cambuſkenneth.

this century, the late Sir John Erſkine, grandfather of the preſent Sir James Sinclair Erſkine, then proprietor, granted feus of a ſmall parcel of ground to ſeveral inhabitants, on which they built a cottage and formed a garden ; and a plan appears to have been deſigned by that gentleman, of building a village in the form of a ſquare, two ſides of which have been actually built. The other houſes appear to have been ſet down, without any regular order, and where a convenient ſpot for a garden could be obtained. About the year 1767, the preſent Lord Alva, reſolving to enlarge the village, granted feus to ſuch as were willing to build ; in conſequence of which, one complete row, conſiſting of about 20 houſes, was erected in one ſeaſon, each houſe having a ſmall garden of a few falls, equal in breadth to the extent of the front of the houſe. A few years after, another row of houſes parallel to the former, and with gardens laid out in the ſame manner, was completed. The rate at which the ground was at that time feued, was at firſt 13s. and 4d. per fall, or 36 ſquare yards ; it advanced by degrees to 15s. and 16s. per fall, as the premium or purchaſe money, together with four-pence the fall of annual feu duty. Taking the medium rate of 15s. it will be found to amount to L. 120 ſterling per acre as the price of the ground, and L. 2 : 13 : 4 as the annual rent to the ſuperior. What proprietor would heſitate to grant feus upon ſuch terms as theſe ; eſpecially, when it is conſidered, that the annual duty may be converted into ſome ſtaple commodity.

The arable ſoil of this pariſh may be properly divided into four different kinds. The firſt, which extends ſouthward from the bottom of the hills, conſiſts of a rich hazel mold intermixed with gravel and ſmall ſtones ; this is ſucceeded by a different kind of ſoil, being a ſtratum of moſs over a bed of clay, and extending from 50 to 100 yards in breadth. In ſome places, this moſs is found to be 7 feet in depth. Next
to

to that, is a ſtrong rich clay, extending a conſiderable way towards the river Devon ; then follows what is called haughing
ground, ſuch as is uſually found upon the banks of rivers ;
the banks of Devon being generally overflowed twice or
thrice every year, great quantities of ſand are left on the
ground as far as the inundation extends. The ſoil at the bed
of the river appears to be in many places above 20 feet deep.
The grounds of this pariſh produce the uſual crops of wheat,
barley, peas, beans, oats, clover, and potatoes.

The whole arable grounds within the pariſh, have been
incloſed, ſeveral years ago, with ditches and hedges. Thoſe
fields, which lie immediately below the houſe of Alva, at
the bottom of the Wood-hill, and extending near to the banks
of Devon, were incloſed, and planted with rows of oaks,
aſhes, and other foreſt trees, by the late Sir John Erſkine,
about 70 years ago, and were probably among the firſt incloſures in this part of the country. Theſe have been chiefly
in grafs for a great many years, and are let annually to graziers, at the rate of from 25 to 30 ſhillings per acre. The
general ſtate of agriculture, in this, as well as in all the
neighbouring pariſhes, was very rude and wretched, till
within the laſt thirty years. And although the ſoil muſt be
allowed to be equal at leaſt, in quality, to that in the moſt
fertile parts of Scotland ; yet truth requires us to acknowledge,
that thoſe who were employed in cultivating it, were late in
arriving at any conſiderable improvements. Wheat, juſtly
eſteemed the moſt beneficial of all crops, was not cultivated in this pariſh, till within the laſt fifteen years.
Clean ſummer fallow, and proper dreſſing with lime and dung,
were rarely, if ever attempted. Good example has at laſt
opened mens eyes; and experience has demonſtrated that the
ſoil, when properly cultivated, is capable of the higheſt improvement, and is fit for producing wheat, and all the ſtrong-
eſt

eſt grain. The tenants begin now to perceive the importance
of fallowing, liming, and cleaning their lands, to obtain good
returns, and the advantage of having broad clover for ſummer
food for their horſes, and being able to work them conſtantly,
inſtead of ſending them (as they did formerly), to graze for five
months idle on the hills, at a conſiderable expence. Any perſon who has been acquainted with the ſtate of farming in this
pariſh and its immediate neighbourhood thirty years ago, muſt
have been led to aſcribe the ſlow progreſs of improvement, in
a conſiderable degree, to the very ſmall number of acres, of
which the far greater part of the farms conſiſted. The ſtock of
the farmer, may be conſidered, as in general, proportioned to
the extent of his farm, which at that time did not commonly exceed thirty or forty acres. It was well, if, according to the mode
of culture practiſed at that time, he could pay his rent, and
provide a mean ſubſiſtence for himſelf and his family. Another circumſtance, which affected in a very particular manner the ſtate of farming in this pariſh, and its neighbourhood, was the practice of driving coals from the coal pits on
the ſouth banks of Devon, to the ſhore of Alloa. To this
labour, the farmers on the eſtates where the coals were raiſed,
were bound by their leaſes ; and without entering more particularly into the ſubject, it muſt be obvious, how pernicious
the effect of this practice muſt have been, with reſpect to the
proper and neceſſary operations upon the farm. Such, however, is the contagion of example, that ſome of the farmers
in this pariſh, who were under no obligation to be carriers on
the eſtate of another proprietor, and excepting during one
very ſhort period, when coal was worked within the pariſh,
had no occaſion to be concerned in it, from ignorance and
unſkilfulneſs reſpecting their proper employment, and from
the deſire of a little gain, earned at the expence of ſevere
labour to themſelves and horſes, with the *tear and wear* of

carts,

carts, rude and ſimple as they were at that time, were fooliſh
enough to join the farmers in their neighbourhood, and employ themſelves during a conſiderable part of the ſummer, in
carrying the great coal to the port of Alloa. They were at
laſt however, wiſely prohibited by Lord Alva, the late proprietor of this barony, from following this abſurd and unprofitable occupation ; indeed when they began to acquire a
taſte for improving their farms, and to reap the benefit of
their improvements, they were ſoon convinced of the inu-
tility of their ancient practice ; and very probably would have
abandoned it of their own accord. The extent of the farms
has been, within the laſt twenty years, conſiderably enlarged ;
the conſequence of which has been, that beſides imitating the
example of the gradual improvements in agriculture, the farmer has been enabled to make a more reſpectable appearance
than formerly. It is evident from the writings of thoſe, who
have treated of the ſubject of agriculture, that it has been
conſidered as a difficult problem, to ſtate the juſt and reaſonable extent of a farm, or to fix the number of acres, that one
farm ſhould contain ; and from the different opinions which
have been given, it may be inferred, that perhaps no general
rule can be laid down. A general obſervation however, may
be offered ; that the farm ſhould at leaſt be ſo extenſive, that
the profits of the ſtock employed in cultivating it, ſhould
enable the farmer to live decently and comfortably, and in a
manner above the other country tradeſmen who ſurround
him. In a ſmall farm of 40, or even 50 acres, allowing it to
be as productive as can be ſuppoſed, and the rent moderate ;
ſtill the profits ariſing to the farmer, cannot poſſibly be ſo
great, as to raiſe his ſtate much above that of the lower claſs
of manufacturers, who inhabit country pariſhes. According
to the diviſion of farms that has hitherto taken place in this
pariſh, which has been from 30 to 60, or not more than 70
acres,

actes, they can hardly be deemed fo large, as to place the farmer in a refpectable fituation.

From the defcription already given of the fituation of the lands of this parifh, they are naturally divided into arable and pafture ground. The three hills are incomparably the moft beautiful in every refpect of the whole range of the Ochills, from Glen devon on the eaft, to their termination, near the bridge of Alloa on the weft. They are cloathed with the richeft verdure, at all feafons, and produce grafs of the fineft quality, and in the greateft variety. They are not fo fteep, fo rugged or inacceffible, as thofe immediately weftward in the parifh of Logie ; and they prefent a more regular, nobler, and bolder afpect, than any of thofe that lie immediately on the eaft. They have been now for many years, divided into two feparate farms, for fheep ; one comprehending the Weft-hill, the other the Middle-hill, together with that part of the Wood hill, which lies behind the fence, or wall, that furrounds the brow of that part of the hill, immediately above the houfe of Alva. 'Tis fuppofed that the former of thefe is capable of maintaining about 100 fcore of fheep, and the latter from 90 to 95 fcore. The rent of the Weft hill, has been greatly increafed, fince the year 1759 *. On the higheft and back-lying ground, where the parifh of Alva marches with an eftate belonging to Mr Murray of Abercairney, in the parifh

* The rent of the Weft-hill in the year 1759, was very inconfiderable. There was then little demand for butcher-meat in this country ; and the profits of grazing were very low. When the next leafe was granted in 1775, when the demand for fheep and wool began to increafe, the tenant was taken bound to pay more than twice the former rent. From the rapid progrefs of manufactures and of luxury, and from the high character of the wool and of the fheep fed on the Alva hills, it is believed that thofe fine fheep-farms are ftill capable of a confiderable advance of rent.

pariſh of Blackford, the ſoil is moſſy, and produces heath in great abundance, together with a ſtrong and coarſe graſs. This however is reſorted to by the ſtronger and older part of the flocks; and theſe, 'tis ſaid by the ſhepherds, are ſeldom obſerved to quit their wild retreat, or to come forward in queſt of the tender and more kindly graſs, excepting perhaps when compelled by the rigour of the ſtorm, to ſeek ſhelter on the fore ground, or lower part of the hills. At the ſame time, it muſt be remarked, that ſnow never lies for any length of time, on the face of thoſe hills *. It is remarkable however, that at the bottom of a ridge of rock, near to the ſummit of the high hill called Ben-cloch, where it is ſheltered from every wind, ſnow is frequently ſeen lying till the month of June. What is obſerved to reſiſt ſo long the ſummer's heat, from the ſingularity of its extended but narrow form to the ſpectator's eye who views it at a diſtance, has received the appellation of Lady Alva's web.

It has never been the practice of the ſheep-farmers here, to breed young ſheep on theſe hills. Although they have generally a few ſcores of ewes on their farms; yet their lambs are commonly ſold to the butcher. Of late years indeed, ſome attempts have been made to rear a few young ſheep, but theſe bear no proportion to the number of their ſtock. The farmers go every year about mid-ſummer, to the markets

at

* Snow ſeldom lies here more than two or three days; and even during that time, the ſheep brouze on the young furze, and are in as good condition, as if they had been fed on hay. The flocks have ſo much ſhelter from the ſituation of the hills, and from the plantations, that they have never materially ſuffered from the heavieſt falls of ſnow. In January 1794, ſo fatal to the ſheep and cattle in the ſouthern parts of Scotland, and in the north of England, the farmers in the hills of Alva were ſo fortunate as ſcarcely to loſe a ſheep.

at Linton, and purchafe fheep of a year old. Thefe, according to the cuftom of the fheep-farmers in the fouth, have been fmeared with tar, but that practice is not found neceffary in this diftrict. After they have been fhorn three times white, as they exprefs it, they are fold about Auguft and September, as fit for the butcher's ufe.

The next thing that is worthy of notice in this parifh, is the ftate of the woollen manufactures. Thefe have been carried on in the village of Alva, for more than a century at leaft. They confift chiefly of Scots blankets and ferges. The former are made from 9d. to 1s. the Scots yard, and the latter from 10d. to 15d. and a few from 16d. to 18d. per yard. It is more than probable, that this fpecies of manufacture had flourifhed a great many years ago, in the neighbouring village of Tillicoultry; as an evidence of this, it is at this day, known among the fhopkeepers of the Lawnmarket of Edinburgh, by the name of Tillicoultry ferges. The number of looms conftantly employed at prefent in this village is 67. The length of each web may be reckoned at 80 yards, and taking the average value at 10d. or 11d. per yard, the grofs produce will amount to from L. 7000 to L. 8000 fter. annually. The manufacturers make ufe chiefly of Englifh wool in their ferges and blankets, and this partly fhort, and partly combed wool. That which is produced from the fheep that pafture on the Ochills, is commonly manufactured by the people of the country for their own private ufe. A very confiderable fum is annually expended by the weavers in this place, in purchafing wool, which it is impoffible to afcertain with any degree of precifion. Thefe ferges are fold not only in Edinburgh, but likewife in Stirling, Glafgow, Greenock, Perth, and Dundee. The fineft kinds of ferges are fometimes dreffed and dyed by the traders in Stirling, and fold as

coarfe

coarſe ſhalloons. A conſiderable quantity of the coarſer ſizes, have of late years been purchaſed by ſadlers as a neceſſary article in their buſineſs. This trade is at preſent in a very flouriſhing condition, and from this circumſtance the manu-facturers here are able to pay 50s. rent for an acre of land, and many of them 40s. for a cow's graſs. It were to be wiſhed, perhaps, that a ſpecies of manufacture more valuable and more extenſively uſeful were introduced, ſuch as an imi-tation of the flannels manufactured in England. But it has always been found exceedingly difficult to give a new direc-tion to habits long eſtabliſhed and confirmed ; and until ſome perſon poſſeſſed of an enterpriſing ſpirit together with a con-ſiderable ſtock ſhall ariſe, an alteration of the preſent mode of carrying on the manufactures here, cannot reaſonably be expected.

Population.—The number of inhabitants in this pariſh, from a late accurate ſurvey, is found to be 612. And of theſe, there are

From 10 years of age and under - -	165
———— 10 to 20 - - -	132
———— 20 to 30 - -	84
———— 30 to 40 - -	94
———— 40 to 50 - -	52
———— 50 to 60 - -	52
———— 60 to 70 -	27
———— 70 to 80 -	4
———— 80 o 90 - -	2
	612

Lift of Births and Burials from 1720 *to* 1791.

From the begin-ing of 1720 to the end of 1729	Mar-riages	Births.			Burials.				
		Males	Females	Total	Males	Females	Total	Adults	Chil-dren
end of 1729	45	113	122	235	28	29	57	34	23
—1730 to 1739	46	93	88	181	81	75	156	99	87
—1740 to 1749	33	47	80	147	68	98	166	110	56
—1750 to 1759	46	87	88	175	58	43	101	66	35
—1760 to 1769	64	103	113	216	81	99	180	101	79
—1770 to 1779	53	122	109	231	72	76	148	94	54
—1780 to 1791	70	144	142	286	127	115	242	119	123

The numbers of this parifh have not increafed in any confi-derable degree fince the year 1760, as appears from lifts re-gularly made up every four or five years from that period.

Church, Stipend, &c.—The parifh of Alva was, long before the Reformation, in the diocefe of Dunkeld, and under the ec-clefiaftical jurifdiction of the bifhop of that fee. From an extract taken from the Chartulary of Cambufkenneth, in the neighbour-hood of Stirling, it appears that the church of Alva was a menfal church, as it is called, belonging to that abbacy, and that the monks performed duty there, from the want of a fufficient fund for the maintenance of a regular clergyman to refide in the parifh. In the 1260, Richard, Bifhop of Dunkeld, made a donation to the monks of the church of St. Mary at Cambufkenneth, of the church of Alva " with all its legal pertinents," and dif-penfing with their employing a vicar to officiate ftatedly. The following reafon is then affigned ; " virorum religioforum ab-" batis et conventus de Cambufkenneth, paupertati compa-" tientes, —— charitatis intuitu, et propter tenuitatem ec-" clefiæ de Alveth." By another extract from the fame Chartulary, it appears that Alexander, ftiled Dominus de Striveling, Miles, made a grant of one acre of land, to God, the

Virgin

Virgin Mary, to St. Servanus, and to the church of St. Servanus de Alveth, deſcribing it particularly as lying near the
well of St. Servanus, " et inter ipſum fontem et ecclefiam."
This charter is dated, A. D. 1276. This well is ſtill within the
limits of the miniſter's glebe, and although its conſecrated name
has been long forgotten, it continues to fend forth a copious
ſtream of the pureſt and ſweeteſt water. About 20 years after the Reformation, and after Stirling, with a few pariſhes
around it, were provided with ſtated paſtors, the Preſbytery
of Stirling was erected on the eight day of Auguſt 1581 *, in
conſequence of an order from the General Aſſembly, to that
effect. The firſt miniſter of this pariſh, was Mr Robert
Mainteith, who was afterwards depoſed for incapacity.

> *Pudet hæc opprobria nobis,*
> *Et dici potuiſſe, et non potuiſſe, refelli.*

From this time and downwards to the year 1632, this pariſh appears to have been united with the neighbouring one of
Tillicoultry, the miniſter of Alva officiating in both; the
livings of each hardly affording a decent ſubſiſtence; the
ſtipend of Alva not exceeding 300 merks Scots, or L. 16 : 13 : 4
ſterling. The fabric of the preſent church was built in the
year 1631, by Alexander Bruce, then proprietor of Alva;
who, after making a ſmall addition to the ſtipend, procured a
disjunction from the pariſh of Tillicoultry. Although the
fabric of the church is ſtill good and found, yet it appears
never to have been completely finiſhed within ; the walls and
roof are not plaiſtered, and the ſeats are in a very ruinous
condition. The windows are too ſmall and ill-placed. As
the ſtructure is ſufficient, it might be repaired at a moderate
expence ; and, without any enlargement of the area, might be
rendered

---

* Records of the Preſbytery of Stirling.

rendered a very commodious and elegant church. The prefent manfe, was built in the year 1762, upon a very neat and
commodious plan. In the year 1765, the prefent Lord Alva,
then proprietor of this barony, fenfible of the fmallnefs of the
living, very generoufly, and without any application from the
incumbent, gave an augmentation in victual to the amount of
L. 22 fterling, at the ufual converfion ; by which means the
ftipend now confifts of L. 34 fterling in money, including the
allowance for communion elements, together with 40 bolls
of barley, and 32 bolls of meal. But what efpecially deferves
to be remembered by the prefent incumbent, to whom this augmention was given, is, that Lord Alva, not only of his own
accord refolved to give it, but actually executed a fummons
againft himfelf, as fole heritor of the parifh, in name of the
minifter without his knowledge, as the firft ftep towards
perfecting, what he had fo generoufly refolved on. The
glebe confifts of nine acres, a fmall part of which is meadow,
and which, if completely drained, might be very beneficial.
Had Virgil himfelf vifited the Ochills, and compofed his firft
paftoral on this fpot, he could not have defcribed it more
graphically than he has done in the following lines ;

> *Et tibi magna fatis : quamvis lapis omnia nudus,*
> *Limofoque palus obducat pafcua junco.*

Let no future poffeffor of this glebe dare to murmur, after
what Maro has fo fweetly fung !

School.—The falary of the fchoolmafter is 200 merks, or
L. 11 : 2 : 2⅔ fterling. This is the maximum appointed by law
for the falary of a parifh fchool. When it is confidered, that
by act of parliament *, the heritors and liferenters of a parifh,

are

---

* Vide Acts W. and M. Par. 1. Seff. 6. Chap 26.

are allowed to obtain relief for the one half of that ſum from the tenants, it may be juſtly wondered, that ſo very few country pariſhes have availed themſelves of it, and ſtill allow their ſchoolmaſters to be ſo meanly provided. To this good and wiſe inſtitution of parochial ſchools, and to the aſſiduous labours of that moſt uſeful claſs of men, our country ſtands indebted for its celebrity in learning and ſcience.

Poor.—The poor in this pariſh are not numerous. At preſent there are not more than ſix perſons, who receive relief from the public charity. Occaſional ſupply is at times given to others, as their neceſſities demand. They have hitherto been maintained by the ordinary collections, together with the intereſt ariſing from a ſmall fund, and the common dues of the pariſh mort-cloths; without any aſſeſſment upon the heritor, or inhabitants. There are examples, more than one, of perſons, who have declined accepting this charity, chooſing rather to ſuſtain their hardſhips with patience, than to receive it from the public. This ſerves to confirm the remark, that when the funds of public charity are increaſed to any great degree, there is generally leſs delicacy in receiving it.

Minerals.—This pariſh has been diſtinguiſhed by the diſcoveries which have been made, in this part of the Ochills, of various metals, and particularly of ſilver. In the neighbouring pariſhes of Logie on the weſt, and Tillicoultry and Dollar on the eaſt, veins of copper and lead have been, at different periods, wrought to a conſiderable extent; and though veins of theſe metals, and alſo of iron ore, have been found in the hills of Alva, yet no experiments of ſuch conſequence have been made, as to aſcertain their true value. Some time between the years 1710 and 1715, Sir John Erſkine, of whom mention has been already made, by means of ſome miners from Leadhills,

Leadhills, difcovered a very valuable vein of filver, in the glen that feparates the Middle-hill from the Wood-hill. It made its firft appearance in fmall ftrings of filver ore, which being followed, led to a very large mafs of that precious ore ; part of this had the appearance of malleable filver, and was found upon trial to be fo exceedingly rich, as to produce 12 ounces of filver from 14 ounces of ore. A fum not greater than L. 40, or, at the moft L. 50, had been expended when this valuable difcovery was made. During the fpace of thirteen or fourteen weeks, it has been credibly affirmed that ore was produced to about the value of L. 4000 *per* week, and it has been conjectured, that Sir John drew from L. 40,000 to L. 50,000, befides much ore, which was fuppofed to have been purloined by the workmen. When this was exhaufted, the filver ore began to appear in fmaller quantities ; and fymptoms of lead, with other metals, were difcovered. The confequence of which was, that all further refearches were at that time laid afide. There are ftill in the poffeffion of Lord Alva, Nephew of the late Sir John Erfkine, fome exceedingly rich pieces of filver ore, which had been got at that time, and which evidently fhew how very valuable that mafs of ore muft have been *.

Thefe have been examined by many of Lord Alva's friends, who have admired, not merely the richnefs of the ore, but its beauty ; the pure *native virgin* filver being obferved to adhere in flender ftrings to the fpar, in a variety of fanciful and irregular forms.

About

---

* In the year 1767, Lord Alva, of fome of the remains of that ore in his poffeffion, caufed a pair of Communion Cups to be made, for the ufe of the Church of Alva ; on thefe, the following infcription is engraved. Sacris, in Ecclefia, S. Servani, apud Alveth, A. D. 1767, ex argento indigena, D. D. C. q.—JACOBUS ERSKINE.

About the year 1759, the late Charles Erſkine, Lord Juſtice Clerk, father of Lord Alva, having a few years before,
purchaſed this barony from his nephew, the late Sir Henry
Erſkine, revived the working of the ſilver mines in this place.
A company conſiſting of ſome gentlemen, kinſmen and friends
of the family, was formed, and a moderate capital ſubſcribed. Theſe carried on the work, with conſiderable induſtry ;
they purſued the courſe of the vein, where the ſilver ore had
been found, a very great way beyond the old workings,
which had for many years been abandoned. Their ſucceſs,
it muſt be regretted, was not in proportion to the vigour of
their exertions ; for although the appearances in the vein
were favourable, and ſmall ſtrings of metal ſometimes diſcovered, theſe however were not followed by any thing of ſufficient importance, to encourage them to continue their re-
ſearches.

A ſhaft or ſump, as the miners term it, was made to the
depth of ſeveral fathoms, immediately below the bottom of
the waſte, from whence the rich maſs of ore, above mentioned, had been taken, and a drift carried on, in the direction of the ſilver vein, upon that level ; but neither did this
attempt anſwer the expectation which had been formed of its
ſucceſs. To facilitate theſe operations however, it had been
reſolved, to drive a level at a conſiderable diſtance, nearer
the bottom of the hill ; for the purpoſe of draining the water
from the works above. In executing this part of their ſcheme,
they had not advanced a great way into the ſide of the hill,
when a large maſs of ore was diſcovered ; at firſt, this was
imagined to be ſilver ; but upon an accurate trial, made by a
gentleman, diſtinguiſhed for his chemical knowledge, it was
diſcovered to be cobalt. A very conſiderable quantity of this
was brought out, of which a great part was uſed in a manufacture of porcelain, that had been erected much about that
                                                      time,

time, at Preftonpans in Eaft-Lothian. When the cobalt is deprived of the arfenic with which it is ftrongly impregnated, and in other refpects properly prepared, it produces a powder of a beautiful deep blue, and with this, a great variety both of ufeful and ornamental pieces of china and glafs were coloured ; which clearly fhewed that the cobalt found in the mines of Alva, was in no refpect inferior in quality to that procured from the mines in Saxony. In confequence of this difcovery, the appearances of cobalt being now fully known, very confiderable quantities of it were difcovered among the heaps of rubbifh, that had been taken out of the mines, at the time when they were worked by the late Sir John Erfkine. This had remained undifturbed, for about fifty years ; when Lord Alva caufed a great part of it to be wafhed, after the manner practifed by miners ; and obtained an additional quantity to that which had been already procured from the level. The work was carried on a great length from the place where the mafs of cobalt had been found ; but fpar and other vein-ftuff appearing, the further working of the mines in this place was totally abandoned.

During the time that thefe works were carried on, a very accurate furvey of all the different veins of metals that had been difcovered in the hills of this parifh, was made by the agent for the company, who poffeffed a very confiderable degree of fkill in the practical part of mining. The feveral appearances and fpecimens of the different ores, which were found in confequence of the trials which were made in the veins; together with the precife direction which thefe take into the hills, with a variety of circumftances relating to them, which it would be improper to enumerate here, were all accurately taken down by their agent, in a regifter or journal, and which is in the poffeffion of Mr Johnftone, the prefent proprietor of this barony. It is efpecially worthy of being remarked, that the perfon

ſon employed to make this ſurvey, and to digeſt the obſervations reſulting from it, was particularly diſtinguiſhed for his
integrity ; and therefore the accounts of the mines, contained
in the regiſter now mentioned, may with ſafety be relied on,
as juſt and accurate, and ſtrictly correſponding to appearances,
as he had not the ſmalleſt tendency to exaggerate his deſcriptions. Although an extenſive knowledge of this ſubject is altogether diſclaimed, yet there is one obſervation, which preſents itſelf ſo frequently to any, even the moſt careleſs, inqui-
rer, that it may be fairly hazarded : That, were new trials to
be made, nearer the ſurface of the veins than thoſe made formerly, there is a probability of their being more ſucceſsful ;
as, in ſome of thoſe veins, maſſes of rich and beautiful ſpar attract the notice of the haſty traveller, and ſeem to invite him
to examine them with ſome degree of attention. This is happily confirmed, by the reſult of thoſe experiments, an account
of which has already been given, which were undeniably more
ſucceſsful than any of thoſe that ſince that time have been
made. It appears from thoſe regiſters of the mines, that there
are not fewer than fourteen or fifteen veins diſcovered in the
hills of Alva, which, from the trials made, are found to contain ſpecimens of ſilver, lead, copper, iron, and cobalt.

On the ſouth ſide of the water of Devon, immediately oppoſite to the lands of Alva, in the eſtate belonging to Lord
Cathcart and Mr Erſkine of Mar, it is well known that the
fineſt coal in all this country is produced. It has now been
worked during a long period of years, and has always been
held in the higheſt eſtimation, on account of its ſuperior quality. The ſame ſeams of coal have been found on the north
banks of that river, in the eſtate of Alva, and extend from one
extremity of the pariſh to the other. It was worked by the
late Sir John Erſkine, about ſixty years ago, and a conſiderable quantity of coal was then brought out. The pits and o-
ther

ther veſtiges of his works, are ſtill to be ſeen. And ſo noble a ſpirit of enterpriſe did that gentleman poſſeſs, that he cut a canal, a conſiderable way along the banks of Devon, in order to convey his coal to the banks of the Forth, to be exported from thence to a proper market. The remains of this canal can eaſily be traced. More than twenty years ago, accurate ſurveys, of the different levels of the water of Devon, were taken as high up as the pariſh of Dollar, with a view to facilitate the tranſporting of coal, belonging to the different proprietors on the banks of the river, by means of a canal intended to have been made where it ſhould have been requiſite ; as, in many places, the current of the river is ſo ſmooth and gentle, as to render one entire canal altogether unneceſſary. Although this projeft was laid aſide, yet in ſome future period it may perhaps be reſumed. It is highly probable, that the preſent proprietor of this pariſh, will judge it proper to begin without delay to work the coal upon his eſtate, for this good reaſon, that the demand for that article is daily increaſing ; and there is every proſpeft that it will continue to increaſe, in conſequence of the prodigious conſumption of Lord Cathcart's coal, by an iron work, lately erefted on that Nobleman's eſtate, near the banks of Devon. No part of it is now ſold for the uſe of the country.

In a deſcription of this kind, it would be inexcuſable to omit taking notice of the beautiful plantations of trees, which ſurround the houſe of Alva ; which are planted in the hedge rows of the ſeveral incloſures, and on the brow of that eminence, on which the houſe ſtands. On this, there is a ſmall foreſt, conſiſting of many different kinds of trees, ſuch as oaks, elms, aſhes, beeches, larches, and pines of different ſorts. Many of theſe, the oaks in particular, ſeem to be of conſiderable

rable age. Some of the afhes too, are remarkable on account
of their fize; and one oak, juftly claims the appellation of the
" Monarch," of *this* wood, not in refpect of its age, but on
account of the tallnefs and ftraightnefs of its trunk, and of the
regularity with which its boughs are extended on every fide.
It is extremely probable, that this little foreft had been at
firft planted by the hand of fome former proprietor; but far
beyond the reach of memory. Moft of the trees, which fur-
round the inclofures below the houfe, were planted by the
late Sir John Erfkine, and as is fuppofed, fome time before the
year 1720. The eaft and weft fides of the hill, immediately
above the houfe, were planted by Lord Alva, more than 20
years ago, to which very large additions have been made
every year, by Mr Johnftone, fince he became proprietor.
It is computed, that not lefs than 98 acres of this hill, are
planted with trees of various forts; and that the policy, as it
is called, and the plantations around the houfe, extend to fifty
acres. The road from the houfe to the church, which is
little lefs than a meafured mile, has a row of trees on every
fide, which renders it a very pleafant and delightful walk.
It is worthy of obfervation, that the trees on this eftate, have
this remarkable property of being exceedingly clean and pure,
in the fkin or bark; and that few or none of thofe moffy ex-
crefcencies, are to be found on the bodies of the trees here,
which are ufually feen adhering to trees that grow in low
and fwampy grounds; which is an evidence not only of a
dry and pure atmofphere, but alfo of the happy quality of
the foil for raifing trees. 'Tis believed, that the fame
obfervation will hold true with regard to the trees that
grow on the fame range of hills, having the fame expofure, and very probably, the foil nearly of the fame quality; while at the fame time, it is but fair to remark, that
few,

few, if any, of the trees, either in the parifhes on the eaft
or weft, are equal either in age or fize, to the trees of this
parifh.

Few fituations afford more ample fcope for the difplay of
elegance and tafte, in the way of rural ornament, than this
place prefents. Nature is feen here in fome of her grandeft,
as well as moft pleafing forms; and a correct tafte, by lopping off fome luxuriancies, and beftowing fome additional
touches, where thefe are requifite, might contribute greatly to heighten the beauty of the fcenery. A rivulet of the
pureft water, pours along the middle of that glen where the
mines were wrought; when obftructed in its courfe by oppofing rocks, it forces its way, and falls in three beautiful
cafcades; where the ground is foft and flat, it forms a capa-
cious pool; it is fhaded on both its banks, with an extenfive
plantation of thriving timber, and forms a convenient recefs
for the purpofe of bathing. Even Diana herfelf, with all
her attendant nymphs, might here boldly plunge into the
cool " tranflucent wave," and not dread the unhallowed eye
of any favage or licentious intruder.

In the eaft end of the church, a monument, plain, and
without ornament, is erected by Lord Alva, in memory of
his father, late Lord Juftice Clerk. The following Epitaph
is infcribed on a marble plate, which, for claffic elegance,
and purity of ftile, is furpaffed perhaps by few modern com-
pofitions of that kind. It is hoped, that it may not be
difagreeable to the few furviving friends of that refpectable and truly amiable man, to recognize a character in
which they delighted, thus elegantly and juftly defcribed by
his fon.

Parenti

Parenti optimo,

Carolo Areſkine, Car. Areſkine de Alva, equitis, filio,

Qui,

Juventute, doctrina plurimum exculta ;

Ætate provectior,

In jure reſpondendo dicundoque

Feliciter verſatus ;

Senectute ſerena placidus,

Summis in Republica muneribus,

Ad LXXXIII, uſque annum,

Gnaviter expletis.

Vita honorifica ſatur,

In ſede tandem avita,

Oſſa juxta paterna,

Heic lubens quieſcit.

Carolo quoque, fratri multum deſiderato,

Familiæ ſuæ, Patrioque, ſi fata tuliſſent,

Decori eximio ;

Londini, in ædicula coenobii Lincolnenſis,

Sepulto,

H. M. P. C. JACOBUS ERSKINE,

1763.

PARISH of BALDERNOCK.

(Presbytery of Dunbarton, County of Stirling, Synod of Glasgow and Ayr.)

By the Rev. Mr. James Cooper, *Minister.*

Name.

In the beginning of the reign of Alexander the II. the lands of Cartonbenach were conveyed to Maurice Galbraith by charter from Malduin Earl of Lennox. Soon after, in the year 1238, we find the fame barony granted by a new charter, under the name of *Bathernock,* to Arthur fon of Maurice Galbraith, with power to feize and condemn malefactors, on condition that the convicts fhould be hanged on the Earl's gallows. From the Galbraiths of Bathernock, chiefs of the name, defcended the Galbraiths of Culcruich, Greenock, Killearn, and Balgair, which eftates have all, except the laft, paffed, by females, long ago into families of other names. The family of Bathernock ended alfo in an heirefs, and the eftate, about the beginning of the 14th century, paffed by marriage to David, fon of Lord Hamilton,

and

and anceſtor of the preſent John Hamilton, Eſq; of Bardowie. From that time, the proprietor of the barony appears to have taken the title of Bardowie ; and the title of Bathernock (now written Baldernock,) dropped by the family, was probably revived and perpetuated by beſtowing it on the pariſh, when it came to be erected. But when that erection took place, or when the name Bathernock came to be written Baldernock, as at preſent, is uncertain. If a conjecture may be hazarded with reſpect to the name, we ſhould rather ſuppoſe, that Baldernock was not a new name, but the original one revived, of which Bathernock was a corruption ; and that Baldernock is alſo a corruption of Baldruinich, (*i. e.* Druidſtown) it being highly probable, that this was a Druidical place of worſhip, as will appear from a remarkable monument of Druidiſm to be mentioned afterwards.

Situation and Surface.—It it is ſituated within the county Stirling, in the presbytery of Dunbarton, and ſynod of Glaſand Ayr. The ſurface is various. On the South, where it is bounded by the river Kelvin, there are ſix or ſeven hundred acres of rich flat land. The inundations of this river frequently blaſted the hopes of the huſbandman, by dammaging, or ſweeping away his luxuriant crops. To prevent ſuch diſaſters, the proprietors, about 16 or 18 years ago, united in raiſing a bank upon the brink of the river : but there are ſeaſons ſtill, when it breaks over, or burſts through its barriers, to reſume for a little its former deſolating ſway. From South to North there is a gradual aſcent, pleaſantly diverſified by round ſwelling hills. The flat ground, before mentioned, is a rich loam ; the riſing grounds towards the Eaſt, are a clayey ſoil over till ; and thoſe towards the Weſt, a a light ſharp ſoil over whin rock. On the North ſide there is ſome mooriſh ground, but the greater part of the pariſh is arable.

arable. Towards the South Weft lyes Bardowie Loch, covering about 70 acres. In it are plenty of pike and perch, of a good fize and quality. The banks are pleafant, upon which is fituated the houfe of Bardowie, within a few paces of the lake.

Climate and Difeafes.—The air, on the high grounds efpecially, is extremely falubrious, and the inhabitants healthy. There are no difeafes uncommon, or peculiar to the place, nor any, for a long time paft, that could be called epidemical, unlefs we fhould rank flow fevers under this clafs. They make their appearance fometimes in the fpring, but more frequently in the autumn, and fpread through whole families, and from family to family. This is obferved to happen chiefly among thofe whofe houfes are fmall, dirty, and not properly ventilated. It is to be regretted that the abfurd, and not altogether innocent practice, of expofing themfelves and their families, by unneceffary vifits to thofe who have been feized with this infectious difeafe, but too much prevails. And it is alfo a fubject of juft regret, that the prejudice againft innoculation of the fmall-pox ftill keeps hold of the minds of many in this part of the conntry. The poor children are thereby expofed to the danger of that difeafe in what they call the natural way; but the innoculation is equally well entitled to be called the natural way. The one way differs from the other in this only, that, by the innoculation, the infection is, by the tender and prudent care of the parents, communicated in that way which, by long experience, has been found moft fafe and eafy; whereas, without the inoculation, the infection is, by carelefs and fuperftitious parents, left to be communicated from their own cloaths after vifiting children under the difeafe, or by accidental intercourfe of their children with perfons who have the infection about their

cloaths,

cloaths, in that way which experience ſhows to be moſt ſevere and fatal.

Population, &c.—In the month of April 1794, the number of families was 137, of perſons 620, of whom there are,

Under	10	years of age	136
Between	10 and 20		133
———	20 and 50		242
———	50 and 70		98
———	70 and 85		11

Total   620

There are at preſent in this pariſh no inſtances of remarkable longevity.

Bachelors from 20 to 40	45
——— ——— 40 to 60	7
——— above 60	2
Widowers from 20 to 60	0
——— Upwards of 60	10
Yearly average of baptiſms	13
——— ——— — Marriages	6

Occupations.—The greater part of the inhabitants of this pariſh devote their time to that moſt innocent and moſt uſeful of ſecular employments, the cultivation of the earth. There are 45 farmers, including 12 feuars, who cultivate their own grounds; 36 labourers, 43 male ſervants, all labourers, 38 female ſervants, almoſt all labourers, 10 weavers of houſehold cloth, 1 taylor, 3 ſhoe-makers, 3 maſons, 3 carpenters, 2 millers, 2 gardeners, 2 ſmiths, 1 engraver, 1 flax-dreſſer, 4 miners, and one man who exerciſes the ſeveral occupations of weaver, conſtable, phyſician, ſurgeon, apothecary, and man-midwife.

Character.—The people are, in general, remarkable for a ſober and regular deportment; an advantage, in a great

measure,

meafure, to be afcribed to their occupation, and to want of manufactures, whofe boafted benefits make but a poor compenfation for their baneful influence on the morals of the people.

Rent of the Parifh.—The valuation of the parifh is 1744l. Scots. It is not eafy to afcertain the real rent, becaufe a number of the proprietors cultivate their own ground ; but it is fuppofed that it wiil not be over-rated at 3000l. Sterling. Arable land is rented from 10s. to 2l. per acre : and befides their rent to the landlord, the tenants are generally bound by their tacks to pay all the public burdens upon the lands they poffefs. Moft of their farms are alfo thirled to a particular mill, and pay, fome of them fo high as the 16th or 17th part of all the grain which they have occafion to grind ; a difcouragement to induftry now altogether unneceffary, and which every landholder, who wifhes to advance the value of his property, by encouraging the induftry of his tenants, ought if poffible to remove.

Mode of Cultivation.—The farms are in general fmall, inclofed and fubdivided ; and the prefent race of farmers are fuppofed to furpafs their fathers in fkill and induftry. Clearing the ground of ftones, draining, levelling the inequalities of the furface, ftraightening the ridges, laying on lime, and guarding againft the common miftake of overcropping, may be efteemed the chief improvements. . The Scotch plough, drawn by 3, and fometimes by 4 horfes, is that in moft common ufe. Oats and barley are the kinds of grain chiefly cultivated. The plough goes little before the beginning of March ; and the farmers feem not anxious to have the fowing of oats finifhed before the end of April, and the barley before the 20th of May. After liming their ground, they generally take two

crops

crops of oats, and one of barley. With the barley, rye-grafs
and clover are fown, of which hay is made in the enfuing
fummer, and fometimes for two fummers. They afterwards
pafture for two or more years, as they judge requifite to
give the ground a fufficient reft, before the fame rotation
be repeated. In the flat lands, wheat has been tried with fuccefs, and has been found to fuffer lefs damage than other
crops, by the floods, from which thefe grounds are, notwithftanding the embankment, not yet effectually fecured. Potatoes are raifed fufficient for home confumpt, and fome to
fpare for the Glafgow market, where they generally draw
from 8d. to 1s. per water peck. From the few trials that
have been made, there is much encouragement for the cultivation of turnip. The black cattle are moftly fmall, and the
farmers not very attentive to improve the breed of their milk
cows.

Roads.—The multiplicity of roads renders it impoffible, by
the converfion of the ftatute labour, to put them all in a proper ftate of repair. It deferves therefore the attention of
both mafters and tenants, how far the improvement of the
country, and their own private intereft, might be promoted,
by fhutting up fome of the roads that are of leaft public utility, and by making an extraordinary exertion for a year or
two, to put the reft once in good repair, after which the
road-money would be fufficient to keep them fo. A good
turnpike road has lately been made, paffing through the fkirts
of this parifh, from the thriving and now populous village of
Balfrone to Glafgow. It is thought that, by directing it
nearer the centre of this parifh, a faving of a mile and a half
at leaft might have been made in a diftance of nine miles.

Price of Labour and Provifions.—A good ploughman receives, befides his board, from 5l. to 7l. per half year, and a
                                                    fervant

fervant woman from 35 to 50 fhillings. The common wages
of a labourer are 14d. per day ; and when they work at piece
work, they generally earn from 1s. 6d. to 2s. per day. They
are better cloathed and lodged, and in every refpect live more
comfortably than thofe of the fame rank, half a century ago.
Old people remember that, in their early years, there was
not a cow killed for beef by any one in the parifh, excepting
in gentlemen's families, and by one or two more ; but now
there are few families that cannot attain to half a cow at
leaft. The price of all kinds of provifions is nearly the fame
with that of the Glafgow markets.

Ecclefiaftical State.—There are 110 families belonging to
the Eftablifhed church, 11 to the Relief, 19 to the Burghers,
2 to the Antiburghers, 3 to the Cameronians, and 1 to the
Bereans.

The prefent incumbent was admitted in 1783. His predeceffors, fince the Revolution 1688, were Meffrs Wallace,
Colquhoun, Garrick, and Taylor. The King is patron of
the parifh. The living confifts of 63 bolls of oat-meal, 33l.
in money, a manfe, and a glebe of 10 acres, whereof 7 are
arable. The church has been built at different times. The
laft enlargement was probably made before the beginning of
this century, with a view to accomodate the inhabitants of
the lands annexed by decreet 1649. The manfe was built
about 50 years ago, and has undergone feveral repairs.

State of the Poor.—The average number of poor in this parifh
is about fix. They are fupported, according to their exigencies,
in their own houfes, from the weekly collections at the church
door, and from the intereft of a capital of 420l. which has
accumulated by the donations of charitable perfons, and from
the furplus of the weekly collections. None of the poor of
this

this parish are difpofed to beg, either in this or neighbouring
parishes ; but much is given away by the inhabitants in alms
to beggars which fwarm from other places, efpecially from
manufacturing towns and villages.

Minerals and Fuel.—This parish abounds in coal and lime-
ftone. The coal refembles that of Newcaftle, caking together, and making a ftrong fire, when properly put on, and allowed to reft three or four hours before it be ftirred. It is
generally found in a ftratum of from 3 to 4¼ feet thick, between two ftrata of lime-ftones. The upper ftratum of lime-
ftone is called the *blue lime*, and the lower the *white lime*,
which laft has generally been efteemed of an inferior quality
to the blue. Thefe ufeful minerals, in places where there is
no great thicknefs of ftrata above them, are come at by removing the fuperincumbent foil : but where they lie deep,
the coal is wrought firft by miners, and afterwards the upper or blue lime is feparated from the roof by wedges or
gunpowder. The coals are fold at the pit for 3d. per hutch,
five of which may be drawn in a cart, by an ordinary horfe,
and fix by an able bodied horfe. The only coal in the parifh wrought for fuel, is the property of Robert Dunmore,
Efq; of Ballindalloch, whofe exertions for the improvement
of his own eftate, and of the country in general, cannot be
mentioned with too much praife. He works the lime alfo to
a very confiderable extent. Befides his, there are three other
limeworks going in the parifh, but upon a fmaller fcale ; and
there is lime-ftone, more or lefs, through almoft all the high
grounds. In it are found petrified fhells of a variety of kinds,
ftimulating the conjectures of naturalifts concerning the re-
volutions of this globe. There is abundance of freeftone of
a good quality for building, and a little iron-ftone ; but, at
the place where it hath been obferved, the ftratum is fo thin

as

as not to be worth working. A small rivulet in the East end of the parish makes a very plentiful deposition of ochre, which, if proper means were used to collect it, might turn to some account. Peats can easily be procured for fuel, but few of them are used, the coals being found less costly. A considerable quantity of them was formerly required by the farmers for kiln-drying their victual; but by the introduction of kilns with brick heads, they have become less necessary, coals answering the purpose equally well.

Antiquities.—Upon the high ground, in a commanding situation, at the North West corner of the parish, stands an old ruinous tower, being all that now remains of the mansion house of the Galbraiths of Bathernock, which appears to have been a large building surrounded with a ditch. Its antiquity must be very considerable, but how great, even tradition does not venture to determine. Not far from thence, to the eastward, are several of those large loose heaps of stones called Cairns, some of them oblong, and others of a circular shape. One of the circular ones, which has not yet been broken up, is about 80 yards in circumference. From two that have been broken up, it appears that they are composed of loose stones carelessly thrown together; but at the bottom are large flags placed on edge, in two parallel rows, at the distance of between 3 or 4 feet, lidded over with flags laid across, the cavity thus formed is divided by partitions into cells of 6 or 7 feet long. In one of the long cairns lately broken up, were found several fragments of a large coarsely fabricated urn, and some pieces of human bones. Tradition says, that in this place, called Craigmadden moor, a battle was fought with the Danes, in which one of their princes was slain. The farm in which these cairns are, is named Blochairn, which may be a corruption of Balcairn, *i. e.* the town

of

of the cairns. But the moſt curious remain of antiquity in this pariſh, is a ſtructure called the *Auld wife's lift*. It is ſituated near a mile North from the church, on very high ground, in a little flat of about 100 paces diameter, ſurrounded by an aſcent of a few yards in height, in the form of an amphitheatre. It conſiſts of three ſtones only, two of which, of a priſmatic ſhape, are laid along cloſe by each other upon the earth ; and the third, which was once probably a regular paralellopiped, and ſtill, notwithſtanding the depredations of time, approaches that figure, is laid above the other two. The uppermoſt ſtone is 18 feet long, 11 broad, and 6 deep, placed nearly horizontally with a ſmall dip to the North. Its two ſupporters are about the ſame ſize. It can hardly be matter of doubt, that this is one of thoſe rude ſtructures erected by the Druids in their ſacred groves. Its ſituation, in a very ſequeſtered ſpot, on an eminence, ſurrounded by a grove of oaks, ſtumps of which trees are ſtill viſible, correſponds exactly to every deſcription we have of theſe places of worſhip. The figure of the ſtones themſelves, and their poſition, bear a ſtrong reſemblance to others which antiquarians have not heſitated to pronounce monuments of Druidifm. The name by which they are called ſeems no ſmall confirmation of the truth of this opinion. A Druidical ſtone in Ireland, mentioned by Cambden, is called the *lifted* ſtone ; and there are ſome in Poitiers in France, known by the name of Pierres levées. But beſides that the ſtones under conſideration have the name of lift, which appears to be the general appellation of ſuch Druidical ſtones, the ſpecific part of their name, viz. Auld wives, is eaſily accounted for, on the ſame ſuppoſition. Upon the authority of Tacitus and Mela, we know that female Druids, generally pretty far advanced in years, lived together in ſiſterhoods, in ſequeſtered ſpots, devoting their time to the offices of the Druidical worſhip. Theſe

Thefe were by the people held in high efteem, and called *Senæ*, or *venerable women*, words nearly fynonymous to the Scots word *Auld wives*. Hence we are induced to conclude, that this is one of thofe lifted ftones, Pierres levées; and that it is called the Auldwive's lift, becaufe it was the lifted ftone where the Senæ, or fifterhood of venerable female Druids refiding here, paid their devotions. Upon the fuppofition, alfo, that this was a feat of the Druid worfhip, we have fuggefted to us a very probable etymology of the name of the parifh. *Bal*, in the Gaelic language fignifies *town*, and *Druinich*, of or belonging to the Druids. The prefent name, Baldernock, is not a greater corruption of Baldruinich, *i. e.* Druidftown, than might be expected in the lapfe of eighteen hundred years.

PARISH OF BALFRON.

(County of Stirling.—Synod of Glasgow and Ayr.—Presbytery of Dumbarton.)

By Mr James Jeffrey, *Miniſter.*

Name, Extent, &c.

BALFRON is a word of Gaelic derivation, and is ſaid to ſignify " the Town of Sorrow." On what account the place obtained this name is not certainly known. The form of the pariſh is nearly an oblong ſquare. Its length, from eaſt to weſt, is ſomewhat more than 8 miles; and its breadth, from north to ſouth, from 1 to 2 miles. It is bounded by the pariſhes of Drymen, Killearn, Fintry, Gargunnock, and Kippen. The greater part of the grounds in this pariſh have the advantage of a fine ſouthern expoſure, riſing gradually from the water of Endrick.

Climate, Soil, &c.—The climate is wet, but not unhealthy, ſeveral of the inhabitants living to a great age; and there are few inſtances of epidemical diſeaſes. An epidemical fever, indeed, prevailed in the winter and ſpring of 1791, and carried off, in the village, upwards of 40 grown up people. But this mortality may be aſcribed, not ſo much to the unhealthineſs of the climate, as to the intemperance of the people at the time, and the damp ſtate of many new houſes, houfes, which were occupied as foon as they were covered in, and plaftered.

The foil is various. In fome places it is light and fandy, but, for the moft part, wet and tilly.

Agriculture is here in a ftate of infancy. The principal corn crop is oats. Barley is raifed but in few places; and green crops are feldom attempted. Among the difadvantages that have hitherto retarded agricultural improvements, may be reckoned the badnefs of the roads, the diftance from foreign manure, and efpecially the poverty of the greater part of the farmers to whom the land is at prefent let, in very fmall portions. Their rents are from 5 l. to 35 l.; two or three of them about 70 l.; and one only up to 100 l. Sterling. But the difadvantages under which the parifh has hitherto laboured, are now in the way of being removed, or fufficiently compenfated, by the extraordinary advantages arifing from fome new manufacturing eftablifhments; and, in as far as their influence has hitherto extended, to improvements in agriculture, as foil has appeared very fufceptible of melioration. There is abundant reafon, indeed, for fuppofing, that a fpirit for fuch improvements will not be difficult to excite; for, of late, many fubftantial inclofures have been made in different parts of the parifh, and particularly on the eftate of Ballindalloch, where, in addition to thefe, there have been feveral plantations of wood formed, with an equal regard to beauty and utility.

Manufactures, &c.—About the beginning of the year 1789, Robert Dunmore, Efq; of Ballindalloch, introduced a colony of cotton weavers into the parifh. For thefe, he, at firft, built a few houfes, at his own expence, in the neighbourhood of the church, and let them out at a fmall yearly rent. This branch of manufacture was immediately carried

on

on to ſuch an extent, that the value of goods manufactured, during the currency of the year 1792, amounted to the ſum of 7676 l. Sterling.

In the ſpring of the year 1790, the public ſpirited exertions of Mr Dunmore having been already directed to this corner, he applied himſelf, with ſucceſs, to procure the erection of a cotton mill in the neighbourhood of his new village; and a happy ſituation having been choſen on the banks of the water of Endrick, the work was carried on, through his means, with ſuch aſtoniſhing diſpatch, that, in the month of June of the ſame year, yarn was ſpun in it. This branch of manufacture, in December 1792, gave employment to 390 people. Of theſe, 120 were men; 90 women; 180 children, from 6 to 16 years of age.

The cotton mill, thus erected, fully anſwered the purpoſe of extending and improving the village. Mr Dunmore readily feued out ground, to the new ſettlers, for the ſite of a houſe and garden, moſt commonly to the extent of a quarter of an acre, and, at firſt, upon ſuch eaſy terms as to afford them ample encouragement; but here, as in many other caſes, well directed liberality proved good policy; for the conſequent proſperity of his village, and its manufactures, ſoon enabled him to raiſe the rate of his feu-duty from 2 l. to 4 l. per acre, without retarding the progreſs of building, or at all diſtreſſing the people. The houſes, in general, are ſubſtantial. Moſt of them are covered with ſlate; and ſome of them are three ſtories high. The village now conſiſts of 105 new houſes, in which there are upwards of 430 rooms with fire places.

For the rapid riſe, and increaſe of the population of this new village, we are partly indebted to a printfield and bleachfield, which Mr Dunmore, with the ſame patriotic views, procured to be eſtabliſhed upon the oppoſite banks of the

water

water of Endrick, and in the adjoining parifh of Killearn; for, although the neceffary works connected with thefe eftablifhments, be feparated from this parifh by the river, yet almoft all the people belonging to them have their dwellinghoufes in the village of B.ltron, and a confiderable part of the grounds originally intended for carrying on the bleaching and printing operations, are on the Balfron fide of the river.

Roads.—Till within thefe few years, the roads of this parifh, during the winter months, were almoft impaffible ; but in this refpect alfo, we have derived much advantage from the introduction of our manufactures, and the fpirited exertions of the gentlemen who has fo laudably patronized them. In this particular line of improvement, indeed, the other landed proprietors, not immediately connected with the mercantile or manufacturing interefts, readily afforded him the moft liberal and manly fupport, and thereby materially promoted both the particular interefts of the manufacturing eftablifhments, and the general good of the country ; in which view Peter Spiers, Efq; of Culcreuch, a confiderable heritor in this parifh, ought to be particularly mentioned with honour. In confequence of thefe exertions, a bridge of two arches, at Ballindalloch, has been thrown over the Endrick, which, when *fwelled*, is a rapid and dangerous river. A turnpike road has been made from Glafgow to the village of Balfron, and leading from it into the military road between Stirling and Dumbarton. Another turnpike road has alfo been made, which, paffing through the eaft end of this parifh, leads from Kippen to Glafgow. Good crofs roads are begun to be formed, and confiderable progrefs has been made in them. Arches have been thrown over all the ftreams of water, and hollow places ; fo that there is now the certain profpect of having good roads through every part of the parifh.

Population,

Population, &c.—The return to Dr Webſter in 1755, amounted to 755 fouls. The population of the pariſh has been in a fluctuating ſtate, in ſo far as regards the village, ſince the year 1790, ſeldom remaining ſtationary for a ſingle week. In December 1792, there were in the pariſh 1381 fouls. Of this number the village contained 981, and of theſe 930 were new ſettlers.

Of the above number, 805 were of the Eſtabliſhed Church, 459 Antiburgher Seceders, who have had a place of worſhip in the pariſh about 60 years, 64 Papiſts, 18 of the Relief Perſuaſion, 17 Cameronians, 9 Burgher Seceders, and 9 of the Church of England.

There were beſides about 200 people, including all ages, imported to the village at Whitſunday 1793, when the printing and bleaching commenced; ſo that, at that period, there were in the village about 1181, and in the pariſh 1581 fouls.

The people employed at the printfield and bleachfield, are almoſt wholly of the Relief and Burgher Perſuaſion; and, beſides theſe already mentioned as reſiding in the village in December 1792, there were ſeveral families of the ſame perſuaſions who had given a temporary adherence to the Eſtabliſhed Church; but at Whitſunday 1793 being joined, all at once, by ſo many of their ſect, each party immediately ſet up a tent for themſelves, and have ever ſince been contending, with much animoſity, for the honour of making proſelytes. It is not, therefore, eaſy to aſcertain the preſent ſtate of the pariſh, with reſpect to ſectaries; and it is ſtill more difficult to ſay what it will be a few years hence.

Till very lately, there was no regular record kept of births, deaths, and marriages. From Whitſunday 1792 to Whitſunday 1793, there were 67 births, 46 deaths, and 30 marriages.

Church

Church and Stipend. Poor. School.—The manfe and offices were built new from the foundation in 1789, and the church, which is neat, and even elegant, in 1793. The value of the ftipend is from 70 l. to 80 l. Sterling, according to the rife or fall of grain, part of it being paid in meal and barley. The glebe confifts of about 18 acres. The Earl of Kinnoul is patron.

The poor have hitherto been well provided for, out of the collections made at the church, dues of mortcloths, and the intereft of about 100 l. Sterling of poor's money; but that they will continue to be much longer fo, out of thefe funds, confidering the great influx of inhabitants, is very doubtful. There are no vagrant poor in the parifh.

The fchoolmafter's falary is 100 l. Scotch, out of which he pays, annually, 2 l. Sterling for a perfon to teach a fchool in a diftant part of the parifh. Befides the parifh dues, which are now pretty confiderable, the fchoolmafter has fomewhat more than an acre of land, originally fued by the feffion for his behoof. This piece of ground was lately exchanged for an equal quantity, with much advantage to the fchoolmafter, by Mr Dunmore, as it ftood in the way of fome of his improvements. Upon the ground Mr Dunmore gave in exchange, he built, at his own expence, a neat and commodious fchool room, with a lodging for the mafter, of 4 rooms, all under one roof.

Mifcellaneous Obfervations.—Peat and turf, of which there are great abundance in the parifh, were, previous to 1790, almoft the only fuel ufed; but, fince roads were made, coal is chiefly burnt, at leaft by the people in the village. It is brought from Campfie or Baldernock, the carriage being upwards of ten miles. Red and white freeftone are found in great plenty. There is alfo lime-ftone. Repeated attempts

have

have been made to find coal, of which, in the opinion of
good judges, there are the moſt flattering appearances, tho'
hitherto without ſuccefs. The price of labour, of all kinds,
is of late advanced more than a third. In many inſtances,
it is doubled. In the year 1787 the wages of an ordinary
man ſervant were from 4 l. to 6 l. a-year. In 1794 they are
from 8 l. to 10 l. A day labourer, in 1787, could have been
hired for 7 d. or 8 d per day; but in 1794 they require 1 s.
or 1 s. 6 d. or 1 s. 8 d. From the vicinity of Glaſgow, and
the eaſy acceſs to it, the price of proviſions is now, in a great
meaſure, regulated by the Glaſgow market. There is no
public houſe in the pariſh, excepting in the village, where
there are a tolerably good inn, and two reſpectable public
houſes. There are, beſides, a great many low public houſes,
which deal only in whiſky and which are productive of the
worſt effects, both to the health and morals of the people.

PARISH OF BOTHKENNAR.

(COUNTY AND PRESBYTERY OF STIRLING.—SYNOD OF PERTH AND STIRLING).

By the Rev. Mr DAVID DICKSON, *Minister.*

Situation, Extent, &c.

THE writer of this account has not been able to difcover the origin of the name Bothkennar. This parifh is fituated in that track of country commonly called the Carfe of Falkirk; is about a mile and a half in length, and nearly of equal breadth. It is bounded on the north by the parifh of Airth; on the weft, by the parifh of Larbert; on the fouth, by the parifhes of Falkirk and Polmont; and on the eaft, by the river Forth. It feems antiently to have been bounded on the fouth by the river Carron, but that river having changed its courfe, now interfects both the parifhes of Bothkennar and Falkirk, leaving part of the former on the fouth, and a fmall part of the latter upon the north fide of it. The parifh contains 96 oxgangs of land, which, at the computation of 13 acres each, amount in whole to 1248; the yearly valuation of which, including cefs, feu-duty payable to the family of Marr, and minifter's ftipend, is 3591 L. 12 s. 6 d. Scotch. The real rent of the parifh cannot be fo exactly

exactly afcertained, as it may vary according to the value of the ground, or the date of the leafes; at a medium, it may be reckoned at leaft at 2 l. 5 s. per acre, which would amount to 28c8 l. Sterling; and when the price of grain is high, it may be confiderably more.

Soil, Produce, &c.—The foil is moftly of a deep clay, and the land, which is believed to have been antiently covered by the waters of the neighbouring Frith, is, in general, very rich, and produces plentiful crops of oats, peafe, and beans, barley, wheat, grafs, and potatoes. Mr Nimmo, in his hiftory of Stirlingfhire, informs us, that as early as the 14th century, (when, in comparifon, little improvement had been made in agriculture), the yearly feu duty paid to the Crown, out of the parifh of Bothkennar alone, was no lefs than 26 chalders of victual, befides 6 chalders paid to the Abbacy of Cambufkenneth. About that time, or probably at a later period, the price of grain was fo very low, that the proprietors of land in the parifhes of Airth and Bothkennar, had it in their option, when paying the feu-duty, to pay either a merk Scotch or a boll of wheat. The former wifely chofe to pay in money, which they ftill do; and the latter in grain, which, inftead of a merk Scotch, has, for many years paft, been equal in value to 20 s. 25 s. or fometimes even 30 s. Sterling. This parifh is almoft a continued flat; there is fcarcely the leaft rifing ground to be obferved through the whole of it, and not a ftone to be feen, unlefs brought from other places. Excepting the roads, there is not a fpot of ground uncultivated. The method of cultivation, the time of fowing and reaping, the wages of fervants, tradefmen, and day-labourers, the prices of coal, grain, and provifions, are in general nearly the fame as in the parifhes of Airth and Polmont, to the ftatiftical accounts of which the reader is

here

here referred. There are 12 orchards in this parish, the largest of which is about 3 acres in extent. They produce chiefly apples and pears, and, in good fruit seasons, bring the proprietors a plentiful return.

Population, &c.—According to a list of the inhabitants, taken by the present minister in 1783, the number of souls was then about 730; but since that time it has considerably decreased, owing, among other causes, to the shipping having been. in a great measure, removed from Carron shore to Grangemouth, on which account, several houses in this parish have been taken down, and others are left without inhabitants. In the year 1793, another list was taken, from which it appears, that there are now only 144 families, and in all about 600 inhabitants, of whom 303 are males, and 297 females; 164 married, and 436 unmarried; among which last, 45 are widowers and widows, and 133 children below 10 years of age. The number of marriages, baptisms, and burials, for the last 10 years, according to the parish register, which, during that time, has been very regularly kept, is as follows:

Years.	Marriages.	Baptisms.	Burials.
1783	5	21	15
1784	2	23	9
1785	8	12	7
1786	2	20	9
1787	6	23	10
1788	7	17	16
1789	8	23	10
1790	12	10	9
	50	149	85

Years.	*Marriages.*	*Baptiſms.*	*Burials.*
	50	149	85
1791	5	23	7
1792	5	11	15
	60	183, of which 101 males, and 82 females.	107, of which 57 males, and 50 females.

There are 38 farmers, and about 86 ſervants, 2 maſons, 3 wrights, 2 journeymen and apprentices ditto, 3 coopers, 3 weavers, 1 journeyman ditto, 3 ſhoemakers, and 1 cobler, 2 tailors, 6 ſmiths, 3 innkeepers, 1 baker, and 1 apprentice ditto, 1 barber, 1 exciſe officer, 8 ſhipmaſters, 6 ſailors, 3 carpenters, and 10 day labourers; 1 clergyman, 2 ſtudents, and 1 ſchoolmaſter. The people, in general, attend the Eſtabliſhed Church; of thoſe who do not, there are about 9 Burghers, an equal number who are connected with the Relief congregation in Falkirk, 8 Antiburghers, 2 Cameronians, and 2 Epiſcopalians. The inhabitants are, for the moſt part, ſober, induſtrious, and kindly affectioned one to another, maintaining a decent and becoming reſpect to the ordinances of religion; whilſt, among the few diſſenters from the Eſtabliſhed Church, there is very little of that narrow bigotted ſpirit, for which the ſectaries in other corners have been too frequently blamed.

Climate, &c.—Notwithſtanding the low ſituation, the climate is uncommonly healthy. It is obſerved to be even more ſo than the higher ground in the adjacent pariſhes. As a proof of its ſalubrity, among thoſe who have died within the laſt 10 years, 11 were above 60; 14 above 70; 5, 80 and upwards; and 1 above 90. At preſent there are living in the pariſh 23 between 60 and 70; 9, 70 and upwards; and 4 above 80. The moſt prevalent diſeaſes are rheuma-

tiſm

tifm and hyfteric complaints. The former may be owing to many of the houfes having only earthen floors; the caufes of the latter, we leave to men of medical knowledge to determine. The ague, which about 30 years ago was very frequent, is now fcarcely known, which may be attributed partly to the ditches being kept more open, and partly to the different manner of living. The frequent breezes from the Frith may contribute not a little to the health of the inhabitants; and fome have fuppofed, that even the fmoke from Carron Work, though in other refpects difagreeable, may ferve to difpel thofe noxious vapours, which, in other places, particularly in low countries, are often fo prejudicial. Inoculation for the fmall-pox is ftill far from being general; but, when practifed, has almoft univerfally been attended with fuccefs.

Church, Manfe, &c.—The church was rebuilt in a modern form, in the year 1789, and is now a very neat place of worfhip, fufficient to accommodate 5 or 600 people eafily. The manfe and office houfes are at prefent repairing at a very confiderable expence. The glebe is about 4 acres of very good land. The ftipend, partly in money, and partly in victual, is generally about 100 l. Sterling. There have been only 4 prefbyterian minifters in this parifh fince Epifcopacy was abolifhed. The firft, viz. Mr Lindfay, afterwards tranflated to Perth, was fettled here in 1721-2; was fucceeded by Mr Penman, in 1744; after him, Mr Nimmo, author of the Hiftory of Stirlingfhire, was ordained in 1765. The prefent minifter was admitted in July 1783. The heritors are 22 in number, of whom only 10 refide within the bounds of the parifh. The principal are, Lord Dundas of Afke, Mr Ogilvie of Gairdoch, and the heirs of the late much refpected General Thomas Dundas of Carronhall, all

of

of whom are non-reſident. The patronage belongs to the family of Airth, who have always exerciſed that right in a manner that does them the higheſt honour. The late Mr Graham, who had a particular pleaſure in promoting the happineſs of thoſe around him, (although not a member of the Eſtabliſhed Preſbyterian Church), was accuſtomed to indulge the people with the choice of their own paſtors; by doing ſo, he obtained juſt and univerſal eſteem while he lived, and on this account his memory will long be highly reſpected. If other patrons were of the ſame diſpoſition, the law of patronage, ſo long complained of, would ceaſe from being a grievance; and inſtead of that frequent diſcord and animoſity, which are ſo deſtructive to the civil and religious intereſts of our country, peace and harmony would every where prevail.

School and Poor.—There is only one ſchool in this pariſh, at which 50 or 60 children are yearly taught Engliſh, writing, arithmetic, Latin, Greek, &c. The ſchoolmaſter has a houſe and ſmall garden. His ſalary is only 100 merks Scotch, which, together with voluntary contributions from ſome of the heritors, his ſchool wages, and perquiſites as ſeſſion-clerk, ſcarcely exceed 20 l. Sterling *per annum*. It is much to be wiſhed, that, in this age of liberality and improvement, ſomething were done for the encouragement of ſchoolmaſters, many of whom, having families to ſupport, muſt often be ſtraitened to obtain even the neceſſaries of life. —The poor in the pariſh are not allowed to beg from door to door. The number upon the Seſſion roll is at preſent 7, who receive a weekly allowance, beſides a few who get occaſional ſupply. They are ſupported by the weekly collections, with the intereſt of 130 l. Sterling, which together amount at an average, for 10 years paſt, to 34 l. 10 s. yearly.

A

A few poor fcholars alfo have their fchool wages and books paid from the fame fund.

Roads and Improvements.—The roads in this parifh, which old people remember to have been once fcarcely paffable, are now in general good, unlefs for a fhort time during the winter, when the ground is very wet, or when covered with water, owing to the tide and land floods meeting together. Within thefe few years, a confiderable extent of ground has been gained in this parifh and neighbourhood from the Frith, which, though defended at a great expence, will foon become a valuable acquifition to its poffeffors. There is a bridge foon to be built over the river Carron, a little above Grangemouth, and a new road to be carried from thence acrofs this parifh, towards Alloa and Stirling, which are likely to be of great advantage to the inhabitants, and will open a nearer and more agreeable communication both to the north and fouth.

PARISH of BUCHANAN,

(County of Stirling, Synod of Glasgow and Ayr,

Presbytery of Dunbarton.)

By the Rev. Mr David Macgibbon.

Name, Extent, &c.

BUCHANAN was formerly called *Inchcailloch*, the name of an iſland in Lochlomond, where the church was till the year 1621, when a conſiderable part of the pariſh of Luſs, at that time on this ſide of the loch, was annexed to the pariſh of Inchcailloch. Some years after the annexation, the walls of the church in Inchcailloch failing, and the people likewiſe not finding it convenient every ſabbath, eſpecially in ſtormy weather, to be croſſing over to the iſland, worſhip was performed in a church near the houſe of Buchanan, which was originally a Chapel of Eaſe belonging to the pariſh of Luſs. From this chapel, which was called the church or chapel of Buchanan, the whole
united

united parifh came by degrees to be called the parifh of
Buchanan. Inchcailloch fignifies " the ifland of the Old
" Women;" fo called, becaufe in former times there was
a nunnery there. The parifh of Buchanan has been reckoned 18 computed miles long, and 6 broad. The cultivated
part of the fouth end lies eaft and weft between the moor of
Buchanan and the river Endric. A long tract lies along
the north fide of Lochlomond to the upper end of the parifh, near which there are two glens croffing the parifh from
eaft to weft, Glendow and Glenarclet, both of which are
inhabited.

Rivers.—The Forth has its fource in the upper end of
this parifh. From feveral fprings, and from rains in thefe
high grounds frequently falling, there is collected a fmall
burn or rivulet, which runs down Glenguoi into Glendow,
and by the addition of feveral large burns in that glen it
is confiderably increafed: At the lower end of the glen it
is called the water of Dow, and below that the water of
Duchray, (as it paffes by the place of Duchray), and not
till it paffes by the church of Aberfoil is it called the Forth.
This river takes its courfe through Monteith by Stirling.
The river Endric, which is the boundary of this parifh in
the fouth, has its fource in the weft end of Dundaff, or
Fintry hills, and runs through the parifhes of Fintry, Kill-
cairn, and Drumen, till it reaches the parifh of Buchanan,
where it flows in beautiful curves through the fertile haughs
(or flats) of Buchanan and Kilmaronock, and falls at laft into
Lochlomond. This river in the winter feafon, when the
loch is full, covers a great part of the lower grounds on
both fides of the parifhes of Buchanan and Kilmaronock,
and when the water lies dead and goes off gradually it enriches the ground; but the floods have often proved hurtful

in

in the ſpring after the ſeed was ſown, and oftener in harveſt, both before the corns were cut down and afterward, carrying ſome away and greatly damaging the reſt. In harveſt 1782, in a flood, the haughs of Endric, in this pariſh, were covered with water, and immediately after, there came ſnow and intenſe froſt, ſo that in ſome places people walked on the ice above the ſtanding corn.

Caves.—In Craigroſtan there are ſeveral caves in which lawleſs people uſed to ſkulk and hide themſelves; thoſe are known by the names of the moſt remarkable perſons who uſed to frequent them. There is one commonly known by the name of King Robert's cave. What gave it that name was, that King Robert Bruce, after his defeat at Dalrec, in the weſt end of Strathfillan, paſſed that day, with very few with him, down the ſtrath, croſſed the water of Falloch, and came down the north ſide of Lochlomond to Craigroſtan. Night coming on, when he arrived at this cave, he ſlept there; next day he came to the laird of Buchanan, who conducted him to the Earl of Lenox, by whom he was preſerved for ſome time, till he got to a place of ſafety. The report is, that the night in which King Robert ſlept in the cave, he was ſurrounded with goats that uſed to lie there in the night, and that when he aroſe in the morning, and found himſelf ſo comfortable, he was ſo well pleaſed with the goats as his bed-fellows, that, when he came to be king, he made a law that all goats ſhould be graſs-mail (or graſs-rent) free.

Hills.—The Grampian hills run through this pariſh from S. W. to N. E. and divide the lower from the higher grounds. There is one pretty high hill in the midſt of theſe called the Conic hill: But the higheſt hill, in this
part

part of the country, is in the upper end of the parifh, called Benlomond, which is about 1080 yards above fea level. The afcent to the top of this hill directly weft is fteep, but from the fouth it is more gradual, till near the top, and then it is fomewhat fteeper. From the top of this hill there is, in a clear day, a very extenfive view to the eaft as far as E-dinburgh, to the fouth as far as Ayr, with the frith of Clyde, and the iflands in it, Arran, Bute, &c. as alfo to the weft fea and the iflands of Iflay, Jura, &c.

Lochs or Lakes.—Though Lochlomond cannot be faid to be in any one parifh, yet as the parifh of Buchanan extends 14 or 15 miles up the fide of the loch, and feveral of the inhabited iflands make a part of it, the greateft fhare of the loch may be faid to fall to the parifh of Buchanan. This beautiful lake, lying from S. to N. has always been reck-oned 24 computed or 36 meafured miles in length. The breadth towards the fouth end is from 8 to 10 miles ; to-wards the north end it is not near fo broad. The north end is confiderably deeper than towards the fouth end; the depth at the foot of Benlomond is about 120 fathoms ; in the fouth end it is about 20, and in many places not a-bove 14. All above Rowerdennan the loch never freezes, however intenfe the froft be ; but what is fouth of Rower-dennen frezes, fo that men, and even horfes with their loads, have travelled upon the ice, when covered with fnow. As there are feveral rivers which pour a great quantity of water into the loch, and as there is but one way by which it empties itfelf into the fea, the loch, in rainy feafons, rifes to a confiderable height, fo that from it loweft ebb it has been known to rife upwards of 5 feet. In this loch they reckon about 30 iflands, but there are only 13 or 14 that can be faid to be of any value, the reft being very fmall,

and

and fome of them but the points of bare rocks. The moſt valuable iſlands are divided between the families of Montroſe and Lufs ; 4 of them, belonging to the Duke of Montroſe, are in the pariſh of Buchanan ; 3 of theſe, namely, Inchailloch, already mentioned, Inchfael, which fignifies " the " Long Iſland," and Incheruin, " the Round Iſland," have a tenant in each of them with arable and paſture ground ; but by far the largeſt and the beſt of all the iſlands, and which likewiſe belongs to the family of Montroſe, is Inchmurin ; in this iſland the Duke of Montroſe keeps his deer, and a foreſter to take care of them. This iſland, it is faid, belongs to no pariſh, but the people in it get church privileges, when they apply for them, at Buchanan. In the fouth end of this iſland, the ancient family of Lenox had a caſtle, but it is now in ruins. There are alſo three ſmall lakes or lochs within the pariſh, namely, Dulochan, Locharclet and Lochamnancairn. In Dulochan there are fome pike, in Locharclet there are pike and large trout, in Lochlomond there are falmon-trout, eel, perch, flounder, pike, and a fiſh peculiar to itfelf, called pollac. This fiſh is of the ſize of a large herring, and at times is caught in great quantities on this fide of the loch with draught nets ; they are beſt in the months of July and Auguſt. Salmon was more plentiful laſt year on this fide of the loch than for many years paſt, owing to the ſtakes and nets upon the mouth of the Leven to prevent the fiſh from coming up, being pulled out ; and yet falmon fold laſt year dearer than before, owing to the carriers attending more regularly than formerly, and carrying them off to Glaſgow, &c. Salmon, which uſed to be fold at 2 d. and 3 d. the pound, fells now at 5 d. and 6 d.

Woods.

Woods.—Near the houfe of Buchanan there is an old oak wood ; great additions have been made to which within thefe 40 years paft. The prefent Duke of Montrofe is planting a great deal of different kinds of trees in the bottom of Buchanan, which in procefs of time, if properly taken care of, muft turn out greatly to the advantage of the family, as well as to the beauty of the place. In the ifland of Inchcailloch there is a large oak wood. From the Grampian hills to the north end of the parifh, along the fide of the loch, is one continued wood, confifting of fome afhes, alders, hazels, but moftly oaks. Woods are of late become very valuable on the fides of Lochlomond, as the timber and bark are eafily tranfported by water to Glafgow, Port-Glafgow and Greenock, and fometimes are carried to Ireland and the weft of England.

Climate and Difeafes.—This country in general is rather wet, not however unhealthy. Fevers are rare, and generally brought from other places, efpecially from the towns, and from the public works that are going on at no great diftance from hence, as bleaching, printing cloth, and fpinning cotton ; the children or connections of people in this parifh turning fickly in thofe places, are brought home, and fometimes the neighbours are infected by them. In that way alfo the fmall-pox was brought into this parifh in winter laft. The difeafe fpreading faft, about 30 of the young people in the neighbourhood where it was, took it ; 10 of whom died. All the parents whofe children had not taken it, (two or three excepted), as if it were with one confent, inoculated their children at one and the fame time ; fo that there are juft now under inoculation in this parifh 128. Several of whom I have feen ; many of them appeared to be pretty eafy ; others had a good

deal

deal of the pox, but are now in a fair way of recovery. Two only died.—What we reckon old people in this
parifh live till they are between 70 and 80 years; fome
reach 85 or 86; only 5 that I can remember, fince I came
to this parifh, reached 90, 2 of whom died going 98.
There is one living at prefent who is going 99; he is remarkably healthy, rifes every day by 7 or 8 in the morning, and if it is a good day, takes a fhort walk before
breakfaft; he has no complaint of his fight, hearing or memory, and his hand is as fteady as when he was a young
man; he was in arms in the year 1715 with his countrymen the Highlanders, and is the only man alive in this
part of the country who was out at that time.

Agriculture, &c.—The foil is of different kinds. The
haughs of Endric are deep, and very fertile for grafs or
corn. The rifing grounds towards the moor of Buchanan,
are partly gravel, partly mofs, and partly till, with
rocks and ftones, both above and below ground, in the way
of the plough. Upon the fide of Lochlomond above the
pals, the ground is drier than below, but rocky and ftony.
The crops are oats and barley. Some few peas are fown,
which do very well where the ground is limed, but they
are in danger of fuffering in harveft in this rainy country.
Some few have tried turnip; they would grow very well,
but they require more attention in the feafon that the people of this country are providing turf or peats, than they
can well beftow upon them. They all plant plenty of
potatoes, and the common people feed at leaft one half of
the year upon them. Oats, if the feafon anfwers, are fown
in the beginning of April, barley through the month of
May, and fometimes in June. There is little flax raifed,
and none but what is for private ufe. A greater quantity
of

of grain than was neceffary for the maintenance of the inhabitants, was raifed; but of late years a great part of the richer grounds being put under grafs, has confiderably diminifhed the produce in general. The generality of the tenants keep near a third more of cattle than they have pafture for; which, though they will not believe it, turns out more to their lofs than their profit. There are 5 entered ftills in the parifh, which do more than confume all the barley that grows in it. The common Scots ploughs are generally ufed; but inftead of being made by the farmers themfelves as formerly, they are now, for the moft part, made by fuch wrights as are moft remarkable in the country for making them, fo that they are not now fo clumfy and heavy as ufual. But by far the greater part of this parifh confifts of hill or moor ground, and is covered with rocks, mofs and heath. For 6 miles up the fide of the loch, each farm has a fhare of the moor which is contiguous to itfelf; but feveral miles of the north end of the parifh have of late years been all put under fheep-pafture. There are only 27 ploughs going in the parifh this year.

Till of late there was rather a want of induftry in this parifh, owing to what the farmers alleged, the fhortnefs of their tacks, which gave them no encouragement to improve, and the difficulty of getting manure: But a lime quarry being fome years ago found out in the moor above the pafs, near a mofs where they get peats for burning the lime, the farmers in the neighbourhood make lime there every year, which they bring to their grounds. This has proved of confiderable advantage to their farms. The farms below the pafs the Duke has inclofed and fubdivided, partly by ditch and hedge, and partly by ftone fences: By building the ftone fences, the farmers who were employed in providing ftones, had an opportunity of clearing their grounds of a

great

great many ftones, which they ftood very much in need of.
And fome of them fince in their wet grounds have been
cafting drains and filling them with ftones, by which their
grounds receive a double advantage. The multures for
fome time paft have been converted into money, fo that
there is little more given now than what is necefflary for
working the grain.

Population.—According to the return made to Dr Webfter, the numbers were 1699. The inhabitants have decreafed confiderably fince fome part of my predeceffor's
time. In one of his lifts, the number was between 1500
and 1600; according to the laft lift which I took of them,
they were only 1111 fouls, and the number is not increafing. There is no regifter of marriages kept; but the regifter in order to the proclamation of banns is regularly kept; and by the fame it appears, that the number
of proclamations from the beginning of the year 1760 to
the beginning of 1790, is 241; from 1760 to 1770, is 82;
from 1770 to 1780, is 83; and from 1780 to 1790, is 76:
The yearly average upon the whole, is 8. The numbers
of births from 1760 to 1790, is 409; from 1760 to 1770,
is 147; from 1770 to 1780, is 143; from 1780 to 1790,
is 119. The yearly average is about 13.

There are no manufactures in this parifh. There are in
it 6 weavers, 3 fhoemakers, 2 tailors, 1 fmith, 2 boat-car-
penters, 2 millers, no wrights nor mafons, except fuch as
work conftantly to the Duke of Montrofe. All the fervants in this parifh are domeftic or houfehold, except fuch as
work to the Duke, who have each of them who go under
the denomination of his workmen, a houfe and garden, a
cow's grazing-park, for their accommodation, with 4 a-
cres of ground. The wages of labouring fervants are daily
increafing,

increafing, owing greatly to the public works going on in the neighbourhood, the enlarging of farms, and the turning off of cottagers. Men fervants get from L. 7 to L. 9 in the year, and fome of them more. Women fervants get L. 4, and fome of them more. A man to work a day's work, or a *darger*, as they are called, is not eafily had; and when got, he takes 10 d. a-day with his victuals. Tailors get 8 d. and victuals.—Some years ago there were feveral Roman Catholics, and a few of the Epifcopal Communion; but there are none of thefe denominations now, fo far as I know, at leaft as common refidenters.

Stipend, School, Poor, &c.—The living confifts of 24 bolls oat-meal, together with L. 62 : 8 : 2, with manfe and glebe. The Duke of Montrofe is patron. The minifter, it is faid, is titular. There are 6 heritors, 5 of whom have a fingle farm each; the reft of the parifh belongs to the Duke, who is alfo fuperior of the other five.—There are 2 fchools, which for feveral years paft have been regularly taught; the parochial fchool, and a fchool appointed by the Society for propagating Chriftian Knowledge. The parochial fchoolmafter has a falary of L. 8 : 6 : 8, with a houfe; for every marriage he has 13 d.; for every baptifm, 4 d.; for teaching to read Englifh, 1 s. 6 d. the quarter, and for writing and arithmetic, 2 s. The charity fchool is kept at Sallochy, about 6 miles above the church, for 3 years; and then at Inverfnaid, about 7 miles farther up the country, for other 3 years, alternately. The charity fchoolmafter has a falary of L. 10 as fchoolmafter and catechift; he has alfo quarter wages from fuch as are able to pay, which I underftand turn out to about L. 4; but he is obliged to teach the poor *gratis*.—The number of poor upon the lift is about 40, fometimes 1 or 2 more. I fay upon

the

the lift, becaufe we only mark down the principal head of the family who receive charity, and are fupplied by the country and the parifh, though in fome families there may be the hufband and the wife, and in others fome fmall children befide the hufband and wife, or a widow with a fmall family in ftraitened circumftances; fo that if every individual were to be put in the lift, the number would be pretty confiderable. There is no provifion made in this parifh for the poor; they are obliged to beg from houfe to houfe through the year, and get their proportion of what collections are gathered on the Sabbath days, to buy cloaths and other neceffaries; and when any of them come to be in ficknefs, or infirm and unable to go about, they have to depend upon the charity of their neareft neighbours, and what can be given them extraordinary of the poor's money. Several years ago the county of Stirling attempted to confine their poor within their refpective parifhes; and after feveral meetings about it, all the parifhes, as far as I know, except Drumen and Buchanan, agreed to the plan; by which means the poor of the parifhes who agreed to it were better fupplied, and the people freed of a good deal of trouble in ferving them at the door; and befides, were not liable to get their goods ftolen, as formerly, by vagrants who went about begging. The poor are every day becoming a heavier burden upon the inhabitants of this parifh, occafioned by the beft growing farms in the lower end of the parifh being put under grafs, and the fmall farms in the head of the parifh, many of them being united together and put under fheep, and let out to people in other parifhes who give nothing for the fupport of the poor, but leave them a burden upon the refidenters. There is about L. 280 belonging to the poor of the parifh, moft of which has been given in different donations by the family of Montrofe.

Manners

Manners and Morals.—The people are generally fober. There are no villages in the parifh, nor even what deferves the name of a clachan at the church. There are only 3 licenfed public houfes : It is an advantage to the morals of the people that there are fo few. The people are hofpitable, and very charitably difpofed towards the poor. They live in peace and harmony among themfelves, and are very ready to oblige and affift one another when need requires. I cannot now recollect one law procefs between the inhabitants before the fheriff or commiffary, fince I came to the parifh ; any difference among them ufed to be made up at the barony court, and there have been very few differences even before the barony court for many years paft. There has no murder been committed time immemorial; no perfons have been committed to prifon, or banifhed for any crime, except one family who came to refide here, finding it inconvenient to live any where elfe, and one individual who came from the fouth, when purfued in his own country, took fhelter here for a few days, and afterwards fuffered at Edinburgh.

Advantages.—One great convenience which this parifh has, is, that almoft every farm has mofs in the moors belonging to itfelf or contiguous to it ; fo that in moderately dry fummers the people may have plenty of good peats. But after all, confidering the time that is fpent in cutting the peats, fetting and keeping them to the drought, and carrying them home, which is a great part of the fummer's work, befides the danger of lofing them all, or moft of them in rainy feafons, I leave it to my neighbours to judge whether it would not be better to caft fewer peats, and ferve themfelves partly in coals, efpecially fince they have now got a turnpike road to the coals. One great advantage

tage which the lower end of this pariſh has received of late
years, is a new line of road from Drumen to Rowerdennan,
which (the ferry intervening) joins the great road from
Dunbarton to Inverary on the ſouth ſide of Lochlomond.
There is always a ferry-boat kept by the family of Montroſe at Rowerdennan, and another by the family of Arrochar on the oppoſite ſide. The ferrying place on this ſide
has, of late years, been made pretty convenient for paſſengers ; a quay has been built both for the ſafety of the boats,
and for the conveniency of horſes getting into and out of
the boats ; as alſo a convenient public houſe. The line
of road from Drumen to Rowerdennan was begun and formed by the ſtatute work ; bridges were built on the burns,
partly by the vacant ſtipend, partly by the bridge-money
got from the county, and partly by the Duke's money·
This road while carried on by the ſtatute work, went on
very ſlowly ; though begun above 30 years ago, it could
not be ſaid to be finiſhed till laſt year ; but now that it is
finiſhed, it muſt greatly attract the attention of travellers,
being for ſeveral miles up the ſide of the loch, highly beautiful and pictureſque ; interſperſed with woods and beautiful fields of graſs and arable grounds ; commanding at the
ſame time an extenſive and delightful proſpect of Lochlomond, and of the principal iſlands in it, as alſo of the
many fine ſeats around the loch.

Miſcellaneous Obſervations.—In the lower end of the pariſh is the houſe of Buchanan, the preſent ſeat of the family
of Montroſe. This place for near 700 years belonged to
Buchanan of that ilk, and was the ſeat of that ancient family, but has been now for ſome time in the poſſeſſion of
the family of Montroſe.—At Inverſnaid in the upper
end of the pariſh, there was, about 80 years ago, a fort
                                                    built

built near mid-way between Lochlomond and Lochcatrine; the defign of which was to guard the pafs between the two lochs, and prevent the cattle and goods of the people in the lower parts of the country being ftolen and carried away northward, as alfo to be a check upon the country around it; the people thereabout being as ready as any o-thers to take away their neighbour's goods. This fort was burnt in 1745, but was afterward repaired. There ufed to be a company of men ftationed there fome time ago; but, for feveral years paft, it has been fupplied with a few men from the caftle of Dunbarton.

The people on the fouth fide of the Grampian Hills, fpeak nothing but Englifh; on the north fide, fuch as have been born and brought up there, fpeak the Englifh and Gaelic. Of late years, feveral tenants from the fouth fide, have removed to farms on the north fide; thefe fpeak Englifh only. All the names of places within the parifh are Gaelic: as, *Coldrach*, ' The Back of the Oaks;' *Blar-vokie*, or ' Plain of the He-Goat;' *Stronmacnair*, ' The ' Point of the Hill, belonging to the Son of the Heir;' *Benlomond*, ' The bare green Hill.'

PARISH of CAMPSIE,

(PRESBYTERY OF GLASGOW, SYNOD OF GLASGOW AND AYR, COUNTY OF STIRLING.)

By the Rev. MR. JAMES LAPSLIE, *Miniſter.*

Situation and Name.

THE pariſh of Campſie meaſures eight Engliſh miles in length, and ſeven in breadth, following the two great lines of road which interſect the pariſh nearly at right angles; the mean length is about ſix miles, and the mean breadth ſix, containing 36 ſquare miles; and allowing only 400 acres to every ſquare mile, the amount will be 14400 acres; it contains 101 plough gates of land, and is valued at 6429 pounds Scots. §

It

§ This pariſh, previous to the disjunction in the 1649, made a particular diſtrict of country by itſelf, not a little marked by peculiar manners and cuſtoms. It was bound on the North, by a range of hills running parallel to the Strath for near ten miles; on the South, by the river Kelvin, which, in theſe days, formed a ſwamp impaſſible in winter; on the Eaſt, the Gurrel Glen became another natural barrier; on the Weſt, Craig-Maddie Muir and the Brawzet Burn ſeparated this diſtrict from Srathblane and Baldernock.

Campſie

It is bounded on the North, by the pariſh of Fintry ; on the Weſt, by Srathblane and Baldernock ; on the South by Calder and Kirkintilloch ; and on the Eaſt by Kilſyth ; forming a diſtinct commiſſariot along with Hamilton, ſtiled the commiſſariot of Hamilton and Campſie.

It is preſumed, that the winding appearance of the ſtrath in general, and particularly of the glens near which the pariſh church is ſituated, has given riſe to the name Campſie, or Camſi, which, in the Celtic language, is ſaid to ſignify crooked Strath or Glen.—Of courſe, the Clachan of Campſie, is, the place of worſhip of the crooked glens.

Indeed, if we attend carefully to the appearance which this diſtrict preſents to thoſe who view it from any of the neighbouring ſtations, particularly the bending of the hills in the form of an amphitheatre, above the village of Clachan, from which five ſtreams, pouring down from five winding glens, form

Campſie, in its original ſtate, was eleven Engliſh miles long, from Weſt to Eaſt; its breadth varied on the Weſt march, from Calder houſe to the Earl's ſeat, it was at leaſt nine Engliſh miles ; whereas, on the Eaſt march, its breadth was ſcarcely ſix.

It contained 150 plough gates of land and was valued at 9670 pounds Scots. It may be oberved that Campſie is ſituated in the Lennox, and formerly made the eaſtern diviſion of that ancient territorial thaneſhip. In the year 1649, the Lords Commiſſioners for Valuation of Teinds, diſjoined all that part which lay betwixt Inch-Wood Burn and the Garrel Glen on the Eaſt, annexing it to the pariſh Monniabrugh, now better know by the name of Kilſyth, which portion contained 30 plough gates of land, and is rated at 2000 pounds Scots valution. In like manner they diſjoined all that portion on the South Weſt, which is ſituated betwixt Balgrochan and the Brawzyet Burn, annexing it to the pariſh of Baldernock, containing 21 plough gates of land, and valued in the county books at 1241 pounds Scots. Theſe two diſjunct portions will no doubt be deſcribed by the miniſters of the reſpective pariſhes to which they belong.

form the water of Glazert, this etymology of Campſie will not appear unnatural.

External Appearance and Soil.—It would not be eaſy to reduce the ſuperficial appearance of this pariſh to any regular figure ; it can neither be ſaid that it is a ſquare, a parallelogram, or a triangle ; the irregular bending of the hills prevents the eye from comprehending it in one view, and the bounding lines of the pariſh have never been accurately meaſured : in looſe terms, it may be ſaid to conſiſt of two hills, with a conſiderable valley or ſtrath between them ; the South hill being the continuation of the Kilpatrick Braes, ſloping gently down upon the Glazert and Kelvin ; the height is about ſeven hundred feet, arable to the top.—Between this South brae and the North hill, (better known by the name of Campſie Fells,) there is a conſiderable ſtrath, narrow indeed on the Weſt, but as it runs Eaſt, it widens into an open champaign country. The ſurface of the ſtrath is uneven, excepting a few haughs on the Kelvin, and Glazert.—Not that the land can be ſtyled rugged or broken ; for almoſt on every ſide of the gentle ſwells, with which this ſtrath abounds, ſome ſmall rivulets collect the waters from the riſing grounds; ſo that, even ſuppoſing the arable part of the pariſh to be in the higheſt ſtate of cultivation, the huſbandman would neither find it eaſy nor expedient to plow the ridges long in one direction.—One meets with boggy, ſtannery, croft, and clay ground, almoſt in every farm.—The haughs which ly upon the Glazert and Kelvin, are compoſed of carried earth, brought down from the hills in floods; of courſe, thoſe upon the Glazert, as being nearer the hills, contain a conſiderable quantity of gravel, and are better calculated for raiſing potatoes, and turnip. The Kelvin haughs, on the other hand,

being

being formed of the ſleigh which the river depoſits on overflowing its banks, muſt be better adapted for the culture of
beans and wheat ; and as the Kelvin, by the new cut which
is making, will ſoon be confined within its proper channel, it
is to be preſumed, that the farmers will then make the moſt of
the excellent ſoil which lyes upon that river. At the kirk of
Campſie, there is a haugh of near three hundred acres, capable of producing all ſorts of green crops, at leaſt equal to
any in the county. *

Climate.—The climate of this pariſh, like every other part
in the Weſt of Scotland, confiſting of hill and dale, is exceedingly variable ; at the ſame time, there is reaſon to believe,
that more rain falls at the kirk of Campſie than in any of the
neighbouring pariſhes to the South and Eaſt : Nor is it to be
wondered that the climate ſhould be wet, when the ſituation
of

* Although the ſoil of this pariſh be ſo exceedingly varied, nevertheleſs
that part of it which contains coal and lime, uniformly appears to be clay,
forming two belts of unequal breadth ; the one upon the North of the water of Glazert, is nearly a thouſand yards in breadth, commencing about a
mile Eaſt from the church, and continuing all along the baſe of the hills to
the eaſtern boundary of the pariſh. The other belt encircles the South braes,
and its breadth is ſomewhat greater ; ſuch is the appearance of the ſurface
in the Strath. As to the Campſie Fells, which make about two fifths of the
whole pariſh, they run parallel to the Strath, from one end of the diſtrict to
the other. The face of the hill is ſomewhat broken with craigs and glens :
the ſummit and back part is a deep muir ground, interſperſed with moſs
hags ; the ſoil on the face of the hills produces a ſhort feeding graſs, equal to
any brae ground in the kingdom ; while the muirs are thought to be well
calculated for the rearing of young black cattle in the more marſhy parts,
and for keeping ſtocks of ewes upon the drier ground. In general, it may be
ſaid, that the ſoil in the Weſt end of the pariſh, and particularly North of the
Glazert, is moſt adapted for paſture ; whereas the land on the South and Eaſt
ſide, ſeems fitter for grain.

of the place is confidered; the Campfie Fells being fituated betwixt the Friths of Forth and Clyde, the vapours which collect from either fea, as they float along, are ʻintercepted by the high ridge of the mountain; and being thus compreffed, they defcend in fhowers upon the valley; neverthelefs, it being a light gravelly bottom, the Strath being well ventilated, and the ftreams of water, owing to the great declivity, running off quickly, the parifh is, upon the whole, uncommonly healthy. Perhaps the great plenty of coal, which enables the meaneft cottager to obtain a hearty fire, along with the uncommon purity of the fpring water, may not a little contribute to the falubrity of a climate which in other refpects might be prejudicial to health from its dampnefs. Whatever other obfervation one might be difpofed to make on the weather in this diftrict, it muft be allowed, that it is remarkable for variety; we have often feen fnow in a morning, rain at mid-day, and froft in the evening, and this alternately for feveral days.—Of courfe, it would be impoffible to fay, as it is faid in fome parts of the ifland, that fuch a month is dry, or fuch a month is warm; the drought of Auguft we have often witnefsed in November, and the tempeftuous fhowers of February are often experienced in July.

Water

† Old people pretend to fay that the feafons are altered, and particularly that they have become colder; and in corroberation of their opinion, they adduce the very flattering but fallacious teftimony of what they felt in their youth, and how the corn ripened fooner on the braes than now : The teftimony of an old man, about what he felt in his youth, when his blood was warm, and his fpirits high, can by no means be confidered as an unequivocal proof of the ftate of the weather; nor is the circumftance of the corns on the high ground ripening fooner than at prefent, an index of the alteration of the feafons. For we all know, that where the foil is thin, and often ploughed, the fcanty meagre crop will be difpofed fooner to whiten, even if

the

Water, Wood, and Mountains.—This parifh may be faid to be uncommonly well watered : In the greateft drought, the number of fprings from the hills afford fuch quantities of water, that the machinery at the different print-fields have a conftant fupply. There is properly fpeaking but one river in the parifh ; and even this one is on a fmall fcale ; it is formed by three ftreams, uniting below the kirk of Campfie : it then receives the name of Glazert, which is faid to fignify in Gæ-lic, the water of the gray, or green promontory, alluding perhaps to the greennefs of the hills from whence the ftreams flow. The Glazert, allowing for all its windings, runs a-bout five Englifh miles, before it joins the Kelvin oppofite to Kirkintilloch. It runs with confiderable rapidity ; the fall from the kirk of Campfie to the Goyle-bridge being fomewhat

more

the climate fhould be wetter and colder, than upon well-refted rich land. As far, however, as we can pronounce any thing certain, relative to the climate, it may be faid that we have fcarcely any permanent froft, till after Chrift-mas : we have feldom wind from the North and Eaft, except in the time of a ftorm of froft and fnow, and ufually for a few days about the beginning of May, when in general it is accompanied with an Eaftland charr, very deftruc-tive to bloffoms of fruit trees. Our rain in general is from the South Weft ; and we fcarcely ever fail to have our Lammas floods, and our Equinoctial ftorm, the firft calculated to lodge our corn, before they are ripe, and the laft to rot them in the ftuke. Summer 1781 was remarkable for a cold drought, which continued feveral weeks withering the grafs, and introducing a black fly upon the corns, which prevented the grain from being fo plump as ufual. 1782 was remarkable for being a backward feafon, fo that fome of our corns were buried below the fnow on the 31ft of October. Summer 1783 was re-markable for a thick fog, whereby the fun was fcarcely vifible for three weeks ; we felt that fummer a flight fhock of an earthquake. Our fum-mers, upon the whole, for thefe fix years bygone, have been rather cold ; our winters, on the other hand, have been open and frefh, as it is termed. So wet have our fummers been, as almoft to countenance the fanciful opinion of old people, that the climate was altogether changed. Summer 1794 has been remarkably warm.

more than 100 feet, above 20 feet per mile. Beſides the
Glazert, there are no leſs than 19 ſmall burns which fall into
it. Perhaps to people who have been accuſtomed to reſide
chiefly in a level country, few ſcenes will appear more truly
picturefque than that of the ſtreams of water ruſhing down
the ſides of the Campſie Fells in a flood, while the top of the
mountain is perfectly hid in the blue miſt. This ſtream of
water, though highly picturefque, and exceeding uſeful, is ſtill
accompanied with ſome inconveniences: In the 1ſt place,
when there is a great drought, the ſpring water is apt to be
impregnated too much with mineral water coming from the
coal-levels, which muſt prove highly prejudicial to the bleach-
er. In the 2d place, The leaſt ſhower brings down ſuch a quantity of moſs from the hills, as to prove very troubleſome in the
finer operations of preparing the cloth : the manufacturers,
however, have contrived in a great meaſure to remedy both
defects, by filtrating the water through the fine beds of gravel, upon which their works are ſituated ; there is one accident which happens, againſt the bad effects of which there
is no guarding, but by turning off the water altogether from
the works; and that is, when the ſtagnating water in ſome
old coal-waſte breaks out, it will tinge every ſtone in the river, for miles, and kill every fiſh which comes within its
poiſonous influence. We have ſeen the trouts, after ſuch an
irruption, floating on the ſurface, gathered in baſkets full, and
eaten by the country people, yet no bad effect following from
eating ſuch poiſoned fiſh *. This diſtrict originally muſt
have been much better wooded than at preſent, as is evident
from

---

* The Glazert, in former times, was a great depoſit for ſalmon ſpawn,
whereby an uncommon quantity of fry was yearly produced, for recruiting
the fiſheries on the Clyde, the number of its fords and ſand banks being well
calculated for ſuch a nurſery. It is ſaid that the raiſing of the Damhead at
Dartick

from the remains of large trees occafionally dug up in the fwamps, and of the fcattered copfe-woods in the glens and braes. There are ftill three confiderable woods in the parifh ; the three together contain at leaft one hundred and ten acres of ground, and confift of oak, aller, birch, faugh, and afh ; though the timber of thefe woods be reckoned good, they are but of flow growth ; the woods upon the banks of Lochlomond arrive at fuller maturity in 18 years, than the Camppfie wood in 28.

The different articles made from thefe woods are fold at the following prices on the fpot : Stobs at 4s. the hundred, four feet long ; kebbres for houfes at 3s. per dozen, if made of birch, and 6s. of afh ; cart-trees at 1s. and 1s. 4d. the pair. A woodman receives 1s. 2d. for cutting and making the hundred ftobs ; and peelers of bark, if men, 1s. per day, and women 8d. Bark fells at 15s. the boll, 12 ftone weight ; and the

Dartick mills, upon the Kelvin, is the fole caufe why the fifh come not up in rodding time to the Glazert. Perhaps there is fome truth in faying that one great reafon of the fcarcity of falmon in the Clyde, is the little regard paid to the young fry.

It would at leaft be an object to the country at large, and particularly to that city, that greater attention fhould be paid to this article, fo that the tributary ftreams which formerly fupplied the Clyde with fry, fhould not be rendered totally ufelefs. I have not heard of a fingle falmon being feen in our river for 18 years; whereas, in former days, they were fo plenty in fpawning time, that it was cuftomary, though unlawful, for the country lads to go out with torches made of the dreffings of lint, and with long fpears to kill confiderable quantities of thefe foul fifh.

Although fometimes the water from the coal-waftes deftroys the trouts in the Glazert, yet as the glen and burns, at the head of the parifh, are well ftocked, the river is quickly replenifhed.

Our trout feems to be of two diftinct fpecies ; the muir trout, with the black back, is a poor, lank, infipid fifh ; the Kelvin trout is yellow in the fkin, and much plumper and richer in the fifh. There is only one loch in the parifh, containing about 32 acres, where there is a confiderable quantity of perch.

the reſpective proprietors are bound by their leaſes to drive
it to market. Although the ſtrath of Campſie be remarkable
for growing barren-timber, there is much leſs planting, either
in belts or in hedge-rows, than might have been expected :
To ſay that the ſpirit for planting is only beginning in the end
of the eighteenth century, in a country ſo calculated by ſoil
and ſhelter to produce fine timber, is not ſaying much to the
praiſe of our induſtry. As to fruit trees, it may literally be
affirmed, that there is not one orchard in the whole pariſh ;
therefore it cannot be ſaid, from recent experience, whether it be a ſoil adapted for the production of apples or not.
Conſiderable attention of late, however, hath been paid by the
gentry to their kitchen gardens ; it is to be hoped, that the
ſpirit of gardening, ſo long dormant, will exert itſelf in the
formation of orchards, and the laying out of plantations : Indeed, in a country where grazing is ſo much practiſed, it is
rather matter of ſurpriſe to the proprietors themſelves, that
ſelf-intereſt long ere now ſhould not have led them to form
ſhelter for their cattle in winter *.

Wild Beaſts, and Birds.—There are two ſpecies of badger
found among the looſe rocks of Campſie Fells, the one ſome
what reſembling a ſow, the other a dog ; the firſt is more arched in the back, and is not ſo nimble in turning itſelf ; there
has occaſionally been hams made of it in this place. The
fox too is a native of this pariſh ; the huntſman ſays, that the
three

* As to ſmall vegetable productions, they are both exceedingly numerous
and varied : moſt of the Scotch plants common to glens, woods, and rocks,
are to be found in this diſtrict. Our ingenious friend, Mr David Ure, declares
that he hath enjoyed conſiderable pleaſure in ſearching for plants in our ſequeſtered vale ; and that his curioſity was not a little gratified. Particularly
all the different ſpecies of the lichen is found here.

three different kinds peculiar to Britain are found here : The gray-hound-fox, with the long bufhy tail, white on the top; fkulks on the Fells, and is particularly deftruƈtive to the lambs. The other two fpecies lurk in woods and old wafte coal-pits ; the one is low and thick made, of a very dark brown ; the other very fmall, of a lively red and a black tip on its tail ; the laft are the moft mifchievous to our poultry. There are likewife weafles, otters, polecats, hedgehogs, wild cats ; and, of late, feveral martins have been feen among the rocks. As to birds of prey, there are four fpecies of hawks ; one pair of the gentil falcon breed regularly every year, in the Craig of Campfie, a fpecies much fought after by fportfmen ; we have likewife the kiftril, that fpecies which we perceive fo frequently in the air, fixed in one place, as it were fanning with its wings, and watching for its fport : The Gofs-hawk, which builds its neft upon trees in fequeftered places, is likewife a native of this parifh ; it dafhes through the woods with vaft impetuofity after its prey ; and the fparrow-hawk is fo common in the upper parts of the ftrath, that the children of the villagers amufe themfelves by taming them ; both the fluggifh inaƈtive buzzard, and the foaring glade or kite, are natives of this diftriƈt : So common is the glade with us, that its various modes of flight are confidered as an almanack for the weather, and its note is a fymbol of moral conduƈt ; we obferve, when it foars high in the air, it prognofticates good weather ; and every boy will tell you that it is not for nothing that the glade whiftles ; alluding to the note of that bird when it glides though the air, watching for its prey. The golden eagle ufed formerly to build in our rocks, though of late it has difcontinued the praƈtice ; but we have a vifit of them annually for fome months in the fpring and early part of the fummer ; they are commonly known among

among the ſhepherds, by the name of the earn, a viſit of which amongſt the flock is dreaded as much as that of the fox. But of all the birds of prey amongſt us, the hen-harriers, or white aboon-glade, as he is called, is the moſt deſtructive to game, both partridges and muirfowl. They breed on the ground a-mongſt ruſhes in the muirs, and fly low along the ſurface of the earth in ſearch of prey; the corbie or raven, the hooded or carrion crow, rooks, jackdaws, and the red legged crow, are natives of this diſtrict. There are about ſix pairs of ravens, which breed annually in the rocks, and are exceeding deſtructive to young lambs in a bad ſpring. I have ſeen, again and again, a raven attack a lamb, beat with its wings about its head, till the poor creature fell headlong over a precipice; and before the ſhepherd could climb to the ſpot, the raven had picked out its eyes. The red legged crow is but ſcarce with us; we ſeldom meet with above a pair or two in the whole range of the Campſie Falls; when we do meet with them, it is amongſt the jackdaws, of which there are a con-ſiderable number which haunt our rocks. A very curious ſcene is frequently exhibited in our hills. If it ſhould happen that a fox leaves his hole, and baſks himſelf in the ſun, among the rocks, immediately all the birds of prey within a mile of him will aſſemble, and flutter, and ſcream over the ſpot where the thief is lurking; eagle and hawk, raven and kite, and jack-daw forget their animoſities, ſeemingly combining in a mu-tual league to diſturb the retreat of reynard, ſo that the huntſ-man conſiders theſe birds as infallible guides to his ſport. It may be obſerved, that beaſts of prey are every day becoming ſcarcer. Till within theſe two years, we had a regular bred huntſman, who hunted this diſtrict; his ſalary was paid by the tenants, at ſo much per plough, which huntſman and dogs were kept and fed by each tenant in his turn. The father

and

and ſon-in-law performed the office of public huntſman, from the year 1715, till 1792, a period of fourſcore years : They were ſaid to poſſeſs ſome of the largeſt fox hounds in the three kingdoms ; they were ſlow but remarkably ſtaunch.—The cry of the hounds, and the animating blaſt of the buglehorn, re-echoed by every rock along the range of Campſie Fells, will be long remembered by the natives of this ſtrath.

Now there are ſcarcely as many beaſts of prey in the whole diſtrict, as to afford amuſement to the graziers in an idle winter day ; the only reaſon which has been aſſigned, is, the converting of ſheep paſture into grazing for black cattle, whereby there is leſs food for ſuch ravenous animals ; of courſe, the large fox has migrated to the high lands, where his food is more abundant. In proportion as the beaſts and birds of prey, have left this diſtrict, the ſinging birds have increaſed ; ſeveral ſpecies have appeared of late, which were formerly unknown, particularly the bulfinch and the wood-lark. It is perhaps at the Clachan of Campſie, which is ſituated in the neighbourhood of copſewoods and retired glens, that a perſon is enabled to comprehend the meaning of a proverbial expreſſion in this county, the ſcreich of day light ;—here and there, the lark begins the ſong, which is ſoon heard and accompanied by all the little feathered choiriſters within reach of its note ;—The air ſeems to vibrate with the ſound.— As to our migrating birds, the ſtatement in the following table is founded on the obſervations of ten years :

NAMES.

Names.	Arrives.	Disappears.
The *White Breasted Swallow*,	from the 7th to the 8th of May.	September 24th till September 28th.
The *Cuckoo*,	27th of April to the 2d of May.	becomes silent about the end of June.
The *Wood Cock*,	about the 26th of October.	about the beginning of March.
Gray Plover or Lopwing,	about the 26th of March.	about the end of July.
Water Wag tail,	about the 1st of April.	about the 1st of October.
Stone Checker,	about the 1st of May.	about the middle of August.
Curlew,	about the 1st of March	about the 1st of October.

In former times, particularly during a hard winter, it was customary for wild ducks, wild geese, and even swans, to visit the swamps of this parish ; these being now drained, such fowls are scarcely to be seen. There are plenty of grouse in the Campsie muirs ; at the same time partridges have of late become uncommonly scarce ; many causes have been assigned for the rapid decay of this species of game, such as the wet summers, and the pretended increase of the birds of prey, which is not fact.

Perhaps it will be found, that this country at present is rather in an unfavourable state for nursing patridges ; the broom, and furze, and briers, being mostly grubbed out, and the land formerly waste, put under cultivation ; whereas artificial shelter by belts of planting is not yet produced ; while the number of idle boys, belonging to the public works, let loose upon a Sunday, strolling about the fields with their tarrier dogs, ferreting out the patridge nests by the smell, may be an additional cause of the uncommon scarcity of this game in the parish.

Strata, Minerals, Lime and Coal.—The hills of which in part the parish of Campsie is composed, are according to the distinction

tion of naturalfts, of two fpecies, *primary* and *secondary;* in the firft, it is faid that coal and lime are never to be found, whereas the fecond abounds with both.

The higheft ridge of the Campfie Fells, is about 1500 feet above the level of the fea, and about 1200 from its bafe; where, properly fpeaking, the mountain commences, the afcent is very rapid; and from examining the glens, and gullys formed on its fides, it feems to be compofed of the following ftrata: At the bafe of the hill, immediately after the coal is cut off, you meet with feveral layers of camftone, (as it is termed with us,) which is eafy burned into a heavy lime. Immediately above the camftone, you find at leaft a dozen ftrata of ironftone, of different thicknefs, with a foft flate interveening betwixt the layers; it is faid by thofe who have examined the ironftone, that it is of an excellent quality. Thefe different feams make up 200 feet of the bafe of the mountain. Then 15 ftrata of muirftone rife above each other to the fummit of the Fells, where they jut out; in the face of the braes, they go by the name of daffes or gerrocks. Betwixt thefe ftrata of muirftone, you meet with various coloured ftuff, fometimes of a copperifh, fometimes of an ironftone colour; and it is faid, there are appearances of copper; but the working of it has not as yet been attempted. Lately, when forming the new turnpike-road along the fide of the hills, feveral veins of fpar and chryftal were found, not unlike thofe which accompany lead-mines; and perfons who had wrought at the different lead-mines in Scotland, declared, that the appearances of that metal were both frequent and favourable: no attempt as yet hath been made to follow out thefe appearances. In the whole range of the Campfie Fells, there is only one place where the rocks affume a bafaltic appearance; and by thofe who admire fuch columnar appearances,

ances, they are ſaid to be very beautiful. Here and there, there were dug out, when forming the turnpike-road on the hills, ſeveral ſtrata of moſt excellent clay marle, both white and ſpeckled ;—it has not as yet become an object of attention to the country people. Beautiful pebbles have been found among the rocks, of which a gentleman lately procured as many as, when poliſhed, furniſhed a ſet of elegant buttons for a coat. About the middle of the ſtrath, you meet with excellent quarries of free ſtone, calculated for all the purpoſes of the builder ; but the minerals of which we have the greateſt reaſon to boaſt, are the inexhauſtable ſeams of lime and coal, which merit a particular deſcription. The coal and lime in this pariſh are generally found in the ſame field : The coal, throughout the whole pariſh, poſſeſſes a caking quality ; at the ſame time it is very foul and ſulphurous, leaving, when burned, an uncommon quantity of ruſty coloured aſhes, which make excellent manure for certain ſorts of land.

The coal on the North of the Glazert, takes on about a mile Eaſt from the Clachan of Campſie, and continues without much interruption to the eaſtern extremity of the pariſh ; it runs parallel to the Fells, and ſeldom exceeds a quarter of a mile in breadth : The field on the South ſide of the river, which forms a belt around the South braes, is conſiderably broader, and is of much ſuperior quality to the other. The coal is found of different depths from the ſurface ; on the North ſide, from ſeven to fifteen fathoms ; on the South, from fifteen to twenty two ; the ſeam throughout the whole pariſh, is, at an average, from forty two inches to four feet in thickneſs, with two ſmall bands, of an inch and an inch and half, running through it. The ſtrata above the coal is found uniformly in the following manner : After the ſoil there is found a ſpecies of till, interſperſed with ſtones ; after which comes a blaze, as it is termed, and which continues to a conſidera-

ble

ble depth ; then flate, which, at a medium, is from feven to
eight feet in thicknefs ; after which, there is uniformly lime-
ftone, being a feam of four feet ; then a flate, and then the
coal : Such is the regular ftrata in Campfie in finking for
coal ; with this difference, however, that the flate in the North
of Glazert, betwixt the lime and coal, is fifteen feet in thicknefs ; on the South, it is fcarcely four ; below the coal, there
is eighteen inches of a ftuff, which the workmen term *dalk* ;
then the white lime, of an inferior quality to the other, and
as yet but feldom wrought.

The coal in this diftrict is full of irregularities, ftiled by
the workmen *coups*, and *hitches*, and *dykes ;* the truth is, the
coal partakes a good deal of the irregularity of the ground
above, which is very uneven. If one was to fpeak in general terms of the whole coal in the parifh, as one field, it might
be faid, that the depth was to the South Eaft, and the rife
to the North Weft ; fuch really being the afcent and declivity of the lands in this diftrict ;—but as there are a number
of gentle fwells in the ftrath, it will happen, that according
as the pit is put down on this fide of the fwell, or upon the
other fide, the dip and rife of the coal will appear favourable,
or the contary.—The dip is fometimes fo fudden as to be
one foot in three, in other places, only one in twenty. Befides thefe coups and hitches, which are found where the ftrata above and below the coal fuddenly approach, or retreat
from each other, by this means couping the coal out of its
regular bed, there are complete breaks in the ftrata, termed
dykes, which cut off the coal entirely in various directions ;
thefe dykes are fometimes obferved upon the furface of the
earth, from which they fink down to an unfathomable
depth ;—There are two of thefe dykes in this diftrict, which
are remarkable, and feem to be uniform throughout : *Firft*,
There is a coup-dyke, which runs from Weft to Eaft ; North

of this coup-dyke, the coal dips about fifteen feet, and then they may work about three hundred yards into the hill, where they ſeem to be cut off entirely by a whinſtone dyke ; ſo there are two great barriers which intercept the ly of the coal upon the North of the Glazert ; the coal on the South of the coup-dyke, takes on almoſt within ſix feet of the ſurface, and is not above ſix inches thick, with ſomething like a clay roof.

Manner of Working.—There is reaſon to believe that coal has been wrough in this diſtrict for ſeveral centuries ; but the working of it ſeems to have been carried in a very aukward irregular manner, taking advantage of the ly of the ground : They uſed to make large excavations upon the ſurface, which they termed creeping heughs ; from theſe excavations, they drove a road into the coal heads, and by this means brought the coals to the hill, dragging them on their ſmall ſledges up the declivity, which was not very great, as the excavation was always made as much to the dip ſide of the hill as poſſible : It is evident, that in this manner they could only work the crop of the coal, where the water created little diſquiet ; a method, however, highly prejudicial both to the landlord and the public ; the next ſtage of working was by ſinking perpendicular pits, ſtiled windlaſs heughs. On the North of the river Glazert, theſe pits were in depth from ſixty to ninety feet ; but they ſo contrived it, that theſe pits were placed near ſome gully or burn, where, by running a level from a certain part of the burn, all the coal round the pit bottom became drained ; and in the ſinking of every new pit, they muſt always do it with a retroſpect to their former level ; ſtill, however, the coal upon the dip ſide might be lying under water ; for although the declivity in the ground favoured greatly

greatly there imperfect short levels, there were many fields
of coal which could not thus be drained but at a moft enormous expence, in driving fubterraneous mines : In this ftage
of carrying on the work, there were employed at leaft two
men at the windlafs, putting up the coals in fkiffies, termed
hutches ; and it is more than probable that they had likewife
to pully up the water for a confiderable time every morning,
before the workmen had got the coals raifed ; the coal bufinefs in this diftrict was carried on in this flovenly manner
during this century : The country was ill fupplied ; the landlords complained that they never made a fhilling of their
coal, while every perfon was furprifed, that a diftrict, poffeffing fuch natural advant ges, fhould make fo little good ufe
of them. About two years ago, coal becoming exceedingly fcarce, and the price rifing fuddenly, there became an abfolute neceffity of working it in a better ftyle ; accordingly,
Mr Dunmore of Ballindalloch, a gentleman to whofe activity and patriotifm this part of Scotland is much indebted, becoming the leffee of feveral works in the parifh, he immediately erected gins, driven by horfes, for pulling up the coals ;
which improvement is anfwering the purpofe, and is either
already, or will be quickly followed by the other proprietors ;
fo that now we have every probability of this neceffary article of life being wrought in a ftyle far fuperior and more expeditious than hitherto experienced.

All the coalliers in this parifh now work with the pick and
wedge : this, however, is only a late improvement ; they pool
in the middle of the feam, where a fmall band of ftone, about
an inch of thicknefs, lyes, called the pooling band, and then
fhear down what is above, ftiled the roof coal, and drive up the
foal coals with wedges ; they carry on their drifts or rooms eight
feet by fourteen, leaving ftoops eight feet by twelve ; but this
varies

varies according as the coal is foft or hard ; every coallier may
be faid to be his own drawer ; feldom or ever has he any perfon
to affift him ; they commonly go to their work at four in the
morning, and continue until two in the afternoon ; formerly
the coals were put out by the *dark*, confifting of twenty eight
hutches, for which dark the coallier received one fhilling and
eight pence, and the proprietors had for lordfhip one fhilling
and ten pence ; an active workman could very eafily put out
two of thefe darks per day, making three fhillings and four
pence ; thefe hutches becoming more and more uncertain as to
the quantity contained in them, both the landlord and public
being impofed upon, it became neceffary to adopt fome new
regulations relative to the meafure ; which has been done
accordingly ; fo that now we compute by loads ; each load
contains 2184 cubic inches, equal to twenty one Scotch pints
and a half, water meafure ; fix of thefe loads make an exceeding good cart, which fhould weigh betwixt twelve and thirteen hundred weight ; the price, at the pit mouth, being eighteen pence per cart, or threepence per load ; a tolerable workman can put out twenty four loads per day, for which he has
three fhillings ; and the landlord the other three fhillings. In
order to afcertain the quantity of coals raifed at the different
pits, of which there are no lefs than fixty going this month of
December 1793, we fhall calculate the average out-put of the
coaliers : There are, in all the different pits, forty fix coalliers;
allowing three carts and a half per day to each, makes one
hundred and fixty one carts per day, fuppofing them only to
work five days in the week ; the out-put per week will be eight
hundred and five carts ; reckoning the coalliers weeks in the
year only to be fifty, the out-put in the year will be forty
thoufand two hundred and fifty carts ; fuppofing that the
meafure, at a medium, does not exceed eleven hundred weight

per cart, the out-put in the year will be 22135 tons and a-half; the price at the hill is fomewhat better than 2s. 6d. per ton; the total value is 2750l. Sterling, of which the coalliers receive 1375l; the remainder goes for lordfhip, and to fupport the hills-men and gin-boys, along with the tear and wear of the work.

According to the calculation of men fkilled in coal-mines, thefe 20,000 tons will at leaft exhauft three acres of coal annually, a wafte, which, great as it may appear, we are able to fupport for 150 years to come; but in reality we are raifing this feafon, at leaft, double of what was raifed formerly, nay, 10 times more than what was put out about 20 years ago; this great quantity of coal is ufed in the following manner: The two printfields confume annually 3500 tons; above 2100 tons is ufed in burning lime; and the remainder in fupplying the parifhes of Campfie, Fintray, Balfrone, Kilairn, Strathblane, Baldernock, and partly Kirkintilloch and Kilfyth. It is doubtful if even yet the coal in this diftrict be wrought to advantage; in reality, we are as yet but working the crop of the coal; it being abfolutely neceffary that they fhould either drive their levels, or erect their fteam engines upon the dip fide, fo that they might work to the rife. Many great fields at this moment ly buried under water, owing to this defect ¶.

It

¶ No map being made of thefe fubterraneous works, and no documents being in the poffeffion of the proprietors, to point out when and how fuch a field of coal was wrought, it is only by fome vague tradition, handed down from one generation of coalliers to another, that we pretend to judge whether the ground be wafted or not; fo that too often the pit is put down upon a trouble, or wafte, to the great detriment of the adventurer; which miftake might be eafily rectified, by each proprietor getting an accurate chart made out of thefe fubterraneous works, for the benefit of pofterity; befides many lives might

It has been obferved that limeſtone is always found in the
fame field with the coal; it is in general a ſeam from three
feet to five in thicknefs, and is wrought in the following manner : They take off the earth from the furface, called tirring,
which is from 10 to 30 feet; feldom or never have they as
yet wrought the lime-ſtone by mining. The probability is,
however, that they will foon be compelled to it; the workmen take tirring at 3d. the fquare yard; they put out the
lime ſtone at fo much per chalder, and by experience they
know what number of fquare yards of broken ſtone, makes a
chalder

might be faved, which are unfortunately loſt by the workmen ſtriking through
upon old waſte; as was the cafe February 1789, when five coalliers were killed in the Newk coal-pit of Campfie. I confider the wages of the coalliers,
as by no means in proportion to the wages of other labourers in the parifh ;
the labourer having only fixteen pence per day : Allowing the coallier a third
more on account of the danger and difagreeable nature of the work, viz. two
fhillings, then there would be one third of the wages, which he receives at
prefent, faved to the public·

Coal, in every inland diſtrict in Scotland, fhould not be confidered as an
article of commerce, which the landlord as a merchant, may fpeculate upon
for his own advantage : It fhould be confidered as an article of the firſt neceffity : Propietors of land fhould recollect, that every circumſtance which
increafes population, ultimately benefits their eſtates ; wherever water is plenty and firing cheap, there the manufacturer and labourer will always refort.
Campfie, at prefent, is confpicuoufly bleffed with both ; and it will difcover
the folly of the landlords, if ever they permit coals to become much dearer ;
it is not the richnefs of the foil which always brings the higheſt rent to the
proprietor ; fome particular local advantage acts in his favour ; and perhaps
there is none to furpafs the advantage of cheap fuel.

A fmall farmer (fuch as we have in this diſtrict) confiders good oat meal
and a good fire as great luxuries ; and while the tenants poffefs thefe, they will
make a confiderable fhift to pay their dear rents.

It is with pleafure that we take notice of the public fpirited attempts made
by feveral gentlemen laſt year, to prevent the coals from rifing in this diſtrict ;
and they have fully fucceeded : They have perhaps funk a little money, but
their tenants and dependants have reaped the benefit, and the public hath paid
them every refpect which an elevated mind can defire.

chalder of lime ; the lime is burnt chiefly in fmall kilns, holding from 10 to 15 chalders, the ftone being more completely burnt, than in thofe of a larger fize ; the layers of ftone
and coal are made alternately in the following proportions :
1ft, Six inches of coal, then 20 inches of lime-ftone, broken
to the fize of a two-penny-loaf. Two firlots (wheat meafure) of burnt ftone make four firlots of flacked lime ; of
courfe, 32 firlots make a chalder of lime, fold, till within
thefe two years, at 4l. Scots, at the quarry, now, 8s. the ready money price ; formerly it was fold with at leaft 6 months
credit. It is doubtful if the ftate of the country as yet will
permit this alteration, fmall as it is ; it requires 6 or 7 loads
of coal to burn the chalder of lime. There were employed
this fummer (1793) 40 workmen in the different lime quarries in the parifh, who raifed at leaft 3000 chalders of
flacked lime ; the Campfie lime is reckoned of an exceeding
rich quality, much fought after by plaifterers ; in common
building, to every boll of lime one boll of fand is required,
to make proper mortar. The great facts relative to our coal
and lime work, are ftated in the following table :

No. of COALLIERS	46	Wages, 3s per day, or 1375l. per annum.
—— Carts	42,250	per annum, at 18d. per cart.
—— Tons	22,135	per annum.
Price -	18d.	per cart confifting of fix loads.
Weight -	12	hundred weight.
LIME-STONE	3d.	per fquare yard, tirring.
Chalder	1s. 8d.	the putting out.
Price -	8s.	per Chalder, when burnt at the kiln.
——	8d.	per ditto for fetting and felling lime.

Coal

Coal	-	3500	Tons conſumed by the printfields.
----	-	2100	conſumed in the burning of lime.
----	-	16,465	conſumed by this, and neighbouring pariſhes.
Value	L.	2750	of out-pit this year 1793.
Lime	-	3000	Chaldrons burned and ſold in the year. 6 Loads of coal, to the burning of 1 chalder of lime : ſo that every chalder, beſides tirring, coſts the tackſman in expence of putting out, in ſetting, and in coals, 3s. 6d. before he can bring it to market.
Men	-	40	employed in working lime.

State of Property.—This pariſh contains one hundred and one ploughgates of land, 73 of which are poſſeſſed by eight great proprietors; the other 28 ploughs are poſſeſſed by 37 feuars, or portioners, holding charter and ſeiſin; the valuation of the whole pariſh, being 6429l. 4900l. is poſſeſſed by the eight great proprietors, in the following proportions :

	Valuation.
William Lennox of Woodhood -	922
John Lennox of Antermony, -	888
Sir John Stirling of Glorat, - -	800
Sir Archibald Edmiſton of Duntreath, -	686
John Macfarlane of Kirkton -	537
John Buchanan of Carbeth, - -	403
John Kincaid of Kincaid, - -	417
John Stirling of Craigbarnet, - -	300

They all reſide in the pariſh, except Sir Archibald Edmiſton, who poſſeſſes large eſtates in the pariſhes of Kilſyth, Strathblane,

Strathblane, Kilpatrick, and Dumbarton : Mr Buchanan of Carbeth, Mr Stirling of Craigbarnet, and Sir John Stirling of Glorat, poffefs, each of them, likewife landed property in other parifhes ; of this property there are 2260 pounds Scots entailed, and in all probability there will be more added by the prefent proprietors. The fmall proprietors are feuers of the families of Montrofe, Keer, Glorat, and Bardowie, and beame fo at the following periods :

Feuers of Montrofe 1632 ; feuers of Keer 1714 ; feuers of Glorat 1742 ; feuers of Bardowie 1713. Landed property in this diftrict hath changed its mafters as feldom as in moft parts of Scotland ; whether this be an advantage to the country, or not, is a queftion upon which fpeculative men have differed ; but this at leaft is certain, that the following families ; viz. Kincaid of Kincaid, Stirling of Craigbarnet, Stirling of Glorat, Lennox of Woodhead, and Edmifton of Duntrath, were, in the year 1470, proprietors of the fame lands which they poffefs at this day ; the eftate of Auchinreoch fell by fucceffion, in the beginning of this century, to the Buchanans of Carbeth, an ancient family in the parifh of Killern : Macfarlane of Kirton, a cadet of the family of Macfarlane, became proprietor of Kirton in the year 1624 ; the eftate of Antermony is the purchafe of Captain John Lennox of Antermony, a younger fon of the ancient family of Woodhead. Perhaps this circumftance, which may pleafe the pride of family, is one great reafon why the improvement of land is fo very backward in this diftrict ; wherever families refided long upon an eftate in Scotland, the object of our Scotch ambition was to poffefs a numerous tenantry, live as they may. The laird fought other means of bettering his fituation, than by the flow returns of agriculture ; whereas,

if

if an eftate often changed its mafter, it became in reality an object of commerce, and every new proprietor made it fomewhat better for his own intereft.

It is curious to obferve the progreffive rife of the land rent in this parifh, fince the year 1642 ; the rent of the plough-gate in thofe days, was about one hundred merks, befides feu fervices : and there is reafon to believe, that the valuation in Cromwel's time, in this diftrict, was made as high as the land could really afford in rent ; during the firft years of the Reftoration, land feems to have rifen, (as appears from fome old tacks :) From the 1680, till the year 1715, it appears that the rife was but trifling ; after this period it rofe confiderably ; and, in the year 1748, was about 1500 l. Sterling ; the next rife was in the year 1763 ; and, confidering the value of the land in the natural poffeffion of the fmall proprietors to keep pace with the tenantry, it rofe to about 3000 l. Sterling. The land-rent this prefent year, is betwixt feven and eight thoufand *per annum*, upon leafes, or in the natural poffeffion of the fmall proprietors.

Years.	1642	1715	1748	1763	1793
Value.	500	800	1500	3000	7000

By this ftatement, it is evident, that land gives fourteen times more rent in money than it did 150 years ago ; allowing for the fervices and other preftations payed by the tenants in thofe days, perhaps we ought not to reckon fo highly ; whether this rife, however, is to be afcribed to the gradual improvement of landed property, or the depreciation of money, becomes another queftion ; and perhaps the landholders will not have fo much reafon to boaft of their advanced rents, if the enquiry be fairly made ; in this rental, that of cot-houfes is not comprehended, which is at leaft five hundred

dred *per annum*; thefe houfes have increafed their rents four times the fum of what they were in 1745; even fo late as 1760, four pounds Scots was the rent of a cottage with a fmall yard annexed to it; fuch houfes rent now at twenty fhillings; but, from the improvement made on cot-houfes, the rent of a room and kitchen, or what in the language of the place is ftiled a *but* and a *ben*, gives at leaft two pounds Sterling; fo that the fame clafs of people pay for lodging fix times more than they did thirty years ago; this increafe arifes chiefly from the introduction of manufactures; now, if the rent of the coal and lime, together with that of the cot-houfes, be added to the land, the total rent of the parifh may be ftated to be eight thoufand four hundred pounds Sterling *per annum*.

Prefent State of Agriculture.—It is not poffible to fay exactly what number of acres there are arable, and what not, as there is no map of the parifh, nor has the whole ever been accurately meafured: If the parifh contains fifteen thoufand acres, it will be found that five thoufand of thefe are arable; of the other ten thoufand, confifting of brae, of muir, and pafture land, three thoufand more may be made arable:—Of courfe, it is about fifty acres of arable land to each plough.

There are ninety-fix heads of families, who live on this property, either as tenants or feuers; and whofe employment is either grazing or agriculture; but it is to be obferved, that there are eighteen heads of families in this lift, who do not make agriculture their chief employment; poffeffing only a few acres of land, and who principally employ themfelves as mafons, or carriers, or road makers; there is another diftinction to be made of thefe heads of families, who employ themfelves in agriculture; 28 of them are feuers, who farm their

own

own lands, the remainder are tenantry; ſeven of theſe laſt make grazing their chief employment.

The following is a table of the rents paid by the different graziers and farmers in this diſtrict, in 1793.

No. 1   L. 600   No. 1   L. 400
    1   167   1   100

comprehending the feuers who farm their own land. The rents of others run betwixt twenty and ſeventy pounds, excepting upon the forfeited eſtate of Bancloich, where ſome tenants pay as low as five pounds *per annum*, they having got leaſes of three nineteen years in 1748.

The labour of theſe hundred plough gates of land was performed in 1793, by ſeventy ploughs, drawn by 222 horſes, yoked in the following manner:

    20   ploughs drawn   4 horſes. each.
    24   ditto   drawn by   2 horſes.
    26   ditto   drawn by   3 horſes.

The following table exhibits the manner in which the five thouſand acres of arable land was cropped in the year 1793, viz.

    2000 acres in tillage and ſown grafs, of which were,
    200 acres in barley.
    100 acres in potatoes.
    30 acres in lint.
    200 in ſown grafs.

1500 in oats; of which, we may deduct 20 for peaſe and beans; the remaining 3000 acres in ley paſture for milk cows, and young beaſts.

There were not ten acres fallow, in the whole pariſh; neither were there above four acres in wheat or turnip. Perhaps there is no country in Scotland more calculated for raiſ-

ing

ing turnip than Campſie ; at the ſame time, I rather think they do not ſtand the winter well in this diſtrict ; I have ſaid 20 acres for peaſe and beans, the wet climate rendering theſe a very unprofitable crop with us, growing all to the ſtraw, without any pods : The produce per acre, at an average, is about ſix bolls ;—ſmall as this may appear, it is at leaſt one third more than it was thirty years ago : If a ſtranger was to view our crop at Lammas, when growing, or even in the ſhock, he would be apt to conclude the product to be a great deal more ; the truth is, our moiſt climate produces much ſtraw and little corn ; I believe, it may ſafely be affirmed, that at an average there is not above fifteen pecks of meal out of the boll ; the barley produces better, the ſoil being adapted for that grain ; and it is ſaid to malt remarkably well ; but the fault lies more in the ſtyle of farming, than in the ground itſelf ; ſo late as the year 1763, the farms were poſſeſſed in run rigg ;—there was ſcarcely any incloſing ; the moment that the crop was ſeparated from the ground, the cattle of the neighbouring tenants grazed in common, till next Whitſunday ; the diſtinction betwixt out-field and in-field, was kept up with the moſt ſcrupulous exactneſs ; there was no rye-graſs and clover ſown, for making hay ; and the bulk of the farmers ploughed their land with what is ſtiled the broad plough, the four horſes yoked abreaſt : Theſe peculiarities are now worn out ; at the ſame time, farming, both as to ſcience and practice, is yet but in its infancy in this pariſh. *

Tacks

---

* It is true, that the climate is not good, but the ſoil is excellent ; and as the crops might be adapted to the climate, there are great hopes entertained, that we ſhall one day excel in farming : The following defects in our mode ſeem to be moſt flagrant : 1ſt, The land being full of ſprings guſhing out, wherever any change of the ſoil takes place in the farms ;—of courſe, nothing

Tacks in this pariſh are commonly let for nineteen years, with a clauſe that the tenant ſhall bear the public burdens, which, conſidering the land tax, the ſtatute labour, and ſometimes the miniſter's ſtipend, at leaſt the vicarage, and ſchoolmaſter's

ing but underdraining can clear the ſoil of ſuch a nuiſance ; and yet unfortunately it is but little practiſed : 2*dly*, Our incloſures are little better than rickle dykes, built of ſtones, gathered from the land, without any mortar ;—of courſe, totally incapable of meliorating the ſoil by keeping it warm; which would be the caſe, if the incloſures were made with of quick-ſet hedges, and belts of planting, for which the pariſh is ſo remarkably calculated; theſe dykes give the pariſh a cold and uncomfortable look. 3*dly*, A great proportion of our arable land is laid down in the moſt miſerable manner without ſown grafs, and impoveriſhed by three ſucceeding crops of oats; by this management, it is in a moſt wretched condition, indeed, when broken up to dergo anew the ſame rotation of crops of oats. 4*thly*, Our land, from being in general a light ſoil, and ſituated in a moiſt climate, is much addicted to weeds ; it is foul even to ranknefs ;—Of courſe, as the corns grow much to ſtraw, the ſtalk of corn is kept conſtantly wet at the root by the weeds ; it ſoon rots, and the leaſt blaſt of wind in Auguſt, lodges the corn on the croft-lands before they are ripe ; whereas, if ſummer fallowing was practiſed, there cannot be the ſmalleſt doubt, but our crops would be clean and much earlier; yet ſummer fallowing is ſcarcely ever practiſed in this pariſh : Along with theſe defects, I muſt mention two other cauſes, which have not a little contributed to retard our progreſs in agriculture : In the *firſt* place, an over attachment to grazing; which hath led the farmers to ſtudy more the raiſing of fodder, than the raiſing of grain ; by this means, the early-feed oats have never received much countenance in this diſtrict ; but, if we conſider the moiſtneſs of the climate, there is no pariſh which requires them more; and from the experiments we have had of ſowing early oats, upon land well cleaned from weeds by ſummer fallowing, there is every encouragement to proceed ;—the grain was fully ripe and early houſed. 2*dly*, I am not ſure but the proprietors themſelves have, in ſome meaſure, contributed to the little progreſs which agriculture hath made in this diſtrict. From an opinion that land was always upon the increaſe, it has not been their object to grant ſuch long leaſes, as to encourage the farmer to ſink money in improving the land : The opinion that has gone abroad amongſt landlords,

master's falary; the poor man's rent is confiderably augmented by fuch items.—Thefe things I don't mention as grievances, for the tenant fubfcribes to them with open eyes; nor
can the landlord be called an oppreffor, becaufe he receives
them; they are all preftations of a fair contract; and of
courfe, if the proprietor did not exact them, he would be
entitled to more rent: I fimply ftate them as defects in our
mode of hufbandry; and which it would be the intereft
both of landlord and tenant to have removed.—Let the tenant know determinately what he is to pay, and let him have
the complete ufe of his time, and the complete management
of the product of his farm. As to a regular rotation of crops,
it is but little known in this diftrict. The old mode of allowing the land to ly ley for three years, and then liming it,
and taking three crops of oats, is, indeed, faft wearing out;
but no regular fyftem is as yet introduced in its ftead.

The rent of the arable land per acre, is ftated in the following table:

For

lords, that the raifing the rents of their lands forced the tenants to be more
active, might be productive of fome good effect; providing that indolence
was the only impediment to a flourifhing ftate of agriculture in this parifh:
Compulfion is but a bad argument, when the object of that compulfion
has not ftrength to obey: I could wifh that fuch an idea was exploded; for
it is no longer the intereft of this country to confider the tenantry upon an
eftate, as part of that eftate.

In England, things feem to be better managed. There are ftill feveral
fervitudes remaining in this parifh, annexed to the leafes of lands, fuch as
kain hens, and the driving of the lairds coals; thefe are indeed but fmall to
what took place about 30 years ago; but, even thefe are fetters upon the induftry of the tenants;—of more hurt to them than of benefit to the landlord;
and it is to be hoped, from the many inftances of an enlightened mind which
the prefent proprietors have fhown, that all fuch cafualities will be abolifhed
on the firft opportunity.

For potatoes	from 4l. to 7l. per acre.	A flying crop.
For lint -	ditto ditto	ditto
For good arable	a guinea and a half.	on leafe.
Ordinary arable	1l. per acre. -	ditto

There is fcarcely any land in the ftrath of the parifh let below 1l. per acre. The brae farms, and the pafture land, are let by flump; it is impoffible to fay what they rent per acre.

It may be proper here to take notice, that lime, though in fuch great abundance in this parifh, was made but little ufe of as a manure till very lately; the inhabitants pretended even to fay that it fpoiled the ground by raifing weeds : the truth is, the objection lay in their injudicious management; there is not the fmalleft doubt, where ground is foul, as is the cafe in the foil and moift climate of Campfie, that lime puts the weeds in vegetation; but if the land had been fallowed, or even permitted to lie long in ley, till the ground was properly fwarded, there is no country in Scotland, where liming produces a better effect, than in this diftrict : As fome recent experiments have fhewn, we now lime at the rate of from fix to eight chalders per acre. Such being the ftate of agriculture in this parifh, it may be faid, without difparagement, that it is, as yet, but in its infancy; and yet it is but doing juftice, both to the proprietors and tenants, to obferve, that the improvements are going on with great fpirit and fuccefs.

Grazing.—There is confiderable attention paid in this diftrict to the management of black cattle, both for the purpofes of the dairy, and likewife for that of the butcher. The following table exhibits the number of cattle and fheep kept in the parifh in 1793.

Milk

Milk cows,	-	-	749
Calves and queys	-	-	503

Fat cows and young beafts for the Falkirk market, and
the butcher,   -   -   917

Winterers, being moftly grazed next fummer for the
butcher   -   -   300

Sheep, being moftly brood ewes,   -   1600

Thefe 749 milk-cows are kept by 177 people; there are ten principal dairies, which confift of betwixt 14 to 20 milk cows; the remainder are fplit down in fmall dairies, containing from 4 to 10 cows. It is not eafy to fay what milk at an average is given per day by the cows of this diftrict; I fhould think from 7 to 11 Scotch pints; below 7 they are not thought worth keeping for the dairy: above 11 they are confidered as remarkable.

About 60 of thofe perfons who have cows, may be confidered as tradefmen and manufacturers; it may be doubted, whether it be of any ufe to fuch a perfon to keep a cow or not; fome are apt to imagine that it is calculated to inftill habits of idlenefs into the minds of their children, who may be employed in herding them by the dykes-fide: no doubt, it will be confidered as an eye-fore by the farmers, to allow the children of tradefmen to feed their cows on the road-fide, to the prejudice of his turnips and peafe; on the other hand, it is of the utmoft importance to the ftate at large, that the children of tradefmen and fedentary people fhould be healthy: I know of nothing more calculated to promote that end than plenty of frefh milk. Our milk cows, within thefe 30 years, have increafed confiderably in bulk; at an average, if fattened, they would weigh 20 ftones, Tron weight. In general, they are the breed of Highland bulls; hence they have a tendency to take on flefh, more than to

give

give large quantities of milk; at the ſame time it muſt be owned, that the milk is remarkably rich; it being very common for a cow, which only gives 8 Scotch pints per day, to produce nearly a pound of butter from that milk per day. Campſie has been long remarkable for making excellent butter: Till of late, it was only ſkimm'd milk cheeſe which they made, of courſe it was not very rich: Now, however, there are ſeveral dairies, which make cheeſe equal to any from Dunlop; and from the price which they receive for ſuch cheeſe, they conſider this plan as more profitable than to make butter.

There are about 1600 muir-ewes kept in the pariſh, whoſe lambs are ſold to the Glaſgow butcher in the ſeaſon, from 6s. to 8s. per head; they are commonly taken away by the butcher during the month of June, and the firſt two weeks of July. Perhaps we have the beſt ſtock of black faced ewes that are to be met with in Scotland; they are completely muir ewes, and yet they weigh twelve Tron pounds per quarter, twenty two ounces and a half to the pound: They are ſold at a guinea per head when fat; the flock which I allude to belongs to Mr David Dun, grazier, and they are paſtured upon the muir-lands of the eſtate of Kirkton, belonging to John Macfarlane, Eſq; In former times, there were at leaſt 4000 ſheep in the pariſh; they were of two ſorts: the black faced ſheep, with coarſe wool, bought at the market of Kilbryde and Linton; and the ſmall country ſheep, with white and yellow faces, and remarkable fine wool. From what the writer of this account recollects, the country ſheep muſt in a great meaſure have reſembled the Shetland breed:—they were the common breed of the country; it being wedder-hogs and Dinmonts alone, which were bought at Kilbryde and Linton market. By ſome ſtrange fatality, this Southland breed hath crept in, though the creature is leſs hardy and

courſer

courser in the wool; at this moment there is not the smallest vestige of our country breed remaining, all the stock ewes in the parish being black faced and coarse wooled: Two causes have been assigned for the total neglect of the native breed: 1st, Since the rise of the flesh-meat took place, it hath been the object of the graziers to pay more attention to the bulk of the carcase than to the fineness of the wool. 2dly, About the year 1763, a new mode of grazing was introduced; the face of the hills being appropriated to the feeding of black cattle, it was found that our native breed of sheep were not fond of the course grafs in the muir, constantly seeking after the short bite on the Campsie Fells, it became absolutely neccessary, therefore, if we were to follow this system of grazing, to procure such a breed of sheep as were fitted for the muir ground.

At present, the wool in this parish I believe to be as good as any wool of the Tweedsmuir breed of sheep; when smeared with tar and butter, it sells betwixt six and seven shillings per stone;—white, as it is termed, sells at ten shillings per stone; we expect eight pounds of clean washed wool out of the stone of that which was smeared; and twelve pounds from the white wool It is chiefly sold to the country people in the neighbourhood. The grazing of black cattle upon brae ground, is perhaps as well understood in this parish, as in most places of Scotland; above 900 are fed annually in this district, either for the butcher, or the Falkirk market; perhaps 300 of these may be wintered; the remainder bought in at the Whitsunday markets.

The winterers graze in the open fields, during the whole winter season, and are fed once or twice a day with coarse hay, made of sprats and grafs,—gathered in autumn amongst the cows feet in their pasture; the graziers commonly begin

to

to fodder, as they term it, about Chriſtmaſs, (It is conſidered as a ſevere winter, when they are forced to begin before
Chriſtmas,) and continue till about the beginning of April,
when the cattle refuſe it. There are few cattle grazed with
us but Highlanders, and we prefer thoſe from, Argyleſhire,
and the iſles : North country cattle are rejected, as they are
conſidered by the graziers as four and difficult to feed : grazing of Highland cattle upon brae-ground in this diſtrict, owes
much of the perfection to which it has been brought, to Mr
David Dun, a native of this pariſh.—He has ſpent the better
of his life in the profeſſion of a ſhepherd, grazier, and breed-
er of cattle ; and his countrymen acknowledge, with pleaſure,
the obligations they are under to him for his ſkill and attention in theſe particulars.—He has, with ſome propriety, been
ſtyled the Scotch Bakewell ; for ſeveral years, he gave 1400 l.
per annum for grafs-lands, and at that time did not ſo much
as grow a cabbage plant ; at preſent, he pays about 800 l. *per
annum* on current leaſes ; he has been known, again and a-
gain, to ſell cattle of the Highland breed, of his own rearing,
at twelve and fourteen pounds Sterling *per* head, to the butchers ;—he has brought his breed of muir ewes to ſuch perfection, as often to ſell his tup-hogs at a guinea *per* head, to
the Highland ſhepherds for brood rams : —He has ſold forty
or fifty at this rate, in a ſeaſon. Beſides, the uncommon ſkill,
which, from long experience, he muſt have acquired in the
judging of cattle and ſheep ; there are certain uniform principles which he goes upon in grazing, which may be proper
to mention : In the 1ſt place, never to ſtock his land ſo hea-
vily as his neighbours, or even perhaps as the land could bear ;
by this means, his cattle have always the choice of grafs, and
he is enabled to gather enough amongſt their feet to fodder them in winter. The cattle by this means are fully fed,
which gives him the option of merchants. 2*dly*, By having

farms of different complexions, he has it in his power to fort his cattle in fuch a manner, as to fuit each farm.—He has it in his power to vary their food, and to change them from farm to farm, as he perceives them healthy, taking on flefh, or the contrary. 3*dly*, In the manner of buying his cattle from the Highland dealers, he is very particular : he muft have the worft and oldeft, draughted again and again from the drove, before he will purchafe it ; by this means, he acquires none but healthy cattle ; perhaps they may coft him a few fhillings more *per* head, but it is foon repaid.—Scarcely ever any of his cattle die ; and they are fo evenly, that it is hardly in the power of the butcher to challenge a bad beaft ; by this management, his profits are uniform over the whole head ; whereas, when cattle are fhot, as it is termed, the profits are greately diminifhed. §

We are not to imagine that the profits of graziers in our brae lands are very great ; when the cattle are bought in at Martinmas, and kept for one year in the pafture, two guineas per head is expected as grafs-mail ; when bought at the Whitfunday market and kept till Martinmas, one guinea is expected per head ; when thefe profits are deficient, it is confidered as a bad year by the grazier ; and when they exceed, it is confidered as good times. *

Roads.

§ This gentleman hath been unfortunately killed by accident, fince writing this account. It happened on the 27th of May 1794, as he was attending on fheep fhearing:—Leading a fheep acrofs a wooden bridge, the rail of the bridge gave way ; and he was thrown into the river ; falling upon a ftone, he was killed on the fpot.

* Notwithftanding the diftrict of Campfie feems to be fo well adapted for the grazing of cattle, perhaps there are fome defects attending their plan, which it may be proper to mention : 1*ft*, It feems to be the misfortune of the Scotch in general, and particularly of the people of this diftrict, that when

they

Roads.—Great attention and ſkill have been ſhown in this article ; the pariſh is interſected by two great roads, the one a turnpike; leading from the military road at Kippin to Glaſgow, the other from Eaſt to Weſt, joining the great Edinburgh road

they obſerve their neighbours thriving in any profeſſion, they immediately run into it, without conſidering whether they have induſtry or talents to ſucceed ; ſuch has, of late, been too much the caſe in the grazing line; ſo that now, the utmoſt induſtry and talents can ſcarcely enable them to live. The country banks afforded abundance of credit to every adventurer ; from ſuch a competition amongſt theſe *would-be-graziers*, the graſs-farms are too high rented ; the cattle are dear bought from their rearers; and the reſult has been, that notwithſtanding the cry of the goodneſs of the times, very little profit has been made by the people embarked in this profeſſion ; for theſe ten years paſt, many bankrupcies have taken place among that claſs of men; It indulges the adventurous ſpirit of the people, and therefore will always be a favourite profeſſion, let the profits be what they will. 2*dly*, The rage for Highland cattle is too great, more ſo than theſe cattle deſerve ; it is true, where ground is high and much expoſed, ſuch cattle is more adapted for the paſture, than the cattle which the low country produces; but perhaps it would be the intereſt of the grazier, to turn all our brae ground in ſheep paſture, and the grounds of the valley into graſs farms, for lowland cattle, where, if once winter food were produced, and the land either protected by planting, or ſhades built where they might be fed with turnip in the open air ; the proſpects of greater profits upon the fattening of beaſts· would be procured, than by the imperfect mode of buying either winterers at the Down markets, or lean cattle at Belting, and ſelling them at Martinmas. 3*dly*, There is another defect which attends the preſent ſyſtem of grazing in this country, and which tends to render the beef of Highland cattle too dear to the conſumer ; there being no leſs than three different claſſes of people who muſt have their profits within the year : There is the drover, who collects theſe cattle in ſmall parcels from the rearer, and ſells them at fairs, at an advanced price to the graziers ; the grazier, again, very often ſells his cattle to the *couper*, who runs them at fairs to the conſumer, and ſometimes exacts a profit almoſt equal to that of the grazier : In ſhort, there is too much of the ſpirit of adventure in this profeſſion, whereby both the grazier and conſumer are loſers.

road at Auchinreach house on the East, and the turnpike
road by Strathblane to Glasgow, on the the West; besides
these two great lines, the turnpike road from Edinburgh to
Glasgow by Falkirk, passes through Campsie for two miles;
and there are two crofs branches which strike off to Kirkintilloch; so that there are in all 20 English miles of road in
this distrièt, 10 of which are kept up by the converted statute labour: It will be easily believed that there are few districts more complicably interfeèted, and, it may be added,
fewer still where the roads are better kept in order. The
roads in this distrièt, before the aèt for converting the statute
labour took place, were miserable indeed; for although the
labour of 101 plough-gates, according to the mode of three
days of a man and horse in spring, and as much in autumn
for each plough, might appear adequate to the purpose; still,
from the awkward and carelefs manner in which they
wrought, the roads were hardly passable in winter; at the
same time, I am convinced that this was as much owing to
the want of skill in the overseers as to the want of dexterity
in the labourers. As to any positive advantage gained to the
public, from the conversion aèt, 12s. per annum is by no
means equal to the labour of six days of a man and a horse.
The sum levied in this parish varied exceedingly of late years,
owing to the increafe of inhabitants; every cotter or house-
holder paying 2s. per annum, it hath amounted to 70l. per
annum, 50 of which is paid by the farmers and landholders,
and the other 20l. by the cottars. Till within these 3 years,
this sum was expended in making and repairing, and keeping up 18 out of the 20 miles of road the parish contains:
Now, by one great line of road being made a turnpike, the
whole money will be expended in future, in improving and
keeping up 10 miles, and in making such crofs-cuts to the

great

great branches, as the farther improvement of the diſtrict ſhall ſuggeſt; one of which improvements is evident to the moſt carelefs obferver; viz. in cutting a line of road from Campſie kirk to the Crow road, the diſtance is not much more than 600 yards, and yet to the people who travel to Stirling from this part of the county, it muſt ſhorten the road fully 3 miles.

Confidering that the roads were made upon no determined plan, but ſometimes altering and mending the old lines, as circumſtances occurred, it is wonderful, that in a diſtrict where the ground is ſo uneven, and particularly when it is confidered that one of the roads croſſes part of a mountain 800 feet high, that there ſhould be ſo few pulls in it; feldom or ever is the rife more ſudden than that of one foot in 20 ||.

Upon

|| As fometimes it hath been propofed to carry a turnpike road from Kilfyth to the military road near Buchanan houfe, the feat of the Duke of Montrofe, through the ftraths of Campfie, Strathblane, and Killearn; and if a bridge was thrown over the Leven, at the boat of Ballach, there cannot be the fmalleft doubt, that the great line of travelling from the Weft Highlands to Edinburgh, muft be through the valley of Campfie, it being much nearer than either by Glafgow or Stirling : (fince writing this account, a bill has paffed, qualifying the heritors of Stirlingfhire to carry this Eaft and Weft direction through the valley of Fintray, to the North of Campfie hills, and through the valley on the river Blane. It may not be improper to obferve here, that the people who grumble moft in paying money inftead of the ftatute labour, are the cottars and tradefmen ; and yet they are the greateft gainers : They don't recollect, that wherever good roads exift, raw materials are eafily imported, and manufactured articles have ready accefs to the market : fuch local advantages, along with the circumftance of cheap fuel, have been the great reafons of encouraging manufacturers to fettle amongft us : the truth is, the public, or the truftees for the public, may be faid to have made a bad bargain when they agreed (as the act of Parliament expreffes) to receive two ſhillings from a cottar in lieu of four days labour, although

the

Upon the different lines of roads, there are no leſs than 19 ſtone bridges, 4 of which are a-croſs the Kelvin. It may be obſerved, that there are ſeveral old cauſeways in the pariſh, on the line of road leading to the pariſh church, which, tradition ſays, were made by offenders in ancient times, by way of penance ; particularly the cauſeways made by the ſeven brothers of the name of M'Donald ; theſe ſhew the ſtile in which roads were formed in thoſe early days ; as far as can be perceived, they conſiſted of one large whinſtone in the middle, with ſmaller ones on each ſide in rows, the breadth of the road being about ſix feet. There is one radical defect attending the roads of this diſtrict ; the ſoil being gravelly, when a ſudden thaw comes after a ſevere froſt in winter, the ground becomes ſo ſpungy, as to be almoſt impaſſable, which can only be rectified by making a layer of beat whinſtone below the water gravel, a practice ſeldom followed. The following table exhibits the ſtate of our roads, and the prices levied at the toll-bar :

	Miles.	£.	s.	d.
Total line of road —	20			
Turnpike road —	10			
Country road - -	10			
Money levied per annum in the pariſh -		70	0	0
From the ploughgates -		50	0	0
From the cottars - -		20	0	0
Price of cattle at the toll-bar -		0	0	0
Horſe and cart - -		0	0	2
Single horſe - - -		0	0	1
The ſcore of cows, ſheep, lambs, &c. -		0	0	5

Manufacturers.

the act expreſſes, that all thoſe receiving public charity ſhall be exempted; perhaps it might be an improvement, if women and men, after a certain age, ſhould be excuſed from paying pariſh burdens; it would pleaſe them, and the public would not be great loſers by ſuch mitigation.

Manufaċures.—At preſent the leading feature of this pa⸗
riſh is its manufactures: Two very extenſive printfields
have been erected within theſe nine years; the one in the
1785, at the French mills, ſtiled the Kincaid printfield, the
firm, Henderſon, Semple and Company, upon a farm which
they have rented from the laird of Kincaid, at three pound
per acre: They have conſtructed not only the moſt elegant
machinery for the calico printfield; but have likewiſe com⸗
pleted a ſet of works for the manufacturing all ſorts of grain;
the fall at this printfield is 22 feet; the grounds are laid
out with great taſte; and in order to obtain ſoft pure water,
they have dug a reſervoir of 120 yards in length, and ſeven⸗
ty in breadth, with a ſmall iſland in the middle, planted
with ſhrubs.

The other was erected in the year 1786, containing a farm
annexed to it of about thirty acres; likewiſe at three pound
per acre, where works uncommonly commodious have been
erected: The firm of this ſecond, is Lindſay, Smith and
Company; both fields are upon a leaſe of 99 years.

Both theſe works have been carried on with ſpirit, and, it
is believed, with conſiderable ſuccεſs. Two circumſtances
induced the manufacturers to ſettle in this pariſh; viz. plen⸗
ty of pit-coal, and the uncommon ſupply of water in all ſea⸗
fons; perhaps the circumſtances of being ſituated in the neigh⸗
bourhood of Glaſgow, and of the Canal, might not a little
contribute to fix their choice. There are about 306 perſons,
young and old, employed at each field; each employs 37
tables for block printing, and 17 copperplate preſſes; they
in general bleach their own cloth for printing.

At the Lennox mill print-field, there is another field laid out
for bleaching lawns, which there is every reaſon to believe will
ſucceed perfectly well. The work people at the Weſter
field,

field, are commodiously lodged at the new village of Lenox-
town; and at the Kincaid, or Easter Field, several of the printers have feued steadings on the grounds; so that there is every probability of a neat village being built, for the convenience of its servants: At first, (as was to be expected in
all new works,) the operative people were a little turbulent;
and considering that they were a collection from all the different corners of the country, enjoying high wages, and carried away by the licentiousness of the times, their turbulence
was not to be wondered at; but that is now all over; and
there are scarce any works in the country, where the people
behave more circumspectly towards their employers, and are
more regular in their deportment.

These public works employ each of them two Excise officers; and they pay of revenue to Government about four
thousand pounds each per annum.

It may be proper to notice, that although the wages of calico printers seem to be the highest of any in the country;
no doubt, when the long apprenticeship is considered, along
with the unwholesome nature of the work, the wages perhaps should be greater than of most other operative people;
at the same time, when it is considered, that the highest wages do not always make the wealthiest tradesman; perhaps,
if some method could be fallen upon to reduce the prices,
both the tradesman and the public would be gainers.

The following table exhibits the present situation of one
field, as far as is known to the public. There being nearly
the same workmen at both, the same table may apply to each.

DESIGNATION.

DESIGNATIONS.		WAGES PER WEEK.	
Block Printers . .	36	from	18s. to 21s. per week.
Copperplates ditto .	22	from	17s. to 21s. ditto.
Pencillers . . .	160	from	4s. to 6s. ditto.
Tearing Boys . . .	34		2s. ditto.
Bleachers	26		8s. ditto.
Engravers	16	from	18s. to 22s. ditto.
Miln Wrights . . .	2		12s. ditto.
Labourers . . .	6		7s. ditto.
Furnace Men . . .	8		7s. ditto.
Excife Officers . .	2	50l.	per annum.
Revenue to Government.		8000l.	per annum.

It may be obferved, that as the greateſt number of block printers at each field are apprentices, ſo, of courſe, their wages are ſmall in proportion : Their maſters are only bound, by their indentures, to allow them 3s. per week, for the firſt four years, and 4s. per week, the laſt three years ; but, owing to the briſkneſs of trade for ſome years by gone, it was cuſtomary to allow the apprentices to work for as much as they could make, giving them the half of the journeyman's prices ; at preſent, the wages of the calico printers in this diſtrict are ſomewhat fallen, owing to the great number of turn-overs (as they are termed,) from thoſe fields which have ſtopped payment. Whether this depreſſion of their wages ſhall continue or not, the ebbs and flows of the trade muſt determine. Theſe two printfields pay annually about nine thouſand pounds Sterling in wages. This pariſh may now be ſaid to poſſefs a ſpirit for carrying on manufactures of different ſorts ; there being no leſs than 105 operative weavers in it ; 9 of which are employed by private families ; the remainder weave to the manufactures in Glaſgow, and, as far as can be well afcertained,

ιained, earn, at an average, from twenty pence to two fhil⸗
lings per day. †

† It will not be improper, to take notice of a fpecies of manufacture which
has exifted in this parifh for fome ages : We know that it was manafactur⸗
ed, to a confiderable extent, as early as the reign of James the 6th, which
goes by the name of the Campfie gray ; and was then confidered as the fta⸗
ple of the country. It may be proper to defcribe it : It was fpun about the
grift of nine cuts out of the pound of wool, each cut confifting of fixty threads,
fix quarters long ; it was dyed a blue colour in the wool, and wove for a pen⸗
ny farthing the ell, in a ten porter or two hundred reed ; they feldom made
it broader than half an ell and a nail of dreffed cloth ; and they fold the
double ell from half a crown to three fhillings ; fo that the weaver had for the
fingle yard little more than fifteen pence : It was fpun by the women in
private families during the fummer ; it being cuftomary for each family to
have two of thefe webbs, one of which was got dreffed againft Martinmas,
and fold to pay the mafter's rent ; the other againft New-years-day ; the pro⸗
fits of which went to fupply the demands of the family. The fairs of Kil⸗
fyth were the great markets for the difpofal of thefe gray webs ; the fervant
lads ufed to collect from all the neighbouring parifhs, in order to fupply them⸗
felves with fuits of Campfie Gray ; which they would eafily do, at the mo⸗
derate expence of nine pounds Scots ; and perhaps, few countries ever fupply⸗
ed a more cheap, decent, and profitable cloathing for working people.—It
was all fpun, as it is termed, upon the *muckle* wheel ; and a woman ufed to earn
three pence per day befides her victuals : It would be improper to pafs over
the breaking of the gray web, a fcene of joy and gaiety, which will not
foon be forgot in this part of the country : If a private family was to have
their wool prepared for fpinning, a number of country laffes were invited in
order to card it ; they generally affembled in the barn ; during the day, a
large piece of cheefe was cut from the kebbock, and wrapt up in a white
cloth, and hid by one of the damfels ; at the gloming, the young lads ufed to
affemble, in order to fearch for this cheefe, and peculiarly fortunate was that
young man confidered to be, who (having received a watch word from fome
of his fair friends,) found out the cheefe, and had the opportunity of dividing
it amongft the fimpering damfels. Both the manufactures and days of inno⸗
cent amufement are gone ; nor has the manners introduced by public works
repaired the lofs ; it muft be owned, however, that fince manufactures were
introduced, there is an uncommon degree of activity which pervades this dif⸗
trict, and which accompanies the people in all their operations ; and perhaps,
indeed, I would rather be difpofed to pronounce the character of the people
in this place inclined to merchandife and adventure.

Population.—This preſent year, 1793, when the numeration was made, there were 2517 ſouls. The p pulation of this pa-riſh has increaſed 900, ſince December 178 , the number then being 1627. In Dr Webſter's account it is given up at 1400. From ſeveral facts in the poſſeſſion of the writer of this ac-count, the population of this pariſh ſeems ſomewhat to have deeclined from the Revolution till the year 1763. The chief cauſe which has been aſſigned for this circumſtance, was the throwing ſeveral ſmall tenements together, making one large farm, whereby a number of families were thrown out of bread, and obliged to emigrate to large towns for their daily ſub-ſiſtence The number of houſeholders or reeks, previous to the 1783, I cannot mark poſitively ; in that year there were 317; population then being ſomewhat better than five to a family ; in the preſent year, there are 609 houſeholders, or people who keep reeks, ſo that the number of ſouls have not increaſed in the ſame proportion as that of houſeholders : the reaſon is obvious : ſeveral young people, printers and pencil-lers, at the different printfields, keep houſe, either ſingly, or perhaps, though married, have not as yet more than one child ; ſo that the population in this pariſh, even ſuppoſing the houſeholders not to increaſe, is not come to its juſt level. To ſhew the proportions from the Revolution to the year 1763, I have ſubjoined the following table ; each ſtatement containing the average of baptiſms for five years :

It

Years.	Baptiſms.	Average.	Years.	Baptiſms.	Average.
1696	49		1732	32	
1700	47		1733	43	
1701	47		1734	28	
1704	41		1735	44	
1705	49		1736	43	
—		46	—		38

Years.	Baptisms.	Average.	Years.	Baptisms.	Average.
1750	37		1773	33	
1751	51		1774	39	
1752	39		—	—	37
1753	42		1781	38	
1754	37		1782	40	
—		41	1783	42	
1760	37		1784	50	
1763	26		1785	46	
1764	44		—	—	43
1765	34		1789	94	
1766	29		1790	79	
—		34 *	1791	75	
1770	36		1792	89	
1771	44		1793	115	
1772	35		—		90

It may be observed that the register of marriages seems to confirm the same opinion, that the population had decreased from the Revolution to the year 1763 †:

Years.	Marriages.	Average.	Years.	Marriages.	Average.
1696	17		1790	26	
1697	19		1791	34	
1698	22		1792	27	
1706	18		1793	26	
1707	28		—		28
—		21			

It is not so easy to ascertain the average of deaths, as no register seems to have been kept, previous to the year 1790, but for these last four years it stands thus:

Years.

* This period seems to have been the lowest, as is likewise evident from the register of marriages.

† It appears, as far as the register of marriages is entire, that the number decreased to about 12; it is now about 28 annually, as appears from the list of the 4 last years.

Years.	Deaths.	Average.	Years.	Deaths.	Average.
1790	38		1792	32	
1791	41		1793	34	36

Allowing our regifters to have been accurately kept, which I believe to be as much the cafe as in moft country parifhes; it is evident that they are regulated by no general rule: The fudden influx of inhabitants have varied thefe regifters exceedingly. The following table exhibits all the facts relative to the prefent ftate of population:

DESIGNATIONS, &c.		Of the three laft years of burials, the difeafes ftand thus:	
Houfcholders,	609		
Inhabitants,	2527	Died of fevers,	8
Males,	1234	Small-pox,	15
Females,	1292	Confumptions,	26
Below 10 years,	882	Palfy,	2
Born in the parifh,	1334	Afthma,	1
Incomers,	1190	Chincough,	6
Baptifms,	90	Bowelhive, (vulgarly ftiled.)	1
Marriages,	28	Meafles,	6
Burials,	36	Child-bed,	1
Above ninety,	0	Still-born,	1
Above eighty,	5	Mortification,	1
Above feventy,	100	Old age,	26

What is now ftiled confumption, feems to have been unknown in this diftrict about 60 years ago; and I believe generally unknown in Scotland: Many caufes have been affigned for this fact, by medical men. Where people were cloathed in plaiding, which fomewhat refembles flannel, as was the cafe till very lately in this diftrict, and where they feldom were confined to work in warm houfes, as is now the cafe, great colds, the forerunners of confumption, would not eafily affect them.

Of

Of this population we have fubjoined the following table, fhewing how they were employed fpring 1792

Of the 882 below ten years of age, there were, at the four different fchools in this parifh, . 200

The remaining were infants in their parents houfes, capable of no employment, . . 682

The remaining 800 males above ten years of age, are employed in the following manner :

Gentlemen who live on their rents	8
Minifter of the Eftablifhment	1
Minifter of a Relief meeting houfe	1
Surgeon . .	1
Farmers and graziers .	96
Weavers . .	105
Tailors . .	8
Houfe-carpenters .	11
Miln-wrights . .	6
Black-fmiths in four fhops .	9
Shoe-makers . .	5
Excife-officers who refide in the parifh . . .	2
Block-printers . .	74
Stocking-makers . .	6
Copperplate prefs-printers	22
Tearing boys . .	70
Coalliers . .	46
Lime-quarriers .	40
Hill-men at the different pits	10
Carters and Carriers .	10
Labourers . .	20
Houfe fervants to the gentry	11
Farmers and graziers fervants	90
Publicans . .	17
Schoolmafters . .	4
Students . .	4
Grave-digger . .	1
Millers . . .	7
Lint-dreffers and glovers .	7
Shop-keepers and chandlers	11
Bleachers . .	60
Dyers . .	16

A Table,

Shewing how the 800 females are employed in 1793.

Wives to the different houfeholders . .	410
Daughters, refiding in their parents families .	170
Servants in gentlemen's families	26
Menial fervants to the farmers and different houfeholders in the parifh . ,	110
As fempftreffes and mautua makers . .	12
Midwives . .	3

The remaining feventy-one are either widows or unmarried women, who refide in cot-houfes 71 Of the married women and young perfons, refiding in their parents houfes, there may be about one hundred and fixty who pencil calico to the print-fields.

Poor.

Poor.—Every attempt hath been made by the heritors and ſeſſion to diſcourage begging ; as yet their efforts have proved abortive ; and although at this moment there is not a ſingle perſon in this pariſh underſtood to be a common beggar, we are ſtill peſtered with vagrants. The poor which we countenance as ſuch, generally reſide along with their children, or ſome near relation ; they receive their allowance on the firſt Monday of each month ; 6s. per month is the higheſt ſum given ; none receive leſs than three ; at an average there are 20 conſtantly upon our liſt. The funds from which they are paid are the collections at the church door, the mortcloth fees and proclamation money, together with the intereſt of 570l. of which 500l. is ſecured on heritable property at 5 per cent intereſt, payable twice in the year : The other 70l. is lodg in bank, payable on demand in caſe of an emergency ; from thoſe funds we have been able as yet to ſupſupply the wants of our poor. The collections at the ſacrament, including the preparation and the thankſgiving days, are applied to the relief of thoſe indigent houſeholders, whoſe ſiſituation is not ſo preſſing as to make them objects of the ordinary charity. Although it is believed that the law allows kirk feſſions to take poſſeſſion of the effects belonging to the paupers, ſo ſoon as they grant them ſupply ; we have anxiouſly avoided being too ſtrict in this particular ; for, callous as the relations of the pauper may be, it is ſtill an inducement for them to affiſt a little ; whereas, if they had no proſpect of ſucceeding to the trumpery, ſmall as it is, the whole care of their relation would be thrown upon the pariſh ; and it is well known that 18d. per week is not adequate to all the neceſſities of lodging, clothing, and feeding a pauper. The Engliſh ſyſtem is to ſupport the poor, the Scotch to affiſt them.

The

The feffion in this parifh has hitherto taken the complete management of fupplying the poor; the heritors meet once in the year, or two years, as it fuits them, to examine and pafs their accounts; and it may be faid here, as in every parifh in Scotland, that it is the cheapeft and beft managed public fund in Great Britain; the only expence incurred with us is of one guinea per annum allowed to the feffion-clerk, for keeping the books. Befides the public parochial charity, there are two other charitable inftitutions, which have lately been founded in the parifh, the one known by the name of the Campfie Benevolent Society, inftituted in the year 1786, and whofe capital already amounts to 110l. which Society allows 3s. to its members per week if bed-rid, and 2s. per week if merely incapable of work; the other inftitution is connected with the Lennox-Kilwinning mafon lodge; its capital is 70l.; it likewife allows liberally to its indigent members.

The annual difburfements by the feffion are between 60 and 70l. Sterling per annum. This parifh, confidering its riches and its population, could afford its poor a great deal more, providing an affeffment took place; the mode of provifion by collections at the church-doors, has been confiderably hurt by a Relief meeting-houfe, which hath lately been erected in the parifh; the collections made at thefe houfes being either employed to pay their minifters, or to pay the debts incurred in building their chapels, none is given to fupport the regular poor; fuch houfes, therefore, upon their prefent footing, are extremely prejudicial to the Scotch mode of providing for the indigent ‖.

‖ From the opportunity that the writer of this account has had, as a native of this parifh, of attending to the ftate of the poor in this diftrict, he cannot help taking notice of a remarkable trait of the degeneracy of the prefent age.

Of the Church.—Campſie was a parſonage ; the parſon of Campſie was the Sacriſtan of the Cathedral of Glaſgow ; of courſe, he muſt have been one of the reſidentary canons ; he had a houſe in the Ratten-row of Glaſgow, ſaid to be ſtill in exiſtence ; and was accuſtomed to ſerve the cure at Campſie by a vicar. As this pariſh, in Roman Catholic times, contained above 150 plough-gates of land, from which the parſon drew tithes ; the probability is, that the living was conſiderable.

Attending

age. About 35 years ago, it would have been conſidered as diſgraceful to children to have allowed their parents to be ſupported by the ſeſſion, or even the more diſtant relations of brethren or nephews, to have heard of their ſiſters or uncles caſt upon the box, as they termed it ; it is now aſtoniſhing with what greedineſs people receive public charity ; they ſomewhat conſider it as a penſion, to which they are entitled. It is not uncommon to perceive children enjoying high wages, and indulging in many of the gaieties of life, neglecting their aged parents : ſuch unnatural conduct was not congenial once with Scottiſh independence, and that dignified pride, which characterized our forefathers, in their more virtuous days. When a pauper dies, it is cuſtomary for the ſeſſion to provide the coffin and winding-ſheet, and mortcloth, gratis. And if there ſhall be no relation of the deceaſed in the pariſh, to contribute for the little entertainment neceſſary at the funeral, which ſeldom happens, 5s. is allowed for ſuch expence. As it might tend to throw more light upon the political ſituation of a country, to examine at what age, and what are the claſs of people of which the paupers of a pariſh are compoſed, I have ſubjoined the following table, comprehending the different periods of admiſſion, and the ſums given.

No. of paupers on our liſt,	25
Of theſe there are females,	16
Males,	9
Above ſixty years of age,	19
The average of the years of their receiving charity,	8
Of this number of paupers, there are no leſs than five facile in their mind,	5
The higheſt ſum given is per month,	6s.
It would appear that it is only the hundredth part of the whole inhabitants who require public charity,	
Of theſe twenty five paupers, eight are unmarried women.	

Attending to that diftinction of bifhops churches, and menfal churches, it was one of the bifhops churches gifted by Donald, Earl of Lennox, to the See of Glafgow, in the year 1270. Thofe who delight in magnifying the riches of the church of Rome, take particular pleafure in pointing out the yard where the parfon of Campfie's corn-ftacks were arranged, and the fite of the mill which was conftantly employed in grinding his grain. There is reafon to believe, that he was not the leaft wealthy heritor of his parifh. Previous to the Reformation, we know that Lamberton and Beaton were parfons of Campfie, and afterwards both of them bifhops of St. Andrews, men who made fome figure in their day *.

The

* Since the Reformation, the names of the clergy who filled that charge, and the dates of their admiffion, have been preferved in the presbytery records of Glafgow ; and they furnifh us with a pretty good fpecimen of the fpirit of the times. There is reafon to believe, that the clergyman of this parifh continued Roman Catholic, and accafionally performed this facred function in the parifh, till the year 1572 ; he is faid to have been a branch of the family of MARR : about that time, we find a Mr William Erfkine, a relation likewife of the MARR family, parfon of Campfie ; he was afterwards titular Archbifhop of Glafgow ; he is faid never to have been in holy orders : How long he continued parfon of Campfie, we know not ; but we find,

1/*, Mr Stoddart, presbyterian minifter of Campfie, on the 3d of November 1581.

2d, Mr James Stewart is fettled affiftant and fucceffor the 25th of March 1607.

3d, Mr John Crichton was admitted the 23d of April 1623 : He was depofed for what was called corrupt doctrine : There is a tradition in the parifh, that he was fuch a remarkable ftout, well breathed man, that he could walk in forty minutes to the top of the Campfie Fells, eating a peafe bannock, to a fpot which, to this day, goes by the name of Crichton's Cairn.

4tb, Mr Alexander Forbes was admitted the 16th of December 1629 ; and was depofed for not conforming to the Synod of Glafgow, on the third of April 1639.

5tb,

The progress of the stipends of this parish, I have not been able to ascertain accurately prior to the year 1618 : It is then declared to be two chalders of meal and 600 merks : In the year

5th, Mr John Collins was admitted the 2d of November 1641; he was murdered in returning from the presbytery about Martinmas 1648; the suspicion fell upon the laird of Balglass, a small heritor in the parish, who was obliged to fly the country to avoid punishment.

6th, Mr Archibald Denniston was ordained the 30th of March 1649 : He was deposed by the protesters in 1655, about which deposition Principal Baillie, in his letters, makes the following remark : He was restored in the year 1661, and died 1679 ; there is a traditionary anecdote mentioned of him, which somewhat marks the character of the man.—In the year 1655 he had begun a discourse on a text, and half finished the first head.—In the year 1661, when restored, he took up the second, prefacing his discourse, by saying, that the times were altered, but that the doctrines of the gospel are always the same.

Principal Baillie, in his letters, speaking of Mr Denniston says, " he was " deposed by the protesters in 1655 ; for his part, he saw nothing evil of the " man. The protesters, says he, put in his room a Mr John Law, a *poor, baxter callon*, who had but lately left his trade, and hardly knew his grammar; " but they said he was *gifted*."

7th, Mr John Law was ordained by the protesters in 1656 : He was ejected 1661, and was restored 1688 ; he never officiated again in Campsie.

8th, Mr George Miln was instituted 24th June 1681 : He was turned out at the Revolution, and was exceedingly ill used ; the worthless part of the parish having risen in a mob and broke his furniture, and threatened his person ; this gentleman, however, by way of retaliation, carried away the records of the parish.

9th, Mr John Govan, who had been imprisoned in the Bass, in James the 7th's time, was ordained minister of Campsie on the 5th of December 1688; he died a batchelor the 17th of September 1729.

10th, He was succeeded by his nephew Mr John Forrester, a brother of Forrester's of Dinovan ; he died in September 1731, at the age of 25.

11th, He was succeeded by Mr John Warden, a son of the minister of Gargunnock ; he was ordained the 3d of April 1732 ; which gentleman was translated to Perth, and afterwards to the Canongate of Edinburgh. He was succeeded by Mr William Bell, a native of Eclesfechan, Dumfriesshire ; who

was

year 1649, an augmentation of a chalder of meal, and one hundred pounds Scots, was granted; and in the 1785, a new augmention was granted; fo that the ftipend now is 80 l. Sterling in money, two chalders of meal, and one chalder of barley: It would appear, that very foon after the act paffed, ordaining glebes to the reformed clergy, that four acres and a half of arable land was allocated to the minifter of Campfie: In the year 1646, when a disjunction and annexation took place, three acres and a half more were allocated for pafture; but, owing to the turbulence of the times which followed, the minifter never feems to have been in poffeffion of them; fo that at prefent the glebe of Campfie is deficient in pafture; the heritors, about 30 years ago, bought an acre of land, adding it to the four acres and half, without fpecifying whether it was in part of pafture or not. Till lately, it was cuftomary for the minifter to ufe fome overt act to prevent prefcription running againft him, anent the three acres and a half which had been allocated for pafture. For fome time after the Reformation, it would appear that the clergyman had lived in the vicar's houfe. In 1627, a houfe was built alenarly for the purpofe of lodging the minifter; it was a fmall houfe of two ftories, thatched with ftraw: In 1727, a new houfe was built on the fame fite; which houfe, along with the ocffies, was repaired in the year 1785, at the very moderate expence of one hundred and twenty nine pounds. The church

confifted

was ordained the 24th of September 1747, and died the 8th of May 1783.

13*th*, He was fucceeded by the prefent incumbent. Thirteen clergymen have therefore officiated in this parifh fince the Reformation, at leaft fince the year 1582; which, at an average, is nearly 16 years to each incumbent; but what is very aftonifhing, out of that number no lefs than five were ejected on account of the turbulence of the times, and one faid to have been murdered; facts, which fhould lead us to value the peaceable and happy times in which we live.

conſiſted originally of three parts : 1*ſt*, What they called the kirk ; 2*d*, the quire ; and, 3*d*, the veſtry; which correſponded to the uſes required in the Roman Catholic times ; it was repaired in the year 1772 : At preſent it would be by far too ſmall for the pariſh, if a relief meeting-houſe had not been erected. The kirk of Campſie, like moſt of the churches in popiſh times, is ſituated at the end of the pariſh ; whether this was from accident, or from choice of the clergy, to fix it in the moſt deſireable ſpot, is not eaſy to determine. If, however, the population of this diſtrict continues to increaſe, there will be an abſolute neceſſity of building a more commodious church in a more centrical ſpot, for the better accommodation of the inhabitants. I obſerved, that in the 1649 there was a disjunction and an annexation of conſiderable portions of this pariſh to Kilſyth and Baldernock ; it appears, however, by a diſpute which lately took place betwixt the miniſter of Baldernock and the heritors of Campſie, anent the augmentation of the ſtipend of Baldernock, that the part disjoined was only annexed *quoad ſacra*; and the probability is, that the proportion annexed to Kilſyth is in the ſame predicament. All the lands in the pariſh are now valued, and the free unpropriated tithe is better than 600 l. Sterling annually, as the fund from which the clergymen may have future augmentations. Mr Campbell of Shawfield is titular, in virtue of his being the purchaſer of the eſtate of Kilſyth, from the creditors of the York-building There is an opinion entertained by ſome people, that if an act of Parliament does not render all miniſters ſtipendiaries, that on account of certain peculiar circumſtances, the miniſter of Campſie is ſtill titular of the tithes.

The duties of this pariſh conſiſt in viſiting and regularly examining the congregation once in the year, beſides preaching three diſcourſes every ſunday, from the 1cth of April till

the

the 10th of October ; and in winter, two difcourfes, one of them always a lecture : The facrament is given once in the year ; three difcourfes on the faft day, two on Sunday, two on Monday : The action fermon in the church, and the evening fermon ; befides preaching at the tent. People have complained, that the tent preaching was prejudicial : I am inclined to believe the contrary from experience : 1*ft*, On account of its bringing a confiderable collection for the poor ; and, 2*dly*, it accuftoms a number of people to meet together in a decent, cheerful, and refpectable manner.—I have never heard either the fober, or the ferious, or the induftrious, complain ; and confidering the fimplicity of our fervice, in moft other refpects, I have all along been accuftomed to confider thefe public religious meetings as beneficial to the manners of the country. The eclefiaftical difcipline of this parifh is ftill kept up. As for difcipline againft fornicators, two days doing public penance in the church, are required, befides a fine of a crown, for each guilty perfon, to the poor. There has been an opinion entertained, that this public penance has been productive of very bad effects in fociety ; fo far has an idea gone forth of this fort, that, for this reafon, fome writers have pretended to fay, that fo long as doing public penance was permitted, no perfon fhould be put to death for child murder : I am inclined to believe, that it would be much more the intereft of the community, in a political light, that the laws of difcipline fhould be more rigidly adhered to ; for if once the vulgar of any country, confider incontinency as a venial fault, they are almoft ready for the commiffion of any crime ; and as I can eafily fee, that the fhame of doing penance operates to deter others ; in this point of view, it is to be confidered as anfwering the ends of edification. Public baptifm is regularly adhered to ; parents requiring private baptifm for their children, pay half a crown to the poor·

Schools.—There are in this parifh two eftablifhed fchools. The parifh fchool was erected in the year 1661, according to the form therein required, under the patronage of John, Archbifhop of Glafgow ; the legal falary was fixed at 100 pounds Scots : It is remarkable, that in the deed of erection, there is an exprefs claufe, declaring, that the fchoolmafter, in all time coming, fhould teach Latin ; and that the fchool fhould be conftantly held at the Clachan of Campfie. There was another fchool erected in 1727, on a mortification of fifty pounds, left by one Young, a pedlar in Glocefterfhire : It is fituated at the diftance of four Englifh miles from the o-ther. The heritors of Campfie have, fomehow or other, per-mitted the half of the falary belonging to the parifh fchool-mafter, to be added to the further emolument of this fchool, of the eaftern diftrict.—It is to be expected, in a little time, this miftake will be rectified, and that the parifh fchoolmaf-ter will receive his legal falary ; and, at the fame time, the other fchoolmafter be fufficiently provided. Befides thefe two fchools, there was a third erected lately at the new vil-liage of Campfie, for the benefit of the inhabitants ; the teach-er has no falary : at the fame time, they have always found teachers ready to accept the office upon the bare emolument of the fchool wages : In the fummer feafon, in the South quarter of the parifh, there is commonly a fourth fchool taught by fome young man from Glafgow, who finds it con-venient to keep fchool during the vacation of the College; fo that at, an average, there are fomewhat above 200 children educated annually in the parifh : There are at leaft one fifth part at fchool of thofe who are below twelve years of age. The inhabitants of this parifh are, upon the whole, rather

rather difpofed to give their children a good education ; at the
time this account was wrote, there were thirteen Latin fcholars at the two parifh fchools; the other children are certain
of being taught to read Englifh, write and caft accompts ;
the common ftyle of education is carried on in the following manner : They learn the founds of the letters, and the u-
nion of fyllables, in the fmall fpelling book ; then they receive
the large fpelling book ; then they get the New Teftament,
and the Bible, in which they commonly read fome time ; and
then the Collection : they get a queftion in the common cate-
chifm to repeat every morning: there is a public repetition
on Saturday, with a pfalm on Monday. There being feveral public works in the parifh, the night-fchool is confiderable, being wholly made up of grown perfons, who attend for
the purpofes of writing and arithmetic, &c. The wages are
fixed for the parifh fchools by the heritors and feffion, at 1 s.
6d. per quaiter for children, half-a-crown for writing and a-
rithmetic, and 3s. for Latin per quarter, befides what they
voluntarily give as a new-year's-gift. It is evident that the
encouragement is too low ; perhaps it would be the intereft
of Government that they fhould have fome little addition of
falary given to them ; let the wages remain as low as poffible, to induce the people to fend their children to fchool ;
from this circumftance of the want of encouragement, and
likewife from being in the neighbourhood of an Univerfity,
from whence ftudents come to be our fchoolmafters, who
have farther profpects, there have been no lefs than thirteen
fchool-mafters in the parifh fchool, fince the year 1759.
Upon the whole, I would ftyle the common education of
Scotland, partly religious, and partly philofophical ; It would
not be our intereft to fee it violently broken in upon ; it is
this mode of education which gives the Scotch nation fuch an
attachment to fpeculation in religion ; it is only following
out what they have been taught in the early period of their
lives.

lives. There are in this pariſh, three ſtudents of divinity, one preacher and two gown ſtudents *.

Character, Morals, Genius, &c.—The inhabitants of this diſtrict, during the laſt, and early part of this century, were ſomewhat conſpicuous for drinking and fighting with their neighbours : If any perſon in this pariſh, however mean his ſituation, had received an injury or affront from an inhabitant of another pariſh ; his neighbours conſidered themſelves bound to ſupport him, and to avenge his quarrel : ſuch conduct, however, ſeems to have proceeded more from pride and

* The peculiar cuſtoms of this pariſh are faſt wearing out. It was cuſ-tomary, till within theſe few years, when any head of a family died, to invite the whole pariſh : They were ſerved on boards in the barn, where a prayer was pronounced before and after the ſervice, which duty was moſt religiouſ-ly obſerved : The entertainment confiſted of the following parts : *Firſt*, there there was a drink of ale, then a dram, then a piece of ſhort bread, then another dram of ſome other ſpecies of liquor, then a piece of currant-bread, and a third dram, either of ſpirits or wine, which was followed by loaves and cheeſe, pipes and tobacco : This was the old funeral entertainment in the pariſh of Campſie, and was ſtiled their ſervice ; and ſometimes this was repeated, and was then ſtiled a double ſervice ; and it was ſure of being repeated at the dredgy. A funeral coſt, at leaſt, a hundred pounds Scots, to any family who followed the old courſe. The moſt active young man was pointed out to the office of ſerver ; and in thoſe days, while the manners were ſimple, and at the ſame time ſerious, it was no ſmall honour to be a ſerver at a burial. However diſtant any part of the pariſh was from the place of interment, it was cuſtomary for the attendants to carry the corpſe on hand ſpokes. The mode of invitation to the entertainment, was by ſome ſpecial meſſenger ; which was ſtiled bidding to the burial, the form being nearly in the following words : You are deſired to come to ſuch a one's burial to morrow, againſt ten hours. No perſon was invited by letter : and though invited againſt ten of the clock, the corpſe was never interred till the evening ; time not being ſo much valued in thoſe days. It was cuſtomary for them to have at leaſt two lyke-wakes (the corpſe being kept two nights before the interment) where the young neighbours watched the corpſe, being merry or ſorrowful, according to the ſituation or rank of the deceaſed.

and ruftic gallantry, than from a fettled malevolence of difpofition. The more improved manners, and a more general
intercourfe with fociety, have, in a great meafure, done away
this turbulent difpofition ; ftill the natives of Campfie may be
confidered as a keen tempered people, by no means averfe to
expofe themfelves to bodily danger at any time : the young
people have no objection to a military life, being fond of novelty and adventure ; during the prefent war, no lefs than 28
have enlifted in the land fervice, and feven have entered on
board the navy ; thefe remarks chiefly apply to the lower clafs
of people. The gentry, for at leaft thefe 40 years, have been
remarkable for their fobriety, decent behaviour, and œcono-
mical habits ; of courfe, they are all in profperous circumftances ; rigid œconomy was not the virtue of their forefathers *.

Eminent

* About ten years ago, the fudden tranfition from ftrict to loofe manners
was felt very remarkably in this parifh ; a number of wandering people, from
different parts of the kingdom, having fettled amongft us at the different
printfields :—people, to fay no worfe of them, not over attentive to regularity of conduct ; thefe perfons, however, have now for the moft part, left the
place. The more fober and induftrious have been retained ; the younger part
of the workmen being now natives of the parifh, and more immediately under the eye of their parents and relations—I confider therefore the morals of
the manufacturing part of the community, as more regular than they were e-
ven five years ago.

The people of Campfie cannot be faid to be of a litigious difpofition : It is
true, from their apparent keennefs, you would be apt to imagine that they
fhould be conftantly engaged in lawfuits.—The reverfe is the cafe : The high.
er born and better informed clafs of people, ftudioufly avoid litigation. A.
mongft the other defcription of the inhabitants, much threatening, and a few
hafty words, generally terminate the difpute. Neither writer nor meffenger
at arms refide in the parifh ; at the fame time, confidering the number of the
tranfactions which muft inevitably take place in a rich and populous diftrict,
(even though no law-fuit intervenes) a great deal of bufinefs is afforded to
both profeffions. Although I could not take upon me to fay that the inhabi.
tants

Eminent Men.—This pariſh has produced no eminent men whoſe hiſtory hath arreſted the attention of world, except Mr Bell of Antermony, a gentleman well known to the learned, on account of his travels to China and Perſia ; this gentleman poſſeſſed an uncommon faculty for ſpeaking the modern languages of Europe ; nor was he leſs remarkable for an amiable ſimplicity of manners, in private life, and the moſt ſacred regard to truth in all he ſaid or did. He was a native of Campſie, having inherited a conſiderable paternal eſtate : he died in the 1780, at the venerable age of 89.

Prices of Proviſions and Labour.—Proviſions of every ſort in this pariſh are regulated by the Glaſgow prices ; the common people have ſuch an inveterate cuſtom of carrying their eggs, poultry, and butter, to town, that we could often buy theſe articles cheaper at the croſs of Glaſgow than in the pariſh of Campſie. I have ſubjoined a table of the prices of proviſions and of labour, for the year 1794.

	L.	s.	d.
Ducks per pair	0	3	0
Hens per pair	0	3	4
Eggs per dozen, for four months 8d ; for eight months, 6d.	0	0	6
Chickens per pair, ready for the ſpit	0	1	4
Butter per Tron lb. 9d ; during two months 11d.	0	0	9
Butter-milk per Scotch pint	0	0	$\frac{1}{2}$
Potatoes per peck, corn meaſure	0	0	$4\frac{1}{2}$

Beſt

tants of this diſtrict are fond of literary purſuits, it would be doing them injuſtice, if 1 did not ſay they were people of capacity and genius; at the ſame time, the tendency of their mind is rather towards an active than a contemplative life.

	L.	s.	d.
Beſt beef per lb. Tron weight, at an average	0	0	6
Ditto ditto in the ſpring months from 7d. to 8d.			
Lamb per quarter, at an average in the ſeaſon	0	1	8
Fed veal no fixed price			
Oat meal, per peck, at an average theſe two years	0	1	2½
Barley at an average per boll - - -	0	18	6
Straw per thrave for thatching - -	0	3	6
Cheeſe of ſkimmed milk per ſtone -	0	4	6
Tarry-wool per ſtone - - -	0	7	0
White-wool per ſtone - -	0	10	0

Milk new milked per mutchkin ½, and ſkimmed, at ½ per choppin.

It will appear, that living of all ſorts is equally dear with any of the great towns in the kingdom ; and, I believe, from the following table, that labour will appear equally high.

	L.	s.	d.
Wages of a man ſervant per half year with board, &c.	5	0	0
Wages of a woman per half year, including ditto,	2	10	0
A common labourer per day, 1s. 4d. in ſummer; in winter 1s. 2d.—average,	0	1	3
Taylor, beſides board per day, -	0	0	10
Servants at the printfields per day, during the whole year - - - -	0	1	0
Miln-wright, - - - -	0	1	8
Maſon, per day, -	0	1	10
Horſe and cart per day, -	0	3	6
Digging ground, building dykes and ditching, is done at ſo much per piece, equally high with any part of Scotland,			
Women ſpin wool per day, with victuals,	0	0	4
Linen yarn ſpun out of the houſe per ſpindle,	0	1	6
Digging potatoes per peck, corn meaſure,	0	0	0½

Bark

	L.	s.	d.
Bark-peelers per day,	0	0	10

The hire of women per day is regulated by the prices given at the printfield.

Appearance of the Inhabitants, and Diseases.—The inhabitants of this district may be considered as uncommonly healthy ; they are a clean limbed, well made people, rather lean of flesh, in general from five feet seven to six feet high ; one half of the young men being above five feet ten, scarcely any above six feet : There are a few who live to a very great age ; although, in general, the heads of families live to the age of seventy ; which circumstance would induce me to style the place more healthy than if we found extraordinary instances of longevity : there is one circumstance to be taken notice of, which is, the uncommon number of accidental deaths, being somewhat more than two per annum ; during the last ten years there were no fewer than twenty three. †

A TABLE, *pointing out the manner of their deaths.*

† Killed in a coal pit by the choak damp, July 1783,	3
Killed in a coal pit February 1785, by damp,	5
Killed by falling down a coal pit,	3
Killed by the stroke of a horse,	1
Killed by the machinery of the different milns,	3
Killed in a quary,	1
Killed by a falling of a tree when cut down,	1
Killed by a the fall from a bridge,	1
Killed by the storms when travelling through Campsie Fells,	2
Drowned,	3

Of course, one eighteenth part of the deaths in this parish may be styled accidental ; and if we were to carry back the calculation for thirty years, there would be found the same proportion

Antiquities.

Antiquities.—There are few in this diſtrict which merit
deſcription, except two Caledonian Forts ; and even theſe
ſcarcely arreſt the attention, unleſs ſo far as they prove that
the Caledonians choſe to occupy places of ſtrength directly
oppoſite to the Roman wall, no doubt with the deſign of
watching the motions of the legionaries.—Theſe mounds
are perfectly circular, with regular foſſes ; the one is ſtyled
the *Meickle Reive,* in the language of the country, and is a-
bout a hundred yards in diameter : The other is ſtyled the
Maiden Caſtle, about twenty yards diameter : They are both
ſituated at the foot of the Campſie Fells, to which the natives could eaſily fly, if attacked ; and ly due North, at the
diſtance of two computed miles, from the peel of Kirkintilloch, ſaid be be one of the chief Roman ſtations on the wall.

There have been ſeveral urns found in the pariſh, containing aſhes and burnt bones ; the urns were about five inches
in depth, and fifteen in diameter ; made of courſe clay, apparently baſked in the ſun ; a ſpecies of freize work encircles
the lower edge ; they have been found in cairns, generally
placed between two flags.

It may not be improper to mention, that Campſie, (before
the disjunction and annexation took place,) extended for
eleven Engliſh miles along the Roman wall ; and, of courſe,
many ſkirmiſhes muſt have taken place in this ſtrath, betwixt
the legionaries and Caledonians : after a particular examination of the country, I have not the ſmalleſt doubt, but that
the ſecurity of this Roman barrier, depended more upon the
almoſt impaſſable ſwamp formed on the North ſide, than on
the ſtrength of its forts ; even at this day, it would be no difficult matter to lay the whole valley under water from Bonny, to Balmully bridge, where Graham's dyke croſſes the river Kelvin : And the names of the different farms in Campſie,

ſie, ſuch as Inchwood, Inchterf, Inchbreak, and Inchbelly, evidently point out, that they were once ſurrounded by water: Inch, it is ſaid in the Gaelic language, ſignifies an iſland: thus, the Caledonians would find it impoſſible to approach the wall on foot; and it is preſumed, that the moraſs was not ſufficiently covered by water, to permit them to croſs it in boats. Many people, unaquainted with the ſituation of the country, have expreſſed ſurpriſe that the Caledonians were ſo ignorant of the art of war, as to be unable, for ſo long a time, to penetrate through Antoninus's wall; the truth is, it could not be attacked, but at the extremities. The natives found it eaſier to paſs over the Friths of Forth and Clyde, than to get acroſs the almoſt impaſſable ſwamp oppoſite to Graham's Dyke; ſo that when any incurſions were made into the Roman province, it is ſcarcely poſſible to conceive that theſe inroads could take place from that quarter which is now known by the name of the pariſh of Campſie; from the top of the Barrhill, where there was a conſiderable Roman Fort, any perſon at this day, taking a view of the country, will concur in the above opinion.

About five years ago, a conſiderable quantity of ſilver coin, chiefly of the coinage of Elizabeth, James and Charles I, mixt with a number of Daniſh and Dutch pieces, were found by one of the *portioners* of the lands of Birdſton, when digging a ditch through a moraſs; they were ſuppoſed to have been hid in the moraſs, about the time when the battle of Kilſyth was fought betwixt Montroſe and the Covenanters; the marauding parties of Montroſe's army having ſtretched as far Weſt as Birdſton, the inhabitants, flying from their depredations, muſt have hid this treaſure, and have forgot where it was depoſited, when they came afterwards to ſearch for it.

Miſcellaneous

Miscellaneous Observations.—It may be here proper to mention a remarkable fact, which marks very much the turbulence of the times, and the impotence of the laws, fo late as they ear 1744. The father of the prefent minifter of Campfie paid *black mail* to M'Grigor of Glengyle, in order to prevent depredations being made upon his property ; M'Grigor engaging, upon his part, to fecure him from fuffering by any *hardfhip*, as it was termed ; and he faithfully fulfilled the contract ; engaging to pay for all fheep which were carried away, if abone the number feven, which he ftyled *lifting* ; if below feven, he only confidered it as a piking ; and for the honour of this warden of the Highland march, Mr John Lapflie having got fifteen fheep lifted in the commencement of the year 1745, Mr M'Grigor actually had taken meafures to have their value reftored, when the rebellion broke out, and put an end to any further payment of *black mail*, and likewife to Mr M'Grigor's felf created wardenfhip of the Highland borders.

The laft inftance in this diftrict of a Baron of Regality exercifing the jurifdiction of pit and gallows over his dependents, is faid to have been exercifed by the Vifcount of Kilfyth, in the 1793 ; having condemned one of his own fervants to be hanged for ftealing filver plate from the houfe of Bancloich : the fellow was executed upon a hill on the barony of Bancloich, ftyled the Gallow-hill ; a part of the gibbet was lately found lying in a fwamp, adjoining to this field of blood.

Lunardi, an Italian, the celebrated aeronaut, alighted from one of his aerial excurfions in Campfie ; having afcended in a balloon from St Andrew's church yard, in the city of Glafgow, upon the 5th of December 1785. At two o'clock in the afternoon, he defcended in this parifh, at twenty minutes

past

paſt two, the diſtance being about ten miles ; the ſpot where the baloon firſt touched the ground was upon the property of Sir Archibald Edmonſton, Baronet, of Duntreath, on the farm of Eaſter Muckcroft.

Although this pariſh has been always conſpicuous for its attachment to its ſovereign ; whether of the Stewart family, as in the laſt century, or of the Hanoverian family, as in the preſent century ; having raiſed a militia both in the years 1715 and 1745,—ſtill I cannot help taking notice, in this Statiſtical Account of a remarkable faĉt relative to the conduĉt of ſome of the inhabitants of this diſtriĉt, which one would almoſt ſay contradiĉts the opinion of their loyalty. In the midſt of the moſt profound peace, and, I may ſay, of the moſt unparalelled proſperity ; all at once, as it were by inchantment, the operative part of this community conceived themſelves to be groaning under the moſt abjeĉt ſlavery. They immediately aſſociated themſelves under the appellation of the Friends of the People : The firſt ſociety was conſtituted at the Milton of Campſie, I think, upon Thurſday the 8th of November 1792 ; the ſecond was conſtituted at New Birbiſton of Campſie, the Saturday thereafter : Two other ſocieties were attempted to be formed in other parts of the pariſh : I believe, however, they did not ſucceed : The two former met often, kept books, ſubſcribed ſmall ſums of money for purchaſing political pamphlets, and ſent delegates to the different Conventions met at Edinburgh. Concerning the impropriety of ſuch ſocieties, the laws of our country hath already given ample teſtimony. It may not be improper, however, in the Statiſtical Account of this pariſh, to give ſome deſcription of the people which compoſed theſe ſocieties : They were chiefly formed from amongſt the journeymen and apprentices at the different print-fields, and a few operative weavers in the village of New Birbiſton, moſtly

lads

lads from 17 years of age to 30 : There might be amongſt them a few half educated people, whoſe vanity conſiſted in raiſing the aſtoniſhment of their more ignorant companions, by a detail of political grievances, which had never entered into the hearts of the other to conceive ; various cauſes co-o-perated to render Campſie a proper hot-bed for ſuch folly.

In the *firſt* place, a conſiderable degree of licentiouſneſs had begun to prevail in this diſtrict, owing to high wages ; and as the influx of ſuch wealth had been rather ſudden, due ſubordination of rank was almoſt totally forgot. In the *ſecond* place, a Relief meeting, about 10 years ago, being e-rected in this pariſh, which had drawn off a conſiderable num-ber of people from the Eſtabliſhment, and rendered them, in ſome meaſure, hoſtile to the the powers that be ; and I am doubtful but the ſpirit of innovation was encouraged in a certain degree, by their public teachers, with a view to in-creaſe the adherents to their own tabernacle. In the *third* place, Mr Muir, advocate, the unfortunate gentleman who was tried for ſedition, having ſome connexions, and being well acquainted in the place, was naturally induced to try the power of his eloquence upon the inhabitants ; and he ſucceed-ed. If to theſe cauſes we add the particular circumſtance of the character of young people at the different printfields ; men, who have abundance of time in the evenings to cabal together; men, too, from their profeſſion, rather given to wan-dering, and fond of novelty, and ſomewhat naturally addic-ted to form aſſociations againſt their maſter's authority ; we will not be ſurpriſed that Campſie ſhould be ſo often men-tioned as friendly to theſe Jacobin ſocieties.

Nevertheleſs, I am entitled to ſay, that the farmers and the inhabitants in general, (there being no fewer than 2527 people in the pariſh,) were remarkable for their loyalty, and attatchment to Government : They very early formed themfelves

ſelves into conſtitutional ſocieties, for the defence of Government, and publiſhed reſolutions. Notwithſtanding all the buſtle which was occaſioned by their folly, the different Jacobin ſoceities in this pariſh altogether, never contained above ſixty perſons.

Relative Situation of the Pariſh.—If we compare the ſituation of the inhabitants this year with certain periods, either in the beginning or middle of this century, it will appear remarkably improved. I have ſubjoined a table, containing the moſt remarkable facts, relative to pariſh œconomics, taken at four different periods: The two firſt I cannot ſpeak of from my own obſervations; at the ſame time, from the opportunities I have had of being made acquainted with them, as a native of this pariſh, I can affirm that the facts are fairly ſtated.

Year 1714.

1ſt, Only three cows ſaid to have been killed for winter beef in the whole pariſh, the gentry excepted.

2d, The wages of a man-ſervant for half-a-year, 9l. Scots; ſome of the beſt get 12l. Scots; a woman-ſervant, 6l. Scots for half-a-year.

3d, No wheaten bread eat in the pariſh.

4th, No incloſure whatever in the pariſh, except about gentlemen's gardens or woods.

5th, No cart or chaiſe; the gentry rode to church on horſeback.

6th, All broad ploughs, the horſes yoked abreaſt.

7th, The men wore bonnets and plaids, and plaiding waiſtcoats, and plaiding hoſe; no Engliſh cloth whatever was worn by the inhabitants, the gentry excepted.

Year

Year 1744.

1*st*, The better fort of farmers joined and got a cow for a winter mart, betwixt two of them; the price then being thirty five or forty fhillings only for a fat cow.

2*d*, No chaife was as yet kept in the parifh; fome few carts, but thefe were only ufed to carry out manure in the fpring; the wheels were not fhod with iron; and the moment the manure was carried out, thefe timber wheels were taken down till next fpring.

3*d*, Perhaps about five or fix inclofures were made in the parifh: it muft be owned, though few, they were moft fubftantially built; they remain entire and firm to this day.

4*th*, No wheaten bread, no Englifh cloth ufed by the inhabitants.

5*th*, A man fervant's wages were from thirty fhillings to two pounds per half year; a woman's, from nine pound Scots to one pound Sterling; fervants in this period uniformly got a pair of hofe and fhoes befides their fee.

6*th*, No potatoes, carrots, or turnips, &c. were ufed by the inhabitants, only a few kail were planted in their yards, for the pot.

Year 1759.

1*st*, Carts were become more numerous, there being then about twenty in the parifh, their wheels fhod with iron.

2*d*, The broad plough ftill continued in many places, though, in general, the horfes were now yoked, two and two; ftill there were no fanners for the milns or barns, the farmers being obliged to winnow the corn in the fields.

3*d*, A man-fervant came now to receive fifty fhillings and three pounds Sterling per half year; and a woman twenty five or thirty fhillings only per half year.

4*th*, There were now two wheeled chaifes in the parifh; and Englifh cloth began to be worn occafionally by the bet-

ter

ter ſort of people, along with worſted ſtockings, and buckles in their ſhoes.

5*tb*, Potatoes ſtill were only cultivated in *lazy* beds.

6*th*, Very decent farmers thought it neceſſary to have ſome part of a fat cow or a few ſheep ſalted up for winter ſtore.

7*th*, By the leaſes granted by the proprietors of land at this time, the tenants were taken bound to incloſe ſome part of the farm ; ſtill there was no ſown graſs in the pariſh, and the cattle grazed promiſcouſly in the winter ſeaſon.

8*th*, There were no clocks in the pariſh, except in the houſes of the gentry and principal inhabitants.

Year 1794.

1*ſt*, There are nearly two hundred carts in the pariſh, per-fectly equipped for any draught.

2*d*, There are four poſt-chaiſes, and three coaches, and one two wheeled chaiſe, kept by the gentry, in the proper ſtyle.

3*d*, The wages of a man-ſervant is betwixt five pounds and ſix pounds per half year ; and a woman's from two to three pounds ditto.

4*th*, Potatoes is now univerſally uſed by all ranks of peo-ple, for at leaſt ſix months in the year.

5*th*, Wheaten bread is now univerſally uſed by every de-ſcription of people ; there being no leſs than two bakers ſta-tionary in the pariſh, beſides ſome hundred pounds value of wheaten bread brought annually from Kirkintilloch and Glaſ-gow.

6*th* There have been near three hundred fat cows killed annually about the Martinmaſs time for winter proviſion ; beſides the mutton, beef, and lamb, killed through the ſeaſon, by two butchers reſiding in the pariſh.

7th, Every lad now dreffes in Englifh cloaths and fancy vefls, with thread or cotton ftockings ; and every girl in cotton ftuff, black filk cloaks and fancy bonnets.

8th, The quantity of liquor drunk in the feventeen public houfes in this parifh muft be very great indeed ; as, I have been told that four and five pounds, at a *reckoning*, have been collected from a company of journeymen and apprentices on a pay night.

9th, The houfes of every decent inhabitant of this parifh, confift at leaft of a kitchen and one room, generally two rooms, ceiled above, and often laid with deal floors, with elegant glafs windows ; and I believe, few of the tradefmen fit down to dinner without flefh meat on the table, and malt liquor to drink : Such is the relative fituation of a parifh in the year 1794, when fome defigning people ufed every effort to convince them, that they were poor, and miferable, and *enflaved*.

Advantages and Disadvantages.—The advantages of this parifh have been confidered as of a very fuperior kind : The foil is naturally dry ; the ftreams of water for bleaching and driving machinery are numerous ; the quantity of coal and lime is inexhauftible ; it is completely interfected by excellent roads ; and, it is believed, that it is able to fupply itfelf with all the neceffaries of life ; and, confidering the number of ftrangers which take up their refidence amongft us, we are led to believe, that few places are more comfortable to the inferior clafs of people ; Glafgow affording a ready market for the produce both of their farms and their induftry.

On the other hand, it may be confidered as one of the deareft places in Scotland for all forts of living, and particularly fo for thofe who live upon fixed incomes ; and I am likewife inclined

inclined to believe, from the turn that the young people have
taken to manufactures, that farmers have rather found it difficult to procure ſervants and labourers for the purpoſes of
cultivating the land : Perhaps it will be the intereſt both of the
landlords and the farmers, to fall upon ſome mode of management which may counteract this growing evil.

PARISH OF DENNY.

(COUNTY OF STIRLING.)

By the Rev. MR. THOMAS FERGUS.

Name, Situation, &c.

THE origin of the name of Denny is unknown.————The pariſh lies in the county and preſbytery of Stirling, and fynod of Perth and Stirling.—It is about 4 miles in length, and 2¼ in breadth.—The ſoil, about the town, or village of Denny, and indeed throughout the greater part of the pariſh, is dry and ſandy; but in ſome places, it is wet, and has a good deal of clay in it.—The air is reckoned pure and healthy, and many of the people attain a good old age. Some, however, are much troubled with rheumatic complaints; and fevers fre- quently prevail, and are often fatal.

Proprietors, Agriculture, &c.—— A fourth part of the pa- riſh belongs to one great proprietor, and another has a confi- derable ſhare of it. The reſt is the property of about 100 ſmaller heritors, feuers, or portioners; many of whom culti- vate their own lands.—— Of late years, the farmers make uſe of a good deal of lime, which they chiefly bring from the pa- riſh of Cumbernauld, and ſome from the pariſh of Dunipace.
—Oats

—Oats are the grain ufually fown, with fome bear and peafe, but no wheat. A good many potatoes, a quantity of flax, and fome clover and rye-grafs, are alfo raifed.

Population.———The population of the parifh of Denny, in 1755, as returned to Dr Webfter, was 1392 fouls. The number is now reckoned about 1400. There are, at an average, 60 births, 20 burials, and more than 12 marriages each year.

Church, &c.—The Crown is patron.——The ftipend is 80 bolls in meal, and L. 38 fterling, in money. The church, manfe, and offices, are not in good repair.—After the Seceffion began, more than one half of the inhabitants, at that time, became Seceders of the Antiburgher perfuafion ; and they have had, for upwards of 40 years, a meeting-houfe, at Loan-head, about 2 miles fouth from Denny. More than a third part of the people are ftill Seceders, of one denomination or another. A few are Cameronians. There are no Papifts nor Epifcopalians.

Mifcellaneous Obfervations.—There are no begging poor, belonging to the parifh, but there are a number of houfe-keepers in indigent circumftances, who receive occafional fupplies from the collections, made at the church-doors, on Sunday.— The men are almoft all engaged in hufbandry, and the women generally in fpinning.———A number of boys and girls are employed at a print-field, and cotton manufactory, in the neighbouring parifh of Dunipace, A large tract of land here, is called Temple-Denny, which formerly belonged, it is faid, to the Knights Templars, fo famous for their crufades againft the Saracens.———The roads, through this diftrict, in general, are in good repair.—There is abundance of ftone for

building;

building ; and coals are got in quantities, ſufficient not only to ſupply the inhabitants, but alſo a good part of the neigh-bourhood.————The Carron, which divides this pariſh from that of Dunipace, furniſhes us with ſome trout.——The great canal, between the Forth and the Clyde, which runs along the ſouthern part of the pariſh, is alſo, in many reſpects, of great benefit to the people.

PARISH OF DRYMEN.

(County of Stirling—Presbytery of Dumbarton—Synod of Glasgow and Ayr.)

By the Rev. Mr. DUNCAN MACFARLAN,
Minister of that Parish.

Origin of the Name.

THE name, *Drumen*, or, as it is more commonly written, *Drymen*, is obviously derived from the Celtic word, *Druim*, corresponding to the Latin *Dorsum*, a *ridge* or *eminence*. It is peculiarly descriptive of the appearance of considerable part of the parish, which is frequently intersected by deep ravines, or water courses, with rising grounds between them. The same word is also to be met with, as a component part in the names of many places, as *Drumquhastle, Drumdash, Drumliagart, &c.* The etymology of these, and almost all the other names in the parish, is purely Celtic.

Extent.

Extent.—It is extremely difficult to give an accurate idea of the fituation of this parifh, as it is of great extent, and its outlines are exceedingly irregular. The utmoft length of the inhabited part is about 15 miles ; but the moors extend confiderably farther. The greateft breadth is about 9 miles.

Surface, Rivers and Fifh.—In fome places, the country is rugged and mountainous ; in others, flat and level ; but, for the moft part, it is an irregular flope, between the high moors and the rivers, cut up by a great number of fmall, but rapid ftreams. The principal rivers, are, the Duchray, the Forth, and the Enrick. The Duchray is one of the moft confiderable branches of the Forth, and divides this parifh, for fome miles, from that of Aberfoil. Near the church of Aberfoil, it joins another confiderable ftream ; and the united river is then known by the name of Forth. Previous to their confluence, the parifh of Drymen leaves them at a confiderable diftance ; but afterwards joins the Forth, near Gartmore, about 5 miles to the S. E., where the winding courfe of that river, for fome miles, divides it from that of Port. The Enrick takes its rife in the hills of Dundaff, about 15 miles from Drymen, to the eaftward. It feparates this parifh from that of Killearn, and afterwards runs through it for about 2 miles. It then forms the boundary between this and the neighbouring parifh of Kilmaronock ; and, about 4 miles farther on, difcharges itfelf into Lochlomond. Thefe rivers abound in trouts, par, perch, pike, eels and flounders, with fome falmon.

Soil.—In fuch an extent, there muft neceffarily be a great diverfity of foil. The banks of the Forth are, in general, covered with a deep mofs ; but, where that is removed, the induftry of the farmer is rewarded, by a very rich clay, pro-

ducing

ducing large crops of grain. The lands near Enrick are, in general, light, dry, and gravelly, a foil by no means unfavourable in a moiſt climate. By far the moſt common foil in the pariſh is poor, wet, and tilly, extremely improper for cultivation.

Climate, Fuel, Cultivation, Produce, &c.—The progreſs of agriculture here has been much retarded, by a variety of unfavourable circumſtances, the chief of which are the climate and local fituation. The weather, as might be expected in the vicinity of high mountains, and at no great diſtance from the weſt coaſt, is in general very wet; which renders the feed time and harveſt exceedingly precarious. But the principal diſadvantage is the diſtance from markets and manure. The neareſt market town is Dumbarton, about 11 miles from any part of this pariſh; and next to it Glaſgow, which is at leaſt 18.—There is fome limeſtone to be had in the neighbourhood, but of an indifferent quality. It is but little uſed, as the country affords no proper fuel for burning it. The farmers, in general, bring their lime from Kilpatrick, at the diſtance of 12 or 13 miles. Coals, which of late have been pretty much uſed, are brought from the fame place. Peats and turfs are ſtill, however, the moſt common fuel; but as in moſt parts of the pariſh, they are brought from a diſtance of feveral miles, and as they require an uncommon degree of attention in cutting and drying, they are nearly as expenſive as coals.—The people, in general, have no idea of reſting their land; but plow, without intermiſſion, for many fucceſſive years, to the great detriment of their farms. The common crops are oats and barley. The barley is chiefly fold to diſtillers; and the average price is from 16s. to 18s. per boll. Oat meal fells at from 14s. to 16s. per boll.

Village,

Village, &c.—There is only 1 village in the parifh, which lies near the church. The inhabitants are moftly tradefmen and day labourers, who depend for employment upon the neighbouring country, excepting a few weavers, who work for the manufacturers of Glafgow. There are Diffenters of various denominations; but none of them have a place of worfhip within the bounds of the parifh. A confiderable number fpeak the Gaelic language; and there are 3 or 4 who do not underftand Englifh.

Population.—Since the year 1756, the population of this parifh has greatly decreafed. This decreafe is partly owing to the prevalence of large farms. In feveral parts of the parifh, 1 family now occupies what was formerly in the hands of 7 or 8. Another caufe of the diminution is to be found in the progrefs of manufactures. Though none of thefe have as yet been eftablifhed in this parifh, they are carried on, at no great diftance, to a very confiderable extent. The bleachfields and printfields upon the river Leven, near Dumbarton, are perhaps the moft extenfive in Scotland : and fome large cotton mills have been lately erected in the neighbouring parifh of Balfron. Thefe give employment to a great number of hands, at wages fo high *, that the farmers find it almoft impoffible to procure fervants at any expence.

STAT-

* About 20 years ago, the wages of a man fervant were about 4l. a year ; they are now about 10l., and frequently a good deal higher. The wages of female fervants have increafed in an equal proportion. At that period, day labourers received 8d. or 10d. a day. They can feldom be got now under 1s. 6d. As the prices of grain, and the other productions of the country, have rifen very little, the natural confequence is, that all the lands are thrown into pafture, in which ftate they require fewer hands, and can be managed at lefs expence.

STATISTICAL TABLE of the Pariſh of DRYMEN.

Population as returned to Dr. Webſter, in 1755, - - - - 2789
Ditto, in April 1792, - - - - - - - 1607

Decreaſe, - - 1182

Number of families in the vil- lage, - - - 40	Number of weavers, - - 60
—————— inhabitants in ditto, 215	—————— tailors, - - 6
—————— reſiding heritors, 20	—————— ſhoemakers, - 15
—————— non-reſident ditto, 20	—————— wrights, - - 16
—————— clergymen, - 1	—————— inn-keepers, - 3
—————— diſſenters, about - 400	—————— ale-ſellers, - 6
—————— members of the eſta- bliſhed church, - 1207	—————— corn mills, - - 6
	—————— flax ditto, - - 3

Annual Average of Births and Marriages * in the Pariſh of Drymen.*

	Births.	Mar.
From 1ſt January 1743, to 1ſt January 1753, - -	46	15
From ditto 1753, to ditto 1763, - - - -	49	16
From ditto 1763, to ditto 1773, - - - -	52	12
From ditto 1773, to ditto 1783, - - - -	30	11
From ditto 1783, to ditto 1792, - - - -	32	10

Heritors

* *The above are carefully extracted from the parochial records ; but as they appear to have been kept with very little attention, during a conſiderable part of the period, their accuracy cannot be poſitively depended upon. Till very lately, no regiſter of deaths was kept.*

Heritors and Rent.—There are 40 heritors in the parish, of whom about one half reside. The Duke of Montrose, and Mr. Graham of Gartmore, are the principal proprietors. The valued rent in the cefs books is 5069l. 10s. Scotch.

Church.—The church is situated near the S. W. extremity of the parish, about half a mile from the river Enrick. It was built about 20 years ago, and is a very commodious and substantial edifice. There are two other places of worship in the parish, each about 6 miles distant, where the clergyman officiates twice a year. The present incumbent was settled in February 1792.

Poor.—There are 38 poor upon the roll at present, many of whom are altogether incapable of doing any thing for their own support. The public funds are entirely inadequate to their maintenance, seldom exceeding 20 l. per annum. As no affessment for their relief has been laid upon the heritors, they must depend, in a great measure, upon private benefactions; and, in this respect, the truly necessitous are much injured by the great number of vagrant beggars, who, through some egregious defect in our police, are permitted to infest the country, without any restraint or interruption.

Diseases and Longevity.—The climate, though moist, is by no means unhealthy. The most common diseases, are nervous fevers, and complaints in the stomach and bowels. There are few remarkable instances of longevity in this parish. The oldest persons now living, have only completed their 87th year. In one family, there are four persons at present alive, whose ages, taken together, make 324 years.

Eminent

Eminent Men.—This pariſh is ſaid to have been the birth place, and at times the reſidence of the famous NAPIER of MERCHISTON, the celebrated inventor of the Logarithms.

Antiquities.—The only mark of antiquity, now to be diſcerned, is a large earthen mound, at a place called *Caſhlie,* near which, it is ſaid, the veſtiges of a Roman Camp were formerly to be ſeen, though now no traces of it are to be found.

PARISH OF FALKIRK,

(County of Stirling, Synod of Lothian and Tweeddale, Presbytery of Linlithgow),

By James Wilson, M. A. *Minister of the Parish.*

Boundaries, and general Description.

THE parish of Falkirk is ·between 7 and 8 miles in
length from E. to W. and in some parts more than
4 miles in breadth. It is bounded on the E. by the frith
of Forth and the parish of Polmont; on the S. by the parishes of Polmont and Slamannan; on the W. by Cumbernauld and Denny; and on the N. by the river Carron,
which separates it from the united parishes of Larbert and
Dunipace. ˙ By the changes which the course of this river
has undergone, a few houses belonging to this parish are
now on the Larbert side; and a few, which are connected
with that parish, are on the Falkirk side of the river.

From

From a reference to the parish of Falkirk, in an action with respect to the patronage of the church and parish of Oldhamstocks, in the presbytery of Dunbar, which was depending in the year 1748 between the King and Mr Hay of Lawfield, it appears that the parishes of Denny, Slamannan, Muiravonside, and Polmont, constituted formerly parts of the parsonage of Falkirk. The three first of these parishes must have been very early separated from Falkirk; but it was not till the year 1724 that Polmont was formed into a parish. The minister of Polmont has not only stipend from his own parish, but also from those of Falkirk and Denny.

The estate of Callander having been confiscated immediately after the commotion in the year 1715, it was sold about the year 1720; and such tithes as were not conveyed with the estate, were disposed of by the commissioners and trustees of the forfeited estates in Scotland to Mr Hamilton of Dichmond, under this express stipulation, that they should be subject to the stipend of a minister for the new parish, which was to be taken off the parish of Falkirk. This circumstance explains by what means it happened that stipend is paid both out of this parish and Denny to the minister of Polmont.

Falkirk is situated on the north road between Edinburgh and Glasgow, and it is nearly at an equal distance from both. The road to Stirling and the North Highlands also passes through this town. Falkirk was once denominated *Ecclesbrae*, that is, the Church on the Brow; and the name is truly descriptive of the situation, for the town stands on an eminence, which has a declivity on every side. In the Gaelic language it is called an *Eglais bhris*, but more commonly an *Eglais bhrec*. The former of these phrases signifies the Broken Church, which some think is not improperly translated Falkirk, that is, the Fallen Church. Certain

tain it is, that the church of Falkirk, as it now ftands, has not all been built at the fame time. In the year 1166, it was given * to the monaftery of Holyroodhoufe by the Bifhop of St Andrew's; and as the parifhes belonging to thefe religious foundations were often not properly attended to with refpect to religious inftruction and accommodation, fo it is not improbable that the church of this parifh might have been permitted to fall into ruin, and thence the name under confideration might have taken its rife.

An Eglais bhrec, the latter of the Gaelic defignations which I mentioned, fignifies the Spotted Church. To this name Buchanan, who underftood the Gaelic language, gives his fupport, for in his Hiftory of Scotland he calls Falkirk, " Varium Sacellum." It is fuppofed by fome, that it got that defignation from the party-coloured appearance of the ftones in the building.

As the wall of Antoninus, which will afterwards be defcribed, paffed very near the church, and where a part of the town is built, fome are of opinion, that the prefent name of this place is derived from *Vallum* and *Kirk*, which by an eafy tranfition, became Falkirk, thereby fignifying the Church upon the Wall.

The greater part of this parifh is inclofed and fubdivided, as well as enriched by trees, villas, and gentlemens feats. The numerous fine trees which are in Callander park and its neighbourhood, together with the wood belonging to the fame place, add much to the pleafantnefs of the town of Falkirk; as it is fituated in the immediate vicinity of thefe rural and enlivening objects. From the manfe, and other places on the north fide of the town, the profpect is delightful, and comprehends a fertile and well-cultivated country of 12 or 14 miles fquare, which is bounded by the

Ochil-

---

* Nimmo's Hiftory of Stirlingfhire, page 136.

Ochil-hills and elevated fituations in the counties of Stirling, Fife, and Linlithgow. Toward the N. W. the tops
of fome of the Highland hills are to be feen, involved in
clouds, and at certain feafons of the year covered with
fnow, when none of it is to be feen elfewhere within the
whole compafs of our profpect. A part of the frith of
Forth, prefenting itfelf to view, and the veffels, paffing on
the canal, within a mile of Falkirk, enhance confiderably
the beauty of the fcene.

When this profpect is involved in the darknefs of night,
the flafhes of light from the iron-works at Carron, appear
in awful and fublime majefty. When a fall of rain or
fnow is foon to happen, the light is refracted by the thick
and moift atmofphere, and confiderable illuminations appear in the air above the works. Thefe are feen at a confiderable diftance, and great flafhes of light are thrown into
the houfes in this neighbourhood, which have windows toward the Carron works. Upon the eminence on the S.
of Falkirk, the profpect not only comprehends the whole
view which I have defcribed, but alfo the fcenery about
Callander houfe, to which I have already alluded; the veffels in the harbour of Grangemouth; the mafts of thofe in
that of Borrowftounnefs; the ruins of the palace of Linlithgow; the fteeples of that town, and thofe of Dunfermline; together with a variety of ftriking objects on
both fides of the frith of Forth, as well as thofe which appear in other points of the profpect.

Population, and Ecclefiaftical State.—The parifh of Falkirk contains about 8020 inhabitants. In the town there
are 3892; in the village of Camelon there are 568; in that
of Briansford *, 758; in the village of Grangemouth, 410;
and in that of Lauriefton, 858; in the country part of the

parifh

---

* Commonly called Bainsford.

parifh the inhabitants are about 1534 in number *. Among a people fo numerous, we mult expect to find different fentiments refpecting religion, as well as about every other fubject which comes under their confideration; but it is no fmall confolation to fee, that the bitternefs of ill-directed zeal is faft giving way to charity, and the natural influence of progreffive improvements. Nothing will ftand the teft of time and experience, but that which is founded on truth. Error and prejudice will pafs away; and it behoves us to rejoice, that amongft the wreck of falfe or unimportant fpeculations, virtue will remain without a blemifh, and completely fecure. It is the effence of true religion; it is the point where men of worth meet; and it is the centre from which every ray of excellence proceeds. The jarrings of intereft may, on occafions, difturb the calmnefs of human life; but if reafon direct the thoughts, and conduct the actions, the effects on the whole muft be harmony and peace.

In the town of Falkirk, there is one chapel for the Burghers, two for the Antiburghers †, and one belonging to the Relief intereft. In Laurieftown, there is a chapel for the moft ancient Prefbyterian Diffenters in Scotland, who are generally known by the name of Macmillanites. The congregations of thefe different meeting-houfes are compofed

---

* The annual number of births, taken upon an average from January 1. 1784 to January 1794, is 272. The annual number of marriages taken in the fame manner, for the fame term of years, is 62. But it appears, that the population of the parifh is increafing, for the average of marriages for the laft eight years is 72.

† There is a difference fubfifting between the two congregations of Antiburghers in this town, which arofe chiefly from the manner of fetting apart the elements in the Lord's fupper.

compoſed of people from this and other pariſhes. In this pariſh there are a few of the Epiſcopal perſuaſion, who have an opportunity of attending divine ſervice every fortnight at Carron. The Roman Catholics are very few in number here, and have no place of worſhip in the neighbourhood.

The church of Falkirk is the only place of public worſhip in this pariſh for thoſe who belong to the religious eſtabliſhment of Scotland. The building is in the form of a croſs, and far from being ſufficient for the accommodation of thoſe who wiſh to attend ; but it is hoped ſomething will ſoon be done to provide a remedy for this inconvenience.

Before the Reformation, the pariſh of Falkirk belonged to the ſee of St Andrew's. Immediately after that period, and before the Preſbyterian mode of worſhip had aſſumed its preſent form, there were ſuperintendents appointed for the different diſtricts of the country. Falkirk was within the bounds of Mr Spottiſwood's inſpection, who was parſon of Calder-Comitis *, and father of Spottiſwood, who ſucceeded the ſuperintendent in the parſonage of Calder, was Archbiſhop of Glaſgow after Epiſcopacy was re-eſtabliſhed in Scotland, wrote a hiſtory of the Church, and, after enjoying many honours, died Archbiſhop of St Andrew's.

While he preſided over this ſee, that part of the dioceſe which was ſituated on the ſouth ſide of the frith of Forth was erected into a biſhoprick, and called the ſee of Edinburgh. St Giles's was the cathedral, and the miniſter of Falkirk was one of the twelve prebends. His ſalary for this office was L. 80 Scotch, which is L. 6 : 13 : 4 Sterling. A perſon of the name of Forbes was the firſt Biſhop of this

---

* This pariſh is now divided into two, which are called Mid and Weſt Calder.

this diocefe. He is reprefented as having been a man of learning and piety, but rather fufpected of being a friend to Popery. His ftudies were chiefly directed toward antiquities; and being reclufe in his manners, he was little acquainted with the world. It is faid that it was no uncommon thing for him to preach five or fix hours at a time *.

After the benefice of Falkirk was beftowed upon the monaftery of Holyroodhoufe, the living of this parifh became a vicarage. The great tithes, which formerly belonged to the parfon, were then claimed by the religious order to which they had been given, and the minifter of the parifh was paid with the fmall; and the parfon of Falkirk ftill receives fome fmall fums of money as vicarage-dues. The ftipend of this parifh confifts at prefent of 32 bolls of barley, 64 of oat-meal, and about L. 65 : 14 : 2$\frac{7}{12}$ of money, together with a manfe, garden and glebe. The minifter of Falkirk alfo claims a right of getting from the eftate of Callander all the coals which are made ufe of by his family, without any other expence than that of paying for cutting them from the ftratum in the pit, and bringing them home. Among feveral donations which King David I. made to the monaftery of Newbottle, was that of fuel and pafture for cattle in the wood of Callander †, and it was upon this grant, I prefume, that the privilege under confideration was founded.

The King is patron of this church, and has the right of prefenting minifters to all the parifhes of which the Earl of Linlithgow and Callander was patron before he was attainted of high treafon. The patronage of the church of Denny appears, by the deed of conveyance, to have been

fold

---

* Burnet's Hiftory of his own times, vol. i. p. 31

† Nimmo's Hiftory of Stirlingfhire, p. 135.

fold along with the barony of Herbertſhire in the year 1632. This tranſaction was ſanctioned by charters of confirmation from the King in the years 1654 and 1680. However the King, as well as Mr Muirhead, claims the right of preſenting, and the matter has not yet been brought to a final deciſion.

Schools.—The grammar-ſchool of Falkirk is juſtly held in great reputation. Beſides the ſchool-wages, the maſter enjoys a ſalary and conſiderable emoluments as ſeſſion-clerk. We have here a ſchool for Engliſh, to which there is alſo a ſalary annexed, the maſter whereof has no ſmall degree of merit in the line of his profeſſion. There are other ſchools in Falkirk which do honour to their maſters; and, upon the whole, our youths have good opportunities of laying the foundation of future uſefulneſs and importance.

In the village of Camelon there is a dwelling-houſe and ſchool-room provided for the encouragement of a ſchool-maſter, but no ſalary. Lord Dundas of Aſke gives to a ſchoolmaſter in Grangemouth a houſe to dwell in, a ſchool-room, and L. 5 a-year. In Laurieſton he gives a dwelling-houſe and ſchool-room, but not any ſalary. One of the name of Scott, ſome years ago, left a ſmall ſum of money for the encouragement of a ſchool at Bonny-bridge, which is toward the weſt end of this pariſh.

Though populous and flouriſhing ſituations like Falkirk yield a decent competence for the ſupport of reſpectable ſchoolmaſters, yet in few ſituations are they paid in proportion to their uſefulneſs in ſociety.

Country ſchools, where the inhabitants are neither rich nor numerous, require at this time peculiar attention. Pariſh ſchools in general ought to have their ſalaries increaſed, as every thing neceſſary for the comfort and ſupport of life is riſing in value, except money, which muſt of

courſe

courfe fall in proportion. Parifh fchools have been the great
nurferies of that general knowledge which is fo commonly
to be found even among the peafants of Scotland ; and from
them fome of our moft illuftrious charaĉters have fprung forth.
But I am afraid, if additional encouragement be not foon
given, that thofe fources of improvement and wifdom muft
foon be abandoned to the direĉtion of the illiterate. Men
of learning and ability will not chufe to languifh in obfcu-
rity and indigence, but will feek for employment in fome
of the more lucrative fituations of civil life; and then the
nation will be prevented from being adorned and improved
by thofe luminaries, which opportunities of education
would have formed and drawn out to public view.

Poor.—The number of perfons in this parifh who are at
one time upon the poors roll, may be eftimated at an average at fomewhat more than 150. They are fupplied with
fmall fums of money, according to their circumftances,
from 1 s. to 5 s. or 6 s. a-month. The money which is
thus expended on the indigent of this parifh arifes from
funds belonging to the poor, from offerings at the church-
gates on days of divine fervice, from other voluntary contributions, and from an affeffment which the landholders
annually lay upon themfelves of L. 1 Sterling for every
L. 100 Scotch of valued rent in the parifh. As many
perfons, from the nature of their property, are little or in
no degree expofed to the affeffment, there is an annual,
voluntary and liberal fubfcription in the town of Falkirk,
and in the villages of the parifh.

There is alfo in the town of Falkirk an hofpital for the
fupport of four aged and infirm perfons. It was founded
and endowed in 1640 by Lord Livingfton of Almond and
Callander. This deed was amplified and confirmed by him
in the year 1668, after he was created Earl of Callander.

Upon

Upon certain parts of the eſtates which then belonged to his Lordſhip, there is ſecurity given for the fulfilment of the obligation. Moreover, if his Lordſhip, or any of the ſucceſſors to his eſtates, ſhould neglect or refuſe to fill up any vacancy in this hoſpital, it is provided by the forefaid act, that, if this neglect or refuſal be perſiſted in, after notice ſhall have been given in due form to the perſon or perſons then poſſeſſing the Callander eſtates, then the miniſter of Falkirk for the time being is authoriſed to preſent a proper object of this charity to fill any vacancy which ſhall be in the circumſtances now deſcribed. Mr Richard Callander, then miniſter of Falkirk, and his ſucceſſors in that office, were, in the above ſpecified deed, made, conſtituted and appointed patrons of this hoſpital, and were lawfully authoriſed to nominate and admit proper poor perſons to the benefit thereof in all caſes where the ſaid Earl or his ſucceſſors ſhould refuſe or illegally delay to do their duty.

There are ſeveral ſocieties in this town and neighbourhood for the ſupport of the members thereof, when they are ſeized by ſickneſs, infirmity or old age ; but it is much to be lamented, that inſtitutions of this kind are not more common and extenſive. When the labourer is in health, he finds ſufficient demands for his money, and too ſeldom thinks of making a little retrenchment in his expences, in order that he may prepare for the evil day. The Legiſlature have turned their attention to thoſe uſeful and important ſocieties, but much ſtill remains to be done, in order to inſure their extenſion and ſucceſs.

Agriculture, and rural Improvements.—The land immediately about the town of Falkirk is let in ſmall pieces, and produces a rent of L. 2, 10 s. to L. 3, 5 s. *per* acre, Scotch meaſure *. The Carſe farms, upon an average,

may

* The Scotch acre contains 54,760 ſquare feet, and the ſtatute acre

may be ftated at L. 2 an acre; more or lefs, according to circumftances. Good land, which is not of Carfe quality, is alfo let at a very high rent; but in fome parts of the parifh, where the foil is poor, wet, and fpungy, the value of the acre is very fmall.

In the Carfe, the crops of grain and hay are fo luxuriant and produ&ive, that the farmers have but a fmall portion of their land in pafture; and of courfe they have no more cattle than are neceffary for the family and the farm.

The rotation of farming in the Carfe of Falkirk confifts in general of fix parts: Firft, the ground is fallowed; fe-condly, it is fown with wheat; thirdly, with beans and peafe; fourthly, with barley; fifthly, it produces a crop of grafs for hay, the feeds of which had been fown the pre-ceding year with the barley; and fixthly, it is fown with oats.

The valued rent of the parifh, by which the land-tax, parifh affeffments, &c. are paid, is L. 13,521 : 8 : 6 Scotch money *. The rental of the parifh, about fourteen years ago, was eftimated at L. 6,277, 9 s. Sterling; but owing to the improvements which have taken place fince that pe-riod, the rental cannot now be lefs than L. 9000. Houfe-rents are not taken into the account in either of the above valuations.

Soon after the eftates of the family of Linlithgow and Callander were forfeited, they were purchafed by the Company which undertook to raife water from the river Thames into the York-buildings, for fupplying a part of the city of London. The affairs of that Company having foon after gone into diforder, their whole eftates were fold for the benefit of their creditors by the authority of the Court of Seffion; and thofe of Callander and Almond were

* A pound Scotch is twenty pence Sterling; but all payments in this country are now made by Sterling money.

were bought by William Forbes, Eſq; the preſent proprie‑
tor.

The whole eſtates, together with ſome other farms
which were purchaſed by him about the ſame time, a‑
mounted to about 8000 Scotch acres; almoſt 7000 of
theſe are in this pariſh. Excepting about 500 acres, it
was all arable; but little more than 200 of it were inclo‑
ſed. The whole farms were out of leaſe, and the tenants
were all removed as ſoon as they could provide themſelves
with other ſituations, in order that there might be no ob‑
ſtruction to the intended improvements.

Almoſt the whole of theſe eſtates is now incloſed and
ſubdivided. The fences are, as much as poſſible, drawn at
right-angles to one another; the ridges are ſtraightened;
and the wet parts are drained, or in the train of being
done with all convenient ſpeed. The incloſures which are
near the town of Falkirk or the villages adjoining, contain
each from three to four Scotch acres of land; but thoſe
which are in different ſituations, comprehend from ſeven to
eight acres of the ſame meaſure.

About 2000 acres, which are near the canal and in the
vicinity of Falkirk, were limed upon the green ſward, and
let to tenants for the ſpace of two years, who were bound
to lay them down with graſs-ſeeds in the laſt year of their
leaſe. A conſiderable part of the land, which was over‑
run by heath, broom and furze, was let to tenants alſo, who
were to plough it five times. This in like manner was to
be laid down for graſs; but in both caſes the graſs-ſeeds
were to be provided by the proprietor, and at his expence.

Theſe improvements will not only add much to the
beauty of a diſtrict already delightful; but when comple‑
ted, will add much to the richneſs of this neighbourhood.
It is one diſtinguiſhing feature in the improvements of Mr
Forbes, that they are intended to be completed before he

let

let the land in long leafes ; whereas it is common to carry on improvements after the farms are in the poffeffion of tenants.

Of Servants Wages, Prices of Food, &c.—A good ploughman gets about L. 12 a-year, together with his bed and board ; and a common female fervant expects from L. 3, 10 s. to L. 4 *per annum*, independent of food and lodging. A man who engages to labour by the day, has 1 s. 2 d. in fummer, and 1 s. in winter. During harveft the wages are higher. Great quantities of grain, efpecially barley, beans, and peafe, are fold in this market. Carfe barley is held in fuch high eftimation, that it brings, in general, two or three fhillings *per* boll more than barley from other parts of the country. During thefe feveral months, the price of grain has been extravagant; barley has been fold at L. 1 : 12 s. *per* boll, wheat at L. 2 : 12 : 6, and oat-meal at 1 s. 4 d. a-peck. It is worthy of obfervation, that in former times of fcarcity, the people of Scotland looked up to England, as well as to foreign countries, for fupply ; but in the prefent feafon, when the people of England are in want, we have not only plenty within our .borders, but have been enabled to relieve them in their neceffity.

Markets, &c.—Befides feveral fairs in the year, and three tryfts *, there is a market every week on Thurfday. At thefe three tryfts there are, at an average, 60,000 black cattle. As moft of them are of the fmall Highland breed, the medium price may be fixed at L. 4 each. Thus at thefe meetings, it is fuppofed, L. 400,000 Sterling are put into circulation. Not a fmall proportion of this money paffes through the Falkirk Bank. There are alfo horfes and fheep difpofed of at thefe markets.

By

* Tryft is a Scotch word for an appointed meeting.

By the favour of Mr Longmoor, a very accurate farmer, I have it in my power to lay before the public a ſtatement of the prices which the Carſe wheat, barley, and oat-meal, brought for the ſpace of 40 years preceding the crop of 1794.

Prices of Kerſe Grain for 40 *years preceding crop* 1794.

	Wheat *per* boll.			Barley *per* boll.			Meal *per* boll.		
Crop 1754	L.o	14	0	L.o	11	8	L.o	10	6
1755	0	15	10	0	14	4	0	13	8
1756	1	3	0	1	0	0	0	16	8
1757	1	0	0	0	16	8	0	9	0
1758	0	14	6	0	10	8	0	9	0
1759	0	14	6	0	11	0	0	9	4
1760	0	16	0	0	11	8	0	10	4
1761	0	15	10	0	12	9	0	14	0
1762	1	1	0	0	17	0	0	15	0
1763	1	0	0	0	16	6	0	12	6
1764	1	1	0	0	16	6	0	15	0
1765	1	1	6	1	1	3	0	17	6
1766	1	1	6	1	2	0	0	16	10
1767	1	2	0	1	1	8	0	12	0
1768	1	2	0	0	16	4	0	15	0
1769	0	18	0	0	16	8	0	15	0
1770	0	18	6	0	17	6	0	15	0
1771	1	2	0	1	0	4	0	17	0
1772	1	4	0	1	1	8	0	16	10
1773	1	4	0	1	1	0	0	16	0

Medium price from 1753 to 1774, being 20 years,

Wheat, *per* boll, - L.o 19 $5\frac{6}{12}$
Barley, —— - 0 16 $10\frac{3}{12}$
Meal, —— - - 0 14 $1\frac{3}{12}$

Crop

Prices of Kerſe Grain continued.

Crop	Wheat per boll.			Barley per boll.			Meal per boll.		
1774	L. 1	1	0	L.0	19	0	L.0	15	0
1775	0	19	0	0	17	0	0	12	8
1776	0	19	0	0	15	3	0	12	8
1777	1	1	0	0	16	6	0	14	6
1778	0	19	0	0	15	9	0	13	0
1779	0	15	0	0	15	3	0	12	0
1780	1	1	0	0	15	3	0	14	4
1781	0	19	0	0	14	10	0	14	3
1782	1	6	0	1	6	6	0	17	6
1783	1	0	0	1	0	6	0	18	8
1784	0	19	6	1	1	6	0	13	4
1785	1	0	0	0	16	0	0	16	0
1786	0	18	0	0	19	6	0	16	0
1787	1	1	0	0	19	0	0	16	0
1788	1	0	6	0	16	9	0	13	6
1789	1	4	0	1	0	0	0	17	0
1790	1	3	0	0	19	0	0	16	8
1791	1	1	6	1	2	0	0	15	3
1792	1	2	0	1	4	0	1	0	0
1793	1	4	0	1	0	6		18	0

Medium price from 1773 to 1794, the laſt 20 years,

Wheat,	-	L. 1	0 8
Barley,	- -	0 18	8 [3]
Meal,	-	0 15	3 [9]

Our markets are well ſupplied with butcher-meat of excellent quality. It is ſold by the Scotch Trone weight; the pound of which, as it is uſed here, is to that of the Avoirdupois, as 7,000 are to 10,450.

Forty years ago, not more than one heifer, cow, or bullock, together with a few ſheep and lambs, were expoſed to ſale in the weekly market of Falkirk. As to veal, it was ſcarcely to be found, but in the ſpring. But I am authoriſed

thoriſed to ſay, that there have not been ſold in the ſhambles of this town, during the courſe of the laſt year, fewer than 2000 black cattle, 6000 ſheep and lambs, and calves in proportion.

Forty years ago, few of the common people were in the habit of eating butcher-meat, except a little with their greens in winter. This ſcanty portion they ſalted about Martinmas, and conſequently, about that ſeaſon of the year, more butcher-meat than common was brought into the market. But now all deſcriptions of the people are more in the praſtice of eating animal food.

It appears from Dalrymple's Annals of Scotland, that the price of a hen in 1295 was only one penny ; but now one that is well fed will coſt fifteen or eighteen pence.

Forty years ago, the price of butcher meat in this market was only about 2 d. *per* pound ; but now it is from 4 d. to 6 d. or 7 d.

Forty years ago there were but 3 ſurgeons in the town of Falkirk ; but at preſent there is 1 phyſician, 5 ſurgeons, and 2 druggiſts.

About 60 years ago this town and neighbourhood were chiefly ſupplied with wheaten bread from Edinburgh and Linlithgow. There were then only 3 bakers in Falkirk, and they were but occaſionally employed. Hence it is, that the people in the remote parts of the country, when they come to procure bread for feaſts or funerals, do ſtill enquire of the bakers if their ovens be heated.

There are now 18 bakers in the town of Falkirk, and 6 in the different villages within the pariſh. They make excellent bread, and the price is regulated by the Edinburgh aſſize.

At the period above alluded to there were not more than 200 bolls of wheat *per annum* reduced into flour for the uſe of the Falkirk bakers. It was ground in common

mills,

mills, and boulted by hand-fieves. Now, about 7000 bolls are made ufe of annually; it is ground in mills, which are made for the purpofe of preparing flour; it is boulted, and the different kinds feparated by machinery, which is conftructed according to the lateft improvements. Seven of thefe mills are within a few miles of the town.

Forty years ago there were but 2 grocers in Falkirk; they complained of little bufinefs, and one of them was alfo a tallow-chandler. They had all their grocery goods from Borrowftounnefs, and imported nothing themfelves. We have now 22 in that line of bufinefs; fome of them carry on an extenfive trade, both in wholefale and retail, and import wine, &c. from foreign parts.

It appears, that in the reign of Charlemagne, there was but one clock in Europe, and it was fent to him by Abdalla King of Perfia *. How different is the fituation of arts and improvements now, when there are four clock and watchmakers in the town of Falkirk itfelf!

There are two lodges of free-mafons in Falkirk. One of them is fo ancient, that it is marked No. 18. in the books of the Grand Lodge. The lodge of Carron alfo meets in a houfe within the precincts of this parifh.

Falkirk was formerly a burgh of regality, and I have now before me a burgefs-ticket, figned by one of the Earls of Linlithgow and Callander. I find no veftiges of any magiftrates which have been invefted with the powers of the burgh, except the bailiff of barony, who, in former times, before the hereditary jurifdictions were taken away, had an extenfive jurifdiction both in criminal and civil cafes. We have ftill a baron-bailie, who is nominated by the lord of the manor. But the power of life and death is not now attached to any barony. He can, within the bounds of his jurifdiction, enforce the payment of rents to

any

* Andrew's Hiftory of Great Britain. vol. 1. p. 93.

any amount, and decide in difputes about money affairs, provided the fum do not exceed L. 2 Sterling. The debtor's goods may be diftrained for payment, and, if not fufficient, he may be imprifoned for one month. He can, for fmall offences, fine to the amount of 20 s. and put delinquents into the ftocks in the day-time for the fpace of three hours.

We ftand much in need of a police-bill for regulating the affairs of the town, and making thofe improvements which the ftate of its increafed population requires. Much to the honour of the people, it may be mentioned, that though there is no place of confinement in the county nearer than Stirling, which is eleven miles diftant, yet there are few inftances of riot or diforder. It has been obferved, that a confiderable part of the bufinefs which comes before the Court at the Stirlingfhire affizes, &c. proceeds from this quarter of the diftrict; but it ought alfo to be attended to, that the population of Falkirk, and three or four miles round it, bears a great proportion to that of the whole county.

A confiderable part of thofe aftonifhing improvements, which, within thefe 40 years, have been made in this parifh, and in the adjoining country, has been owing to the great canal, which is cut from the frith of Forth to the river Clyde. As Scotland is almoft cut into two parts by the frith and river, which have juft been mentioned, an idea was formed as early as the reign of Charles II. of opening a communication between the eaft and weft feas through the medium of a canal. In 1723, a furvey of the intended track was taken by Mr Gordon, who is well known as the author of the " Itinerarium Septentrionale." In the year 1762, Mr Mackell, at the expence of Lord Napier, took another furvey of the projected canal, and gave alfo an eftimate of the money which would be neceffary to

carry

carry the defign into execution. Mr Mackell's report attracted the attention of the Board of Truftees appointed for the Encouragement of the Fifheries and Manufactures of Scotland ; and at their requeft, Mr Smeaton in like manner took the bufinefs under his confideration, and gave in an eftimate of the expence.

After various attempts, a bill was fanctioned by Parliament, which gave powers for raifing a ftock of 1500 fhares for the purpofe of making a canal between the Forth and Clyde. Each fhare was to confift of L. 100, and the whole capital would thus amount to L. 150,000.

On the 10th of July 1768 this great work was begun under the direction of Mr Smeaton. The operations commenced at the eaft end, and the late Sir Laurence Dundas of Kerfe, Baronet, cut and removed the firft fpadeful of earth which was taken from the canal. The fpade is yet kept in Kerfe houfe in memory of that tranfaction, which was the beginning of an undertaking, great in the defign, and difficult in the execution ; but happy in its effects, and likely to be of unfpeakable advantage to fucceeding generations.

On the 10th of July 1775, the canal was fit for navigation as far weft as Stockingfield, which is within a few miles of Glafgow. About two years afterwards a fide branch was cut, by which veffels could go ftill nearer Glafgow, and a bafon, together with granaries, and other buildings, were prepared. By this time the Company's public funds were exhaufted ; for the making of canals being then in its infancy in Britain, the manner of doing the bufinefs in the eafieft way was not underftood, and confequently the work was carried on at a much greater expence than it could be done for now, although the value of labour is much increafed.

The

The canal remained in this languiſhing and unfiniſhed ſtate, till by the aſſiſtance of Government, the managers were enabled to begin their operations again in July 1786. The work was conducted by Mr Robert Whitworth, and on the 28th of July 1790, the navigation from ſea to ſea was opened. When, by the intervention of the canal, a communication between the eaſtern and weſtern ſeas was completed, the event was ſignalized by the characteriſtic ceremony of pouring a hogſhead full of the water of the frith of Forth into the river Clyde *, amidſt the ſhouts and approbation of an aſtoniſhed multitude.

When we conſider the novelty of the undertaking, and the difficulty of the enterprife, we ſhall not be ſurpriſed to find, that it was 22 years and 18 days in being finiſhed. The canal in its courſe paſſes through marſhes, and over rivers, rivulets, and roads. There is a conſiderable aqueduct bridge, which conveys it over the Glaſgow and Stirling road, a little to the weſtward of Falkirk. But the moſt magnificent is that having four arches, which conducts it over the river Kelvin, where the valley in which it runs is 400 feet wide, and the depth from the ſummit of the middle arches to the channel of the river is more than 65 feet.

The ſide cut, which has already been mentioned, was carried forward to within half a mile of Glaſgow. Larger and more commodious baſons were made ; neceſſary buildings were erected; there is land to be ſold for building a village, and the place is called Port Dundas, in honour of Lord Dundas. From this port there is a junction made with the Monkland Canal, which is a ſmall cut running 12 miles into the country on the eaſt of Glaſgow, for the purpoſe of conveying coals into that city.

The

* Edinburgh Magazine for April 1793.

The length of the great canal is 35 miles; the collateral cut to Glafgow 2¾; and that from Port Dundas to the Monkland Canal, 1 mile; in whole, 38¼ miles. This extenfive track of a canal is fupplied with water by fix refervoirs, which cover about 409 acres of land, and contain about 12.679 lock-fulls of water; and the Company have it in their power to increafe the number of refervoirs. The fummit of the canal is 141 feet above the level of the fea *. The number of the locks is 20 on the eaft, and 19 on the weft. The length of the locks between the gates is 74 feet, and the width between the walls 20 feet. The medium breadth of the canal at the furface is 56 feet, and at the bottom 27. Veffels of 80 or 90 tons, properly conftructed, may be navigated through, and are fit for

voyages

* The fummit of the canal was at firft but 140 feet. One foot in height was afterwards added to all the lock-gates, which has made fome people conclude, that as 20 locks are on the eaft, the fummit muft now be 160 feet. But though the water throughout the canal be one foot deeper, yet the fummit is only raifed 12 inches. The firft lock from the fea does now elevate veffels 8 feet; but the increafed height of this lock raifes the water on the next one foot; thus the upper gate of the 2d lock, which was 7 feet above the level of the water on the lower fide, is reduced to 6 feet, and confequently, when a foot is added to its height, it only, as formerly, raifes the veffel 7 feet. The fame thing happens to the third lock, and fo on through the whole; and when you arrive at the fummit, the boat is only one foot higher than it would have been before the addition was made to the gates, and this foot was gained at the firft lock.

The circumftance of there being 20 locks on the eaft fide of the fummit, and only 19 on the weft, may be accounted for as follows:—On the eaft, the canal terminates in the Grangeburn, where there is fo little water, that the veffels are left nearly dry at ebb tide; whereas on the weft, it ends in the Clyde, where the water is 8 feet deep without the help of the tide, and thus one lock is faved.

The revenue arifing from the canal was annually increafing from the commencement till 1792, when it amounted to about L. 14.000. By the ftagnation of trade in 1793, it did not reach L. 12,000; but in 1794, it was fomewhat more than L. 12,000.

Government have fhares in this canal to the extent of L. 50,000.

voyages by fea. The tonnage dues are 2 d. *per* ton every mile, with fome exceptions, refpecting lime, &c. The direction of the canal is under a Governor, Council in London, and a Committee at Glafgow, who meet monthly. They are chofen annually, by a general meeting, which is held in London every month of March.

The extenfive trade carried on through this canal fuggefted to Sir Lawrence Dundas the propriety of building a village and quay near the eaft end of it on his own eftate. The place which he fixed upon for this purpofe was the angle which is formed by the junction of the river Carron and the canal. They were begun to be built in the year 1777; the village is now of confiderable extent, and is called Grangemouth.

Veffels bring into this port timber and hemp, deals, flax, and iron, from the Baltic, Norway, and Sweden, and grain from foreign markets, as well as from the coafts of Scotland and England. The trade to London is carried on by the Carron Shipping Company, who in their veffels convey to that place goods which are made at Carron, together with other articles of commerce; and when they return, they bring grocery goods dye ftuffs, &c. for the fupply of Glafgow, Paifley, Greenock. Falkirk, Stirling, and many of the inland towns of the weft country

The tonnage at this port is, at a medium. nearly as follows: Veffels belonging to England, which bring cargoes from foreign places, about 5000 tons annually; ditto, from England, which carry on a coafting trade about 4000 tons annually; thofe belonging to Scotland, which are employed in foreign traffic, about 10,000 tons annually; thofe which carry on the coafting trade are about 9000 tons annually; the Carron Shipping Company require about 9360 tons; the veffels belonging to foreign nations, which come annually to Grangemouth, may be eftimated in their tonnage

at

at 2000. Great quantities of herrings made their appearance laft winter in the·frith of Forth, and many of them were caught at the very mouth of the river Carron. More than 120 fail from Greenock, Rothfay, Stranraer, &c. came through the canal to fifh, and they returned homewards with full cargoes.

At Grangemouth, there is great need of additional warehoufes and fhades. But what is moft of all wanted is a cuftomhoufe, or branch thereof. Borrowftounnefs having till of late been the principal place of trade in this neighbourhood, a cuftomhoufe was eftablifhed there, and fufficient attention has not yet been paid to the fituation of Grangemouth. Thofe at this port, who have bufinefs to do in the cuftomhoufe, are obliged to travel to Borrowftounnefs, which is eight miles diftant ; and when the river Avon is not fordable, they are under the neceflity of going round by Linlithgow-bridge, which lengthens the journey four miles.

But the Carron iron-works have in a peculiar manner tended to improve this town and neighbourhood. They are fituated on the northern banks of the river Carron; and though they are not in this parifh, yet many of the workmen live in it, and as they are not two miles from the town of Falkirk, the fhops and markets thereof are generally reforted to by thofe who are employed in the various operations of that extenfive manufacture.

The Carron Company have a charter for employing a capital of L. 150,000. It is divided into 600 fhares, and no perfon can have a vote in the management, unlefs he be poffeffed of ten fhares. Thefe works were firft projected and eftablifhed by Dr Roebuck, and Meffrs Cadell and Garbet. They were joined by other gentlemen of refpectability, and the Company are now in a very flourifhing
condition.

condition. The works are under the immediate direction of Mr Joſeph Stainton, who is alſo a partner.

They are ſupplied with iron-ore from Lancaſhire and Cumberland; and with ironſtone from Banton, Denny, and Bonnyhill, &c. in this vicinity, and from the county of Fife, &c. They have limeſtone from Burntiſland, &c. and coals from Kinnaird, Carron-hall, and Shieldhill. All the materials, which are made uſe of at theſe works are brought to them by water-carriage, except coals, and theſe are found in their neighbourhood. At an average they uſe 800 tons of coal, 400 tons of iron ſtone and ore, and 100 tons of limeſtone *per* week. The ironſtone is firſt calcined in an open fire; but the iron-ore needs no preparation in order to be fit for the blaſt furnace.

There are five furnaces of this deſcription, which are ſupplied with ſtrong currents of air from caſt iron cylinders, inſtead of bellows. Theſe cylinders are conſtructed ſomewhat like forcing pumps, and are not only more durable than bellows, but have more power, and produce a better effect. They have three cupolas, which receive a proper ſupply of air by means of pipes connected with the forcing cylinders. There are alſo fifteen furnaces, which are kept in action by the external air, without the aid of any artificial blaſt.

At Carron all kinds of caſt iron goods are made in the beſt manner. A ſhort kind of cannon called Carronades were invented there; and, in certain ſituations, they are conſidered as of great importance. They are moved in grooves; and thus the increaſed friction more effectually oppoſes the force of the recoil. The caliber of the cannon is bored out of the ſolid metal, and thus the hole is more ſmooth and juſt in its direction, than when caſt with a core, and the piece is leſs ready to burſt in time of action. The

outſide

outſide of the cannon is turned by proper inſtruments, and the whole is not only neat, but ſubſtantial.

At theſe works bar iron is alſo made ; and in accompliſhing that buſineſs, the following method is purſued :

The pig iron is melted in a finery, where coke is uſed; while hot, it is beaten out into plates about an inch in thickneſs. Theſe plates are afterwards broken into pieces about two inches ſquare, for the convenience of ſcouring them, &c. They are then ſcoured in an iron cylinder, which is connected with the water-wheel, and when they are properly prepared by this operation, they are put into pots, which are made of fire clay, and in an air-furnace they are brought to a welding heat ; in this ſtate of preparation they are put under the hammer, and wrought into blooms ; the blooms are heated in a chafery, or hollow fire, and then drawn into bars for various uſes. In this condition the iron is equal in goodneſs to that which is imported from Ruſſia under the name of new ſable iron.

The machinery is moved by the water of the river Carron, and for a ſupply in time of drought, they have a reſervoir to the extent of about 30 acres. But as this precaution is not enough in very dry ſeaſons, they have moreover an engine for throwing back the water that it may be uſed again, and this engine raiſes 4 tons every ſtroke, and makes about 7 ſtrokes in a minute. If we take into the account, along with the people who are directly employed in the manufacture at Carron, thoſe alſo who are engaged in the mines and pits, together with thoſe who carry materials to the works, and goods by ſea and otherwiſe immediately from them, we may eſtimate the whole at 2000 people.

Nobody is admitted to view the works on Sundays, except thoſe who are properly recommended, or known to be worthy of attention. Mr Burns, the Ayrſhire poet,

not

not knowing, or not attending to this regulation, made an attempt to be admitted, without difcovering who he was, but was refufed by the porter. Upon returning to the inn at Carron, he wrote the following lines upon a pane of glafs in a window of the parlour into which he was fhown :

We cam na here to view your warks,
   in hopes to be mair wife :
But only, left we gang to hell,
   it may be na furprife.

But when we tirl'd at your door,
   your porter dought na bear us ;
So may, fhould we to hell's yetts come,
   your billy Satan fair us *.

                              Remarkable

---

* William Fullarton, Efq; of Fullarton, in the county of Ayr, North Britain, has obtained a patent for making caft and malleable iron after a new method. He calcines the iron-ftone or ore, if it be neceffary, redu-ces it to powder, bolts it, feparates the extraneous matter, and then puts it into a furnace, along with a fufficient quantity of coke, or charcoal. The furnace is intended to act as a crucible ; and the metal, when fluid, is not to be drawn off, and caft into pigs, but is to remain as a loop at the bottom. When it is taken out thence, it does not require to be melted again, but after being heated may, without any other procefs, be beaten into bars.

The principal advantages, which appear to attend the method, pro-pofed by Mr Fullarton muft arife from his manner of preparing the iron ftone or ore, and from permitting the metal to cool gradually in the furnace ; to which may be added the removing of the flag, which he takes care to do while the fufion is going forward. From the fpecifica-tion which he has given, it feems as if pulverifing the iron ftone or ore, and freeing it of extraneous matter, precludes the neceffity, and faves the expence of ufing limeftone as a flux ; and cooling the metal gradually, prevents that brittlenefs which caft iron and fteel poffefs when they are cooled on a fudden ; and thus the loop is in a better ftate of preparation for being put under the hammer.

                                                              But

Remarkable Events.—Margaret, commonly called by hiftorians the Maiden of Norway, died at Orkney, on her way to Britain, where fhe was to have been crowned fucceffor to her grandfather Alexander III. of Scotland. Upon her death there was much agitation in the kingdom, and many competitors fprang up for the Crown. But of all thofe who laid in their claims, the rights of Robert Bruce and John Balliol * appeared to be moft worthy of inveftigation and fupport. On the fide of one or other of thefe opponents were the people of Scotland generally arranged. As the conteft was violent, and not likely to be brought to a fpeedy iffue, it was refolved to fubmit the whole bufinefs to the decifion of Edward I. of England. He accepted of the offer with much pleafure, and took that opportunity

But if I fully underftand the fpecification, Mr Fullarton's method muft be fubject to feveral inconveniencies. Either the furnace muft be very fmall, or it will be difficult to remove the regulus after it has remained there till it be cold, and the work muft fuffer an interruption by waiting fo long before a new charge can be put in. In order to obviate thefe inconveniencies, it might be proper to draw off the metal in the fluid ftate, and having caft it into pigs of the ufual form, put them while hot into a furnace, expofed to a well regulated heat, and fuffered gradually to become cool.

A gentleman, who was taken by the French during the laft American war, having efcaped from prifon, was travelling homeward, and on his way, in paffing through a valley among the Pyrenean mountains, came to a fmall forge, where fome men were making iron from the ore. They fifted it, and having mixed it with charcoal, put it by fmall quantities at a time into a furnace. They let it remain till it was duly fufed. Then they put a bar of iron among the metal, to which a knob adhered, and when it had acquired a proper confiftency, they beat it with a hammer, repeating the operation, till, in a fhort time, they had made a bar of confiderable length. This method is recommended by its fimplicity, and perhaps it may fuggeft fomething for the improvement of making bar-iron in this country.

* Formerly called Robert de Brus, and John de Balliol.

nity of confuſion, uncertainty, and terror, to have himſelf proclaimed Lord Paramount of Scotland; and finding Balliol not unwilling to acknowledge this ſupremacy, he decided the conteſt in his favour. But Edward ſoon hurled him from the throne, under the pretence that he had only put the ſceptre into his hands to be ſwayed in truſt. The troops of the Engliſh monarch ſoon over-ran many of the moſt important diſtricts of this kingdom; and in triumph carried to Weſtminſter the ſtone of Scone, which was made ſomewhat in the form of a chair, in which the Kings of Scotland had been in uſe to be ſeated at the time of their coronation.

In this ſeaſon of national dejection and diſmay, appeared William Wallace, of an ancient, but at that time an obſcure family [*]. He lifted up the ſtandard of liberty, and many flocked around the ſignal. But ſtill there were not a few, who through envy or fear would not join the patriots. But Wallace and his adherents prevailed. They fought and were ſuccefsful. They drove the Engliſh beyond the borders, and entered the countries in the north of Edward's kingdom.

When the King of England was informed of theſe events, he returned from the continent where he had been with an army; and marching into Scotland, he advanced with victorious bands through that country, meeting with little reſiſtance till he came to Falkirk.

Having come within view of the Scotch army, they ſaw them drawn up in battle array, ſomewhat more than half a mile north from Falkirk. Before this time many perſons of eminence and power had joined the party of Wallace. Of thoſe who were preſent with him on the occaſion now

under

---

[*] Of Elderſlie, in the county of Renfrew, which was probably at that time a part of Lanarkſhire. Dalrymple's Annals, vol. 1. p. 286.

under review, the following names are the chief of thofe which have been preferved on record : John Comyn, or Cuming, of Badenoch, the younger; Sir John Stewart of Bonkill, and not of Bute, as tradition has handed it down. This gentleman was brother to the Steward of Scotland, from whom the firname of Stewart, or Stuart, was taken. To thefe we muft add Sir John Graham * of Abercorn or Dundaff; and Macduff, the uncle of the Earl of Fife †.

Wallace had arranged his infantry in four bodies, of a circular form, with the convex fide toward the enemy ; the archers formed a line between the circles; and the cavalry were placed at a little diftance in the rear. The ftrength of Edward's army confifted of cavalry, which were drawn up in three lines; and the third, which was intended to be kept as a corps of referve, was commanded by the king himfelf. Nothing being faid of the manner in which the Englifh infantry were difpofed, we are naturally led to believe, that they were not numerous.

A morafs, which was in front of the Scotch army, but is now drained by the canal, prevented the troops of Edward from attacking the Scotch in front; but wheeling to the right and left, they flanked them on both fides, and the carnage was dreadful. Struck with a panic by the fall of Graham, Stewart, and Macduff, and preffed by the well appointed cavalry of England, they were compelled, after a brave refiftance, to abandon the conflict, and leave the victory in the hands of Edward.

Sir John Graham and Sir John Stewart were both buried in the church-yard of Falkirk. The ftone which was laid on the grave of Sir John Graham had fome fculpture upon it, which the hand of time was faft obliterating. At length another

---

* Generally called in old records, Sir John de Graham.

† Dalrymple's Annals of Scotland.

another ſtone was erected with decorations, and an epitaph, the whole being ſupported by pillars. When the letters of the inſcription were nearly defaced, another of a ſimilar kind was put over it; and when it alſo had ſuffered conſiderably by the lapſe of time, the late William Graham of Airth, Eſq; erected a third, after the ſame manner as the two former. The inſcriptions are as follow :

Mente manuque potens, Vallæ fidus Achates,
Conditur hic Gramus, bello interfectus ab Anglis.

xxii. Julii, anno 1298.

Heir lyes Sir John the Grame, baith wight and wiſe,
Ane of the chiefs who reſcewit Scotland thriſe.
Ane better knight not to the world was lent,
Nor was gude Grame of truth and hardiment.

Not far from the tomb of Sir John Graham lie the aſhes of Sir John Stewart. The place of his reſt is but a few feet from the eaſt end of the church, and near the ſouth corner of it. Though Sir John was nearly allied to the progenitors of the houſe of Stuart, whoſe kindred blood flows in the veins of many illuſtrious families of Great Britain, and alſo in not few of the princes and potentates of the earth, yet his grave is not marked out, except by a ſtone without a name, and is the ſegment of an octagon.

Much has been ſaid with reſpect to diſcontents, which are repreſented as having ſubſiſted among the leaders of the Scotch army on the eve of the battle. The peeviſh departure of the well-tried patriots, Wallace and Cuming, cannot be received but upon the moſt authentic documents. Jarrings might have prevailed among a number of leaders, where the ſubordination of regular government was not obſerved; but from the character of the men, and the circumſtances of the caſe, no fault ſeems to have been com‑

mitted,

mitted, which was either difgraceful to themfelves, or hurtful to the iffue of the day *.

In the reign of Charles I. the Earl of Lanark, who was
afterwards the 2d Duke of Hamilton, together with a perfon of the name of Monro, being friendly to the King, attacked with their troops, near Stirling, the army which
had been raifed by the Marquis of Argyle, and the Earls
of Caffilis, Eglintoun, and Loudon. The former were re-
pulfed, and fled to Falkirk; but a temporary accommodation ftopt for a time the effufion of human blood.

In the battle of Dunbar, Cromwell was fuccefsful, and
he marched forward to give Charles II. battle, who was
encamped with his army at the Torwood in this neighbourhood, and had then been proclaimed King of Scotland. On
his route, Cromwell ftormed, and took Callander houfe,
where Charles had a garrifon.

The Earl of Arran, when Governor of Scotland, did,
with the confent of his party, agree to give Mary, the
young Queen of Scots, in marriage to Prince Edward, the
heir to the Englifh throne. But having at Callander houfe
met with Cardinal Beaton and the Earl of Murray, leaders
of the oppofite party, a negociation was entered into,
which broke the matrimonial treaty.

It appears, that Mary Queen of Scots vifited Lord Livingfton at Callander houfe, *anno* 1565 †.

In the year 1745, when the troops of Great Britain were
in Flanders fupporting the houfe of Auftria againft the arms
of France, the grandfon of James II. who, at the revolution
in this country, had taken refuge at the Court of Verfailles,
afferted his father's pretenfions to the throne of thefe kingdoms. This meafure was, without doubt, agreeable to the
French

---

* Dalrymple's Annals of Scotland, vols. 1. pages 262. and 263.

† Stuart's Hiftory of Scotland, vol. 1. p. 93.

French Court, as it would evidently be the mean of with-drawing our forces from the continent. Perhaps it was even fuggefted by them; and we know that they gave a fmall fupply of money and arms.

Charles, flufhed with the hopes of power, eminence, and royalty, failed from a port in Brittany on the 15th of July, and in a fhort time landed in the Highlands of Scotland. There he inftantly drew together a confiderable number of partizans, and marched directly to Edinburgh. He got poffeffion of the town of Edinburgh, lodged in the palace of Holyroodhoufe, and foon afterwards engaged at Prefton, near Muffelburgh, a few of the King's troops, who were under the command of Sir John Cope. Here he was victorious; and in the anxious expectation of future fuccefs, marched into England, as far as Derby, by the way of Carlifle. Though he had many friends near the road by which he went, yet prudence permitted but a few of them to follow his fortune.

Difappointed in his views, he returned by Glafgow, marched to Stirling, and laid fiege to the caftle. By this time a confiderable number of the King's troops were af-fembled near Edinburgh, commanded by Lieutenant-General Hawley. He marched for the relief of Stirling; and having ftopped to refrefh the troops at Falkirk, he encamped with them between the glebe and the field where Sir John Graham fell in defence of liberty and his country.

On the 17th of January 1746 the alarm was given, that the Prince's followers were advancing by the Torwood. By different means they attempted to deceive the army of the King. They left a ftandard at the place where they had halted on their way from Bannockburn, which, being feen at Falkirk, would, they fuppofed, hufh their opponents into a temporary fecurity. They alfo fent a fmall detachment by the north fide of the river Carron, that it might

appear, if there was any alarm, that they intended to attack the King's camp on the left; but, in the mean time,
the principal body of their forces were led ſtraight forward, and croſſed the ford of Carron, at Dunipace, about
the diſtance of three miles to the weſtward.

No ſooner was this diſcovered than the drums at Falkirk camp beat to battle. But the General not being preſent, they were detained ſo long before his arrival, that the
enemy had gained an eminence, which is about a mile ſouthweſt from this town. The way thither being rugged, the
cannon could not be dragged up time enough for the action; ſwampy ground rendered the cavalry almoſt uſeleſs,
and a tremendous ſtorm of wind and rain blowing directly
againſt the face of the national troops, added to the unfortunate circumſtances of the day. Notwithſtanding the
bravery of Major-General Huſk, and other officers, the
King's forces were worſted; many were killed, ſeveral taken priſoners, and the reſt fled to Linlithgow.

Among the perſons of rank who were left dead on the
field were Sir Robert Monro of Foulis, Bart. and his brother Duncan, a phyſician. Sir Robert, in the retreat, was
ſurrounded by the enemy, and after a deſperate reſiſtance,
yielded to the ſtroke of death. The phyſician, from the
affection which he had for his brother, left the peace and
ſweets of retired life, and followed him through the din of
arms, and the dangers of battle. In the diſcharge of this
amiable office, he fell a victim to kindneſs and brotherly
attachment. They were buried beſide each other in the
church-yard of Falkirk; a ſuperb monument was erected
to their memory; and the circumſtances of their death are
recorded by ſuitable inſcriptions. The number of forces
which were led to action that day was about 6000 of the
royal party, and perhaps ſomewhat more of thoſe in the

intereſt

intereſt of the Prince; but the true amount of his troops has
not been exaɛtly aſcertained.

Hawley found means to vindicate himſelf to his Sovereign; but the impreſſions of his conduɛt which remain
here, are by no means favourable to his charaɛter, as a General entruſted with an important command. If we credit
report, he was dining that day at Callander houſe with
Lady Kilmarnock, whoſe Lord had then declared himſelf
in favour of the young adventurer, and was at that time
aɛtually engaged in his ſervices ſomewhere in the iſland.

The aɛtion began about 3 o'clock in the afternoon, and
by the evening the Prince's army were in poſſeſſion of the
town of Falkirk. One of the ſons of Macdonell of Glen-
gary, when walking in the principal ſtreet, ſoon after he
had arrived from the field of battle, was ſhot from a window by a muſket-bullet. He did not inſtantly die; but
having languiſhed a few days, he expired. His death was
accidental, for it was occaſioned by one of his own men,
whoſe gun had miſſed fire during the engagement, and not
being appriſed of this circumſtance, while he was cleaning
his piece, the ſhot went off at the expence of a life, which
he would have done much to ſave. But ſuch was the violence, zeal and diſtruſt which prevailed, that he was found
guilty, and ſhot in this neighbourhood. Soon after the
battle of Falkirk, the Prince's troops were vanquiſhed and
diſperſed at Culloden. Thus tranquillity was reſtored to
the nation; and we truſt, that the horrors of civil war will
never again prevail in the land.

Eminent and Remarkable Charaɛters.—The Livingſtons
were long conſpicuous and powerful in this pariſh and
neighbourhood. It is ſuppoſed that they are of Hungarian
extraɛtion, and that the family ſprung from a gentleman of
the name of Livingus, who came with Margaret, Queen of
                                                          King

King Malcolm Canmore, about the year 1075. We find, that different branches of this family were employed in fome of the moft important fituations and tranfactions of this country *.

In the progrefs of fociety there arofe among them the three diftinguifhed families of Linlithgow, Callander, and Kilfyth. The Vifcount Kilfyth, and the Earl of Linlithgow and Callander, were found guilty of rebellion in 1715, had their eftates confifcated, and their titles forfeited. The titles of Linlithgow and Callander at this time centered in the fame perfon, and the Earl found means to efcape to the continent, where he died. Sir Thomas Livingfton of Bedlormie and Weftquarter, Baronet, is lineal heir of the family.

Lady Ann, the only furviving child of the laft Earl of Linlithgow and Callander, was married to the Earl of Kilmarnock, who joined the followers of the Prince in the year 1745, and was beheaded for treafon on Towerhill, on the 18th of Auguft 1746, in the 42d year of his age. His infidelity to the King is the more remarkable, as his family had always been loyal, and as he himfelf, at the beginning of the commotions in which he afterwards was an abettor, had exerted himfelf confiderably in behalf of the reigning family.

The truth feems to be, that as he was not in opulent circumftances, he was induced to become an adventurer ; and from his marriage-connection, he was in hopes that if the Prince fucceeded, he would be raifed to the poffeffions and perhaps to the honours of the forfeited and deceafed Earl of Linlithgow and Callander. And this leads me to obferve, that it is politic in a ftate to inflict as few permanent difabilities and punifhments as the nature of government and

* Douglas's Peerage, articles Linlithgow, Callander, and Kilfyth.

and good order will permit. If a man falls a juſt victim to the law, the galling remembrance is gradually deſtroyed among his connections and deſcendents; but if an eſtate be forfeited, or a civil privilege be permanently taken away, there is a perpetual brooding over the misfortune, and from this ſource there often ſprings the bitterneſs of ſtrife.

Our Government have, with much prudence and humanity, reſtored the eſtates which were confiſcated in 1746; and it is much to be lamented, that ſomething effectual has not been deviſed for the heirs of thoſe who ſuffered by the forfeitures in the year 1716. The eſtates having been otherwiſe long ago diſpoſed of, could not be reſtored; but the wiſdom of thoſe in power, among the many reſources which they have, might perhaps find out the means of at leaſt a ſmall compenſation.

The eſtate of Kerſe, in this pariſh, once belonged to the Hopes, a family of conſiderable note and antiquity in this country. John de Hope was one of the barons who ſubmitted to Edward I. of England in 1296, when he had invaded Scotland.

Kerſe, as well as many other eſtates in Scotland, were purchaſed by Sir Thomas Hope, who, as an advocate, made a conſpicuous figure.

In the revolutionary period of the Scotch church, ſix miniſters, who had denied that the King had any power in eccleſiaſtical affairs, were committed to the caſtle of Blackneſs, and for high treaſon were brought to trial at Linlithgow, Jan. 10. 1606. No counſellor of eminence, not even Sir Thomas Craig, the procurator for the church, could be prevailed upon to ſtand forward as their advocate at the bar of the Court. Mr Thomas Hope, for he was not then created a baronet, undertook, though but a young man, to plead their cauſe. His forcible elocution, his ingenious, though unfuccefsful exertions, procured him admiration, and brought him into notice.

He was not only confulted in all difficult cafes by the Prefbyterians, but was efteemed by the Court party, and was King's Advocate, both in the reign of James VI. and Charles I. He had three fons, who were Lords of Seffion, and two of them fat upon the Bench as Judges, while he himfelf was at the bar. The Lord Advocate has a right to plead with his hat on, and tradition fays, that this privilege was introduced in the time of Sir Thomas Hope, as it was thought unbecoming the dignity of a father in his fituation to plead with his head uncovered before his fons. But it is more probable, that the cuftom was introduced as a diftinguifhing mark of refpeft to the King's Advocate.

Sir Thomas, his fecond fon, to whom he gave the eftate of Kerfe, was eminent in the law, and, I believe, the only commoner who ever has been Lord Juftice-General of Scotland; as his father, Sir Thomas of Craighall in Fife, was the only perfon not honoured with a title of nobility, who at any time, in the charafter of Lord High Commiffioner, reprefented his Majefty in the General Affembly of this church. The eftate of Kerfe was fold fometime ago to the late Sir Laurence Dundas, Baronet, father of Lord Dundas, the prefent proprietor.

Antiquities.—In the barony of Seabegs, near the canal, there is an artificial mound of earth, where courts and deliberative councils were formerly held, as appears by the name Mote, which the place yet retains. There is alfo a fmall burying ground, where formerly there was a Roman Catholic chapel.

In different parts of this neighbourhood there have been dug up urns, filled with afhes, and ftone coffins, containing human bones. Somewhat more than twenty years ago,

there

there was found, in a hollow of a freeſtone quarry near Caſtlecary, ſome wheat, which had become black, and was ſuppoſed to have been there, from the time that the Romans poſſeſſed that ſtation.

The ſmall river Bonney, which ſeparates a part of this pariſh from Denny and Dunipace, ſeems to be the Cronan of Oſſian.

Old Camelon *, not *Camelodunum*, but probably *Bede's Guidi*, appears to have been formerly a place of conſequence. There are now few veſtiges of it remaining; but not long ago, foundations of houſes, and the direction of ſome of the ſtreets, were viſible. Much has been ſaid about the importance which it once had; we have heard of the riches and ornaments of royalty which were found there, when it was taken by the Romans. But we have no authentic documents by which we can decide whether it was a habitation of ſome of the ancient tribes of North Britain, or whether it was only a Roman ſtation.

It is alſo reported, that Camelon was a ſea-port town; and in confirmation of this we are told, that an anchor was formerly dug up † in the ground near it. There are circumſtances which authoriſe us to conclude, not only that the river Carron has been navigable farther up than the place where Camelon ſtood, but alſo that the ſea came very near Falkirk, and covered the whole of that diſtrict which is now called the Carſe. The name Carſe in Scotland is generally applied to that land which has been formed by the retreat or excluſion of the ſea. Our carſe lands are very little raiſed above the level of the frith of Forth, and in many places are defended by banks ‡. The Carſe, which

---

* A new village in its neighbourhood is called Camelon.

† Sibbald's Hiſtorical Enquiries, chap. 7.

‡ A few days ago, in the morning of October 30. a tide being uncommonly high, the banks were overflowed by the ſea, and the water not only entered many houſes, but inundated ſeveral hundred acres of the Carſe land.

which is very valuable in quality, might eafily be enlarged
by encroaching farther on the fea. Lord Dundas, by this
method, has lately added about 70 acres to his eftate.
About the beginning of this century, a Dutchman, who
was well acquainted with operations like thefe in Holland,
propofed to the Duke of Hamilton to gain for him 2000
acres off the fea, adjoining his eftate of Kinneal, in the parifh of Borrowftounnefs, provided he fhould be allowed to
poffefs it rent free for forty years, and be furnifhed with
timber, &c. from the Duke's wood in the neighbourhood.
The propofal was rejected ; and the fea continues to roll
its tides over thofe fhallows, where fruitful fields might
now have been yielding an annual income of L. 4000 or
L. 5000 to the proprietor, and a confiderable quantity of
provifions for the fupply of this populous part of the
country.

But the moft prominent feature of antiquity in this parifh is the Roman wall, built in the reign of the Emperor
Antoninus Pius, under the direction of his Lieutenant Lol-
lius Urbicus. It in general follows the track where Agricola had previoufly erected a chain of forts. It is more
than 1600 years fince the wall was built, and yet in feveral parts, both in this parifh and elfewhere, its form and
courfe are vifible. It extends from the frith of Forth to
the river Clyde, and was about 40 Roman, or 37 Englifh
miles in length. Carriden, Kirneal, and Blacknefs, on the
eaft, Dumglas and Old Kirkpatrick on the weft, have, by
different people, been fuggefted as its boundaries. Bede
fays, that it began two miles from the monaftery of Abercorn, and ended at Alcluith, which appears to be the fame
place which is now called Dumbarton *. If the wall terminated

* Camden's Britannia by Gough, article Lennox.

minated at Old Kirkpatrick, Dumbarton was probably a fort belonging to the Romans; and we know, that on the eaft coaft their forts and ftations were carried far beyond the end of the wall *.

This wall, or rather defenfive work, confifted of a ditch on the north, and a wall on the fouth. It varies as to the breadth of the ditch; but is never lefs than 12 or 15 feet wide, and the wall was about 12 feet thick at the foundation †. The ditch was deep in proportion to its breadth; and the wall was high in proportion to its width. Notwithftanding what has been faid by fome authors, no part of this wall appears to have been built of ftone, except in fwampy places, where the nature of the ground required it. Forts or ftations, and between thefe, turrets or watchtowers, were erected for the accommodation of foldiers to defend it; and as they were at no great diftance from one another, a general alarm could be given at the approach of danger. Hence the vulgar belief that the wall was hollow, and that the found of a trumpet which was blown at one end could be heard at the other. Caftlecary, Roughcaftle, and Camelon, were the moft remarkable forts or ftations in this neighbourhood. The fite of the two former are ftill to be feen.

Much light has been thrown on the hiftory of this wall by ftones with infcriptions, which have been dug up in various parts of it. A confiderable number of thefe ftones are in the College of Glafgow, &c.; one in Sir John Clerk's collection, and one in Callander houfe, with the following infcription:

VEXI
LEG XX
PRIMIG

From

* Sibbald's Enquiries.

† The ditch in Callander park is above 40 feet wide; in fome other places it is not fo much by half.

From thefe different ftones it appears, th at the wall was chiefly made by the 2d and 20th legions, and the vexillations of the 6th and 20th, together with a cohort of auxilliaries *. Every 100dth part of a legion was called a century, and had a vexillum, or pair of colours. To guard thefe, ten of the beft foldiers were allotted for each vexillum, and thofe guards, which in every legion amounted to 1000 men, were called its vexillation.

This rampart is denominated by Buchanan, in his Hiftory of Scotland, the wall of Severus. Other writers have alfo given it the fame name ; but though it may have been repaired by Severus, as it was by different people, yet the wall which he built was not in this diftrict of the country, but was drawn between the Solway frith and Newcaftle, nearly in the fame direction in which Adrian had formerly built his.

The wall of Antoninus is generally known in this country by the name of Graham's Dike. Some are of opinion, that it derived this name from a powerful leader of that name, who broke through this famous line of defence, and routed the Britons on the fouth fide of it, who were then abandoned by the Romans. Others affirm, that in the reign of Malcom II. one Gryme, who was connected with the royal family, afpiring to the throne, drew together fome followers, and in order to fettle the commotion, the pretender got a grant for the term of his life of all that part of Malcolm's kingdom which was on the north fide of the wall, and that the line of feparation was from this event called Gryme's Dike; hence, by an eafy tranfition, Graham's Dike. It has alfo been fuggefted, that as the building of this wall has been attributed to Severus, fo by tranflating Severus into Englifh, you have Grim ; and in a country

* Henry's Hiftory of Great Britain.

country where the ſirname of Graham is ſo common as it is here, it was very natural to find the appellation Grim's Wall, converted into Graham's Dyke *. The name itſelf is of little conſequence, but the wall is a ſtriking monument of Roman activity.

The ſoldiers of the Roman empire were not allowed to be enervated by idleneſs. They were conſtantly employed, and often engaged in ſevere manual labour. Not only the walls which have been taken notice of, but alſo the various roads which they made in Great Britain are clear proofs, that they were called forth to exertion, and kept in active life. Along the ſouth ſide of Graham's Dyke, a cauſeway was formed for the more expeditious and comfortable travelling of the ſoldiers from one part of it to another.

Nearly oppoſite to Callander houſe, an earthen wall of conſiderable height and thickneſs branches off from Graham's Dyke, runs through Weſt-quarterhouſe garden, and reaches the old caſtle of Almond. From that toward the eaſt, there are few or no certain traces of it to be ſeen ; but we may preſume, that it once ended at Linlithgow, where there was a Roman camp, on the very place where the King's palace was afterwards built. This wall has no foſſe, and being broad at the top, was probably intended to be a road, as well as a line of defence.

* Dyke in the Scotch language means a wall.

The

The following corrections and additions to the Statistical Account of the parish of Polmont are here inserted, at the request of the Rev. Mr William Finlay :

The parish of Polmont is not *interfected*, but bounded by *the frith of Forth*, on the north, and by the river *Avon* on the east. A small part of it is interfected by a *short cut* from Grangemouth, which is now the only navigable communication betwixt the great canal and the Forth. The iron stone is sold by the proprietors of land to the Carron Company, not at *tenpence per stone*, but at *tenpence per ton*. The annual amount of the funds for relief of the poor is not L. 28, but about L. 55, and the expenditure nearly the same. By an interlocutor of the *Teind Court*, June 1793, the stipend of this parish is ordained to be 111 bolls, 2 firlots, 1 peck, and 2 lippies of bear, 56 bolls of meal, and L. 152 : 10 : 10 Scots money, with L. 60 money forefaid for furnishing the communion-elements. The real rent of the parish is about L. 4000 Sterling *per annum*.

PARISH OF FINTRY.

(County of Stirling——Presbytery of Dumbarton——Synod of Glasgow and Ayr.)

By the Rev. Mr. GAVIN GIBB, *Minister of* STRATHBLANE.

Name, Situation, and Extent.

THE name of this parish is of Gaelic origin, and signifies *Fair Land.* Contrasted with the bleak and precipitous rudeness of the adjacent moors and mountains, its grassy hills, its fertile and well watered valleys, entitle it to this appellation.——Fintry is situated in the midst of that range of hills, which reaches from Stirling to Dumbarton, and behind that particular district of them usually denominated *the Campsie Fells.* It lies 17 miles due N. from Glasgow, 12 miles W. by S. from Stirling, and 21 or 22 miles E. by N. from Dumbarton. It belongs to the commissariot of Glasgow. It extends from E. to W. 5 miles, and from N. to S. more than 4; though the only parts of it, which are inhabited, are a small valley on the banks of the Endrick, and another on the banks of the Carron; both of which rivers have their source in this parish.

General Appearance.——The general appearance of the country is hilly. The hills are small; they are clothed with re-
freshing

freſhing verdure ; and their ſhapes are finely diverſified. Covered with ſheep, they ſuggeſt many paſtoral images. The
eaſtern part of the pariſh conſiſts of three ranges of hills, with
ſcarcely any intervening plain. Between the two ſouther-
moſt of theſe ranges, the Carron bog or meadow commences ;
the largeſt perhaps in Scotland. Beginning in Fintry, it runs
E. between the pariſhes of Kilſyth and St. Ninian's to the
extent of 4 miles ; is in ſome places 2 miles in breadth, and
in no place leſs than 1 ; containing about 500 ·acres in one
continued plain. It affords ſuſtenance during the winter to
the cattle of the ſurrounding farms. This remarkable meadow, beſides its utility, adds great livelineſs and beauty to
the general face of the country. The ſcene it exhibits during the months of July and Auguſt, of 20 or 30 different
parties of people employed in hay-making, is certainly very
cheerful : And during winter, the greater part of it being
overflowed by the Carron, which runs through the middle of
it, and which is then induſtriouſly led over its whole extent,
to fertilize it for the enſuing crop, it aſſumes the appearance
of a large and beautiful lake. In both ſituations, it affords an
agreeable relief from the bleakneſs of the country around it.
Towards the weſt end of the pariſh, the hills are more rocky
and rugged. The valley through which the rapid ſtream of
the Endrick runs, widens gradually to the extent of a mile.
Several groves, recently planted, beginning to lift their heads
along the banks of the river ; the cultivated fields on its margin ; the hedges and hedge rows round the encloſures on the
eſtate of Culcruich ; an extenſive plantation behind the manſion-houſe of that name ; and ſome well-diſpoſed clumps of
trees on the ſides of the oppoſite hills, gratify the traveller,
not only with a view of beauty, but of well-directed induſtry.
Above theſe, the ſummits of the mountains on both ſides, broken, and preſenting abrupt precipices, and ſometimes covered
with

with clouds, add grandeur and dignity to the fcene.——The profpect, however, is confined within narrow limits, excepting towards the weft, where it is terminated by Benlomond, that rifes with eminent dignity above the neighbouring Grampians. Thus fenced and fequeftered, the little hills and valleys of Fintry fuggeft ideas of tranquil and undifturbed feclufion. Nor can any thing of the kind be more agreeable than when in fummer, the fun fetting by the fide of Benlomond, throws a blaze of parting radiance on the romantic banks of the upper Endrick.

Soil.—The foil in thofe parts of the parifh which are fit for agriculture, is light, quick, and fertile ; agrees better with dung for manure than lime ; and, when enriched with the former, produces excellent crops. Some recent experiments however have fhewn, that when the ground is paftured for two years, then limed and allowed to reft another year, it will thereafter yield better crops, than by any mode of hufbandry hitherto practifed.

Cultivation and Produce.—In agriculture, however, the inhabitants have made but few improvements. They follow fervilely the ancient mode *of pafturing, and of fowing oats*, for two or three years alternately on their out-field, and of uniformly fowing as much land with bear as the winter's dung will cover ; and from which they afterwards take two fucceffive crops of oats. However a few of the farmers are now beginning to get the better of thefe prejudices, and find their account in altering the mode of cropping. In making this change they have been inftructed and prompted by Mr. Spiers of Culeruich, who, fince his refidence on his eftate, has fet the example of clearing the ground with turnips, and has introduced the fowing of grafs and clover feeds for hay. The beneficial

ficial effect of this method, has encouraged ſome of his own
tenants to follow his example ; and there is no doubt but
the practice will become general in all thoſe farms upon
which the encloſures are fencible againſt ſheep. The method
alluded to conſiſts, as was mentioned, in cleaning the ground
with turnips and potatoes ; in ſowing next year bear with
grafs ſeeds ; in raiſing hay for two years ; in paſturing one
or two ; in ſowing oats for two years ; and then in returning
to the turnips. This routine anſwers very well, and, with
the ſingle improvement of taking only one crop of each
kind, and paſturing two years, is beſt adapted for this ſoil,
which, being light, is ſoon impoveriſhed by a continuation of
crops, and if not regularly cleaned by paſturing and crops of
turnips, is apt to be over-run with the *creeping wheat-graſs*,
known by the vulgar name of *felt*, or pirl-grafs. There is
no ſoil better adapted for raiſing potatoes, of which the inhabitants plant conſiderable quantities ; after which they
commonly ſow flax-ſeed, which ſucceeds very well, yielding
from three to four ſtones from each peck ſown.

Cattle.—But the attention of the inhabitants is, with very
few exceptions, confined to grazing *, which is by far the
moſt

* Under this article it is but juſtice to mention the name of DAVID DUN, a
man whoſe exertions, in improving the mode of grazing, are truly laudable, and
to whoſe example its preſent advanced ſtate, through a conſiderable part of the
weſt of Scotland, is in a great meaſure owing. He has the merit of firſt improving the breed of black cattle and ſheep, by raiſing them to a greater ſize,
and feeding them more thoroughly, than was ever done before upon grafs alone.
This he has accompliſhed, by judiciouſly ſelecting the moſt choice cattle, to ſtock
his farms with, and by keeping his grafs lighter, i. e. by putting fewer cattle
upon the ſame ſpace of ground, than what had been uſed in former times.——As
a ſpecimen of his ſucceſs in this branch, the writer ſtates the following facts,
which are well atteſted. At one time he ſold a Highland ſtot, which was killed

moft beneficial mode of ufing the ground in this parifh, where
hill and vale equally afford moft excellent pafture for black
cattle and fheep. They ufe the plough therefore chiefly with
a view to the fuftenance of their cattle through winter, as
fodder is the great object of labour. In fome of the farms
the rent is folely paid from the produce of milk cows; indeed butter and cheefe form the ftaple produce of the parifh.
Feeding of cattle is alfo generally practifed. In the month of
May, each farmer buys a number of Highland cows, proportioned to the extent of his farm, which he fattens during
fummer, and again fells off in the months of September and
October. When markets are brifk, and fales ready, this is by
much the moft convenient and advantageous method of ufing
the ground in this parifh, as the excellence of the pafture
during fummer, enfures the fattening of the cattle purchafed,
and the difficulty of procuring fodder for winter prevents the
rearing any more than are neceffary, to keep up the ftock of
milk-cows. Sheep are alfo an object of attention. The
breed is in general good, a confequence of the excellent pafture

ed in Glafgow, and weighed, according to the purchafer's confeffion, 52 ftones
beef, and 10 ftones tallow : the price he received was 25 guineas. At another
time he fold 25 Highland ftots at 12l. each, the lighteft of which weighed upwards of 30 ftones. He fells annually about 60 tup-lambs of a year old, for
which he never receives lefs than a guinea each; and his lambs for killing he
commonly fells in May, at half-a-guinea each. He carries on his plan on a very
extenfive fcale, renting farms in different parts of the country, from one to another of which, he removes his cattle at the proper feafons, according to the quality of the farm, and the ftate of the cattle. His ftots he fells at 5 years old,
but calves of his own rearing fometimes equal his beft cattle, at three years old,
and are accordingly fold at that age. When he dealt to the greateft extent he
paid rents to the amount of 1800l. per annum; the largeft proportion of which
he paid to the Duke of Montrofe. His annual ftock at that time was 470 black
cattle, and 2740 fheep, of which 200 were ewes, as a permanent ftock, from
which he has frequently fold in a year 300 lambs.

ture on which they graze, as well as of the care which is taken to improve the ſtock, by croſſing the breed, and rearing
none but the beſt *ewe-lambs.* Lambs are alſo frequently
brought from the ſouthern parts of Scotland, which improve
greatly on this ſoil. The wool is of a very good quality.
Lambs generally ſell at 6l. per ſcore ; wool ſells at from 5s.
to 7s. per ſtone. The following table will ſhew the number
of cows and ſheep kept in this pariſh :

Milk Cows,	-	-	-	263
Fat ditto,	-	-	-	370
Sheep,	-	-	-	2470

Population.—The population of this pariſh, like that of
moſt other grazing countries in Scotland, has decreaſed very
much within theſe 40 years. Since the return to Dr. Webſter, in 1755, it has decreaſed more than a third part. There
are ſeveral farms in the pariſh, upon which from 14 to 20
familes formerly lived, where only from 5 to 8 families now
reſide. This depopulation is evidently cauſed by throwing
ſeveral ſmall farms into one, which enables the poſſeſſor to
pay a greater rent to the proprietor, and at the ſame time to
live better in his own family, than when parcelled out in
ſmall portions. Nor is this counted diſadvantageous to thoſe
who are ejeċted, as the great demand for hands by manufacturing companies, affords them a ready reception; where they
and their children can earn more, and live better, than upon a
ſmall farm. But, notwithſtanding preſent opinions, it ſtill
remains a doubt, whether this revolution in the ſtate of a
country, will in the end prove a national advantage. Whether a pallid and ſickly race, brought up in the confined air
of cotton mills, with few attachments, and little education,
will compenſate for the ſturdy ſons of our hills and mountains,

tains, or afford a fet of as loyal and virtuous fubjects, is a queftion which we leave pofterity to determine.—The prefent ftate of the population is as under. }

POPULATION TABLE *of the Parifh of* FINTRY.

Population in 1755, - - 891	Between 50 and 70, - 55
Ditto in 1793, - - 543	——— 70 and 100*, - 17
———	Weavers, † - - 5
Decreafe, - 248	Tailors, - - - 3
Of thefe there are,	Smiths, - - - 2
Males, - - - 273	Shoemaker, - - 1
Females, - - 270	Average of births for the laft 15
Under 10 years of age, - 136	years, - - 16
Between 10 and 20, - 110	Ditto of deaths, - - 8
——— 20 and 50, - 225	

Manufactures and New Village.—This parifh is on the eve of experiencing a great change, by the introduction of manufactures, on a very large fcale. A cotton mill is juft erected on the eftate of Culcruich, 156 feet in length, and 40 feet wide; which, when finifhed, will employ 1000 hands. A handfome village, upon a rifing ground along the fide of the Endrick, is already feued off, and building for the reception of the work people. The houfes, according to a regular plan, are to ftand in one row, and to confift of two ftories and garrets. Thus fituated, the village will be well aired, dry and healthy; and very pleafant, having the gardens in front, *feparated from the houfes by the turnpike road,* dreffed on a floping bank down to the river.

Proprietors

* It is worthy to be recorded, that there died, a few months previous to taking up this lift, one man above 80, and another 103 years old.

† Some of thefe have apprentices and journeymen; and they are fupplied with work from manufacturing companies. Men fervants wages are 4l. and 4l. 10s. in the half year; women fervants from 1l. 10s. to 2l.

Proprietors and Rent.—The whole property of the pariſh is veſted in the Duke of MONTROSE, and Mr. SPIERS of Culcruich ; the former of whom is patron of the pariſh, and the latter is the only reſiding heritor. The preſent rent is between 1500l. and 1900l.; but it may be expected to riſe conſiderably.

Church, &c.—The church was built before this century : Part of it appears to be of a very ancient date. The manſe was built in 1732, and has undergone ſeveral repairs. The ſtipend conſiſts of 44 bolls of meal, 5 bolls of bear, and 24l. 10s. Sterling in money; excluſive of the glebe, which contains 9 acres, 4 of which are arable.

Poor.—The poor of this pariſh are ſupported by the weekly collections, and the intereſt of a fund, which has accumulated to 200l. Sterling and upwards, chiefly by donations from the family of Montroſe. The preſent number on the poor's roll is 7, and varies from that 10. They receive, individually, according to their neceſſities, from 1s. to 3s. weekly. Beſides this ſtated diſtribution, attention is paid to clothing the moſt deſtitute, and ſupplying them with fuel. Theſe ſupplies are adequate to their wants ; infomuch, that there is not, nor has been for many years paſt, a ſingle inſtance of a poor perſon, belonging to the pariſh, going out to beg. This attention to their own poor, however, does not by any means free the inhabitants from the burden and plague of mendicants from other places. Crowds flock thither, from the great towns and populous villages, for the ſpace of 30 miles round, who frequently repay the charity they receive, by making nightly depredations upon their humane landlords.

Fuel.—The fuel which has been principally uſed hitherto in this pariſh, is peat; in cutting, drying, and carrying home which, the whole ſummer is ſpent, from the end of ſeed-
time,

time, till the beginning of the hay harveft. This, were there no other obftacle, is a powerful bar to agricultural improvements, as the only time of the year, in which the farmers can carry lime, is fpent in preparing and fecuring their fuel. It is to be hoped, however, that this obftacle will foon be removed. An attempt is juft now making to find coal upon the eftate of Culcruich, and appearances have hitherto been favourable. Whatever may be the ultimate iffue of this fearch, great praife is due to Mr. Spiers for his indefatigable exertions, in promoting every meafure that can contribute to the profperity of the parifh*.

Roads and Bridges —Till within thefe two years, the accefs to Fintry was extremely difficult on all fides, infomuch, that had it not been rendered eafier, no improvement could have made its way thither. The difficulty was even fo great as almoft to forbid any attempt to remove it. A hill, almoft perpendicular, over which horfes could fcarcely crawl with half a load, cut off the communication with Campfie and Glafgow, from which fide coal could only be got; and deep moor and mofs obftructed the approach on the N. and W. Thefe obftacles, feemingly infurmountable, are now happily overcome,

---

* The MODE OF BORING, which he has adopted, is fuch as muft afcertain, without a doubt, whether there be coal in the country or not, and may ferye as a leffon to others, who may have occafion to make trial for coal in hilly countries. The top of the hill confifts of a very thick bed of whin ftone, below which there is a bed of free-ftone equally thick. Beginning at the bottom of the free-ftone, which is half a mile up the hill, with a 10 fathom bore, he takes the level of the bottom of this bore down the fide of the hill, making allowances for the dip and run of the metals, where he bores again to the depth of 10 fathoms, and fo on, continuing till he reaches the level of the river. In one of thefe bores there was found laft week a fmall crop feam of coal, which it is to be hoped is the forerunner of one of greater confequence. If the attempt fucceeds, it will be of the utmoft importance, to a tract of country for 10 miles round, the greateft part of which lies at prefent 20 miles from coal.

overcome, by the public ſpirited exertions of Mr. Spiers and Mr. Dunmore. The gentleman laſt mentioned, has formed, as it were, a new creation on the water of Endrick, and given life and ſpirit to a country which, 4 years ago, ſeemed condemned to perpetual dullneſs; having, in that ſpace, brought from different parts of the country, to the neighbouring pariſhes of Balfron and Killearn, no fewer than 1100 perſons. Both theſe gentlemen, with much private expence, obtained an act of parliament for a new diſtrict of roads, in the weſtern parts of Stirlingſhire; and, with a promptitude of execution, equal to their zeal in moving the meaſure, have furniſhed this part of the country with as good roads as any part of Scotland. The *Craw Road*, a mile in length and upwards, which was formerly 1 foot of aſcent in 7, and in ſome places 1 foot in 5, is now reduced to 1 foot in 20, in the ſteepeſt place. This line of road reaches from Glaſgow through Fintry, and joins the military road between Stirling and Dumbarton, about 6 miles to the N. of this place. The county road to the W. is alſo now put into a ſtate of repair ; ſo that, from being the moſt difficult of acceſs, Fintry is now eaſily acceſſible on all ſides.—The bridges, on this line of road are numerous, and add very much to the eaſe of the communication ; as the deep ravines formed by the mountain ſtreams, which were formerly very difficult to paſs, are all arched over, and filled up to the level of the adjacent banks. The bridge over the Endrick conſiſts of 4 arches, 2 of which are 26 feet wide, and the other two 12 feet each. The bridge on the old line of road, about a mile farther up the river, conſiſts of one beautiful arch of 47 feet wide, and another of 15 feet.

Rivers, Fiſh, &c.—The *Endrick* has its ſource in the hill of Fin on the northern ſide of the pariſh. It runs E. a little way, takes a ſudden turn to the S., forming the eaſtern boundary

of

of the parifh for 2 miles; then turns due W., rufhing over the *Loup of Fintry*, and inclofing part of the parifh within 3 fides of a fquare. After receiving the river *Blanc*, and other plentiful ftreams, in its courfe, and forming 2 beautiful cafcades at GARTNESS, the fpot where the famous NAPIER of MERCHISTON invented his logarithms, it lofes itfelf in Lochlomond, about 14 miles below Fintry. This river abounds with trout and par. The trout are reckoned to be of a fuperior quality, and may be taken in great numbers, even by an unfkilful angler; upon which account it is very much reforted to, by perfons fond of that amufement. Salmon, likewife, make their way in great numbers into the mouth of this river; fome of which, when the water is high, come as far up as Fintry. The *Carron* rifes in the W. end of the parifh, on the S. of the Endrick, and runs E. in a ftraight direction, watering the Carron Bog in its paffage; leaving which, it rufhes over the *Auchinlily-Linn Spout*, a tremenduous cataract, correfponding to an interefting defcription in the tragedy of Douglas,—

" Red came the river down," &c. &c.

From this it continues its courfe eaftward, through the Carfe of Falkirk, and falls into the Forth, about 3 miles from that town. It abounds with fmall and large trout; fome of which, taken in the pools in Carron Bay, meafure 20 inches in length.

Natural Curiofities.—The only curiofity which is univerfally remarked in this parifh, is the above mentioned *Loup of Fintry ;* a cataract of 91 feet high, over which the Endrick pours its whole ftream. In rainy weather, and more efpecially after a thunder fhower, or a water fpout, which frequently happen

happen in thefe parts, the *Loup of Fintry* may be mentioned along with what is moft magnificent in this kind of object. —There is alfo in this parifh a grand range, or colonnade, of bafaltic pillars, which rife in a hill called *Dun*, or *Down*, at the end of the hill of Fintry. The range confifts of 70 columns in front, which are of a gigantic ftature, fome of them feparating in loofe blocks, others apparently without joints from top to bottom. They ftand perpendicular to the horizon, and rife to the height of 50 feet. They are fome of them fquare, others pentagonal and hexagonal. A block, feparated from one of the hexagonal columns, meafured by an accurate furvey as follows:

		Feet.	Inches.			Feet.	Inches.
1ft fide,	-	2	1	5th fide,	-	1	2
2d do.	-	1	8	6th do.	-	0	10½
3d do.	-	1	5¼	Its greateft diameter,	2	11
4th do.	-	1	3¾	Its leaft ditto,	2	3

On the E. fide of the range, the columns ftand feparated one from another, by an interftice of 3 or 4 inches. This interftice leffens gradually towards the W. fide, till nothing but a feam is difcernible, and then all is blended in one folid mafs of rock, which is very much honey-combed, and has the appearance of having been ignited. The mountain above mentioned, confifts of very extenfive beds of red ochre.

PARISH OF GARGUNNOCK.

(COUNTY OF STIRLING.)

By the Rev. Mr JAMES ROBERTSON.

Situation.

GARGUNNOCK, or Gargownno (as it is called in ſome old records), is ſituated about ſix miles weſt of the town of Stirling, on the ſouth ſide of the Forth, by which it is ſeparated from the pariſhes of Kilmadock, and Kinkardine. It is bounded on the eaſt and ſouth, by the pariſh of St. Ninians, and on the weſt, by Kippen, Balfron, and Fintry.

Name.—It ſeems of no great importance, to aſcertain the preciſe meaning of the word Gargownno. Different etymologiſts will give different explanations of the names of places, in which there is often more imagination than knowledge. Gargownno is probably of Celtic origin ; deſcriptive of the particular ſpot, on the banks of the Forth, where a ſmall fort ſtood, of which there is ſome account in the Hiſtory of Sir William Wallace. There we read of the * Peel of Gargownno, in which

---

* Peel ſignifies a fort.

which an Englifh party was ftationed, to watch the paffage of the Frew, in its neighbourhood. Wallace with a few followers, took the fort by ftratagem in the night, while the Englifh were off their guard. The curious ftranger may be conducted to the ground which it once occupied; and may perhaps regret, that fcarcely a ftone is now left to tell its ftory. There is fomething fo venerable in the abodes of our anceftors (though in ruins), that it is much to be wifhed, the frequent practice of carrying them away, for the purpofe of making dykes, or fences, was for ever abolifhed. The remains of the bridge of Offers, about a quarter of a mile weftward of the Peel, by which Wallace croffed the Forth, on his way to the mofs of Kinkardine, are ftill in exiftence; and for feveral years, it has been in agitation to rebuild it, which would greatly facilitate the communication betwixt the parifhes on both fides of the river, and encourage tenants to give an additional rent for their farms.

Extent.—This parifh extends about three miles and an half, from eaft to weft, and from north to fouth it meafures fix.

Divifion of Lands.—All the eftates confift of muir, dry field, and carfe farms. On the fouth is the muir, which is part of a hilly tract of ground, ftretching out from Stirling to Dumbarton. That portion of the muir which belongs to this parifh, confifts of about 3000 acres, of which each heritor has a divifion, lying in a direct line with his other lands.

The muir has of late become an object of greater confideration, than in former periods. The demand for fuch pafture is much increafed; and this has naturally led the proprietors to fet a higher value on it, than they were accuftomed to do a few years ago. Every one has his own

proportion

proportion accurately meaſured; and its worth is now ſo well underſtood, that ſometimes it is no eaſy matter to ſettle a diſpute about a few acres; which perhaps, in other times, would have gone for nothing. That part of the muir, which is connected with the eſtate of Gargunnock, was let, laſt year, at almoſt double the former rent; but the proprietor hath this year taken it into his own hands; and having pe-ruſed Sir John Sinclair's pamphlet on the ſubject, hath been induced to ſtock it with the Cheviot breed of ſheep. The ſhepherd, who has been brought from that country, is hopeful the experiment will ſucceed to a wiſh, although all the ſheep farmers here are ſtrongly prejudiſed againſt the ſcheme; and predict its total failure, during the winter months. The ſupe-rior quality, and price of the wool, is a ſufficient juſtification of the attempt; and if the plan is ſucceſsful, it will certain-ly turn out one of the moſt beneficial of all our improvements. Men of property alone are qualified to engage in deſigns of this nature. If they are ſucceſsful, they will ſoon be follow-ed by others; and ſociety at large will reap the good fruits of their labours. Or, ſuppoſing the undertaking ſhould prove abortive, they are ſufficiently able to ſuſtain the loſs. That man is deſerving of praiſe, who employs his ſubſtance in ſuch laudable purſuits, as according to his beſt judgement may be uſeful to the community, as well as to himſelf.

It would be of great advantage, both to the landlord and te-nant, if care was always taken to annex to the muirland farm ſome low lying fields, of better paſture; as, where this is not the caſe, the farmer is often obliged to ſend his flock du-ring the winter to a great diſtance, which muſt be attended with inconvenience. Col. Eidingtoun of Gargunnock is well provided in this reſpect; a circumſtance favourable to his purpoſe of rearing the Cheviot breed. The tenants of the muir of Boquhan, in this pariſh, are alſo well accommo-dated.

dated. They poſſeſs ſome good paſture ground, immediately below the hill, which adds much to the value of their farms, both with reſpect to convenience and profit. They are at pains never to overſtock thoſe fields, in ſummer; and the ſheep find abundant proviſion in them, in winter. By this means, the muir is covered by the ſheep which it has bred; and the farmer ſays, that ſuch as have been thus reared at home, turn out much better than thoſe which he hath brought, at any time, from other parts of the country.

It is ſeldom that any part of the muir is cultivated for raiſing grain. Attempts have been made this way, but moſt frequently with little or no ſucceſs. A few acres near the houſe of the farmer, have been ſown with oats or barley, but a good crop was never expected. The ſoil and climate forbid the uſe of the plough. There are extenſive meadows; which, after having been covered with water in the winter, and had a little manure thrown upon the ſurface, produce abundance of excellent hay; and hay-making, which is generally in the month of Auguſt, is the principal harveſt.

The whole of the muir is without inhabitants, two families excepted, which poſſeſs that part of it belonging to General Campbell of Boquhan. Gargunnock-muir, as has been ſtated above, is in the hands of its own proprietor; but the other diviſions are rented by ſheep farmers in neighbouring pariſhes. To reſide at a diſtance from the farm muſt always be attended with diſadvantage. It is impoſſible the neceſſary attention can be given to the flock. Or, if the truſt is committed to a ſhepherd, whoſe viſits are only occaſional, and who cannot be conſtantly at hand, eſpecially amid the ſtorms of winter, when much exertion is often requiſite to ſave the animals; it is eaſy to ſee the riſque muſt be greater, than when the maſter himſelf, or ſome ſuch intereſted perſon, reſides on the ſpot.

The two muirland houſes have nothing in appearance to recommend

commend them; and yet the low roof, the ſort of door which obliges a perſon for the ſake of his head to make a profound bow as he walks in, and the pitiful window, which ſcarcely affords him ſufficient light to ſhow him where he is, are inconveniencies ſoon forgotten, when he is placed by the fire ſide. The inhabitants though dwelling in a deſert, have a civility of manners which does them honour. An old ſoldier who came to their door, was kindly received, and continued for years to make their houſe his home. All the return they could expect, was a little amuſement in the winter evenings, while he rehearſed the ſtory of ſieges and battles.

If houſes for the entertainment of the public cannot be expected in a country that is thinly inhabited, this diſadvantage is ſo much the leſs felt, that the people are remarkable for hoſpitality. There is a kindneſs to the ſtranger, which is ſeldom to be met with in larger and more poliſhed ſocieties. If there is little ceremony, there is much good will.

In many places of the muir, there are roots of trees diſcovered, of a large ſize, from which it appears to have been once a foreſt; but now a tree cannot be diſcerned. While aſcending the hill, a little copſe-wood may be perceived upon the edge of the rock, which the ſheep cannot reach.

The acceſs to the muir is by narrow paſſes called ballochs *. General Campbell of Boquhan has, lately, at no ſmall expence, made an excellent road from the ford of Frew, to his muirland. This road, ſix miles long, has opened up an eaſy communication with the low country. Carts can now approach the heights to carry down peats, the fuel in common uſe, or to receive the dung that would otherwiſe be thrown into the water.

* Balloch ſignifies *road.*

ter. In forming this road he met with oppofition from the tenants of the muir. The many advantages derived from it have now corrected their miftakes and prejudices, in oppofing what was fo evidently intended for their benefit.

It is delightful to look down from the hills to the cultivated plain below. The profpect is extenfive and beautifully diverfified. The windings of the Forth, the fertile valley, adorned on both fides with the feats of the proprietors, and ftretching from weft to eaft farther than the eye can reach ; and the range of mountainous country on the north and fouth, ferving as a wall to fhelter it from the ftorms, form altogether one of the moft picturefque fcenes in Scotland. The beauty of the landfcape is greatly increafed of late, by the very extraordinary improvements in the mofs of Kincardine, belonging to Mr Drummond; where many families, encouraged by the liberal terms held out to them by that gentleman, have fettled and live comfortably. As their number is daily increafing, and each family is bound to remove a certain portion of the mofs yearly ; it is underftood, that the period is at no great diftance, when upwards of a thoufand acres of carfe land will be added to his eftate, while in the mean time thofe who clear the ground of the mofs have an ample reward. The plan has fucceeded beyond every expectation. There is no object of curiofity, in this part of the country, equal to the improvements in the mofs of Kincardine.

The inhabitants of this parifh look to the hills for figns of the weather, and are feldom difappointed. The fetting fun, fhining on the face of the mountain, indicates fair weather ; while the fudden falling of mift on the top of it, foon after he has arifen bright, is confidered as the fure mark of a rainy day.

Several rivulets flowing from different quarters of the muir, and at length uniting, form a fucceffion of cafcades, over

craggy

craggy precipices, which after heavy rains, are feen and heard at a great diſtance. The beſt view of them is from the riſing ground, at the weſt end of the village of Gargunnock.

Dryfields—The dryfields occupy the intermediate fpace, between the muir and the carfe grounds. Their name fuppofes that they are not fubjeᴄt to thofe floods, which frequently cover the carfe, a flat low-lying country. Befides their being confiderably raifed above the level of the carfe, and their gradual afcent to the bottom of the hills, which makes it impoffible for water to remain upon their furface; they are alfo for the moſt part of fuch a light fandy foil, as quickly abforbs the rain, and fhews the propriety of the name they bear.

The greateſt part of the dryfields, until of late, lay waſte and wild, overrun with furze and broom. Few of them were fubdivided or inclofed or cultivated in any confiderable degree. Plantations were not in ufe, and excepting on the fides of the glens, fcarcely any thing like a tree was to be feen. But now it is quite a new fcene. All the heritors have united in a regular plan of inclofing with dykes and hedges. Many of the uncultivated fpots are covered with thriving plantations. The country is adorned and the farms fheltered.

In giving fome account of the prefent ſtate of the dryfields, Boquhan, the property of Lieut. John F. Campbell claims particular attention, as his unwearied exertions, in executing an extenfive plan of improvements for thirteen years paſt, have beautified and enriched his lands, in a high degree.

The plan has been carried on at an expence, exceeding at times the rental of the eſtate; and yet fuch expenditure is not loſt, if by this means the value of the ground is proportion-

ably

ably increafed, and bread is given to the induftrious poor. Fifty or fixty day labourers, and occafionally a greater number, are employed in planting, hedging, draining, ditching, rooting out whatever might obftruct the plough, making good roads from farm to farm, and fencing the young hedges and plantations againft injury from cattle. Twenty five pounds fterling *per* week, laid out in this manner, have not only fertilized many wafte and barren fields, but have alfo afforded the means of fubfiftance to not a few families in the neighbourhood. Every one muft have fome amufement, and there are amufements which pleafe not on reflexion ; but, when agricultural improvements are viewed merely in the light of an amufement, (though they were attended with no other advantage), it is certainly one of the moft rational that can be conceived, and to a generous mind it muft give real pleafure, as every ftep taken to cultivate the country, contributes to the general advantage of the community.

A pamphlet lately publifhed by the General himfelf, entitled " Notes refpecting the Situation and Improvements of " the Lands of Boquhan", defcribes in a lively, entertaining, inftructive manner, the change produced on the dry fields, fince they came into his poffeffion.

Thefe improvements may not appear fo ftriking to thofe who faw their commencement, and have been accuftomed to obferve their progrefs from day to day, as they muft to every one, who may now return to Boquhan, after an abfence of feveral years. Strangers, as they pafs along, are charmed with the fcene, and furvey at leifure that rich variety of natural and artificial beauty which furrounds them.

There is only one thing regretted, by fome of the inhabitants. It was neceffary, to pull down a confiderable number of cottages. Three or four fmall farms are thrown into one, by which means, the population of the dry fields is diminifh-

ed ;

ed : but when it is considered that the lands are now cultivated to much better purpose than formerly, that they are doubly
fruitful, and that wherever a family is possessed of a few
acres only, even the necessaries of life must be procured
with difficulty; when to this it is added, that such persons
find no worse subsistence as day-labourers, than as tenants of
what do not merit the name of farms, it must be owned,
that the method which is now almost universally adopted, of
having fewer tenants, but larger farms, is of advantage to
the country, while it is attended with no permanent loss to
any individual.

Better houses are also obtained, than could be expected
were the farm to consist of little more than twelve or twenty
acres.   And this must uniformly be the case, wherever farms
are extensive, and let to substantial tenants; as when one
farm-house only is required, where three or four perhaps
were formerly necessary, the farmer will be better accommodated, in every respect, in a style of elegance unknown in
former times, and with less expence to the landlord.

Dr Moir of Leckie, whose lands are situated eastward of
Boquhan, has also commenced a plan of improvement, in the
dry fields, by inclosing and planting such spots of ground, as
are but little adapted to cultivation.   When the gentleman,
whom he lately succeeded, came to the estate, it was incum-
bered with heavy debts.   He instantly resolved, that his income whatever it might be, should exceed his expenditure,
until he gave every one his own.   He lived long enough to
see his laudable purpose fulfilled.   The plan he had laid
down, however, made him unwilling to engage in any expensive scheme of improvement; and when the period at length
arrived, which brought him the accomplishment of his wishes,
he was then so far advanced in life, as to find no enjoyment
in pursuits which require all the vigour and activity of youth.

On

On this account, it muſt be acknowledged, that the lands of Leckie are far behind ſome other eſtates in the pariſh, with reſpeċt to thoſe elegant improvements, which uſually diſtinguiſh the reſidence of men of fortune and taſte.

The preſent proprietor has already done much to remedy this defeċt, and laſt year, more than double the uſual number of labourers was employed. The place is beginning to aſſume a new aſpeċt. A garden is to be immediately formed, in a field very favourable for ſoil and expoſure ; and when the family make the houſe of Leckie their ſtated abode, which it is expeċted will ſoon happen, there is every reaſon to believe that rapid progreſs will be made in many other uſeful and ornamental improvements.

About a mile to the eaſtward of Leckie, the road from Stirling to Dumbarton paſſes over a riſing ground, and there the dryfields of the barony of Gargunnock are viewed to advantage. The ſpeċtator is charmed with the proſpeċt. The caſcades from the hills, the glens covered on each ſide, ſome with natural wood, and others with regular plantations, the village, the church and manſe, the chimney tops of Gargunnock-houſe juſt diſcerned above the wood, the well dreſſed fields, ſome for paſture, and others for crops of various kinds, and all incloſed with dykes and hedges in excellent repair, form altogether a very fine landſcape. The incloſures however, which are immediately under the hill, and have been long in paſture, are over-run with furze and broom, which are almoſt their only produce, when not cultivated for ſeveral years. Fields of this nature, it has been ſaid by ſheepfarmers, are exceedingly uſeful in the winter, as the ſheep feed on furze. But as fields in graſs are ſuperior in every reſpeċt, the proprietor has begun to clear away this kind of ſhrubbery. Burning or rooting out furze and broom, does not anſwer ſo well, as cutting them a little above the ſurface

of

of the ground. The root foon withers and dies. Nothing however can do the bufinefs fo effectually, as the plough; and when the grounds are again thrown into pafture, the cattle will prevent them from relapfing into their former wild ftate, for a long courfe of years.

Gargunnock-houfe, now the feat of Col. Eidingtoun, ftands on an elevated fituation, near where the dry-fields are united to the carfe; and commands an extenfive profpect. Though of an irregular figure, it contains good accommodation for a genteel family. Some parts of it are evidently of ancient date. On the eaft wing, there is a fort of tower, which gives it a dignified afpect on that quarter; and until a few years ago, there was a high wall, and ftrong gate in front of it, which indicated that it was defigned as a place of ftrength. It is probable the Peel, which was at a little diftance, having been abandoned, or fallen into decay, it became neceffary that the manfion of Gargunnock fhould be fo conftructed, as to become a place of fafety to its inhabitants.

The barony of Gargunnock, for near a century paft, belonged to the family of Ardkindlas; and the late Sir James Campbell, whofe memory will be long dear to the parifh, having refided chiefly here, was at great expence, in making improvements both on the houfe, and the adjoining fields. The removal of the wall and gate, marked the manners of the times. The garden and orchard, which were immediately under the windows, were alfo removed; high grounds were levelled; an addition was made to the houfe, in a modern ftyle: A floping bank was formed on the eaft and fouth, where the garden formerly was, and where fheep now feed; and from the high road, to which he gave a new direction, an approach was made to the houfe, far fuperior to any in this part of the country.

The

The houfe of Gargunnock has acquired an additional grandeur, from the fine front built by Col. Eidingtoun in fummer
laft.

There is one general remark to be made, refpecting the
dryfields. No portion of them is now allowed to lie neglected. They are almoft entirely inclofed throughout their
whole extent, to the bottom of the mountain; and the heritors vie with each other, in decorating and fertilizing this
part of their property.

Carfe.—Etymologifts explain this word, as fignifying rich
or fertile. This account is juftified by fact, for fuch lands,
when properly cultivated, produce luxuriant crops. About
forty years ago, the carfe grounds lay almoft in a ftate of
nature, unprofitable to the landlord, for it was difficult to
find men who would venture to poffefs them. Bad roads,
fields uninclofed, the ftiffnefs of the foil, ignorance of that kind
of farming which is fuited to the carfe, prefented great difficulties when any attempt was made towards improvement.
But now it is aftonifhing to obferve the effects of better hufbandry. The rivulets flowing from the hills, through the
carfe, have been confined within their proper channel, fo as
to prevent the overflowing of the fields, excepting upon very
rare occafions, after exceffive rains; many of the farms are
fenced with hedges, in a thriving condition; the old divifion
of the lands into outfield, and infield has been abolifhed.
The practice of liming is followed, with great fuccefs; a regular rotation of crops has been almoft univerfally adopted;
and from 4 fhillings fterling per acre, there has been of late
a rife to upwards of a guinea, and in fome inftances, to 30
fhillings fterling.

The whole carfe it is believed, was originally under water.
Beds of fhells, fimilar to thofe which are now in the Frith of
Forth,

Forth, have been difcovered in feveral places. This feems to juſtify the opinion, that the carfe has, at fome diſtant period, been gained from the fea. In later times, it was covered with what has been called the Caledonian foreſt; at leaſt it is certain, that when the Romans were in this neighbourhood, the carfe was filled with trees of a large fize, which they cut down, to diflodge the Scottiſh army that took refuge there.

The carfe property of Mr Graham, an heritor of this pa-rifh, ſtill goes by the name of Micklewood, which evidently re-fers to a former period of its hiſtory : For although there are fome uncommonly fine trees, chiefly oaks, near his houfe, which muſt have been there for fome centuries, Micklewood undoubtedly fignifies a wood much more extenfive, than can now be difcerned in this country. The probability is, that not only the whole carfe of this and the neighbouring parifhes, but the dry-fields alfo were a foreſt; as large roots of trees, which are manifeſtly of very ancient date, are every where found, efpecially on the fides of the glens.

It appears that after the foreſt was cut down, what is now called carfe, became mofs. Not long ago, about two acres ſtill remained in this fituation, in the carfe of Boquhan, to fhew what the whole once was; and at the prefent day, there are upwards of 1000 acres of mofs, in the carfe of Blair-drummond, in the parifh of Kinkardine, direѰly north of the lands of Micklewood. This mofs, as has been mentioned above, is daily diminifhing. Trees of extraordinary bulk are found in it. The trunk feparated from the root, and lying at a little diſtance, with the marks of the ax upon it, proves not only the exiſtence, but the cutting down of the foreſt. Upon this the mofs gradually grew ; fcarcely any part of it is deeper than another. The cleared grounds are on a level with the fields in culture around them, and fo fertile is the land thus won from the mofs, that after burning the furface, it bears

plentiful

plentiful crops of oats, for feveral years, without any fort of manure.

The proprietors of Boquhan and Micklewood are the only heritors of diftinction who refide in the carfe ; and their houfes and plantations appear beautiful from the heights. The venerable oaks of Micklewood, attract the attention of every vifitor. Nor can we omit to mention the row of firs, where herons, time immemorial, have built their nefts, and brought forth their young. Thefe firs of Micklewood are the only trees of the kind in the parifh to which they refort, and Mr Graham allows thofe trees to remain chiefly on their account.

All the roads in the carfe (excepting that of Boquhan and Micklewood), are fo extremely bad, that during the rainy feafons they are almoft impaffible. At fuch times, carts cannot be ufed. Every thing muft be carried on horfeback, and even in this way it is with difficulty that the bufinefs is accomplifhed. When the farmers are fpoken to individually upon the fubject, they are conftantly complaining of their roads, and feem anxious to affift in repairing them. But no one choofes to fet about the work alone. When the time is convenient for one, it is inconvenient for another. Fair weather comes, the road is dry and firm, and the matter drops. In fhort the proverb holds true ; " What is every body's bufi-" nefs is no body's."

The beft way would be, that the landlord fhould make good roads to all the farms, and affefs the tenants for the intereft of what money may be expended. This mode would be acceptable to them all, and of great advantage to the proprietor ; as when leafes expire, eafy accefs to the farm will be always one of its moft powerful recommendations.

The houfes on the carfe farms are not good. There are two circumftances which muft always prevent them from being fo. The firft is, the farms are fmall, fome twenty, and few

more

more than forty acres. Can good houses be expected in such cases ? The second is, the house is built by the tenant who is only allowed some timber by the landlord. It is of consequence fitted up as superficially as possible. If it serves the purpose of a dwelling during the currency of the lease, nothing more is expected. For these reasons, it seems probable, that farm houses will be mean and uncomfortable, wherever they are built at the expence of tenants of a few acres. Upon the farm of Redhall, in this parish, consisting of 100 acres of carse and as much of dryfield, the property of Mr Seton of Touch, there has been lately built an exceeding good house of two floors and with a slate roof and handsome offices, at the expence of the proprietor. Such houses, though for the present expensive, last for ages, without the necessity of those repairs, which are incessantly required for those thatched cottages of half stone and half clay, which begin to decay almost as soon as they are reared. It is to be acknowledged, however, that poor as the carse houses still are, they are much better than they were twenty years ago. They consist at least of two apartments, each having a chimney and a tolerable window : Nor are the cattle now permitted as formerly, to enter at the same door with the family. If the dunghill, which in many instances is still in front of the house, were removed to a proper distance behind it, this would be another step to cleanliness and health.

Soil.—There are few fields, either dryfield or carse, uniformly of the same soil. In the dryfields the soil is chiefly light and sandy, not unfrequently with a red tilly bottom ; but in some places it is a rich loam, resembling the low or flat grounds on the banks of the Forth. In the carse there is clay of all colours, but blue is the most prevalent, which is also

I   the

the beft in quality. In a dry fpring feafon, after an open
winter, the clod is fo hard, that there is great labour and fatigue before the harrows can make any impreffion. A good
deal of froft in winter, and occafional fhowers in fpring, are
favourable to the carfe; but, if there has been little froft, or,
if there is great drought after it is ploughed, the clay becomes
impenetrable as the rock, and it is not without much toil
that the feed is covered. The nearer the banks of the Forth,
the land becomes fo much the more pliable. The clay mixt
with gravel and fand, form thofe rich flat fields on the fides
of the river, which are in high repute both for corn and
pafture.

Farming.—The method of-farming now generally obferved,
proves its fuperiority by its effects, while new attempts are
made from year to year, by thofe of fpirit and enterprize in
the way of farther improvement. The ufe of lime to the
amount of 8 chalders per acre in the carfe, and 5 in the dryfields, and the fyftem of having a regular rotation of crops in
every field, are the chief circumftances which have produced
the very material difference betwixt the prefent and the former quantity of grain in the parifh. It is no unufual thing
now to find 10 bolls of wheat or barley upon an acre, which
once produced almoft nothing but thiftles. The carfe is fown
with wheat, beans, barley, and grafs feeds, and after hay has
been cut for two years, the field is next in oats, but in fome
places pafturing is preferred, as it contributes much to
enrich the ground.

The late Mr Graham of Micklewood, who had a thorough
knowledge of farming, and who pointed out the way to the improvement of the carfe, fcrupuloufly obferved the following
rotation of crops, as what he judged the beft, and exprefsly
appointed a particular farm to be fo cultivated in all time

coming;

coming; perſuaded that experience would prove the excellence of his plan. A farm, ſaid he, ought to conſiſt of twelve incloſures, and be managed as follows. Summer fallow, wheat, beans, barley, hay, paſture three years, oats, beans, barley, oats, ſummer fallow, &c. This order is found to anſwer ſo well, that the farm of Woodyett which exactly obſerves it, has always a better crop than any other in the pariſh. The three years paſture is the chief thing which diſtinguiſhes his plan, and probably contributes moſt to give it full effect.

The wheat and barley land for the following year, is begun to be ploughed about the end of harveſt; and, if the weather is at all favourable, the whole of this buſineſs is concluded before the winter ſets in. Wheat is ſown about the middle of September, thereafter, when the field has been ploughed five or ſix times. The lee intended for oats, is ploughed during the winter months, if the weather permits. Beans are ſown about the end of February, and beginning of March, although in a climate ſo inconſtant as ours, the ſeed time is uncertain. Beans ſown and ploughed down on the 9th of January produced one of the beſt crops perhaps we ever ſaw, and ſo wet was the ground a few years ago, that it was not till the 6th day of April that any ſeed was ſown in this country. The uſual time for ſowing oats is from the 20th of March to the end of April. The barley is ſown after this, and the laſt in order, though not the leaſt profitable, is the turnip, a ſpecies of huſbandry introduced of late by ſome of the heritors, in which the tenants do not ſeem diſpoſed to follow their example.

Beans are not ſown in the dryfields, as the ſoil is not ſufficiently ſtrong to bear a crop of this nature. Peas are ſometimes tried to advantage, but for the moſt part they run to ſtraw, without grain. The rotation of crops in the dryfields

is

is commonly this; oats for two years in fucceffion, and barley the third year with grafs feeds, hay for two years, and pafture for three or four. Potatoes are alfo raifed in confideraable quantities, and there is not a crop to which the foil is better fuited. The return is very encouraging. A boll and a half, and often two bolls are digged where one peck was planted. Some lay the fets in drills, which undoubtedly is the beft way, as by this means the rows are diftant from each other near 2 feet, the plough can be ufed among them, throughout the fummer, and while this anfwers every purpofe of fummer fallow, the earth is raifed about their roots, which makes them dry and mealy, and promotes vegetation. A field in potatoes is a fine preparation for wheat or barley. None of the red kind are here ufed, excepting the yam, which grows to a very large fize, and affords good food for cattle.

The carfe farmers are careful to procure horfes of fuperior fize and ftrength. For the moft part the ploughing, fummer fallow excepted, is conducted with two horfes, without a driver. Four muft at times be employed in fummer fallowing. Lefs progrefs perhaps may be made with two horfes than with four, but the work is better done, as two properly trained, and acquainted with the ploughman's voice, will proceed with more fteadinefs, and in a ftraighter direction than four, drawing unequally, and injudicioufly driven by an ignorant boy.

In each farm there is a field in wheat, well dreffed and limed. It has been found that dung is more advantageous to the wheat than lime, and feveral farmers now give lime to the barley fields, and dung to the wheat. One of them this year gave the wheat field a part of both, and the return is luxuriant.

Laft year, not quite an acre and a half of the minifter's

glebe, which had been in paſture for three preceding feaſons, was ploughed only once about the end of October, and fown with wheat without lime or manure of any kind, and the crop produced L. 20 : 11 : 6. On boll was fown and fifteen were reaped.

The huſbandman is at pains to find good feed for his lands. If the fame grain is inceſſantly uſed it ſoon degenerates. This defect is remedied ſometimes by exchanging that of the carſe, for what grew in the dryfield. But the chief improvement this way is the introduction lately of the early red oats from the fouth, which produces more meal, and ripens almoſt a month ſooner than any other known in this country, This promiſes to be a great acquiſition to thoſe whoſe crops are frequently in danger from a late and a wet harveſt.

The drill huſbandry is not practiſed here. Attempts were made to introduce it at Boquhan, and premiums were offered by the proprietor to the tenants who ſhould uſe it ſuc-ceſsfully. Some had not the ſpirit to engage in it, and thoſe who began had not patience to perſevere.

Great improvement is made in the art of ploughing. Prizes are annually given by the gentlemen in the neighbourhood to thoſe who excel, and the young men eagerly contend for this honour. The old Scottiſh plough is moſt generally in uſe, but Small's is beginning to be in great repute. The old plough is frequently made by the farmers themſelves, and at little expence, which is an almoſt irreſiſtible argument in its favour.

The threſhing machine which abridges the labour, and en-ables the farmer to prepare his grain with great ſpeed for the market, is now ſet up, not only by ſome of the heritors, but alſo by ſuch of the tenants as have large farms. This is acknowledged to be one of the moſt uſeful inſtruments of huſbandry, that has ever been invented. It has no other in-convenience,

convenience, than that when a great quantity is threfhed out at once, the ftraw is lefs relifhed by the cattle, than when it is frefh from the flail.

Kilns, with heads made of caft-iron, in which twelve bolls of oats can be dried in the courfe of 6 hours, have been built laft year, by the chief heritors. Care muft be taken not to over-heat them, and to turn the grain often, as in fome inftances where thefe precautions were neglected, the whole has been loft.

The farmer juftly complains of the heavy tax, which bears the name of multure. It is indeed a real oppreffion, when many of the farms are bound to pay the miller the eleventh peck of meal, and in fome cafes, a fimilar quantity of beans, and barley. The tenants of Leckie are now free from this bondage. The miln is in the hands of the proprietor, and arable land is affeffed at the rate of one fhilling fterling per acre for defraying every neceffary expence, to which the tenants have chearfully fubmitted.

It would be of great benefit to the country, if all that variety of fervice ufually demanded by heritors, befides the proper rent, were relinquifhed. Great inconvenience arifes from the obligation to which the tenants are fubjected; to pay fowls, to drive coals, peats and dung; and in harveft, to cut down the proprietor's grain. By being thus in a ftate of requifition, the tenant is often incapable of attending to his own affairs. On fome very important occafions, the opportunity on his own farm is loft, and never returns.

There is an eftablifhed market in Stirling, for all forts of grain, to which the neighbouring farmers refort; and they find a ready fale. The price is ufually regulated by the Edinburgh and Haddington markets.

The whole fecret of farming, feems to ly in preferving the land dry and clean, in obferving a regular rotation of crops,

taking

taking care not to impoveriſh the ſoil, and to be ſeldom from
home, eſpecially in ſeed-time and harveſt, ready to ſeize the
favourable opportunity when it occurs. " The hand of the
" diligent maketh rich".

Population.—It appears that there has been little variation in
the population of the pariſh, for many years. The cotton mills
at Balfron and Down, and the great demand at Glaſgow a few
years ago, for weavers, maſons, and day-labourers, conſiderably diminiſhed the number of ſouls in this pariſh. The hope of
regular employment, and better wages, enticed ſeveral families
to ſettle in thoſe places; where the young and the old were conſtantly occupied. By the late ſtagnation of trade, however,
many have been obliged to return to their former occupations.

Additions made to ſome farms, and the ſpirit of improvement prevailing among the heritors, which has led them to
keep a great part of their lands in their own poſſeſſion, have
baniſhed many inhabitants from the dryfields, where the
ruins of cottages are frequently to be met with; but in the
mean time, the village of Gargunnock, which in the memory of ſome ſtill alive, confiſted only of 3 or 4 houſes, now
contains about 400 ſouls.

Number of ſouls	-	830	Perſons above 80 years of
Males	- -	403	age - - 2
Females	- -	427	Do. betwixt 70 and 80 9
Families	- -	178	Do. betwixt 60 and 70 58
Belonging to the Eſtabliſh-			Do. betwixt 50 and 60 83
ed church	-	808	Do. betwixt 40 and 50 78
Epiſcopalians	-	3	Do. betwixt 30 and 40 104
Seceders	- -	14	Do. betwixt 20 and 30 147
Relief ſociety	- -	2	Do. betwixt 10 and 20 182
Cameronians	- -	3	Do. Under 10 - 167

Total 830

The

The population of this parifh in 1755, was 956
In 1793, it is   -   -   -   830

The number of fouls diminifhed   -   126

Heritors 8, clergyman 1, fchoolmafter 1, ftudents 2, farmers 55, weavers 10, fhoemakers 2, taylors 7, mafons 3,
wrights 4, baker 1, innkeepers 3, fmiths 4, cooper 1, day-
labourers 28, carriers to Edinburgh and Glafgow 2, widowers
11, widows 38, batchelors above forty 8, unmarried women
above forty 9, men-fervants 94, and maid-fervants 62.

Regifter of Marriages.

No.	No.
A. D. 1744—10	A. D. 1784— 8
1745— 6	1785— 7
1746— 8	1786— 9
1747— 6	1787— 5
1748— 8	1788— 5
1749—13	1789—10
1750— 7	1790— 9
1751—14	1791—10
1752—12	1792—12
1753— 4	1793—11
Yearly average — 8	- 8

Regifter

Regiſter of Baptiſms.

No.	No.	No.
A.D. 1639—25	A.D. 1744—36	A.D. 1784—24
1640—35	1745—28	1785—23
1641—33	1746—19	1786—20
1642—28	1747—32	1787—22
1643—35	1748—48	1788—19
1644—27	1749—31	1789—20
1645—39	1750—36	1790—26
1646—26	1751—30	1791—14
1647—22	1752—32	1792—15
1648—26	1753—36	1793—20
Yearly average—29	- - —34	- - —20

Regiſter of Deaths.—No correct account can be given of the number of deaths, in this pariſh; as not a few of the inhabitants have their burying ground in other pariſhes, and it is only when the mort cloth is required, which only happens when the funeral is in the pariſh burying ground, that the death is inſerted in the regiſter. The tax on baptiſms and deaths was paid reluctantly. The one on marriages did not occaſion ſo much alarm, although it was thought ſome kind of reward ought rather to have been offered by the legiſlature, to thoſe who entered regularly into that connexion. All have agreed, that there is wiſdom in the repeal of thoſe taxes.

Poor.—The number of poor who receive a ſtated monthly allowance from the Parochial funds, is ſixteen, all of whom, one excepted, reſide in the village. It is uſual alſo, in the winter ſeaſon, to give occaſional ſupplies of meal and coals, to families who may be in difficult circumftances, but whofe names are not on the poor's roll.

There is now no affeffment for their maintenance. This has been unneceffary for fome years paft, as fupplies abundantly fufficient have been obtained another way.

George Moir, Efq. of Leckie, now deceafed, generoufly added 100 guineas to the poor's ftock in 1788. Being of the Scotch Epifcopal communion, he feldom attended the Eftablifhed church. He faw however, and he had the humanity to acknowledge, that the poor of the parifh fuffered a lofs, by his abfence ; and when he gave the fum above mentioned, he faid, " he was only paying what he owed them." It is to be wifhed, that wealthy heritors who either do not refide upon their eftates, or who are too much in the habit of being abfent from church, would imitate him, in this inftance, and confider the cafe of the poor, who muft fuftain a lofs, when thofe in affluent circumftances withhold their weekly collections at the church. The chief refource for fupplying the poor in this parifh, and in almoft every parifh in Scotland, arifes from the collections made at the church on the Lord's day.

At the fame time, there are perhaps few country parifhes in Scotland, where there is more ample provifion for the neceffities of the poor, than in Gargunnock. The capital ftock belonging to the Kirk Seffion, amounts to L. 365 Sterling, the intereft of which, together with the collections, mortcloth-money, the fees paid at marriages, baptifms, &c. afford the widow, and the fatherlefs, the aged and infirm, a confiderable portion of the neceffaries of life *.

The

* An addition was made to the funds of the poor in 1784, by a very fingular circumftance. Two old women, fifters, who lived in the village of Gargunnock, had for many years, every appearance of extreme indigence ; though

The care of the poor is laid on the Kirk Seſſion. A committee is appointed to enquire into the circumſtances of thoſe who petition for ſupply; and more or leſs is granted, according as the caſe ſeems to require. Few have leſs than half a crown per month; while, four, five, ſix, and in ſome caſes, even ten ſhillings are diſtributed to thoſe, who are abſolutely helpleſs. A perſon muſt reſide in the pariſh, at leaſt three years, before he can be entitled to the public charity.

No public begging is allowed. We are often harraſſed by vagrants from other places; but they are not permitted to acquire a reſidence in the pariſh. One ſeldom gives them any thing, without having cauſe to repent it. They ſpend every thing they receive at the firſt ale-houſe; and for the reſt of the day they become a public nuiſance. The conſtables are called, who ſee them out of the pariſh; but this does not operate as a puniſhment, while they are ſtill at liberty. It would be of great advantage, if in every pariſh, there was ſome place of confinement for people of this deſcription, to keep them in awe, when they might be inclined to diſturb the peace of the town, or of the neighbourhood.

Church,

though without making any application for aſſiſtance from the pariſh. One of them at laſt, applied to be received on the poor's liſt; and as no doubt was entertained of her poverty, ſhe received four ſhillings per month. She died about ſix months after the commencement of her penſion. On examining her bed-cloaths, one purſe (of gold and ſilver), was found after another, till the ſum amounted to upwards of forty pounds ſterling. Some old cheſts and barrels were found ſtored with beef, meal, cheeſe, and various other kinds of proviſion; and it was evident that *the poor women* had lived in great affluence. The relations of the deceaſed, on hearing of the diſcovery, came from a diſtance, to lay claim to her effects. But according to the ſettled rule of the pariſh, ſhe had bequeathed all her effects to the poor, at the time ſhe was received on the poor's liſt. One half was allowed to be the property of the ſiſter, who had received no penſion from the pariſh. The

other

Church, &c.—The church was rebuilt in 1774, is very neatly fitted up, and in excellent repair. On the top of the eaſt gable, there is the figure of a croſs, and on the weſt, that of a creſcent. Theſe were upon the gables of the old church, and have been replaced upon the new. This might have given offence a century ago; but the people are now wiſer than to quarrel with a ſtone of any ſhape or appearance.

The manſe, which was built for a bachelor, is too ſmall for the accomodation of a family. Few houſes of the kind, however, are more pleaſantly ſituated. There is a good garden. The ſoil and expoſure are ſo favourable, that crops and fruits, of various kinds, are reaped from it earlier than from any other in the pariſh. The ſtipend is about L. 80 ſterling, with a glebe of 6 acres. Col. Eidingtoun, the proprietor of the eſtate of Gargunnock, is the patron.

Pariſh School.—The ſchool-houſe is ſituated on a riſing ground, at the weſt end of the village. It has two floors, the firſt for the ſchool, the ſecond for the habitation of the ſchool-maſter. During the winter ſeaſon, there may be 50 or 60 ſcholars; and yet the whole income, including ſalary, perquiſites as Seſſion-clerk, and ſchool fees, ſcarcely amounts annually to L. 16. The reading of Engliſh is taught for a merk Scots per quarter, writing and arithmetic for 2 ſhillings; fees, which are by no means adequate to the troubleſome taſk of the maſter. When a man decently qualified ſubmits to the drudgery of training up children in ſeveral important branches of education, common ſenſe muſt revolt at the idea

of

other half became the property of the Kirk Seſſion, to the great mortification of the relations; who certainly deſerved this diſappointment, as they had taken no notice of the deceaſed, while ſhe lived.

of his being in a worſe ſituation than the day-labourer. It is
hoped ſomething will be done for a better proviſion to the
maſters of pariſh-ſchools.

Village.—The village, conſiſting of about 90 houſes, chiefly
of one floor, and thatched, is ſituated on the ſide of a hill,
part of the barony of Gargunnock. The military road from
Stirling to Dumbarton, paſſes through it. The beſt inn upon
the road is here, few houſes of that kind are kept in ſuch
good order. It is kept remarkably clean and neat, a circumſtance not very common in houſes of the ſame deſcription.

Each inhabitant has a ſmall garden. The one half of
the property belonging to the village was fued out about fifty
years ago, at the rate of 20 ſhillings ſterling per acre, the o-
ther half at a later period was fued at 40s. There is no kind
of trade or manufacture in the village; not even a grocery
ſhop that deſerves the name. Supplies of all the neceſſary
articles are got from Stirling weekly, or by carriers from
Edinburgh or Glaſgow. There are ſome weavers, taylors,
and ſhoemakers, and the other inhabitants are chiefly day
labourers.

Much inconvenience aroſe from the want of a ſurgeon, but
this is now removed. Dr. Moir of Leckie the firſt heritor,
and a gentleman of great eminence in his profeſſion, is ever
ready to give his advice and aſſiſtance to the villagers without
a fee. There is no writer or attorney among them. When
any diſpute ariſes, which is very ſeldom, it is either ſettled by
the Miniſter, or by Mr Graham of Micklewood, a juſtice of
the peace, in whoſe judgement parties acquieſce.

Antiquities.—A little ſouthward of the village, there is a
conical height called the Kier-hill, which is evidently artificial, and ſeems to have been a military work. There are remains

mains of a ditch or rampart of a circular form, which proves that it is not of Roman origin. It is probably of later date, and appears to have been the place from which Sir William Wallace fallied forth on the night when he took by furprize the Peel of Gargunnock.

In one of the dryfields of Boquhan, fome pieces of brafs armour and points of fpears were found a few years ago by a tenant, when digging for limeftone. A great quantity of human bones were alfo difcovered in the fame fpot, the remains probably of the flain at the battle of Ballochleam, which was fought in the adjoining fields.

There is no object of natural curiofity in this parifh equal to the glen of Boquhan. The road made on the eaft fide by the prefent proprietor, leads to a moft romantic view. But, if a perfon has leifure and perfeverance to defcend and walk along the bottom of the glen, at the field of Old-hall, he will be furprized at every ftep, with a fcene perfectly wild, as though nature were in ruins.

Local Difadvantages.—This parifh is fituated on the north fide of the hill. In the higher parts of the dryfields, the fun is not feen during the winter months. Coal muft be brought from Bannockburn, 10 miles diftant; for although marks of coal can be obferved in feveral places within the parifh, no attempts have been made to difcover it. The tenants on the banks of the Forth have boats, but thefe in their prefent ftate are found inconvenient and dangerous for horfes and loaded carts. A bridge is much wanted near the lands of Micklewood. The one at the ford of the Frew, does not fufficiently accommodate the inhabitants of a tract of fertile country, for many miles on both fides of the river.

Roads.—The military road from Stirling to Dumbarton, made betwixt 30 and 40 years ago, and which paſſes through the centre of this pariſh, is now by Act of Parliament to have a new line of direction, and to be made a turnpike road. It is hoped the truſtees will confine the exercife of their power to what is immediately ufeful and neceſſary. Any alterations in order to avoid heights, or to leſſen the diſtance, where that can be conveniently done, would be readily fubmitted to by all, from the evident advantage refulting from them. But, if new lines of confiderable length are propofed, where the grounds muſt be purchafed and re-inclofed ; or, if the road ſhall be fo formed as to render plantations and improvements ufelefs, which have been carrying on for years in the faith that the prefent line of road was to be permanent ; if it ſhall be fo directed, as to abandon a number of thriving villages, or fo unneceſſarily widened as to break in upon many beautiful ſtrips of planting, by which means a debt muſt be incurred that can only be repaid by a heavy toll on the grain, the coal and the lime, it is doubtful, whether the good or the evil of fuch alterations would preponderate. The truſtees have no intereſt but to act for the general advantage of the country, and there is no reafon to doubt that this will be the object of their chief attention.

Game, &c.—In this pariſh there are the heath-fowl, hares, and partridges.

The commencement of partridge ſhooting, as early as the beginning of September, is very often a caufe of their fcarcity, as the tenants are tempted to deſtroy the eggs for the fake of the crops, which are fometimes much injured by the fportf-men and dogs.

The cleft of Ballochleam is ſtill remarkable for the hawks,

for

for which it was in great requeſt in former times, when fal-
conry was in faſhion.

A crow perfectly white, was found laſt ſpring on a tree at
Boquhan.

The farmer ſuffers a real loſs by flocks of pigeons which
cover his fields in ſeed time, and make frequent viſits to his
wheat before it is cut down; and thinks a tax on pigeon houſes
would be a wiſe meaſure.

Diſeaſes.—Rheumatiſm, fevers, conſumptions, are the chief
diſorders of the more aged inhabitants, and the ſmall-pox, the
meaſles, and hooping cough, of the young. Not a few are
afflicted with the ſcrophula, but the people have little con-
ception of its effects on their poſterity. There is ſtill an un-
lucky prejudice againſt innoculating for the ſmall-pox, while
the people have a ſtrong inclination to frequent the houſe
where the diſeaſe exiſts, not perceiving, that by doing ſo they
communicate the infection to their children as effectually, and
a thouſand times more fatally than by the lancet. Dr. Moir
innoculates gratis, and has had conſiderable influence in re-
conciling the common people to a practice, which God in his
providence hath remarkably bleſſed for the preſervation of the
human race.

It is difficult to determine whether the carſe or the dryfield,
be moſt favourable to health. Some have lived to a great
age in both; but it is certain, that as the tenants of the carſe
have the greateſt ſhare of labour, ſo they ſeem moſt capable
of enduring it; and if a greater degree of labour ſupported
with vigour indicates health, or promotes it, it may be conjectured, that the carſe is fully as healthful as the dryfield.
It would perhaps be of advantage, if thoſe who are moſt expoſed to fatigue, to cold, or to moiſture, would uſe a cotton,
inſtead of a linen ſhirt. It might contribute to prevent
thoſe

thoſe rheumatic complaints, to which they are ſo often
ſubject.

Price of labour, wages, &c.—A few years ago, a man ſervant for the farm, who lived with the farmer, could have been
found for 5 or 6 pounds ſterling per year, but now L. 10 or 12
are given. Women ſervants who lately were engaged at
L. 2 10s. are now ſcarcely ſatisfied with L. 4. Their purſe
is juſt as empty as before, but there is a material change in
the article of dreſs. The day labourer who once wrought at
ſix-pence or eight-pence per day, now receives a ſhilling, and in
ſeed time and harveſt, his victuals beſides. Laſt harveſt, 1794,
the wages roſe to ſixteen and eighteen-pence per day, beſides
victuals, which is by far the higheſt rate of wages remembered
in this country.

The day-wage-men for the whole pariſh reſide in the village. They are called forth to their labour in the morning,
by the ſound of pipe or drum, and have the ſame ſignal when
they retire in the evening. They are a ſober induſtrious contented ſet of men, and though their food be ſimple, and their
dreſs and dwellings mean, it is believed that they have more
real enjoyment, than thoſe who are in the more elevated
ſituations.

Food and dreſs.—The aged inhabitants are ſurprized at the
change in the article of living, and what is evidently a proof
of the wealth of the country, is unreaſonbly the ſubject of
their lamentation. It is ſeldom that any of them live beyond
their income. The other extreme ought alſo to be avoided.
More is expected than the pooreſt fare, and the meaneſt dreſs
from men of opulence. When the farmer is only careful
how he may lend his money, and add to his ſtock, and lives
at home as penuriouſly as when he had nothing, he denies
himſelf

himfelf the proper ufe of the bounty of Providence, and is really poor in the midft of his profperity. There are few fuch in this parifh. They all affemble at church, clean, and in decent attire ; many of the women in black cloaks and bonnets, and the younger fort adorned with ribbons. It gives general difguft, however, when the drefs is unfuitable to the ftation. There is fometimes a contention for pre-eminence in gaudy fhew, which is feverely cenfured, efpecially when the maid fervant cannot be diftinguifhed from the miftrefs.

All the men, with a very few exceptions, wear hats, and what may be thought remarkable, there is only one wig in the whole parifh. Tea is univerfally ufed. Even the pooreft families have it occafionally, and the laft cup is qualified with a little whifky, which is fuppofed to correct all the bad effects of the tea. There are few families without fome butcher meat laid up for the winter. All agree, that they are better clothed and fed than their forefathers ; and feem contented with the lot affigned them.

Price of Provifions.—Oat meal is from 15s. to 17s. Sterling per boll ; peas and barley meal about 10s. do ; potatoes, corn meafure, 5s. do ; butter 12s per ftone ; common cheefe 4s, and a better kind made on Saturday's evening 5s. 6d. per ftone ; poultry at a reafonable price. A good fowl may be got for 1s fterling ; eggs at 4d. per dozen. The price of neceffaries in this parifh varies according to the demand at Stirling on the market days.

Great fcarcity was apprehended in 1783, through the failure of the preceding crop ; but upon the return of peace, a large quantity of white peas being commiffioned from England by a man of public fpirit, and grinded into meal, affifted the other expedients which were then adopted to prevent a famine in this part of the kingdom.

Character

Charaĉter, Manners, and Cuſtoms.—The charaĉter of the inhabitants of the pariſh is ſobriety. They profeſs to fear God, and honour the king. In their deportment they are grave, and in their ſpeech conſiderate. They are remarkably attached to the inſtitutions of religion, and all of them, (22 perſons excepted), worſhip together at the pariſh church. During the late attempts of deſigning men to throw the country into confuſion, not an individual in this pariſh joined the clubs of pretended reformers, or ſhewed the leaſt diſaffeĉtion to our happy conſtitution. The only reform they wiſh, is in their own perſons and families, where they acknowledge there are many things which need to be correĉted ; but they leave affairs of ſtate to thoſe who are lawfully appointed to govern. There has been no one here charged with any capital crime, for a long courſe of years. The miniſter's garden is ſituated near the high road, and might be eaſily plundered, and yet he cannot ſay that he has been robbed of a ſingle apple, ſince he came to the pariſh, upwards of 7 years ago. There is very ſeldom occaſion for church diſcipline ; no cauſe has been carried from the ſeſſion to the preſbytery for many years.

The ſacrament of the Lord's Supper is diſpenſed twice in every year. And as there is no ſtated allowance to defray the expence of the communion in winter, the pariſhioners chearfully contribute for this purpoſe.

Young and old are diſtinguiſhed for polite attention to ſtrangers. Men of ſuperior rank have a reſpeĉtful bow from every one they meet ; for people here have not been taught the new doĉtrine of liberty and equality.

It is ſeldom there are ſocial meetings. Marriages, baptiſms, funerals, and the concluſion of the harveſt, are almoſt the only occaſions of feaſting. At theſe times, there is much unneceſſary expence. Marriages uſually happen

in

in April and November. The month of May is cauti-
oufly avoided. A principal tenant's fon or daughter has a
croud of attendants at marriage, and the entertainment lafts
for two days at the expence of the parties. The company at
large pay for the mufic.

The manner of conducting funerals in the country needs
much amendment. From the death to the interment, the
houfe is thronged by night and day, and the converfation is
often very unfuitable to the occafion. The whole parifh is
invited at 10 o'clock in the forenoon of the day of the funeral, but it is foon enough to attend at 3 o'clock afternoon.
Every one is entertained with a variety of meats and drinks.
Not a few return to the dirge, and fometimes forget what
they have been doing, and where they are. Attempts have
been lately made to provide a remedy for this evil ; but old
cuftoms are not eafily abolifhed.

The dregs of fuperftition are ftill to be found. The lefs
informed fufpect fomething like witchcraft about poor old
women ; and are afraid of their evil eye among the cattle.
If a cow is fuddenly taken ill, it is afcribed to fome extraordinary caufe. If a perfon, when called to fee one, does not
fay, " I wifh her luck," there would be a fufpicion he had
fome bad defign. It is but juft to fay, that the generality of
the people are fuperior to thefe vulgar prejudices, though the
traces of them are ftill to be found.

There is one prevailing cuftom among our country people ;
which is fometimes productive of much evil. Every thing is
bought and fold over a bottle. The people who go to the
fair, in the full poffeffion of their faculties, do not always
tranfact their bufinefs, or return to their homes, in the fame
ftate.

It is but juftice, however, to fay, that a difpofition to virtue,

tue, induſtry, loyalty and peace, characterizes the inhabitants of the pariſh of Gargunnock.

Valuation.—The valuation of the whole pariſh is L. 4127 :
15 : 2. Scottiſh money; but the real rental is above L. 3000
ſterling. About 30 years ago, it was only the half of that
ſum. There is now an increaſe at every term. No farm is
now let without an additional rent. Applications are made
for the farm, long before the leaſe expires. The ſeparate
eſtates, which comprehend the whole pariſh, are Leckie and
Kepdarroch, Boquhan, Gargunnock, Micklewood, Redhall,
and Culmore.

PARISH OF KILLEARN,

(County of Stirling, Synod of Glasgow and
Ayr, Presbytery of Dumbarton.)

By the Rev. Mr David Ure, M. A. *Minifter, Glafgow.*

Situation and Extent.

THE parifh of *Killearn* forms the weftern extremity of
the Strath of Blane. This beautiful valley exhibits
a landfcape, replete with a great variety of ftriking objects.
It is fkirted by two ridges of hills, fome of which are of
confiderable height. The fore ground is enriched by the
water of Blane, meandring through fertile paftures and well
cultivated fields ; whilft the diverfified profpect, extending
over the parifhes of Killearn, Drymen, Kilmaronock,
Buchanan, *&c.* comprehends Lochlomond, Benlomond,
Benliddie, the Grampian Hills, *&c. &c.* and at length
is loft among the far diftant mountains of Argyle
and Perthfhire, mingling their azure-coloured fummits
with the clouds. Vaft maffes of bafaltic pillars, exhibiting
extenfive colonnades, arranged in almoft every poffible direction,

rection, come into view on the one hand, and a limpid ſtream, forming a delightful caſcade, on the other. Here a verdant wood, in variegated windings, ſkirts the ſides of the hills ; and there a deep glen, hollowed out by the work of many ages, lays open to view not a ſmall part of the bowels of the earth. In one point of light may be ſeen the ruins of an ancient caſtle *, once the well fortified habitation of a rich and powerful family ; and in another, a numerous flock, ſcattered like ſnowy ſpecks on the verdant declivities of the mountains. Few places in Scotland afford a greater diverſity of the grand and picturefque ſcenes of nature, grouped together in ſuch pleaſing varieties. This pariſh is bounded by the pariſhes of Strathblane and Campſie, on the S. E. ; by New and Old Kilpatricks, on the S. and S. W. ; Drymen and Dumbarton, on the W. ; Balfrone, on the N. ; and Fintrie, on the E. It is by computation about 12 miles in length, from N. E. to S. W. and $2\frac{1}{4}$, at an average, in breadth.

Population.—It is inhabited by 206 families, 56 of whom live in the village of Killearn, which contains 223 perſons. The 150 families reſiding in the country, reckoning five individuals to each, will include 750 inhabitants, making in whole 973 ſouls. The population in the year 1755 was 959. Soon after this time it greatly decreaſed, owing chiefly to the demolition of cottages, to each of which was commonly annexed a paffle of two or three acres of land. Lately, however, from the rapid advance of trade, the population has been greatly on the increaſe. By the following table of births, as they ſtand inrolled in the parochial records, it will appear that the preſent population is not ſo great as at a century ago.

TABLE

* Duntreath, the property of Sir Archibald Edmonſtone of Duntreath, Baronet.

TABLE OF BIRTHS.

Dates.	Births.	Dates.	Births.
1695,	37	1740,	30
1696,	32	1760,	11
1697,	22	1780,	16
1698,	47	1790,	10
1700,	35	1791,	26
1720,	30	1792,	27

Gentlemens Seats, &c.—About a mile and a half ſouth of the village is the *Place of Killearn*, anciently the ſeat of a cadet of the Montroſe family, but lately of *Robert Scott of Killearn, Eſq;* and now the property of *the Right Hon. James Montgomery, Lord Chief Baron for Scotland.* The preſent edifice, which is far from being large, was built in the year 1688. Numerous plantations, regularly diſpoſed in form of clumps, belts, and wilderneſſes, beautify and ſhelter an extenſive tract of pleaſure ground round the houſe.

Croy, ſituated about a mile from Killearn place, received the greateſt part of its preſent improvements, about 30 years ago, from its then proprietor, *Robert Muirhead, Eſq; merchant, Glaſgow.* About 50 acres around the manſion-houſe are laid out in planting, diſpoſed in the moſt advantageous manner for ſhelter and ornament. Amongſt the natural beauties of Croy may be mentioned *Dualt glen.* The ſides of this delightful receſs are very ſteep, and, for a long courſe, exhibit a great variety of trees and ſhrubs, grouped together in almoſt every conceivable form, whilſt the under herbage diſplays not a few rare indigenous plants in great perfection. Foot paths, cut out alongſt the windings of the banks, command, in various points of light, many beautifully diverſified proſpects. The head of the glen is terminated by a freeſtone rock, nearly perpendicular, about

6c

60 feet in height, over which the rivulet of *Dualt*, falling precipitately into a deep Linn, forms a delightful cafcade, which adds not a little to the grandeur and folemnity of the fcene. About half a mile from Dualt glen, and in the eftate of Croy, is *Afhdow*, which exhibits a fcenery in many refpeɢs peculiarly ftriking. It confifts of a high rock, over which the water of *Carnock* precipitately falls, and, by the work of many ages, has cut out for itfelf a deep and winding paffage. The projeɢing rocks, on both fides the water, are wild beyond defcription. Nearly meeting at the top, in fome places, they widen below into beautiful curvatures, naturally hollowed out in various direɢions. The romantic appearance of the rocks is fet off to advantage by trees and fhrubs hanging, in great profufion, over the clefts. The rivulet dafhing over the precipice, and rumbling through the deep-worn channel ; the united harmony of a great variety of the feathered tribe ; and the dark fhade, which perpetually refts upon a great part of this piɢurefque fcenery, confpire to fill the mind of the beholder with the moft pleafing ideas of the grand, the delightful, and the folemn. The eftate of Croy, now the property of *William Richardfon of Croy, Efq; Profeffor of Humanity in the Univerfity of Glafgow*, is receiving daily improvements.

Ballikinrain, the property and fummer refidence of *Robert Dunmore of Ballindaloch*, Efq; occupies one of the moft pleafant fituations in this part of the country. The manfion-houfe, which is of a modern conftruɢion, is by far the moft elegant and commodious dwelling-houfe in the parifh. The eftate, before it came by marriage into Mr Dunmore's poffeffion, belonged for feveral centuries to the *Napiers of Ballikinrain*. The laft proprietor, John Napier of Ballikinrain, Efq; was the *fixteenth* of the name and family of Napier, who, in fucceffion, poffeffed the eftate. It is now enriched with many agricultural improvements, efpecially

inclofures

incloſures and planting, which are highly ornamental as well as profitable.

On the eſtate of *Balglaſs*, likewiſe the property of Mr Dunmore, and adjoining to Ballikinrain, is a large dwelling-houſe or caſtle, of an antiquated conſtruction. It is reported that this place was anciently well fortified, and that *Sir William Wallace of Elerſlie*, the brave defender of his country, once found it a ſafe retreat in time of danger. This place is rendered conſpicuous by the *Corries* or *Curries of Balglaſs*. They are ſemicircular excavations, naturally hollowed out in the weſtern extremity of that ridge of hills, commonly known by the name of Campſie and Strathblane Fells. Some of the Corries are very ſpacious, being more than a mile diameter. In ſeveral places they beautifully exhibit the various mineral ſtrata, of which the mountains are compoſed.

At no great diſtance from Ballikinrain are *Balquhan* (vulgarly *Bohan*) and *Carbeth*; the former, belonging to *Thomas Buchanan of Balquhan, Eſq*; and the latter to *John Buchanan of Carbeth, Eſq*. Around the manſion-houſes on both eſtates are plantations and incloſures to a conſiderable extent.

No ſpot in the pariſh, or perhaps in Scotland, has a better claim to the attention of the public, than the indiſputable birth-place of GEORGE BUCHANAN, the celebrated poet and hiſtorian. That great man, whoſe name is deſervedly famous through Europe, was born at a place called the *Moſs*, a ſmall farm-houſe on the bank of the water of Blane, and about two miles from the village of Killearn. The farm was the property of George Buchanan's father, and was for a long time poſſeſſed by the name of Buchanan. It is now the property of Mr William Finlay of Moſs, and holds of the family of Drummikill, from which

which George's anceftors defcended. The place is called
the *Mofs*, becaufe it is fituated in the vicinity of a peat-
mofs, which is part of the farm. The dwelling-houfe, confidered as a building, is very far from being confpicuous ;
although it is no worfe, and probably never was worfe than
the ordinary farm-houfes in this part of the country. Its
appearance of meannefs arifes from its being very low, and
covered with ftraw thatch. Part of it, however, has been
rebuilt, fince the year 1506, when George was born. Mr
Finlay is highly to be commended for preferving, as much
as poffible, the ancient conftruction and appearance of this
far famed and much honoured houfe. The moft fuperb
edifice would fink into oblivion, when compared with the
humble birth-place of George Buchanan. Long may the
Mofs of Killearn afford mankind a ftriking proof that the
Genius of learning does not always prefer the lofty abodes
of the great and powerful. It muft, however, be remarked,
that the parents of Buchanan, although not very opulent,
yet were not in abject or indigent circumftances. The
farm, which confifts of a plough of land, was able, by the
aid of induftry and œconomy, to keep them eafy. A place
in the neighbourhood is, to this day, called *Heriot's Shiels*,
fo denominated from Buchanan's mother, whofe name was
Agnes Heriot, and who firft ufed that place for the fhield-
ing of fheep. It is reported, that he received the firft rudiments of his education at the public fchool of Killearn,
which was for a long time in great repute, and much frequented. He afterwards, by the liberal affiftance of his
uncle George Heriot, after whom he was named, went to
Dumbarton, Paris, &c. &c. to complete his ftudies. A
confiderable number of old trees yet remain adjacent to
the houfe; and are reported to have been planted by
George when a boy. A *mountain afh*, famous for its age
and

and ſize, was blown down a few years ago; but care is taken to preſerve two thriving ſhoots that have riſen from the old ſtool.

The gentlemen of this pariſh and neighbourhood, led by a laudable ambition to contribute a teſtimony of reſpect to their learned countryman, lately erected, by voluntary ſubſcription, a beautiful *Monument* to his memory. By ſuch public marks of approbation beſtowed upon good and great men, the living may reap advantage from the dead. Emulation is thereby excited, and the active powers of the mind ſtimulated by an ardour to excel in whatever is praiſeworthy. Buchanan's monument is ſituated in the village of Killearn, and commands an extenſive proſpect. It is a well-proportioned *Obeliſk*, 19 feet ſquare at the baſis, and reaching to the height of 103 feet above the ground. In the middle is a cavity of 6 feet ſquare at the bottom, gradually diminiſhing until it reaches the height of 54 feet, where it becomes ſo narrow as to receive the end of a Norway pole, which is continued to the top of the obeliſk. To this pole, the machinery for raiſing up the materials for building, was fixed. Owing to this peculiar mode of conſtruction, the monument is believed to be much ſtronger than if it were ſolid. The foundation was laid, in the month of June 1788, by the Reverend James Graham, miniſter of the pariſh. In the foundation-ſtone was depoſited a *cryſtal bottle* hermetically ſealed, containing a ſilver medal, on which was engraved the following inſcription:

In

In Memoriam,

Georgii Buchanani,

Poetæ et Hiſtorici celeberrimi:

Accolis hujus loci, ultra conferentibus,

hæc Columna poſita eſt, 1788.

Jacobus Craig, architeĉt. Edinburgen.

This beautiful ſtruĉture is built of a white millſtone-grit found a little above the village of Killearn, and in the eſtate of the Lord Chief Baron. The quarry from which it was taken has been wrought for a long time paſt, and is very extenſive : It was known by the name of the Lettre-hill Quarry, from the name of the ground ; afterwards it was called the Mill-ſtone Quarry, becauſe mill-ſtones were frequently taken from it ; then the Houſe of Montroſe Quarry, becauſe it afforded ſtones for the Duke of Mon-troſe's houſe at Buchanan ; now it is called the Monument Quarry. The ſtone is not of a very courſe grit, but is ex-tremely hard and durable.

Gartneſs.—The *Pot of Gartneſs*, in the water of Enrick, has, for its beauty and ſingularity, always attraĉted the at-tention of ſtrangers. It is a deep linn, ſhaped like a cal-dron or pot, whence the origin of the name. It is occa-ſioned by the fall of the water over a rock that lies acroſs the river ; the fall is not perpendicular, but is interrupted by three or four breaks. . This romantic and well known ſpot affords no little entertainment to the angler ; as the ſalmon and trout from Lochlomond, being frequently un-able to force their way over the rock, which requires two or three great leaps quickly made, are detained in the linn,

and

and taken ſometimes in great numbers.—At this place, but on the Drymen ſide of the water*, is *Gartneſs mill*, which has long maintained a high reputation for grain ‚and lint. The remarkable ſervices done the public by this mill during the great froſt in the year 1740, were ſo ſeaſonable, that they will not for a long time be forgotten. It fortunately happened, that in 1739 the mill received a new wheel of a very good conſtruction. It was made of black ſaugh (willow) that grew at Touch, a few miles from Stirling. This kind of wood, of all others, was then preferred for making mill-wheels ; its excellency was ſuppoſed to conſiſt in toughneſs and durability. Owing to the ſtrength and other properties of the wheel, Gartneſs-mill was, by the aid of a conſtant fire, kept a-going during the ſeverity of the froſt, when all other mills, for a great way round, were entirely ſtopped. Corn at that time was brought to Gartneſs from great diſtances, and thereby many families were kept from ſtarving.—Adjoining the mill are the remains of an old houſe in which JOHN NAPIER of Merchiſton, inventor of the logarithms, reſided a great part of his time (for ſome years) when he was making his calculations. It is reported, that the noiſe of the caſcade being conſtant, never gave him uneaſineſs, but that the clack of the mill, which was only occaſional, greatly diſturbed his thoughts. He was, therefore, when in deep ſtudy, ſometimes under the neceſſity of deſiring the miller to ſtop the mill, that the train of his ideas might not be interrupted. He uſed frequently, in the evening, to walk out in his night gown and cap. This, with ſome things which to the vulgar appeared rather odd, fixed on him the character of a *warlock*. It was firmly believed, and currently reported that he was in compact with the devil ; and that

* The Enrick at this place divides Killearn from Drymen pariſh.

that the time he fpent in ftudy was fpent in learning the *black art*, and holding converfation with *Old Nick*. But John Napier was not the only great man who, in days of ignorance, was fuppofed to be a wizard ; nor were the vulgar in this neighbourhood the only people who believed in witchcraft.

Quadrupeds, Birds, &c.—This parifh is not remarkable for any of the more uncommon productions of nature. The fox, badger and foumart, are no ftrangers to fome of the glens and rocks. Afhdow is particularly noted for the haunts of owls, hawks, kaws, and wild cats. The currie of Balglafs has long been remarked for an eagle that hatches her young in that fequeftered and rocky fpot. Herons have their periodical haunts in feveral places of the parifh, as at Balglafs and Corbeth, where in tall fir-trees they annually bring forth their young. The king's-fifher has been obferved at Croy, on the banks of the Blane, a river much refembling the muddy and flow-flowing waters chiefly frequented by that beautiful bird. Jays, magpies and bulfinches abound in the plantations at the hill of Killearn, and fome of the neighbouring banks.

Fifh.—Few places in Scotland afford better entertainment for the angler than this parifh, there being a great number of rivulets and brooks abounding with trout, of which Lochlomond affords in great plenty a perpetual fupply. Salmon, pike, and eels of different kinds, frequent the Enrick and Blane ; but no fifh in greater numbers, at a certain feafon of the year, than the braife (*roach*, Eng.) Vaft fhoals come up from Lochlomond, and by nets are caught in thoufands. Their emigrations from the loch, however, are only for the fpace of three or four days about
the

the end of **May.** The parr is, through the whole year, an
inhabitant of the Enrick ; but it is in greateſt perfection
about the beginning of harveſt. Some of them more than
a foot in length, have been caught at Gartnefs.

Plants, Trees, &c.—Great varieties of indigenous plants
ornament the numerous glens, rocks, and muirs. The Juniper grows in fome places to a great fize, and is commonly very prolific. The ſtone bridge over the Blane, at
the Mofs, is founded upon a layer of juniper buſhes. It·is
believed that this plant, when in a wet fituation below
ground, refiſts corruption for a very long time. It was believed, during the plague in Scotland, that people who
lived in the immediate neighbourhood of places abounding
with juniper, or who burned it plentifully in their houfes,
were not readily, if at all affected with the plague. The
Scottiſh Gaul, *(Myrica Gale, Linn.)*, a valuable vermi-
fuge, abounds in feveral places of the pariſh. Were the
qualities of this oderiferous ſhrub more generally known,
its cultivation would probably be attended with confiderable profit. Amongſt the plants which are not generally
very common, are the Feſtuca *ovina vivipara ;* Echium
vulgare, Imperatoria *Oſtruthium,* Parnaſſia *paluſtris,* Poly-
gonum *Penſylvanicum,* Adoxa *Mofchatellina,* Eryſimum
Barbarea, Chryfofplenium *Alternifolium,* Saxifraga *hyp-*
noides, Matricaria *Parthenium,* Empetrum *nigrum,* Afple-
nium *Scolopendrium,* A. *Ruta muraria,* Polypodium *Lon-*
chitis, P. *phegopteris,* P. *fragile,* Lycopodium *clavatum,*
L. *Selaginoides,* L. *Selago,* L. *Alpinum.*

The Sambucus *nigra* (elder tree, Eng.) is no ſtranger
in many places of the pariſh. Some of the trees are very
well ſhaped, and by the natural bending of the branches
caufe an agreeable ſhade, or bower, exhibiting an example
of the propriety of the name given to that fpecies of plants

in

in Scotland, namely, the *Bower-tree.* A great number of beautiful oaks ornament the eſtate of Ballikinrain. The largeſt, and probably the oldeſt in the pariſh, grows in full vigour at Killearn place. The trunk is 12 feet circumference, and ſupports many ſtately branches that widely diſplay a foliage uncommonly pleaſant. No produ&ion of the vegetable kingdom in this pariſh is, however, more remarkable than two large yew trees at Ballikinrain. One is the berry bearing kind, the other not. The trunk of the former is 8 feet in circumference, of the latter, 10 feet 8 inches. They are only 9 feet ſeparate from each other, making the appearance, at a diſtance, of a ſingle tree only; they are about 60 feet in height. Nine large branches ſtrike off from the male plant, at the height of 6 feet from the ground : they make a beautiful curve downwards, ſo that their extremities touch the earth, and cover an area of 18 yards diameter, forming a moſt agreeable ſhade, impenetrable at all times to rain. As there is no account, even by tradition, when they were planted, their age muſt be great. They are frequented by a conſiderable number of the golden creſted wren, *(Motacila Regulus)*, the ſmalleſt bird in Europe, and, except the humming bird, probably in the world. They build their neſts under the curving extremities of the branches, where the foliage is thickeſt. Their neſts are conſtru&ed with exquiſite art, and are ſuſpended under the twigs, like ſo many little baſkets from the ceiling of a room.

This part of the country is far from being deſtitute of exotic plants in a high degree of perfe&ion. This is particularly the caſe with reſpe& to the larix, a great number of which adorn the banks and incloſures at the houſe of Killearn. They are about 60 years old, being among the firſt of the kind that were planted in the open field in Scotland; they are generally 3 feet diameter at the thickeſt,

and

and have grown to the tallneſs of nearly 100 feet. For beauty and ſize very few, if any of the kind in Scotland ſurpaſs them. In the vicinity of the larixes are many beautiful ſpruce and beech trees, of uncommonly large dimenſions. The oriental mapple, the ſweet cheſnut and tulip trees have, in this place, arrived to great perfection and beauty.

Minerals, &c.—With reſpect to the mineral kingdom, few things in this pariſh merit particular attention. The higher parts of the hills conſiſt chiefly of a decompoſible whinſtone, containing, in ſome places, ſmall veins of an hæmatitical iron ore ; but the quantity yet diſcovered is too ſmall to become an object of importance. In ſome places on the ſides of the hills, are found many ſucceſſive ſtrata of till and limeſtone. Theſe are beautifully diſplayed in ſeveral places where large excavations have been made by means of water. The limeſtone is of two kinds, and is wrought but in ſmall quantities. The preferable kind is not diſpoſed in regular compact ſtrata, but rather in irregular maſſes, imbedded in a reddiſh clay blotched with white. The inferior kind is called camſtone, from its being chiefly found in glens. It is diſpoſed in thin, but numerous regular ſtrata, ſeparated from each other by a bluiſh till, that, when acted upon by the weather, falls down into clay. The camſtone, when broken, has a ſmooth ſurface ; it contains a great proportionable quantity of clay in its compoſition ; and after it is ſufficiently burnt, and whilſt red hot in the fire, it muſt be ſlacked with water poured upon it, otherwiſe it will not readily fall down into lime. The ſtrata are ſo thin, that they are not thought to be worth working. Fragments of the ſtone, which fall down from the ſides of the glens, are occaſionally gathered for uſe. Some varieties of it, which crumble down by expoſure to the weather, might, without being burnt, ſerve for the

purpoſe

purpofe of manure. An extenfive ftratum of an excellent millftone grit enriches the eftate of Balglafs, and fupplies the country to a great diftance with millftones. The quarry began to be regularly wrought about 40 years ago ; it is now cut down to the depth of 24 feet, and can afford ftones of any fize, and of 3 different qualities. A very thick ftratum of foft freeftone, the grit not fine, prevails in all the lower grounds of the parifh; its depth has not yet been difcovered. It is of a red colour, but variegated with blotches, and ftreaks of white and grey. It is not of the beft quality for building, and affords no fymptoms of any valuable mineral in the vicinity. Several trials, by *boring* and *fhanking*, have been made to find coal, but unfuccefsfully ; and I do not think that any where in the parifh the fymptoms of that ufeful foffil are favourable. Amongft the ftones in this parifh may be mentioned a jafper, which abounds in the banks of Enrick, and likewife in the parifhes of Buchanan, Balfrone, and Fintry. The colours are brown, red and green intermixed, in the form of blotches and ramifications ; fome nodules refemble the bloodftone, whilft others contain a confiderable portion of the zoned agate, which abounds in many places of Scotland. The jafper takes a fine polifh, and has been cut into feals, buttons, &c.

Climate.—The climate is wet and cold, but the air is not infalubrious. The inhabitants are not remarkably fubject to any epidemical difeafe. Many of them live to a confiderable old age : There are four perfons at prefent between 80 and 90 years of age. John Buchanan of Provanftoun, aged 104, died here *anno* 1792.

Agriculture.—The moft of the hilly part of the parifh is yet in a ftate of nature, having never been plowed ; but

the

the lower grounds are generally arable. The former contains feveral extenfive moors and moffes, which are chiefly
occupied in fheep-walks ; the latter, (not the half of the
extent of the parifh), is for the moft part inclofed with
ftone-dikes and hedges. The foil is, for the moft part,
of a ftiff clay that becomes exceffively hard when dry, and
generally has a wet cold tilly bottom. In fome diftricts,
however, are a few fields of a loamy foil, which produce
good crops of oats, barley and peafe. The climate is very
unfavourable for the culture of wheat ; but the cultivation
of lint, potatoes, ryegrafs and clover, is attended with profit. There is, however, more cropped with oats than with
all the reft put together. The cultivation of turnip in the
open field is not practifed, although, from fome few trials
that were made on that profitable root, there is reafon to
believe that it might be attended with confiderable advantage in feveral thoufand acres in the parifh. Extremely
few of the lately improved implements of hufbandry have
here been brought into practice. The common Scotch
plough, wrought with four horfes, is in general ufe. The
farmer, before agriculture can be brought to any tolerable
degree of perfection, muft direct his care to free his land
from under water, which almoft univerfally prevails. But
the practice of draining, although very much needed, meets
here with fmall attention.

Few places afford better opportunities for irrigation than
this parifh. The country is abundantly fupplied with excellent water that pours down from the adjacent heights in
fprings and fmall rivulets, which could eafily be directed
over the numerous declivities. This mode of improvement
was a few years ago tried with fuccefs in Mr Dunmore's
eftate. The land over which the water was made to flow,
produced grafs uncommonly luxuriant, and retained through
the whole year a fine verdure.

Attention

Attention is beginning to be paid to the breeding of milch-cows by crossing the Ayrshire with the native breed, which approaches nearly to the Highland. The native cows are generally of a black colour, with white faces; and weigh, when fat, about 16 stone heavy weight. The milk of a cow *per* day in summer, is commonly about 4¼ pints Scotch. The milk is mostly made into butter, that brings at an average 9 d. *per* lb. The skimmed milk is made into cheese that is sold from 4 s. to 5 s. *per* stone. Grazing cattle for slaughter is, in many parts of the parish, carried to a confiderable extent, and is attended with profit. The moorland farms are stocked with about 1400 score of the black and grey faced sheep. A few Spanish sheep were, in the beginning of 1793, brought by Mr Dunmore to Ballikinrain, and are thriving very well. Horses for the draught are of the Lanarkshire breed, and are chiefly purchased at Glasgow and Rutherglen markets. Not a few of the farmers, however, are in the practice of rearing horses on their farms. Two-wheeled carts, and waggons with one horse, are very generally used; but sledges are found to be necessary in the moorland farms.

The arable land is in general divided into farms of about 60 acres each. These are let in leases chiefly of 19 years duration. The lands in the estate of Killearn are, for the encouragement of the farmer, generally let in leases of three 19 years; and the consequences are far from being bad, for the tenants are, on the whole, doing very well. Care, however, is very properly taken by the Lord Chief Baron, to give this encouragement only to persons of active and industrious habits, and who have a spirit for agricultural improvements. Long leases to an indolent farmer, even although at certain terms there may be a proportionated rise in the rent, only encourages his insuperable indolence. He seeks no more than merely to scrape together as much as will

barely

barely pay the rent, and keep his family in life. The land is worn out to the laſt; his domeſtics are trained up in habits of negligence and ſloth ; a bad example is ſet before the community ;—and Poverty ſtares with her meagre countenance, in the houſe and in the field.

The moorland farms are ſeveral hundred acres in extent. The great diſparity of ſoil and ſituation, occaſions a ſimilar diſparity of the rent of land. From 10 s. to 15 s. *per* acre is a common rent for arable land ; but ſome of it is no higher than 6 s. or 7 s. Some places, eſpecially on the banks of Blane and Enrick, where the ſoil is very good, are uſually rented at L. 1, 10 s. *per* acre ; but in many parts of the moors an acre is not worth more than 6 d. and in the moſſes not worth 1 d. The increaſe of manufactures in the neighbourhood, and the advancement of agricultural improvements, for which there is great room in the pariſh, will probably raiſe conſiderably the value of land. The pariſh is ſupplied with ſeven corn-mills and two lint-mills, which have abundance of water all times of the year. To theſe mills the moſt part of the pariſh yet continues to be aſtricted.

Trade.—Every encouragement is given the farmer by having a profitable and ready market in *Balfrone*, to which he has an eaſy acceſs. The late rapid population of that newly erected village, has greatly improved the adjacent country. This pleaſing alteration ariſes wholly from a variety of manufactures, recently introduced into the neighbourhood, chiefly by Robert Dunmore of Ballindalloch, Eſq. This public-ſpirited gentleman, inſpired with the ambition of doing good to mankind by employing them in uſeful induſtry, began his improvements in the year 1788, by eſtabliſhing a muſlin manufactory at Balfrone. This village, which is in the immediate neighbourhood of Kil-

learn,

learn, and which formerly contained no more than fix or feven families, was at that time laid out according to a regular plan, and now contains no fewer than 220 families. The houfes, many of which are 2 ftories high, are in general covered with flate. The *Ballikinrain* cotton-mill was erected by Mr Dunmore in 1792. It is conftructed for fpinning woollen as well as cotton; the former for the carpet, the latter for the muflin manufacture. This work, at prefent carried on under the management of Mr Robert Macmorran from Douglafs, employs about 100 perfons, moft of whom refide in the neighbourhood of the mill. The greateft manufacturing work in the parifh is *Enrick printfield*, which was begun in 1792. The operative part of the bufinefs is carried on by Mr J. F. Moriar, a Swifs, under the firm of Meffrs Monteith, Warren, and Company, Glafgow. The buildings are conftructed to contain 16 printing preffes, to go by water, and 72 tables for block-printing, befides boiling-houfes, dye-houfes, &c. for executing bufinefs on a very extenfive fcale. Every part of the apparatus is new, and of the moft approved conftruction, efpecially the wafhing wheels, which are not furpaffed by any in Europe. One of the bleaching-fields, confifting of a plain of 15 acres, is fecured from the inundations of Enrick by an artificial bank, the raifing of which coft a confiderable fum of money. Bufinefs was begun here in the month of June 1793. But unfortunately an entire ftop was almoft put to the work by the prefent ftagnation of trade, which has communicated its baneful influence through all this country. The whole work at prefent (Sept. 1793) employs no more than 250 perfons, the moft of whom refide in Balfrone.

Manufactures, Wages, &c.—The manufactures in the parifh, befides what are carried on in the places already mentioned,

mentioned, are not very confiderable. Their ftate may, in general, be known from the following lift of tradefmen and artificers :—Blackfmiths, 4 ; coopers, 4 ; dyers, 4 ; flax-dreffers, 3 ; gardeners, 2 ; hofiers, 11 ; mafons, 7 ; fhoemakars, 12 ; tailors, 5 ; weavers, 28 ; wrights, 14.— Mafons and wrights receive 1 s. 8 d. a-day, during fummer, and from 1 s. to 1 s. 2 d. in winter. Tailors work in their employers houfes, each receiving, befides his victuals, 10 d. for his day's work. The hofiers are all employed by manufacturers in Glafgow, and are paid by the piece. A day labourer has from 8 d. to 1 s. a-day, with victuals; and 1 s. 3 d. or 1 s. 4 d. without victuals. A man-fervant for country work has from L. 3 to L. 5 Sterling, *per* half-year, befides bed, board and wafhing ; a woman-fervant has about L. 2. All the fhoemakers are engaged in *cuftomary work*, a common expreffion for home confumpt. In this alfo all the weavers are at prefent employed. That fo many looms fhould be engaged in cuftomary work for fo fmall a number of people, ceafes to be a wonder when it is confidered that very little cloth of foreign manufacture is worn in the parifh. The inhabitants continue the practice of making cloth for their own wearing. The men are decently clothed, both for *kirk and market*, with well-dreffed *Scots cloth*, commonly of a brown, grey, or blue colour. In this they think themfelves to be warmer and more comfortable than in the beft Englifh fuperfine. The womens apparel is chiefly a variety of ftuffs of their own manufacture ; as *Bengals*, a kind of cloth of linen warp, and cotton weft ; *drugget*, compofed of linen warp and woollen weft ; *harns*, and other coarfe linens of various kinds, befides plaiding, both tweeled and plain, for gowns and petticoats. Their bed-cloaths, as blankets, ticking, &c. are wholly of their own making. The linen yarn they fpin from lint of their own raifing, and the woollen from fleeces the product

duct of sheep farms in the parish. They practise the arts of scouring and bleaching their woollen and linen, which, for the safety of both yarn and cloth, they prefer to the methods used in some bleachfields. A lye made of breckins (*pteris aquilina*, LINN.) is of great use to them, both for washing and bleaching. The method of preparing this lye is very simple. The breckins are cut when arrived at their full growth, and always when dry. As soon as convenient after being cut, they are mixed with dried broom ; both are laid in a heap, and burned. No more broom is used than what is necessary to assist in thoroughly burning them. Along with the broom is sometimes added the dried roots of cabbages and green kail. The ashes of the whole are carefully collected, and boiled in water until all the alkali is dissolved ; then the lye is poured off for use. In this lye the yarn or cloth is boiled for a certain time ; and the bleaching is thereby greatly accelerated. Not a few of the inhabitants dye a considerable variety of colours, from materials the product of the country. In the proper management of their cloth, however, they are greatly assisted by *Mr William Jamison*, dyer and clothdresser at Runroy near Gartness, who has brought the dyeing and dressing of Scots cloth to a considerable degree of perfection. Cloth is sent him to be dyed and dressed from Glasgow, Stirling, and all the country round. Mr Jamison manufactures plaids, duffles, blankets, &c. &c. for sale ; and his demands are daily increasing.

In addition to what the industrious women of Killearn make for their family wear, they bring a considerable quantity of cloth to the market. As much usually of every web is exposed to sale, as defrays the out-laid expences for weaving, &c. For this overplus they find abundance of customers, either in the city of Glasgow, or at three fairs annually held in the village of Killearn. Scots cloth is ſold from 10 d. to 5 s. 6 d. *per* yard; harn from 8 d. to 1 s. 5 d.; linen from 1 s. 6 d. to 3 s.

By a community ſo actively employed, little time is waſted in idleneſs, intemperance, or political cabals. There are, however five public houſes in the pariſh, but they are chiefly frequented by travellers. Two turnpike-roads, lately made through the pariſh, are of great ſervice to the inhabitants. The ſtatute-labour, which is moſtly raiſed in money at 18 s. Sterling *per* L. 100 Scots of valued rent, is applied to private roads, which are ſtill far from being in a good condition.

The greateſt impediment to improvements in this part of the country is the ſcarcity of good fuel. The neareſt coal is in Campſie or Baldernock, at the diſtance of 10 or 12 miles. The price at the hill is 1 s. 6 d. the cart-load, containing about 12 cwt. The carriage comes to about 4 s. The ſcarcity of coal is ſupplied by *turf* and *peat*, for obtaining which the feuars and tenants have a ſervitude on the moors. The turf is procured by ſetting fire to the graſs and heath about the month of June, and then raiſing the ſurface with what is called a *ſlaughter ſpade.* This practice greatly injures the moors by depriving them of their verdure, which neceſſarily requires ſeveral years to be renewed. The loſs, however, is in ſome meaſure repaid by the great quantity of aſhes for manure, procured from this kind of fuel.

Religion.—With reſpect to the ſtate of religion, few obſervations occur that merit the attention of the public. The people in general regularly attend divine ſervice in the pariſh church. There are only about 12 adherents to the different parties of Seceders. Several reſpectable clergymen, ſince the reformation from Popery, have ſucceſſively been miniſters of the pariſh, as Meſſ. Forſter, Gilleſpie, Sempell and Craig,

Craig, before the Revolution in 1668. Since that time the people have been happy under the fuccefsful miniftry of Meffrs George Park, James Bain, James Morrifon, and the prefent incumbent, James Graham, who was ordained *anno* 1768. The church was rebuilt in the year 1734, and is conveniently feated. Mr John Finlayfon has, for nearly 40 years, officiated as parochial fchoolmafter. The falary is L. 8, 13 s. yearly. The wages for Englifh, writing, and arithmetic are only 1 s. 6 d. *per* quarter. Three or four private fchools have, for fome time paft, been kept in different parts of the parifh ; the numerous rivulets and deep glens by which the country is interfected, render, to children living át a diftance, the accefs to the parochial fchool always dangerous, and often impoffible.

State of the Poor.—Paupers ufually on the feffion-lift are from 10 to 15, who, according to their need, receive from 4 s. to 16 s. *per* quarter. A few indigent families receive, after the facrament, a little fupply, as the minifter and elders fee proper. The funds for anfwering thefe charitable purpofes amount annually to about L. 30, the moft of which is collected in boxes handed by the elders through the church, immediately before pronouncing the bleffing in the forenoon. None of the poor are permitted to beg. To be fo poor as to need affiftance from the kirk-feffion is in this, and moft other places of Scotland, where poor taxes are not eftablifhed, accounted a difgrace, as fuch a ftate is commonly confidered as proceeding, for the moft part, either from indolence or mifmanagement. Every attempt to eradicate, or even to weaken fuch a fenfe of fhame, is doing a manifeft injury to fociety.

Mifcellaneous Obfervations.—Superftition yet continues to operate fo ftrongly on fome people, that they put a fmall
quantity

quantity of ſalt into the firſt milk of a cow after calving, that is given any perſon to drink. This is done with a view to prevent *ſkaith*, if it ſhould happen that the perſon is not *cany*. A certain quantity of cow dung is forced into the mouth of a calf immediately after it is calved, or at leaſt before it receives any meat ; owing to this, the vulgar believe that witches and fairies can have no power ever after to injure the calf. But theſe, and ſuch like ſuperſtitious cuſtoms, are every day more and more loſing their influence.

At *Blareſſen Spout-head*, if we believe tradition, a bloody battle was fought between the Romans and Scots ; ſeveral ſtones ſet on edge have continued ever ſince to diſtinguiſh the ſpot. The tenant, a few years ago, would have carried all the ſtones away, had he not been ſtrictly prohibited by Mr Buchanan of Carbeth, the proprietor of the ground, who had got notice of his intentions.

A very large cairn ſome time ago was demoliſhed in the muir of Killearn, and the ſtones uſed for building dikes. This ancient ſepulchral *tumulus* concealed, in the bottom of it, a coffin, compoſed of ſtones ſo very large that they could not eaſily be removed, without being firſt broken in pieces.

A phenomenon not unworthy the attention of the public, is an old woman, who, owing to exceſſive grief, about 20 years ago, became deranged in her judgment. She was then about 50 years of her age. The hair of her head ſoon afterwards became thin and very grey, in which ſtate it continued till about 5 years ago, when it gradually turned black, thick, and ſtrong. She generally goes with her head bare, and has not yet recovered the right uſe of her reaſon.

The *kippering* of ſalmon is ſucceſsfully practiſed in ſeveral parts of the pariſh. All the blood is taken from the fiſh immediately after it is killed ; this is done by cutting
the

the gills; it is then cut up at the back, on each fide the bone or chain, as it is commonly called. The bone is taken out, but the tail, with two or three inches of the bone is left; the head is cut off; all the guts are taken out; but the fkin of the belly is left uncut; the fifh is then laid, with the fkin undermoft, on a board, and is well rubbed, and covered over with a mixture of equal quantities of common falt and Jamaica pepper. Some of this mixture is carefully fpread under the fins to prevent them from corrupting, which they are exceedingly ready to do, efpecially if the weather is warm. A board with a large ftone is fometimes laid upon the fifh, with a view to make the falt penetrate into it more effectually. In fome places, as Dumbarton, inftead of a flat board, a fhallow wooden trough is ufed, by which means the brine is kept about the fifh; fometimes two or three falmon are kippered in the fame veffel at the fame time, one being laid upon the other. The fifh, with the board or trough, is fet in a cool place for two or three days; it is then removed from the board, and again rubbed with falt and pepper, after which it is hung up by the tail, and expofed to the rays of the fun, or the heat of the fire. Care is previoufly taken to ftretch out the fifh by means of fmall fticks or hoops placed acrofs it from fide to fide. After it has remained in the heat a few days, it is hung up in the kitchen, or other dry place, till ufed. Every method is taken to keep the fifh from putrefaction. It is an error to fuppofe, as fome have ignorantly done, that kippered falmon means corrupted falmon.

Some people, in order to give the kipper a peculiar tafte, highly relifhed by not a few, carefully fmoke it with peat reek, or the reek of Juniper bufhes. This is commonly done by hanging it up fo near a chimney in which peats, or Juniper bufhes are burnt, as that it receives the fmoke.

ſmoke. There it remains two or three weeks, by which time it generally acquires the taſte. Salmon kippered in this manner uſually ſells 2 d. *per* lb. higher than when freſh.

This pariſh and neighbourhood were, for a long time, unhappily expoſed to the plundering inroads of large companies of migratory freebooters, who for ſafety lurked in the borders of the Highlands. Theſe depredators made frequent incurſions into the pariſhes of Buchanan, Balfrone, Killearn, Dumbarton, Kilpatricks, &c. and carried off all the cattle they could find. This infamous practice was continued ſo late as the year 1743, and perhaps later. Long before that, however, ſome gentlemen near the border of the Highlands, undertook, for certain ſums of money, to protect the property of their neighbours, or to make a full recompence for what was ſtolen from them. The money paid for this protection was called the *Black Mail*, and was paid agreeably to a bargain concluded upon by the two contracting parties. One of the original contracts remains in the poſſeſſion of Mr Dunmore at Ballikinrain. As this contract is not only a literary curioſity, but is perhaps the only contract of the kind now exiſting, and as it exhibits a true picture of the ſtate of the country ſo late as the year 1741, and likewiſe leads us to form an idea of the happy alteration that has ſince taken place, the ſubjoined copy of it *verbatim* will not, it is preſumed, be unacceptable to the public, eſpecially as the report of the Black Mail is ſo generally, yet ſo imperfectly known *.

---

* Copy of a Contract for keeping a Watch on the Borders of the Highlands. *anno* 1741.

It is contracted, agreed, and finally ended betwixt the parties underwritten, to witt; James and John Graham elder and younger of Glengyle, on the one part, and the gentlemen, heritors, and tenants, within

the

the fhires of Perth, Stirling, and Dumbarton, who are hereto fubfcribing, on the other part, in manner following : Whereas, of late years, feveral perfons within the bounds aforefaid have been very great fufferers through ftealing of their cattle, horfes, and fheep ; for preventing whereof the faids James and John Grahams, with and under the conditions, provifions, and for the caufes after fpecified, hereby bind and oblige them, conjunctly and feverally, their heirs executors, and fucceffors, that the faid James Grahame fhall keep the lands fubfcribed for, and annexed to the refpective fubfcriptions, fkaithlefs of any lofs, to be fuftained by the heritors, tenants, or inhabitants thereof, through the ftealing and away taking of their cattle, horfes, or fheep, and that for the fpace of feven years complete, from and after the term of Whitfunday next to come ; and for that effect, either to return the cattle fo ftolen from time to time, or otherwayes, within 6 moneths after the theft committed, to make payment to the perfons from whom they were ftolen, of their true value, to be afcertained by the oaths of the owners, before any Judge-ordinary; providing always, that intimation be made to the faid James Graham, at his houfe in Correilet, or where he fhall happen to refide for the time, of the number and marks of the cattle, fheep, or horfe ftolen, and that within 48 hours from the time that the proprietors thereof fhall be able to prove by hable witneffes, or their own or their herds oaths, that the cattle amiffing were feen upon their ufual pafture within the fpace of 48 hours previous to the intimation, as faid is; and declaring, that it fhall be fufficient if the heritors or tenants, be-fouth or be-eaft the town of Drymen, make intimation in writing at the houfe of Archibald Strang, merchant in Drymen, of their loffes in the before mentioned, to a perfon to be appointed by the faid James Graham of Glengyle to attend theire for that purpofe, and in his abfence to the faid Archibald. And further, it is fpecially condefcended to and agreed upon, that the faid James Grahame fhall not be bound for reftitution in cafes of fmall pickereys ; declaring, that an horfe or black cattle ftolen within or without doors, or any number of fheep above fix, fhall be conftructed to be theft, and not pickerey. And with regard to horfes and cattle ftolen within the bounds aforefaid, and carried to the fouth, the faid James Grahame obliges him, that he fhall be as ferviceable to the gentlemen fubfcribers in that cafe as he poffibly can ; and if he cannot recover them, he fubmits himfelf to the difcretion of the heritors in whofe ground the theft is committed, whether he fhall be liable for their value or not.

And it is hereby exprefsly provided and declared by both parties, That in cafe of war within the country, that this prefent contract fhall thenceforth ceafe and become void ; for the which caufes, and on the

other

other part, the heritors and tenants hereto fubfcribing, with and under the provifions and declarations above and under written, bind and oblige them, their heirs, executors, and fucceffors, to make payment to the faid James Grahame of Glengyle, or to any perfon he fhall appoint to receive the fame, of the fum of L. 4 yearly during the fpace forefaid, for ilk hundred pound of ye valued rent of the lands annexed to their refpective fubfcriptions, and that at two terms in the year, Whitfunday and Martinmas, by equal portions, beginning the firft terms payment thereof at the faid term of Whitfunday nixt, for the half year immediately following, and fo furth, to continue at the faids terms during the continuance of thefe prefents: provideing always, like as is hereby fpecially provided and declared, that it fhall be leifome and lawful for both parties to quitt and give up this prefent contract at the end of every year if they think fit, intimation being always made on the part of the faid James Grahame at the refpective kirk-doors within the bounds aforefaid, on a Sabbath day, immediately after the forenoon's fermon, a moneth before expiration of the year: and on the part of the heritors and other fubfcribers, by a letter to the faid James Grahame from them, and another from him, acknowledgeing the receipt thereof, or the atteftation of two wittneffes, that the letter was left at his houfe, or was delyvered to himfelf two moneths before expyring of the year; it being always underftood, that any fubfcriber may quitt and give up the contract for his own part, whether the reft concur or not at the end of each year, as faid is. And both parties bind and oblidge them and their forefaids to perform the premiffes *hinc inde* to others under the penalty of L. 20 Sterling, to be payed by the party failzier to the party obferver, or willing to obferve their part thereof, attour performance. And moreover, for the faid James Grahame's further encouragement, and for the better reftraining the evil practices above mentioned, the fubfcribers hereby declare, that it is their intention that all fuch thieyes and pickers as fhall be apprehended by the faid James Grahame of Glengyle, or occafionally by any other perfon within the bounds aforefaid, againft whom there is fufficient proof, fhall be profecute according to law, and brought to juftice. And for greater fecurity, both the faids parties confent to the regiftration hereof in the books of Council and Seffion, or others competent, that letters of horning on fix dayes, and other executorials needfull, may pafs hereon as effeirs. And to that effect they conftitute

their procurators, &c. In witnefs whereof, both the faids parties have fubfcribed thefe prefents, confifting of this and the preceding fheet, written on ftamped paper, by Andrew Dick, chyrurgeon in Drymen, at Balglas,

glas, the tuentyeth day of Aprile Im vije and fourty-one years, by Robert Bontein of Mildovan, before William M'Lea his fervant, and Mr William Johnfton fchoolmafter at Balglas, the faid Robert Bontein having filled up his firft date, and witneffes names and defignations. At Ballikinrain the tuintie-firft day of forefaid moneth and year, by James Napier of Ballikinrain, before Alexander Yuill his fervant, and Gibert Couan, tenant in Ballikinrain, the faid James Napier having filled up this fecond date, witneffes names and defignations. Att Boquhan the tuenty-fecond day of Aprile, moneth forfaid, and year, by Hugh Buchanan of Balquhan, before thefe witneffes, John Paterfon and Robert Duncan, both tenants yr. Att Glins, the tuenty-feventh day of moneth and year forefaid, before thefe witnefes, Walter Monteath of Keyp, and John Buchanan younger of Glins. Att Eafter Glins, the tuenty-feventh day of moneth and year forefaid, before thefe witneffes, Walter Monteath of Keyp, and Thomas Wright younger of Eafter Glins, fubfcribet be Alexander Wright of Peufid. Att Ammere, the firft day of Mey feventin hundred and fortie-one years, befor thees witnes, Arfbelt Leckie of Arnmere, and Walter Menteath younger of Keyp, Walter Monteath, att above place, day, date, year, and witneffes, by James Key portioner of Edenbelly, month, date, place, and year aforefaid, before thefe witneffes, Walter Monteath therein, and Walter Monteith younger of Keyp, and by Robert Galbraith at Fintrie, fourth May, before Robert Farrie of Balgrochan, and James Ure, tenant in Hilltowne of Balgair.

Will. Johnfton, witnefs.
William M'Lea, witnefs.
Gilbert Cowan, witnefs.
Alexander Yuill, witnefs.
John Paterfon, witnefs.
Robert Duncan, witnefs.
Walter Monteath, witnefs.
John Buchanan, witnefs.
Thomas Wright, witnefs.
Archibald Leckie, witnefs.
Walter Monteith, witnefs.
Alexander Wright, witnefs.
Archibald Leckie, witnefs.
Walter Monteath, witnefs.
Walter Monteath, witnefs.
Robert Farrie, witnefs.

Robert Bontein of Mildovan, for my lands of Balglas in the paroch of Killern, being Three hundred and fifty pound of valuation; and lands of Provanftoun, in the paroch of Balfron, Ninety-feven pound feven fhilling valuation.
James Napier of Ballikinrain, for my lands in the paroch of Killern, being Two hundred and fixtie pound of valuation. And for my Lord Napier's lands in faid paroch, being Three hundred and twentie-eight pound of valuation. And for Culcreuch's lands in the paroch of Fintrie, being Seven

James

James Ure, witnefs.
John Buchanan, witnefs.
James M'Grime, witnefs.

hundred and twentie feven pound of valuation. And for faid Culcreuch's lands, in the paroch of Balfrone, being One hundred and ten pound of valuation.

Hu. Buchanan of Balquhan, for my lands of Boughan and Brunfhogle, in the paroch of Killearn, being One hundred and feventy-three pound of valuation.

Mofes Buchanan of Glins, Two hunder fextie-two pund valuation.

John Wright of Efter Glins, Sixtiefix pound val.

Alexander Wright of Pufide, On hundred and foure pound and fix fhiling and eghtpenny Scot valuation.

Walter Monteath of Kyp, Three hundred pounds valuation.

James Key, portioner of Enblioy, for fextiey-fix pond Scots valuation.

Robert Galbraith, portioner of Edinbely, for thritie-three pound Scots valuation.

Alexander Buchanan of Cremanan, for my land of Cremanan, in the paroch of Balfron, and
being Two hundred and fixty-eight pound of valuation.

And the faids James and John Grahames have fubfcribed thefe prefents at Buchanan, the eleventh of June Iaj vij and fourty-one years, before David Græme of Orchill, and John Smith writer in Buchanan : Declareing, that notwithftanding of the date of the faids James and John Grahame's fubfcription, yet it fhall be underftood, that the obligations on both partys by this contract fhall and do commence from Whitfunday Iaj vij and fourty-one, in regard it was agreed betwixt the partys, that the faids obligations fhould commence at that term. The date, witneffes

neffes names and defignations, with this declaration, being wrote by the faid John Smith, and declared to be part of this contract.

> Da Græme, witnefs.   Ja. Grahame.
>
> John Smith, witnefs.   John Graham.

It would appear, from the following letter, that this contract was not difadvantageous to Mr Grahame:

> Sir,   *Balikinrain, May* 25 1743.
>
> Notwithftanding of the contract entered into betwixt feveral gentlemen of the fhyres of Stirling and Dumbarton, you and I, annent keeping of a watch, whereby you was to pay yearly four *per cent.* of valuation; yet I now agree with you for three *per cent.* for the lands you have contracted for; and that for the firft term of Whitfunday, and in time comeing during the ftanding of the contract. And I am, Sir, your moft humble fervant,   JA. GRAHAME.

Leaving the reader to make what reflections on this curious contract he pleafes, I fhall only obferve, that Mr Grahame, in this affair, is to be confidered as a more fuccefsful keeper of the peace, defender of juftice, and guaranteeing power, than moft who have affumed thefe characters; for by his activity and vigilance, in a few years, juftice, honefty and peace were, in this part of the country, eftablifhed on a firm and lafting foundation, and continue to operate without the aid of contracts, watches, or guarantees.

PARISH OF KILSYTH.

(COUNTY OF STIRLING.)

By the Rev. Mr ROBERT RENNIE.

THIS pariſh conſiſts of two baronies, the eaſt and the weſt. The former for many ages has been called Monaebrugh. The latter Kilſyth ; but till the year 1649, it belonged to the pariſh of Campſie.

Origin of the Names.—The etymology of the names is uncertain. It ſeems even dubious whether they are of Latin or Gaelic original. If the name Kilſyth be derived from the Latin, it may perhaps have been a compound of *cella*, a church, chapel, or burying ground, and *Cetæ*, a Romiſh ſaint. And it was certain that there was a chapel in that diſtrict ; for though it is now raſed to the foundation, the place ſtill bears the name of Chapelgreen, being the ſite of a ſchool.

If the name be of Gaelic original, it is moſt probably derived from *cuil* a cell or burying ground, and *ſcoth*, peace. This derivation is equally plauſible as the other. For near Chapelgreen, which is almoſt in the centre of the weſt barony, ny, there was formerly a tumulus or cairn of ftones. That this tumulus was a burying ground or funeral pile, is certain; for an urn and afhes were fome time ago found in it. And there is a faint tradition, that it was erected over the dead, flain in a memorable battle, fought between the natives and the Romans; which was the forerunner of a *peace.* It is but juftice to fay, however, that the fame tradition bears, that the natives were furprized unarmed, and therefore, had recourfe to the firft offenfive weapon that offered, which was their *fcyths* or *fickles.* And from this circumftance, it is faid, the diftrict derived its name.

The etymology of Monaebrugh, is as uncertain. Gentlemen acquainted with the Gaelic fuppofe it to be a compound of *monaugh, hilly,* and *ebroch,* a place full of rivulets. And it muft be acknowledged, that this is defcriptive of the general appearance of that diftrict. For it confifts of an endlefs fucceffion of hill and dale, from one end to the other, and it is interfected by a great variety of rills.

Others have fuppofed it to be of Latin original. If fo, it is perhaps a compound of *mona,* a monk, and *Ebroch,* the name of a fmall rivulet which runs through this diftrict. And in confirmation of this, there is a tradition in this parifh, that a certain faint, whofe name is not recorded, had a hermitage in a fequeftered glen upon this very rivulet.

Situation.—The whole parifh is fituated in the county of Stirling. But it is the fouthermoft extremity of it. The form of it is an irregular oblong fquare, running in length along the great high way, leading from Edinburgh to Glafgow, 7 miles. The breadth is nearly one half of its length. Of courfe, it contains nearly 24 miles fquare, or about 15000 acres. The rivers Carron on the north, and Kelvin on the fouth, Inchwood burn on the weft, and the Bufh burn on the eaft, eaſt, form the natural boundaries of the pariſh ; and it lies contiguous to Denny on the eaſt, and Campſie on the weſt, to Fintry and St. Ninians on the north, and Kirkintulloch and Cumbernauld on the ſouth. I never ſaw a ſeparate map of the whole. But there is a very elegant beautiful and cor- rect plan of the eſtate of Kilſyth, in the poſſeſſion of the pro- prietor. And in the map of Stirlingſhire, in Atlas Blaviana, there is a very minute and pretty accurate delineation of this pariſh.

The general appearance of the whole to a ſtranger is ra- ther bare and bleak. A child may number the trees ; but there are a few ſmall copſe woods. The eaſt barony has very much the appearance of a highland diſtrict or ſtrath. Even the weſt is very uneven in its ſurface, and much in want of planting and proper incloſures. There is not a ſtrip of planting in the pariſh. It forms altogether an ex- tended ſtrath between two lines of hills ; in ſo much, that at one point, it ſeems to be part of a great ditch, interſecting the kingdom, terminating at the Frith of Forth on the eaſt, and Clyde on the weſt ; being at nearly equal diſtances from either. It ſends ſeveral ſtreams to both. For near the centre of the pariſh is the ſummit or higheſt part of the whole ſtrath, from whence iſſues the Kelvin, running weſt, and Auchencloch burn running eaſt. The Dullatur bog, through which they both run, is almoſt on a level with the water in the great canal, which cuts it into almoſt equal parts. And the canal is at that place 160 feet above the level of the Forth, at Grangemouth.

Though the ſurface of this pariſh is rough, broken, and uneven, being almoſt an uninterrupted ſucceſſion of hill and dale, yet we have no mountains of any note. The higheſt form a part of that ridge which riſes at Greenock, runs through Kilpatrick, Baldernock, Campſie, Kilſyth, and
Denny,

Denny, and thus interfects the whole kingdom. To us they seem to rife to a confiderable heighth, and to form a natural shelter from the northern blaft; but none of them are more than 1200 feet above the level of the valley, or 1368 above the fea. From the fummit of the higheft there is one of the moft extenfive, beautiful, and variegated views in Scotland.

The firft thing that arrefts the attention, is the amazing extent of profpect that opens all around. At leaft part of 14, if not 16 counties, and perhaps one half of Scotland, is under the eye at one glance. Though not nearly fo beautiful and variegated as that from the top of Benlomond, the view is richer, and more extenfive. For, being nearly at equal diftances from the Atlantic and the German oceans, the whole extent of the Ifland from eaft to weft is viewed at once. Towards the fouth and north, the profpect is ftill more extenfive. At a moderate calculation, the area of the whole may be 12000 miles.

The ftriking contraft between the Highlands and Lowlands is the next thing that attracts the attention. If you turn your eye fouthward from the Frith of Forth to Clyde, and from Pentland and Galloway to the Ochils and Kilpatrick hills, the whole feems one extended fertile plain; or rather, like a beautiful garden fheltered on all hands by the furrounding mountains, and divided into numberlefs beautiful inclofures, like the compactments of a flower garden.

Nothing can poffibly be a more ftriking contraft to this, than the profpect to the north. For 70 or 80 miles, it appears to be an endlefs fucceffion of hill upon hill, overtopping one another till they are loft in the diftance of the profpect, and blended with the blue clouds or azure fky. In a foggy day, or frofty morning, the profpect is truly picturefque. Being raifed entirely above the fog, the whole plain to the

fouth

ſouth appears like the ſea in a calm ; while the hills on the north ſeem to raiſe like iſlands out of the main, or like the tumultuous waves of the ocean in a ſtorm.

Though there is ſcarcely a peep between any of the hills to the north, yet there is an infinite variety of ſcenery of every kind to the ſouth. The friths of Forth and Clyde, with the iſlands they contain ; a vaſt variety of lakes and rivers, woods and wilds, with innumerable rich corn fields and incloſures ; the great canal, and villages, towns, cities, and ſhires, add beauty, variety, and grandeur to the whole.

Soil.—Where there is ſuch an uneven ſurface, there muſt of courſe be a great variety of ſoil. In general a light ſandy or gravelly bottom is moſt prevalent ; excepting in the rich, beautiful, and extenſive valley weſt of the town. It conſiſts of a rich loamy fertile ſoil, from 2 to 2¼ feet thick ; and con-tains upwards of 600 acres. The weſt barony is upon the whole the richeſt; approaching often to clay : the eaſt is more gravelly. In ſome places the ſurface is almoſt entirely covered with ſmall ſtones, from the quarter of a pound to two or three pounds weight. Theſe, however, are not ſuppoſed to be inju-rious, but rather an advantage to the ſoil. They are ſaid to pre-vent the ground from heaving and caſting the ſeed in ſpring,— to ſhelter the tender blade in ſummer. They are ſuppoſed like-wiſe to prevent the ſcorching rays of the ſun from withering the corns,—to retain the moiſture in great drought ; and, by retaining alſo the heat all the ſummer night, to promote ve-getation. Perhaps the principal advantage is generally over-looked ; which is, that they throw off a kind of laminous rind or ſhell, like the coats of an onion, which, being mixed with calcareous earth, moulders down and meliorates the grounds. The ſandy ſoil which prevails here, though light and ſhallow, is generally productive ; always eaſily cultivated,

and

and fufceptible of much improvement at a moderate expence. Being naturally dry, it fuits beft with a wet fummer; and would almoft require a fhower every day.

Climate.—Of courfe, it is very well adapted to our climate, which is rather watery. As we lie along that line of hills which reaches the Atlantic on the weft, we are expofed to frequent heavy fhowers from that quarter; efpecially when the wind is wefterly, which it generally is for nine months in the year. The hills at Greenock attract the clouds that rife from the Weftern Ocean. And, if the wind is high, it conveys them along the whole line of hills. If there is only a gentle breeze, which veers a little to the N. W. the clouds follow the line of the Clyde, and leave that of the hills at Dumbarton or Kilpatrick. This, of courfe, is the point to which the hufbandman, in hay time and harveft, looks with eager fufpence: And it is a kind of barometer which feldom fails. For, if the clouds leave the hills at Kilpatrick, and follow the line of the Clyde, we may reft affured, that we fhall efcape the fhower; but we can feldom efcape, when the clouds follow the direction of the hills.

But though the climate is in a certain degree moift, it is far from being unhealthy. The air is in general pure and falubrious; perhaps more fo than either near the eaft or weft coaft. For as we lie at an equal diftance from both, we are of courfe free from the peculiar inconveniences of either. We are feldom vifited with the fogs which prevail in the eaft; and are not expofed to the almoft inceffant rains, which predominate in the weft. The fogs feldom rife fo high; and the clouds are often expended before they reach us. Hence, in fummer and harveft the fky with us is often clear and ferene; when at Greenock it is cloudy, dark, and lowring, and on the frith of Forth thick and foggy; as may be feen at a diftance from our
hills;

hills ; and this too not for a day or two occaſionally, or in a few inſtances, but frequently, and for conſiderable periods of time.

Rivers.—The rivers in this diſtrict are not very remarkable. The Carron, both for ſize and claſſic fame, claims our firſt attention. It is, as its name denotes, *a winding ſtream* ; eſpecially in as far as it is the boundary of this pariſh. The *bonny links of Carron water* are well known, and well deſerve the appellation. For upwards of 3 Engliſh miles, that river runs, in a ſlow ſerpentine courſe, through one of the fineſt, richeſt, and moſt extenſive meadows perhaps in Great Britain. I ſuppoſe it may contain near a thouſand Scottiſh acres. In ſummer, during the hay-making, it preſents one of the gayeſt and grandeſt ſcenes of the kind to be ſeen any where.

The next in order is the Kelvin. It takes its riſe near the centre of this pariſh ; and it runs weſtward through the valley, in a ſlow, oozing, ferpentine courſe, upwards of four Engliſh miles within this pariſh. Hence, it was formerly always gorged up at every turn the river took, and overgrown with flags, ruſhes, and water-lillies ; ſo that it frequently overflowed the adjacent valley, giving it the appearance of a great lake, or conſiderable arm of the ſea. By this means, the hay in ſummer, and the corn in harveſt, were often flooded ; and all the lands that lay within water mark were greatly injured.

About three years ago, Sir Archibald Edmonſtone, Bart. of Duntreath, who is proprietor of the lands on the north of the river for upwards of 4 miles, propoſed to the heritors on the ſouth, to have a new cut made, as wide and deep as to contain all the waters ; and as nearly in a ſtraight line as the ſituation of the grounds, and the courſe of the river, would allow. Fully ſenſible of the advantages of this undertaking, and eager to promote and encourage it, he generously offered to be at two thirds of the whole expence; although, in justice, it could only have been expected that the one half should have fallen to him. Yet, at first, only a few of the numerous heritors on the south, accepted even of these advantageous terms; so that, for the first summer after the contract was made, there was only a mile and three quarters of the new cut formed.

The advantages even of this partial improvement were soon experienced. The river, in place of oozing through a muddy crooked course, at the rate of a quarter of a mile in the hour, runs within the same time, with a steady equable and full current of two miles; and easily discharges all the water, without the least danger of overflowing its banks.

Even though this had been the advantage, it would have been more than sufficient to compensate the proprietors for the expence of the work. But this, though a great is one of the least of the advantages they now reap. Formerly the valley on both sides, being nearly on a level with the surface of the river, even when there was no flood, was of course, gorged with water; so that the meadows were almost impassable for cattle at any time. Even part of the arable lands was often almost in the same state; and was of consequence unproductive, unless in very dry seasons. At all times, the crops of hay and corn, before they could be prepared for the stack or the barn, were dragged from the fields to a dryer situation, with prodigious labour, and considerable expence; and what was of as much consequence, with great loss of time. Now it is otherwise, the cattle have access to the meadows at all times. Even in winter, when they were formerly like one continued lake, they are now fit for pasture. And in summer, the hay may be made where it grows, and waggons drive along the grounds which were formerly a *morass*. As there is a fall of about 18 feet in the course of

the

the whole new cut, and as it is generally four, though in many places fix feet below the furface of the adjacent grounds, it ferves as a *general drain* to the whole valley. So that every furrow which was formerly a little water ditch, and every ditch which was formerly gorged up to the brink, is, or may be eafily drained; by this means, 300 acres of meadow may be turned into arable land; 60 acres of mofs-into meadow, and 500 acres of the fineft arable land in the parifh, may be rendered of double value, in the courfe of a few years; and that too, at very little expence.

Thefe advantages were feen by all the moment the firft part of the cut was finifhed. So that it was an eafy matter to procure the concurrence of all the heritors of the fouth, for extending it nearly two miles farther, the following fummer; and that too, upon more equal terms. Of courfe, the advantages arrifing from the work were extended in proportion.

The plan was formed, and executed under the infpection of Mr Robert Whitworth Engineer. And like all his other undertakings in this country, gave great and general fatisfaction. To prevent all difputes, and if poffible any law fuit, two arbiters were mutually chofen by the heritors on the fouth and north, to mark out the line of the new cut, in confiftency with the plan propofed, to judge of and determine any difference, and to afcertain the comparative value of any little parcel of ground that fell to be exchanged, or to be fold.

The dimenfions of the cut are various, in proportion to the quantity of water it receives. For a mile at the top, where there is only a fmall river, it is only from 18 to 20 feet wide at the furface, by 10 or 12 at the bottom. But as it receives new acceffions of water, it was proportionally enlarged. So that the fecond mile, it is 22 or 24 at the top,

by

by 14 or 16 at the bottom. And the loweſt and remaining part of it, is 28 by 16 or 18. Of courſe, the whole cut is of a regular form, ſloping gradually on each ſide, and happily proportioned to the quantity of water it is meant to diſcharge.

The expence of the whole was not above L. 600 ſterling; a ſum which is indeed very inconſiderable, when compared with the advantages of the work. The ſame contractor undertook both parts of the cut, but at different prices. The firſt part he engaged to cut for 2d a cubic yard. But in that caſe, he was not bound to form the banks into a regular ſloping ridge, but only to lay down the earth regularly, at leaſt a yard diſtant from the edge of the cut. And it was underſtood, that each tenant or proprietor, would at his leiſure, and at very ſmall expence, form it into a regular bank. As this was neglected by many, it was therefore judged moſt adviſeable, to contract not only for cutting the remaining part, but for forming the banks. Of courſe, 2d¼ the cubic yard was offered, and accepted : and as the whole courſe was either a fine rich ſolid mould, from two to three feet deep, or a ſtiff clay mixed with moſs, it was found to be a reaſonable allowance. The bank on either ſide is three feet from the edge of the cut, and for the moſt part upwards of three feet high. And as they ſlope equally both ways like a ridge, they may be ploughed at pleaſure, or ſown with graſs-ſeeds. If at any future period it ſhould be neceſſary, they may eaſily be raiſed a foot or two feet higher at the ſummit ; leaving a water courſe, of from 30 to 40 feet wide, from bank to bank, ſo as to contain double the quantity of water. For one foot at top would nearly contain as much as four at bottom.

It may be worthy of obſervation, that as ſoon as the work was contracted for, numbers from England and Ireland, as

well

well as Scotland, flocked to it. So that it was finished in the course of a few months. The Scotch and Irish for the most part, used the spade and wheel-barrow; and by their amazing perseverance, working from sun rise, till sun set, they made great wages, and greatly expedited the work. But in wet weather they were much retarded. The planks became slippery, their spades and wheel-barrows were all clotted over with mud and clay, so as to become very cumbersome. Though they excelled the English at other times, by their perseverance, they were in wet weather far behind. For the English seldom or never used the barrow; but only a light narrow spade, about 18 inches long, and 6 inches wide: and scooped or hollowed out in the mouth. With this they threw out wedges of earth and clay, from the deepest part of the cut, over their shoulder, with the greatest ease and expedition, to the distance of 6 or 10 yards. This appeared to me a simple, safe, and very expeditious method; and peculiarly adapted to such a work, in such a soil.

The whole cut has now the appearance of a small canal. And if the banks were planted with willows, or even one hedge row of them, they would soon adorn the whole plain; and become a valuable article to the proprietors.

Excepting these two rivers, there are none else in this parish; though there is a variety of rills, rivulets and burns. The most remarkable of these is the Garrel burn. This, as its name denotes, is a *rough, rapid, turbulent stream*. Its whole course is in this parish, and does not exceed 4 miles. Yet in a mile and a half, it falls nearly 1000 feet. So that there is a great number of cataracts, and water falls in its course. But though very romantic, and even awful in times of a great flood, yet as none of them are above 50 feet perpendicular, they are not very distinguished.

This

This burn formerly poured all its ſtream into the Kelvin ; after running cloſe by the north ſide of the town. But about 25 years ago, it was carried off by the canal company, by a ſmall canal, about a quarter of a mile above the town, into a large reſervoir about a mile to the eaſt.

The remaining burns are ſmall in compariſon with this. And they are only diſtinguiſhed by the great number and variety of water falls, and milns erected upon them.

The Inchwood burn is the boundary of this pariſh on the weſt. Next to that, is the Quinzie burn, on which there is a lint and a corn miln. On the Garrel burn, there is a fullers miln, a lint and a buffing, a meal and a barley miln.

In the eaſt barony there is Shaw-end burn; on which there is a threſhing miln near its ſource, and a lint and buffing, a barley, a corn, and a ſnuff miln farther down, and below the great reſervoir. Near the eaſtern extremity of the pariſh, is Auchincloch burn ; on which there is in the courſe of 60 yards, three lint milns, three buffing milns, and a corn miln ; and all of them, are well ſupplied with water.

Bridges.—It is almoſt unneceſſary to ſay, that along the courſe of the great high road to Glaſgow, there are bridges acroſs all thoſe rivulets. On Inchwood-burn, at Inchwood ; on Quinzie burn, at a farm houſe of that name ; on Garrel burn, at the town of Kilſyth; on Shaw-end-burn, at Shaw-end ; and on Auchincloch-burn, at Auchincloch. Along the ſame line of road, there is a number of ſmaller arches, thrown over the ſeveral rivulets that croſs it ; which ſcarcely deſerve to be mentioned. But the bridge of Carron over that river; and of Auchinſtenie over the Kelvin, are the largeſt, and by much the moſt remarkable within the pariſh. The former conſiſts of one large and a ſmall arch. The latter of ſix ſmall arches. Of courſe its appearance is rather ſingular,

and

and it has ſomething of the air of antiquity about it. Perhaps it is not unlike ſome of the Roman aqueducts.

For this reaſon, ſeveral diſtinguiſhed antiquarians of rank
and literature have ſuppoſed it to be a Roman bridge. As
far as I could learn, they have been diſpoſed to be of this
opinion, principally, becauſe it is within half a mile of the
great Roman wall, preciſely at an equal diſtance from the
eaſt and weſt end of it, acroſs the valley, which was the
boundary of their dominions; and at the only narrow place
over which a bridge could conveniently be thrown; at leaſt
if that valley, as was ſuppoſed, was at that time either an
extended lake or impaſſable morafs.

Beſides theſe extrinſic circumſtances, the bridge was ſuppoſed to bear in itſelf evident marks of its being a Roman
antique. It was narrow, being only about 9 feet wide; it
had no edges, at leaſt, none above 4 inches high; and above
all, it had a *ſemita* or foot-path, of hewn ſtone, about 10
inches wide on either ſide.

But all theſe circumſtances put together, though in the
eyes of an antiquarian they may ſeem to amount nearly to
demonſtration, muſt give way to ſtubborn facts.

In cutting the courſe of the Kelvin, not 20 yards below
this bridge, there was found the remains of a paved ford or
cauſeway, built together with wood, which was ſtill entire;
a few horſes ſhoes, and pieces of iron were found in it.
This revived the general ſuſpicion, that the bridge was not ſo
old as was ſuppoſed; and a tradition that about 100 years
ago a man and horſe periſhed in paſſing this ford. But
what put the matter beyond the poſſibility of a doubt, and
confirms the above tradition is, that among the late Lord
Kilſyth's old papers, of which I ſhall have occaſion to ſpeak
afterwards, I find that his Lordſh'p made application to the
quarter Seſſions at Stirling, in the year 1670, for money to
eject

erect a bridge acrofs the Kelvin, at Auchinfterrie. In thefe papers the precife fum is ftated, the name of the mafon who built the bridge, is likewife mentioned ; and there are people alive, who recollect to have feen a ftone on the weft edge of the bridge, with the above date upon it.

Lakes, &c.—There are no natural lakes in this parifh. But the great refervoir above mentioned, is perhaps one of the largeft and moft beautiful artificial fheets of water in the kingdom. It is of an oval form, fully three quarters of a mile long, and fomewhat lefs than half a mile in breadth ; and it covers upwards of 70 acres. The country around it is rugged and uneven, and gives the whole a romantic air. A few firs are planted at the eaft end, and in an ifland near the weft end of the lake. They thrive very well, and add variety and beauty to the whole. The expence of this work was very inconfiderable, in comparifon of the furface and quantity of water it contains. It was originally an extenfive hollow, as if fcooped out for the purpofe, by the hand of nature. At one place only, there was a deep opening, about 100 feet wide at the bottom, and 200 yards at the top. By filling this up to the heighth of about 25 feet, the work was at once completed. And by leaving a fluice in the centre, it can be filled or emptied at pleafure. The whole is finifhed in a mafterly and ingenious manner.

This lake abounds with fifh : and, if it were not occafionally let out in the drought of fummer to fupply the great canal, it would furnifh abundance of perch and trout at all times, and of the very beft quality. The lade that runs from it, and communicates with the canal, is one of the beft ftreams for trouting in the parifh : but it is only a ftream ; and therefore not to be compared with the river Carron. This, in its whole extent, from its rife till it reaches the

Forth, is one of the fineft rivers in Scotland. The quantity, quality, and fize of the trout,—the endlefs variety of pools and ftreams,—and the opennefs of its banks, all concur in rendering it the favourite retreat of the angler : In fo much, that people of all ranks, and from a confiderable diftance, refort to it in the fifhing feafon ; and there is fcarcely a peafant or fhepherd on its banks, who is not eager in purfuit of this amufement, and eminent in the art. Where the river is rapid and turbulent, and of a clear channelly bottom, the fifhes are fmaller and whiter after being dreffed : but in the larger and deeper pools, efpecially as far as it is the boundary of this parifh, where it is for the moft part a large, deep, winding river, they are redder when dreffed, and darker when caught, and much larger in fize. I have feen them two, three, and even four pounds weight ; and from 18 to 24 inches long, and full grown *.

The Kelvin, and all its tributary ftreams, at leaft before it

was

---

* There is a tradition, that fifh were much more abundant 50 or 100 years ago than now. It is even faid, that before the Partick miln-dam was erected over the Kelvin, falmon in fpawning time came up as far as Kilfyth, and were to be found in every pool. It is certain that none have been found fince.

The reafons why the fmall fifh are lefs abundant, may be,

1ft, That there is much more lime ufed as manure than formerly : And it is allowed that the lees of lime are deftructive both to the fifh and their fpawn.

2dly, There is much more flax raifed. Being watered in the rills and rivulets, it pollutes the ftreams, and renders the water noxious to all, and fatal to many.

3dly, Drag-nets and pock-nets, i. e. nets in the form of a bag, are often ufed, though contrary to law : all the larger fifh are by that means deftroyed.

4thly, As none of the heritors refide, fifhing is quite a common privilege with us : It is of courfe the amufement of every idler.

was cut and ſtreightened, furniſhed a conſiderable quantity of fine trout. The pools were numerous and large. But, being a muddy flow running river, it became a harbour for pikes : This voracious animal preyed upon the ſmall fiſh. But now, that the courſe of the river is open and clear, and free of pools, the trout muſt in time become more abundant ; whereas the pike can find little or no harbour.

The great canal, in all likelihood, will prove a very ample ſource of ſupply for all kinds of fiſh that delight in a ſtagnant muddy water. Perch, pike, and brozes, already abound. The firſt, though numberleſs, and caught even by children with the greateſt eaſe, are as yet for the moſt part very ſmall. They ſeldom exceed 6 inches, though I have ſeen them a foot long. The pike are both abundant and fully grown : ſometimes they are from 10 to 20 lib. weight ; but for the moſt part from one to four. They are generally caught by lines baited ; ſeldom or never with the rod and fly : and it is only the amuſement of children to catch them, the true angler ſeldom thinks it worthy of his attention.

Springs.—There is perhaps no diſtrict where there is a greater variety and abundance of ſprings. Along the whole brow of the hills they abound ; and they are equally remarkable for the quantity and quality of the water they ſend forth. There is one or two ſo copious, that during the heat of ſummer they will each fill a pipe of 3, perhaps 4 inches diameter ; and the water of almoſt all of them is as pure as cryſtal. Two have been conſecrated to their tutelar ſaints, and ſtill bear their reſpective names ; the one is called St. Tartan's, perhaps a contraction of St. Tallertan's ; the other, which ſeems to have attracted the attention of our forefathers for many generations, is called St Mirron's. There is a third that goes by the name of Kittyfriſt well. There is no ſuperſtitious veneration paid, nor any virtue aſcribed to the waters of any of them. The laſt mentioned is rather regarded as noxious ; And the waters of it are ſaid to have proved fatal to the unwary traveller : But this ſeems to be a vulgar prejudice. The water appears pure and ſalubrious ; but as it lies upon the hilly road to Stirling, and near the very ſummit of the hill, perhaps ſome traveller, in the fervid noon of a ſummer's day, overheated with the fatigue of climbing, may have raſhly taſted or drunk liberally of the cooling ſpring. This, at all events, muſt have been dangerous. Perhaps, at one time or another, it may have proved fatal.

There is one mineral ſpring in this pariſh, about a quarter of a mile above the town, and near the old manſion-houſe of Kilſyth. It ſeems to be a ſtrong chalybeate ; and is ſaid to have been much reſorted to in former times, and deemed medicinal in certain nervous affections of the ſtomach It is now ſo totally neglected, that it is not eaſy for a ſtranger to diſtinguiſh the place where it was. I know of no chemical analyſis having been made of the water ; but, as it taſtes and ſmells ſomewhat like rotten eggs, or the ſcourings of a foul gun, as it makes ſilver black, and wood of a reddiſh yellow, I am diſpoſed to think it is impregnated with a conſiderable quantity of ſulphur.——In one of our lime quarries there are evidently ſome ſprings of a petrifying quality, but none of any note.

Minerals.—The mineralogy of the pariſh would fill a volume ; and might engage the attention of the natural hiſtorian for a life time. As I do not pretend to be an adept in that ſcience, I ſhall only give a general glance at the ſubject.

The firſt article I ſhall mention, is the iron-ſtone. In both extremities, and near the centre of the pariſh, this has been found ; and there are favourable appearances in a variety of other places: excepting at Banton, in the caſt barony, it has not been wrought to any conſiderable extent; but it is upwards of 25 years ſince it was firſt wrought there by the Carron Company; and it continues to be wrought to a conſiderable extent, ſtill furniſhing generally about 5000 tons every year. The number of miners has been various, but in general from 50 to 60; and as there is ſtill a great field remaining, it may employ as many hands, and furniſh as great a quantity for many years to come. It conſiſts in general of ſeveral ſtrata, from 4 to 14 inches thick; ſeparated from each other by their ſeams of clay or dalk, and ſubdivided by perpendicular fiſſures into ſmall ſquare wedges, from ſix inches to two feet.

Theſe ſeams are principally the property of William Cadell, Eſq. of Carron-park; though ſome part of them belongs to the Carron Company.

In the weſt barony belonging to Sir Archibald Edmonſton, there is a very uncommon collection of ball iron ſtones; theſe are of a beautiful form, and exquiſite richneſs and quality. They are uniformly of one ſhape; reſembling a round flat topped loaf of bread, or an apple pudding; but they are of all ſizes from a quarter of an inch to 12 inches diameter.

When broken or cut aſunder, they exhibit within a great variety of ſquare partitions; theſe are generally filled with white ſpar, which the old foſſiliſts call ſeptaria. But I have ſeen them quite empty; and beautifully excavated like a honeycomb. Being pretty hard, they receive a fine poliſh; and they have been wrought up by marble cutters into ornaments, in-laid work, or cabinets. Some of them are truly beautiful; but their intrinſic value conſiſts in the fine quality and great quantity of iron which they contain; they are ſuppoſed to be the richeſt that have ever been found. The Carron

ron Company, who buy up all the iron-ftone in this parifh, and in almoft all this county, pay for this at the rate of 9s per ton delivered at their works, or on the banks of the great canal. But this is generally allowed to be a price very inadequate to its value, which is comparatively great. For the moft part thefe balls are found in a deep bank of blaes. They lie in regular ftrata, at unequal and irregular diftances. But the balls of each ftratum are generally of the fame fize ; towards the top of the bank, they are fmaller, and larger below. Though the balls, when collected, are valuable, yet the quantity of blaes is fo great, in comparifon with the quantity of iron-ftone, and the ftrata are at fuch a diftance, that it never can be wrought to a great extent with much advantage. Yet, as it lies on the courfe of a rapid burn, and as the blaes is foft and friable, there are confiderable quantities of it wafhed down daily, but efpecially at every flood ; while the balls are left behind. It is in this way chiefly that they have been hitherto collected.

Immediately under the bank of blaes in which this ball iron ftone is lodged, there is a very fine poft of lime-ftone. In fome places it is only 3 or 4, but for the moft part 7 or 8 feet thick. It is a conglomeration of fmall fhells, of all fizes, from an inch diameter, till they become fo fmall as to be invifible to the naked eye. Their form is as various as their fize : but for the moft part, they are long and cylindrical, and fomewhat like a fcrew. I believe the technical name for fuch is orthoceratitæ. They are generally fuppofed to be an extraneous foffil ; for the original fhell has not yet been difcovered in any of the frequented feas. The greateft part of thefe are very fmall ; though I have feen fome an inch in diameter ; and 3 or 4 inches long.

At one time, I had occafion to pick up a petrifaction rather of an uncommon fhape, fize, and colour. It was lodged

ged in the clay above the lime ; and it reſembled much an elephant's tooth, at leaſt it was of the colour of ivory, and as ſmooth. It was preciſely of the form of a large tooth or ſmall crooked horn, about an inch and a half diameter at the baſe, and tapering till it terminated in a ſharp point. The water that oozes through the fiſſures of this poſt of lime is clearly of a petrifying qualityₜ And all theſe apertures are filled with clay and petrified ſhells. Where this poſt is thickeſt, which is at a place called Weſtſide, it has been wrought for ſome years by mining, and has been burnt in draw-kilns. As the roof is good, the poſt generally 7 or 8 feet thick, and divided into ſquare cubes by horizontal and perpendicular fiſſures, it is wrought to much advantage, at a very moderate expence. It may be wrought for ages, for the poſt ſeems inexhauſtible. And it is nearly 700 feet above the level of the valley, and muſt therefore always be level free.

As it conſiſts almoſt entirely of ſhells, it is of courſe, of the beſt quality ; and contains the greateſt quantity of calcareous earth, and the leaſt proportion of ſand of any lime perhaps in Scotland. Therefore the demand for it is great, and increaſes every year. Conſiderable quantities of it have been ſent to Glaſgow, by the great canal. But the greateſt part is employed in this pariſh, and in the pariſhes of Kirkintulloch, Cumbernauld, and Cadder. Upwards of 1000 chalders have been ſold this ſummer; though the work is properly ſpeaking, in its infancy. It is ſold at ſo low a rate as 8s the chalder, or 6d per boll, and is the cheapeſt lime in this neighbourhood, though it is the beſt. The boll is equal to three firlots of corn meaſure.

Below this, about a quarter of a mile, and in the courſe of the ſame burn, there is another poſt of lime. It is of a very free grain ; and of a duſky marble colour, capable of a fine poliſh. But as the poſt is thin, not exceeding 45 inches,

and

and is covered with a deep bank of blaes, from 10 to 30 feet thick, and without a proper roof, it can never be mined, nor even removed without conſiderable expence.

In a variety of other places, there are favourable appearances of lime; eſpecially in the eaſt barony. Near the centre of it, at a farm called Berry-hill, there are ſeveral ſtrata of lime, which have been wrought to advantage. But it is much more ſandy, and contains leſs calcareous earth; and is in every reſpect, of a coarſer quality. Yet, as there is a good roof, and, as it may at all times be wrought level free; as it conſiſts of ſeveral ſtrata, of above 6 or 8 inches thick, with interſtices of clay about the ſame thickneſs; and as it is divided into ſmall ſquare wedges by perpendicular fiſſures, it is wrought with eaſe and little expence; ſeldom or never requiring the force of powder. But the road to it is ſteep, and in bad repair; therefore the demand for it has not been great, except from the immediate neighbourhood.

I ſuppoſe however, that there may be at leaſt 1500, if not 1800 chalders annually thrown out from the three poſts put together.

Beſides theſe, which have all been turned to account, there is about a quarter of a mile above Weſt-ſide, a vein of copper, which was wrought about 60 or 70 years ago, by order of the York building company. Of this, I could not have given any diſtinct account; unleſs it had been examined by the ingenious Mr Raſpe, in the year 1791. As his report is very accurate, and now before me, I ſhall ſtate it in his own words, in the note below *.

In

* " I examined a drift, which had been driven into the ſide of the hills " near Corri, many years ago. And found in it a vein of reddiſh heavy ſpar, " or vitriolated barytes. It has been very prepoſterouſly ſhut up, with a view " as it would appear of preventing or diſcouraging any further trial. For as " the

In a variety of places, but efpecially in the farm of Dun-
trocher, about a mile above the town of Kilfyth, and in the
valley

" the drift was horizontal, it could not occafion any danger to cattle. I had
" it opened for me, juft wide enough for me to creep in, on all fours. I
" found the drift within very narrow, 8 fathoms upon the run of the vein,
" which is north and fouth. At the forehead a fhort crofs drift appeared eaft
" and weft, full of a ruffy clay as it were, upon a crofs goffan, or clay vein,
" the thicknefs of which remains as yet undetermined. The heavy fpar vein,
" feems here to be interrupted by it; though it may probably con-
" tinue a good way beyond it. For it appears clearly, in the face of
" the brae, many fathoms fouth and fouth weft, the other way : fo that there
" is no doubt of its being a regular fpar vein of a confiderable length and
" width. In the drift, it is about 2 feet, and in the above mentioned fouth
" or fouth weft end, rather more than that even at the grafs."

" Confidering that this kind of heavy fpar is the conftant matrix and at-
" tendant of metals of all the veins and works which I have feen and ex-
" amined in the Ochil hills and Highlands ;—that the vein is favourably
" fituated in high ground, on the very edge of the hill; that confequently, it
" may be undercut very deep by fhort flanking levels; and chiefly, that
" in fome parts, it is thinly fprinkled with copper ore, I think it my duty, to
" recommend a flight trial of it, by a couple of trial pits of 3 or 4 fathoms, as
" alfo by a couple of cofteening pits or trenches, upon and beyond the crofs
" goffan, or clay vein in the forehead of the old drift."

" The coft of this trial will probably not exceed L. 25 fterling. And the
" refult of it whatever it may be, will be fatisfactory ; whether ore be found,
" or only the nature of the vein afcertained fully, as a road for fpirited fpe-
" culators to venture upon hereafter."

The above report is fo accurate and important, that I truft it will not be
thought tedious. And the following claufe, I think, merits attention.

" Higher up in the Haleftain burn, I faw large maffes of grey, and variegat-
" ed, dull coloured flint ; yellow and red jafper, with nodels of agate
" and porphyry. If the jafper could be traced here to a regular body, which
" is not unlikely, lapidaries might be fupplied from hence, very cheap ; or
" rather, lapidary milns might be fet up in the burn, or at Kilfyth, to great
" advantage. For this jafper is of a very fine grain ; and fome how or other
" finds its way already to the lapidaries and fcal engravers, at Edinburgh
" and London."

valley alſo, there are favourable appearances of a clay marle. But as no trial has been made of it, I cannot ſpeak with certainty, either of its quantity or qualities.

About a quarter of a mile ſouth of the town, within 30 yards of Auchenſterrie bridge, and 100 of the great canal, there is a valuable and inexhauſtible quarry of baſaltes.

The whin-ſtone rock is from 20 to 30 feet high; and as there is very little ſurface upon it, it may be wrought at a ſmall expence; more eſpecially, as it is in many places interſected by horizontal and perpendicular fiſſures, whereby it is cut into blocks of all different ſizes. It is peculiarly adapted for cauſeways, or paving the ſtreets of any populous city. The ſtone is ſolid, compact, and durable; yet though extremely hard, and therefore capable of receiving a very fine poliſh, it is very free, and eaſily formed into almoſt any ſhape. The prevailing colour of it is a ſlate blue, beautifully freckled with little white nodules.

The demand for this ſtone has been conſiderable. Several thouſand tons have been annually conveyed up the great canal to Glaſgow, and the neighbourhood; and it is ſaid to be equal in quality to any ſtone that has been found. Though at the diſtance of 14 miles, as it is conveyed by water, it can be furniſhed at as cheap a rate, as if it were within 3 or 4 miles of that city.

I may add, that near the centre of this pariſh, in the Garrel glen, about half a mile above the town, there is one of the richeſt, fineſt, and moſt beautiful poſts of free-ſtone in

Great

I have ſeen ſome of theſe myſelf, they are beautiful indeed. Specimens of each are in the poſſeſſion of Mr Robert Wilſon at Banton, who has with much labour and ingenuity, made a beautful and pretty complete collection of the minerals and foſſils of this pariſh. It would be a happy circumſtance if there was in every pariſh a cabinet or collection of the ſame kind.

Great Britain ; and happily it is inexhauſtible. The colour
of it is exquiſite ; for the moſt part, it is a beautiful white,
with a tinge of yellow. But ſome of it is finely variegated
with brown and yellow veins, like marble. Other parts of
it are decorated with the moſt delicate vegetable impreſſions,
as black as coal. Some of theſe are as ſmall as a hair, and
when the ſtone is finely poliſhed, they are a beautiful contraſt
to the reſt of the maſs. I believe no free-ſtone is capable
of a finer poliſh. For though it is ſoft and eaſily wrought
when firſt brought from the quarry, it becomes daily whiter and harder when expoſed to the weather. It becomes
hard, white, and of a fine conſiſtence ; and ſo durable, as to
ſtand all weather, and ſuit every climate. Of courſe, it is
equally calculated for building above or below the ſurface of
the earth or water ; and for the fineſt ornaments, and ſtrong-
eſt and coarſeſt pieces of architecture. In the erection of
bridges, where it is expoſed to the conſtant attrition of the
water, and in paving ſtreets, it is particularly uſeful. Of
courſe, it is much eſteemed in Glaſgow, and wherever it is
known. Many ſtreets in the New Town of Glaſgow are
paved with it ; and it has been formed into ſome of the
fineſt ornaments, ſuch as vaſes, columns, and fretted work.
The demand for it is great, and it is ſold at a reaſonable price. Even when delivered at Glaſgow in blocks,
it is only 2s the yard for pavement ; and there are upwards
of 1000 tons conveyed to Glaſgow by the great canal every
year *.

I am convinced if its value were known, there would be
a greater demand for it than there is from many places of Scotland,

---

* This quarry is ſet at L. 40 ſterling annually. Each quarier is allowed 7d¼
the yard, for his work. Land carriage to the canal coſts 3 pence per yard ;
for lordſhip 3 pence ; trackage and tonnage in the canal are trifling.

land, but especially from England. For if free-stones are conveyed to London from the country north of Aberdeen on the east coast, and from Stevenston in the county of Ayr on the west, they certainly might be conveyed with equal advantage from Kilsyth. The great canal passes within less than a mile of this quarry; and I am persuaded, that a load of Kilsyth free-stone either roughly formed or in the block, would be a valuable commodity of the kind. For if sold in London at L. 1 : 12s. the ton, as free-stone of inferior quality is, it might furnish a very liberal freight, or as ballast prove a profitable branch of trade.

The post is generally from 10 to 15 feet, and lies upon a seam of coal about as many inches thick. There are a great variety of coal stalks, rising from this seam, like trees from the surface of the earth. Some of them are 6, 10, or 20 feet long in proportion to the depth of the free-stone; and they differ as much in diameter as in length, being of all sizes from an inch to 2 feet. These are justly esteemed by philosophers objects of great curiosity. And they have furnished matter for much speculation; they resemble exceedly a petrifaction: and yet the substance is not calcarious earth, but solid free-stone of similar texture with the circumjacent rock. I have in my possession, one the largest and most beautiful that has hitherto been found. It is nearly 16 inches in diameter, and 6 feet 9 inches in length, of a compact solid mass. For the original stem when entire was upwards of 12 feet long; but the top, as is generally the case, was less solid, and mouldered down or was easily broken when exposed to the open air. In shape, colour, and appearance, it precisely resembles the trunk of a thorn tree; in so much, that every stranger at first view supposes it to be one. It seems to be of equal solidity with any part of the mass; and the surface of it is beautifully fretted with regular indentations

much

much like the ſurface of a fir top. Beſides theſe, there are likewiſe longitudinal ſeams from end to end, reſembling the trunk of an old yew, or thorn tree. It is unneceſſary to ſay, that the circumjacent caſe bears a ſimilar impreſſion, only reverſed. But it deſerves to be mentioned, that within the ſame trunk, and at different angles, there lie a variety of ſmaller ones, from two to three inches diameter. Theſe are ſeldom parallel to one another, and cannot be extracted without deſtroying the large trunk ; but when extracted, they ſhew beautiful impreſſions ; finer by much than the larger trunk. Theſe ſometimes branch out into regular ramifications at top, as they almoſt always do at bottom ; and the ſmaller the branch the finer and more delicate the impreſſions upon its ſurface ; in ſo much, that the ſmalleſt will bear and almoſt require to be examined by the microſcope. I gave one of them lately to a gentleman, who promiſed to ſend it to Weir's muſeum.

It is unneceſſary to add, for I believe it is a common thing, that there are uniformly vegetable impreſſions along the baſe of the coal and ſurface of the dalk or blaes. Theſe are ſo endleſsly varied, that I cannot pretend, nor would it be proper to attempt an enumeration of them.

Coal.—The only article that remains to be mentioned, is the coal. This has been wrought for ages ; and is ſtill abundant, I truſt inexhauſtible. The ſeams are various, and of very different quality. The coal in the weſt barony, is one of the beſt I ever ſaw. It burns clear, laſts long, gives a good heat, and cakes, ſo that the very droſs of it is valuable ; and makes a better fire than moſt other coals. Happily for us this ſeam is now wrought to a conſiderable extent, and promiſes to be a laſting benefit to this pariſh and the neighbourhood. Robert Dunmore, Eſq. of Ballakinrain, is at preſent the taokſman ;

and as he is a gentleman of a liberal mind, and public ſpirit, I have no doubt that he will carry on the work with ſucceſs and to a great extent. This ſame ſeam has been wrought for generations in different places of the weſt barony ; but it was given up for many years, till lately the work was re-vived.

The coal in the eaſt barony, eſpecially at Banton and Glen Garrel, is of an inferior quality. But for that reaſon, it is uſeful for a variety of purpoſes which the other could not ſo well ſerve. It gives an uncommon heat, but upon being ex-poſed to the air, it moulders down into droſs. And when thrown into a chimney, it is ſo brittle, that whenever it is touched, it turns into a powder or mere gum. But in an oven, or furnace, or ſmith's forge, it is of great ſervice : and is one of the beſt coals for theſe purpoſes in the kingdom. Of courſe, there is a great demand for it from printfields, and other public works, and from ſmiths, for 6, 10, or 12 miles round.

None of thoſe coals are far below the ſurface. Of courſe, they are eaſily kept level free. In the weſt barony, the ſeam is generally from 4 to 12, and in the eaſt from 12 to 16 fathom deep. The ſtrata in Glen Garrel, where coal has been wrought for 50 years without interruption, lie generally in the following order :

1ſt, Soil and rubble.

2d, A thin bed of blaes, or ſometimes channel.

3d, A poſt of free-ſtone, from 10 to 20 feet thick.

4th, Indurated ſhivers, blaes, or ſometimes in its place a thin ſeam of coal 11 inches thick.

In the eaſt end of the pariſh, at a place called Buſh, is the richeſt and beſt ſeam of coal ; but it is not level free, and therefore would require a fire engine. It has been wrought to a conſiderable extent. I find that Lord Kilſyth,

ordained

ordered it to be opened in the year 1670. There are nearly 100 coal pits that have been wrought.

In general, the dip of all the coals is to the fouth eaft.
But when it meets with what are called hitches, the dip alters
in every direction. In one place at Balcaftle, the coal was found
in the form of a trough, rifing up in all directions.

The manner in which they are wrought is by pick and
wedge ; boys, and fometimes girls are employed to draw the
fkiffies, below ground. The men enter about 4 in the
morning, and their day's work is generally over by 2 in the
afternoon.

Each load may be about 2420 cubic inches. It is fold at
7d$\frac{1}{2}$ at the hill. Four of thefe make a tolerable cart ; it is faid,
they will weigh upwards of 1200 weight.

There are generally from 8 to 12 conftantly employed as
colliers ; each of thefe at an average, will put out 10 or 12
loads per day : though fome can put out more. For each
load they have 3 pence, fo that in general, they can earn
from 2s. 6d. to 3s. a day. There may be about 120 loads,
that is 30 carts put out daily, or about 180 carts every week.
Allowing 50 weeks in the year, there will be 9000 carts,
or 36,000 loads, annually put out. This is equal to 10,800,000
hundred weight, or 871,200,000 cubic inches. At half a
crown the cart, the fale in a year may be equal to L. 1125
fterling. But the expences attending the work are very
confiderable ; fometimes 9 or 10 men are conftantly employed, befides colliers : fo that the weekly expences are generally from L. 9 to L. 16.

It is to be hoped, that a great deal of this will be faved.
For there is a fmall fteam engine immediately to be fet up.
This will eafily do the work of a number of men, and fave an
enormous expence.

If

If ſo, it may be expected, that the prices may fall ſomewhat; at preſent the poor find them to be very high. And
what is ſurpriſing, for 100 years, that is, from 1670,
till 1770, the coals kept nearly at the ſame price, from
3d. to 4d. the load. Since that period, they have become
too much an article of commerce. Speculation has run
ſo high, that they are now double the price they were 20
years ago. It were to be wiſhed, that gentlemen would conſider this.

It is ſuppoſed that there are many ſeams below the
one that has been wrought. It ſeems only the cropt
coal. But as it abounds, no attempt has been made to ſearch
deeper.

Vegetables.—The vegetables of this pariſh are not very
remarkable. Yet our ſequeſtered glens furniſh abundance
of amuſement for the botaniſt. Thoſe who are verſant in
that ſcience inform me, that there are not a few of the
rarer indigenous plants. Broom and furze abound in e-
very incloſure. There are a few plants of the black berry
tree. The floe tree is in almoſt every glen. The hawthorn, hip thorn, the wild raſp, and elder, with all the
varieties of the bramble, are frequently to be ſeen. In
every glen and copſe wood, the hazel prevails. There
are a few crab apples to be found, ſcattered up and down :
but chiefly in the neighbourhood of the decayed and ruinous
old orchards of the family of Kilſyth. Perhaps they may be
the produce of ſeed dropt from thoſe gardens, or carried by
wild birds. There is a variety of the willow tribe, though
no great quantity any where. The birch is one of our moſt
beautiful plants. The mountain aſh, and ſmall cherry tree,
either in bloſſom or full bearing, are both a beautiful ornament
to our glens. The largeſt trees are the aſh, the elm, the
alder,

alder, the ſycamore, and oak : but they are very thinly ſcattered.

The few fruit trees which we have are ſometimes very prolific, but the produce is always precarious. There is a great variety and very conſiderable quantities of gooſeberries, raſps, and currans. And few, if any country pariſhes can boaſt of as many flower gardens, or a more curious and complete collection of flowers.

Animals.—The animals of this pariſh are ſuch as are common over all the neighbourhood.

Foxes, badgers, polecats, weaſels, and hedgehogs, abound. A few otters and rabbits may be found alſo ; and the hare is frequently to be ſeen.

The birds of prey, are in no reſpect ſingular or remarkable. The moſt common are the kite, and the hawk, and the raven-crow. The owl is alſo to be found. But the moſt deſtructive of all, is the grey *glade*, or kite, as it is commonly called. The eagle once frequented our rocks and hills, while paſtured with ſheep. But ſince black cattle have come in their place, the eagle is never ſeen. Even the foxes and ravens, on the ſame account, are not ſo numerous as heretofore. The moor fowl and wild duck, the partridge and wild pidgeon, the heron, the magpie and ſkylark, are all to be found in their ſeaſon. The ſnipe, the ſparrow, the redbreaſt and wood-pecker, the bat, the common green moor, and red breaſted or roſe linnet, the blackbird, the thruſh, the goldfinch, the chaffinch, the wren, &c. with all the varieties of ſmall birds, are common here.

In winter, wild geeſe in amazing flocks, to the number of 200 or 300 at a time, appear in the valley. The northcock
and

and ſnow bird, only appear in ſevere ſtorms, like that of winter 1795.

The birds of paſſage, with the uſual time of their appearance and departure, will appear from the following table.

	Appearance.	*Departure.*
The cuckow, about	25. March;	when barley begins to ſhoot.
The ſwallow,	28. April;	1. October.
The lapwing,	20. March;	26. July.
The curlew,	10. March;	10. October.
Woodcock,	21. December;	various as the ſtorm riſes.

Church, Living, Manſe and Glebe.—It is impoſſible to ſay, when there was a church firſt erected at Monaeburgh. In all likelihood, it was very ſoon after the Reformation; perhaps before it. At all events, it was before the year 1586. For at that time, Mr Alexander Livingſtone, a near relation of the family of Callendar, was parſon of this pariſh. The ſucceſſion of miniſters, and ſeveral particulars relating to the church, are inſerted in a note; which was chiefly taken from an old volume of the records of the preſbytery of Glaſgow, which was ſometime ago diſcovered at Dumblane; and has very lately been deſtroyed by an accidental fire in Glaſgow *.

Mr

* The time of Mr Livingſtone's admiſſion is not recorded; but in the year 1592 he was ſo aged and infirm, that he could neither preach, adminiſter the ſacrament nor exerciſe diſcipline, ſo that the preſbytery upon a viſitation adviſed him to get a helper. It would appear, however, that he was unwilling to take this advice. For in the year 1594 the Preſbytery applied to the Synod for a helper to Mr Livingſtone. What was the conſequence of this application we are not told. But in the year 1597 Mr Livingſtone was depoſed for *inhability in his perſon of ſpiritual graces, to teach the kirk, and for inhability to uſe diſcipline in the ſaid kirk as becomes.* In this ſentence he ſeems to have acquieſced, for he confeſſes

Mr James Robe was admitted minister, 24th April 1713. He had received a presentation from the Viscount of Kilsyth. And

confesses the charge. Perhaps he was the more ready to do so, because the Presbytery at the same meeting took Mr William Livingstone his son on trials for the living. The reason assigned for their doing so, was, that he perceived himself to be inwardly called to the ministry.

Accordingly in the year 1599, having on July 3. received a presentation from Lord Livingstone, (I suppose the Earl of Callendar), he received inauguration, on the 17th, imposition of hands, collation and confirmation. At this time he was a considerable heritor in the parish; being proprietor of the lands of Monaeburgh. The boundaries of that estate are not well known, but it is certain that the grounds upon which the village stands were a part of them. For Sir William Livingstone of Kilsyth, one of the Lords of Session, purchased them from the parson for the express purpose of extending the village, which stood at that time on the banks of the *Ebroch.* Those new feus were granted along the *Garrel Burn,* which meets the Ebroch nearly opposite the centre of the village; and of course the new town was called Burnside. The parson seems to have been a man of considerable influence at that time, and in the year 1604 he used all that influence with the greatest zeal in opposing the restoration of the bishops. For which cause, and for his nonsubmission to the canons and ceremonies, he was deposed, and by his Majesty's authority, deprived of his ministry both at Monaeburgh, and also at Lanark.

After this period there seems to have been a vacancy for some years. At last, in the year 1615, Mr Archibald Graham was admitted minister. Soon after his admission he disposed of a part of the glebe, though it appears that he did not pocket the money; but in all likelihood allowed it to go to repair the church. At all events, we find that he expended a considerable sum in repairing the easter gabel, building a belfry, and purchasing a bell. This bell was only taken down this summer, and had a date upon it corresponding to this, viz. 1626. All that Mr Graham required in acknowledgement of this donation, was, that his name might be cut upon the vane of the belfry, and A. G. the initials of his name still remain as a memorial of his liberality. Mr Graham seems to have breathed much of the spirit of his predecessor. For even in the year 1636 he had not practised the canons and constitutions. And therefore he was called before the high Commission Court to answer for his conduct. That court seems to have been much incensed, for though

a

And ſo tenacious was his Lordſhip of his right, that neither
he nor his Lady would allow a call to be moderated in his
favour.

a very favourable teſtimonial was given him by the pariſhioners, and even by
the Preſbytery, he was depoſed.

The ſollowing year Mr Gabriel Cunningham was admitted. He ſeems
to have been leſs ſcrupulous. Taking warning from the fate of his two immediate predeceſſors, he conformed to epiſcopacy, after the reſtoration. At
the time of his admiſſion the ſtipend of Monaeburgh was only 5 chalders of
victual, meal and barley 100 lb. Scots, and 16 ſtone weight of cheeſe. In the
year 1665 the money ſtipend was, however, augmented to 350 merks. At the
ſame time the manſe was conſiderably repaired But principally at the parſon's own expence. This was the more remarkable, as he had paid 500
merks for it to his predeceſſor. After theſe repairs, it was valued by tradeſmen as worth 1160 merks. His glebe, after the ſale his predeceſſor had
made of a part of it, conſiſted only of 7 acres or little more. In all likelihood,
the Sacrament of the Lord's Supper was not adminiſtered in this pariſh, till
about this period. For it is recorded, that in the year 1665, communion
table cloths, cups, and tickets, were obtained, and a baſon for baptiſm, but no
ſlaggons, nor even a church bible The people repeated the creed, ſaid the
Lord's prayer, and ſung the doxology after the pſalms.

About this period, the village was conſiderably increaſed. A new town
was built, not along the banks of the Ebroch or Garrel Burn as formerly, but
on a riſing ground about 200 yards ſouth of thoſe ſtreams, which at that time
was called *Moat Hill*, as the Lord of the manor had been accuſtomed to hold
courts of juſtice in that place. This new town of courſe was called by the
title of the proprietor, Kilſyth. And from that period the whole village obtained that name. Though the pariſh for upwards of 40 years retained ſtill
the old name Monaebrugh. The village about the time that this new addition
was made, or at leaſt ſoon after it, being removed at ſome diſtance from the
ſmall rivers, and in all likelihood ill ſupplied with water, that precious article
was brought in earthen pipes, from a neighbouring ſpring about a quarter of a
mile from the town; And a well or ciſtern was made near the centre of the
new town, which ſtill bears date 1676 Since that period, other ciſterns ſupplied by the ſame ſpring, have been erected in different parts of the town, e-
ſpecially in the year 1716.

It would appear that Mr Cunningham died miniſter of this pariſh. For
in the year 1666 Mr James Gartſhore was admitted to the charge. But he
did

favour. The prefbytery, being affured that the prefentee was acceptable to the parifh, difpenfed with that form, and ordained

did not continue in that office long. For he was tranflated to Cardrofs in the year 1673.

Two years after this, Mr Walter M'Gill, the laft epifcopal clergyman that officiated here, was admitted minifter, being tranflated from Wigton. He was a man of uncommon meeknefs and moderation ; and a great favourite of all ranks and denominations of people in the parifh ; infomuch, that when it was declared vacant by the Prefbytery in the year 1690, an uproar enfued. The patron and his lady, and a great and powerful party in the parifh efpoufed his caufe ; and when the Prefbytery met at the church, the patron fent down the chamberlain to refufe them admittance, and lock up the doors. The populace even offered violence to the Prefbyterian clergyman who was to officiate. The friends of the Prefbytery were exafperated by this ; and a fcuffle enfued, in which many were wounded, and one killed. Mr M'Gill's partizans at laft prevailed. And the Prefbytery themfelves feem to have been at a lofs what fteps next to take ; infomuch, that they defifted from farther procedure, and even declared that they could not take any other meafures. They were foon refcued from this dilemma. For in Feb. 1691 Mr M'Gill formally gave in his demiffion of the charge. When the Prefbytery met at this time, they called for all the books of difcipline, and regifters of baptifm. The latter were delivered up ; and are on the whole regular and diftinct from the year 1620 till that period. They are ftill in good prefervation, as will appear from the extracts I make from them. When the clerk was ordered to deliver up the books of difcipline, he faid, they were in the hands of Mr M'Gill. When he was interrogated, he faid, he had left them in the manfe; the beadle who had charge of the manfe, being called, faid, that fome perfon or other had deftroyed them. So that it would appear all the three were willing to have prevented them from falling into the hands of the Prefbytery. All the bills, bonds, and papers refpecting the poors funds were neverthelefs recovered, as well as the utenfils and veffels belonging to the church.

A vacancy enfued for fome time, during which period the Prefbytery vifited and ordered repairs upon the church, manfe, and offices, to the amount of L. 212 : 1 : 4 Scots.

On the 29th of Dec. 1682, Mr James Hay, the firft prefbyterian minifter, was tranflated from Kilmalcomb, and admitted to this charge. During

ing

ordained him without a call. The principal occurrences during his incumbency, are recorded by himfelf in his own narrative, and by other contemporary writers; and it would be both un-neceffary, and improper for me to enumerate them. At the fame time, I cannot altogether pafs in filence, what has been termed, the extraordinary work at Kilfyth, Cambuflang, and fome other parifhes, in the year 1742; efpecially as there were even then fome who called themfelves Chriftians, fo blinded by prejudice, or by party zeal, as to affirm that it was a work of the Devil. Had they been fatisfied with reviling the honoured inftruments of that work, even though they did call them *limbs of Satan*, or *ambaffadors of hell*, I fhould have only pitied them, and been willing to bury their railing in oblivion: But they were fo deftitute of that charity, " which thinketh no evil, " which rejoiceth not in iniquity, but rejoiceth in the truth;" as to perfift in afcribing to diabolical influence, the effects pro-duced among the people. I think myfelf therefore obliged to make fome remarks on their conduct. And therefore I cannot pafs their conduct in filence. If there are men of the prefent time, who can view the fubject in the fame light, I reply to both, in the fpirit of meeknefs, " that a kingdom divided a-gainft itfelf cannot ftand;" and that if their reprefentations have

ing his incumbency the church received confiderable repairs. The whole roof was renewed, the north aifle and the vault or burying ground under it, was like-wife repaired in the year 1697. And the parifh was affeffed in the fum of L. 1266 : 13 : 4 Scots for that purpofe. Mr Hay being confiderably advanced in years before he was admitted, foon became unable to officiate. Infomuch, that on the 1ft of July 1710, he teftified to the feffion his defire of having an affiftant And in the fame day Mr James Stewart was elected by unanimous confent of the minifter, feffion, and congregation to be affiftant, and that as long as he was pleafed to cont'nue among them. In that capacity he officiated till the death of Mr Hay in July following.

A confiderable vacancy again enfued. So that for nearly three years the Prefbytery regularly fupplied the charge once in the fortnight.

have been juſtified by the facts, it is certain that at leaſt, in this pariſh, " Satan was divided againſt himſelf."

Others, with more candour and charity, have conſidered the remarkable circumſtances to which I allude, as more the effect of enthuſiaſm, than of deluſion. A great part of the eſtabliſhed church, who were not eye witneſſes of what really happened, were of this opinion at the time; and it is perhaps a common opinion ſtill.

They have endeavoured to account for the unuſual agitation and religious concern which then appeared among the people, by the influence of natural cauſes alone. They have aſcribed them to the influence of paſſion, of hope, and fear, and ſympathy, and example, or to all theſe cauſes united. They have told us, that the inſtruments of that work addreſſed the paſſions of men, more than their underſtandings; that thoſe on whom the chief impreſſion was made, were almoſt all affected in the ſame way, and expreſſed themſelves in ſimilar language; that the agitation of one was communicated to the multitude, and acted like a charm on their ſympathetic feelings.

This repreſentation is plauſible, but it is only plauſible. With the candour of a Chriſtian, and the affection of a brother, I would aſk thoſe who have urged it:

1ſt, Is it poſſible to preach the goſpel in its native ſimplicity and purity, without addreſſing the hopes and the fears of mankind? Where theſe paſſions have been addreſſed, has the effect been uniformly the ſame, as at Kilſyth in 1742? The reverſe is certainly the truth, though we are all men of like paſſions with our fathers. Why are men who are addreſſed in the ſame manner, ſo much more cold, and careleſs, and lukewarm, than the people who were diſtinguiſhed at that time? And why was it that under the *ſame miniſtry and the ſame means,* the ſame effects were not produced, even in 1742,

and

and the following years ? We can adopt no concluſion with candour or conſiſtency, but that the remarkable circumſtances of that time, are not to be aſcribed to thoſe who were the inſtruments of producing them, or to any peculiarity in the means which they employed ; but to the real efficacy of the doctrines of Chriſt, and to the power of God which accompanied them.

2dly, Let it be allowed, that all were affected in the ſame way, and that they expreſſed themſelves in the ſame, or in ſimilar words ; let it be granted that all ſighed, and groaned, and cried ; though Mr Robe in his narrative, laſt edition, page 128, ſays, that thoſe who diſcovered ſuch appearances, were by far the feweſt in number, being not one out of ſix, of thoſe who felt this religious concern. But, may not an honeſt mind reaſonably conclude, that the ſame cauſe ſhould produce ſimilar effects ; and that the ſimilarity in different perſons, indicated the operations of the ſame ſpirit in them all.

3dly, The power of ſympathy is undoubtedly great ; no man denies it to be ſo, who knows any thing of the human frame. It is not improbable that its influence was conſiderable on the people of that time. But he, " who has the " hearts of all men in his hands, and who turns them as the ri- " vers of waters whitherſoever he will," " who makes the very " wrath of men to praiſe him," might or did employ, even this as the means of " turning many to righteouſneſs." But whatever energy we aſcribe to the means, let us not forget the hand which directs them to their end, or " the power " which worketh all in all !" without the agency of God, the influence of the moſt powerful means is ineffectual. Neither is he that planteth any thing, nor he that watereth, but God who giveth the increaſe. I have no doubt that there were both enthuſiaſts and hypocrites diſtinguiſhed in 1742. Mr Robe acknowledges this in his narrative, page 271. But

I

I am happy to have it in my power to fay, that there are perfons yet alive in this place who have proved by the uniform
tenor of their lives, that they were not of the number,
though their religious impreffions were received at that period.
By their fruits they may ftill be known, and the effects of
converfion on men's practice is the only true teft and criteri-
on by which we ought to judge. Whatever were the means,
whether hope, or fear, or fympathy, or example, they experienced at that period a great and important change, which
has formed and decided their characters through life. And
" if the fabbath of the Lord, which was formerly defpifed, was
" then held honourable ; if the ordinances of religion, which
" were formerly neglected, were then ftrictly obferved; if the
" old and the young became fervent and frequent in family
" and private prayers ; if drunkennefs and licentioufnefs were
" then difcountenanced, curfing and fwearing difcontinued ;
" and if filthinefs and foolifh talking, gave place to the pious
" and pure effufions of a grateful heart ; if, in a word, ftrife
" and contention, wrath and malice ceafed, and love, and
" peace, and long fuffering, and forbearance, and forgive-
" nefs of one another prevailed, if the thief ftole no more,
" but made reftitution ; and a whole parifh at once, became
" decent and devout, fober and ferious ; and that they did
" fo, is attefted by paftor and people *, heritors, elders, and
" Magiftrates, in 1742, and by all the wife and worthy men,"
of the congregation of Kilfyth, who were eye witneffes to the
events of that year, and are ftill alive; call this enthufiafm, or call
it by any other name, I pray God, that I may ever feel its influence, and bear teftimony to its power among this people !

I

---

* See Mr Robe's narrative, p. 3d.

I pray God, that it may reach every kindred, and people, and tongue, and nation ! fay, that it is the influence of fear, or hope, or fympathy, or example, its effects are worthy of the doctrine of falvation, and indicate the power which renders it effectual.

On the 21ſt March 1754, Mr John Telfer was ordained miniſter, he died on the 29th of March 1789. And on the 3d of September following, the prefent incumbent was admitted. The crown is patron ; and what is perhaps remarkable, there has not been a miniſter introduced into the parifh fince the revolution, who has not had the unanimous concurrence of the people. The living was augmented about three years ago, and now confiſts of 67 bolls 3 firlots of meal, 11 bolls 3 firlots of barley, L. 52 : 16s. in money and 16 ſtone weight of cheefe.

In the year 1787, the glebe alfo was augmented ; fo that it now contains in arable and paſture lands by decreet 14 ac. 2 r. 15 f. befides an acre and a half Scots meafure, which has been poffeffed by the miniſter time immemorial ; and is allowed to belong to the church.——The glebe is at prefent in a variety of lots, of courfe not inclofed. But an excambion will foon take place, by which it will be thrown into one lot, and all inclofed of courfe. The manfe was built about 8 years ago : it is a good houfe, well finifhed, and in good repair.

School.—The parifh fchool was diſtinguifhed for many years, and though it has lately been on the decline, it is to be hoped, that it will foon be equal to what it has ever been. At leaft the heritors of the parifh have contributed all in their power to make it refpectable. They have affeffed themfelves in a handfome fum for building an elegant dwelling-houfe and fchool for the teacher ; it is nearly finifhed. And as they

have

have elected a young man of a liberal education, abilities, and character, it is to be hoped, he will meet with every encouragement and be eminently uſeful. At preſent he has two boarders, and will have accommodation for a few more. His ſalary is now increaſed to 100 lib. Scots; he receives quarterly for teaching Engliſh 2s. 2d. for writing and arithmetic 3s. for Latin, Greek, and French, 4s. 6d. Beſides he is appointed ſeſſion clerk : for which he receives annually in name of fee L. 2: 10. ſter. for each proclamation 2s. for every baptiſm 6d. and for a certificate 6d. beſides other trifles.

The town is populous, the ſchool large, and manufactures in a flouriſhing condition, and therefore it is probable that he ſhall meet with ſuitable encouragement. At the ſame time, it is much to be regretted, that men of a liberal education, who devote their time and talents to the inſtruction of the riſing generation, ſhould be ſo much neglected and meet with ſuch inadequate ſalaries.

A common tradeſman, if ſober and attentive, is much more independent, and may in general earn a better livelihood than the moſt part of pariſh ſchoolmaſters. While this continues to be the caſe, few men of abilities or character will aſpire to the office, or rather doom themſelves to the drudgery to which it requires them to ſubmit, with the aſſurance of poverty attached. If they are driven to the office by neceſſity, they muſt ſoon dwindle into inſignificance, and by becoming deſpicable in the eyes of the ignorant and worthleſs becauſe poor, muſt loſe their influence and their uſefulneſs of conſequence. But it is to be hoped, that the wiſdom of the legiſlature will ſee the impending evil, and ſpeedily interpoſe their authority to ward it off. If the ſalary of each parochial teacher were doubled, it would be only a trifle to the landed intereſt, and a mutual benefit to the teacher and the taught. Or, if this ſhould not be though adviſeable, might not every eſtabliſhed

ſchoolmaſter

ſchoolmaſter be appointed poſtmaſter if he reſides in a poſt town, or land ſurveyor for the pariſh in which he officiates ; neither of theſe employments would engroſs too much of his attention. And either of them might be a handſome addition to his income. Beſides the parochial ſchool which is very properly placed in the centre of the village, there are two, ſometimes three private ſchools in it, beſides one in the centre of the eaſt, and one in that of the weſt barony.

The latter of theſe at Chapelgreen was erected in the year 1723, in conſequence of a donation of L. 60 ſter. from Mr. John Patrick merchant in London, and a native of this pariſh. That ſum according to the terms of the donation, was devoted to the purpoſe of building the ſchool and endowing the teacher with a yearly ſalary not exceeding L. 3 ſter. in order that he might be enabled to teach the poor ſcholars gratis. The ſeſſion are nominated truſtees of the fund under the inſpection of the preſbytery ; and they are likewiſe patrons of the ſchool.

The ſchool in the eaſt barony is at Banton ; it is generally well attended, though the encouragement to the teacher is not very great. He has a dwelling houſe ; and William Cadell, Eſq. proprietor of the eſtate of Banton, has very liberally contributed to the ſupport of the teacher from year to year. There may be at an average 260 ſcholars taught annually within the bounds of the pariſh.

Poor.—The poor belonging to this pariſh, are not numerous ; excepting in years of great ſcarcity, or want of employment. They are of courſe, liberally ſupplied.

The funds are raiſed chiefly from the weekly collections, though in part from occaſional donations. There is beſides this, a ſum collected annually for the uſe of the mortcloths. As our burying ground is in much requeſt by ſtrangers, as well as the inhabitants of the pariſh; that ſum becomes often a conſiderable and very ſeaſonable ſupply.

By act of parliament, 1597, thoſe funds are entruſted to the Kirk Seſſion; and they never can be committed to better hands. Though the management is entirely a labour of love, and a great labour too, often attended with much obloquy, and ſeldom or never rewarded even by the grateful acknowledgement of the heritors; yet, as it involves the intereſt of the poor, it is regarded by every elder as a ſacred depoſit. With diligence and diſcretion they conſider the caſe of the needy. By aſſociating with every claſs of people, they become acquainted with the real wants and diſpoſitions of the widow, the orphan, and the fatherleſs, the feeble, the aged and infirm, and ſpeedily adminiſter relief. Upwards of L. 100,000 ſter. at leaſt, is entruſted to the elders of the church of Scotland; and by them diſtributed with a degree of fidelity and public ſpirit, which reflects the higheſt honour upon their office. Yet though the landed intereſt are relieved of a burden, which they themſelves could not ſubmit to, and from a duty which men of high rank could ſcarcely diſcharge, it is ſeldom that they will allow a Seſſion houſe, or even a ſhade for collecting for the poor; or if it be granted, it is often with reluctance. And yet I ſuppoſe, that the greateſt part of them would ſooner erect ſuch a ſhade at his own expence, than ſubmit to the danger and drudgery of ſtanding a whole hour, even one ſunday of the year, in a cold bleak winter day in the open air, to collect the mite which every worſhipper offers.

That the funds of this pariſh have been collected with ſuch trouble, managed with ſuch fidelity, and diſtributed with ſuch diſcretion, as I have now hinted, will appear from the following particulars.

At

At the Revolution, the whole funds delivered over to the Seſſion, amounted only to L. 19:10. ſterling. The weekly collection at that time never exceeded 1s and 8d; yet there is now in land and heritable bonds and caſh, a fund near L. 300 ſterling, for the ſupport of the poor; and that too raiſed, not by a parſimonious hoarding up of the poor's funds, not by withholding *what was meet*, or granting the needy only a penurious pittance, but by a prudent faithful diſcharge of their duty, in collecting and diſtributing. That the Seſſion of Kilſyth, was not in uſe to deny the relief which was neceſſary; and that theſe funds have been managed with ſuch prudence and care, will appear from the following table.

		Receivings.				Diſburſements.		
Years.		£.	s.	d.		£.	s.	d.
1720	-	8	16	8	-	10	6	4
1721	-	28	8	4	-	25	6	8
1740	-	24	0	0	-	20	12	8
1747	-	32	0	0	-	31	0	0
1749	-	43	8	0	-	37	0	0
1750	-	36	0	0	-	29	10	0
1765	-	42	10	0	-	41	0	0
1770	-	57	0	0	-	37	10	0
1772	-	22	10	0	-	16	2	0
1782	-	63	0	0	-	60	0	0
1784	-	56	0	0	-	55	0	0

For the laſt ten years, the average of receivings, is annually L. 70, diſburſements, L. 65.

The table is only given as a ſpecimen. In all of thoſe years, the treaſurer gave in a diſtinct account, for the preciſe term of a year. And therefore his receivings and diſburſements,

burſements are clearly ſtated for that preciſe term. In the interveening periods, the account was ſometimes taken in 6, 9, or 15 months, ſo that the annual rate cannot be ſo very accurately aſcertained. But the ſame proportion between the receipt and diſburſements holds, and therefore it is unne-ceſſary to be more particular. But in a pariſh like this, where moſt of the heritors do not reſide, and ſome have ſeceded from the church, and where none of them interfere with the poor's funds, the above facts ought to be made known to all. Eſpecially when it is conſidered, that the above ſums have been collected literally from the poor, or from the lower or-ders of the people, that is, from farmers and tradeſmen, and the few reſiding heritors who attend divine ſervice in the eſta-bliſhed church. Of courſe, the weekly collection has been ne-ceſſarily ſmall, though great in proportion to the circum-ſtances of the inhabitants : And had it not been for the ſe-ceſſion, it might have been one fifth more ; for in the year 1736, and after that period, when the ſeceſſion had firſt commenced, there is a great defalcation ; and there was a greater ſtill, about the year 1770, when the ſociety of relief was eſtabliſhed in this place. For it cannot be concealed, though it is with ſincere regret I mention it, that when the people of that communion withdrew themſelves from the eſ-tabliſhed church, they ſeem to have ſhut up their bowels of com-paſſion from their poor brethren ; at leaſt they have witheld their hand from relieving them. But it is to be hoped, at leaſt it is devoutly to be wiſhed, that they may ſpeedily ſee it to be their duty to aſſiſt, if not altogether to ſupply the poor of their own perſuaſion, and not caſt them off when helpleſs. They will certainly loſe nothing by doing ſo, either in their character as men, or as chriſtians. On the contrary, they will have the approbation of the pious and the pure of every perſuaſion, and the bleſſing of the poor who are attached to their communion.

To

To the honour of all denominations of chriſtians in this pariſh, they are always ready to contribute in a *private* capacity, when the circumſtances of the poor require them to do ſo. During the inclement winter 1795, when every labourer was entirely idle, and almoſt every claſs of tradeſmen, a ſubſcription was opened for the feeble, the aged, and the infirm, and for the honeſt and induſtrious, who could not find employ-ment, but were unwilling to come upon the pariſh. In the courſe of a few days, upwards of L. 11 were collected from the common orders of the inhabitants of every different communion; and by the concurrence of the heritors, it was raiſed at laſt above L. 30. The non-reſiding heritors not only concurred in this deſign, but have agreed to give a handſome ſum yearly, for the ſupport of the poor; an example truly laudable and worthy of imitation.

The ordinary poor which are not very numerous, are chiefly ſupported by the weekly collections at the church. But there are ſeldom above 10, and never above 15 upon the weekly liſt; theſe receive from 2s. 6d. to 4s. 6d. monthly, each according to their ſeveral neceſſities. But by far the greateſt ſum goes to the ſupply of the occaſional poor. And that none may be overlooked, the ſeſſion meets weekly all the year round; and in winter they meet always twice, ſometimes thrice, for the purpoſe of giving more liberal ſupplies than can be afforded weekly. At Martinmaſs, New-years-day, and Candlemaſs, they diſtribute from L. 3 to L. 4 ſter. either in money or in coals, or cloaths, to all without diſtinction who ſtand in need of them. Sometimes this occaſional ſupply amounts to L. 20 ſter. in the winter; beſides what is expended in the education of ſome orphans and many poor children.

Yet our funds have hitherto been ſufficient; ſo that there has not been an aſſeſſment in this pariſh for a century paſt,

excepting

excepting in the year 1740, as that was a year not only of want approaching to a famine, but of great ficknefs and diftrefs, the feffion very judicioufly took advantage of the act of parliament 1672. In the terms of that act, they called a meeting of the heritors, gave up a lift of all the poor within the parifh, and a ftate of the funds for their fupply : calling upon them to affefs themfelves to make up the deficiency. Yet after all, the fum exacted was only L. 5 on each 100 lib. Scots valuation, which was certainly very trifling : and little felt either by heritor or tenant, as it was equally paid by both.

The above, however, is only an account of our parochial fund. Befides thefe, the weavers and mafons have each a friendly fociety, and a common fund for the fupport of their brethren. Thefe focieties have given confiderable relief to multitudes; infomuch, that without them or fomething fimilar to them, this parifh muft have been affeffed long before this time to a confiderable amount *.

Population.

---

* The fociety of weavers was inftituted in the year 1760. At that time the manufacturing bufinefs was only in its infancy. And of courfe, the operative weavers were not numerous ; yet their numbers every year increafed, and multitudes joined the fociety, who knew nothing of the craft ; fo that there are now upwards of 350 belonging to it. Each member either pays 7s. 6d. upon admiffion, and one fhilling yearly ; or one pound two fhillings fter. at once, and he is for ever exempted from any future contribution, except a voluntary one, and entitled to all the privileges of the fociety. Thefe privileges are confiderable : if confined to bed by ficknefs, every member receives 3s. weekly ; if only unable to work, though walking about, he receives 2s. befides. At his death, there are L. 2 fterling allowed his widow or family, or friends, for funeral expences. Thefe and all their other regulations, feem to be wifely and well calculated to promote the common intereft of the fociety : efpecially as every member has an honeft pride in fupporting himfelf and his family, and a great averfion to come upon the funds, unlefs when neceffity urges him. The funds though fmall at firft, have by proper

and

Population.—The population of this pariſh may be very accurately ſtated. For in the year 1790, an exact liſt was taken of
every individual in it : at that time it contained preciſely 2450
ſouls, but the three following tables will give the moſt con-
ciſe view of this ſubject.

The

and prudent management, increaſed to what is to them a conſiderable ſum.
In houſes, bills, and bonds, their property may amount to upwards of L. 300
ſterling.

They meet annually upon the 1ſt Friday of Auguſt to chuſe their deacon,
and other office bearers, who meet regularly every quarter, or as often as
occaſion requires, to receive petitions, ſupply the poor brethren, and ſettle
the private affairs of the ſociety.

The maſon lodge was inſtituted about the ſame time : they hold of the
grand lodge of Edinburgh; every member at entry, pays 7s. 6d. if the ſon of
a member, if a ſtranger 10s. 6d. and all pay 4d. quarterly thereafter. Their
number is likewiſe on the increaſe, and may amount to about 120, their funds
will of courſe be enlarged ; at preſent they exceed L. 100 ſter. in houſes, bills,
and bonds. They have a very convenient lodge well fitted up ; they are able
in ſome meaſure to contribute to the ſupport of their poor brethren : if unable to work, they allow each member 2s. 6d.; if confined to bed, he receives
3s. weekly. And a guinea is likewiſe allowed for funeral charges; ſo that when
a poor man is connected with the ſociety both of maſons and weavers, which
is often the caſe, he has a very liberal allowance.

The miners of this pariſh propoſe likewiſe to eſtabliſh a friendly ſociety ;
but it have not yet taken place, though I hope it will very ſoon.

Of all charitable inſtitutions, thoſe friendly ſocieties ſeem to be the beſt : for
they are not only happily calculated to relieve the poor, but to maintain that
honeſt ſpirit of independence, which is the ſure mark of an honeſt and inge-
nuous mind. They therefore deſerve encouragement from all ranks and denominations ; but eſpecially from the landed intereſt, who have it in their
power to be liberal. It would be for the intereſt of every heritor to encourage
them; perhaps it is not unworthy of the legiſlature itſelf to interpoſe in their
behalf. Their funds might be exempted from all duty on bills and receipts :
or in caſes when they come in competition with other creditors, they might
be allowed a preferable claim to all ; except the crown and the landlord.

But

The firſt exhibits at one glance, a diſtinct view of the number of houſes, families, heads of families, widows, widowers, children, farmers, and male and female ſervants, in each diſtrict ſeparately. For I think it more confiſtent with the object of a ſtatiſtical account, to give a detail of the proportion of inhabitants in each diſtrict apart ; than merely to ſtate the number of the whole pariſh. By this means it will be an eaſy matter to ſay in any future period, whither the town or country part of the pariſh is increaſing or decreaſing : and in what proportion and denomination of inhabitants.

The ſecond table exhibits a diſtinct view of the number of children in each family of every diſtrict ; that are at the time alive.

The third repreſents the number of each denomination, and of every claſs of inhabitants.

TABLE

But a part, if not a principal part of theſe funds ought to be eſtabliſhed by law, as a ſupport for the widows and children of the reſpective members of each ſociety. Or, if the funds already collected are found inſufficient for that purpoſe, why, might not each member become bound to pay a ſmall additional ſum for the purpoſe of eſtabliſhing a widows fund ? A trifling ſum annually from each would ſerve the purpoſe. But perhaps the wiſeſt meaſure that could be adopted, would be to unite the friendly ſocieties into larger bodies, and the tradeſmen of the ſame craft throughout the kingdom into one ſociety. The common ſtock, if allowed to accumulate for a few years, would ſoon be ſufficient to anſwer all the purpoſes of their widows and their poor, and more effectually than the funds of ſmall and ſeparate ſocieties.

TABLE I.

Names of Districts.	Houses.	Families.	Heads of Fam.	Widows.	Widowers.	Children.	Farmers.	Men-servants.	Maid-servants.
Dundaff,	12	13	22	3	1	46	14	5	2
Auchinrivoch,	16	15	23	1	2	53	16	8	4
Cobziumboa,	23	23	44	1	2	78	15	5	4
Tomfin,	12	15	28	1	0	39	9	6	8
Auchincloch,	35	41	82	3	2	91	6	5	9
Banton,	43	45	62	3	2	114	8	7	6
Round the town,	22	17	37	0	0	63	14	6	9
Balmalloch,	17	18	31	5	2	57	14	5	5
Drumbreck,	29	30	50	5	2	53	12	5	8
Old place,	18	18	30	3	0	65	9	8	6
Quinzie,		18	74	14	4	97		4	6
North west, ⎫			35	11	2	120			4
South-west, ⎪ Quarter.	104	150	8	9	2	128		8	4
South-east, ⎬			92	7	2	123			5
North-east, ⎭						117			
New-Town,	59	96	126	7	2	213		4	2
Total.	**408**	**506**	**902**	**82**	**28**	**1458**	**118**	**68**	**99**

TABLE II.

Families, containing each [children].

	1,	2,	3,	4,	5,	6,	7,	8,	9,	10
Dundaff, ⎫	4	1	2	3	2	1	1	1	0	0
Auchinrivoch, ⎪	0	1	0	0	4	3	2	0	0	0
Cobziumboa, ⎬ East barony	3	6	9	4	5	2	0	0	0	0
Tomfin, ⎪	3	2	3	2	1	1	2	0	0	0
Auchincloch, ⎭	0	6	1	4	4	3	1	0	0	0
Banton, ⎫	6	4	9	4	2	2	2	0	0	0
Round the town, ⎪	2	6	4	4	1	0	0	0	0	0
Balmalloch, ⎬ W. barony	0	1	1	4	4	4	4	2	1	0
Drumbreck, ⎪	3	6	9	4	5	0	1	0	0	0
Old place, ⎭	3	2	2	3	3	1	1	1	0	0
Quinzie, ⎫	0	4	0	5	2	1	2	0	0	0
North west, ⎪	4	4	3	4	4	2	1	3	0	0
South-west, ⎬ Town	13	12	6	6	3	5	2	0	0	0
South-east, ⎪	7	8	6	4	3	3	2	3	0	0
North-east, ⎪	10	12	5	2	4	1	1	0	1	0
New-Town, ⎭	9	12	16	5	3	8	3	1	1	0
	71	**71**	**79**	**54**	**43**	**35**	**24**	**10**	**5**	**1**

TABLE

T A B L E III.

Weavers	- -	400	Clock-maker	- 1
Tambourers	-	280	Pensioners-chelsea	- 4
Taylors	- -	15	Publicans	- - 12
Masons	- -	10	Labourers	- - 24
Wrights	- -	12	Grocers	- - 23
Coopers	- -	2	Coalliers	- - 6
Carters	- -	5	Miners	- - 40
Flax-dressers	-	4	Excise-officer	- 1
Gardners	- -	3	Sheriff-officers	- 3
Nailers	- -	2	Stocking makers	- 7
Smiths	- -	10	Bakers	- - 2
Wheel-wrights	-	3	Surgeons	- - 2
Butchers	- -	5	Seamstresses	- 4
Shoemakers	- -	12	Drummer	- - 1
Millers	- -	5	Stampmaster	- - 1
Toll-keeper	- -	1	Carriers	- - 2
Sickle-makers	-	6	Teachers	- - 5
Students	- -	6		

Besides the distinction of employment, they may be distinguished likewise by their religious professions, thus:

Minister of the Establishment	- - 1	Adherents to the Relief	207
		To the Secession -	270
Do. belonging to the Society of Relief	- 1	Cameronians -	9
		Glassites -	1

The remainder adhere to the Established church, viz. 2000.

There may be about an hundred families or householders, that have no children. And upon the whole, there are not quite 3 children alive to each family.

In moſt places, there are more children to a family in the country than in the towns. But upon an examination of the 2d table, it will appear that the reverſe is the fact with us : this is undoubtedly rather ſingular, but it may perhaps be eaſily accounted for. The manufacturing claſs of people, generally marry younger than farmers and labourers ; becauſe they are much ſooner upon an independent footing. A weaver, the moment his apprenticeſhip is over, can earn a decent livelihood, and after ſerving as a journeyman for a ſhort time, generally marries or begins houſe-keeping. Whereas a ſervant, or even the ſon of a reſpectable farmer, unleſs he turns to ſome other profeſſion, is not ſo ſoon independent : the ſon, if his father is alive, is dependent on him, and in ſome meaſure his ſervant ; and the ſervant as he changes his maſter and his reſidence often, cannot ſo conveniently marry. As this is the caſe, and as the farmers and labourers are the moſt numerous claſs in the country, as the manufacturers are in the town, it is natural to ſuppoſe, that the latter ſhould marry ſooner, and of courſe, ſhould ſooner become the fathers of families.

I ſhall not preſume to ſay poſitively, whither the population of this pariſh has been on the increaſe or decreaſe : it ſeems to have been always on the increaſe. If Dr Webſter's account be accurate, the increaſe is very conſiderable indeed, ſince the period in which he enumerated them. At that time, there were only according to his account 1346; ſo that in the courſe of 40 years, there are no leſs than 1104 ſouls added to this pariſh.

The chief cauſes of this increaſe are doubtleſs the following : 1ſt, That manufactures have been, eſpecially ſince that period, in a flouriſhing condition : 2d, That of courſe, many from the remote highlands, and ſome from almoſt every quarter,

ter, have reſorted to this diſtrict : 3d, That the greateſt part of the farmers younger ſons have become tradeſmen or manufacturers : of courſe, they do not leave the pariſh, but reſort to the village ; and, by marrying, ſoon add to the number of ſouls. It corroborates this opinion much, that there are upwards of 900 ſouls in the old, and 300 in the new town : whereas the country part of the pariſh is not much more populous than it was laſt century : ſo that all the increaſe of population is in the town. Indeed it is certain, that it contains 300 ſouls more than it did even 10 years ago ; that is, before the new town was begun. And as the ſituation is highly advantageous—and the encouragement to new ſettlers liberal, it muſt in all likelihood continue to increaſe. Eſpecially, if a cotton miln, a bleachfield, printfield, or any public work be eſtabliſhed among us ; in that caſe, the increaſe muſt be rapid, and the population doubled in a very ſhort time.

But in a ſtatiſtical account, as little as poſſible ſhould be left to conjecture. Therefore, without entering upon uncertain ground, I ſhall give as full a table of births, or rather baptiſms, as I can. And fortunately I have been enabled to collect the materials for upwards of a century.

Years.

Years.	Marriages.	Males.	Females.	Not of this Parish.	Total.	Births.
1688	2	14	5	3	24	19
1689	4	5	4	1	14	9
1690	0	5	3	0	8	8
1691	9	6	9	0	24	15
1692	9	9	11	0	29	20
1693	13	26	28	2	69	54
1694	15	34	20	3	72	54
1695	24	31	11	3	69	42
1696	19	20	29	1	69	49
1697	17	24	23	1	65	47
Average	$11\frac{2}{10}$	$17\frac{4}{10}$	$14\frac{3}{10}$	$1\frac{4}{10}$		$40\frac{7}{10}$
1698	14	24	18	1	57	42
1699	19	22	22	4	67	44
1700	12	20	12	1	45	32
1701	23	30	20	1	74	50
1702	12	29	18	0	59	47
1703	14	25	27	1	67	52
1704	15	27	22	2	66	49
1705	14	16	21	1	52	37
1706	10	29	35	1	75	64
1707	13	32	21	3	69	53
Average	$14\frac{6}{10}$	$25\frac{4}{10}$	$21\frac{6}{10}$	$1\frac{5}{10}$		47
1708	14	27	18	1	60	45
1709	20	34	25	4	83	59
1710	13	25	27	5	70	52
1711	15	17	22	1	55	39
1712	14	22	19	0	55	41
1713	13	30	25	0	68	55
1714	11	23	25	1	60	48
1715	12	24	31	3	70	55
1716	9	33	25	3	70	58
1717	16	26	22	4	68	48
1718	16	35	32	4	87	67
Average	14	$27\frac{1}{10}$	$24\frac{4}{10}$	$2\frac{4}{11}$		$51\frac{6}{10}$

Years.

Years.	Marriages.	Males.	Females.	Not of this Pariſh.	Total.	Births.
1719	23	25	29	3	80	54
1720	8	31	31	3	73	62
1721	17	35	23	4	79	58
1722	16	31	28	16	91	59
1723	19	35	26	17	97	61
1724	23	32	23	17	95	58
1725	10	36	33	22	101	69
1726	26	28	32	14	100	60
1727	25	33	36	8	102	69
1728	13	26	29	0	68	55
Average	18	$31\frac{2}{10}$	29	$10\frac{4}{10}$		$60\frac{5}{10}$
1729	10	32	30	3	75	62
1730	17	22	18	2	59	40
1731	26	26	31	4	87	57
1732	12	31	36	1	80	67
1733	20	30	21	1	72	51
1734	18	37	32	8	95	69
1735	13	28	21	5	67	49
1736	17	23	35	2	77	58
1737	11	37	33	2	83	70
1738	6	28	22	3	59	50
Average	15	$29\frac{4}{10}$	$27\frac{9}{10}$	$3\frac{1}{10}$		$57\frac{3}{10}$
1739	11	34	30	3	78	64
1740	10	26	26	2	54	52
1741	6	22	20	3	51	42
1742	12	28	20	2	62	48
1743	17	32	25	1	75	57
1744	14	27	23	3	67	50
1745	11	35	27	2	75	62
1746	8	27	25	1	61	52
1747	13	22	42	3	80	64
1748	17	28	24	3	72	52
Average	$11\frac{9}{10}$	$28\frac{1}{10}$	$26\frac{1}{10}$	$2\frac{3}{10}$		$54\frac{3}{10}$

Years.

Years.	Marriages.	Males.	Females.	Not of this Parish.	Total.	Births.
1749	15	41	29	6	91	70
1750	21	24	25	0	70	49
1751	16	28	22	1	67	50
1752	17	31	19	2	69	50
1753	17	21	25	4	67	46
1754	9	32	29	0	70	61
1755	20	33	17	0	70	50
1756	14	19	27	0	60	46
1757	14	20	20	2	56	40
1758	12	27	17	0	56	44
Average	$15\frac{5}{10}$	$27\frac{2}{10}$	23	$1\frac{5}{10}$		$56\frac{6}{10}$
1759	8	26	20	0	54	46
1760	15	24	19	0	58	43
1761	21	35	24	0	80	59
1762	22	28	25	0	75	53
1763	24	34	23	0	81	57
1764	13	30	36	0	79	66
1765	13	23	27	0	63	50
1766	19	40	34	0	93	74
1767	17	23	38	0	78	61
1768	12	23	20	0	55	43
Average	$16\frac{4}{10}$	$28\frac{6}{10}$	$23\frac{6}{10}$			$55\frac{2}{10}$
1769	24	27	36	0	87	63
1770	31	28	36	0	95	64
1771	18	44	41	1	104	85
1772	19	42	46	0	107	88
1773	15	38	33	1	87	71
1774	13	32	28	1	74	60
1775	15	37	29	0	81	66
1776	10	37	27	6	80	64
1777	12	31	32	2	77	63
1778	19	28	23	2	72	51
Average	$17\frac{6}{10}$	$34\frac{4}{10}$	$33\frac{1}{10}$	$1\frac{3}{10}$		$67\frac{5}{10}$

Years.

Years.	Marriages.	Males.	Females.	Not of this Pariſh.	Total.	Births.
1779	13	27	32	0	72	59
1780	0	20	23	0	43	43
1781	14	38	29	0	81	67
1782	8	37	19	0	64	56
1783	4	44	26	0	74	70
1784	3	28	21	0	52	49
1785	13	30	28	0	71	58
1786	12	29	31	0	72	60
1787	3	36	28	0	67	64
1788	7	31	38	0	76	69
Average	$7\frac{7}{10}$	32	$27\frac{5}{10}$			$59\frac{5}{10}$
1789	8	37	30	2	77	67
1790	11	31	34	1	77	65
1791	14	37	31	0	82	68
1792	11	45	27	1	84	72
1793	9	34	25	0	68	59
1794	9	29	24	0	62	53
Average	9	$35\frac{3}{6}$	$28\frac{3}{6}$	$\frac{4}{6}$		64

The following Table, will ſhow the proportion between the males and females for 10 years, by an average.

Years.	Males.	Females.
From 1688 to 1698	17	14
——— 1698 to 1708	25	21
——— 1708 to 1718	27	24
——— 1718 to 1728	31	29
——— 1728 to 1738	29	27
——— 1738 to 1748	28	26
——— 1748 to 1758	27	23
——— 1758 to 1768	28	23
——— 1768 to 1778	34	33
——— 1778 to 1788	32	27
——— 1788 to 1794	35	28

The

The average was nearly from 28 to 26 during the above period; ſo that the number of males born has always been greater than the number of females.

At an average of 100 years, there are twins twice every three years: At preſent, there have been twins in four different families, within the courſe of a few months.

N..B. The following Table ſhows the number of children born in every month.

	In the year 1754.					In the year 1774.			
	Marriages.	Males.	Females.	Total.		Marriages.	Males.	Females.	Total.
January,	1	2	1	4		1	1	3	5
February,	1	2	2	5		2	3	2	7
March,	1	3	1	5		0	4	2	6
April,	1	2	6	9		1	1	1	3
May,	0	3	2	5		1	6	4	10
June,	0	6	2	8		2	3	2	7
July,	0	3	3	6		0	1	4	5
Auguſt,	0	3	3	6		3	0	4	7
September,	1	2	1	4		1	4	1	6
October,	1	3	4	8		0	5	1	6
November,	1	1	2	4		0	2	3	5
December,	2	2	2	6		2	2	1	5

	In the year 1764.					In the year 1784.			
January,	2	2	4	8		1	1	0	2
February,	0	2	1	3		0	0	3	3
March,	1	5	5	11		0	2	3	5
April,	1	2	1	4		0	4	3	7
May,	1	1	3	5		0	4	4	8
June,	0	2	3	5		1	1	1	3
July,	0	1	2	3		1	2	2	5
Auguſt,	0	1	1	2		0	2	0	2
September,	1	4	4	9		0	1	0	1
October,	1	3	4	8		0	1	1	2
November,	5	0	3	8		0	3	1	4
December,	1	7	5	13		0	7	3	10

I have been more particular in the above extract, becauſe I think it one of the moſt important articles in a ſtatiſtical account ; and becauſe the regiſters of this pariſh have
been kept with uncommon care.

Therefore, as it may be depended upon as correct, it may
ſerve many uſeful purpoſes in time to come : and at preſent
may furniſh a very plauſible if not a certain ſtatement of the
proportional increaſe or decreaſe of the population of this
pariſh during all the above periods.

A few remarks upon this ſubject, may tend to ſet it in a
clearer light. It is generally ſuppoſed, that if we multiply
the annual births in a pariſh by 26, the product will give the
number of inhabitants. But in this pariſh at leaſt, this will
not hold at preſent : and 1 think, I can aſſign very ſufficient
reaſons for this.

1ſt, The ſtill born children, and thoſe who die before baptiſm are not regiſtrated.

2dly, Since the feceſſion at firſt took place, a number, if not
the greater part of feceders, neglect to regiſtrate their children.

3dly, Since the duty was impoſed upon baptiſms, a ſtill
greater number have neglected to do ſo, in order to evade the tax.

4thly, In a manufacturing village like this, there are a
great many ſtrangers who come to reſide : and in proportion to
the encouragement they meet with, the number muſt increaſe.
For theſe or other reaſons, we muſt multiply the number of
baptiſms at preſent by 38, to give the number of inhabitants :
and the reaſon is, that upon an average, there are at leaſt 8, if
not 10 children born annually, who for one or other of the
above reaſons, are not regiſtrated.

Yet, if we multiply the births for every period by 38, I
fear this rule may be fallacious. For before the feceſſion took
place, and manufactures were introduced into this pariſh, or a
duty impoſed on the pariſh regiſter, the record was unqueſtion-
ably more complete.

I

I ſhall therefore endeavour to make an allowance for this in the following calculation.

For the firſt 10 years after the Revolution, the average of births annually, was about 40.

Multiply this Nº.	40 by 30 the Nº. of inhabts.				1200
For the ſecond 10 years	47 by 30	-	-	-	1410
For the third	51 by 30	-		-	1530
For the fourth	60 by 30			-	1800
For the fifth leſs *	57 by 35	-		-	1995
For the ſixth leſs	54 by 35		-		1890
For the ſeventh	56 by 35	-			1960
For the eighth	55 by 35	-		-	1925
For the ninth †	67 by 36			-	2412
For the tenth	59 by 38				2242
For the laſt 6 years	64 by 38		-	-	2432

Here it will appear, that I have made an allowance for ſtill born and unbaptiſed infants, even at the earlieſt period. In place of 26, I have taken 30, allowing 4 annually. After the ſeceſſion, I have allowed 5 more annually, which I think may be a reaſonable allowance for thoſe of that perſuaſion, who neglected to regiſtrate their children. After the relief ſociety was eſtabliſhed here, a few more would neglect to do ſo : eſpecially conſidering the duty on baptiſms ; therefore, I have from that period allowed 3 more.

After much minute inveſtigation, I ſuppoſe the above may give a pretty accurate idea of the progreſſive increaſe of population.

Mr Robe mentions in his narrative, that there were in the year 1742, 200 communicants in this pariſh. At preſent there are no leſs than 515 in full communion with the church.

Table

* After the ſeceſſion.
† After the relief ſociety was eſtabliſhed here.

T A B L E I.

Showing the number of deaths in every month, for ten years.

	1785	1786	1787	1788	1789	1790	1791	1792	1793	1794	Total.
January,	1	1	4	5	3	3	4	27	11	7	66
February,	3	2	3	4	7	2	7	15	6	4	53
March,	4	5	12	11	0	1	1	12	8	7	61
April,	8	6	8	3	4	5	4	8	6	4	56
May,	2	6	10	7	1	6	3	4	4	5	48
June,	6	7	6	4	3	2	3	1	4	6	42
July,	1	6	2	2	6	6	2	3	1	4	35
Auguſt,	2	3	3	1	1	2	2	2	2	2	20
September,	1	3	2	3	0	6	7	2	1	4	29
October,	3	4	1	2	2	4	9	2	5	4	36
November,	6	11	5	2	5	3	5	0	2	8	47
December,	4	2	7	4	2	5	12	3	2	0	4
Total.	41	56	63	48	34	45	59	79	52	53	

T A B L E II.

Showing the number of adults, male or female, old or young, in the above period.

	1785	1786	1787	1788	1789	1790	1791	1792	1793	1794	Total.
Old men,	5	12	6	7	10	4	10	8	5	8	75 *
Old women,	5	5	13	6	10	8	8	10	13	9	87 *
Young men,	3	3	4	4	2	3	4	2	9	4	38 †
Y. women,	7	7	4	5	4	2	2	6	7	6	50 †
Children.	10	18	30	16	4	21	18	53	0	10	190 ‡

The

* From 60 to 90.

† From 15 to 30.

‡ From 1 to 10.

The following may serve as a bill of mortality for the above period, as the diseases are distinctly marked out.

T A B L E III.

	1785	1786	1787	1788	1789	1790	1791	1792	1793	1794
Small pox,	9	19	15	8		1	6	30		3
Innoculate do.			2				1			
Old age,	7	16	16	10	14	9	12	20	15	9
Measles,						1		2	1	
Consumption,	4	3	6	4	3		5	3	2	6
Cancer,			1				2		1	1
Bowels,				1	1	4	2	2		5
Croup,				2		11	3	5		
Flux,				1	1		3	5		
Fever,				2	3		2	3	12	6
Throat,								1	1	
Accident,		1	2			2	1		2	1
Child-bed,	1				1				1	
Teething,										1
Water in the head,										3
Epilepsy,										1
In drink,									1	
Hooping cough,			5				2	4		
Suddenly,				2		2	1			
Jaundice,						1			1	
Bleeding at the nose,							2			
Unknown,	9	6	10	8	7	5	2		6	3
Total.	30	45	57	38	30	36	43	76	43	39
From other parishes.	11	11	6	10	4	9	16	6	9	14

The following remarks will in fome meafure explain the above tables, and they are neceffary to prevent miftakes.

Although the firft table is an accurate ftatement of the numbers enrolled in the mortcloth keeper's books, yet there are a few annually die, who are not enrolled. All who are ftill born, and even a few infants have not the ufe of the mortcloth ; but to counterbalance this on the other hand, fuch children as are ftill born or not baptifed, are not included in the foregoing regifter of baptifms.

From the firft of thefe tables, fuppofing them to be accurate, it will appear, that on an average of 10 years, about 51 die annually : and that January, February, March, April, and May, are the moft fatal months ; next to them is June, November, and December ; and on the other hand, July, Auguft, and September, are in general the moft healthy months.

From the fecond table, it will appear, that in the fame period, two thirds of the mortality bill confifts of children : and two thirds of the remainder of old men and women : and that there is a very fmall proportion of young men and young women that die, that is between the age of 15 and 30.

From the third table, it will appear, that the fmall pox are by much the moft fatal of all the difeafes to which we are liable. When this difeafe prevails, the mortality bill rifes for that year, and *vice verfa*.

Heritors, &c.——The heritors of this parifh are not very numerous, and few of them have property in it to a great extent. Sir Archibald Edmonftone, of Duntreath, Bart. is proprietor of five fixths of the parifh, and fuperior of the whole, except a valuation of L. 80 Scots. He is alfo titular of the tiends.

The

The following liſt of the heritors and their reſpective valuations, as it is extracted from the ceſs books, will give a pretty accurate idea of the proportion of landed property, which belongs to each. Though I ſhall not preſume to point out their reſpective rentals, as that would be extremely indelicate and improper. I ſhall only give the ſuppoſed rental in *cumulo.*

Heritors Names.	*Valuation.*		
	L.	s.	d.
Sir Archibald Edmonſtone -	3108	10	0
William Cadell, Eſq. Banton -	281	15	10
Carron Company -	120	15	10
His Grace the Duke of Montroſe -	80	10	7
The Town of Kilſyth feuers -	75	0	0
Mr P. Marſhall, Townhead - -	75	0	0
Mr D. Patrick, of Weſter Auchincloch -	40	5	3
Mr John Miller, of ditto.	35	4	9
Mr A. Laing, of Ruchhill -	30	0	0
Mr William Ranken, of Bogſide -	24	3	3
Mr J. Bow, of Auchinruoch -	20	0	0
Mr John Graham, of Auchincloch -	14	1	4
Mr Young, of Brockyſide -	7	10	0
Mr P. Bow, of Auchinclock - -	4	0	6

Scots L. 3916 17 9

Suppoſed rental ſter. L. 2950 0 0

Beſides cot-houſes, feus, &c. which may be 150 more. The firſt four are non-reſiding heritors. All the reſt reſide, except Mr Young. And the greateſt part of them farm their

own

own property; ſo that there is no fixed rent put upon it.

Farmers.—The farmers in this diſtrict are in general a ſober, virtuous, and reſpectable claſs of men : they are equally
free from the licentiouſneſs of the proud and wealthy, and
from the growling and diſcontented temper of the leſs ſober
and leſs induſtrious poor. It muſt be acknowledged, however, that they do not in general much excel their neighbours
in the art of farming : like the tenants of moſt of the forfeited eſtates in Scotland, they are perhaps rather indolent,
becauſe they are independent ; and they make but few
ſpirited exertions, becauſe their rents are ſmall and their
leaſes long. Perhaps the principal cauſe why they are behind in ſome improvements, is, that their farms are in general very injudiciouſly laid out. They conſiſt of a long narrow ſtrip, beginning in the valley and riſing to the ſummit of
the hill ; ſometimes one, two, or three miles long, and not a
quarter of a mile broad. At the time when the leaſes were
granted, that is, about the beginning of this century, this
might be attended with many conveniences. The great object at that time for every farmer, was to have every thing he
needed within his own farm : and by this diviſion, he had his
proportion of moſs, and meadow, paſture, and arable ground.
Whereas, had the farms been regularly laid out, this could
not have been the caſe. This, however, is now a great bar to
improvement. For the rich low grounds in the valley and its
vicinity, by being interſected, and every farm by being intermixed with another in this irregular manner, cannot be incloſed
to advantage ; of courſe, cannot be improved, from circumſtances which are rather the misfortune than the fault of the
tenants. For unleſs a general excambion were taking place,
and every farm were new modelled, which is next to impoſſible,

ble, while the present leases last, the valley must lie open, and uninclosed ; and, therefore, continue to be poached all the winter : for this cause it is, that the worst, that is the high lying cold ground, which is allotted for pasture, is all inclosed : while the low, warm, rich valley, lies open ; a circumstance this, which is surely very uncommon in the present period.

It is chiefly owing to this circumstance, that every farmer is in some measure a grazier, though there are but few who follow that line to any great extent ; at the same time, it is much more attended to, than it was 40 or 50 years ago. Before the rebellion 1745, a great proportion, perhaps one tenth of the arable part of the parish, was cultivated. From the valley to the very brow of the hills, upwards of 800 feet above the level of the sea, almost every inclosure was ploughed in regular rotation. Whereas now, it is very uncommon to see one acre in 20 of those high grounds cultivated. The reason is obvious, and every one who looks at the grounds must see it. The fields are steep, and of course, very expensive in the culture : every plough requires 4, in some places would require 6 horses, and never less than two men. After all this labour and expence, the produce must be scanty, and the harvest late ; in some cases so late, as to endanger the crop, if not ruin it altogether. Besides, as lime is at a considerable distance, and the roads bad, and as dung cannot be conveyed from the valley, where the farm houses in general now stand, there is little probability of improving them to much advantage. For the expence of seed, labour, and manure, it is feared, would exceed the produce ; the high wages of men servants, the advanced price of horses, and of every utensil that is necessary, and the amazing expence of carrying manure in sufficient quantities to those high fields, are circumstances sufficient to discourage the farmer

from

from making the attempt, or at leaſt to account for his un-
willingneſs to hazard it. But let it not be ſuppoſed that the
high fields are uſeleſs, or of little value : on the contrary,
they are rich and productive to the farmers ; they are perhaps
more productive than a great part of the ploughed land.
They yield great abundance of the richeſt and earlieſt paſture
in the weſt of Scotland ; and being of a ſouth expoſure and
uneven ſurface, they afford every variety of ſoil and ſhelter,
either for ſummer or winter. The beautiful green hills, are
covered with the ſweeteſt paſture ; the valleys, or rather interveening marſhes, which are likewiſe numerous, produce
abundance of coarſe hay : and every little hill or incloſure,
has its little rivulet. The demand for fat cattle has increaſed,
and ſeems to be increaſing, and the high grounds have for many
years been entirely employed to feed cattle. It is generally
allowed, that there is no ſtrath in the weſt of Scotland more
favourable for the purpoſe than the ſtrath which lies weſtward
from Kilſyth, through Campſie, and Strathblain *.

Horſes,

---

* The graziers in this pariſh are an active induſtrious and reſpectable claſs
of farmers : they ſeem to know their buſineſs well ; and puſh it with conſiderable ſpirit. If they are liable to any errors, it may perhaps be the following :

1ſt, That they rather overſtock their grounds, ſo that the cattle have not
ſufficient choice of the beſt paſture : and beſides the coarſe hay is thus greatly
injured.

2d, In purchaſing their cattle, they are not always at due pains to pick the
beſt out of the flock ; whereas, if they were to exclude all the ſhots, it would
be ultimately for their intereſt, though the cattle were dearer in the mean
time.

3dly, They run too much upon highland cattle : doubtleſs, they take on
the beef faſt, and feed very quickly, and when fed, are ſweeter than larger
cattle. But, perhaps, it would be the intereſt of the grazier, to buy up
large

Horſes, Sheep, &c.—From the circumſtances which have
been mentioned, the number of plough horſes muſt be greatly diminiſhed, more eſpecially as the two horſe plough upon
Small's conſtruction, is generally uſed in the low grounds.
The number of milk cows, but eſpecially of fat cattle, muſt
be in proportion increaſed; how much I cannot ſay. The
following table, however, will exhibit a correct view of the
whole live ſtock of the pariſh, and its ſuppoſed value, eſtimated by a proper judge.

		Suppoſed value on average.			Total.		
		L.	s.	d.	L.	s.	d.
N°. of Sheep	1000	0	10	6	525	0	0
Horſes	290	12	0	0	3480	0	0
Milk cows	750	4	10	0	3375	0	0
Fattened do.	720	4	10	0	3240	0	0

Total L. 10620 0 0

But beſides the above, there is a great number of young
cattle and horſes, and likewiſe a few ſwine, which will at leaſt
raiſe the general value of the ſtock to L. 11000 ſter. A milk
cow yields from 8 to 12 pints of milk daily.

Produce,

large country cows for the richeſt of his paſture; and reſerve the hilly grounds
for the highland cattle.

Theſe things, however, are more attended to now than heretofore.

The profits are of courſe greater. Each cow for ſummer graſs meal, is allowed to yield from 20s. to 30s. at an average: when fed both in winter and
ſummer, each yields from 35s. to 45s.

But in this account, I make no allowance for the loſs of cattle, &c. &c.
which is ſometimes conſiderable.

Produce, &c.—The produce of the arable lands conſiſts principally in oats, though partly in barley, potatoes, beans, rye graſs, and hay. It is difficult to ſay, what proportion of acres there may be in each kind; there are not 2 acres in fallow, nor 3 in wheat and turnip, in the whole pariſh. But the following will be found to be a general eſtimate of the produce.

	Acres.	Aver. Nº. of bolls p. acre.	Higheſt produce, bolls.	Nº. bolls.	Price per boll.			Total va-lue.		
					L.	s.	d.	L.	s.	d.
Oats,	1600	5	10	8000	0	15	0	6000	0	0
Barley,	100	8	10	800	1	0	0	800	0	0
Potatoes,	200	80	120	16000	0	4	0	3200	0	0
Hay,	180	160	250	28800	0	0	4	480	0	0
			ſtone.							

Suppoſed produce of the pariſh L. 10480 0 0

Our oats yield from 12 to 16 pecks of meal in the boll. And it is univerſally underſtood, that a warm ſummer makes the crop yield well, and *vice verſa*, though the fodder be plenty.

The table is not taken from an accurate meaſurement: but the produce per acre may be depended on. It is but ſeldom that the average riſes above it, though in ſome fields it is e-qual to the laſt column.

Rye is ſeldom ſown, at leaſt in any quantity. I have never ſeen above an acre in one field: but the little that is raiſed, is uncommonly good. Wheat has been attempted, but we have not acquired the art of cultivating that precious grain to ad-vantage: though our rich valley is peculiarly adapted to the purpoſe,

purpoſe, yet as it is not incloſed or ſubdivided, it cannot be ſown with wheat to any advantage : for the winter poaching would ruin the crop. Much of the riſing ground, if incloſed, ſummer fallowed, and properly manured, might likewiſe produce abundant crops of wheat. Flax is raiſed in ſmall quantities, but chiefly for private uſe, and ſeldom for ſale : and the quality of it is at all times more remarkable than the quantity. It is generally allowed to be of the fineſt grain and colour, of any in Stirlingſhire *. Rye graſs and clover have been introduced about 10 years ; and as they have turned out to great advantage, they are much run upon, at leaſt by all who have proper incloſures for the purpoſe : though they are ſometimes ſown even for paſture in open fields.

But potatoes are the favourite produce of this pariſh, and it has been juſtly and long famous on this account:—I ſay juſtly and long ; for it not only gave birth to the gentleman who firſt introduced the culture of potatoes into the fields, by dibbling and hand-hoeing, but it was the ſcene of his earlieſt experiments : and, if the name of any man deſerves to be handed down to ſucceeding ages, with honour and gratitude, it is that of *Robert Graham, Eſq ; of Tamrawer*. He, with a ſpirit truly patriotic, and a mind active and indefatigable, ſet vigorouſly to work in the cultivation of potatoes in the year 1739. Before that period, he and others had raiſed them in gardens : but there was a vulgar and a common prejudice,

---

* This laſt ſeaſon, I knew 20 ſtone weight of flax raiſed from 4 pecks, and ſold at 14s. the ſtone : as eight pecks are allowed to ſow an acre, this was a produce equal to L. 28 ſter. per acre. Beſides that, 18 pecks of ſeed were ſaved off the above half acre, and ſold at half price.

It was conſidered as a remarkably good, though not an uncommon crop.

prejudice, that they could be raiſed no where elſe to advantage. Mr Graham, to ſhow the abſurdity of this opinion,
planted about half an acre of ground in the croft of Neilſtone,
where he then reſided. This excited the attention of the
neighbourhood, and the report of it was ſoon ſpread far and
wide: infomuch, that people of all denominations, and
ſome noblemen of the higheſt rank, (among whom was the
unfortunate Earl of Perth), came to witneſs the plantation.
And had they known the amazing benefit that was to accrue
to the nation, from this fortunate attempt, they would have
doubtleſs hailed the auſpicious event, and erected a monument to Mr Graham on the ſpot. Regardleſs of the ignorant
ridicule to which his firſt experiments expoſed him, he proſecuted
his favourite purſuit, with increaſing ardour and ſucceſs : and
by his perſevering induſtry, and uncommonly happy talent
for proſecuting every ſpecies of improvement, he raiſed the
cultivation of potatoes in the neighbourhood of Kilſyth, to
a pitch ſcarcely yet, if at all ſurpaſſed any where ; and to
promote the ſame ſpirit, and ſpread the bleſſing far and wide,
he rented lands in the vicinity of Renfrew, and Perth, Dundee, and Glaſgow, Leith, and Edinburgh ; and for many
years obtained the premium for cultivating potatoes, till at
laſt no competitor was found ; all were compelled to yield
the palm to him.

This will not perhaps appear ſo ſurpriſing, if the following
facts are attended to.

After an endleſs variety of experiments, which he very properly recorded, but the record of which is unfortunately loſt,
he, in the year 1762, planted one peck of potatoes with the
dibble, and in October following, raiſed from the ſame peck,
16 bolls and $\frac{1}{4}$ boll, or 264 pecks.

As this may appear ſurpriſing, if not incredible to ſome,

I

I am exceedingly happy to have it in my power to eſtabliſh the fact upon the moſt unequivocal evidence. The gentlemen who were called to witneſs the planting and raiſing of the potatoes, very properly publiſhed an account of the whole operation in the Newſpaper of the day, for the benefit of the public. And happily the original atteſtation is now in my hands.

A copy of it will ſurely be acceptable, and deemed ſtrictly ſtatiſtical; more eſpecially, as it points out the manner in which the operation was carried on, and the very high ſtate of improvement to which Mr Graham had arrived.

" We John Marſhall of Townhead, Henry Mar-
" ſhall of Ruck-hill, and Alexander Maxwell preſent
" bailie of Kilſyth, went at the deſire of Robert
" Graham of Tamrawer, and attended his ſervants upon
" the 21ſt of April 1762.

" We ſaw them meaſure an exact peck of potatoes,
" which we ſaw them plant with the dibble and draper.
" Each ſet was diſtant 18 and 21 inches length-ways
" of the ploughed ridge, and between 12 and 15 inches
" acroſs the ridge.

" And upon the 26th of October following, we
" did alſo attend Mr Graham's ſervants, while raiſing
" the produce of the ſaid peck of potatoes, which we
" then ſaw meaſured on the ground, amounting to 16
" bolls and a half, which is 264 pecks, ariſing from
" the ſaid one peck. The truth of all which is atteſted
" by us, and

" Signed JOHN MARSHALL,
    " HENRY MARSHALL,
        " ALEXANDER MAXWELL."

If

If the man who makes a ſingle pile of graſs or corn to grow, where there was none before, in the eyes of Dean Swift, deſerved more of his country than all the politicians that ever lived, we leave it to the learned to weave a laurel crown for Mr Graham.

The method in which his operations were carried on, were ingenious and ſingular, and might have been deſcribed.

There is no branch of huſbandry more attended to, nor proſecuted with more ingenuity and ſucceſs by all claſſes, than the cultivation of potatoes. Every year there is ſome real, or imaginary improvement introduced; and it is eagerly adopted and proſecuted with much care and perſeverance. I have known many try 8 or 10 ſpecies of ſeed in one ſeaſon. This ſpirit they partly have imbibed from Mr Graham; but the ſucceſs is principally owing to local circumſtances. The ſoil is not only highly favourable, but every feuer has, and almoſt every inhabitant lays his account with taking, a ſmall lot of ground, for the expreſs purpoſe of raiſing potatoes. They have beſides time and inclination to beſtow great care, and attention, in planting, weeding, and dreſſing them. And their endeavours are generally crowned with ſucceſs [*].

Our

---

[*] The following ſeems to be the reſult of endleſs experiments.

1ſt, That the kidney potatoe is the beſt feed, moſt productive, and pleaſant to the taſte at the ſame time.

2dly, That ground which has never been broken up before, or at leaſt, never produced potatoes, is by much the moſt productive; though not better manured than other ground.

3dly, That potatoes ought to be planted each ſet at the diſtance of 1 foot 6 inches, from each other; at leaſt in the ridge, even when they are not drilled.

N. B. It is univerſally agreed, that potatoes when frequently repeated, or even oftener than once in 7 years on the ſame ground, are a very ſcourging crop; if once in two years, they ſpeedily reduce the ſoil to a *caput mortuum*.

4thly, That

Our feed time is rather late in general. In the laſt week of March, or firſt of April, the oats are for the moſt part fown; though fometimes fown confiderably later. Potatoes are planted,

4thly, That each plant ſhould be carefully boxed up with the hoe, if not drilled, or otherwife with the plough; as in that cafe, it becomes greatly more productive. For every time the earth is thrown up, the plant ſtrikes out new fibres: and a fucceffion of crop may thus be obtained. The loweſt tire may be ripe and ready for eating, while the higheſt are fcarcely formed. But where this is attempted, as it was often by Mr Graham, the plants ought to be 3 feet diſtant from each other, in all directions.

5thly, It is allowed that if the ground be lea or grafs, the dung ought in that cafe, to be fpread in harveſt preceding; or at leaſt, early in the fpring; that it may in fome meafure be incorporated with the foil; before it be ploughed. Even in ſtubble it is deemed advantageous.

6thly, It is generally allowed that lime is very unfavourable for the cultivation of potatoes. It is even faid, that the bad effects of it are experienced for 10 or 20 years. One of thefe is, that the crop of potatoes though large, is almoſt always fcabbed or foul.

7thly, The feed is generally cut in pretty large fets, and kept a week or two if poffible, before it be fet. This is faid to be a great advantage, particularly in wet grounds. It is faid to make the potatoe fpring fooner, and to prevent the feed from rotting. For being ſhrivelled and dryed, and covered with a kind of tough rind, it is more capable of refiſting the moiſture, and at the fame time, has an equal tendency to vegetate quickly.

8thly, A moſt productive crop may be raifed of early potatoes, before the middle of July. And either turnips, greens, or grafs-feeds, may be raifed as a fecond crop. Yet the potatoes may yield of clear profit per acre, from L. 10 to 12.

9thly, In gardens and fmall plots, the ſtocks of greens and cabbage, are one of the beſt manures for potatoes. If dug in drills, and the ſtocks be laid in regularly, they both enrich the ground, and keep the foil open; and thereby give room for the ſhoots to fpread.

Laſtly, Great crops have been raifed out of the young ſhoots, in place of fets.

planted, and the barley sown in the last week of April, and first of May.

The old people make a general remark, that the spring is much later, and the summers a great deal colder, than they were 40 or 50 years ago. Of course, that the harvest is not only later, but much more precarious.

One remarkable summer is mentioned about 40 years ago, in which the heat was so great at seed time, that the labourer could not endure it at noon. So that it was a common thing to sleep the greatest part of the day, and labour in the night. From barley seed-time, till barley harvest, there was not a shower, but copious dews; yet the crop was the most productive of any since that period; though the straw was short, and the sheaves few, and scarcely a stack to be seen in a barn-yard, the barns containing almost all the grain and fodder.

Price of Provisions.—As to the price of provisions, it is generally low. Beef, mutton and veal, are at least a penny per pound lower than in Glasgow; sometimes even two pence; lamb and butter always two pence. Eggs and poultry of all kinds are lower in proportion; so that it is needless to be more particular. It will doubtless serve the purpose of a statistical account better, to point out the comparative value of as many articles as possible, at different periods. And as I had occasion to consult an old memorandum book, belonging to Mr Cornwall of Banton, who was chamberlain to Lord Kilsyth in the year 1670, I find the precise price of the following articles, stated at that period; and in another manuscript of a private gentleman belonging to this parish, I find the same articles rated in the year 1745. I shall therefore state the account.

Prices in the year 1670,				In 1745,				In 1795,		
	L.	s.	d.	L.	s.	d.		L.	s.	d.
A boll of feed corn,	0	7	0	0	10	0		0	18	0
—— of barley,	0	8	0	0	11	8		1	12	0
—— of oat-meal,	0	10	0	0	8	4		0	18	0
—— of lime *,	0	0	6	0	0	6		0	0	6
A pound of butter,	0	0	4	0	0	3		0	0	9
A load of coals,	0	0	2	0	0	3		0	0	7½
A leg of mutton,	0	1	1	0	1	0 average	0	2	6
A pair of ſhoes to his Lordſhip,	0	1	8	0	2	6		0	7	6
Do to his fervant,	0	1	6	0	2	4		0	6	6
A ſcore lean highland cows, each	0	13	4	1	18	0		3	12	0
A cows hide,	0	2	6	0	3	6 average	0	18	0

There are beſides the above, a number of articles rated in Mr Cornwall's memorandum, but not in year 1745. A table of theſe may be acceptable.

Rate of articles in 1676, and in 1795						
	L.	s.	d.	L.	s.	d.
A pound of tobacco,	0	1	6	0	0	0
powder, -	0	0	8	0	2	2
ſhot, -	0	0	3	0	0	4
A pint of wine, I ſuppoſe Scottiſh,	0	1	6	0	6	0
A barrel of herring, -	0	16	8	1	7	0
A ſtone falt butter,	0	5	8	0	13	0
A pair worſted ſtockings to my Lord,	0	2	2	0	6	6
of gloves to do.	0	1	4	0	3	0

A

* The meaſure was much larger than at preſent, each boll being a horſe load.

	L.	s.	d.	L.	s.	d.
A yard of linnen for ſhirts to my Lord,	0	0	10	0	3	6
Making 6 ſhirts to do.	0	1	0	0	6	6
A ſtone of lint,	0	10	0	0	14	0
To dreſſing a ſuit of cloaths, and making ſtockings to my Lord,	0	1	8	0	0	0

The following rate of wages and annual fees, &c. is mentioned alſo, in the ſame period.

	L.	s.	d.	L.	s.	d.
His Lordſhip's groom's fee,	5	8	0	18	0	0
A thicker a day with meat,　　-	0	0	5	0	1	8
A dyke builder do.　　　　-	0	0	6	0	1	8
A coallier do.	0	0	10	0	3	6
A labourer do.	0	0	6	0	1	6
A tradeſman do.	0	0	8	0	2	0
A leg of beef	0	5	0	1	0	0
A cow's tongue,	0	0	4	0	1	0
A horſes hay and corn all night in Glaſg.	0	0	9	0	1	8
To one horſe ſhoe and 3 removes,	0	0	7	0	1	3

In the following articles the compariſon cannot be ſo eaſily
ſtated, but they are diſtinctly marked in the ſame record in
1676.

	L.	s.	d.
An advocate's retaining fee for my Lord,	20	0	0
The chamberlayn's allowance,	44	0	0
A year's board for my Lord at Glaſgow college,	82	0	0
A phyſician from Glaſgow for a viſit,	1	4	0
Do. do.　　　from Edinburgh do.	4	10	0
A ſurgeon's viſit from Glaſgow,	0	7	3
To the phyſician's man	0	4	3
A furniſhed velvet hunting cap to my Lord,	1	5	0

A

	L.	s.	d.
A hat to my Lord,	0	12	0
A gun to do.	0	16	8
A pair pocket piſtols,	1	13	0
Do. hulſters furniſhed	0	18	0
A ſuit of cloths for his Lordſhip's page,	0	15	0
A ſaddle and bridle furniſhed to my Lord,	1	0	3
Matriculating his Lordſhip's arms,	1	8	0
Small ſeeds for his Lordſhip's garden yearly,	0	4	10

	L.	s.	d.
A ſtone of ſkimmed milk cheeſe,	0	4	6
Do. of ſweet milk not ſkimmed,	0	8	0
A threave of ſtraw for thatch,	0	3	0
A ſtone of do. do.	0	0	2
A ſtone of tarry wool,	0	7	0
Of white do.	0	9	6
A mutchkin of ſweet milk,	0	0	0 $\frac{1}{2}$
A Scottiſh pint of churned do.	0	0	0 $\frac{1}{4}$
Weaving a yard of linnen,	0	0	8
A man, a horſe and cart per day,	0	5	0
A ſpindle of linnen yarn ſpun,	0	1	6
A peck of potatoes dug for,	0	0	0 $\frac{3}{4}$
A wood cutter a day,	0	1	3
A pealer do.	0	0	8
A ſtone of bark,	0	1	6
100 ſlabs 3$\frac{1}{4}$ feet long,	0	3	6
Do. 4$\frac{1}{4}$ feet long,	0	4	6

The rent of lands bore much the ſame proportion. At the above period, I find the very beſt lands in the valley, ſet from year to year, at the rate of 10s. ſter. the acre. At this moment, they yield from 50s. to L. 3 ſter. A great part of the valley is ſet at that rate : but, I ſuppoſe it would not

yield

yield fo much upon a leafe of 19 years. In general the rents are very low in this parifh as the leafes were many of them granted about the beginning of this century. An acre in potatoes or flax, if prepared for the crop, lets at L. 6 fterling.

The wages of fervants have rifen in a ftill greater proportion. They are nearly triple to what they were even 40 years ago. Independent of his food, a ploughman expects from L. 10 to L. 12; a maid fervant from L. 3 to L. 4. A hay cutter a day charges 2s. 6d. a reaper in harveft 2s. a female do. 1s. 6d. When engaged by the week and finding his own provifions, a man receives 9s. and a female 7s weekly. A weaver can earn from 1s. 6d. to 2s. 6d. a day at an average.

Antiquities, &c.——The antiquities in this parifh are not very remarkable : yet a few deferve a place in this account.

This diftrict muft have been the fcene of contention, and the field of blood for many generations ; perhaps from the days of Agricola, till the civil war in 1646. It feems to have been without the fixed limits of the Roman empire. For the fouth boundary of the parifh runs nearly parallel to Graham's Dyke for upwards of 6 miles. In that diftrict of the wall, it is never more than half, nor lefs than a quarter of a mile fouth of this parifh. At Wefterwood, and Bar-hill, there are two diftinct Roman Forts ; and of courfe, two Pictifh forts in this parifh correfponding to thefe : Cunny park to the former, and Balcaftle to the latter. The laft mentioned is by much the moft remarkable. It is perhaps the moft beautiful, regular, and entire of any Pictifh fort in Scotland. It is placed in the angle of two fmall rills, near a farm houfe called Caftle town,

or

or Balcaſtle, on that account ; and, it riſes regularly on all
ſides at an angle of 45 degrees, ſo that the form of it reſembles the top of a hat ; but it is not equally high all a-
round.   On the ſouth it is about 40 feet, on the north only
20 perpendicular : and it has been ſurrounded on all ſides by
a foſs, which might eaſily be filled with water by the
rivulets on either ſide.   At the baſe it is nearly 100 yards
in diameter ;   at the ſummit, which is flat, it is ſcarcely 50,
and is quite circular.   There is a tradition that it is hollow
within ;   and ſome pretend to have ſeen the mouth of
the mine open, which leads to the cavity.   But, if there
ever was ſuch a mine, it is now entirely ſhut up, and
there is not the ſmalleſt veſtige of any ſubterraneous paſſage
at preſent.

The ſloping ſides of this mound are covered with broom
and bruſhwood.   The top, though once overgrown alſo, is
now cleared, and often cultivated, and produces excellent
potatoes and oats.

The other fort at **Cunny park** ſeems not to have been ſo regular or large.   At leaſt it is not now ſo entire :   and ſcarcely
deſerves to be mentioned.

Beſides theſe, there have been other Roman antiquities
found in this pariſh and neighbourhood.   For an account of
theſe, I refer the reader to Horſeley's Britannia, and
Henry's hiſtory.   They are moſtly lodged in the univerſity of
Glaſgow.   That learned ſociety have thrown off copperplate impreſſions of all the Roman antiques in their poſſeſſion.

There are ſeveral circular fortifications, called cheſters,
which bear evident marks of great antiquity.   The moſt remarkable are at Auchincloch, Auchinvillie, and Townhead.
They are all ſimilar to each other, and much about the ſame

ſize ;

fize; being nearly 40 or 50 yards diameter. The outer wall or inclofure, for fome of them have evident marks of fmaller, but irregular inclofures within, confifts of a rude mafs, of large and fmall tumbling ftones, built without any regularity or order; and without mortar of any kind. In times of ignorance and barbarifm, they may however have been places of confiderable ftrength. Though it feems very uncertain for what purpofe they were at firft erected.

That they were ftrong holds, or places of defence, or fhelter, feems unqueftionable. Indeed the name they bear, feems to indicate this much; for chefter in Gaelic, fignifies a *camp.* And as the name is of Gaelic original, for this as well as other reafons, I am difpofed to think they are of greater antiquity, than even Agricola's wall, or Graham's dyke. Perhaps they are coeval with the Roman forts; and it is generally allowed, that thefe were formed before the wall.

If this be the cafe, in all probability, thefe chefters may have been intended as places of refuge, for the women and children, and the defencelefs and unarmed inhabitants of this diftrict. To them they would naturally fly for fhelter, in cafe of an unexpected defeat, or fudden incurfion of the Roman invaders. The fituation and ftructure of thefe fortifications, feem both to favour this conjecture. They are fituated at no great diftance from the Roman wall; lying along the north fide of the valley, which was the boundary of that empire. Befides this, they contain a number of fmall fubdivifions, like the ruins of rude huts, which might have ferved for fhelter from the ftorm; as the great outer wall was for fafety from the invader.

This at leaft feems a more plaufible conjecture, than that they were intended as a place of fecurity for cattle, and the other ftock and moveables of the natives. They are too fmall to contain any confiderable number of cattle. And befides

the

the neighbouring mountains, furniſh in a thouſand different places, proteċtion, as well as paſture for cattle, to much better purpoſe. Nor is it likely, that they were intended as a defence from the wolves, and ravenous beaſts. The wall that ſurrounds them, ſeems to be a work of much greater labour and ſtrength, than was neceſſary for this purpoſe.

But if we ſuppoſe, as is ſurely very likely, that the Caledonians had a ſtanding army always along the line of the Roman wall, they, though fearleſs of danger, and diſdaining all ſhelter, but the ſtrength of their own arm, muſt neceſſarily have been attended with a number of women, and defenceleſs followers. Theſe needed, and naturally ſought for a place of refuge. And ſuch a refuge, the cheſters might afford *

But

* Nature ſeems to have marked out this ſtrath, as the boundary of the Roman Empire. Whether it was pitched upon from neceſſity or choice, I cannot ſay. But the following particulars will make it appear, that it was the moſt eligible place for raiſing up a barrier againſt the native Caledonians.

1ſt, It is by much the narroweſt place in the whole Iſland. The Frith of Forth and Clyde interſeċt the kingdom for many miles on either ſide.

2dly, It is beſides the north boundary of the lowlands. The whole country to the north, appears to a ſtranger, to be an endleſs ſucceſſion of bleak and barren mountains.

3dly, The whole ſtrath of Kelvin, ſeems to have been an impaſſible moraſs. In ſome places, I ſuppoſe the whole valley was covered with water: From this weſtward to the Clyde, it was therefore a natural barrier of itſelf. From the Dullatur bog eaſtward, it ſeems to have been entirely under water. Camelodunum ſeems to have been a ſea-port town. If it was ſo, the whole valley to Kilſyth pariſh, muſt have been an arm of the ſea, though not navigable, yet next to impaſſible. Had it not been for theſe natural advantages of ſituation, the Roman wall muſt have been a feeble defence againſt the hardy, brave, and free ſons of Caledonia.

In more than one place, there ſeems to have been artificial mounds raiſed in the valley, to throw it under water.

The

But this is given merely as a conjecture. For though many of the ftones have been removed, there never has been found the fmalleft veftige of any infcription, nor even of any character whatever upon them.

The *tumuli* in this parifh are probably of equal antiquity with the chefters. Thefe however, have never been numerous, or confiderable ; and they have all been rafed to the foundation, for many years. The larger ftones have been ufed for building inclofures, the fmaller for the highways. I have been able only to trace the fite of two of thefe tumuli. The one at a field near Auchincloch, which I am told in Gallic, fignifies a field of ftones. The other about 600 yards eaft from Chapel-green. That they were erected as monuments over the dead is generally allowed, as urns containing the afhes of the dead, have been found in moft, if not in all that have been examined.

But the queftion ftill remains, by what nation were they erected ? If by the native Caledonians, why have urns been found in them, with evident marks of the bodies having been burnt ? If by other nations, whence came they ? For though fome may be fuppofed to be Roman, they cannot all be fo, as the greateft part of them are beyond the Roman boundary. And yet there is a very ftriking fimilarity in the ftructure of them, which would argue they were the work of one nation. But for what end were fuch mighty piles huddled together, in fuch a rude confufed mafs, and with fuch immenfe labour and drudgery, upon the fummit of very high hills too, where

fcarcely

The Ban-hill, feems to me to have been the moft important fort. It is nearly centrical; and commands a view of the wall for nearly half its length ; and it overlooks the whole ftrath to the north. Befides, it is nearly oppofite to the only narrow place of the valley; where a paffage could be forced with the greateft expedition.

ſcarcely a ſtone was to be found? If it was merely to commemorate the atchievements of the dead, or as a monument to his praiſe; how comes it that there never has been found any inſcription, or even hieroglyphic, to point out the names, deſignation, charaćter, or country of the deceaſed? If it was merely to defend the body from the ravenous wolves, and wild beaſts, one tenth, in many caſes, one hundredth part of the pile might have ſufficed. And beſides, the body ſeems to have been burned; ſo that there was no danger from that quarter. It ſeems, however, certain, that theſe were the works not of any individual, or family; but of a whole ĉlan, or tribe, or nation. Perhaps they were the work of ages. All nations pay veneration to the aſhes of the dead; and I believe there are none ſo rude and uncivilized, as to have no monuments. In early ages, the natives of this iſland, might fall upon this method of diſtinguiſhing the graves of great heroes, and eminent ſaints. As a tribute of eſteem, every traveller as he paſſed, would naturally add his ſtone to the heap; ſo that although ſmall at firſt, it would increaſe from year to year, in proportion to the veneration that was paid to the deceaſed. In evidence of this, it is ſaid, that a ſimilar cuſtom ſtill prevails in the highlands of Scotland; and almoſt every cairn or tumulus, has its reſpećtive name, as Angus-cairn, &c.

One of the cairns in this pariſh, likewiſe records the name of ſome ſaint or hero. It is near a place called Kelvin-head. Now, as *kel*, or *cuil*, or *cella* ſignifies a cell, or burying ground; ſo *vean*, or *bean*, which in Gallic are the ſame, is the name of a Culdee ſaint; or, according to ſome, of *Fingal*, the Caledonian hero. At all events, this tumulus ſeems to have been the burying place of *Vean*. And hence the origin of the names in the neighbourhood of it, as *Bean-ton*, or, as it is now contraćted, Banton; Beanenyre; Tom-vean,

or

or *bean*; and *Kelvin* is the name of the river, which riſes very nearly where the cairn ſtood.

There are both in the eaſt and weſt barony a few monuments of feudal tyranny. In the *Bar-wood*, (from whence it doubtleſs derived its name,) there is an eminence ſtill called the *Court hill*, where the haughty Barons were wont to ſit in judgement. And near Quinzie-burn in the weſt barony, there is an eminence called the *Gallow-hill*, where the ſentence was put in execution. The very place where the gallows ſtood, is ſtill pointed out. Theſe ſerve only to recall to mind the days of cruel deſpotiſm, when, at the call of a lawleſs tyrant, the defenceleſs, perhaps innocent victim, was dragged from his peaceful lowly cot, and in one ſingle day, without evidence of his guilt, or an opportunity of acquittal, was arraigned, tried, condemned, and executed! And while we heave a ſigh over the ſorrows of our fathers, the very recollection of that ſlavery under which they groaned and bled, makes us lift up our eyes in grateful homage, and bleſs indulgent heaven, that we are happy and free!

At different periods, and in a variety of places in this pariſh, there have been a number of ancient coins found. But the greateſt part by far has been concealed from the public. Of thoſe that have been ſeen, part have been of gold, part of copper, but the greateſt number of ſilver, and of all ſizes, from a three penny piece, to that of a crown. A few may ſtill be recovered, and at a very trifling expence, for they are regarded only as bullion; and as far as I have ſeen, would not be much eſteemed by the antiquarian.

The greateſt part have been found along the field, where the battle of Kilſyth was fought. It belongs not to me to give any detail of that engagement in this place. Suffice it only to ſay, that every little hill and valley, bears the name, or records the deeds of that day. So that the ſituation of

each

each army can be diſtinctly traced. Such as the Bullet and Baggage-know, the Drum-burn, the Slaughter-how or hollow, *Kill e many butts*, &c. &c. In the Bullet know and neighbourhood, bullets are found every year; and in ſome places ſo thick, that you may lift 3 or 4 without moving a ſtep. In the Slaughter how, and a variety of other places, bones and ſkeletons, may be dug up every where; and in every little bog or marſh for three miles, eſpecially in the Dullatur bog, they have been diſcovered in almoſt every ditch. The places where the bodies lie in any number, may be eaſily known; as the graſs is always of a more luxuriant growth in ſummer, and of a yellowiſh tinge in ſpring and harveſt. The hilt of a ſword, and part of a ſaddle, with a variety of coins, have been found in different places; and at one time, a gold ring with an eſcutcheon was diſcovered; but it is now loſt, or in the poſſeſſion of ſome perſon unknown to me.

The little hill where the gallant Graham encamped the night before the engagement, is ſomewhat remarkable. The tents have been raiſed with ſod, and it is eaſy at this day, to diſtinguiſh the place where they ſtood, and the form and ſize of each. The ſtation was extremely well choſen, and gave him every advantage over the enemy, perhaps in a great meaſure enabled him to decide the combat.

The carnage muſt have been dreadful. And the conſequences were fatal, and long felt by the defenceleſs inhabitants. Like every other civil war, it was carried on with the keeneſt contention, and unrelenting cruelty. Many of the peaſantry were butchered, and many more plundered. To this day, numberleſs ſcenes of blood and cruelty are recorded. One in particular is mentioned. A poor country man having fled with his four ſons, was overtaken by a flying party. Being ſuſpected by them, they inſtantly fell upon the old man, though feeble and unarmed. The generous youths
clung

clung around their aged fire, either to plead for, or defend him. In this posture it is said, they were all cut to pieces, and now lie in one tomb.

On this article I may mention, that there is a very fine arched vault, or burying ground, under the church. This was originally erected by the family of Kilfyth; and it has been their burying ground for many generations. As the estate was forfeited, and the title became extinct in the year 1715, it has never been used as a burying ground since that period. The unfortunate Viscount himself fled to Flanders; and though he returned more than once, *incog.* in the habit of a common beggar, and as such, lodged with several of his tenants, and secured a considerable quantity, if not the whole of his silver plate, yet it is certain, he was not buried in Kilfyth. The tradition is, and it is said to be confirmed by a variety of people, and even by some papers and letters lately found, that he and a number of the unfortunate Noblesse, were either murdered, or died by a sudden accident in Holland, about the year 1717.

The last that was buried in this place, was his lady. She is said to have been of the family of Dundee *. Her body being

---

* Jean, daughter of Lord William Cochrane, son and heir of William Earl of Dundonald. She was first married to John Viscount of Dundee; then to the Viscount of Kilfyth. Her son died in infancy.

See Crawford's Peerage, Dundee, Dundonald.

Lady Kilfyth with her infant son, was smothered or killed in Holland, or Flanders, by the falling of a roof, along with her husband. It has been supposed that the thing happened not by accident, but design; that several considerable persons who had been concerned in the Rebellion 1715, were involved in it, as well as the family of Kilfyth; and that only two of the whole company escaped, by being seated in a window. That this account is in general true, may be seen from letters lately found (in 1780), among the papers in the Advocates library, which refer to Kilfyth. The fact is detailed besides

in

being embalmed, was ſent over to Scotland ſoon after, and buried in great pomp, at Kilſyth. It was incloſed, firſt in a leaden coffin, nicely cemented; that again with a very ſtrong wooden coffin. The ſpace between the two coffins, was filled up with a white matter, ſomewhat of the conſiſtency and colour of putty; but of a rich and delicious aromatic flavour. It is but a few years ago, ſince this matter was laid open, by the decay of the wooden coffin. And a few weeks ago, the lead coffin was perfectly entire. But ſome rude thoughtleſs people, having gone to viſit the tomb, with ſacrilegious hands tore up the lead covering. To their great ſurpriſe, they found under it a board of fir, as clean and freſh, as if it had been formed yeſterday. This being looſened, by the removal of the lead, they, to their utmoſt aſtoniſh-ment, found the body of Lady Kilſyth, and her child, as entire as the hour they were entombed.

Every feature, and every limb, is as full, nay the very ſhroud is as clear and freſh, and the ribbans as bright, as the very day they were lodged in the tomb. What renders the ſcene truly intereſting as well as ſtriking, is, that the body of her ſon and only child, the natural heir of the titles and eſtates of Kilſyth, lies at her knee. His features are as compoſed, as if he were only aſleep. His colour is as freſh, and his fleſh as full, as if in the perfect glow of health. He ſeems to have been an infant of the age of 3 months.

The body of Lady Kilſyth, is equally well preſerved : and it would not be eaſy for a ſtranger to diſtinguiſh with his eye, whether ſhe is dead or alive. For, with the elegant

ſtyle

---

in Dalrymple's Memoirs. The wound which Lady Kilſyth received was on the right temple; and is ſtill as diſtinct, as on the day ſhe received it. The child ſeems to have received no other injury, than that of being ſmo-thered in the arms of its mother.

ftyle in which fhe is dreffed, the vivid colour of the ribbans, the frefhnefs of her looks, and the fulnefs of her features, fhe arrefts the attention, and interefts the heart. And unfeeling as the grave muft that heart be, which doth not heave a figh at the fight.

For my part, it excited in my mind a thoufand melancholy reflections. But above all, the deepeft regret, that fuch violence had been offered to her afhes, as to lay them open to view.

Happily there is not one fold of her fhroud difcompofed, nor a fingle feature or member yet impaired. But I fear, that being now expofed to the open air, and the fine aromatic fluids within the coffin daily evaporating, the body muft foon moulder into duft. To prevent this, the coffin has been clofed with as great care as poffible, and the accefs to the tomb is fhut.

The liquid in which the body has been preferved (and the coffin feems to have been full it, for the whole fhroud is faturated with it), feems to be a pure ardent fpirit, of the colour and confiftency of brandy, or rather fpirit of wine. But though perfectly pure, it has entirely loft all its pungent qualities, and feems now quite vapid.

The tomb is an arched vault 16 feet fquare and quite fhut up ; but, from what it contained, the air of it is as fweet, pure, and odoriferous as a ball room.

I have only to add, that there is in my poffeffion an old manufcript, much mutilated, which feems to be a chronicle of Scotland. Much of it is yet legible. It takes up the hiftory of Scotland at the chriftian æra ; and contains a regular feries of all the remarkable events in every king's reign, with the name of the kings, down to the year 1565. I have compared it with many memoirs, hiftories, and annals of Scotland, but as far as I can yet learn, it is an original, and not a copy. I think it may be valuable.

This

This parish has in common with others experienced years of scarcity, on which a few remarks are subjoined in a note *.

Miscellaneous

* Great scarcity approaching to a famine. The most remarkable was during the 7 last years of the last century. And for that reason, they are called the 7 dear years. There may perhaps have been one, or even two years successively of as great scarcity since that period: but there never has been more. Of course, the evil was more lasting and more generally felt at that time, than ever since : and in all probability accumulated every year; till at last the absolute necessaries of life could scarcely be got for any money. The price of provisions was exorbitant. Barley meal, though very inferior in quality, was sold at a merk the peck; oats rose to the enormous sum of L. 30 Scots the load, while oat meal was not to be purchased. For though several of the more opulent inhabitants went to Falkirk, the richest corn country within 30 miles, they could procure no supply at any price. Greens boiled with salt, became a common food. Fodder was as scarce as grain. Many of the cattle perished at the stall, and many of them who were driven out to seek a scanty pittance expired in the field. Mothers fell down dead with their infants at their breasts. Even many of the people who survived, were feeble and emaciated, and became a prey to numberless and fatal diseases. The mortality was so great, that a pestilence seems to have succeeded the famine.

The causes of this scarcity are not known. But it is said, that the harvests were late, and the winters early ; so that the frost and snow blasted the growing corns,

Various shifts not known since, were tried in order to ward off the evil. Among the rest it is mentioned, that snails were collected in summer with great care, and salted for the winter's store.

Indulgent Heaven has been more liberal to us. So that this generation has never known want, like that which our fathers experienced. The year 1740, was a year of scarcity, perhaps equal to any one of the 7 dear years. Oat meal rose to the exorbitant price of 2s. the peck : and at one time could scarcely be procured for money. Every other necessary of life was in proportion dear : yet few, if any, died of absolute want. As money, however, was scarce, and manufactures almost unknown among us, numbers whose situations gave them no reason to expect it, were through want of employment reduced to the humiliating necessity of craving a scanty pittance from door to door. Others were supplied from the poors funds, in a more private manner. The number of Paupers was thus greatly increased ; and their necessities and demands increased in proportion. Of course, the parish funds were deemed insufficient, and an assessment became necessary. Yet this is the only year since the Revolution, that the session were driven to this expedient.

The

Mifcellaneous Remarks.—A few remarkable phenomena which have appeared in this parifh, are likewife fubjoined in a note *.

Eminent

The caufes of this fcarcity are generally known. The harveft was late. The corns of courfe were greatly injured by the winter froft, which fet in early and fevere. Potatoes, though introduced into this parifh, were only cultivated in very fmall quantities by Mr Graham. Even thofe that were raifed, were not preferved with fuch care as to protect them from the ftorm, which was uncommonly fevere. Many fowls, fome cattle, and a few of the wild animals, were frozen to death. Many of the people were froft bitten. And much of the furze, broom, and brufhwood, and of courfe, all the greens and garden ftuffs, decayed and became ufelefs.

It is almoft unneceffary to mention, that there was a confiderable fcarcity in the year 1782. I believe it was generally felt ; and in other diftricts more fenfible than here. The potatoes though a moft luxuriant cropt were rather late, and they were totally loft. The corn harveft was alfo late. The winter was early ; fo that a great part of the oats were never ripened. And no fmall part was rotted in the field after it was reaped. Even that part which was preferved, was not productive. The following year added to the calamity, for the feed being generally bad, and equally fcarce, the produce of courfe was fmall. The poor had lefs to fow, and what was fown was much lefs productive ; fo that upon the whole, that year was not much more abundant than the former. And, had it not been for a very feafonable fupply of white peafe, both the poor and the rich muft have been in a deplorable condition. Even the refpectable farmers, who have generally meal enough and to fpare, were reduced to the neceffity of buying one peck of meal after another. Yet the price never much exceeded 1s. 6d.

The inhabitants of the village, efpecially the fociety of weavers, very wifely laid out a part of their funds, for purchafing that neceffary article, at the loweft wholefale prices : and retailed it at prime coft. This proved a great relief to multitudes. For meal was thus almoft always to be had here, and at a lower price than could naturally have been expected. The fociety loft little or nothing ; at the utmoft only the intereft of their money for a few months.

In the year 1793, and 1794, the great ftagnation of trade, and the almoft total want of employment, bore hard on the manufacturing clafs of inhabitants. And had the fame circumftances operated in fame degree for a fingle year more, all ranks and denominations muft have felt the confequences.

* In the year 1733, on the 27th June, there was a very remarkable thunder ftorm. The morning was fair : the fky clear : the fun bright. About

Eminent Men.—This pariſh has produced a few eminent men, whoſe names ought to be recorded.

" Sir William Livingſtone of Kilſyth, was a man of much
" penetration

11 o'clock, A. M. a gleaming, but gloomy darkneſs overſpread the ſky. The ſun was ſhorn of his beams, and put on a diſmal dark copper colour.

The cloud that overcaſt the ſky, aroſe in the ſouth weſt. At firſt it appeared very ſmall : but as it approached, it became darker and larger, and gleamed with lightning. And as the darkneſs increaſed, the flaſhes became more vived.

About one o'clock, this cloud reached our hills. The lightenings flaſhed inceſſant : the thunder roared tremendous, and the mountains ſeemed to ſhake. At firſt, a few dropping fragments of broken ice of great ſize fell. This was a happy warning to all who were in the fields to fly for ſhelter. Had they remained without, they muſt have been greatly hurt, for ſome of the hail meaſured 3 inches in circumference ; ſome ſay a great deal larger. And it fell in ſuch quantities, as to cover the ſurface ſome inches deep. It was noon next day before it melted away.

The damage done by the hail was very conſiderable ; and by the flood from the hills ſtill more ſo. The barley which was beginning to ſhoot, the flax, which was then in the bloom, and the peaſe and beans, which had begun to bloſſom, were almoſt irrecoverably loſt, being cut and daſhed to the ground, by the hail. The corns in the vallies were greatly injured by the rapidity of the flood, though it was only of a few hours duration. As if a water ſpout had fallen, and ſome ſuppoſe this was the caſe, the face of the hills, which an hour before were parched, was covered with numberleſs torrents, ſo as to have the appearance of a great collection of cataracts. Every rill became a river, ſweeping houſes, bridges, corn, and cattle, all before it, with irreſiſtible fury. The conſequences of this flood were felt for years, and the devaſtation it occaſioned may yet partly be ſeen. Several acres in the vallies, were overlaid with ſtones of all ſizes, from ſtones of 20 tons, to the ſmalleſt gravel. In ſome places this layer was 4 or 6 feet deep ; and a part of them ſtill remain. At a moderate calculation, the damage done in this pariſh, though fortunately it extended only to this, was upwards of L. 1000 ſterling. See beginning of Mr Robe's narrative.

Happily no lives were loſt, though many narrowly eſcaped. A woman and

" penetration and confiderable learning. Being efpecially
" eminent in the knowledge of the law, he was appointed
" one of the fenators of the College of Juftice in 16c9. And
" having diftinguifhed himfelf in that office by his affiduity
" and abilities, he was in a few years admitted to be one of
" his Majefty's Privy Council, and conftituted Vice-Cham-
" berlain of Scotland. He died about 1627."

" Mr

and child in her arms, were flightly injured by the lightning fitting at her
own fire, while a cat was killed at their feet. Some women who were
bleaching clothes in the valley, narrowly efcaped the rapidity of the torrent,
by climbing up a thorn tree which was hard by. This thorn ftill ftands
in the valley. Many cattle were fwept away, along with the houfes in which
they ftood. It is faid, that fome of thefe were left alive, when the flood
fubfided. It is even faid, that an infant in a cradle was carried feveral hundred yards along the ftream, and yet was found fafe.

In the years 1769 and 70, when the great canal was cut through the Dullatur bog, there appeared a very fingular phenomenon. Myriads of fmall toads,
each about the fize of a nut, or fmall turkey bean, were feen hopping over all the
adjacent fields, to the extent of feveral miles fquare. Ten, fometimes twenty or thirty, might be collected in one fquare yard. So that when you looked
along the furface of the ground, they appeared hopping like hail ftones.
What was very fingular, they were all going in one direction, directly
north ; yet they were never feen beyond the fummit of the hill ; nor
any where in any quantity the enfuing fpring.

It is fuppofed they came originally from the Dullatur bog, which is a large
and very deep morafs ; and in all likelihood it has once been a lake. For at
prefent, it is only covered with a thin matted turf, or fward. Under that,
there is in moft places, a great body of water, though in fome, of flow mofs.
And near the weft end of it, there is a fmall dry rifing ground covered with
wood, which is called the *ealan*, or in Englifh the ifland. From all which I am
difpofed to think, that in the time of the Romans, perhaps fince that period,
it was one deep extenfive lake. Yet it never fent forth at any other period in
the memory of man, any fuch fwarm of reptiles. Thefe, though innumerable,
were all of one age and fize. If it were to fend forth fuch a fwarm annually,
the whole country would foon be overrun.

" Mr John Livingſton was likewiſe a native of this pariſh.
" He was born in the year 1603. His father was a relation
" of the family of Kilfyth, and poſſeſſed a ſmall eſtate in
" the eaſt barony. It would appear, that the name of this
" eſtate was Monaeburgh. The greateſt part of the village
" is built upon it, though the boundaries of it are not well
" known."

" Mr Livingſton was a man of letters and piety. Early
" in life, he devoted himſelf to the ſtudy of divinity. He
" held a charge in the miniſtry firſt in Ireland. After
" ſpending a number of years in this charge, he was tranſ-
" lated to Stranraer, and next to Ancrum near Jedburgh.
" He was intelligent, active, zealous, and ſucceſsful in
" promoting the intereſts of pure and undefiled religion.
" His memory is ſtill dear ; and though the memoirs he
" wrote are in few hands, they are eagerly read by the inha-
" tants of Kilfyth."

" His life, tranſactions, and death, are narrated at ſome
" length. He died in the year 1672."

" I have had occaſion to mention, that Mr Robert
" Graham of Tamrawer, was a native of this pariſh ; and
" that his name deſerves to be handed down to poſterity,
" on account of his very ſucceſsful experiments upon the cul-
" tivation of potatoes."

" It may perhaps deſerve to be mentioned, that there
" is a family of the name of Stevenſon, who for many
" generations have been eminently uſeful, and much em-
" ployed in reſtoring diſlocated joints, and dreſſing bro-
" ken limbs. Though in a great meaſure ignorant of
" the theory, they have at leaſt acquired the practice ; and
" in all generations, as well as this, have been often ſuc-
" ceſsful."

Mode of Living, &c.——A great variety of changes in the external appearance and mode of living of the inhabiants, have taken place within the laſt 50 years. The moſt obvious and remarkable of theſe may be mentioned.

In their dreſs, there is a very viſible change. Formerly, the moſt reſpectable farmers, uſed to wear nothing but Scotch cloth, generally of their own making, plaiding hoſe, and blue bonnets. Now, the ſervant men on holidays wear nothing elſe than Engliſh cloth, cotton and thread ſtockings, and hats. The females formerly, wore nothing but a linen head dreſs, and tartan worſted plaids, which covered the head, or at beſt red ſcarlet cloaks. Whereas now, every maid ſervant wears a ſilk bonnet and cloak, and generally muſlin or printed gowns, and thread ſtockings. So that the men and women ſervants, are now much more gayly dreſſed, than their maſters and miſtreſſes were formerly.

In their mode of living, ſimilar if not greater changes have taken place. Formerly no wheat bread was uſed, excepting by the family of Kilſyth, or on extraordinary occaſions, ſuch as marriages, funerals, or perhapson a fair or market day. Whereas now, it is almoſt univerſally uſed, by all denominations, at leaſt to breakfaſt. Oat meal, milk, cheeſe, and butter, were the principal food of all, and of many the only fare. Little or no beef, mutton, or veal, was uſed. Even opulent farmers thought it extravagant to ſalt the carcaſe of a whole cow, for winter. And the moſt reſpectable tradeſmen never uſed more than a leg of beef, in the year. So that in the whole village, there were not 12 cows killed; and probably not twenty-four in the whole pariſh. Whereas now, every tradeſman has his mart; and every farmer uſes one, many two or three, in the year. So that, at an a-

verage,

verage, there are 160 killed in the village, and 280 in the pariſh every year, beſides a very conſiderable number of ſheep, calves, and lambs in their ſeaſon.

Tea was not known in this pariſh 40 years ago. Whereas now, it is almoſt univerſally uſed, and by a great many both in the morning and afternoon.

The employments of the inhabitants are very different from what they were. The females formerly devoted by much the greateſt part of their time to ſpining flax ; the reſt was ſpent in preparing the flax and tow, and working in the fields in ſpring, hay time, and harveſt. Now, ſpinning is much diſuſed, eſpecially by the young. Their are ſeveral hundreds of young girls from 8 to 14, who never ſpin at all. Perhaps the greater part of them, have never learned that uſeful art. Tambouring is now the chief employment. Every ſpecies of needle work occupies the reſt ; excepting a few mothers and younger children of manufacturers, who are employed in preparing the yarn for the loom. Only a few of the farmers wives and ſervants are employed in ſpinning linen yarn.

The males in the town for the moſt part were labourers; though there were a few tradeſmen. Now there are a very few labourers, but a great proportion of tradeſmen of all denominations, eſpecially of weavers; and every perſon may now find employment.

This may account for a ſtriking change that has taken place, and been much obſerved by the older claſs, that this generation marries in general much younger than the former; eſpecially the tradeſmen. Many of the males marry below 20, and the greateſt part below 25 ; whereas formerly they ſeldom married below 30. The moſt part of the females marry below 20; whereas formerly 25 or 30 was the

ordinary

ordinary age. The reason of this may be, that a numerous family of children *all idle*, necessarily became burdensome; whereas now every child, male or female, above 6 years of age, can find employment; and a numerous thriving family is a great support to a sober industrious tradesman.

The common utensils of a family are very different from what they were 50 years ago. At that period, there were no tea kettles, tea dishes, bellows, nor watches, and very few clocks. Now, every family can furnish these articles. There were few spinning wheels, still fewer check reels; in place of these, the *rock* and hand reel were used. There were no lint nor barley milns; of course, the lint was dressed at home, in each family; and the barley bruised in a stone mortar. Every farmer had his own kiln for drying his corns. A common kiln is now erected near each miln, where every farmer gets his grain dried at 6d per boll. There were no carts nor wheel carriages of any kind. All the grain was carried on horseback, or in harvest, upon sledges or cars.

Indeed the roads were at that time so steep, narrow, and rugged, that wheel carriages must have been almost useless. The line of the roads was generally straight, or nearly so, over hill and dale; or if they deviated from this course at any time, it was only to avoid some marsh, or to find a firm bottom. They seem to have thought of little else, at least they never dreamed of a level road. Now the roads are good, and carts and wheel carriages of all kinds abound.

But the most remarkable changes have taken place in the course of 25 years. The introduction of manufactures, and the great canal, have been the principal causes of them.

The species of manufactures most run upon is the muslin. Some of these are only a 1000, others 1700, and even 2000 reed; and of every species. There are at least 350 hands thus employed. Supposing each hand to work 3 yards per day,

day, that will amount to upwards of 300,000 yards annually.
At 6d per yard, which may be the average, that will amount
to L. 7500, as the total earning of that craft yearly. By
this account, every weaver is ſuppoſed to earn about L. 21 : 8s
at an average. And it is an undoubted faƈt, that an ordinary
tradeſman can eaſily earn at leaſt 1s a-day all the year round,
making allowance for ordinary avocations. It is ſaid, that a
ſober, induſtrious, and aƈtive hand, can even earn from 2s to
4s a-day, or at an average all the year round, 1s 6d, making reaſonable allowances for avocations.

N. B. The fly ſhuttle is commonly uſed, and allowed to be
a great improvement.

Allowing him to have 3 or 4 ſons working with him,
though each ſon earn but half the wages of his father, the
amount is very conſiderable, and may enable a tradeſman to
live well ; and at the ſame time, provide liberally for his family. If he has daughters, their earnings at tambouring,
may be very nearly at an average, 4d each day ; though
it is ſaid, when this branch was firſt introduced, they
could make from 1s to 2s a-day. Even now, they ſometimes
can earn a ſhilling. Suppoſing the tambourers to be 280,
their joint earnings at 4d daily, will amount to upwards of
L. 1200 ſterling ; or nearly L. 5 annually each. But this is
doubtleſs a very low eſtimate. I ſuppoſe at an average of old
and young, and making every allowance, they earn at leaſt
L. 6 each *.

Various

* About 3 years ago, Titus Harris from London began the cotton manu-
faƈtory in this pariſh. From very ſmall beginnings, and ſome ſay with no
capital, he, in the courſe of 12 months, raiſed the buſineſs to a conſiderable
heighth, and employed many hands. At one time, he had 10 or 12 ſpinning
jennies employed. But either owing to great miſmanagement or misfortune,
or perhaps to both, he inſtantly gave way ; by which means, a few families in
this

Various other branches of manufactures have been introduced here. But excepting the making of ſickles, they have generally failed. At preſent, there are about 5 or 6 hands conſtantly employed in this branch. Their earnings are not known; and in the ſituation they are at preſent, it would be improper to make them public. They furniſh generally about 1600 dozen of ſickles every year; and ſend them all over Scotland, eſpecially to the north.

The making of files was alſo attempted. And it might have ſucceeded, had it not been owing to accidental circumſtances, which made it be removed elſewhere. The greateſt number that ever were employed in this branch, was 8 or 9. And they furniſhed about 3000 dozen yearly.

The ſtarch manufactory was at one time begun, and there was a fair proſpect of ſucceſs. But by miſmanagement or misfortune, it was given up.

At preſent, there is only one who tans hides in the pariſh. But 30 years ago, there were ſeverals. About that period, there were two breweries likewiſe employed; but they are both given up.

It is ſaid, that there are ſome marks of the truth of the tradition, that, in Roman Catholic times, the parſon carried

on

this pariſh, and many elſewhere, were deeply involved. It may afford ſome picture of the times, and of the credulity of this nation, or at leaſt neighbourhood, to narrate his hiſtory. With his ſtaff in one hand, and his bundle in another, he arrived at Kilſyth altogether a ſtranger. At firſt he ſeemed to have little or no command of caſh; and of courſe little credit. Even for ſome months, he was looked upon with a jealous eye.

But having got ſome how or other credit, or a caſh account on ſome company in London, and his bills being honoured in a few inſtances at firſt, he rapidly roſe in credit, and by addreſs and application to buſineſs, ſeemed to be in a very flouriſhing way. But alas! it was at the expence of many, and to the ruin of a few. The amount of his debts, was L. 4000.

on an extensive brewery. The site of it, and of his stack yard which was very large, were only lately dug up.

Road.—It is not above two years since the new line of road between Glasgow and Edinburgh by Cumbernauld was first opened. Before that period, the principal road was by Kirkintilloch and Kilsyth; and it was very much frequented. Our little village, by being a general thorough fare, was always crowded, and had much the air of a busy thriving place. There is now much less bustle and noise, and more of the appearance of dullness and desertion; yet trade is as brisk, and the inhabitants except a few publicans, are as thriving as at any former period. Two flys, and perhaps 10 or 12 post chaises, and double the number of post horses, used to pass daily. Now there is not a single fly, seldom a post chaise in a week, and perhaps not a post horse in a day. The chief inn in Kilsyth, though almost never clean or commodious, was much frequented. The publican used to keep one, two, or sometimes four post chaises, and from 6 to 12 post horses. Now there is neither chaise, nor almost a post horse, to be found. Of course, the turnpike gate, which was formerly rented at L. 145, is now so low as L. 51, and yet the profit to the keeper is but small.

The post-office, besides affording a salary of L. 15 ster. generally produced between L. 36 and L. 40 yearly. At present, it yields from L. 38 to L. 40, allowing a salary of L. 12 annually to the postmaster. So that in trade, there is no falling off.

Advantages.——It remains for me to mention the peculiar advantages this parish enjoys. And happily these are many and great. The village in point of situation, will yield to none. It stands upon a gently rising ground, a fine dry sandy foil, in the middle of a rich ſtrath, and it is acceſſible at all times, as it is upon the old north road from Glaſgow to Edinburgh ; and what is highly favourable, it is at equal diſtances from Falkirk and Glaſgow on the eaſt and weſt, and from Hamilton and Stirling on the ſouth and north. The air is pure and ſalubrious. There is abundance of ſpring and running water, with both of which the town is copiouſly ſupplied : And there are in the immediate vicinity, a variety of ſituations very favourable for a bleachfield or printfield, and abundance of water-falls for machinery of almoſt any ſize. In one place eſpecially, a fall may be obtained of nearly 30 feet perpendicular, within 300 yards of a good coal, near abundance of fine lime, and upon a beautiful poſt of free ſtone, where the ſtones for the building might be dug out of the foundation. This is within a quarter of a mile of the village, and what is more, within leſs than an Engliſh mile of the great canal. So that there is an open eaſy acceſs to the German and Atlantic oceans, and by them to the whole world. This conſideration is of great conſequence to a manufacturing village. It gives us at once, all the advantages of an inland and ſea port town combined. For we can export our manufactures to any port, and import grain or other commodities from any quarter of the globe, with equal eaſe as at Greenock, or Grangemouth. The rich abundance of the carſes of Falkirk, Stirling, and Gowry, and of the fertile lands of Lothian, Carrick, and Ireland, is brought to our doors, at as eaſy and cheap a rate, as if they were our neighbouring pariſhes, within 6 or 10 miles.

These advantages have induced a great many new ſettlers to come among us. And Sir Archibald Edmonſtone, Bart. of Dunbreath, and proprietor of the eſtate of Kilſyth, with a ſpirit truly liberal and generous, has given them every encouragement,

couragement, and has within theſe 8 years feued a complete new town.

Diſadvantages.—But while we enjoy many advantages, and are abundantly fenſible of it, we labour under a few peculiar diſadvantages, though I truſt we are grateful to heaven that they are ſo few and ſmall. A few of theſe diſadvantages I ſhall ſhortly enumerate.

1ſt, It is doubtleſs a conſiderable loſs, that none of the principal heritors refide in the pariſh. All claſſes and denominations, but eſpecially the poor, muſt feel this.. The tender nurſing hand of a liberal landlord, is to them, a mighty bleſſing.

2d, But it is not only thoſe who feel the loſs. The pariſh at large, but eſpecially the town, have cauſe to regret, that there is not within the pariſh a ſingle juſtice of the peace, commiſſioner of ſupply, or magiſtrate, nor even a baron bailiff : ſo that the ſmalleſt petty offence, or outrage, cannot be redreſſed without applying to ſome juſtice of ſome neighbouring pariſh.

And what is ſtill worſe, every idle, worthleſs vagrant, who can find ſhelter no where elſe, is apt to reſort to this as a place of refuge, where he may ſkulk about and pilfer with impunity. Amazing crouds of ſturdy beggars infeſt us at all times, eſpecially in harveſt, when all the males are at work in the field. At that time they not only crave a reaſonable alms, but often enforce their unreaſonable demand, by frightening the peaceable and induſtrious inhabitants. If there be any evil which calls for redreſs in this place, this is one ; and to redreſs it is ſurely not impoſſible.

3d, It is likewiſe a loſs to this pariſh, that we have no weekly market. The peaſant and manufacturer, whether in the town or country muſt feel this.

4th, The farmers labour under a few inconveniences. But
they

they are only few, and much more than counterbalanced, by the many peculiar advantages they enjoy.

Characters of the Inhabitants.—The characters of the inhabitants of this pariſh, are as various as their countenances; as in every mixed ſociety, the good and the bad are blended together.

To ſpeak in general terms, however, they are punctual in their attendance on religious ordinances, decent and devout in their external appearance, and regular in their manners. They are ſober, active, and induſtrious; open, candid, and even generous in their dealings; loyal to their ſovereign, obedient to all lawful authorities; and they ſtudy to live peaceable and quiet lives, in all godlineſs and honeſty.

Though divided into various ſects, they are to a man ſteady friends to the proteſtant perſuaſion, and live together in the unity of the ſpirit, and the bond of peace.

Upwards of one half of the inhabitants can trace back their parentage, for many generations, all natives of this pariſh. Independent in their circumſtances, and of a more independent ſpirit, they have a high ſenſe of honour, and a great regard to character.

The above will by many be deemed a flattering picture; and I dare ſay, I may be accuſed of partiality. My only plea is, that I have been born and bred among them; upwards of 500 of them are my blood relations. For this cauſe, I am perhaps better acquainted with their feelings and ſentiments than any man, and though partial, I truſt I am too upright to flatter them. On the contrary, I muſt acknowledge, that among the riſing generation, there are many leſs regular in their manners than their fathers.

I have many reaſons to be attached to this pariſh. Where-
ever

ever I turn my eye, I meet with the friends or companions of my youth. Tenderly alive to all they feel, and all they fear, I cannot but have a deep concern, and ardent deſire, for their temporal and eternal intereſts. Happy ſhall I be, if living or dying, I can be the humble inſtrument of turning even one of them to righteouſneſs *.

* There is a very curious collection of old parchments in this pariſh. Some of them go nearly as far back as the Reformation. They principally refer to the affairs of the church, being charters or grants of lands and privileges, from certain abbeys to certain livings. Among the reſt are ſome from Cambuſkenneth near Stirling.

They might afford matter of much curioſity, perhaps furniſh ſome important information.

PARISH OF KIPPEN.

(COUNTIES OF PERTH AND STIRLING.)

By the Rev. Mr JOHN CAMPBELL.

———————

Name.

THOUGH many names of places in this country are un-doubtedly of Gaelic origin, yet it is difficult to procure any etymology of the name of the parish, that may be con-sidered as perfectly satisfactory. *Ceap* in Gaelic, is nearly of the same import with the English word *cape,* or promontory, and resembles it in sound. From this the word *Kippen* is said to be derived ; and the name is supposed to be descriptive of the situation of the village, which stands on an eminence, near the point of the hill, which terminates at Boquhan. The village has exactly this appearance, when viewed from the north west, as from Cardrofs, or the opposite braes of Monteath.

Situation and Limits.—The parish of Kippen lies within the counties of Perth and Stirling ; under the ecclesiastical jurisdiction of the Presbytery of Dunblane, and Synod of Perth and Stirling. It is bounded on the north by the river

Forth,

Forth, which ſeparates it from the pariſhes of Kilmadock, Kincardine, and Port. On the eaſt, it marches with Gargunnock; on the ſouth, with Balfron; and on the weſt, with the pariſh of Drymen. The road from Stirling to Dunbarton paſſes through this pariſh for 7 miles; it is more, however, than 8 miles in length, between the diſtant extremities. Its breadth is unequal; generally from 2 to 3 miles; at the middle of the pariſh, it is nearly 4 miles broad.

Boundaries of Stirling and Perth Shires.—One might have expected that the river Forth, which forms a natural limit to this pariſh for ſeveral miles, ſhould have alſo ſerved as a boundary to the ſhire of Perth. This county however, in two or three places, paſſes over this natural limit, and becomes indented in the county of Stirling; ſo that about one third part of the pariſh of Kippen, lies in Perthſhire, the other two thirds in Stirlingſhire. Such an irregularity ſeems now ſurpriſing. But it is well known, that ancient proprietors had influence to get ſuch portions of their eſtates as they choſe, disjoined from thoſe counties within which they were locally ſituated, and connected with ſuch other counties, as better ſuited their convenience. Other inſtances of this kind, and more remarkable than in the caſe before us, might eaſily be adduced in ſupport of this obſervation *.

General Aſpect of the Country.—From ſome of the higher grounds, an ample and variegated proſpect preſents itſelf to the eye of the ſpectator. At the head of the ſtrath, ſtands

the

* Some lands in the pariſhes of Bonhill and Kilmaronrock, which formerly belonged to the laird of Gleneagles, and of which he is ſtill ſuperior, were once connected with the ſhire of Perth, though they lie at a conſiderable diſtance from the limits of that county.

the houfe of Gartmore, commanding a view of the whole plain below, which extends eaftward for 20 or 30 miles. The houfe and policy of Cardrofs, a few miles farther down the country, greatly enliven the landfcape. The carfe, a rich and beautiful valley, exhibits an inclofed and well cultivated country, embellifhed with numberlefs farms, and gentlemen's feats; and in fummer and autumn, often loaded with luxuriant crops. So rich and extenfive a fcenery is rarely to be feen. The dufky fpots which are covered with mofs, pleafe by contraft; and the imagination is gratified by anticipating the period, when the mofs fhall be cleared away, and its room occupied by the ufeful productions of the earth, and the habitations of men. Stirling caftle, and the rocks of Craig-forth and Abbeys craig, appear on the eaft, like iflands emerging out of the carfe. The braes of Montcath rife on the northern fide, like an amphitheatre. And a rugged range of the Grampian mountains, ftretching from Benlomond to the Ochills, encompaffes the whole. Thus the eye is at once gratified, with a profpect of rude and cultivated nature, and with a furvey of the noble effects of human induftry and art.

Carfe.—The parifh of Kippen is divided by nature into the *carfe* and *dryfield*. The former confifts of the level ground that lies on the fouth fide of the Forth, between that river and the rifing grounds. It is of unequal breadth, from half a mile to a mile, and in fome places more, and forms a part of that extenfive plain, which reaches from Gartmore on both fides of the river, as far eaftward as Borrowftounnefs. In different places in this parifh, it is covered with mofs to the extent of 300 or 400 acres.

Mofs.—There feems reafon to believe, that the greater part

of

of the plain eaftward from Stirling, has at one period been covered with mofs ; and that the arable lands on both fides of the river, have been recovered from the mofs, by dint of labour, in a courfe of ages. It is probable that the whole of this extenfive plain, had been previoufly under water. Shells, both feparate and collected into beds, are found throughout the carfe ; and it is not long fince fifh bones of a confiderable fize, have been met with in the neighbourhood of Stirling. The mafs of clay would naturally be accumulated and levelled by the operation of the tides. The period in which this part of the country was under water, muft be very remote, as on this fubject both hiftory and tradition are equally filent. After the receffion of the waters, the fame fpace muft have been occupied with trees and fhrubs. Thefe would be produced by the fame caufes, which, in procefs of time, cover ground that is left without culture, with various vegetable productions. A foreft would at laft appear ; and by the fall and putrefaction of this foreft, the mofs, in its prefent ftate, has unqueftionably been formed. Oaks of a great fize, are ftill found on the fubjacent earth, where the mofs has been cleared away. Many of thefe are in good prefervation ; when expofed to the air for fome time, they become hard ; and when put to ufe, prove very durable. They are rarely ferviceable for furniture ; but fuit very well for roof timber, ftobs, and bridges over mofs ditches. Other trees, fuch as birch, alder, black-faugh, rowan, hawthorn, and hazle, are alfo found ; hazle nuts are frequently met with. The trunks or bodies of thefe trees, are generally confumed ; but the roots remain. It is natural to enquire, how this great foreft fhould happen to be overthrown. A hurricane of wind occurs at firft, as a poffible caufe of this great effect. But in this cafe it is obvious, that the trees muft either have been broken about the middle, or torn up by the roots, and would

be

be found uniformly lying in the direction of the current. But the roots are generally found standing in the clay; the trunks separated from them a little above the ground, lying in all directions; and sometimes, on the oaks particularly, the marks of an ax or hatchet have been traced. The testimony of several historians of credit, as well as other authentic monuments, lead us to a discovery of the authors of this great catastrophe. When the Romans pushed their conquests into Britain, our ancestors, the Britons and Caledonians, were forced by the victorious legions to retire to their hills, or secure themselves in those extensive forests, with which the island then abounded. From these strong holds they sallied forth as opportunity offered, and by their frequent incursions, not only annoyed the armies of their conquerors, but enriched themselves with booty. From the speech of Galgacus, given by Tacitus in his life of Agricola, it appears that the Romans had been much employed in cutting down forests and draining morasses, with a view to secure themselves against such predatory attacks from the natives. But to put an effectual stop to these depredations, in the last expedition of the Emperor Severus, general orders were issued to cut down all the forests throughout this part of the island. This service was performed by the Roman legions, assisted by those natives whom they had been able to subjugate. Herodian * concisely mentions this fact. Dion Cassius †, whose account is more particular,

informs

---

* Lib. III. c. 48.

† Xiphilin. ex Dione, lib. 39. The passage relative to this subject in the abridger of Dion, is curious and interesting. " Quam Severus, quum veilet omnem in suam potestatem redigere, ingressus est in Caledoniam, eamque dum pertransiret, habuit maxima negotia, quod sylvas cæderet, et loca alta perfoderet, quodque paludes obrueret aggere, et pontes in fluminibus faceret. Nullum enim prælium gessit, neque copias hostium instructas vidit; a quibus proponebantur

informs us, that in this expedition, the Romans loft no lefs than 50,000 men. We need not wonder then at the fpeed and fuccefs, with which this great undertaking was accomplifhed *. In the mofs of Kincardine, a Roman way, 12 feet wide, and regularly formed by trees or logs of wood laid a-crofs each other, is ftill to be traced †. And a Roman camp kettle was found in the year 1768, in the lands of Mr Ramfay of Ochtertyre, which has been prefented by him to the Antiquarian Society in Edinburgh. Such are the grounds on which it is believed that the foreft in this part of the country was cut down by the Romans ; moft probably in the expedition of Severus, A. D. 207, whilft Donald I. reigned in Caledonia. He was the firft Scottifh prince (according to Buchanan ‡), who embraced Chriftianity. The overthrow of this foreft would naturally interrupt the courfe of thofe various ftreams which formerly ran through the valley. This body

---

proponebantur confultò oves bovefque, ut quum ea noftri raperent, ac longe de via declinarent, facile opprimerentur. Ad hæc noftris aquæ valde oberant, difperfifque infidiæ parabantur : quumque non poffent iter facere, occidebantur a fuis, ut ne ab hoftibus caperentur. Itaque mortui funt e noftris ad quinquaginta millia. Neque tamen deftitit Severus, quoufque ad extremam infulam venit.

* Modern hiftorians, relying on thefe authorities, agree in their accounts of the tranfactions of the Romans at this period in Britain. Buchan. Rer. Scot. Hift. Lib. IV. c. 37. Henry's Hift. of Great Brit. Vol. I. chap. 1. Encyc. Brit. edit. 3. Vol XII. p. 388, under the word Moss.

† In Mofs Logan in this parifh, a way has lately been difcovered, which from all accounts, in refpect of breadth and conftruction, exactly refembles that in the mofs of Kincardine. But as the information concerning it was received only fince this account was drawn up, no opportunity has yet offered of examining it fo particularly, as to authorize a more decided opinion refpecting its origin.

‡ Hift. lib. IV. 36.

body of ftagnant water, fwelled from time to time by rains, and melted fnow, and rivulets defcending from the heights, would continue to increafe till it became fo confiderable as to open a paffage for itfelf to the eaft. And thus the valley, at that period, muft have exhibited the appearance of a vaft mo-rafs. The wood and leaves, and other vegetable fubftances, all rotting together, would in time accumulate, and form the great body of the mofs. The confolidation of this mafs of corrupted vegetables would leave room for the water above it, to run off by fuch channels as it could find or form. By fuch a procefs in a feries of ages, it is natural to imagine, that this mofs has been brought into the ftate in which it now appears.

Cafting of Peats.—The foil underneath the mofs is a ftrong rich clay. The mofs is generally from 8 to 10 feet in depth, and confifts of different fubftances, regularly difpofed in ftrata, as follows. Immediately above the clay is a ftratum of fat brown earth, from 9 to 12 inches in depth, fuppofed to have been formed by the incorporation of the clay with the conti-guous mofs, and which feems to have been the vegetable mold, covering the clay when the foreft was cut down. The next bed lying immediately above the former, is the great body of the mofs, which confifts of various vegetable fubftances, cor-rupted, compacted, and matured by age. This is annually cut for peats, and fupplies moft families in this country with fuel through the year. The upper ftratum is a light and fpon-gy fubftance, much paler in the colour than the bed of peat mofs. It feems to be formed chiefly of decayed leaves and ftalks of heath, bent grafs, and other plants with which the furface of the mofs is overgrown, but not yet fufficiently cor-rupted fo as to be formed into mofs. Of this upper ftratum, 3 or 4 feet muft always be pared away, which is generally done

in

in winter, and thrown by the spade into the pit out of which the peats were taken in the preceding year. It then forms the *spreadfield*, or ground upon which the new peats are laid out to be dried. As the whole of it cannot be thus disposed of, the remainder is by means of little canals formed for the purpose, floated down into the Forth. The peats are always cast as soon as possible after feed time, and are carried home in the course of the summer or harvest. It was a remarkable proof of the uncommon wetness of the season 1792, that few peats were got home that year, but remained on the spreadfield till next summer. This circumstance had not happened before in the memory of man, and necessarily subjected poorer families to very great inconvenience.

Clearing away of Moss.—As the carse soil is so valuable, it must be an object of importance to the proprietors, to have the superjacent moss cleared away *. Those portions of land, which in this parish are recovered from the moss, are such as lie under old spreadfields, from which the peats have formerly been taken. This operation is generally performed in winter. The water which comes down from the higher grounds in *burns* or rivulets contiguous to the moss, is by means of small ducts or canals introduced into the spreadfield which is intended to be put away. The spreadfield having been previously interfected with these canals, of a proper depth and width, its substance is, by many hands, thrown into these when water can be had in plenty, and thus carried down into the river. Much yet remains to be done, before the arable land is procured. About a foot of moss, mixt with many fragments of trees and roots,

* Mr Drummond of Blair-Drummond, carries on an undertaking of this nature on an extensive scale. See an interesting account of the process employed for that purpose in Encyc. Brit. 3d. edit. Vol. XII. under the article Moss of KINCARDINE.

roots, fome fmall, many very large, muft be digged up. In fome places this operation muft be repeated oftener than once. Such of thefe fragments as are unfit for any ufeful purpofe, are burnt when dry, generally in the months of May and June. The afhes, with what remains of the mofs, and brown earth formerly mentioned, when judicioufly mixt with the clay, form together one of the beft foils. Some pains are alfo requifite to level the inequalities, which is beft done at firft, to to prevent the water from ftanding in the hollows. The clearing away of the fpreadfield was formerly done for L. 40 Scots, or L. 3 : 6 : 8 fter. per acre ; but fince wages have increafed, it will coft from L. 5 to L. 6 fter. In this manner in a courfe of years, a confiderable quantity of land has been gained from the mofs, worth from 15s. to 20s. fter. per acre. The carfe foil, in favourable feafons, produces rich crops of every kind of grain common in this country ; particularly wheat, beans and peafe, and oats ; barley is not fo certain a crop.

Haugh.—Befides the mofs, and the land recovered from it, there is along the banks of the Forth, a narrow ftrip of haugh or holm, which is very fertile, and equally adapted to tillage or pafture.

Dryfield.—From the carfe, the lands rife at firft abruptly, and then very gradually for about a mile, or more in fome places; continuing flat for a confiderable fpace, they again decline towards the fouth. This elevated part of the parifh, is called the *dryfield;* a term which is by no means defcriptive of the nature of the foil, but is ufed merely to diftinguifh it from the lower grounds or *carfe* Where it firft fprings from the carfe, it is marked by all thofe appearances which the banks of rivers that have been deferted by them exhibit. The interjacent valley between this parifh, and the green

hills

hills of Boquhan and Glinns, is very narrow at the eastern extremity. Towards the west, the country is more open. From the southern boundary, most of the baronies in this parish are laid off, parallel to each other, down to the sides of the Forth. The dryfield of Kippen forms the greater part of that hill, which, commencing at the bridge of Boquhan, and extending through the whole of this parish, and part of the parishes of Balfron and Drymen, terminates about a mile westward from the village of Balfron. The land which lies on its northern declivity, forms the main body of the parish of Kippen, and exhibits a pleasing view of fruitful fields, generally well inclosed, and occasionally interfected with glens and rivulets.

Moor of Kippen.—Towards the summit and southern declivity of the hill, on which it hath been observed, that the greater part of this parish is situated, there is an extensive moor, called the moor of Kippen, which runs the whole length of the parish, and comprehends also part of Balfron. On the south side, the ground which is lighter, and not so good as that on the north side of the hill, slopes gradually for half a mile or more, and is terminated by a small rivulet called the Pow of the Glinns, which divides Kippen from Balfron. This water runs eastward, till it falls into the burn of Boquhan, which again forms the boundary between Kippen and Gargunnock, and empties itself into the Forth, at the bridge of Frew. Another small stream, west from the former, takes a different course, and runs westward into the water of Endrick, which finally goes into the Clyde. Under the mosses in the moor of Kippen, are found some oaks and other trees, though not so large as those in the low moss on the sides of the Forth. It is probable that the whole dryfield has been covered with wood, mostly oak; for on the sides of

the

the glens, through which the water collected in the moor runs down into the Forth, the trees grow thick, and within thefe 50 years, ftocks of oaks with young fhoots growing from them have been feen in different places: thefe however, are now rooted out, and the fields cleared for the plough.

Stones.—The moor abounds with red and white free-ftone. On the fouthern boundary lime-ftone is alfo found. This lime-ftone, containing a confiderable portion of fand, fuits the carfe well, but is not thought fo proper for the dry-field.

Lake.—In the moor, there is a fmall lake or refervoir of water called *Loch-leggan*, about a mile in circumference. A fmall ftream iffues from it, which turns feveral mills. In the middle of the loch, there is a *cairne*, or heap of ftones, fuppofed to be the ruins of an old houfe, of which however, no authentic accounts can now be obtained. There are no fifh in the loch, but a few perches of a fmall fize. Trouts are to be had in the feveral rivulets which run into the Forth: the burn of Boquhan affords them in greateft plenty.

River Forth.—The river Forth has but a mean appearance in this part of the country. It is confined within narrow and deep banks, and except in a few places, its current is fo very flow, as hardly to be perceptible. From Gartmore to Stirling, a line of 20 miles, the fall of the river is faid not to exceed, on an average, a foot in the mile. The banks of the Forth, are from 10 to 20 feet; and in fome places more from the furface of the bank, to the bottom of the river. Many large trees are ftill found in the bottom; and fome appear with their ends projecting from the banks, as the water wafhes away the clay. They are found at different depths, from

6

6 to 20 feet below the furface of the bank; and in all direc‐
tions, fome lying horizontally, others ftanding almoft upright.
The river contains both pike and perch. In former times,
falmon ufed to come up in abundance, but fince the moffes
began to be cleared away, they have not been taken in any
confiderable quantity. There are two bridges over the Forth
in this parifh; one near Cardrofs built in 1772, the other at
Frew, built in 1783; both at prefent are in good repair.

Natural Curiofities.—" The burn of Boquhan, which, de‐
" fcending from the rock of Ballochleam, makes little im‐
" preffion on the ftrata of lime ftone or iron, meets at laft
" with the red fand-ftone, through which it has opened a
" paffage, and wrought its foft materials into a number of
" curious fhapes, fuch as the wells and caldrons of the De‐
" von. It is yet remembered, when it burft through a large
" projection of the rock, and threw the mill with all its ap‐
" pendages, on the other fide of the bank *."—In the garden
of Broich, there is a yew tree, of a regular conical form,
whofe branches fhooting regularly from the trunk, with their
extremities falling down to the ground, exhibits the appear‐
ance of a large umbrella to thofe who ftand under its fhade.
The circumference of the trunk about 2 feet above the ground,
is 10 feet; height of the trunk to the loweft row of branches,
9 feet; height of the tree, about 50 feet; circumference of
the circle overfpread by the lower branches, 140 feet. It is
fuppofed to be 200 or 300 years old; and though it may not
vie with the yew of Fortingal, muft ftill be allowed to be a
beautiful object.

Antiquities and Hiftory.—The names and fituations of feve‐
ral places in the parifh, plainly fhew that in former times, they
have

* Gen. Campbell's notes, page 18.

have been places of ftrength. Thus the caftle of Arnfindlay,
of which no veftiges now remain; the tower of Garden, part
of which, was ftanding 20 or 30 years ago; the remains of
the houfe and caftle of Arnprior, may ftill be traced. The
houfe of Broich too, feems to have been furrounded with a
rampart and foffe. A fmall green mound on the eaftern confines of the lands of Buchlyvie, appears to have been a tumulus. Some human bones, inclofed in flags of ftone, were
lately found in it; but there is no tradition which gives any
account of its origin.—Some years ago, an urn containing
afhes and bones, was found in the Caftle-hill of Dafher.
There are feveral fmall heights in this parifh, to which the
name *Keir* * is applied, which bear the marks of fome ancient
military work, viz. Keir-hill of Glentirran, Keir-hill of Dafher, Keir-brae of Drum, Keir-know of Arn-more, and
Keir-brae of Garden. On the fummit of each of thefe, there
is a plain of an oval figure, furrounded with a rampart,
which in moft of them ftill remains entire. The *Peel of Garden*, (on which there is a work of the fame kind,) is lefs elevated in point of fituation; it rifes but a little above the
carfe. The inclofure however is confiderably larger than that
of the Keirs; and the rampart and ditch, in refpect of form
and appearance, have fuffered lefs from the injuries of time.
None of thefe are of fufficient extent to have ever admitted
of a regular encampment. The circumference of the rampart
on the Keir-hill of Dafher, (which is neither the largeft nor
the fmalleft, and the only one that has been meafured,) does
not exceed 130 yards. Various opinions have been entertained concerning thefe works. The country people fay that
they were Pictifh forts. A different conjecture fuppofes
them

* " Keir, Caer, Chefter, Caftra, are faid to be words of a like import."—
Gen. Campbell's notes, page 17.

them to have been temporary forts, or ſtations erected by
the Romans, for giving ſignals, depoſiting proviſions and
ſtores, and protecting their pioneers from the attacks of the
Caledonians, whilſt employed in cutting down the great
foreſt in the plain below. This conjecture, it is imagined,
receives ſome ſupport from the conſideration, that places of
a ſimilar form are found in other parts of the country, into
which the Romans are known to have penetrated. Others,
unwilling to admit their pretenſions to ſo high antiquity,
believe them to have been formed by the feudal proprietors;
for ſome purpoſes of ſecurity or convenience, which it may
be difficult now to diſcover. It is ſurely matter both of ſurpriſe and regret, that no certain account can now be obtained of the origin and uſe of theſe works; which apparently
have formed a part of ſome extenſive ſyſtem, the develope-
ment of which might ſerve to illuſtrate the ancient ſtate
and hiſtory of our country *.—A diſpute having ariſen between

* There ſeems to be a conſiderable reſemblance between theſe forts, and
the forts of the Firbolgs, of which an account is given in Groſe's Antiquities
of Ireland. The paſſage alluded to, is extracted from that work in the
Monthly Review, for December 1794, page 394; and was not ſeen by the
writer of this account, till after it was prepared for the preſs. The inſer-
tion of the paſſage may perhaps be gratifying to ſome readers. " The forts
" common in this period, will be ſeen to be perfectly conſiſtent with the rude
" ſtate of the military art among the Firbolgs; though very ſuperior to thoſe
" of the Celtes. The Iriſh, who retained the cuſtoms of the latter, Cam-
" brenſis tells us, had no caſtles; their woods ſerved them for camps, and
" their marſhes for ditches. However, they learned from the Firbolgs, to
" take refuge on hills, as Cæſar ſays the Britons did. Theſe were conical
" riſing grounds, which were encircled with a ſingle, double, or triple en-
" trenchment, and which afforded ample protection; ſuch were the infinite
" number of high round forts every where to be met with, and by Cam-
" brenſis, expreſsly aſcribed to the Oſtmen. The ſize of theſe earthen forts,
" varied with the number and power of the clan; ſome are but 13 or 20
" yards in diameter, others cover as many acres."

tween the inhabitants of the baronies of Glentirran and Arnprior, refpecting the courfe of the ftream that iffues from
Loch leggan, the parties met at a place near the loch, determined to decide the conteft by arms. In this affray, feveral
perfons were killed; from which circumftance, the place
bears the name of *Bloody mires.* King James V. who then
refided at Stirling, having taken cognifance of this matter,
ordered the ftream to be taken from both, and turned into
the channel, which it ftill retains. He likewife ordered the
new mill to be built, which, being confidered as a royal mill,
pays a feparate cefs to this day.—During the arbitrary reigns
of Charles II. and James II, the inhabitants of this parifh
fuffered greatly from the perfecution and tyranny which then
prevailed. Mr Ure of Shirgarton, a gentleman of diftinguifhed piety and zeal, underwent various hardfhips, the memory of which is ftill preferved by tradition in the neighbourhood *.—In the year 1676, the Sacrament of the Lord's Supper was difpenfed in the *night,* to a very numerous meeting
at Arnbeg †. The minifters who affifted in difpenfing that
ordinance, were Meffrs. John Law, after the Revolution
minifter at Edinburgh, Mr Hugh Smith at Eaftwood, and
Mr Matthew Crawford.—A chapel formerly ftood near the
eaftern boundary of the parifh, befide the old manfion-houfe
of Glentirran. The remains of it were feen within thefe
few years. It is faid to have been built for the accommodation
of the parifhes of Gargunnock and Kippen, in confequence
of the indulgence granted by King James. A Mr Barclay
then officiated as minifter.—In former times, the highland

clans

* Many particulars refpecting this worthy gentleman, are recorded by
Mr Wodrow, in his Hiftory of the fufferings of the Church of Scotland; fee
efpecially, Vol. ii. page 260.

† Wodrow's Hiftory, Vol. i. page 416.

clans, which were ſituated on the borders of the low country, were accuſtomed to ſubſiſt in a great meaſure, by rapine and plun er. In the year 1691, a party of theſe free-booters viſited this pariſh, to the great terror and loſs of the country. They were commanded by old *Rob Roy*, a robber by profeſſion, who pretended to have a commiſſion from King James " to plunder the rebel whigs." The peaceable inhabitants were obliged to flee for their ſafety, and leave their property to the rapacity of this banditti, who ſeized upon cattle, victual, furniture, &c. and carried away as much as they were able. Only one man, ſervant to Sir James Livingſton, was killed upon that occaſion. This act of depredation was remembered by the fathers of ſeveral perſons ſtill living, and is known by the name of the *herriſhip* * of Kippen.—In the year 1745, the rebel army paſſed the Forth by the ford of Frew on their way to Stirling. The inhabitants were obliged to furniſh proviſions for the ſupply of their immediate neceſſities; but their march was not marked by any other acts of violence.

Population.—It is probable, that the pariſh of Kippen was more populous in former times, than it is at preſent. The enlargement of the farms, neceſſarily occaſioned the fall of the cotteries, which afforded ſubſiſtence to many families. In conſequence of the encouragement offered by the manufacturing companies, lately eſtabliſhed at Balfron, many families as well as individuals have removed to that village. A conſiderable decreaſe has taken place within theſe laſt 10 years.

In 1755, the number of inhabitants, according to Dr Webſter's account, amounted to

In

---

* From the Scots word *herry*, to rob or plunder.

In 1764, the number of examinable perfons, is ftated to have been 1450, which is nearly the fame as at prefent.

In 1783, the number of families was 446; of fouls 1940.

In 1793, the number of families was 399.

———— Males 847, females 930; in all 1777 fouls.

Under 10 years,	343	From 40 to 50,	180
From 10 to 20,	399	From 50 to 60,	145
From 20 to 30,	325	From 60 to 70,	128
From 30 to 40,	190	From 70 to 80,	48
	——	From 80 to 90,	19
	1257		——
			520 Total 1777.

Diftinguifhed according to their Religious Perfuafions.

Of the Eftablifhed Church,	-	-	1266
Antiburgher Seceders,	-	-	491
Burgher, do.	-	-	4
Cameronians,	-	-	13
Epifcopalians,	-	-	3
			——
			1777

Table

Table of Marriages, Baptisms, and Burials in this Parish, for the following years.

Years.	Marriages.	Baptisms.			Burials.		
		Males.	Fem.	Total.	Years.	Males.	Fem.	Tot.
From 1700 to 1709 incluf.	104	229	194	423	1783	3	4	7
1710—1719	170	193	214	407	1784	12	7	19
1720—1729 -	183	194	167	361	1785	14	14	28
1730—1739	188	293	251	544	1786	8	2	10
1740—1749 *		199	178	377	1787	22	10	32
1750—1759 - -		229	160	389	1788	18	16	34
1760—1769 -	158	242	272	514	1789	8	6	14
1770—1779	172	271	237	508	1790	4	10	14
1780—1789 -	161	242	238	480	1791	8	14	22
1790	18	23	22	45	1792	7	10	17
1791 - -	11	19	18	37				
1792 - -	15	20	23	43				

In 1792-3, there were in the parish of Kippen, 24 heritors, of whom the greater part do not reside in the parish; 1 established minister, 1 antiburgher minister, 1 phyfician, 1 writer, 2 schoolmasters, 100 farmers, 88 farming men servants, 8 millers, 6 maltmen, 4 licensed distillers, 1 excife officer, 10 merchants, 37 weavers, 5 journeymen do. 14 apprentices, 1 stocking weaver, 8 wrights, 3 do. journeymen, 6 do. apprentices, 2 wheelwrights, 4 hecklers, 6 masons, 1 do. apprentice, 10 shoemakers, 2 journeymen do. 2 do. apprentices, 1 faddler, 1 journeyman do. 2 tanners, 1 journeyman do. 4 coopers, 14 taylors, 2 journeymen do. 2 do. apprentices, 8 smiths, 2 do. apprentices, 1 dyer, 1 baker, 2 butchers,

* Chafm in the register of Marriages from 1745 to 1758; and the register of Baptisms feems to have been irregularly kept during the greater part of that period.

chers, 8 publicans, 7 carters, 4 sheriff-officers, 47 day labourers.

Parish Register,—There are no records extant previous to the commencement of the present century. From 1700 to 1745, the register of marriages and baptisms appears to have been kept with considerable accuracy. For the 12 following years, the register of marriages seems to have been entirely neglected. From that period too, many parents who had joined the secession, neglected to get their children's names enrolled in the parish register. For this reason, the register, especially of baptisms, cannot be confidered as exhibiting a complete enumeration of the children born in the parish from that time downward *. It may also be observed, that as the names of parties enrolled with a view to proclamation of banns, when they happen to reside in different parishes, are registered in both the parishes to which they severally belong ; this circumstance muft make the number of marriages appear greater than it is in reality. And therefore in calculating the whole population of Scotland, fo far as regard is had to the authority of parochial registers, it may be laid down as a maxim, that the number of marriages will upon the whole exceed, and that of baptisms fall short of the truth. In this, as well as in moft country parishes, no account of burials was kept till within thefe few years ; nor can the register of thefe be considered as perfectly accurate.

Climate, Health, Diseases.—The climate is wet, on account, probably, of the vicinity of the hills, and the prevalence of wefterly winds. A register of the weather was kept for many

years

---

* Of late years, care has been taken to render the register of baptisms more complete than formerly.

years by Dr Leckie, a gentleman of intelligence and observation in this parish, but he found " only a series of capricious " changes, incapable of being classed or connected, so as to " form any useful rule, or any observations on the weather " or seasons that can be depended upon in this country." The climate though wet, does not appear to be unhealthy, which may be attributed perhaps to the frequency of high winds, which prevent the vapours from becoming stagnant. The number of aged persons at present in the parish appears from the preceding tables; within the few last years, two persons have died near the age of 100 —A pleasant and uncommon spectacle of health and industry is seen in this village; an old man, his son, and grandson, all smiths, of one name, dwelling in the house in which they were born, and continuing to follow their occupation in the same shop from day to day. The inhabitants of this part of county are not subject to any disease that can be considered as peculiar to the climate. The ague is said in former times to have prevailed in the carse. It is now extremely rare, at least in the parish of Kippen. Epidemical diseases are not frequent. In the spring months of years 1785 and 1787, a pleuretic fever prevailed, which carried off a number of people. The year 1788 was fatal to some old people and children. Of the uncommon mortality in these years, the openness of the preceding winters cannot properly be assigned as the cause; for they were not more open, perhaps less so, than several succeeding seasons which were accompanied with no such consequences. The small-pox and measles are sometimes fatal to children. Inoculation is rather gaining ground, though slowly. It is surprising that any prejudice should remain against a practice, which experience hath proved to be so salatary. Dr Leckie, (whose practice both in this country and the West Indies, has been very extensive,) declares, " that only two of all those
                                                                " whom

" whom he has inoculated died of the fmall-pox : the one
" of thefe was taken ill with them within 24 hours after be-
" ing inoculated ; the other in lefs than 3 days. He has re-
" fided above 40 years in Kippen, and inoculated above 20
" yearly at an average".

Remarkable Medical Cafe.—It may not be improper in this
place to mention the remarkable cafe of a boy who loft a
confiderable portion of brain, and yet recovered, without
detriment to any faculty mental or corporeal. On the 1ft of
July 1792, William Stewart, a fervant boy, about 14 years
of age, was by a blow from the foot of a horfe knocked to the
ground, and left in a ftate of infenfibility. From a large
wound on the right fide of his fore-head, blood iffued in confiderable quantities, as well as at different times, a confiderable portion of the fubftance of the brain. The boy not only
furvived the accident, but recovered, and was feen perfectly
well, by the writer of this account in the month of November
following. A diftinct account of this cafe, and of the whole
procefs of the cure, was publifhed by Mr Robert Leny, a
young gentleman, practitioner in phyfic, which deferves the
attention of thofe who are curious in phyfiology. It is inferted
in the Medical Commentaries, publifhed by Dr Duncan of
Edinburgh, for 1793, p. 301.

Church, Manfe, &c.—The church is faid to have been
built or rebuilt in 1691. The eafter part of it was rebuilt in
1737. It was completely repaired in 1779, and is now a very
decent and commodious place of worfhip —William Lecbie
of Dafher made a prefent of a very good bell to the parifh.—
The prefent manfe was built in 1706. The ftipend by the
laft decreet of augmentation in 1763 is nearly 89 bolls of
meal, together with L. 34 : 3 : 4 fter. which fum includes the
ordinary

ordinary allowances for communion elements, and graſs mail.
—James Erſkine Eſq. of Cardroſs is patron. Were all patrons, in the diſpoſal of vacant benefices, to ſhew the ſame
regard to the wiſhes of the pariſhioners which this gentleman
has uniformly done, the practical evils which have often been
complained of as reſulting from the exerciſe of patronage,
would not be felt.

Meeting houſe.—A meeting-houſe in connection with the
Antiburgher ſeceders was built at Buchlyvie in 1751. The
miniſter has L. 50 ſter. as ſtipend, ariſing from the ſeat
rents, with a houſe and garden. The congregation is gathered from the ſeveral contiguous pariſhes. The members of
the ſeceſſion have laid aſide much of that moroſeneſs and
acrimony which diſtinguiſhed their predeceſſors, and in general maintain good neighbourhood with their brethren of the
eſtabliſhed church. There is a burying place connected with
the meeting-houſe.

School.—It muſt be obvious that one parochial ſchool is
entirely inadequate to the extent and populouſneſs of this pariſh. To remedy this inconvenience, various plans have been
at different times propoſed. It has long been found abſolutely neceſſary to have another ſchool at the weſt end of the
pariſh. But the heritors felt reluctance to impoſe upon
themſelves the burden of two parochial ſchools. A ſchoolmaſter who was admitted in 1752 was taken bound to provide at his own charge two teachers, the one at Buchlyvie,
the other at the burn of Arnprior, for ſix months in the year;
or to have 50 merks retained from his ſalarly, which was then
L. 100 Scots. It was afterwards propoſed to remove the
parochial ſchool to a convenient ſituation in the center of the
pariſh, and to have only one teacher. At laſt it was determined

mined in 1763 to have two eſtabliſhed ſchools; the ſalary was advanced to L. 115 Scots, of which L. 75 is allotted to the ſchoolmaſter at Kippen, the remaining L. 40 to the other teacher. In the year 1782 a ſchoolhouſe, including a dwelling-houſe for the maſter, was built at Claymires. It is in ſufficient repair and tolerably commodious. The ſchoolmaſter at Kippen is but indifferently accommodated. In former times, a houſe was occaſionally rented for the ſchool, and the maſter was ſeldom accommodated with a dwelling-houſe. The ſchool was held in the church for ſome time previous to its reparation in 1779. Since that time a houſe has been rented, on a long leaſe, for a ſchool-houſe, and dwelling-houſe for the maſter; neither of which, however, are very commodious.——In the ſchool at Kippen, are taught reading, writing, arithmetic, book-keeping, Latin, and church muſic. The whole emoluments of the ſchoolmaſter, including his ſalary and fees as ſeſſion clerk, may amount annually to L. 25 or L. 30 ſterling *. As the diſtance from the two eſtabliſhed ſchools is more than 4 miles, the inhabitants of the intermediate diſtrict find it convenient to employ a teacher during the winter months to inſtruct younger children in the elements of reading and writing. The number of ſcholars laſt winter, when the ſchools were moſt frequent, was at Kippen 60, at Arnprior 36, at Claymires 64.

Poor.—The funds for ſupply of the poor in this pariſh ariſe, from the weekly collections, dues from marriages, from the mortcloth, occaſional fines from delinquents, together with L. 13 : 10, the intereſt at 4½ per cent of L. 300 ſter. which at
different

---

* An addition of two guineas per ann. has been lately made to the ſchoolmaſter, for keeping the record of the meetings of heritors.

different periods has been mortified by individuals for behoof of the poor of the pariſh. Of this ſum 2000 merks, or L. 111 : 2 : 2$\frac{8}{12}$ ſter. was mortified by the late Walter M'Lachlan of Weſter Colbowie, the intereſt of which in terms of his will muſt be diſtributed among the poor in Buchlyvie. The half of this ſum was left to the diſpoſal of the aſſociate ſeſſion at Buchlyvie, whoſe intromiſſions were to be ſubject to the review of the kirk ſeſſion of Kippen ; but they declining to accept of the management on theſe conditions, the whole was given to the kirk ſeſſion of Kippen. On this account a ſeparate book is kept for recording the diſtributions that are made to the poor in the barony of Buchlyvie.——The annual amount of the funds muſt neceſſarily vary. From L. 40 to L. 50 is diſtributed every year. The number of the poor is alſo variable. In 1792 the number of ordinary penſioners on the liſt was generally 22, who received in different ſums, according to their neceſſities, the higheſt L. 2 : 7, the loweſt 9s. or 10s in the courſe of the year. Beſides the ſtated diſtributions, occaſional ſupply is alſo granted to perſons who ſuffer from temporary diſtreſs.—In 1782 the heritors bought, and diſtributed a quantity of oatmeal to the moſt neceſſitous, below the market price. With a view to prevent improper applications, it has ſometimes been required that thoſe who receive ſupply, ſhould aſſign to the ſeſſion for behoof of the poor all the property they may die poſſeſſed of, after the houſe rent and funeral charges are paid. But the neceſſity of this meaſure is not very urgent, whilſt the poor in general diſcover ſo much reluctance to accept of public charity.—The funds are managed by the kirk-ſeſſion, who keep regular accounts of their intromiſſions ; theſe are occaſionally reviſed and homologated by the heritors.——Objections have ſometimes been made to the payment of the ſalaries of the preſbytery clerk and officer, and of the ſynod clerk, which altogether a-

mount

mount to 11s. 2d. per ann. from this parifh. Were any o-
ther fund provided for payment of thefe falaries, the alteration would undoubtedly be proper, and credit would then be
given to the liberality of thofe who brought it forward. But
on what principle of juftice, it fhould be attempted to devolve
this burden on the clergy, it is furely difficult to difcover.
—— On the whole, it is believed that no better plan can be
devifed for taking care of the poor, than that which is generally practifed throughout Scotland. And whilft the members of kirk-feffions continue to act with fidelity and prudence,
their gratuitous performance of a fervice, which is accompanied with confiderable trouble, undoubtedly entitles them
to the gratitude and fupport of their country.

Villages.—The village of Kippen ftands about a mile diftant from the eaftern boundary of the parifh, and contains
76 families. Buchlyvie, which is 5 miles farther weft, is a
larger village, and contains 102 families. The greater part
of the inhabitants of both thefe villages confifts of labourers
and trades people of different defcriptions. There are feveral
merchants alfo, who fupply us not only with rye grafs, clover,
lint feed, and wool, but with moft articles of perfonal and
domeftic confumpt.

Fairs and Markets.—Five fairs are held in the village of
Kippen, and as many in Buchlyvie in the courfe of the year.
Befides which, there is a weekly market in Kippen, in each
Wednefday, for 3 or 4 weeks, in the month of December.
By an Act of the Parliament of Scotland [*], June 15th 1686;
William Leckie then proprietor of the barony of Dafher or
Defhoar,

---

[*] The original extract of the act, figned by Lord Tarbat, then Lord
Clerk Regifter, is in the poffeffion of Mr Graham of Gartmore.

Deſhoar, and his ſucceſſors, are authorized to keep 3 free
fairs in the year, at certain times which are ſpecified, each
to continue 3 days; and alſo a weekly market every Wedneſday, to be holden on the Caſtle hill of Daſher, on which part
of the village of Kippen now ſtands. Two of theſe fairs
ſtill remain. That which was appointed to be held in the
month of September, has been long diſuſed, as alſo the
weekly market; if indeed it was ever obſerved at all. The
weekly markets in December are probably all that remains
of it.

Prices of Labour, &c.—It muſt be of uſe to record the
price of labour, and of the proviſions and various commodities which are produced and conſumed in a country, as no
circumſtance tends more to aſcertain its relative ſituation
with reſpect to other countries, and to itſelf, both in former
and ſubſequent times.—About 40 years ago the wages of
men-ſervants were about L. 2, of women from 15s to 16s 8d
a-year, with bounties. Thoſe who were careful ſaved moſt
of their wages, as the bounties were ſufficient to furniſh them
with cloaths. About 30 years ago, wages had gradually advanced, men's to L. 5 or L. 6, women's to L. 1 : 15 or L. 2 : 5.
Bounties are now generally aboliſhed, and in 1793, from
L. 7 to L. 9, were given to men, from L. 2 : 10 to L. 3 : 10,
to women.—In harveſt, as there is no weekly market, reapers are generally hired by the ſeaſon. Before 1760 men received from 13s 4d to 16s 8d, women from 10s to 13s 4d;
and in 1793 men received 30s, women 20s.—Before 1760,
the wages of taylors and day-labourers, was 4d a-day, with
victuals; 6d was given in 1783, and 10d in 1793. Carpenters and maſons about 30 years ago, got 6d a-day, with victuals; in 1793, they received 1s 2d. Formerly, ſmiths were
paid by the farmers with grain, for ſerving them in work
through

through the year; they are now paid for the piece of work, at certain fixed rates. Within these 10 or 12 years, a considerable rise has taken place, on most of the articles of living. The following table, shews the prices of a few of the most common articles at different periods.

		In 1763.	*In* 1783.	*In* 1793.
Butter per lib. Dutch weight, -		4d or 4d$\frac{1}{2}$	6d or 7d	9d or 9d$\frac{1}{2}$
Cheese,	do.	1$\frac{1}{2}$	2d	2d$\frac{1}{2}$ or 3d
A hen,	-	4d to 6d	8d	10d or 1s
Eggs per doz.		1$\frac{1}{2}$	2d	3d

Mutton, veal and lamb, were formerly sold without being weighed at so much per quarter; they are now sold by weight, and regulated by the Stirling market, which is generally 3d or 3d$\frac{1}{2}$ per lib. Dutch weight. Beef is seldom killed except about Martinmas, and is sold for 4s or 4s 6d per stone. It is hardly necessary to take notice of the prices of grain, which are perpetually varying. It may suffice to mention oat-meal, which in summer 1783 sold at 22s per boll; it had not reached near that price, since the year 1757; in 1785, it fell so low as 13s 4d or 12s 6d; but 15s or 16s, may be considered as its price on an average.

Manufactures.—This parish does not admit of any establishments in the cotton-manufactory, as no situation could be found, commanding at all times a plentiful supply of water. Yet some branches of manufacture in some degree reach even to us. In the village of Kippen 25 or 30 young girls, under the inspection of a mistress, are employed by a company in Glasgow in tambouring muslins. In Buchlyvie, some of the newly invented jeanies for spinning cotton have been

set

ſet up by a company in Balfron. And in both villages, as well
as through the pariſh, a conſiderable number of weavers has
been employed by ſeveral companies in weaving muſlins *.—
Such inſtitutions not only give bread at preſent to many individuals and families, but muſt in time excite a general
ſpirit of induſtry and enterprize amongſt our people.—In
Buchlyvie there is a tan-work, conſiſting of 16 or 20 pools;
and in another place ſheep ſkins are tanned to a ſmall extent.—
Before the commencement of the preſent diſtillery act in
1793, there were 4 diſtillers of whiſky in the pariſh, who
carried on an advantageous trade, as they ſtood on the north
ſide of the line fixed by the former act, to ſeparate the
highlands from the low country. By the preſent act a
change of line has taken place, by which this pariſh is thrown
on the ſouth ſide, and thus cut off from the benefits of the
highland diſtrict. Since December 1793, there is but one
diſtillery of the ſize required by law, which furniſhes the
country with whiſky, and produces a very conſiderable revenue to government. Including the licence and duty on
malt, the proprietor pays about L. 1200 ſterling annually to
the exciſe.

Heritors, Rent, &c.—There are in all 24 heritors. Of theſe
6 are feuars or portioners, not including the ſmall feuars in the
villages. Robert Graham Eſq. of Gartmore is the principal
heritor; there are 9 who reſide in the pariſh. Excepting two
or three eſtates, the whole property in the pariſh has been
changed within theſe 50 or 60 years. The valued rent
amounts to L. 5185 : 8 : 8, Scots. The preſent real rent,
may

* Since this article was firſt written, theſe branches of manufacture have
ſuffered ſome interruption, in conſequence of the late ſtagnation of trade.
This however, it is hoped, will prove but temporary.

may be eftimated at L. 4000 fterling. The rents are generally paid partly in money and partly in victual. Moft of the landlords require alfo kain of fowls, certain carriages of victual or coal; and thofe who refide in the parifh, a certain number of days labour in the mofs when cafting peats; all which it would be better to abolifh, and take the value in grain or money at a reafonable converfion. Thirlage is generally abolifhed; in fome inftances however it ftill remains. This inftitution marks a remote period of fociety, and the remains of it greatly retard improvement.

Land and Produce.—The quantity of land in this parifh cannot eafily be afcertained. According to the moft probable conjecture, the carfe may be fuppofed to contain 1200 acres of arable land, and about 300 of mofs; the dryfield about 5000 acres of arable and pafture land, and about 1500 or 2000 of moor. Land in the carfe is worth from 15s to 20s; in the dryfield, from 5s to 25s per acre. Oats, and barley or bear, form the ftaple produce of this parifh. Oatmeal in confiderable quantities is exported to the weft highlands, the printfields on the water of Leven, the Dunbarton, and the Glafgow markets. The barley is purchafed by the diftiller and the malt men in the parifh; by the latter, malt in confiderable quantities is exported to the highlands. Much more barley than grows in the parifh, perhaps double the quantity, is purchafed by them. Some wheat is fown in the carfes, very little in the dryfield; the wetnefs and latenefs of our climate is peculiarly unfavourable to the cultivation of this kind of grain. Peafe are fown in the dryfield, and beans in the carfe. Moft farmers raife as much flax as fupplies their own families with that ufeful article, but none for the market. The fame thing may be affirmed with refpect to potatoes. Very few turnips are fown.—In the carfe, a kind of

white

white faugh grows to a conſiderable ſize. It will grow to the thickneſs of a foot in diameter in the ſpace of 20 years, and is peculiarly uſeful for farming utenſils and machinery.

Cattle and Carriages.—The number of horſes is ſuppoſed to be about 360, of which the greater part has been reared in the pariſh.—The number of cows is about 1600; about 180 or 200 are annually bought and ſold; the remainder conſiſts of milk cows and young ſtock.—Formerly every farmer kept a number of ſheep, but ſince the farms have been incloſed this practice has been diſcontinued. The number at preſent in the pariſh will not exceed 8 or 10 ſcore.— There are about 165 ploughs, 285 carts, and 3 two-wheeled chaiſes.

Agriculture.—The ancient mode of huſbandry which prevailed throughout Scotland, was alſo practiſed in this pariſh. No attempts to improve it ſeem to have taken place before the middle of the preſent century. A few incloſures were made about 40 years ago. But any improvements of conſequence, have all been introduced ſince the military road from Stirling to Dunbarton was completed. Since that period a very conſiderable change has taken place. Moſt of the lands in the pariſh are incloſed with ſtone dykes or thorn hedges. A good deal of lime is every year laid upon the fields. And a general ſpirit of induſtry has been excited, which promiſes in time greatly to improve the agriculture of the country.

The wetneſs of the climate is a great diſadvantage. This not only injures the crops, but renders our ſeaſons generally late. We are upon the whole three weeks later than Eaſt-Lothian, and often a fortnight later than our neighbours in the vicinity of Stirling. Seldom does the ſeed labour begin before the middle of March, and not unfrequently the end of

that

that month approaches, before the fields are dry enough for the plough. In the year 1789, the bear-feed was not finished before the 8th June. So late a feafon however was rather uncommon. Harveft is feldom over before the middle or end of October, and corn is feen fometimes ftanding out even when the month of November is advanced. On account of the frequent rains, it is but feldom that any labour can be got forward after harveft, or during the winter. The fame circumftance is alfo unfavourable to the practice of fallowing, which however is neglected in this country, more than is proper. It is indeed feldom or never attempted in the dry-field, and in the carfe but fometimes, as a preparation for fowing wheat.

The foil of the carfe has been already defcribed. In the carfe farms, the infield or crofting grounds were formerly kept in a conftant rotation of barley, oats, and beans. A great part of the infield carfe lands has been laboured in this way for time immemorial, without ever being paftured or fummer fallowed. The outfield was fown with three crops of oats fucceffively, and then paftured. Carting clay from the ditches and ends of ridges, and mixing it with dung and mofs, was thought to make excellent manure, though procured with great labour. This compoft however is lefs ufed, and more lime is laid upon the grounds, fince the practice of fummer fallowing and fowing grafs-feeds was introduced. This is found to poffefs great advantages over the former mode of culture.

The whole dryfield of this parifh lies upon a rock, which is immediately covered with a bed of till, and above this is the foil, which is of unequal depth, though generally fhallow. Hence it is generally wet, as the water is not allowed to fubfide. The foil immediately contiguous to the moor is mofly and poor, but it becomes richer farther down the hill. The

crops

crops on thefe high grounds are feldom adequate to the labour and expence beftowed upon them. What fhall we
think of the fituation of that land, and of thofe who labour
it, from which an increafe in the proportion of 3 to 1 is
reckoned an excellent crop? The inferiority of the oats and
barley produced on fuch grounds, is alfo experienced both
at the mill and market. It would certainly be better if
more of the higher part of the dryfield were thrown into
grafs. If the tillage indeed were altogether abandoned, thefe
lands in a fhort time would be overgrown with heath or
broom. But this might eafily be prevented by occafional
cropping.

It would be a great improvement to drain thofe fields
which are moft injured by water. In fome places indeed
the rock comes fo near the furface, that fuch a meafure is
impracticable. But in many places it might be adopted
with great advantage. So extenfive an undertaking however
could hardly be carried on by ordinary tenants on a 19 years
leafe. It would therefore be the intereft of the proprietors
to give them fome proper encouragement. A laudable example of this kind is fet by Mr Stirling of Garden, who
agrees to be at the expence of cafting the ditches, and the
tenants are bound to fill them up with ftones. Wherever
this improvement is attempted, care fhould be taken that the
ditches be of fufficient depth. They ought to be 3 feet deep,
and filled with ftones as near the furface as that the plough
cannot touch them.

Too little attention is paid in general, to a proper rotation
of crops. The dryfield cannot well bear more than two white
crops fucceffively. Thofe therefore who go on to take three
or four, certainly impoverifh their grounds. A greater proportion of the farm fhould be laid down in grafs, and other
green crops occafionally interpofed. This will be more attended

tended to, as improvements in hufbandry advance amongſt us. Some of the more judicious farmers have begun to adopt this plan, and find their account in the change of their practice.

Turnips are but little cultivated in this part of the country. Experience however has ſhewn their utility in cleaning the ground, keeping it in good condition, and furniſhing manure; an objeƈt of great importance, where dung cannot be purchafed. There can be no doubt that in many places of our dryfield, turnips might be cultivated with fuccefs.

As our feafons are generally late, the ufe of earlier forts of feed muſt appear an obvious advantage. The Effex oats and fome other kinds have been tried. But the tendency of thefe to be ſhaken with the harveſt winds, has hitherto difcouraged our farmers from making much ufe of them.

Several of the implements ufed in hufbandry would admit of improvement. The Scottiſh plough is generally ufed, but little attention is paid to its conſtruƈtion. As thofe prejudices againſt all innovations however proper, which diftinguiſhed the ancient farmers of Scotland, are now wearing away, it is to be hoped, that all fuch alterations as reafon and experience prove to be ufeful, will in time be introduced. It is agreeable to obferve that fome ploughs of a better conſtruƈtion have lately been procured; and within thefe two years, no lefs than 8 threſhing mills have been ereƈted in the pariſh. Every corn mill has now a kiln contiguous to it; the kiln-heads are of caſt iron, which occafion a confiderable faving in refpeƈt of ſtraw and fuel. The oats are dried in much lefs time, and the meal produced is equally good as by the ancient method. Formerly almoſt every farmer was accuſtomed to have a kiln of his own, which not only required frequent reparations, but was extremely liable to accidents by fire.

A better method of ploughing, than that which the old farmers

mers practiſed is now generally adopted ; fewer horſes are employed, and in ſome inſtances without a goadman.

The ploughing matches that have been inſtituted in different parts of the country, have been accompanied with very good effects. A plan of this kind has once and again been attempted here. Under the patronage of a number of gentlemen in the neighbourhood, a ploughing match took place on the 22d March 1794, at which 7 ploughs ſtarted, and about L. 12 ſter. was diſtributed in different ſums to the 7 beſt ploughmen, and a ſmall gratuity to the reſt. Such well-judged encouragement muſt ſtimulate our farming ſervants to excel in this important part of practical huſbandry.

Diſadvantages ; and Projected Improvements.—The want of coal is one principal diſadvantage under which this pariſh labours. We have none nearer than Bannockburn and Auchenbowie, either of which is at leaſt 12 miles from the village of Kippen. There ſeems reaſon to believe that coal may be found in the lands of Glinns and Balgair in this neighbourhood. Attempts for that purpoſe have repeatedly been made in theſe places, as well as in the lands of Buchlyvie, but hitherto without the ſucceſs that might be deſired. The acquiſition of coal ſo near would be of vaſt importance to this part of the country.

We have lime at no great diſtance, and even within the pariſh. As the limeſtone however contains a conſiderable portion of ſand, it is thought not to ſuit the dryfield ſo well, though proper for the carſe lands. But as the coal neceſſary to burn it cannot be procured but at great expence and trouble, moſt farmers, eſpecially in the middle, and eaſt end of the pariſh, find it more for their advantage to drive lime from Stirling ſhore, to which it is brought up the Forth from the Earl of Elgin's lime works, or from the eſtates of Sauchie and

Murrayſhall,

Murrayshall, about 12 miles from the village. This lime-
ftone being of a richer quality than that which is nearer us,
is found peculiarly fuitable for the dryfield. The fhells coft
8s. 6d. or 9s. per chalder at the kiln.

The parifh of Kippen raifes much more grain than is neceffary for its own confumpt, but lies far from a good market.
Stirling is abundantly fupplied from its own immediate vicinity, and both Glafgow and Dunbarton are 24 miles from the
village. This difadvantage might be alleviated by making
good roads. The road from Kippen to Glafgow by Campfie
moor, was formerly extremely bad, and often impaffable in
winter. In 1792 it was made turnpike, and the courfe of it
in feveral places altered with advantage. A bill has lately
received the fanction of parliament for making the military
road turnpike likewife. As thefe two great roads interfect
each other at the village of Kippen, the effects of this undertaking muft be extremely favourable to this neighbourhood,
as well as convenient for the public in general, by opening
the communication between the northern and fouthern parts
of the country.

It is the opinion of many of the graziers and dealers in cattle, that Kippen is one of the moft convenient places, perhaps, in Scotland for a cattle market ; and that in the late
fluctuating ftate of the tryfts, it might not have been difficult
to transfer to it a great part of the fpring and autumn markets.
There is a fpacious moor near the village which lies very
convenient for that purpofe. With a view to encourage
their refort to it, Mr Graham of Gartmore, the proprietor, offered it to the dealers in cattle free of cuftom for
19 years.

It is alfo believed that the eftablifhment of a corn market once a week at Kippen might prove very beneficial ; as alfo a weekly market in the time of harveft for

hiring

hiring fhearers. Both of thefe objeʒts feemed in a fair way
of taking place a few years ago ; the defign however was
afterwards dropped *.

When the fcheme of joining the rivers Forth and Clyde by
a navigable canal was firft projeʒted, it was doubted which of
the two was the preferable courfe, viz. the fouthern track,
nearly the fame with what was aʒtually adopted ; or " the
" other, by following the river Forth for fome miles above
" Stirling, and then crofling over by the bog of Bolatt into
" the water of Endrick, down to Loch Lomond, and from
" thence by the river Leven into the Clyde at Dunbarton †."
Though this plan was rejcʒted, yet it deferves the confideration of all the proprietors on both fides of the Forth, whether
it might be proper to have that river rendered navigable as
far up as Gartmcre. It appears from Mr Smeaton's report,
that this is not only a praʒticable undertaking, but might be
executed at no great expence. " Two locks and one dam
" would make an open navigation from Gartmore to the
" Frith of Forth, at all feafons of the year ; and was there
" any trade of confequence up this extenfive valley, would
" be worth the while, independent of a navigable commu-
" nication between the two feas. One lock ought to be placed
" oppofite Craigforth mill, and the lock and dam at the ford
" of Frew. This with a little clearance of the fhoal at Car-
" drofs, would make a navigable paffage over the fame ‡."
The advantages refulting from fuch a plan, in furnifhing us
with coal, lime, &c. in opening new markets for our grain,
and

---

* A frefh attempt to eftablifh a weekly corn market at Kippen, was made
fince this account was written, in fpring and fummer 1795, not without the
profpeʒt of fuccefs.

† Mr Smeaton's report, in Scots magazine for 1767, p. 177.

‡ Ibid. p. 180.

and confequently in raifing the value of landed property in this part of the country, are fo apparent that they do not need to be pointed out.

The moor on the fummit of the hill might better be difpofed of in planting. A quantity of wafte and barren land in Glentirran moor, has within thefe few years been divided into fmall lots, and feued off to a number of people, each of whom builds a houfe on his feu and improves the ground. This land till lately was of very little value; it now brings 20s. per acre to the proprietor, Mr Graham of Gartmore. It is not every fituation however that admits of this improvement. Part of the fame moor has lately been cultivated by General Campbell, whofe extenfive improvements on the eftate of Boquhan are highly beneficial and ornamental to the country.

Character of the People.—The great body of the people in this parifh is entitled to the praife of fobriety. There are few inftances amongft us of notorious profligacy. By means of induftry and œconomy, they in general obtain a comfortable fubfiftence, and fome individuals have raifed themfelves to opulence.———The fame changes with refpect to drefs and manner of living, are obferved here of late years as in other places.

General Reflections on the State of Society.—It feems not unreafonable to apprehend, that fuch a ftate of fociety as appears at prefent in the parifh of Kippen, and other places whofe circumftances are fimilar, is as favourable to happinefs as the courfe of human affairs can ordinarily admit. In a country where improvements are altogether unknown, much happinefs cannot be enjoyed; for there the neceffaries of life are procured with difficulty, or, if they are eafily procured, little

fcope

ſcope is afforded for active exertion. On the other hand, where improvements in agriculture and the arts have been brought to a high degree of perfection, luxury and other evils accompany them, which are no leſs unfriendly than poverty and indolence to the happineſs of man. It is in ſome intermediate ſtate, where improvements have begun, and are ſtill advancing, that the circumſtances of ſociety appear moſt calculated to promote the comfort of human life. Such, it is conceived, is the cafe with reſpect to this neighbourhood, and many other places in Scotland whoſe ſituation is the fame with ours. The truth of this aſſertion will be manifeſt, if we take a comparative view of ſeveral ſtates of ſociety, which are known to have exiſted, or do ſtill exiſt in Scotland.

It is unneceſſary to dwell on thoſe remote periods, when a ſpirit of ferocity and warlike manners prevailed. Surely there could be little happineſs where there was little property, and that which men poſſeſſed was inſecure.

If we look back only to a generation or two, and reflect on the ſtate of the country in the former part of the preſent century, or ſurvey thoſe places, where the recent improvements in huſbandry have not yet been introduced, a ſtate of ſociety is exhibited that cannot be gratifying to a lover of mankind. The lands, ſterile from want of culture, requite their penurious poſſeſſors with penury. Life is indeed protracted, though few of its comforts are enjoyed. Men ſeem patient in enduring hardſhip, but averſe from labour. Strangers to enterprize, the powers of their minds ruſt through mere diſuſe. A harmleſs, torpid race, who might be ſaid to ſleep rather than to live. The farms generally ſmall, juſt enabled them to maintain their families and pay the landlord, but held out few inducements to ſtimulate exertion.

In the ſouthern parts of Scotland as well as in England, where

where agriculture feems to be brought to the higheft ftate of improvement, we fee extenfive farms in the poffeffion of tenants who appear as gentlemen, and are able to live in affluence and fplendour. Experience however undeniably proves that thofe fituations in life which admit of luxury, are unfavourable to happinefs. And in thefe places the diftance between mafter and fervant is fo very great, that though the latter may enjoy a prefent fubfiftence, yet he can have little or no hope of bettering his circumftances to fuch a degree, as to rife to independence, and obtain poffeffion of a farm himfelf. Such extenfive farms are alfo unfavourable to the population of the country.

Let us next attend to thofe places where manufactures have been introduced. There the neceffaries and conveniencies of life are procured with facility. Abundant fcope is given to exertion. And riches pour on all who are willing to labour. But thefe difproportioned rewards of labour generally tend to enervate the finews of induftry, fofter idlenefs, introduce a total relaxation of morals, and confequently lead to poverty and wretchednefs *. Population indeed appears to increafe with rapidity ; but its progrefs is arrefted by difeafe, which feems to fix its abode in thofe extenfive work-houfes that are employed in manufactures. In the cotton-works particularly, children become able to fupport themfelves almoft as foon as they are able to fpeak or walk. But their wan and fickly afpect, occafioned by conftant confinement ; and their unacquaintance with the fentiments of religion and morality, arifing from the want of proper education, and the early infection

of

---

* It is well known that comparatively few operative manufacturers rife to opulence. Their money is diffipated as faft as it is gained. Hence the wretchednefs of fuch multitudes of this defcription, in confequence of the late ftagnation of trade.

of evil company, do much more than counterbalance the profits of infant labour. If ſuch children live till they become
parents, what hopes do they afford refpecting the next generation ? By the wife and humane exertions of ſome benevolent
individuals, theſe evils may be partially prevented or alleviated ; but a general care to guard againſt them is more than
can reaſonably be expected. To all which it may be added,
that the facility with which money is procured by the lower
ranks, tends to generate a ſpirit unſuited to their condition in
life, unfriendly to ſubordination, and menacing eventually
the order and peace of ſociety.

Now if we direct our view to ſuch a ſtate of ſociety as takes
place at preſent in this pariſh, and in other places which have
reached the fame degree of improvement, a variety of circumſtances will appear which combine to promote the felicity of
human life. The farms are not too extenſive, and yet ſufficiently large to offer abundant ſcope to exertion. A comfortable ſubſiſtence is within the reach of every perſon who is able,
and who chooſes to labour. Perſevering induſtry and enterpriſe are crowned with liberal rewards. Not a few of our
moſt reſpectable farmers were once ſervants, and are now e-
qual, perhaps ſuperior in fortune, to the maſters whom they
ſerved. One man might be mentioned, who began the world
with nothing, and, by farming only, reared a numerous family, and lately purchaſed an eſtate in the pariſh for which he
paid 1500 guineas. The trades people in the villages live
more comfortably than thoſe of the fame rank in great towns.
Almoſt every family of this deſcription has a kail-yard, and
keeps a cow ; and thoſe who are able to get a few acres of land
find this a great advantage. Occaſional attention to their land
forms an agreeable and uſeful relaxation from the ſedentary
life of a handicraft, and ſupplies the family with meal and potatoes, and winter proviſion for the cow. Though our ſituation

tion does not admit of eſtabliſhments in manufactures, we are not altogether excluded from a ſhare of the benefits derived from them. The increaſing demand for grain, cattle, &c. is beneficial to the farmer; whilſt the ſmaller erections for ſpinning cotton, tambouring, and weaving muſlins, bring to us theſe manufactures, and the advantages reſulting from them, upon ſuch a ſcale as is not likely to produce any material injury to the health or morals of thoſe employed in them. At leaſt thoſe who have the ſuperintendence of ſuch ſmall manufacturing ſocieties, have it in their power to prevent or to correct abuſes, to a degree that is altogether impracticable in great towns, or larger eſtabliſhments of this kind.

Such are ſome of the advantages enjoyed by a country which hath emerged from the unprofitable indolence of former times, and in which improvements are ſtill advancing, though they have not yet arrived at that ultimate point of perfection to which they naturally tend.

The diſadvantages which accompany an advanced ſtate of ſociety, ſeem to render it no leſs unfriendly to human happineſs, than thoſe earlier ſtages in which improvements are but little known. To prevent or to correct theſe evils, is ſurely one of the nobleſt objects which can employ the exertions of politicians and philanthropiſts. To this deſireable end, the preſent ſtatiſtical inveſtigation of the kingdom, when completed, may be expected in a high degree to contribute. And the writer of this account will think himſelf happy, if theſe remarks ſhall lead the people in this part of the country, and others placed in ſimilar ſituations, to contentment with the lot that Divine Providence hath aſſigned to them, and animate them to a becoming uſe of thoſe advantages which they at preſent enjoy.

Parish of Kippen.

Additional Information, by the Rev. J. Campbell.

The following anecdotes are not only curious in themselves, but throw light on the state of society of Scotland at the time to which they refer. They are transcribed from the Essay on the Family and Surname of Buchanan, by William Buchanan of Auckmar, p. 57—60.

In the reign of King James IV. and for divers ages before, the Meinzieses were proprietors of a great part of the parish of Kippen, and some of the parish of Killearn, though scarce any memory of that name remains in either of these parishes in this age. A gentleman of that name being laird of Arnpryor, at the above mentioned juncture, who had no children of his own, nor any of his name in these parts that could pretend any relation to him, was for some time at variance with one Forrester of Garden, a very topping gentleman of Arnpryor's neighbourhood, who, upon account of his neighbour Arnpryor's circumstances, sent a menacing kind of message to him, either to dispone his estate in his favour voluntarily, otherwise he would dispossess him of it by force. Arnpryor not being of power to oppose Garden, and being loath to give his estate by compulsion to his enemy, judged it the more proper, as well as honourable method, to dispone his estate to some other gentleman who would counterbalance Garden, and would maintain the rightful owner in possession thereof during his life. In this exigency he had recourse to the laird of Buchanan, offering to dispone his estate to one of Buchanan's sons, if he would defend him from any

any violence offered by Garden. Buchanan readily accepted of the offer; and fo far undervalued Garden, that he fent his fecond fon, then only a child, without any other guard than his dry nurfe, to overfee him, along with Arnpryor, to be kept by him as his heir. Upon notice hereof, Garden came to Arnpryor's houfe with a refolution to kill him, or oblige him to fend back Buchanan's fon, and grant his former demands. Arnpryor having gone out of the way, Garden very imperioufly ordered the woman, who attended Buchanan's child, to carry him back forthwith whence he came, otherwife he would burn Arnpryor's houfe and them together. The woman replied, that fhe would not defert the houfe for any thing he durft do; telling him withal, if he offered the leaft violence, it would be revenged to his coft. This ftout reply was fomewhat damping to Garden, who at the fame time reflecting, that he would not only be obnoxious to the laws for any violent meafures he fhould take, but alfo to enmity with Buchanan, which he was by no means able to fupport, therefore followed the fafeft courfe, by defifting for the future either to moleft Arnpryor, or fruftrate his deftination; fo that his adopted heir enjoyed his eftate, without the leaft impediment, after his death.——This John Buchanan of Auckmar and Arnpryor was afterward termed King of Kippen, upon the following account. King James V. a very fociable debonair prince, refiding at Stirling, in Buchanan of Arnpryor's time; carriers were very frequently paffing along the common road, being near Arnpryor's houfe, with neceffaries for the ufe of the King's family; and he having fome extraordinary occafion, ordered one of thefe carriers to leave his load at his houfe, and he would pay him for it; which the carrier refufed to do, telling him he was the King's carrier, and his load for his Majefty's ufe; to which Arnpryor feemed to have fmall regard, compelling the carrier in the end to

leave

leave his load, telling him, if King James was King of Scotland, he was King of Kippen, ſo that it was reaſonable he ſhould ſhare with his neighbour King, in ſome of theſe loads ſo frequently carried that road. The carrier repreſented this uſage, and telling the ſtory, as Arnpryor ſpoke it, to ſome of the King's ſervants, it came at length to his Majeſty's ears, who ſoon afterwards, with a few attendants, came to viſit his neighbour King, who happened to be at dinner. King James having ſent a ſervant to demand acceſs, was denied the ſame by a tall fellow, with a battle-ax, who ſtood porter at the gate, telling there could be no acceſs till dinner was over. This anſwer not ſatisfying the King, he ſent to demand acceſs a ſecond time; upon which he was deſired by porter to deſiſt, otherwiſe he would find cauſe to repent his rudeneſs. His Majeſty finding this method would not do, deſired the porter to tell his maſter, that the *goodman of Ballageich* * deſired to ſpeak with the King of Kippen. The porter telling Arnpryor ſo much, he in all humble manner came and received the King, and having entertained him with much ſumptuouſneſs and jollity, became ſo agreeable to King James, that he allowed him to take as much of any proviſion he found carrying that road, as he had occaſion for; and ſeeing he made the firſt viſit, deſired Arnpryor in a few days to return him a ſecond at Stirling, which he performed, and continued in very much favour with the King, always thereafter being termed King of Kippen while he lived.

* Ballageich is the name of the rock on which the Caſtle of Stirling ſtands.

UNITED PARISHES OF LARBERT AND DUNIPACE.

(*County of Stirling.*)

By the Rev. Mr GEORGE HARVIE.

Situation, Extent, &c.

THE united parishes of Larbert and Dunipace are situated in the county of Stirling, about seven miles distant from the town, lying towards the south-east, and are within the presbytery of Stirling, and synod of Perth and Stirling. Each parish hath its own church and kirk-session. These churches were originally two chapels, belonging to the abbot of Cambuskenneth, near Stirling: But, at the Reformation, they were erected into different charges; and, since that time, have been under one minister. The extent of both parishes, from east to west, is about eight, and from south to north, about two miles. . They are generally level ground; and the soil is partly of a light dry nature, and partly clayey.

Minerals.—There is plenty of free-stone and coal in both parishes; but no coal is wrought at present, except at Kinnaird and Quarrole, which lie in the parish of Larbert.

Population.—In former times, the parish of Dunipace was the most populous; but now the population there is greatly diminished, nifhed, owing to the heritors taking the land into their own hands, and appropriating it to pafturage for large cattle, fheep, &c. The population of the parifh of Larbert has increafed in a very large proportion. There are about 3000 people in it above 12 years of age, confequently about 4000 in all. In Dr Webfter's report, the number is 1864. There are feveral villages in faid parifh, but no market town. The number of handicraftfmen in Larbert parifh is about 1500. In the parifh of Dunipace, there are only about 80. The annual average of marriages in the parifh of Larbert is about 31, which is taken from the records. The births in it are about 60; but, on account of the different fectaries, there are a great many who are not recorded. Of deaths, there are about 38; but there are feveral inhabitants in the parifh of Larbert who have their burying places in other parifhes, and the deaths of fuch are not inferted in our records. At an average of three years, there are, in the parifh of Larbert, 17 baptifms, 5 marriages, and 10 burials.

Manufactories.—The manufactories in both parifhes are very confiderable. In the parifh of Dunipace, there are a printfield, and a cotton-fpinning manufactory. In the parifh of Larbert the famous Carron works are fituated, which is one of the greateft founderies in Europe. There are about 1000 workmen employed, and about 150 carts for driving coals, iron-ftone, &c. The works confift of 5 blaft furnaces; 16 air furnaces; a clay mill for grinding clay and making fire bricks for the ufe of the faid furnace; an engine that raifes 4 tons and a half of water at one ftroke, and, on an average, draws 7 ftrokes in a minute. This engine goes in the time of drought, and confumes 16 tons of coal in 24 hours. Befides the coals confumed by this engine, there are 120 tons burnt every day in the works, and by the inhabitants belonging

belonging to them. Befides the air furnaces, there are 3 cupola furnaces, that go by virtue of the blaft furnaces, by pipes conveyed from the machinery of the blafts. Their bufinefs is much the fame with the air furnaces. There are alfo 4 boring mills, for boring guns, pipes, cylinders, &c. One of the boring mills is adapted for turning the guns on the outfide. They have likewife fmiths forges for making the largeft anchors and anvils, as well as fmall work of various kinds; befides a forge for making malleable iron, and a plating forge: Alfo a forge for ftamping iron, the hammer of which, with the helve, are both of caft metal, and weigh a ton and a half. A nail manufactory is likewife carried on in Larbert parifh to a confiderable extent.

Church.—There are no places of public worfhip, except the eftablifhed churches of Larbert and Dunipace.

Produce, &c. — Neither parifh can fupply itfelf with meal, owing to fo much ground being laid out in pafture. In both parifhes, there are about 50 acres fown with flax, and as much with grafs. There is no ground in common in either, except where the great cattle tryft is held three times in the year. It is a dry muir, belonging to Sir Michael Bruce, where, it is computed, there are between 20,000 and 30,000 cattle collected at the October tryft. The advantages enjoyed by both, are plenty of coal, and, from their vicinity to the great Canal, water carriage to and from the Eaft and Weft feas at an eafy rate. Of courfe, they have plenty of provifions brought to them from many diftant places.

Antiquities.—Near the Carron works once ftood the famous *Arthur's Oven,* called by Buchanan *Templum Termini.* Several Danifh forts, or obfervatories, are in thefe parifhes; one

at

at Larbert, another at Braes, in the pariſh of Dunipace, and a third in Upper Torwood. There are two artificial mounts in the pariſh of Dunipace, near the church. Each of them cover, at the baſe, about an acre of land. They are up-wards of 60 feet high, and raiſed in a conical form. The reaſon of raiſing them is ſaid to be for a memorial of a peace which had been concluded there between the Romans and Scots *. A part of one of the mounts, towards the weſt, was carried away (as Buchanan ſays) by a flood in the river Car-ron. At what time this happened is uncertain; but the courſe which the river had then taken, when it made this encroachment on the mount, is ſtill viſible. The great Ro-man Cauſeway from Carmuirs, (where the Roman camp was, in the pariſh of Falkirk), which croſſed the river Carron by a bridge, weſt of the village of Larbert, and went almoſt in a ſtraight line to the caſtle of Stirling, is ſtill entire in many parts, both in the pariſh of Larbert and Dunipace. In Dunipace pariſh is the famous Torwood; in the middle of which there are the remains of Wallace's tree, an oak which, according to a meaſurement, when entire, was ſaid to be about 12 feet diameter. To this wood Wallace is ſaid to have fled, and ſecreted himſelf in the body of that tree, then hollow, after his defeat in the north. Adjoining to this is a ſquare field, incloſed by a ditch, where Mr Donald Cargill excommunicated King Charles II.

Schools.--In the pariſh of Larbert there are five ſchools, the principal of which is the pariſh ſchool in Stenhouſe-muir. The number of ſcholars, in general, is between 60 and 70. The annual ſalary is 100 l. Scotch, and 1 l. Ster-

ling

---

* The name of the pariſh is ſuppoſed to originate from theſe two hills. They were the *Dunes pacis* or *hills of peace.*

ling as feffion clerk. The perquifites arifing from baptifms, marriages, and certificates, &c. amount in general to 8 l. 10 s. Sterling. In the fchool at the village of Carron-fhore, there are about 40 fcholars, and the fame number in th ichool at the village of Larbert. In another fchool at the colliery of Kinnaird, about 24 fcholars are taught. In the parifh fchool of Dunipace there are about 40 fcholars. The fees *per* quarter are the fame with the parifh fchool of Larbert. The annual falary is 100 merks Scotch; the mafter has 1 l. Sterling *per annum* for being feffion clerk. The perquifites arifing from baptifms, marriages, &c. amount to 1 l. 4 s. 8 d.

Mifcellaneous Obfervations.—The great road that leads from Stirling to Edinburgh, goes through both parifhes, upon which there is a toll bar at the Torwood. This road is maintained by the toll; and other crofs roads are repaired by an affeffment laid upon houfeholders, and the ftatute work of the farmers. The land rent is generally between 20 s. and 30 s. Sterling *per* acre. There are feveral funds in the parifh of Larbert, befides the poor's rates, and collections at the church door. The firft was erected by the Carron Company foon after they began their works, for the benefit of their workmen. The members belonging to this fund are about three hundred and twenty. There are three public houfes in the parifh of Larbert; one at Carron, and two in the village. There is one in the parifh of Dunipace, on the road from Stirling to Glafgow. But alehoufes, or rather what may be called whifky-houfes, are very numerous in both thefe parifhes. In thefe houfes a drink of good ale cannot be got; but aquavitae is to be had in abundance. It has even got the better of fome of the fair fex, who inftead of being admired, then become the abhorrence of fober men. In general it is obferved to be hurtful to the

health,

health, morals, and uſefulneſs of mankind, eſpecially when taken too often, or to exceſs. There are ſix heritors in the pariſh of Larbert, viz. Sir Michael Bruce, Bart. Colonel Dundas, Mr Bruce of Kinnaird, Mr Strachan of Woodſide, Mr Caddel of Banton, and Mr Miles Riddell of Larbert ; and three in Dunipace, viz. Mr Morehead of Herbertſhire, Mr Johnſton of Denovan, and Mr Spottiſwood of Dunipace ; each of whom keeps a four wheeled carriage. It is worthy of being recorded, to the honour of theſe gentlemen, that during the great ſcarcity in 1782 and 1783, they voluntarily raiſed the aſſeſſment upon their property from 20 s. to 30 s. Sterling on the 100 l. Scotch of valued rent, for the ſupport of the poor ; beſides importing grain, which they ſold be-low the market price to all who applied for it. Mr Bruce of Kinnaird, the famous Abyſſinian traveller, has lately erec-ted an elegant monument of caſt metal, over the vault wherein his lady and eldeſt ſon are interred, which is much admired by ſtrangers. There have been 40 houſes built within theſe 10 years, beſides one gentleman's ſeat in the pariſh of Larbert, and only four taken down within that period, Servants wages are very high in compariſon of what they were formerly, being about 10 l. *per annum*, beſides their board ; ſo that between the increaſe of rents, and the high rate of wages, the huſbandman is often put to great dif-ficulties. Such as employ cottagers ſeem to be eaſier, and better ſerved.

PARISH OF LOGIE.

(*County of Stirling.*)

By the Rev. Mr JAMES WRIGHT.

Extent and Situation.

THIS parish is about four miles in length, and nearly as much in breadth, and is situated about two miles north from Stirling, in the presbytery of Dunblane, and provincial synod of Perth and Stirling. The parish lies in three shires, viz. Stirling, Perth, and Clackmannan.

Population.—About 30 years ago, when a computation of the number of the inhabitants was made, at the request of the sheriff-depute of Perthshire, it was reckoned, that the souls contained in each of the three counties, amounted to about 500, making in all 1500. In Dr Webster's report, the number is 1985.

Produce and Soil.—Provisions of all kinds are plentiful. There are four coalhills within as many miles of the church. There is plenty of peat in Mofs Flanders, which is about four miles distant from the church. As to the soil of this parish, the one half of it is strong carse clay ground, and is reckoned to be the richest of any in the kingdom; the other half is dryfield, and hilly ground; the former produces exceeding

ceeding good crops; the latter is fit for pafturing cattle, fheep, and goats: thefe two foils are nearly equally divided by a high-road, at the foot of the Ochil hills, running from Alva to Stirling.

Poor. — Poor's rates are adopted in this parifh, one half of which is paid by the heritors, and the other by the tenants. In the year 1774, the number of the poor was 33, for whom were contributed L. 40 Sterling. L 28 was paid by the heritors and tenants, and L. 12 out of the poor's funds; but in 1775, L. 38 was diftributed, and for fome years paft, the heritors and tenants have advanced only L. 22, which, with L. 12 paid yearly out of the poor's funds, fhows that the expences have diminifhed. The poor live in their own houfes, and none are allowed to beg.

Mifcellaneous Obfervations. — The abbey of Cambufkenneth is the only place of antiquity in this parifh, where King James III. of Scotland was buried. Nigh to this is the Abbey Craig, of confiderable height; upon the top of which is to be feen the form of a battery, faid to be erected in Oliver Cromwell's time, when he laid fiege to the caftle of Stirling, but without effect. There is a high conical hill in this parifh, called *Dunmyatt*, from the top of which, is to be feen part of 12 counties. About half a mile from the foot of this hill to the north, is a very fine well, which iffues from more than 60 fprings, that rife through the fand and channel. It is called the *Holy Well*, and is faid to have formerly been much reforted to by the Roman Catholics. There are appearances of filver and copper mines in this parifh. Some of them have been wrought, but with little profit to the adventurers. The only one that feemed to prove advantageous, was that on the eftate of Aithrey, belonging to Mr Haldane,

Haldane, in the years 1761, 1762, 1763, and 1764, a company of gentlemen from England, along with the proprietor, laid out a confiderable fum of money in working this mine; and they got about 50 barrels of filver ore, of which four barrels made a ton, and each ton was valued at London at L. 60 Sterling. One Dr Twiffe, to whom the ore was configned, became bankrupt, which put an end to the adventure.

PARISH OF MUIRAVONSIDE.

By the Rev. Mr JOHN BERTRAM.

Name, Situation, Extent, Soil, &c.

THIS parish takes its name from the river Avon, which divides the counties of Linlithgow and Stirling. It is situated in the latter, although it belongs to the presbytery of Linlithgow, and synod of Lothian. It is bounded by the parishes of Borrowstounnefs, Linlithgow, Torphichen, Polmont and Slamanan. It is about 6 miles long, and 2 broad. The eaft end is of a light gravelly foil; the rett clay, with a mixture of mofs and moor. A confiderable part of the parifh has been inclofed within thefe few years. The farms are very fmall: The rents commonly are high: The harveft early. There are 50 ploughs in the parifh; and no farmer has more than one. As the farms are fmall, grafs parks are commonly taken from year to year for feeding cattle. More corn is raifed than is neceffary to fupply the parifh. Twenty acres of lint were fown laft year. The rental of the parifh may be about L. 2000.

Population.—The return of the population to Dr Webfter is faid to have been 1469: but there feems to have been a miftake here, as one who knows it well afferts, that there has

been

been no material alteration ſince the year 1745. At preſent, the number of ſouls amounts only to 1065. Of theſe, there are 302 under 10 years of age. The oldeſt man in the pariſh is 90. - The barony of Almond has been all laid out in graſs, and the farm houſes have become ruinous. This may be aſſigned as one cauſe, and it ſeems to be the principal one, of the decreaſe of the population; but that eſtate being now all incloſed, conſiderable plantations made, and to be let out in commodious farms, will add greatly to the beauty and population of the place. The annual average of births is 45; deaths 35; but the Seceders, in general, do not inſert their names in the pariſh regiſter. The number of this ſect here is 65. There are 37 heritors. The greateſt part of them reſide in the pariſh. There are no vagrant poor belonging to the pariſh. There are 20 penſioners on the poors roll.

Church and Stipend.—The church is old. The ſtipend is L. 83 : 6 : 8, at the old converſion of L. 8 : 6 : 8 the chalder of victual. The glebe conſiſts of 4 acres. The crown is patron.

Antiquities.—There ſtill remain ſome ruins of an old abbey, called Manuel, on the ſide of the Avon, about half a mile above Linlithgow bridge. It was built in the 12th century. There is an old caſtle called Almond hard by the church, which belongs to the Callander eſtate, but is not inhabited.

Miſcellaneous Obſervations.—There are ſeveral coal mines, and a great quantity of iron-ſtone in the pariſh. The fuel is coal and peat; but the former is chiefly uſed. There are 17 mills in this pariſh on the river Avon. There is 1 flour
and

and 1 barley mill; 4 corn and 4 lint mills; 2 ſnuff and 2 fulling mills; 1 bark, 1 bleeching, and 1 flint mill. The wages of men ſervants, living in the houſe, are commonly L. 6 a year, and of women ſervants L. 3. Labourers get 10 d. and 1 s. per day.

PARISH OF POLMONT.

(*County of Stirling.*)

By the Rev. Mr WILLIAM FINLAY.

Name, Situation, Extent, &c.

THE pariſh of Polmont was disjoined from that of Fal-kirk in 1724. The derivation of the name is un-certain ; but one of the titles of the Duke of Hamilton, viz. Lord Polmont, i. taken from it. The pariſh is ſituated in the county of Stirling, preſbytery of Linlithgow, and ſynod of Lothian and Tweeddale. Its greateſt length is 5 miles, and its breadth 2. It is interſected by the Frith of Forth on the north, and the river Avon on the eaſt ; and partly by the great canal.

Soil, Climate, Minerals, &c.—A conſiderable part of the pariſh is of a rich carſe ground, and very fertile ; the average rent of which is 2 l. *per* acre. The reſt is high, and of a light ſoil, but moſtly in cultivation, except a ſmall part of moor, and about one eighth, or one tenth, in common. The cli-mate is remarkably healthy, even in the low carſe diſtricts. Seed is ſown in March or April, and harveſt generally takes place in September. There are ſeveral mineral ſprings, im-pregnated with iron, from the great quantities of iron ore in the higher grounds. The ſhore of the Frith (if it may be ſo called)

called), is flat, pretty extenfive at low water, and covered with fleetch. There are feveral confiderable quarries of free-ftone, two of which are conftantly wrought for building, and employ from 12 to 14 men. There are alfo feveral coal mines, chiefly belonging to the duke of Hamilton. The principal one is that at Shieldhill, in the moor fouth from Falkirk, which is let in leafe to the Carron Company, and produces about 500 tons *per* week, of a remarkably fine quality This coal work employs about 250 people, men, women, and children, and from 40 to 50 horfes. It yields, to the proprietor, about 500 l. *per annum*; befides the profit of the iron-ftone, which is wrought from the old coal-pits, and is fold to the Carron Company at 10 d. *per* ftone weight, above the expence of working it, and affords conftant employment to about a dozen of people.

Population.—According to the report fent to Dr Webfter in 1755, the population then amounted to 1094 fouls. It muft therefore have increafed confiderably fince that period, as it now amounts to about 1400. Of thefe the far greater part refide in the country, there being only a few houfes near the church, and about 50 families who have feus on the turnpike road, which lies fouth from it. The average of births, for thefe laft five years, is 64; of deaths, during the fame period, 53, and of marriages, 22. The average number of perfons to each family is 3½, there being 400 houfes in the parifh, and not one of them uninhabited. Of thefe there are ten, which may be properly ftiled villas, being poffeffed by genteel families, but without any great extent of property. The building of thefe houfes, and the concomitant improvements of the country, occafioning a demand for labourers, have been the chief caufes of increafing the population, as well as of preventing emigrations, of which

there

there has not been a ſingle inſtance from this diſtrict, for theſe five years paſt. There are about 200 houſehold ſervants, male and female, in the pariſh, the former of whom get from 5 l. to 8 l. a year, and the latter from 2 l. 10 s. to 3 l.

Church, Stipend, &c.—The living, including the glebe, is worth about 90 l. *per annum* at an average. The Crown is patron. The church was built in 1732, and has had no reparations ſince, except being plaſtered in the roof and walls in 1785. The manſe was built a few years after, and got ſome trifling repairs in 1784, and, in 1785, new office houſes were built. There are about 40 heritors, 20 of whom are of the ſmaller ſort. All the people attend the eſtabliſhed church, except a few Seceders. There are no Epiſcopalians, and only one Roman Catholic. There are at preſent 17 regular penſioners, who receive alms from the poor's funds, beſides thoſe who receive charity occaſionally. The annual amount of the funds for their relief is about 28 l. Sterling.

General Character, &c.—The people, in general, are ſober and induſtrious. None have been indicted for any crime, or baniſhed, theſe many years, one only excepted. They meaſure from 5 feet 8, to 5 feet 10 inches. There is only one individual in the pariſh 6 feet 3. No particular manufactures are carried on in it. The expence of living is rather upon the increaſe of late years. Landed property has not changed often, and what has been ſold lately has drawn 30 years purchaſe, and in general higher. On the whole, the people enjoy the uſual comforts and advantages of ſociety, and appear to be very well contented with their ſituation and circumſtances.

Parish of Polmont.

Corrections by the Rev. William Finlay.

The parish of Polmont is not *interfected*, but bounded, by the Frith of Forth on the north, and by the river Avon on the eaft. A fmall part of it is interfected by a fhort cut from Grangemouth to the Forth, which now forms the only navigable communication betwixt that and the Great Canal.— The *ironftone* is fold by the proprietors of land to the Carron Company, not at *tenpence per ftone*, but at tenpence per *ton*.— The annual amount of funds for the relief of the poor is not *twenty-eight* pounds, but about *fifty-five*, and the expenditure about fifty-two.—By an interlocutor of the Tiend Court, June 1793, the ftipend of this parifh is ordained to be 111 bolls, 2 firlots, 1 peck, 2 lippies bear, 56 bolls of meal, and L.152 : 10 : 10 Scots money, with L.60 money forefaid for furnifhing the communion elements.—The real rent of the parifh amounts to about L.4000 fterling per annum.

The following corrections and additions to the Statiftical Account of the parifh of Polmont **are** *here inferted, at the requeft of the Rev. Mr William Finlay:*

The parifh of Polmont is not *interfected*, but bounded by *the frith of Forth*, on the north, and by the river *Avon* on the eaft. A fmall part of it is interfected by a *fhort cut* from Grangemouth, which is now the only navigable communication betwixt the great canal and the Forth. The iron ftone is fold by the proprietors of land to the Carron Company, not at *tenpence per ftone*, but at *tenpence per ton*. The annual amount of the funds for relief of the poor is not L. 28, but about L. 55, and the expenditure nearly the fame. By an interlocutor of the *Teind Court*, June 1793, the ftipend of this parifh is ordained to be 111 bolls, 2 firlots, 1 peck, and 2 lippies of bear, 56 bolls of meal, and L. 152 : 10 : 10 Scots money, with L. 60 money forefaid for furnifhing the communion-elements. The real rent of the parifh is about L. 4000 Sterling *per annum*.

PARISH OF St. NINIANS.

(COUNTY OF STIRLING.)

By the Rev. Mr SHERIFF.

———————

Name.

THE ancient name of this parish was Eggles The appellation is derived from the eminence of the place of worship, *ecclesia*, by which the parish was distinguished. The modern name, both of the parish and of its principal village, St. Ninians, is derived from St. Ninian, whose history is not certainly known. The following conjecture is, however, sufficiently probable to give some gratification to the curious. According to Buchanan *, Dongardus succeeded to the kingdom of Scotland in the year 452 About this period, the Scottish ecclesiastics were infected with the Pelagian heresy. Palladius was employed by Celestine to oppose the Pelagians : and Ninianus is mentioned among his disciples, as highly distinguished, both by the extent of his learning and the sanctity of his life. The character of those

* Book 5th.

thofe times gives fufficient reafon to believe, that Ninian was afterwards canonized : and as no other faint of that name occurs in our hiftory, it is not unreafonable to conclude, that St. Ninian's Row in Edinburgh, St. Ninian's Well in this place, as well as this parifh and village, received their appellations in honour of this pious reformer.

It is not neceffary to fuppofe that the parifh adopted the name of the faint immediately after his death, or even immediately after his canonization. In our own times, new buildings have affumed the names of ancient faints; whilft a charter, belonging to the abbacy of Cambufkenneth, furnifhes a reafon for limiting the prefent name of the parifh to the latter years of the papal fupremacy in Scotland.

The names of the other villages are generally of Englifh extraction. To this clafs, belong Newmarket, Miltown, Charterfhall, Clayhills, Newhoufe, and Bannockburn. Powmilne and Polmaife appear to be derived from *pou*, a provincial word, fignifying a watery place. From the Gaelic we muft learn the meaning of fuch names as thefe : Touch, Touch-adam, Touch-gorm, Auchenbowie, and Auchenlilly, Linfpout.

Situation.—The parifh belongs to the fynod of Perth and Stirling, and to the prefbytery of Stirling. It is bounded on the eaft by the parifh of Airth; on the fouth, by Larbart, Dunipace, and Kilfyth; on the weft, by Fintry and Gargunnock; the river Forth, if the fmall fpace occupied by the parifh of Stirling be excepted, feparates it on the north from Kincardine, Lecropt, Logie, and Alloa.

Extent.—The road between Powbridge, the eaftern extremity of the parifh, and Randyford, the weftern extremity, meafures between 15 and 16 miles : but as the figure of the
parifh

parifh is irregular, its extent may be computed, at a medium, about 10 miles from eaft to weft, and about 6 miles from north to fouth.

The appearance of the Parifh ancient and modern.—The parifh is naturally divided into three regions. The moft northerly divifion is called the Carfes. The carfes are flat lands lying along the banks of the Forth, from the eaft to the weft end of the parifh : thefe lands, in a plain but a little raifed above the level of the Forth, extend fouthward from one to two or three miles.

The dryfield lands form the middle divifion. Thefe rife fuddenly and confiderably above the level of the carfes, and occupy by much the moft extenfive part of the parifh. The muirlands form the higheft region and the moft foutherly divifion. They rife confiderably above the level of the dryfield grounds, and occupy, it is fuppofed, fomewhat more than a fourth part of the whole extent of the parifh.

It is highly probable, that not only a great part of the dryfield lands, but that a great part of the muirlands alfo was originally covered with wood. The royal foreft of Dundaff muft have covered the high lands, which are ftill called by the name of the lands of Dundaff. The royal foreft of Stirling muft have covered the rifing grounds to the fouth of that town. An extenfive mofs renders it probable, that even the low lands of the parifh, efpecially to the north eaft, were once covered with trees. There can be no doubt, that at an early period, the Torwood occupied much of the lands of the parifh to the eaft and to the fouth eaft.

The limits of the carfe and dryfield lands, ftill affume the general appearance of the banks of a river, and give plaufibility to an opinion, that the carfe lands were originally covered

by

by the water of the Forth. But be this as it may, the hiftory of the battle of Bannockburn, gives fufficient evidence
that the carfes, in the Reign of King Robert Bruce, formed
an almoft impaffible moraf.

It is by no means probable, that the exertions of art were
much employed in improving the original appearance of the
parifh. We have few monuments of antiquity, except the
Roman caufeway which enters the parifh at the Torwood,
and paffes through it in a north-wefterly direction.

The ruins found in the Muirland, near the fource of the
Carron, fhould, with fome others in the parifh, have been
paffed over in filence, were they not generally fuppofed to be
the remains of a caftle, the refidence of Sir John the Graham,
who fell in the battle of Falkirk, defending the liberty of his
country, againft the ambition of Edward.

Prefent Appearance.—The prefent appearance of the parifh
is very different from its former ftate; the face of the country
is naturally beautiful, and the natural beauty of the hills and
vallies is increafed by the windings of the Forth, by innumerable inclofures, by many young thriving plantations, by
a variety of villages, and by feveral genteel houfes, appearing
in different parts of the parifh.

The carfes are now efteemed as valuable as any land in
North-Britain. They have already attained the higheft degree of modern cultivation; and generally produce luxuriant
crops of wheat, barley, oats, peas, beans, flax, and artificial
graffes.

The dry fields are in general arable, and have likewife reached a confiderable degree of cultivation. They produce the
fame crops with the carfes; though the produce of the latter
be generally fuperior to the produce of the former, both in
quantity and quality.

The

The muirlands are in general moſt profitably employed in rearing black cattle and ſheep; though in many places they are arable, and might on every farm ſupply the quantity of corn conſumed by the feuars and tenants.

Agriculture in the Carſes.—*Rotation of Crops.*—A farm is divided into ſix parts. The firſt part is laid down in fallow, the ſecond part in wheat, the third in beans, the fourth in barley, the fifth in graſs, the ſixth in oats. The rotation on each of theſe ſix parts is the ſame, viz. fallow, wheat, beans, barley, graſs, oats. The only difference conſiſts in the crop with which the rotation begins. The firſt part begins with fallow, &c. according to the preſent condition of the land.

Tillage.——The fallow whilſt preparing for a crop of wheat, is ploughed ſix times, if the weather be favourable; the fields for beans or oats once, for barley thrice or four times; graſſes are uſually ſown with the barley.

Manure.——Eight chalders of lime are allowed to an acre. The lime is thrown on the fallow after the fifth plowing, and immediately before the ſixth plowing, when the wheat is ſown. Dung is laid on the ground that is preparing for barley; ſeventy carts are allowed to an acre. No other manure, for the moſt part, is employed during one rotation of ſix years.

Seed and Produce.—Two firlots of wheat ſown on an acre, return from eight to ten bolls. Three firlots of barley ſown on an acre, return ſeven bolls. One boll or five firlots of oats ſown on an acre, return ſix or ſeven bolls. Five or ſix firlots of beans ſown on an acre, return ſeven or eight bolls. Two firlots of rye graſs, with ſix or eight pounds of clover

ſown

ſown on an acre, uſually return about 200 ſtones of hay. The carſe farmers uſually confine themſelves to one crop of graſs.

Seed-time, &c.——Beans are ſown about the beginning of March; oats about the latter end of March; barley about the latter end of April; wheat ſome time before or about the firſt of November.

Harveſt uſually begins about the middle of Auguſt, and ends about the laſt of September.

The cultivation of the dryfield lands is ſomewhat different from the cultivation of the carſes. The ſucceſſion of crops in the dryfield is commonly in the following order: Oats two years, barley one year, graſs one year, paſture two years. Where the ground is very good, peas and beans inſtead of oats are ſometimes ſown in the ſecond year of the rotation.

Land preparing for oats, peas or beans, is ploughed once. Ground for barley twice. Graſſes are uſually ſown with the barley.

Lime is laid on the dryfield lands in the month of Auguſt, immediately after the graſs crop is cut. It is not ploughed down. Seven chalders are allowed to an acre. Dung is laid on the ground, preparing for barley; ſixty carts drawn by one horſe, are allowed to an acre. When beans and peas are ſown, the dung is laid upon the ground preparing for them. Neither more nor other manure is almoſt ever uſed during one rotation of ſix years. There is marle in the pariſh, but the uſe of it has of late been almoſt entirely diſcontinued.

Five firlots of oats ſown on an acre, return ſeven bolls. Three firlots of barley ſown on an acre, return ſeven bolls. Five firlots of peas and beans ſown on an acre, return ſix or ſeven bolls. Half a boll of rye-graſs ſeed, and eight pounds

of

of red, and four pounds of white clover feed fown on an acre, return 200 ftones of hay.

Oats are fown about the middle of March. Barley about the beginning of May. Beans about the firft of March.

Oats and beans are reaped about the middle of September. Barley about the latter end of Auguft.

When wheat is fown on the dryfield lands, which is not generally done, the preparation, excepting two plowings, is the fame as in the carfes.

The carfe land is too wet during winter, for the profitable cultivation of turnips; they are fometimes fown on the dry-fields.

A few potatoes are planted by almoft every farmer, whether in the carfes or in the dryfields. Three bolls planted on an acre return about fixty bolls. A little flax alfo is generally fown after potatoes. Twelve pecks of lintfeed fown on an acre, return thirty fix ftones of lint from the mill. Different kinds of ploughs are ufed. The price alfo varies from 12s. to L. 2 : 12s : 6d. Two horfes are ufually put to a plough; and are fufficient to cultivate a farm of thirty acres.

It need hardly be added, that thefe ftatements have been made at an average, and muft frequently and confiderably vary according to the circumftances of particular feafons, and of different farmers.

Roads.—Seven miles of the great turnpike road from Edinburgh to Stirling, five or fix miles of the turnpike road from Stirling to Glafgow, about twelve miles of the road from Dunbarton to the ferry near Alloa, lie in this parifh. All our roads and bridges are kept in excellent repair by the attention of the country gentlemen. The expences are defrayed by the produce of the tolls, or of the ftatute labour.

About

About twelve years ago, an act of parliament was obtained for the better regulation of the ſtatute work in the county of Stirling. By that act, inſtead of ſtatute labour, leave is given to aſſeſs the land in 18s ſter. for every L. 100 Scots of the valued rent.

Rivers.—The water of Endrick, famous for its trouts, riſes in our muirlands; and after running weſtward through the pariſhes of Fintry, Balfron, Killearn, Drymen, and Buchanan, empties itſelf into Loch Lomond.

Bannockburn (ſo called, *(Majoris Hiſtoria)* becauſe on it was made the meal of the bannocks, or panis cineritius of the Romans; cakes toaſted under the aſhes were called bannocks), receives its water partly from Loch Coulter, and partly from the high lands in the north weſt part of the pariſh. It takes its courſe towards the north eaſt, and falls into the Forth within the bounds of the pariſh. This ſmall river might be employed to great advantage by the manufacturer or artiſan.

The Carron runs along the ſouthern boundary of the pariſh for five miles and an half. The Poems of Oſſian have marked the banks of this river as the ſcene of battle between the Romans and the independent clans of the north.

It has been thought, though it cannot be certainly determined, that the Earl's burn, the Earl's hill, a hill and a rivulet in the muirland part of the pariſh, derived their names from the reſidence of ſome feudal baron or earl in the neighbourhood of the Carron. It is natural to ſuppoſe, that Gillies hill, another hill in the muirland part of the pariſh, derives its name from the name Gill or Gillies. The names both of Gillies and Morifon occur in the muirlands. It is certain, that the fair lady, mother of Gill Morice, " lived on the Carron ſide." This union of facts and probabilities ſuggeſts to the imagination, though it cannot perſuade the judgement

that

that this parifh was the fcene of the tragical fong, known by the name of Gill Morice. The Carron was once diftinguifhed by a cafcade called Auchintillilin's fpout. It is now diftinguifhed by a very extenfive iron manufactory in the parifh of Larbert.

The Forth is the only great river with which we are concerned. It forms the boundary of the parifh on the north. The length of the river from Gargunnock where it meets, to Kerfey where it leaves this parifh, is more than fixteen miles, though the diftance betwixt thefe places does not in a ftraight line exceed half that extent. The windings of the Forth have been remarked and admired by every traveller of tafte; but whilft they beautify the country, they render the navigation of the river peculiarly tedious. A minute defcription of the Forth feems altogether unneceffary, as the Forth or ancient Bodotria is fufficiently known to every ftudent of Britifh hiftory.

Loch Coulter, the only confiderable loch in the parifh, extends about two miles in circumference. It abounds with perches and eels, and lies in the muirland part of the parifh. It is currently reported, on the evidence of witneffes ftill alive, that about twenty-four years ago, by fome convulfion of nature, a ftone weighing nearly a ton was thrown from its bed in the loch to the diftance of fome yards to the northward.

The Carron frequently overflows a confiderable tract of meadow and fome arable land on its banks. Some of the low lying lands on the banks of the Forth are fubjected to the overflowings of the river. A confiderable farm called Bollfor-nought, probably from its being gained from the Forth, is particularly fubject to this inconvenience. The wall with which it is furrounded has fometimes been broken down by the weight of the water, and the greater part of the land overflowed.

It

It may be proper in this place to obferve, that feveral years ago, a remarkable *water fpout* emptied itfelf, partly on the lands of Touch, and partly on the lands of Touch-adam. The water which fell on the lands of Touch, carried off fome cattle, feveral houfes with their furniture. A few of the inhabitants were drowned. The water which fell on the lands of Touch adam, directed its courfe towards the village of St. Ninians and carried off a bridge and two houfes, together with a great quantity of earth from the minifter's glebe and fome other places.

No other remarkable phenomena of this kind are talked off, excepting two fhocks of an earthquake, which in one night, about thirty years ago, were very generally felt in the parifh and neighbourhood.

There are feveral mineral fprings in the parifh; but they are not at prefent much frequented.

We have feveral merchants who retail the articles of ordinary confumption.

We have no great manufactories. Four tanneries employ about 20 hands. Four mafters employ about 113 hands in making nails. One hand works from 1000 to 1200 nails per day.

The moft confiderable manufacture is carried on at Bannockburn. Of late cotton-cloth, and for a long time, all the tartan ufed by the army, has been manufactured at this village.

There are three coal works in the parifh; one at Auchenbowie, one at Pleanmuir, one at Bannockburn. Thefe works taken together, raife about 600 tons of coal per week. They fupply the adjacent country, efpecially to the weft and north, to a very confiderable extent.

The parifh abounds with lime-ftone. At prefent, however, it is not wrought to any confiderable extent, except at Craig-

cnd

end and Murray's hall. At Murray's-hall, from 12 to 13 chalders of lime are wrought by about 17 hands. The burning feafon begins about April, and ends about Martinmas. The lime is wrought under ground, in the fame manner as coal. The feam of lime is from 5 feet 6, to five feet 8 or 10 inches thick. At Craig-end, 16 men and 2 horfes are employed in working yearly about 2000 chalders of lime. The feam at this work, is about 5 feet 8 inches. By a chalder is meant 6 bolls peafe meafure. A chalder of fhells is equal to 18 or 19 bolls of flacked lime. The lime at both thefe works is of the firft quality. An experiment was made at Craig-end; and in 96 bolls of lime, there was found only one boll of fand.

From 50 to 100 hands are ufually employed in malting, and in diftilling aquavitae. There are at leaft 6 diftilleries in the parifh. Some of them at prefent, (November 1794,) are not employed.

Price of Provifions.—Wheat, 21s per boll, Stirling meafure; barley, 19s; oats, 14s; peafe, 17s; beans, 18s; potatoes, 4d per peck; hay, 4d per ftone; beef, 4d½ per lib. mutton, 4d do.; veal, 4d; pork, 3d; a hen, 1s 3d; a duck, 10d; butter, 9d per lib. cheefe, 3d½; milk, per pint Scotch, 2d; eggs, per dozen, 4d; whifky, 1s 6d per pint; ftrong beer, 5d; fmall beer, per gallon Englifh, 4d; coal per ton Dutch, 5s 4d; candle per lib. 6½; cows grafs for fix months, 30s; ftone of fmeared wool, 4s 3d; ftone of white wafhed wool, 7s; falmon from 4d to 1s per lib.

Price of Labour.—A weaver 14d per day; fhoemaker 14d do; ftocking-maker 1s; taylor 10d with victuals; carpenter 9s per week; cart and plough-wright 8s per week; mafon 20d per day; black-fmith 9s per week; tanner 15d per day; maltfter maltſter 12 guineas with victuals, *per annum;* man-ſervant *per annum,* with victuals, L. 9 or 10; nailer 15d per day; wool-comber 15d; maid-ſervant with victuals, L. 4; day-la-bourer 14d; gardener 14d; ſlater 2s 3d per day; cooper per week, with board, 4s; baker, *per annum,* with board, L. 11; ſieve-wright per week, with board, 3s 6d; clock-maker per week, with board, 10s; wheel-wright do, 4s; miner per week, 10s; tanners from 9s to 7s per week.

Rent.——The valued rent of the pariſh certified to the Exchequer in the year 1661, amounted to L. 20,861 Scots. But according to the ſubdiviſion ſtated by the Commiſſioners of Supply, it does not exceed L. 20,710 of the ſame money.

In the year 1775, the miniſter applying for an augmenta-tion of ſtipend, ſtated the real rental of the pariſh at L. 12,663 ſterling. But as it is certain, that the rent of land, of coal, and of lime, has riſen conſiderably ſince that time, the real rental at preſent cannot be computed at leſs than L. 15,000 ſterling.

The landholders amount at preſent to the number of 132; 51 have held their property for 14 years; 36 have ſucceeded as heirs; 45 have purchaſed their eſtates: 25 poſ-ſeſs L. 100 valued rent and upwards; 47 poſſeſs from L. 20 to L. 100 valued rent; 60 poſſeſs from L. 1 to L. 20 valued rent.

Meetings of Landholders.—Theſe proprietors have in the ſchool-houſe a commodious room, where they uſually meet for tranſacting buſineſs. Ten days, ſabbaths not included, pre-vious to a meeting of Landholders, intimation of the time and cauſe of the meeting muſt be made by letter, to ſuch of their number as do not reſide in the pariſh; to ſuch as reſide,

ſimilar

fimilar intimation is given from the precentor's defk, after divine fervice is concluded.

Thefe meetings provide for, and fuperintend the building and repairing of the church, manfe, fchool-houfe, manfe-office-houfes, and the walls of the glebe and church-yard. They have a right to infpect the expenditure of the funds committed to the management of the Kirk Seffion. They have a right to infpect the expenditure of vacant ftipend. They have at prefent the principal management of the provifion made for the poor. They almoft alone nominate to the office of fchoolmafter; and as landholders in the parifh, they have a limited right to vote in the election of minifters, ferving in the church eftablifhed by law. Every caufe is determined by a majority of votes. Records of their tranfactions are kept by their clerk, and appeals may be made to the Court of Seffion, from any decifion fuppofed to be illegal or irregular.

The confiderable eftates, are Touch, Touch-adam, and Polmaife, Sauchie, Bannockburn, Craigforth, Auchenbowie, Stuart-hall, Throfk, Carnock, Grunyards, Plean, and lands belonging to the town and hofpitals of Stirling. Few of the proprietors of thefe eftates refide in the parifh.

Population.——Though the inhabitants of the parifh have been frequently numbered, we are not able by authentic records, to afcertain its ancient population.

In the year 1755, the population returned to Dr Webfter, amounted to 6491. In 1792, it amounted to 7079. It is beyond a doubt, that the population of the parifh is increafing. The decreafe of population by the uniting of farms in the country, is more than compenfated by the increafe of the inhabitants in the villages.

Farmers.——

Farmers.—Some of our farmers have been favoured with a liberal education. A few of them have been inſtructed in the rudiments of the Latin language. Almoſt all of them have been taught writing and arithmetic, as well as to read the Engliſh language with underſtanding and eaſe. Moſt of them from their earlieſt years are inured to manual labour. Nor are the operations of carting, plowing, &c. confined to their earlier years; many of them always, and moſt of them occaſionally, lend their perſonal labour to the cultivation of their grounds.

As our farmers in general do not enjoy the luxuries of affluence, ſo few of them are ſubjected to the miſeries of extreme poverty. Their diet is uſually frugal; but occaſions are not wanting when they enjoy with temperance the comforts of the table. Their mental qualifications are not inferior to their external advantages. This valuable order of ſociety, is in this place diſtinguiſhed by no inconſiderable degree of manly intelligence and general information.

A careful and candid obſerver will not deny, that our farmers are in general frugal, induſtrious, and moderately happy; at the ſame time he muſt acknowledge, that their circumſtances might, in many reſpects, be conſiderably improved. It is not altogether without reaſon, that they complain of the ſmall extent and of the high rents of their farms. Their dwelling houſes, with a few exceptions, are confeſſedly incommodious. Though the veſtiges of their original ſlavery be gradually wearing away, they are not as yet completely effaced. In ſome baronies, the farmers work the hay, and in others, they cart the coals of the landholders. Thirlage is an obvious grievance. Thirlage is a low kind of monopoly by which the tenant is obliged to make all, or ſome part of his meal, at one ſpecified mill. The conſequences of thirlage are ſimilar to the conſequences

of

of all other monopolies : Fraud, extortion, infolence, and inferior workmanfhip. If thefe crimes be feldom committed, the caufe muft be fought in the miller, not in the nature of the monopoly.

Manufacturers and others.—The education and manners of our manufacturers fo nearly refemble the education and manners of our farmers, that a defcription of the latter in a great meafure fuperfedes the neceffity of defcribing the former. Though diftinguifhed by fome peculiarities infeparable from their profeffions, our manufacturers poffefs a degree of enlargement of mind, which reflects confiderable honour on the order.

This happy effect muft chiefly be afcribed to the general caufes which are every where diffufing an ennobling light through the mafs of mankind. In this place, however, fome other caufes contribute a fubordinate influence to enlighten the minds of our people. The abfence of great manufactories, by obliging the individual to tranfact bufinefs for himfelf, prevents the degradation of mind which invariably follows a minute fubdivifion of labour. Many of our manufacturers, as well as of our farmers, are admitted to the office of an elder in the different congregations connected with the parifh. The duties and privileges of the office, tend not only to enlarge the minds of the elders, but enable them alfo in their intercourfe with others, to extend the fphere of general information. Add to this, that the public bufinefs, in moft of our congregations, is conducted on a very liberal plan. The great body of the congregation is frequently affembled and confulted, and the habit of thinking acquires additional ftrength from the opinions which, on thefe occafions, are openly propofed and difcuffed.

But

But be the caufes what they will, the fact is undeniable, that a confiderable degree of intelligence is poſſeſſed by the great body of the people.

Poor.—The poor are well fupported. The number of villages, the vicinity of the coal and lime-works, the eafe with which feuars build houfes, and the low rent at which they can afford to let them, have induced many indigent people to take up their refidence in this parifh. After many attempts to ameliorate the condition of the poor had been made and abandoned by the Heritors and Kirk Seſſion, the prefent fcheme was in the year 1774, adopted by the county of Stirling. The poor live in their own houfes, and receive a monthly penfion, according to their circumftances. A committee of refiding heritors, the minifter, fome elders, and other parifhioners, meet on the firft Thurfday of every month, and fuperintend the payments made to the poor, according to a roll made up by the committee at a private meeting.

The funds are raifed from,

1. An aſſeſſment on the land at a certain rate, per cent. the one half payable by the proprietors, the other by the tenants, according to their refpective valued rents. This rate is fixed at a general meeting, held annually for the purpofe. The rate has never been below 12s per L. 100 valued rent, nor above 16s, except in 1783, when it rofe to 18s.

2. A voluntary contribution from the inhabitants of the villages.

3. The balance of the Seſſion funds, after paying the ufual accounts.

4. The produce of the deceafed penfioners effects, fold by public auction.

5. The

5. The weekly collection at the parish church.

6. Dues from the mortcloths.

The number of pensioners varies every month. The following Table contains the number of pensioners, and the sums expended for 15 years.

			£.	s.	d.
A. D. 1776 -	99 pensioners,		165	11	4
—77 -	104	- -	201	12	1½
—78 -	105	- -	201	18	6½
—79 -	99	- -	197	16	3
—80 -	109	- -	202	6	8½
—81 -	117	- -	197	18	10
—82 -	111	- -	214	6	6
—83 -	119	- -	237	13	3
—84 -	127	- -	256	8	9
—85 -	106	- -	206	19	5
—86 -	111	- -	210	10	7½
—87 -	110	- -	218	8	3¼
—88 -	110	- -	217	13	4¼
—89 -	112	- -	222	4	11
—90 -	101	- -	210	10	11

About two years ago, the Seffion received about L. 1000 fterling, by a will : On a day fixed by the will of the Donor, the intereft of this fum is divided amongft the pooreft inhabitants of the village of St. Ninians.

Ecclefiaftical Eftate.—It appears from the regifters, that from the year 1655, to the year 1732, the office of minifter of the Gofpel in this parifh, was fuccefsively held by Mefsrs George Bennet, William Fogo, James Fullerton, James Forfyth, William Couper, John Logan, Archibald Gibfon.

Mr

Mr James Mackie, was admitted March 1734. This ſettlement was promoted by the Heritors, in oppoſition to a great
proportion of the inhabitants of the pariſh. During this incumbency, about one half, it is reported, of the inhabitants of
the pariſh, left the Eſtabliſhed Church, and joined the Secef-
ſion.

Mr John Gibſon with conſent of all parties, was admitted
May 1754, and till his tranſlation to Edinburgh, 1765, the
pariſh continued almoſt in the ſame ſtate in which he found
it.

The next ſettlement was oppoſed by almoſt the whole pariſh. In June, however, 1773, the eighth year of a proceſs
before the General Aſſembly, the patron prevailed, and Mr
David Thomſon was admitted miniſter. The Eſtabliſhment
was then abandoned by the great body of its adherents. Theſe,
with a few others from neighbouring pariſhes, joined themſelves to the Communion of the Preſbytery of Relief. A
large houſe was erected; a miniſter called and ordained;
and a ſtipend was fixed at L. 100 *per annum.* This ſtipend is
principally raiſed from the produce of the ſeat-rents.

Previous to Mr Thomſon's death in 1787, his hearers were
indulged with the choice of the aſſiſtant preacher. From this
period, the adherents of the Eſtabliſhment were gradually
augmented. In the year 1788, they reſolved from voluntary
contributions, to purchaſe the right of Patronage; though
the price amounted to a ſum, between L. 600 and L. 700 ſter.
the reſolution was ſoon carried into effect, and a young man,
who was appointed to preach in the church during the vacancy occaſioned by Mr Thomſon's death, was admitted miniſter in October 1788.

The right of preſentation is now lodged with a committee
of 9. The committee conſiſts of 3 elders, 3 heritors, and
3 heads of families. The members of this committee, are

choſen

chofen by the people, and hold their places for life, if they continue in full communion with the Eftablifhment. The committee is obliged to prefent in due time and according to the rules of the church whatever candidate is recommended to them by a majority of votes. Every head of a family in full communion with the Eftablifhment, has a right to vote in the election of a minifter.

In 1746, The church, which the Highland army had converted into a magazine, was blown up; but whether by defign or accident, is not known; feveral lives were loft by the explofion. It is remarkable enough, that the fteeple remained entire. It ftands at a confiderable diftance from the prefent church, and never fails to excite the traveller's furprize at fuch an unufual disjunction.

The New Church was built foon after the deftruction of the other. It is 75 by 53 feet within the walls, and at prefent in complete repair.

About 5 miles fouth-weft of the church, there is another place of worfhip. The heritors of the muirland part of the parifh erected this chapel, and the minifter or his affiftant, ufually preaches there on the firft fabbath of every month.

The ftipend was fettled as follows, by a decreet of modification and locality, of date February 1785. " The Lords of " Council and Seffion, modified, difcerned, and ordained, " and hereby modify, difcern, and ordain the conftant fti- " pend and provifion of the kirk and parifh of St. Ninian's, " to have been for the crop and year of God 1776, and " yearly fince fyne, and in all time coming, 4 chalders meal, " 2 chalders bear, and L. 1000 Scots money for ftipend, " with L. 90 money forefaid for furnifhing the Communion " Elements; but have difcerned, and hereby declare, 600 " merks of the faid ftipend fhall be paid by the purfuer, to " an affiftant preacher or helper in the faid parifh, ay and " until

" until a new erection fhall take place. And on fuch events
" happening, the faid 600 merks fhall go to the minifter of
" the faid new erection, as a part of his ftipend; which
" modified ftipend, and modification, for the Communion
" Elements, the faid Lords difcern, and ordain, to be paid
" yearly, locally, to the faid purfuer and his fuccessors in
" office, minifters ferving the cure of the faid parifh, con-
" form to the divifion, and locallity following." The meal
and bear according to the decreet, muft be given in before
Candlemafs, and the money muft be paid, one half at Whitfunday, and the other half at Martinmafs.

The fchool-mafter teaches Latin, Greek, Englifh, book-
keeping, &c. his falary paid by the heritors, is L. 14 : 12.
his other perquifites amount to about L. 20, befides an excellent dwelling-houfe, fchool-houfe, garden, and the ordinary fchool fees.

There are many fmall fchools in different parts of the parifh; together with a Sabbath-evening fchool, in which
the principles of religion are taught gratis, by one of the
elders of the church.

Antiquities.—In early times, that tract of country now called Stirling-fhire, was fituated upon the confines of no lefs
than 4 kingdoms. It had the North Umbrean and Cumbrean
dominions on the fouth, and thofe of the Scots and Picts
upon the north. Probably it belonged fometimes to one,
and fometimes to another; for thefe powers were perpetually
making encroachments on each other. Such a fituation,
puts it beyond a doubt, that St. Ninians muft have been the
field of contention, not only between parties and tribes, but
likewife between nations. An attempt however, to perpetuate the memory of thefe contentions, were equally vain and
fruitlefs. The wifdom of hiftory has configned them to de-
ferved

ferved oblivion ; and to recover them by means of tradition, were only to augument the already too numerous monuments of the weaknefs and folly and crimes of mankind. Their magnitude and confequences, have perpetuated the memory of 3 battles, which the ftatiftical reader will expect in the parifh of St. Ninians.

The battle of Stirling, was fought on the 13th September 1297. The Scots were commanded by Wallace ; the Englifh by Hugh Creffingham, and John Earl of Surry and Suffex. The defeat of the Englifh, effected near Corn-town, on the northern banks of the Forth, was completed at the Torwood. The boundaries of the Torwood are much contracted, and that part of it which lay in this parifh, is almoft entirely removed.

The battle of Bannockburn, was fought in this parifh, on Monday, the 24th June, 1314. The Englifh Reader may find an account of this battle, in any Britifh Hiftorian. The Antiquarian will not be difpleafed with the following authentic defcription of Bafton.

Bafton, a Carmelite friar, and prior of a monaftery in Scarborough, was reckoned one of the beft poets of his age. Edward brought him with the Englifh army to Scotland, that he might witnefs and celebrate the victory, which that monarch expected to obtain. The poet was taken prifoner, but obtained his liberty, on condition of compofing a poem in honour of the victorious Scots. Independently of the tranfaction which it records, the poem itfelf is not the leaft of our curiofities *.

There

---

* *Baftoni metra de illuftri Bello de Bannockburn.*

De planctu cudo metrum, cum carmine nudo.
Rifum retrudo, dum tali themate ludo.
Rector cœleftis, adhibens folamina mœftis,
Verax eft teftis : que profpera ferre poteft his.

Quos

There are several vestiges of this battle in the parish. In a garden at New-house, two large stones still standing, were erected

Quos vincit restis, pro sindoni sordida vestis,
Ploro sub his gestis, perimit quos torrida pestis.
Bella parata fleo, lamentans sub canapeo,
Subque rege reo, nescio, teste Deo.
Est regnum duplex, et utrumque cupit dominari,
Sed neutrum supplex vult a reliquo superari.
Dum se sic jactaut, cum Bacco nocte jocando
Scotia, te mactant, verbis vanis reprobando ;
Dormitant, stertunt, quos irrita somnia mutant,
Fortes te putant, patriæ confinia vertunt.
Explicat exercitus splendentia signa per arva,
Jam sunt dispersi, nimis est virtus sua parva.
Fulminat ad bella præco, clamans dira novella,
Fellea sicut mella, tanta durante procella.
Nunc armatorum disponunt gesta virorum,
Ne gens Anglorum vires enervet eorum.
Tu fer vexillum, quo Scoti terrificentur,
Agmina post illum, belli pro more sequentur ;
Arcetenens arcus tendas, nec sis modo parcus,
Illic transmittas hostes perimendo sagittas ;
Istac tu tela vibris quasi fulgor, anhela,
Non te pro tela, mortem feriendo revila.
Obviet hic illis cum fundis atque lapillis,
Pandens visana, faciendo concava plana.
Et loca tu siste, tendantur ut arte balistæ,
Examen triste populus denunciet iste.
Hastæ tolluntur, patriæ satrapes rapiuntur,
Sic disponuntur, quod multi multa loquuntur.
Format et informat Rex Scotus prælia dira.
Sunt equites pedites ; O quam congressio mira !
Clamat ; Rex animat Scotorum nobiliores,
Citat, et invitat ad bella viros potiores :
Cernit discernit acies pro morte paratas,
Tales mortales gentis confert superatas.

erected in memory of the battle fought on the evening before
the battle of Bannockburn, between Randolph and Clifford.
The

Fatur, folatur turbas populi venientes.
Rifit, derifit Anglorum fœdera gentis,
Fortis dux mortis digitos ad bella docebat,
Cervis protervis, nulla differre jubebat.
Lætus fit coitus, fcitis rumoribus iftis,
Stabit, pugnabit, fic fiet Anglia triftis.
Rex fortes tenet, et cunctis dat fua jura,
Quos armis munit, prædicens bella futura.
Imbre fagittali minuatur ab inguine fanguis,
Turbine lethali ftimulet jaculator, ut anguis
Hafta teres fodiat proceris fpargendo cruorem,
Miffilibus cum pericibus renovando dolorem.
Timba fecuri pectora cruri fcindere curet,
Tela vibrabit, fic fuperabit, fi bene duret.
Mucro latet, nil poffe patet, pro marte valere,
Sors præterit quibus omen erat fupplenda, replere
Machina plena malis pedibus formatur equinis,
Concavas cum palis, ne pergant abfque ruinis.
Plebs foveas fodit, ut per eas labantur equeftres,
Et pereant fi quos videant tranfire pedeftres.
Advena turba vocatur, Scotica gens muniatur,
Prima phalanx fociatur, regia vis comitatur.
Scandere nullus eorum terga valebit equorum,
Fient fic aliorum plures domini dominorum,
Exploratores mittunt hinc inde petentes,
Multos rumores funt inter fe referentes.
Dira dies folis pandit primordia molis
Angligenæ prolis, hinc exit, ab ore fuo lis.
Arrida terra gerit Strivelini prælia prima,
Splendida turba ferit, fed tandem tendit ad ima.
Eft dolor immenfus, augente dolore dolorem ;
Eft furor accenfus, ftimulante furore furorem ;
Eft clamor crefcens, feriente priore priorem ;
Eft valor arefcens, fruftrante valore valorem ;

The place has lately received the name of Randolph-field.
On Brocks-brae, the Bore-ftone, from a hole in its center,

is

Eft calor ardefcens, urente calore calorem ;
Eft gens demefcens, reprobante minore minorem.
Eft ftupor auditus, geminante ftupore ftuporem ;
Eft populus tritus, perdente timore timorem.
Surgit rugitus, fundente cruore cruorem ;
Nunc timor eft fcitus metuente timore timorem.
Atra dies lunæ peftem renovat nocituram,
Quam vi fortunæ facit Anglis Scotia duram.
Anglicolæ, qui cœlicolæ, fplendore nitefcunt
Magnanimi, tanquam minimi, fub nocte quiefcunt.
Expectat, fpectat, gens Anglica quos nece plectat,
Admotos Scotos, ab iis non longe remotos.
Plebs plangit, clangit ; fed quam congreffio tangit.
Nec plangit, frangit vires quas ictibus angit.
Magnifici medici Scotorum funt inimici ;
Munifici medici potuit victoria dici ;
Infultus ftultus prætenuitur ordine cultus ;
Singultus multus erumpit ab aggere vultus,
Defcendens, frendens pedibus, gens Scotica tendens,
Defendens, vendens fua prodit dira rependens.
Hic rapit, hic capit, hic terit, hic ferit ; ecce dolores !
Vox tonat, æs fonat, hic ruit ; hic luit arcta modo res.
Hic fecat, hic necat, hic docet, hic nocet, ifte fugatur ;
Hic latet, hic patet, hic premit, hic gemit, hic fuperatur ;
Hic fremit, hic tremit, hic pavit, hic cavit, ifte ligatur ;
Hic legit, hic tegit, hic metit, hic petit, hic fpoliatur ;
Crefcit inedia, corpora, prædia diripiuntur ;
Heu mulieres, miles et hæres inficiuntur.
Clare comes, venerande fomes Glovernicæ cultor,
Heu moriris, fub ftrage peris, fic fit Deus ultor.
Trux Cliffordenfis mucrone retunderis enfis
Ictibus immenfis ruis hoftibus undique denfis.
Miles Marfcallus Willielmus, in agmine fortis
Scotorum callas tibi pandit vulnera mortis.

Audax

is faid to have fupported Bruce's ftandard. Some catthorps, or fharp pointed irons, have been found in Milton-bog. The Park-mill feems to have received its name from the park of wood, mentioned by Barbour in his defcription of the battle. About a mile from the field of battle, a party of Englifh endeavoured to oppofe the victorious army, and left the name of the Bloody Fold to the place where they fell; perhaps Sir Ingram Umfraville gave his name to Ingram's crook.

On the 11th of June, 1488, the field of Stirling, or the battle of Sauchie-burn, was fought on a tract of ground called

Audax Edmunde Maley, probitate virilis,
Tegens hoftiles fuperat feritates abunde.
Belliger infignis Tibitoyt, quafi fervidus ignis,
Enfibus et lignis cadis, inftat mors tua fignis,
Nobilis argent. pugil, inclite dulcis ægidi,
Vix fcieram mentem cum te fuccumbere vidi.
Quid fruar ambage, de tanta quid cano ftrage,
Vix poterat tragedia pandere fchifmata plagæ.
Nomina bellantum mea mens nefcit numerari,
Quot, quæ, vel quantum mors novit ibi violari.
Multi mactantur, multi jaculis terebrantur.
Multi merguntur, multi vivi capiuntur.
Brolis ftringuntur, et munera multa petuntur.
Jam funt ditati per eos et magnificati,
Qui primi ftrati fuerunt, velut apporiati,
Per gyrum finis loca funt vallata rapinis;
Verba repleta minis replicantur, et aucta ruinis,
Necis quid dicam, quam non fevi meto fpicam,
Linquo doli tricam, pacem cœlo juris amicam,
Qui curat plura, fcribendi fit fua cura;
Eft mea mens dura, rudis et vox, ima litura.
Sum Carmelita, Bafton cognomine dictus,
Qui doleo vita, in tali ftrage relictus,
Si quid deliqui, fi quæ recitanda reliqui,
Hæc addant hi qui non funt fermones iniqui.——FORDUN,

led Little Canglour, on the eaſt ſide of a ſmall brook called Sauchie-burn, about two miles ſouth from Stirling, and about one mile from the field of Bannockburn.

Beaton's Mill, the houſe where James III. was put to death, is ſtill ſtanding, and may be ranked amongſt the numerous monuments of that ambition, which often endangered, and in the end, ruined the Royal Family of Stuart.

PARISH of SLAMANNAN, or St. LAURENCE.

(County of Stirling, Synod of Lothian and Tweeddale, Presbytery of Linlithgow.)

By the Rev. Mr. James Macnair.

———————

IN the year 1470, and reign of James II., it is said, that Lord Livingstone obtained a charter, under the great seal, of the lands of Slamannan. His Lordship's successors, the Earls of Linlithgow, and last of Callander, feued out these lands to different persons, the superiority of which continued in that noble family till the year 1715, when they were forfeited, together with the patronage of the church, and became the property of the crown. But whether the foresaid charter contained a grant of all the lands, or only a part, may be uncertain, as the papers of many of the proprietors bear, that their lands were feued from Lord Torphichen. And as these lands are all sucken to one mill, and the rest of the lands

to

to another mill, though they are interfperfed together, it is probable, that Lord Torphichen once had a right to one half of the lands of Slamannan, and the Earl of Callander to the other.

Name.—Though this parifh bears both the names of Slamannan and St. Laurence, yet the firft of thefe is now univerfally ufed. I find the laft only ufed in the old records of feffion, and in the prefentation iffued forth by his majefty, who is patron of the church, where the words are, " the church and parifh of Slamannan, other- " wife St. Laurence ;" from which I am apt to think, that St. Laurence was not the name of the parifh, but only of the church. It was originally a prebend ; and as a great many old places of worfhip were called by the names of particular faints, this might be called by the name of this faint. There is an excellent fpring of water a little to the fouth-eaft of the church, which ftill goes by the name of Laurence Well ; but what the origin of the word Slamannan is, like moft other proper names, is very uncertain, and merely conjectural. Some fay, it derives its origin from the following circumftance. When the Earl of Callander and Linlithgow, to whom it belonged, firft fent up his fervant to plough part of it, (it being formerly a barren moor), he afked his fervant, how it would work; to which he anfwered, it would *flay man and mare*. Others again fuppofe, that from its vicinity to the Caledonian Wood, it had often been the fcene of battle, where many had been flain. And to ftrengthen this opinion, there is, upon the fouth-fide of the church, at a little diftance, a fmall hill, which is called Caftle Hill, where, they fay, anciently ftood a caftle. There are no remains of it now, only the farm-houfe up-

on

on the weſt ſide of it, goes by the ſame name. And a little to the eaſtward of this hill, there is another riſing ground, where there is the veſtige of a trench, and which goes by the name of Killhills, becauſe of the number, it is ſuppoſed, that were killed there. Beſides, there were anciently here, 2 cones of earth, about 50 yards diſtant from one another, which are ſuppoſed to have been raiſed as monuments of peace, like the 2 at Dunipace; the one of them ſtill ſtands, and is evidently artificial; the other was levelled, and the church of St. Laurence built upon it. Theſe circumſtances, and the names of theſe places, together with others at no great diſtance, ſuch as Balcaſtle, Balquhatſtom, &c., give ſome foundation for the ſuppoſition, that there muſt have been many ſlain here; and hence, probably the name Slamannan. Others ſay, that the name is Gaelic, and ſignifies the Blind Man's Valley, there being a valley upon the north ſide of the church from E. to. W., where the river Avon runs. But as in all the old writings, the word is univerſally ſpelt Slamanna, without the laſt *n*, there appears a great ſimilarity in the two laſt ſyllables to the word Dalmeny; and I think it very probable, they may be of the ſame original. Now, Dr. Robertſon, in his account of the pariſh of Dalmeny, ſays, that the word Dalmeny ſignifies black heath; from which I am apt to think, that Slamanna muſt ſignify ſome kind of heath, perhaps brown or grey, or long heath, for the pariſh hath all originally been covered with heath.

Situation and Extent.—This pariſh lies in the ſhire of Stirling, and is the moſt ſoutherly pariſh in it. Nigh the N. W. end of the pariſh, there is a point where the three ſhires of Stirling, Dunbarton and Lanark meet; and at the

the S. W. end, the fhires of Stirling and Lanark meet with the fhire of Linlithgow. It confifts of the old parifh of Slamannan, and a part annexed from the parifh of Falkirk. The original parifh of Slamannan is from 4 to 5 miles in length, and from 2 to 3 in breadth, and lies upon the fouth fide of the water of Avon, which anciently feparated it from the extenfive parifh of Falkirk, which lay upon the north of the Avon ; but about the year 1730, there was a divifion made of the parifh of Falkirk, when the whole parifh of Polmont was taken off it, and alfo a part of it annexed to the parifh of Slamannan. The part annexed to this parifh lies immediately upon the north fide of the river, and is nearly of the fame length with the old parifh, and about one mile broad ; fo that the prefent parifh of Slamannan, including the annexation, will be from 4 to 5 miles in length, and from 3 to 4 in breadth.

River and Lochs.—The river Avon, which runs through this parifh, from W. to E., takes its rife from a loch in the parifh of Cumbernauld, called Fanny Side Loch. It immediately receives a confiderable addition from a fmall rivulet which takes its rife from a mofs in the Eaft Monkland parifh, about 2 miles diftant, and which fome think is more properly the head of the Avon. Certain it is, there is a farm-houfe very near that mofs, where this rivulet comes from, which is called Avon-Head. There are alfo 3 lochs in this parifh ; one in the north fide of the annexation, called the Ellridge Loch, which fupplies a corn mill with water, and falls into the water of Avon ; the other two are upon the S. W. fide of the old parifh, called the little and the great Black Lochs ; the one of which, namely the little Black Loch, runs E., and the other, the great Black Loch, which is
about

about half a mile W. from the other, and lies upon the
boundaries of this and the Eaſt Monkland pariſh, runs
W.   It hath lately been made a reſervoir to the great
canal between the Forth and Clyde, by the run of the
water of Calder, by which it is carried into the Monkland
canal, and from that, by a cut near Glaſgow, conveyed
into the large canal.   There are ſome trouts in the water of Avon, and alſo in the 2 Black Lochs, and ſome
perches and eels ; but none, I believe, in the Ellridge
Loch.

Valuation and Rent.—The valuation of the old pariſh,
in the ceſs-books, is 2349l. 11s. 7d. Scots, and the annual
rent in the year 1771, was eſtimated at 1040l. 5s. Sterling. The valuation of the annexation is 1066l. 13s. 1d.
S.ots, and the annual rent, in the year 1771, was eſtimated at 527l. Sterling.   There are, at preſent, in the
pariſh, 28 reſiding and 25 non-reſiding heritors ; and in
the annexation, 6 reſiding and 13 non-reſiding ; ſo that
the whole number of heritors is 72.   The moſt of the
reſiding heritors farm their own lands, except a few, who
have conſiderable property ; in which caſe, they let part
of it to tenants.   And theſe lands have been in poſſeſſion
of the ſame families for many generations, perhaps ſince
firſt feued out.

Soil.—The arable lands on each ſide of the Avon, for
about half a mile, are of a light free ſoil ; and, if properly prepared, would produce very good crops, almoſt of
any grain. Theſe are interſperſed with haughs and meadows, which are of a rich loamy ſoil. The haughs produce good crops of oats, and the meadows very good
natural graſs, which is made into hay, and is excellent
feeding for black cattle in winter. Some of theſe lands
are

are let at 1l. the acre, but the moft of them at half of that. The foil lying farther off the water for about a mile, is of a ftrong hard clay, and does not produce fo good crops as the lands above defcribed. The rent of thefe lands may be about 7s. 6d. the acre. The foil in the extremity of the parifh is of a very black moffy bottom, and produces bad crops; as the lands lie interfperfed amongft moffes, the crops feldom come to perfection. The farmers make moft by raifing young cattle and by milk, the grafs not being fit for fattening them. The 2 firft kinds of foil defcribed, may be, and fome of it is improved, but the laft not capable of much.

The farms here are generally fmall, few of them being equal to a ploughgate; the moft of them only the half, and fome not fo much. The higheft rent of a ploughgate does not exceed 30l. Sterling. They univerfally make ufe of the old Scotch plough, and generally have the one half of their ground tilled, and the other lying in natural grafs. They let it lie commonly for 3 years, and then plough it for other 3 years. It is generally milch cows they feed upon their ground, with a few young ones to fupply the place of the old ones; but there are few or no fheep, the foil being rather wet and moffy, and therefore not fo favourable for them. Their wives and daughters, together with a fervant, take care of the milk, of which they make a good deal of butter and cheefe, and by which the tenants generally pay the moft of their rent.

Produce.—The foil produces pretty good flax, not very fine in quality, but ftrong and good of its kind, though they feldom raife more of it than is for their own ufe. There is alfo fome bear raifed, but the principal produce is oats. Sometimes they fow grafs feeds with their bear; but

little

little of the ground being encloſed, it is much deſtroyed by the cattle in the winter, when they are allowed to go at large. The want of proper encloſures, with plan‑tations, is a great hindrance to the improvement of the country. Alſo they lie at a good diſtance from lime, but not indeed at ſo great a diſtance, as that the roads are very bad. They are about 6 or 7 miles from the lime-works of Torphichen or Bathgate, and about the ſame diſtance from thoſe of Cumbernauld. Another great obſtacle to the regular improvement of the pariſh is, that a great number of the proprietors occupy their own lands ; and though they and their families live very comfortably and independently upon the produce, yet they cannot ſpare any money to lay out in improve‑ments. However, there are ſome of them who are both planting and encloſing more of their ground, and making their roads a great deal better. They have, eſpecially of late, made a road through a moſs, called Moſs Candle, more than a mile in length, between this and Falkirk, which makes the communication much more eaſy ; and the propoſed road between Edinburgh and Glaſgow, by Bathgate and Airdrie, it is expected, will be of conſi‑derable ſervice to this part of the country.

Population, &c.—According to Dr. Webſter's report, the population in 1755 was 1209. The number of in‑habitants in this pariſh at preſent is 1010 ; of whom there are 466 males, and 544 females : and of theſe there are 263 under 10 years of age ; 255 between 10 and 20 ; 317 between 20 and 50 ; 126 between 50 and 70 ; 37 between 70 and 80 ; and 2 above 80. There are 223 families, including ſingle perſons who keep houſes by themſelves ; 312 married perſons ; 6 bache‑
lors,

lors, or unmarried men; and 20 unmarried women above 40 years of age; there are alfo 17 widowers and 42 widows. The inhabitants of the annexation were always confidered to be nearly equal to one half of the old parifh; at prefent, however, they are a great deal lefs, being only 272, and the old parifh being 738. This is owing chiefly to fome of the farms in the annexation being of late purchafed by Mr. Forbes of Callander, which are lying in grafs, and the houfes uninhabited.— Since April 1788, there have been about 130 births, and 47 marriages. There has been no regular regifter of the deaths kept; but, by comparing the roll of the prefent year with the one taken up in 1788, I find there are about 70 who have died fince that time. Upon an average, therefore, the births each year may be about 32; the marriages 10; and the burials 18.—There are no manufactures carried on in this parifh, nor is there any village in it; the few houfes which are near the church not deferving that name. The moft of the inhabitants are farmers, except a few employed in the other neceffary bufineffes of life; fuch as weavers, tailors, fmiths, &c. But thefe are only employed in thefe branches by the inhabitants of the parifh; and therefore there are only fuch a number of them as are fufficient for the parifh. There are about 4 fmiths, 10 mafons and joiners, 12 weavers, 12 fhoemakers, 3 tailors, 3 millers, and 1 lint-miller, 3 flax-dreffers, 3 public-houfes, and a few coal-hewers. Thefe laft are employed by the Carron Company, and are fometimes more numerous than at other times. There were more than 20 of them about 2 years ago, and at prefent there are not more than 5. There is 1 clergyman and 1 fchool-mafter; but no furgeon nor writer. There are about

15 heads

15 heads of families connected with the Secession, making in all, with their families, about 78 persons, but many of their families attend upon the parish church [*].

Poor.—The average number of poor upon the session roll is about 12. They are supplied by the collections made on Sunday, together with the interest of a small fund of about 150l., without any assessment. They generally get from 2s. to 4s. the month, and one 5s. Sometimes also families, when they are in distress, receive occasional supplies as they need. But none of those who receive from the session are allowed to beg.

Diseases.—The most common disease I have observed since I came to this parish, appears to be the consumption, occasioned not so much by the constitution of the inhabitants, as by the coldness and dampness of the houses. The bad state of the houses often brings on colds upon those that are young and tender, which, if not speedily removed, ends in a consumption. It is not unfrequent also for old people, when confined much to their houses, and unable to take that exercise which is proper for the circulation of the blood, to be troubled with

[*] The wages of an ordinary ploughman are 8l. in the year, and some of them 10l. They have risen very considerably of late. A woman servant 3l. in the year, and as much ground as sows half a peck of lint-feed in the summer half year. A labouring man used to be hired at 6d. a day, and his meat; but now they ask 8d. As there is no market-town in the parish, the price of vivres is always regulated by Falkirk, which is the nearest market-town, and about 5 miles distant.——There is plenty of fuel in the parish, both coal and peat; but peat is most generally used, as every person hath commonly a right to some moss connected with the lands he possesses, or pays only 1s. for as many as he can cast in a day. The Carron Company, who work some pits in the parish, supply the country with all the coal they need, though most of the heritors have coal in their own lands.

with great fwellings in their legs; and not a few have died of the dropfy, which, it is probable, alfo originates from the fame caufe. What ftrengthens this opinion, is, that thefe complaints are more frequent among the lower clafs of the inhabitants, the few families who are in a fuperior ftation, and have comfortable houfes, not being fubject to them. Otherwife the people are generally pretty healthy; and I have obferved fewer fevers here than in the neighbouring parifhes.

Church, Stipend, &c.—The walls of the church were rebuilt about the year 1753; but the old feating was ftill continued, which indeed is very old; many feats being marked with the year 1632, and fome of them even fo far back as the year 1556. It ftands, therefore, in much need of being renewed. When the annexation was joined to this parifh, they were allowed to build an aile, for their own accommodation, upon the N. fide of the church, at their own expenfe, and to uphold it for 20 years; and the heritors of Slamannan were bound to uphold the old church for the fame number of years; after which they were all to bear any expenfe upon the church and church-yard walls, in proportion to their valuations. But as they were otherwife annexed only *quoad facra,* they pay no part of the minifter's ftipend. The King is patron. The ftipend is 50l. Sterling in money, 2 chalders of meal, and 1 chalder of bear, a manfe and glebe of about 15 acres. There is alfo 3l. 6s. 8d. for furnifhing communion elements, together with the intereft of 500 merks, which is in the hands of the feffion. The manfe was built more than 30 years ago, fince which time it hath not only been frequently repaired, but had a confiderable addition made to it.

TOWN AND PARISH OF STIRLING.

(County and Presbytery of Stirling.—Synod of Perth and Stirling.)

By the Rev. Mr. JAMES SOMMERVILLE, *one of the Ministers of that Town.*

Origin of the Name.

THE town and parish of Stirling have the same name. In all records of any antiquity, it is written *Stryveline,* or *Stryveling* ; and it is conjectured to have derived this name from the Scotch word *stryve,* because of the frequent contentions about the possession of it, which arose among the different clans, in the days of ancient feud and barbarism. This, however, is mere conjecture, as all disquisitions about the origin of names generally are. Buchanan and other Latin authors uniformly call it *Sterlinum.* The town's ancient seal has, on one side, a crucifix erected on a bridge, with this inscription, *Hic armis Bruti, Scoti stant hac cruce tuti.* On the reverse is a fortalice, surrounded with trees, with the inscription, *Continet hoc nemus et castrum Strivilense.* The town has another seal, which contains the arms, viz. A Wolf upon a rock, inscribed *Oppidum Sterlini.*

Extent,

Extent, &c.—The pariſh of Stirling is chiefly confined to the town. The whole land in it does not exceed 200 acres. The caſtle, with the conſtabulary, by which is meant a ſmall portion of land, formerly annexed to the office of conſtable, are not reckoned in the pariſh of Stirling. As little are the Royal Domains, or King's park. They are exempted from all parochial aſſeſſment, and are in the pariſh only *quoad ſacra*, and that only ſince the chaplain ceaſed to officiate, or reſide in the caſtle. The landward part of the pariſh lies between the town and the Forth. It extends along the ſouth ſide of the river, from Kildean, about a mile above the bridge of Stirling, to the eaſt of the town, with ſome parks on the the ſouth of it. Theſe lands, on an average, are rented at 50 s. per acre. The ſmall village, called *the Abbey*, which occupies the place where the celebrated Abbacy of Cambuſkenneth once ſtood, and which is ſituated in a northern link of the Forth, eaſt from Stirling, has hitherto, along with the barony of Cambuſkenneth, in which it is ſituated, been reckoned part of the pariſh of Stirling. What gave riſe to this arrangement is not known, unleſs it was, that the ſervants belonging to the Abbacy worſhipped in Stirling ; or that the Canons, Monks or Friars of that monaſtery, performed divine ſervice, in the church of Stirling, and formed a kind of connexion which continued to ſubſiſt after the reformation. One thing is certain, that it has ſubſiſted ; for there is actually a ſeat in the church of Stirling, allotted for the inhabitants of that village ; and it appears, that an elder from it has ſat in the ſeſſion of Stirling, almoſt uniformly ſince the year 1559. The barony of Cambuſkenneth pays a part of the ſtipend of the firſt miniſter of Stirling ; but it is ſubject to poor's rates in the pariſh of Logie, and to the juriſdiction of the ſheriff of Clackmannan. The commiſſary of Stirling alſo exerciſes his juriſdiction over it, as a part of the pariſh of Stirling ; and

the

the commiffary of Dumblane exercifes his jurifdiction, as lying within the parifh of Logie.

Climate and Longevity.—The fituation of Stirling is alfo
reckoned very healthy. The height of the rock, on which
it ftands, above the level of the flat carfe grounds, no doubt
contributes much to this effect. Epidemical difeafes are
fcarcely known. At this very time there are four or five perfons in Stirling above 90. The *Croup, or Cynanche Trachea-
lis* *, feems to be moft fatal to children; the afthma and palfy
to old age.

Burgh of Stirling.—Stirling is allowed to be a place of confiderable antiquity. Buchanan mentions it again and again,
fo early as the 9th century, but gives no defcription of it :
and to throw any light upon this fubject, from the town's
charters, is impoffible. The moft ancient of thefe records is
granted by King Alexander I. and is dated at Kincardine, the
18th of Auguft, in the 12th year of his reign ; whereas there
is reafon to believe, that Stirling had been incorporated long
before, as the charter of Alexander is not a charter of erection,
but only confers fome additional privileges on the burghers
and freemen. Alexander the I. who granted this charter,
afcended the throne anno 1107, and reigned 17 years. It
therefore bears date in 1120. About the middle of the 12th
century, it would appear to have become a place of royal refidence. David I. kept his court at it, probably that he
might be near to the Abbacy of Cambufkenneth, which he
founded anno 1147, and on which he lavifhed many marks
of his favour. He brought the canons of that monaftery from
the

---

* This is a difeafe of the *Glottis, Larynx,* or upper part of the *Trachea,* attended
with hoarfenefs, and a peculiar whizzing found in infpiration, and a fhrill ringing
found in fpeaking and coughing, as if the noife came from a brafen tube. It feldom attacks children before they are weaned, or after 12 years of age.

the neighbourhood of Arras, in the county of Artois. In ancient charters, they fubfcribe themfelves *Abbates de Stryveling*. Alexander Miln, Abbot of that place, was the firft Prefident of the Court of Seffion, inftituted by James V. anno 1532. The Abbacy now belongs to Cowan's Hofpital in Stirling, having been purchafed from the predeceffors of Mr. Erfkine of Aloa, on whom the property of thefe lands was conferred at the reformation. It is probable, that Stirling grew to its prefent fize, very foon after it became the tempo-rary refidence of royalty; and, from the moft accurate attention to its fituation and circumftances, it may be concluded to have undergone very little change, either in fize, or in the number of its inhabitants, for the laft 600 years, till very lately. But to give an account of the antiquities of Stirling, however defirable, would only be to wander into a labyrinth of conjecture. Mr. Nimmo, in his hiftory of Stirlingfhire, has faid all upon this fubject, that can be ftated with any degree of certainty. There is no regular annal, or regifter, refpecting it, previous to the middle of the 15th century; and the only one that reaches back to that period, or near it, is the regifter of fafines, commencing in 1473. The council records commence in 1597.

Situation and Improvements.—The fituation of Stirling is romantic. Raifed on a rock in the middle of an extenfive plain, in the near neighbourhood of a winding river, which feems unwilling to part from it; and, having the full view of finely cultivated fields, bounded on the fouth by rifing woodlands, and on the north by the Ochil hills, it is fcarcely poffible to imagine any landfcape more beautiful or picturefque. Added to its fituation, which is fingularly beautiful, it has of late received many improvements, exceedingly conducive both to the comfort and conveniency of the inhabitants. Water has been brought from a confiderable diftance to fupply the town.

Commodious

Commodious fchool houfes, in airy fituations, and a fpacious market place, have been erected within thefe few years. A noble walk along the fummit of the rock, at the very root of the fouth wall, from the one end of the town to the other, fhaded from the fun by a fhelving thicket of fine thriving trees, has been lately finifhed at a confiderable expence. This walk, which is perhaps the fineft thing of the kind, that any place can boaft of, was begun, anno 1723, by a Mr. Edmonftoun of Cambus-Wallace, and finifhed only in the year 1791, under the patronage of the prefent magiftrates. Much however, as has been done to improve the beauty of Stirling, a great deal ftill remains to be done. The caftle and Gowan Hills, which admit of great improvement, and which could no way hurt the fortrefs, though improved to the utmoft, remain like all other government property, as barren, rugged, and neglected, as if the ftern Genius of the north had faid, *Let them never be touched by the hand of Art or Induftry.*

From an attentive obfervation of the grounds on which Stirling ftands, and from the beft traditional accounts, Stirling feems to have been neither much increafed nor diminifhed, for feveral centuries. The court raifed it to its prefent fize. When that was withdrawn, neceffity ftimulated to induftry and kept it up. It was erected into a royal burgh, probably as far back as the middle of the 9th century. It holds the fifth place in the rank of royal burghs, and was one of the *Curiæ quatuor burgorum,* a court which gave birth to the prefent *Convention of Burghs.* The jealous and contracted fpirit of *incorporation,* ever tenacious of ancient cuftoms, and hoftile to all novelty and invention, nay, expulfive of the enterprifing ftranger, has kept the inhabitants of Stirling trudging on in the routine of their great-great-grandfathers, as it muft ever do thofe of all places, where improvement is not forced, by peculiarly advantageous local circumftances.

Set or Conſtitution of the Burgh.—The town-council conſiſts of 21 members, 14 of whom are merchants, and 7 tradeſmen, viz. a provoſt, 4 bailies, a dean of guild, a treaſurer, 7 merchant counſellors, and 7 deacons of trade. Beſides the ordinary juriſdiction in civil cauſes, which is common to the magiſtrates of all royal boroughs, and to the ſheriffs of counties, the magiſtrates of this town have alſo an extenſive criminal juriſdiction, conferred upon them by their charters, equal to the power of Sheriffs, within their territories. Prior to the year 1781, the old council elected the new one, 11 members at leaſt of the old council being changed yearly. Six of the 7 trades ſent a leet of 4, and the bakers a leet of 8 to the council, who had power to put a negative upon the one half of each leet. Each incorporation choſe one out of the remainder, as their repreſentative in council. The burgh having been disfranchiſed in 1775, by a ſentence of the Houſe of Peers, confirming the decree of the Court of Seſſion, his Majeſty was pleaſed, in 1781, to reſtore it to its privileges of election, by his poll warrant, in which he made the following alterations on the ſet. The guildry company of merchants, annually elect 4 members of the new council. The trades chooſe their 7 repreſentatives, without ſending leets : only the old counſel previouſly declares 4 of the old deacons incapable of being re-elected for the enſuing year. And there are ſtill at leaſt eleven of the old council changed yearly. By the new ſet, as well as the old, the provoſt, bailies, treaſurer and convener, cannot be continued in their offices more than 2 years at a time. The dean of guild being now choſen by the company of merchants, is neceſſarily changed yearly. The trades incorporated by royal charter are, the bakers, weavers, hammermen, ſkinners, butchers, tailors and ſhoemakers. The maltmen, barbers, and other profeſſions, have no repreſentative in council, nor any royal charter, but only acts of erection

tion from the town-council, about the year 1720, or betwixt 1720 and 1730. Each perſon, upon entering, pays 2 l. 2 s. 6 d. to the funds of the burgh, beſides what he pays to thoſe of his own ſociety or incorporation.

Peculiar Law.—There is a remarkable bye-law of this community, made in 1695, which the members of council muſt annually take an oath to obſerve. By it they bind themſelves, to take no leaſe of any part of the public property, under their management, nor to purchaſe any part of it; neither to receive any gratification out of the public funds, under pretence of a reward for their trouble, in going about the affairs of the borough, or of the hoſpitals founded in it. By this bye-law, alſo, *a board of auditors* is elected annually, for inſpecting the public accounts, conſiſting of 2 members choſen by the merchants at large, and 2 choſen in like manner by the ſeven royal incorporations.

Caſtle, &c.—None can tell, when the caſtle was built, any more than the town. Even the bridge, which is doubtleſs a work of much later date, has no memorial of the date of its erection. The whole town ſtands upon a rock, ſtretching from N. E. to S. W.; and, with the caſtle, ſituated on the utmoſt prominence of the rock, towards the north, very much reſembles the ridge on which the high ſtreet and caſtle of Edinburgh are ſituated. Several of the houſes in Stirling, now ſtanding, are doubtleſs of very ancient date. In one, which was lately taken down, on the ſouth ſide of the broad ſtreet, there was a ſtone marked IIII.—*Mar's Work*, a large and aukward edifice, was begun by the Earl of that name, anno 1570, while he was regent of Scotland, but never finiſhed. The tenement, called *Argyll's Lodging*, was built partly in the year 1637, by Alexander, Viſcount of Stirling.

Churches,

Churches, &c.—The weft church and tower were, it is faid, erected in the time of Alexander III, or at leaft not later than the year 1494, when probably James V. caufed it to be built, for the accommodation of fome Francifcan Friars, whom he had brought into this country, and fettled in a convent, almoft contiguous to this church. It has no date upon it, and though of very beautiful architecture, it is now fo much under ground, and fo low roofed, that no reparation can ever render it a comfortable place of worfhip. Indeed, it has been very little employed for that purpofe fince the reformation, unlefs during the few years that Mr. Ebenezer Erfkine preached in it, when the people of Stirling chofe to have a third minifter. The eaft church, the prefent place of worfhip, was erected by Cardinal Beaton, and is a more fplendid and magnificent fabric, but is very little accommodated to the purpofes of Prefbyterian worfhip. It would need to be almoft totally altered and repaired, to render it either elegant or convenient. The abfurd pretence of its area being private property, held on no better fecurity, than the gift or conveyance of the kirk-feffion, (fome of the poffeffors indeed found upon grants from the town-council, for fome trifling confideration) is the great hindrance to this moft neceffary reparation. The area of the churches ought never to be the property of any but the community at large. Common fenfe, as well as religion, dictates that the poor fhould have an opportunity of hearing the gofpel as well as the rich.

Ecclefiaftical Hiftory.—The charge of Stirling was made collegiate in the year 1651. Previous to that period, we find a Mr. Robert Montgomery, a Mr. Patrick Simpfon, and a Mr. Henry Guthrie minifters of Stirling. Montgomery was depofed by the affembly, for a fimoniacal compact with the Duke of Lennox, about the bifhoprick of Glafgow. Mr. Henry Guthrie was afterwards bifhop of Dunkeld, and wrote " Memoirs

"moirs of Scottifh affairs, from 1627 tothe death of Charles I."
It appears from the council records, that this Mr. Guthrie,
after his removal from Stirling, refided at Kilfpindie. There
he probably wrote his memoirs. In 1661, after the death of
James Guthrie, the council fent feveral deputations to invite
him back to his charge in Stirling ; but he declined it, on account
of bad health. Mr. Nimmo mentions another Mr.
Henry Guthrie, who was executed in the beginning of the
reign of Charles II. on account of his activity in oppofing
the meafures of the court. But this certainly was the celebrated
Mr. James, who was beheaded in the year 1661, und
who was minifter of Stirling at that period, along with a Mr.
David Bennet. There are fome of the faid James's books,
with the chair in which he fat, ftill in the manfe of Stirling.
In the council records, a Mr. John Allan is mentioned as prior
to Mr. Bennet *.

Mr. Ebenezer Erfkine was fettled 3d minifter in 1731,
where he continued, till he was depofed by the General Affembly
in 1738. Upon this, Mr. Erfkine, and three of his brethren,

* By act of council 2. February 1663, Mr. Andrew Kynnier, minifter of Eaft
Calder, was called and collated by the bifhop of Edinburgh as minifter, along
with Mr. Matthias Simpfon, who fucceeded Mr. Bennet. In 1665, Mr. James
Forfyth was firft minifter. In 1668, Mr. Patrick Murray was made 2d. minifter,
in the room of Mr. Kynnier who had died in 1664. But from the public confufion
of that period, the vacancy was not fooner fupplied. An act of 22d January
1676, appoints a commiffioner to go to Edinburgh or St. Andrews, to fpeak to the
archbifhop of St. Andrews, and offer to him the perfon whom the council has
chofen to be firft minifter of this burgh ; and to deal with his Grace effectually
thereanent. The minifter's name is not mentioned.

An Act is recorded 9th Auguft 1679, anent fupplying the vacancy of the 1ft
charge, by the death of Dr. William Pearfone.

28th Auguft 1679, Mr. John Munro is prefented by the Council.

On the 10th June 1682, Mr. James Hunter minifter at Denying, is chofen
3d minifter, in room of Mr. Patrick Murray deceafed.

From this period, to the 1694, there is no mention of the minifters of Stirling
in the records. From the 1694, we have Meffrs Robert Rule, John Forrefter,
James Brifbane, Archibald M'Aulay, Charles Muir, and Alexander Hamilton.

thren, Mr. Wilſon of Perth, Mr. Alexander Moncrieff of Abernethy, and Mr. James Fiſher of Kinclaven, ſeceded from the church of Scotland, and ſtiled themſelves *the Aſſociated Brethren*. About the year 1744, ſome ſcruples were ſuggeſt-ed to theſe brethren, then formed into a ſynod, with others who had acceded to them, about the *Burgeſs Oath*, by Mr. Moncrieff, which, in 1748, produced a ſchiſm among them.

At the head of the Aſſociate Synod remained Mr. Ebenezer Erſkine, and at the head of the other party, who called them-ſelves Antiburghers, appeared Mr. Adam Gibb. Mr. Gibb excommunicated Mr. Erſkine and his aſſociates. The excep-tionable clauſe in the burgeſs oath runs thus : " Here I pro-" teſt before God and your Lordſhips, that I profeſs and al-" low with my heart, the true religion preſently profeſſed " within this realm, and authoriſed by the laws thereof ; I " ſhall abide thereat and defend the ſame to my life's end, " renouncing the Roman religion, called Papiſtry."

The Antiburghers decreed, that it was inconſiſtent with the principles of the Seceſſion, to ſwear an attachment to the eſ-tabliſhed religion, after having deſerted it on account of its corruptions. The above burgeſs oath was uſed at Perth. In Stirling, there never was a word about religion in it, until ſome few years ago, the following clauſe was introduced, at the deſire of ſome of the Antiburghers, to ſcreen them from the cenſure of their miniſter and ſeſſion. " I ſwear to be a " a faithful burgeſs to the burgh of Stirling, to obey the ma-" giſtrates thereof, and town officers having their lawful " commands," The additional clauſe follows : " *In matters* " *purely civil, ſo far as agreeable to the word of God.*

Since the depoſition of Mr. Erſkine, the third charge of Stirling has never been filled *. It was allowed to fall into
                                                            diſuſe

---

* From the 1738, Mr. Thomas Turner, Mr. Daniel Macqueen, and Mr. John Muſchet, in the firſt charge. Thomas Cleland, Thomas Randal, Walter

difuse by the prefbytery. Whether the affembly gave their
fanction to this, is uncertain. A manfe was bequeathed to
the minifter of the firft charge, during the laft century, by a
Colonel EDMOND, who was a native of Stirling, and who, after rifing to rank and affluence, as a foldier of fortune, gave
this teftimony of refpect to the place of his nativity. The 2d
minifter has no manfe. They have each of them 110 l. of
ftipend. The ftipend of the 1ft minifter is paid out of the
tiends, and collected by the town, in confequence of an agreement betwixt the minifter and town to that effect. The ftipend of the 2d is paid by the town, from an impoft on the
malt ground at the town mill. The chaplainry of the caftle,
procured through the intereft of the town, is vefted in the
firft minifter only, during life.

Schools.—At the grammar fchool, which has two teachers,
a rector and ufher, 70 boys, on an average, are educated annually. The prefent rector, Dr. Doig, a man of diftinguifhed eminence in his profeffion, is growing up in years, and
declines the trouble of boarders, otherwife the fchool might
be more numerous. At the writing fchool, the number of
fcholars is annually about 100. There are two eftablifhed
Englifh teachers, and a teacher in Allan's hofpital, permitted
by the town, to receive Englifh fcholars, who may have under their care annually, about 200 children. The falary of
the rector is 40 l. yearly, and a houfe. The other teachers
have from 20 l. to 30 l. Sterling annual falary.

Population.—About 40 years ago, it is faid, fcarcely any
houfe was repaired till it fell. Even then, it was often allowed

Walter Buchanan, and James Sommerville in the fecond, have fucceffively filled
the cure of Stirling.

lowed to lie for several years in ruins. Now, houses are rebuilt before they are totally decayed, and within the last 20 years, more houses have been built and repaired, than was done before in the course of half a century. Though more than 30 new houses have been built lately in the town and environs, some will not admit that the population is increased. The inhabitants, it is said, now choose to occupy more room.—That may be the case ; but by the return made to Dr. Webster, in the year 1755, the souls in the parish of Stirling amounted only to 3051 ; whereas, by a pretty accurate survey, made in the year 1790, there were 1188 heads of families, and 4483 souls.—Besides, in this list, there are above 30 families in the environs of the town, not included. As the inrolment of the year 1790 was deemed incomplete, a new one was made this year, (1792,) and the number of souls in the parish was found to be 4698. Since the commencement of the summer 1792, they are probably augmented to 5000, by the increase of hands employed in the Cotton manufactory.

	Ministers	People
Of these 4698, there are belonging to the Established Church,	2	2795
—————— The Burgher Seceffion,	2	1415 *
—————— The Antiburgher ditto,	1	172
—————— Cameronians,	1	120
—————— Epifcopalians, chiefly Nonjurants,	2	89
—————— The Prefbytery of Relief,		74
—————— Bereans, or the difciples of Mr. Barclay,		33
		4698

Of

* *It will not appear furprifing, that there are fo many Burgher Seceders in Stirling, when it is recollected, that the Seceffion was begun in this place, by Mr. Ebenezer Erfkine, who, by his highly popular talents, drew fuch numbers after him. This fpirit, alfo, when once it is introduced, uniformly becomes hereditary. Befides, from the fcantinefs of room in the church, it is certain, that many take feats in that meeting, who are never in ac-*
ꞇua^l

Of the different Professions there are,

€lergymen,	8	Weavers,	-	68
Phyficians,	- 3	Hammermen,	-	13
Surgeons,	- 3	Skinners,	-	2
Writers,	- 18	Butchers,	-	2
Merchants	- 30	Taylors,	-	14
Bakers,	- 12	Shoemakers,	-	18

Lift of Births, Deaths, &c. for three years preceding 1792.

Years	Baptifms*.	Marriages.	Burials.
1788.	82	43	50
1789.	75	51	4
1790.	67	52	68

Manufactures.—As far back as the end of the 16th century, fhalloons, manufactured in Stirling to a confiderable extent, were fent over to the Low Countries. *Bruges* was then the ftaple port for Scotch commodities. The manufacturers miftaking their own intereft, and debafing the quality of their fhalloons, foon loft, however, the advantages of that gainful branch of trade, and the town became miferably poor. Though the manufacture was greatly hurt by fuch conduct, yet it was never entirely dropt. Coarfe fhalloons continued to be manufactured in Stirling ; and at prefent this branch is confiderably revived. For feveral years paft, perhaps not lefs than 200,000 yards of this commodity have been annually manufactured in Stirling, and its neighbourhood. Towards the beginning of this century, and during the decay of the fhalloon manufactory, that of the Tartan ftarted up in its place. It continued to flourifh till about the year 1760, but is now almoft dwindled away. At prefent, the carpet manufacture flourifhes. For feveral years, one company has employed

tual communion *with them. Perhaps, through length of time, neceffity, more than any thing elfe, obliges many to connect themfelves with thofe, with whom, for a long time, they only feemed to affociate*

* The lift of baptifms is by no means complete.

ployed 12 looms in that work, and produced carpets of very fine colour, and the very beſt quality. Another company employs about 8 looms : and this year a third company has begun work, and mean to employ not lefs than 12 looms. There are in all betwixt 30 and 40 looms conſtantly employ‐ ed. The dyers are reckoned eminently ſkilled in their pro‐ feſſion, and the colouring of the Stirling carpets is allowed to be very fine.

The *cotton manufacture* alſo begins to take place here. Three companies from Glaſgow give out cotton yarn to be woven, and one of them have about 40 little girls engaged at the tambour. Another company have this year got jennies ; and though erected only at Whitſunday laſt, are juſt now em‐ ploying 50 looms to ſpin their own yarn. Near 100 perſons, young and old, are already employed by this new company. There may be in all 260 looms employed in weaving coarſe muſlin. Wool ſpinning is likewiſe carried on to a conſider‐ able extent. There are above 100 employed by one maſter in this work, in teaſing, ſcouring, and combing the wool, and making it ready for the wheel.

The river Forth runs ſo level in the neighbourhood of Stir‐ ling, that mills cannot be erected for the purpoſe of manu‐ factures. In every other reſpect, Stirling is favourable for them. Coals are plentiful ; the rents of houſes are low, and wages very moderate *.

Bunks.

* The wages of a maſon per day, are 1 s. 8 d. ; of a labourer from 1 s. to 1 s. 2 d. Wrights get 1 s. 6 d. ; Taylors 1 s. Shoemakers are paid by the piece. A man ſervant gets, per annum, from 4 l. to 5 l. ; a maid ſervant about 1 l. 10 s. per half year, or from 50 s. to 3 l. per annum. The average price of butcher meat is 4 d. per lb. throughout the year. The bear and bread in Stirling are al‐ lowed to be of the very beſt quality.

Banks.—There are three banks in Stirling. The Bank of Stirling ; that of Campbell and Thomson ; and that of Belch and Company ; befides a branch of the Old Bank of Scotland. The laft, and two firft, do bufinefs to a confiderable extent.

Fifhery.—The falmon fifhery belonging to the town, which, but a few years ago, brought a revenue of 30 l. now brings 405 l. It is let to a company, who fend the fifh chiefly to the London and Edinburgh markets. There was, in the late leafe, no refervation in favour of the inhabitants, which fometimes occafions murmuring, as the falmon is often higher priced in the Stirling market, than even in that of Edinburgh.

Hofpitals, &c.—There are three hofpitals. The firft is that endowed by ROBERT SPITTAL, taylor to King James V. The date of the mortification is not on record. It is fuppofed to have been about 1530. The original fum is not known. It was mortified for the fupport and relief of poor tradefmen. There was a houfe built for their reception, at the foot of Mary's Wynd ; but it is probable they never occupied it, as there is not fo much as a fingle tradition where it ftood. The funds were laid out on lands in the neighbourhood of Stirling. The prefent yearly rent of thefe lands is 221 l. Mr. Nimmo, who fpeaks from report only, makes it 300 l.; and from the fame fource, makes the yearly income of Allan's Hofpital alfo 100 l. more than it really is. At prefent, there are 44 penfioners on Spittal's Hofpital, 16 of whom, who were deacons of trade, receive per week 1 s. 4 d. :—the reft have weekly 1 s. 2 d. The annual expenditure, for the fupport of the poor on this foundation, is about 172 l. Sterling. The managers of this hofpital are at prefent increafing the funds. The charter being loft, the patrons have no rule for diftributing the funds but cuftom. There is no provifion from this hofpital for the

widows

widows of decayed tradefmen. There have been inftances of this, however, though they are never admitted on the penfion lift. This had been a much better charity ; but was unhappily overlooked by the founder. A poor widow, ftripped of charitable fupply, at the fame time that fhe lofes her hufband, muft be poor indeed.

Cowan's Hospital comes next in order. It was founded and endowed by John Cowan, merchant in Stirling, anno 1639, for the fupport of 12 decayed guild brethren. The original mortification was 2222 l. Sterling. There was a neat genteel houfe erected by the patrons, after Cowan's death, for the reception of the brethren on whom he had entailed his charity. The fituation of this houfe is moft beautiful and romantic. But what is furprifing, there were fcarcely any to be found who would accept the benefit of charity, according to the appointment of the founder. The pride of the decayed brethren made them fpurn at the idea of leaving their own houfes, and retiring into an hofpital, to be fupported on public charity. For upwards of 90 years, the funds were allowed to accumulate. The houfe flood empty for nearly the whole of that period, nor was it ever completely occupied. With the accumulated funds, lands were purchafed. Among others, thofe of the old Abbacy of Cambufkenneth. The managers appointed by the founder were the town council, together with the firft minifter of Stirling. They knew not what to do with the revenue of the hofpital. At length, it was refolved, to alter the mode of difpenfing the charity, ftill following out the fpirit of the inftitution. Not only decayed guild-brethren, but their widows and daughters are admitted to a fhare in thefe funds. The prefent income of the lands belonging to Cowan's Hofpital is 1158 l. Sterling. There are above an hundred penfioners on this charity. They receive weekly from 1 s. 6 d. to 2 s. 6 d. each, which amounts annually to about 658 l. Sterling. The furplus is expended in incidental charities, paying public burdens, and the intereft of money lately borrowed to make an additional and advantageous purchafe of lands. The funds are carefully managed, and, notwithftanding the above large expenditures, muft increafe.

JOHN ALLAN writer in Stirling, in emulation, very probably, of the benevolent example of the above mentioned gentleman, would alfo engage in the eftablifhment of an hofpital. He had more experience, and was determined to render his bounty more extenfively ufeful and beneficial. About the year 1725, therefore, he mortified a fum of money, not for the fupport of the indigent fquanderer, the negligent, and the uninduftrious, but for the maintenance and education of the children of decayed tradefmen. The fum mortified was 30,000 merks. The managers are, the town council, and the fecond minifter. They laid out the money on lands. The yearly rental of thefe lands, at prefent, is 298 l. Sterling. There are now 14 boys, maintained clothed and educated on thefe funds. The mafter of the hofpital receives at the rate of 11 l. Sterling annually for each of them. They are admitted at 7 years of age, and kept in the houfe till they are 14. At leaving the hofpital, they are allowed 100 merks to put them to a trade. The annual expenditure upon the maintenance, clothing, and education of thefe boys, is about 164 l. Sterling. According to a claufe in Mr. Allan's will, ordering fupply to be given from thefe funds, to any of his poor relations, who may be in indigent circumftances, there is at prefent about 37 l. Sterling yearly, paid to eight of his relations, at the rate of 1 s. 9 d. per week. The furplus funds, after paying public burdens, &c. go to accumulation.

Befides thefe charitable foundations, the funds of the guildry, or merchant company, defray the expence of educating

the

the poor guild brethren's children, aſſiſt them in purchaſing clothes, and paying their apprentice fees. The Kirk-Seſſion pays to 56 paupers annually about 73 l. Sterling, at the rate of 6 d. *per* week to each. From the town's funds, there are ſix who receive about 16 l. Sterling annually, at the rate of 1 s. *per* week. They alſo pay for teaching 24 or 30 poor children to read Engliſh.

To prevent the nuiſance of begging poor, a ſcheme, by annual voluntary ſubſcription, was ſet on foot ſome years ago, from which about 80 paupers receive annually 156 l. Sterling, at the rate of 9 d. each per week. Beſides all theſe charities, the Kirk-Seſſion diſtributes betwixt 40 l. and 50 l. Sterling a-year to incidental poor. Nearly the ſame ſum, or more, is diſtributed annually by the Burgher Seceſſion ; and the boxes of the different incorporations alſo give charity to a conſiderable extent. It is ſuppoſed, that every 12th perſon in Stirling receives charity.

This may ſeem ſurpriſing ; and it will be neceſſary to mention ſome of the more obvious cauſes, why there are ſo many poor, and ſo great conſumption of charitable funds, in ſuch a ſmall place as Stirling. It is generally ſaid, that Stirling being ſo near the Highlands, and known to be rich in funds, a number of indigent people, while they are ſtill capable of labour, but have little or no proſpect of ſupport at home, ſhould infirmity or old age come on, emigrate annually into Stirling, and take up their reſidence there, till three years are elapſed, when they give in their claim for ſupport, and are of courſe admitted as neceſſitous poor. It cannot be denied, but there may be ſome truth in the allegation, becauſe the greater number of poor on the Stirling penſion liſts, are obviouſly of Gaelic extraction. Their names are almoſt all Gaelic names. Beſides, there can be no doubt, that the report of rich funds has a ſtrong attraction. This circumſtance, of itſelf, chiefly mul-
                                                                    tiplies

tiplies the poor. Increafe the means of dependence, and the the effect is unavoidably increafed. This is more efpecially the cafe, if the funds are legally eftablifhed, and, if a certain age and defcription entitles to a participation of thefe funds. It is more than prefumable, that all charitable fupply, except in cafes of abfolute incapacity of labour, fhould be cafual, exactly proportioned to the deficiency of active power, and dependent on the moft accurate inveftigation of the prefent circumftances of the pauper. If this is not the cafe, it uniformly cuts the nerves of induftry, and is a nuifance to fociety, rather than an advantage. The indolent and the clamorous, looking forward with folicitude to that period, when they fhall undoubtedly be entitled to fupport by certain ftatute, remit every exertion, confume like drones any little property that may remain to them, and fall at length, with eagernefs, into the arms of provided and fecured fupport, with a haughty contempt to this facred dictate of common fenfe, " That he who will not work, fhould not eat."

The managers of the eftablifhed charitable funds in Stirling are perhaps as accurate, attentive, and impartial, as any fuch body of men can be ; but they muft walk by ftatute, and are often obliged to admit upon the funds, thofe who both *can* and *ought* to labour for their bread. This circumftance has an influence extenfively pernicious. Indolence is contagious. They who are capable of labour, being rendered indolent and inactive, through dependence on fecured fupport, gave a tincture to all their immediate connections. They are ever found among the fauntering and the idle, and confequently increafe the number of the poor.

Nor can the ordinary managers of the poor's funds, however attentive, always exclude the undeferving.—They meet too feldom.—They have too little time.—They cannot be at the pains to give incidental aid, the moft ufeful and neceffary of all charity. It is eaſier for them and for their treaſurer, to admit perſons to regular and ſtated penſions. Stated penſions, except to the blind, the lame or the diſeaſed, are always productive of dependence. They continue the demand on the poor's fund; they increaſe the number of the poor. This cauſe indeed is not peculiar to Stirling. It operates in every place where the adminiſtration is not in the hands of the Seſſion, who, from the frequency of their meetings, and their thorough acquaintance with the circumſtances of the poor, muſt ever be the moſt natural and judicious diſpenſers of public charity; and there can be no doubt, but the gentlemen of landed property, who, in many places of Scotland, have contributed to *annihilate* the Seſſions, will ſoon find the puniſhment of their folly, in the enormous weight of aſſeſsment, which they muſt lay upon their land, for the ſupport of the daily increaſing poor.

The great number of low houſes in Stirling augments the liſt of the poor. The proprietors of ſuch houſes, unable or unwilling to repair them, can let them only to the poor, the ſluggiſh, or the depraved. None elſe will take them. In ſuch uncomfortable habitations, the ſpirits of men are broken, or their health impaired; and they ſoon fall unavoidably on the funds of the poor.

The low rate of female labour in Stirling, is another ſource of poverty. The utmoſt a woman can earn by ſpinning wool, is 3 d. a-day. With this they cannot maintain themſelves, pay the rent of a houſe, and get other neceſſaries. Such ſmall encouragement deſtroys induſtry. A female having ſo little proſpect of advantage from her labour, is at no pains to be expert in it. Many of them will rather be idle altogether than turn a wheel. When neceſſity urges, they are incapable of proficiency, and muſt either ſtarve or beg. There are, perhaps, few places in Scotland, where the quantum of female

labour

labour is lefs, becaufe it is fo unproductive. Manufacturers fhould confider themfelves as obliged to increafe the price of female labour.

But perhaps the chief caufe of the numerous poor in Stirling is the caftle. This may feem a paradox, but it is eafy to be explained. The fole ufe of this fortrefs, at prefent, is to be an afylum to invalids. About 100 of thefe are generally ftationed in it. Thefe men, who probably enlifted at firft, from diflike to labour and regularity, do not find, in the army, much opportunity of becoming attached either to induftry or fobriety. Having generally contracted habits of thoughtlefnefs and diffipation, they retire into the caftle, very little qualified to enjoy the advantages of that fituation. Secured in 6 d. a-day, or looking forward to the Chelfea penfion, the low women in Stirling afpire at a connection with them, and think, that when they are wives of caftle foldiers, they fhall never want. When thefe invalids and penfioned foldiers are fober and induftrious, they are very able, with their pay, to provide a decent fupport for their families ; but few of them are of this character. Being generally ignorant, vicious and debauched, they get wives like themfelves, or make them fo. All their income is ufually fpent with the day. They never get their houfes furnifhed. They live amidft meannefs and rags. Their minds are debafed. Their children are trained up under the very worft example. The fathers foon die, worn out with intemperance. They leave their families beggared, unprincipled and debauched. Thefe families are the nurferies of beggars. Nearly one half of the paupers in Stirling fpring from thefe nurferies.

Where there is fo much poverty, there will of courfe be much bafenefs and degeneracy of mind. True religion only can tame the heart, and fweeten the manners of the poor. On them, however, this is generally found to have little influence.

The

The ſtrong cravings of nature lead them another way. Theſe, being but ill ſupplied, produce violence, chagrin, jealouſy, and every ill paſſion. *Give* them, and they are tolerably quiet and orderly ; but withhold or conſtrain, (both of which are often abſolutely neceſſary,) and they are clamorous, ſurly, invidious, and bent on every practice within their reach, however criminal it may be, to obtain what they need. The manners of the inferior ranks in Stirling, muſt therefore be neceſſarily rough, petulant and diſagreeable. Harraſſed with perpetual anxieties about daily bread, they have little or no time to think of ſuperior objects ; and either will not, or cannot come within the reach of thoſe important leſſons of divine truth, which ſupport the mind of man, and render him calm, patient and compoſed, even although the field ſhould yield no corn.

But what ſtill farther induces this unwilling complaint, againſt the manners of the poor, is a circumſtance not peculiar to Stirling, though it takes place there. It is found in almoſt every town, city, and borough, throughout Great Britain, and is ſingularly diſgraceful to a great and enlightened nation. There is generally no room in churches for the accommodation of the poor. They muſt either loiter away the days of public ſolemnity, in ſloth and vicious indulgence at home, which they will very ſoon be inclined to do, or they muſt ſtand at an awful diſtance, in ſome cold unoccupied area, which very ſoon becomes irkſome and intolerable. Beſides, in ſuch ſituations, it is ſcarcely poſſible they can receive much advantage from public inſtruction. Let a remedy be provided for this evil : Let churches be built, or decent places provided for the accommodation of the poor, and their manners would ſoon be corrected, at much leſs expence, and much more effectually, than by thouſands expended on the building of bridewells and correction houſes. Charity employed in

preventing

preventing vice is charity indeed. That which is employed in *correcting* it is often mere felfishnefs.

The manners of the inferior ranks are alfo much hurt and debafed every where, by the great number of tippling houfes, and the low price of ardent fpirits. Of thefe, the number in Stirling has been confiderably diminifhed for fome years paft, but ought to be ftill more fo. In 1782, there were 94 licenfed ale houfes in Stirling. In 1790, there were only 68. The difference has arifen probably from the additional tax. In 1782, a licence coft 1 l. 1 s., In 1790, a licence coft 1 l. 11 s. 6 d. If the legiflature would increafe the tax upon the retail of ardent fpirits, it is probable fuch a ftep would contribute much to prevent the growing depravity of the people. It would diminifh the number of thofe nefts of vitiation. It would leffen their acceffibility, efpecially to the weaker fex, who, from many circumftances, are too eafily led to haunt them. One of thefe muft be particularly mentioned, though not peculiar to Stirling. While females are fervants in families of fuperior rank, or even in the houfes of the better kind of tradefmen, inftead of receiving abundance of plain and wholefome food, which is their due, they are foolifhly indulged with luxuries, which they can tafte no more the moment they become the wives of honeft labourers. Feeling this change of fituation, which occafions difagreeable reflections, and fubjected to the uneafineffes unavoidably connected with their change of ftate, they betake themfelves to ardent fpirits to kill their griefs, and are thus infenfibly led into habits of intoxication, which ruin themfelves, their interefts, and their families in every refpect. There is no caufe of increafing immorality, among the lower ranks of the people, more abundant than this. There is none, which the care of magiftrates and rulers ought to be more employed to prevent. If the mothers of families are corrupted, virtue muft be gone. Mafters fhould have regard to the future interefts of their fer vants, more than to their preſent indulgence. Magiſtrates and rulers ſhould render the venom, which poiſons the morals of the people, as inacceſſible as poſſible.

This is more in their power, and vaſtly more practicable, as well as likely to be more efficient in remedying material evils, than the ſyſtem ſo much in vogue among our preſent ſciolists in government, who are for pulling down every thing, in order, as they pretend, to build up a more perfect and beautiful edifice. Let the revenue laws be reviewed *. By them, the people have been in a manner compelled to uſe ſpiritous liquors, for want of wholeſome beer. The preſent mode of gauging the brewer, and of farming the duties to the diſtiller, has the unavoidable effect of ruining the former, and encouraging the latter. The conſequence is, that the brewery, in moſt parts of Scotland, produces a thin vapid ſour ſtuff, under the name of ſmall beer, which is all that the common people can poſſibly get for their money, unleſs they go to the expence of Engliſh porter, now become the beverage of the more opulent. The poor labourer, finding that the beer he purchaſes neither warms nor nouriſhes him, flies unavoidably to ardent ſpirits, now ſelling at a very reduced price.

Beſides, the diſtiller works, as it is called, *againſt time*, i. e. he pays ſo much annually per gallon, for the contents of his ſtill, and works without controul. It is ſaid, that a diſtiller can now charge his ſtill, no leſs than 25 times in 24 hours, inſtead of once or twice as formerly, when he was regularly ſurveyed. This pours in ſo great a quantity of the commodity to the market, that it cannot miſs being cheap. Hence the labourers take whiſky, with a little bread to their breakfaſt. It inebriates and ſubverts the minds of men, women

and

---

* Sanabilibus ægrotamus malis.

and children, emaciates their bodies, renders them unfit for labour, ruins their perfons, corrupts their hearts, and leads them to think of plots, rebellion and every evil work. Take the tax off the brewery, and lay it on the diftillery, and it is impoffible to fay how much the virtue and morals of the people would be improved. This is an objedt furely worthy of a wife and virtuous adminiftration. Thefe obfervations were unavoidable, from an attentive furvey of the manners of many among the lower ranks of the people.

Charader.—With refpedt to the manners of the inhabitants in general, there is a fobriety, order, and decency among them, fcarcely to be expedted. The great body of the people, in Stirling, even of the principal people, do not yet think it below them to attend religious ordinances ; and, there are few who allow themfelves, in the pradtice of jaunting, or making excurfions on the Lord's day, for the fake either of bufinefs or pleafure. Hence, there is among them, an external decorum and fobernefs of mind, a freedom from giddinefs, extravagance, and diffipation, which refpedt for religious inftitutions alone can produce. Urbanity and focial intercourfe are not unfrequent among them. The only thing which interrupts this is political jealoufy,—a dæmon, which, at certain feafons, unhappily rages too much in almoft every little burgh throughout Scotland. Would magiftracy uniformly maintain the dignity of that fituation, and exert itfelf with fpirit or boldnefs folely for the public good, without any regard to the prolongation of their honour, but juft as it refults from public fuffrage and opinion, this evil would nearly expire. So far as this evil refults from diffentient principles in religion, it is lefs fufceptible of cure. For this, no remedy can be found, but the reftoration of religion itfelf, which always renders men forgiving

ing, affectionate and gentle, and uniformly unites them into one.

Miſcellaneous Obſervations.—Stirling being ſituated on the iſthmus, betwixt the Forth and Clyde, is, by means of its bridge, the great thorough-fare of the north of Scotland. There are only two inns in it which deſerve the name. Theſe are ſpacious and good.—The county meetings are uſually held in Stirling. There is no public room, or hall for this purpoſe —Stirling is one of the ſeats of the Circuit Court.—The only jail in the county is here. The number of priſoners is generally not great. For theſe three laſt years, there have been only two criminal trials. Petty thefts and debt are the ordinary cauſes of impriſonment.—The Falkirk diſtrict of the county, being the moſt populous, and no public magiſtrate reſiding there, it uniformly furniſhes the greateſt number of priſoners.—The banditti always croud to a populous place, where there is no eſtabliſhed authority. There ſhould be, in every county, a public work-houſe, for the confinement of the pilferers and ſorners, who are found to be of that county. Baniſhment only increaſes their neceſſity of ſtealing.

In the council houſe of Stirling is the *Jugg*, appointed by law to be the ſtandard of dry meaſure in Scotland, It is ſtatuted and ordained, that the wheat firlot ſhall contain the full of this jugg twenty one times and one fourth ; and that the firlot for barley, malt and oats, ſhall contain it 31 times. The great number of public tranſactions, which have taken place in Stirling, and in the caſtle, would, of themſelves, fill a volume ; and, if deemed neceſſary to the Statiſtical account, can be found in Nimmo's hiſtory, and the Encyclopaedia Britannica, under the article STIRLING.

PARISH OF STRATHBLANE.

(COUNTY OF STIRLING.)

By the Rev. Mr GIBB.

———————

Name.

THE parish of Strathblane takes its name from the river Blane, which rises in it, and runs through its whole extent. Blane is a contraction of two Gaelic words, signifying *warm river*. The literal interpretation of the word Strathblane, consequently is, " the valley of the warm river;" a name fitly appropriated to this parish, which from its situation, enjoys a peculiarly mild atmosphere. Lying on the south side of the Lennox hills, it is sheltered by them from the inclement winds of the north; while the reflection of the sun's rays from a light sandy soil, produces an agreeable temperature of the air at all seasons.

Situation, Boundaries, &c.—Strathblane is situated in the northwest corner of Stirlingshire, and lies withing the bounds of the commissariot of Glasgow. In ecclesiastical matters it belongs to the presbytery of Dumbarton, and synod of Glasgow and Ayr. It is bounded on the east, by the parish of Camp-

fie,

fie ; on the fouth, by the parifhes of Baldernock and New-kirkpatrick ; and on the weft and north, by the parifh of Kil-learn. It lies 10 miles north from Glafgow, 14 eaft by fouth from Dunbarton, and 20 fouthweft from Stirling. Its form is an oblong fquare, 5 miles long, and 4 miles broad.

Soil, and face of the Country.—This parifh may properly be diftinguifhed into valley and moor grounds. The valley is bounded by high hills on the north, and by a rifing ground on the fouth fide of the river, which afcends about one third of the height of the oppofite hills. This hanging ground on each fide of the river, confifts of a light quick foil, is well culti-vated, and produces excellent crops. Toward the weftern extremity, the valley widens confiderably ; and the foil there, on the level grounds, is clay mixed with a rich earth, depo-fited from time to time, by the overflowing of the river. This foil is fit to carry heavy crops of any kind of grain.

The moor runs parallel to the valley, commencing at the brink of the rifing ground on the fouth fide of the river, and extending in an uneven furface, about a mile and a half in breadth. Here the ground defcends into the parifh of New-kirkpatrick, with a declivity fimilar to that with which it af-cends from the Blane. A great proportion of this confifts of heath ; but in many places, particularly on the fouth border, and in the weftern extremity, it is now cultivated, and pro-duces crops nearly as rich as thofe in the Strath. The foil here, in the parts fufceptible of cultivation, is dry, light, and rocky ; and from the return which it makes, when pro-perly laboured and manured, gives great encouragement to the improver. Befides thefe moor and valley grounds, the hills on the north fide of the parifh afford moft excellent paf-ture for black cattle and fheep.

The

The general appearance of the country is agreeably picturefque. Coming from the fouth, the traveller at firft afcends
from the fertile fields of New-kirkpatrick, into what appears
an extenfive heath ; but which he no fooner enters, than he
finds it interfperfed with cultivated fields, and here and there
obferves a lake of feveral acres. Defcending into the valley, he
is charmed with the verdure of the country, the mildnefs of the
air, and the appearance of chearfulnefs and plenty, which is
difplayed around. Several neat villas fcattered along the bottom of the hills, and here and there a cafcade precipitating
its torrent from their fides, enliven and beautify the fcene.
In fummer, the landfcape is enriched and adorned by the
luxuriant foliage of the woods with which the hills are fkirted,
and the whole receives an air of grandeur, from the abrupt
precipices in which the hills terminate. Toward the weft,
the hill of Dumgoiack, on the Duntreath eftate, prefents a
fingular and ftriking appearance. Infulated in the middle of
the valley, of a conical figure, and compleatly clothed with
wood, it arrefts the attention ; whilft a fhoulder of the oppofite hill, projecting like the pedeftal of an arch, directs the
eye, as it were through an immenfe vifta, to the plains below, when the whole profpect is bounded by the diftant
mountains on the fide of Lochlomond.

Cultivation and Produce.—For many years paft the farmers
have paid confiderable attention to the improvement of their
lands; and perhaps the ftate of agriculture is nearly as far
advanced as the nature of the foil will admit. Already inclofed, for the moft part dry, and originally quick and fertile, it requires only to be manured and laboured, in order to
produce plentifully. The manure chiefly ufed is lime, and
the opportunity of getting it readily from the neighbouring
parifhes of Campfie and Baldernock, has caufed it to be gene-

raily

rally adopted. The quantity laid on at once is but small, being 4 chalders per acre; but this is repeated with equal advantage, after two rotations of crops, or every 12th year. This fact has been ascertained by undoubted experiment. The crops generally raised, are oats, barley, and grafs-feeds. The usual rotation, is 2 years pasture, 2 crops of oats, 2 of hay, and then pasture again. The lime is spread upon the pasture grafs, a year previous to ploughing it up for oats. This gives it time to incorporate with the mould, and both improves the grafs, and meliorates the soil for a future crop, to a higher degree than when laid on in the same year in which the ground is ploughed. The grafs-feeds are sown with the second crop of oats, in the quantity of half a boll of rye-grafs feed, and from 4 to 6 pounds of clover feed to an acre. This course of cropping is uniformly adhered to, and is only varied, in as far as barley is partially introduced for the second crop of oats. As far as this can be done, it is certainly an improvement on the plan; but as barley only succeeds when the ground is well dunged, the sowing of it cannot be extended any farther than the quantity of that manure collected in the course of the year will admit.

This method of croping may be thought too severe, especially the second crop of hay, which is very impoverishing. But as this article brings a good price, being usually sold at 6d per stone, the farmer depends a good deal upon it for his rent; and it yields ready money the second year, without any expence of feed or labour; an object worthy of being attended to.

Of late years, however, the farmer's hopes have in a great measure been frustrated in this respect, by the inattention of the feed merchants, who have supplied them with rye-grafs feed, which remains only one year in the ground. The first appearance of this annual feed, caused a good deal of alarm

and

and difappointment, and various methods have been adopted, to remedy or fupply the defect. Some by preferving and collecting the feed of fuch as remained the fecond year, acquired by degrees, a ftock fufficient for their own fupply. Others, by fowing an additional quantity of clover feed, fecured at leaft, a good bulk of hay the fecond year, though inferior in quality to the rye-grafs hay.

But the hope of an effectual and general relief is now afforded, by the public fpirited propofals of the *Farmers Society* at Glafgow, who have lately taken the matter into confideration. This fociety (of which moft of the farmers in this parifh are members), confifts of the moft noted and experienced farmers in an extent of country of 15 or 20 miles round Glafgow. The exertions of fo many men, eminent in their profeffion, promife to become of general utility. By a private fubfcription among themfelves, they have already raifed a confiderable fund, from which, they give premiums to eminence in agricultural exertions or ufeful improvements. They alfo affift fpirited members of their own body, by lending them money from their fund, toward carrying ufeful projects into execution. It has been propofed amongft them, to commiffion their own grafs-feeds from the beft foreign markets ; by this plan if it fhall be carried into execution, they will not only fecure the beft in quality, but alfo have a faving on the price. When imported to the general depot at Glafgow, each parifh can conveniently get the quantity alotted to it conveyed home. It is by turning the attention of the inhabitants of a country to fuch ufeful and practical objects, that a nation may expect to become truly great.

Peafe and beans have been found to thrive well in feveral farms, and one fpirited farmer made lately an experiment of a wheat crop, which fucceeded to his wifh. From 2 acres, he reaped 32 bolls. The ground indeed was fummer fallowed, and richly dunged. This ſucceſs would have encouraged him to continue the plan, but the ſcanty ſupply of dung prevented him. He therefore now ſubſtitutes a turnip crop for the ſummer fallow, and a barley crop for the wheat; and from an exact calculation, he finds he is a gainer by this latter method. If this practice ſhould become general, it will certainly be more profitable than the method at preſent in uſe.

The following table contains the average quantity of grain and hay ſown, and produced annually.

Annual Average of

	Bolls ſown.	Product of each boll.	Total product.
Oats	486	7	3402
Barley	44	8	352
	Acres.	Stones.	Stones.
Hay	120	product 150 per ac.	18000

Grazing.—Agriculture, however, conſtitutes only one branch of the farmers employment in this pariſh. The rearing and feeding black cattle and ſheep, occupy a conſiderable ſhare of their attention. The excellent paſture afforded by the hills, which can never be turned to agricultural purpoſes, both compels and encourages their exertions in the grazing line.

In this branch, the ſtock of milk cows deſerves to be firſt mentioned. This has been brought to a conſiderable degree of excellence, by the attention which has been given to procure bulls of a good kind, and by ſelecting the beſt and handſomeſt cows to breed from. Accordingly, the breed is much eſteemed in the country toward the weſt and north, and the farmers find encouragement to rear as many as they can, to anſwer the demand that is made from that quarter. The cows reared, are ſold when they firſt become pregnant, which

which is at 3 years old, and they then bring from L. 5 to L. 6 each.

Befides the milk cows or native ftock, a confiderable number of highland cows are fattened upon each farm. Thefe are commonly bought in at the Michaelmafs and Martinmafs markets, and wintered upon the farm, with the affiftance of a little fodder, from New-year's-day, till the middle of April. They are then fed during the following fummer, and fold to the Glafgow and Paifley markets in autumn. At the time they are fold, they generally weigh from 18 to 24 ftones of beef and tallow, which brings, at an average, 6s per ftone.

The fheep ftock confifts of ewes, which are all of the fhort or black faced kind; which the farmers have taken confiderable care to improve, by felecting the beft rams, and fupplying the defect of their ftock, with the beft and ftouteft ewe lambs. In addition to this, they alfo buy in from time to time, good lambs from thofe parts of the country which are famed for keeping good ftocks of fheep. The profits arifing from the fheep ftock, are chiefly derived from the wool and lambs. The fmeared wool fells at 6s per ftone, and white wool from 8s to 9s. The lambs bring at an average 6s each. A few of the worft ewes called *fhotts*, are likewife fold every year about Martinmafs.

The ewes are fo managed, as to begin to produce their lambs about the 10th of April; the moft proper feafon on high grounds. It fometimes happens, that a number of them have twins. When that is the cafe, the ewes are brought down to the low grounds, where the rich pafture enables them to nurfe both. If any ewe happens to lofe her lamb, fhe is confined in a houfe, with a twin lamb taken from another, for two nights; by which time, fhe becomes attached to it, and nurfes it as her own. In the latter end of July, the lambs are weaned; when thofe felected for keeping up

the

the ſtock, are put to a ſeparate part of the farm, where they are kept apart from their dams, till next ſummer. The reſt are either ſold for ſlaughter, or for ſtocking farms in other parts of the country.

In the month of November the whole ſtock is ſmeared; a practice which, although it is both expenſive and troubleſome, is found to be not only neceſſary, but beneficial. The ſalve, a mixture of tar and butter, kilis the vermin with which ſheep are infeſted, and makes the wool adhere cloſely to the animal. This contributes both to its comfort during the winter, and preſerves a better fleece till the ſeaſon of ſhearing, than what is then found on the white or unſmeared ſheep. The wool alſo, though not of ſo fair a colour as the unſmeared, is yet of a better quality. Theſe advantages attendant upon ſmearing, have been aſcertained in the moſt ſatisfactory manner, by a comparative experiment lately made by a farmer in this place. He took 100 lambs of the ſame ſtock, and divided them equally; taking equal care in every reſpect of the two parcels. He ſmeared 50, and left 50 unſmeared. At the ſheep ſhearing ſeaſon, 4 fleeces of thoſe that were ſmeared, weighed a ſtone; whereas, it took 7 fleeces of the unſmeared to produce the ſame weight. The quality too of this laſt was inferior, being coarſe and matted. He perſiſted in the experiment for 5 years, and the older the ſheep grew, the preference in favour of the ſmeared wool became ſtill more decided; till at laſt the merchant could ſcarcely be prevailed upon to take the white wool at the ſame price with the ſmeared. The ewes alſo failed ſooner than the others; ſo that he gave up the attempt, fully convinced of the propriety of ſmearing the wool ſtock.

The ſame enterpriſing ſpirit, however, which prompted the above experiment, induced him to try others, for reducing the expence of ſmearing. After repeated trials of ſundry in-
gredients

gredients mixed with the *tar* and *butter*, in order to reduce the quantity of thefe expenfive articles, he found that butter-milk in a certain proportion, produced this effect. Thus, 2 pints of butter milk, added to 6 pints of tar, Scots meafure, and 12 pounds Tron, of butter, will fmear 4 fheep more than the fame quantity of tar and butter by themfelves. If the butter-milk be a week or two old, it is fo much the better. It makes the tar and butter incorporate more clofely, renders the falve firm, and draws much finer upon the fheep, than without it. Befides thefe advantages, the falve thus prepar-ed, is fit for immediate ufe; whereas, without this ingredi-ent, it requires to ftand fome days after it is made, before it can be ufed.

The horfes kept in this parifh, are entirely deftined for the purpofes of hufbandry, and a very few are reared for fale.

A table is fubjoined, fhewing the numbers of each kind of cattle in the parifh.

Horfes kept for labour,	-	-	100
Do. reared annually,	-	-	26
Milk cows,	-	-	310
Cows rearing under 3 years old,		-	376
Cows fattened annually,	-	-	442
Sheep, confifting of ewes.		-	1200

This article ought not to be concluded, without taking notice of the laudable exertions of Archibald Edmonftone, an extenfive grazier on the Duntreath eftate, to introduce im-provements in his line. Among many other attempts to this purpofe, (to which allufions have oftener than once been already made in this account,) he has lately introduced a few fheep of the true Spanifh breed into his farm. The only hazard of which he was apprehenfive, was that the inclemen-

cy

cy of the weather in winter would hurt them. Of this ap-
prehenſion he has been moſt agreeably relieved. They have
already ſtood two winters, as well as the reſt of his ſtock;
and one of them was the moſt ſevere, that has been known
for many ſeaſons. The only precaution which he uſed, was
to keep them on his low grounds during winter; but in ſummer, they are fond of feeding on the tops of the hills, and
thrive there as well as the native breed. Their lambs are
equally hardy as themſelves, and promiſe to become a great
acquiſition to the country; the wool being much ſuperior to
any ever known in this place. Each ewe produced L. 4, and
the ram L. 5, which brought 3s 6d per pound, and was even
at that price ſold much under value.

Laſt year he croſſed the breed with the Spaniſh ram and
Scots ewes; and alſo with a Scots ram, and the Spaniſh
ewes; and this experiment has ſucceeded beyond expectation.
The lambs thus generated, have wool little or nothing inferior to the old Spaniſh ſheep, and they may be expected to
be even hardier than theſe, as being inured to the climate
from their birth. In ſhort, there is not a doubt, if he had a
ſufficient extent of low ground to winter a large ſtock upon,
that Mr Edmonſtone would puſh this experiment to a degree
which might prove highly beneficial to himſelf, to his landlord, and, *as ſetting an uſeful example,* to the whole country.

In autumn laſt, he alſo procured a few Cheviot ewes,
which he has croſſed with his Spaniſh ram. It is expected
this will produce a hardy breed, and improve the wool to a
ſtill greater degree of fineneſs, than the croſſing with the
common Scots ewes; but on the ſucceſs of this experiment,
time muſt be left to decide.

Manufactures.—Although this pariſh cannot boaſt of extenſive eſtabliſhments in manufactures, yet lying in the vicinity

nity of the city of Glafgow, a portion of that fpirit of enterprife, which poffeffes all ranks there, has diffufed itfelf hither.
Three bleachfields have lately been erected, which employ a
confiderable number of perfons. Thefe belong to companies
ftationed at Glafgow, who fend their goods here to be
bleached. Nothing can excel the foftnefs and purenefs of
the water for this purpofe, being broken by rufhing from the
hills and precipices, and filtered through beds of the cleaneft
fand. The ground alfo on the banks of the river, affords
the moft favourable fituations for fpreading cloth. Confifting
of a warm fandy foil, it contributes towards whitening and
clearing the goods fooner, and to a more exquifite purenefs,
than can be done where the foil below is of a clayifh texture.
The chief employment of one field is bleaching muflins and
pullicates. The other two belonging to inkle factories in
Glafgow, are wholly confined to bleaching tapes and yarn.

Mechanics.—Of thefe weavers conftitute the greateft proportion, as befides the employment they get from the country
people, they are fupplied with abundance of work from the
manufacturing companies in Glafgow. There are about 22
looms employed in this manner; befides 10 inkle looms lately
fet to work, at one of the bleachfields above mentioned. Of
other tradefmen, there are 7 taylors, 3 fhoemakers, 3 hofiers,
3 carpenters, and 1 fmith.

Population.—There being a great many feuars or fmall heritors, who refide upon and labour their own lands, this parifh has on that account been lefs fubject to fluctuation in
its inhabitants, than might otherwife have happened. It has
however experienced fome changes in this refpect. A confiderable diminution of numbers has been produced, within
the laft 20 or 30 years, by the greater proprietors letting out
their

their lands in large farms, which exclude cottagers. On the other hand, an acceſſion of 60 or 70, has lately been obtained by the perſons employed at the bleachfields.

The population as returned to Dr Webſter, in 1755, was 797. In this preſent year 1795, it is found by an actual enumeration, to be 620 ſouls.

Of theſe there are,

Under 10 years of age,—140
From 10 to 20 years,—125
—— 20 to 50   -   —247
—— 50 to 70   -   —68
—— 70 to 100   -   —40

Total   620

Diminution ſince 1755,   177

Average of deaths *per annum*,   -   7
—————— of births,   -   13
—————— of marriages,   -   5

Poor.—The poor are ſupported by the weekly collections at the church, and the intereſt of a fund amounting to L. 220, accumulated by charitable donations from individuals, having property or intereſt in the pariſh. There are at preſent 7 perſons on the pariſh-roll; 5 of whom receive 5s monthly, and the other 2, being bed-rid, receive 10s monthly. Beſides this allowance, they are ſupplied with coals in the winter, and for ſome of them, their houſe rent is paid. Several others, who have not hitherto been admitted on the roll, receive ſuch occaſional aſſiſtance, as their neceſſity requires. Theſe diſtributions are managed by the Kirk Seſſion, without
any

any expence to the fund. To their difcretion alfo, is left the apportioning each poor perfon's fupply, and they keep regular books for the infpection of the heritors. By this management, the poor are kept from public begging, a nuifance wherever it prevails; and with which this parifh, notwithftanding it thus fupports its own poor, is greatly infefted by mendicants from other parts.

Heritors.—The fuperiority of this parifh is vefted in his Grace the Duke of Montrofe and Sir Archibald Edmonftone Baronet of Duntreath; whofe anceftors, at one time, alfo poffeffed the whole property of it. In the beginning of laft century, that part of it which belonged to the eftates of Montrofe was chiefly feued out; the caftle of Mugdock, and the park adjoining, being alone retained in the family. The eftate of Duntreath, formerly one of the greater baronies, in right whereof the proprietors fat in Parliament without election, ftill conftitutes about a third part of the parifh. The anceftors of this family, were twice allied to the Royal Family of Scotland. Their laft marriage into it was between Sir William Edmonftone, Baronet of Duntreath, and Mary Countefs of Angus, daughter of Robert III. and fifter to James I. This Princefs lies buried in Strathblane church. The prefent Sir Archibald is lineally defcended from both alliances.

There are 9 other heritors, who poffefs property in the parifh, from L. 100 to L. 250 each; befides 15 of fmaller note, who refide on, and farm their own lands. The whole rental of the parifh, amounts to L. 2500.

Church, &c.——The church is a mean building, erected in the beginning of the prefent century; and having never been lathed or plaiftered, the bare walls and roof without
cieling,

cieling, preſent a very ſorry appearance for a place of worſhip.

The ſtipend hitherto has been 85 bolls of oat-meal, and
L. 27 : 7 : 11 ſterling in money. A new decreet of modification was obtained at the inſtance of the preſent incumbent,
before the Teind Court, in 1793, converting the money into
grain; which when allocated, will augment the value of
the *living* to L. 130. His Grace the Duke of Montroſe is
patron.

Roads, &c.—This pariſh is interſected with good roads in
every direction. Two turnpikes run through it from ſouth
to north, in parallel lines, at 2 miles diſtance from each
other. The one leads from Glaſgow to Balfron, and a little
beyond that village, joins the great military road between
Stirling and Dumbarton, at the 17th mile-ſtone from Stirling.
The other line leads from Glaſgow to Drymen, where it alſo
joins the military road, at the 11th mile from Dumbarton.
Beſides theſe roads, which interſect the pariſh at right angles,
there is another which cuts it diagonally, from ſoutheaſt to
northweſt, forming a junction between the Edinburgh road
near Kilſyth, and the above-mentioned military road at Drymen bridge. The weſtern part of this line, which was formerly impaſſible, is juſt now converted into an excellent
turnpike road. If the bridge over the Leven at the mouth of
Lochlomond, which is at preſent in contemplation, be built,
the ſtraight road from the weſt highlands to Edinburgh, will
run through Strathblane, thereby avoiding the compaſs by
Stirling on the one hand, and by Glaſgow on the other.
To theſe advantages, it will add that of being more level,
there being no ſenſible aſcent from the Leven, to Kilſyth.
All theſe roads have received very material improvements
within the laſt 6 years. From being ſo ſteep and rugged,

that

that a horfe could not draw half a load upon them, they
are now rendered fmooth and level, fo that a carriage of any
weight may pafs with eafe. This improvement we owe to
Robert Dunmore of Ballendalloch Efqr, the original mover
of it; a gentleman to whofe public fpirited exertions this diftrict of country ftands indebted for many real and permanent
advantages.

There are many bridges over the ftreams which fall from
the mountains; but none of any note. They all confift of 1
arch, of about 12 feet fpan. Of thefe, there are 7 within
the parifh, which render the communication eafy and fafe at
all times.

Wells, Lakes, &c.—The hills, which form the northern
boundary of the parifh, conftitute part of that range anciently
known by the name of " the Lennox hills." In former times,
the noble family of that name had extenfive poffeffions in
this part of the country; and the diftrict itfelf was denominated Lennox. The fhire itfelf is now partitioned between
the counties of Dumbarton and Stirling; but the range of
hills will tranfmit the name to pofterity.

The " Lennox hills" reach from Dumbarton to Stirling,
beyond which the range is continued from the Forth to the
Tay, under the name of the Ochils. Throughout the whole,
ftupenduous piles of bafaltic rocks are found. In Fintry, which
lies in the midft of this range, about 8 miles eaftward, a
moft magnificent colonade of thefe pillars prefents itfelf; of
which a particular defcription is given in the Statiftical Account of that parifh. In this parifh, the front of a precipice
for the fpace of a furlong is lined with ftately columns of
the fame kind. They confift of 4, 5, and 6 fides, are from
2 to 3 feet in diameter, and 30 feet high. They rife from
the horizon with a little inclination from the perpendicular,

and

and ſome of them are apparently bent in a ſegment of a curve line.

The higheſt hill in the pariſh is the *Earl's ſeat*, elevated above the reſt of the range, with a conical top. Here the Blane has its ſource, whence it runs in a ſouthweſt direction for 3 miles, and is then precipitated from the ſouth ſide of the hill, over ſeveral very high falls. The moſt remarkable of theſe is the *ſpout* of *Ballagan*, a caſcade of 70 feet. This, when the river is ſwelled, puts on a very grand appearance. Leaving the ſpout, the Blane turns due weſt; when after running 8 miles in this direction, it loſes itſelf in the Endrick, which falls into Lochlomond. It may here be obſerved, that the Blane, with the whole diſtrict through which it runs, has been omitted to be marked in Ainſlie's map of Scotland.

At the ſpout of Ballagan a very remarkable ſection of the hill is preſented. The ſide of it, cut perpendicularly by the water, diſcovers no fewer than 192 alternate ſtrata of earth and lime-ſtone. Near the bottom of the ſection are found ſeveral thin ſtrata of alabaſter of the pureſt white. There were found alſo near the ſame place, among the rubbiſh thrown up by the river in a late inundation, ſome fragments of antimony, which when tried by a chemical proceſs, turned out to be very rich ſpecimens. The ſource however, whence theſe were dug, has not been diſcovered. If it ſhall be found, it may probably prove a valuable mine.

There are 6 lakes in the pariſh, the largeſt of which does not exceed half a mile in length, and a quarter of a mile in breadth. Theſe lie in the moor-land part of the pariſh, and contribute to render that a chearful proſpect, which would otherwiſe be bleak and dull. They abound with pike, perch, and trout. They are alſo frequented by wild ducks, and other aquatic fowls. In the Blane likewiſe, there are

plenty

plenty of fmall and fome large trout; and falmon make their way up in confiderable numbers, at fpawning time.

Buildings.—The caftles of Mugdock and Duntreath, efpe-cially the former, have been anciently places of confiderable ftrength. There is no tradition concerning the time when they were built; nor do they bear any infcription from which that can be afcertained. Their conftruction, however, deter-mines them to have been built about the fame time, and for the like purpofe, with many others of the kind in Scotland, viz. to defend the chieftains who poffeffed them from the fudden incurfions of a hoftile or enraged neighbour. The caftle of Mugdock feems to have been a regular fortification. Covered on the eaft and north by a lake, the waters of which were drawn around it by a ditch, whereof the fcite is ftill apparent; it muft have been inacceffible to any force, which could be brought againft it in thofe days. The fquare tower which is ftill entire, has fomething peculiar in its conftruc-tion. After rifing to the height of the outer wall, the weft and fouth fides of it fpread fo as to form an obtufe angle at the corner, over the great arched gate-way. This would ap-pear to have been done with a view of more eafily obferving from within the motions of an affailant. By this conftruc-tion alfo, miffive weapons might be difcharged from both thofe fides of the tower, upon an enemy approaching the gate.

Oppofite to this tower, at the diftance of 300 yards, is heard a very extraordinary echô. It repeats any fentence of 6 fyllables, in the exact tone, and with the very accent, in which it is uttered; waiting deliberately till the fentence is finifhed, before it begins; and it will reverberate even a whifper.

Trees.—

Trees.—Two oak trees adjoining to the public road at Blar-quhoſh, in the weſtern extremity of the pariſh, attract the notice of paſſengers, as being unuſually large in this part of the country. The trunk of the largeſt, meaſures 15 feet in circumference, and its branches form the radii of a circle 30 yards in diameter. As the public road paſſes underneath it, it falls within the notice of every traveller. The other grows near it, and though not quite ſo large, is a more beautiful tree, having a taller trunk, and being more cloſely covered with foliage.

Inundations.—Owing to the vicinity of the hills which at-tract the clouds, the Blane is frequently ſubject to ſudden ſwellings. It has however, only riſen twice to an alarming height, withing the memory of perſons now living. About 60 years ago, a water ſpout is ſaid to have burſt at its ſource; which poured ſuch a torrent from the hill, as threatened unavoidable deſtruction to the plains below. Happily how-ever, as the Blane falls into the valley, at a place whence it declines to both the eaſt and weſt, the waters, burſting from their accuſtomed channel, were diſcharged eaſtward. By this circumſtance, the country was ſaved at that time, from the effects of the deluge. The waters turning in this direc-tion, where the valley is wide and level, they ſtagnated upon it. Here alſo, they could do little damage, the ground to-ward the eaſt for 2 miles being marſhy.

The accounts, however, which old people gave of the mag-nitude of that inundation, were ſuch as appeared fabulous; till they were again formidably exemplified, during a thunder ſtorm on the 13th of Auguſt laſt, 1795. About 8 o'clock on the evening of that day, the clouds which during the after-noon had hung in threatening aſpect around the ſkirts of the horizon, were condenſed above the Earl's ſeat. Here they

burſt,

burft, and fell, as was evident from the effects, in entire
fheets. The fpout of Ballagan appeared as an opening,
whence the bowels of the mountain were iffuing in water:
reaching the plain, the torrent burft the banks of the river on
each fide, and difcharged itfelf in nearly equal quantites to
the eaft and weft. That which run weft, tore up every thing
before it. Corn fields were laid wafte. Oats, barley, and
potatoes, were deftroyed to a great amount. Much damage
was done to the bleachfields below. It carried ftones of 3
tons weight a confiderable way into the open field. At one
place, it forced a paffage for itfelf along the public road,
which it tore up like the channel of a river. In fhort, it prefented fuch a fcene of devaftation, as muft appear incredible
to thofe who have not feen it. It is computed, that there
was at leaft 6 times the quantity of water ever feen in the
river, during the greateft ufual floods; and had it not been
for the circumftance of a part being difcharged to the eaft, it
would have fwept the houfes fituated on its banks before it.
It lafted 4 hours, during which time, the thunder and light-
ening were tremenduous.

Hiftorical Anecdotes.—The name of Rob Roy M'Gregor, a
famous Highland free-booter, is familiar to every inhabitant
of this part of Scotland. The depredations which he and his
defcendants committed are ftill related with wonder. The
following copy of an order of the Juftices of the Peace, met
in quarter feffion at Stirling, a little after the middle of laft
century, will fhow the manner in which he held the country
under contribution. It is taken verbatim from the original
manufcript, fent at that time to be publifhed at the kirk of
Strathblane.

" AT

" AT Stirling, in ane Quarter Seſſion, held be the Juſ-
" tices of his Highneſs Peace, upon the 3d day Febru-
" ary, 1658—9. The Laird of Touch being Chyrſ-
" man.

" Upon reading of ane petition given in be Captain M'Gre-
" gor, makand mention that ſeveral heritors and inhabitants
" of the paroches of Campſie, Dennie, Baldernock, Stra-
" blane, Killearn, Gargunnock, and uthers within the ſher-
" rifdom of Stirling, did agrie with him to overſee and pre-
" ſerve thair houſes, goods, and geir, frae oppreſſioun, and
" accordinglie did pay him; and now that ſum perſones delay
" to maik payment according to aggriement and uſe of pay-
" ment; thairfore it is ordered, that all heritors and inhabi-
" tants of the paroches aforeſaid, maik payment to the ſaid
" Captaine M'Gregor, of thair proportionnes, for his ſaid
" ſervice, till the firſt of February laſt paſt, without delay,
" All conſtables in the ſeveral paroches, are heirby comman-
" dit to ſee this order put in executionne, as they ſall anſwer
" the contrair. It is alſo heirby declared, that all who have
" been ingadgit in payment, ſal be liberat after ſuch tyme
" that they goe to Captaine M'Gregor, and declare to
" him, that they are not to expect any ſervice frae him,
" or he to expect any payment frae them. Juſt copie ex-
" tracted be

" JAMES STIRLING, Clk. of the Peace."

" FOR Archibald Edmonſtoune, Bailzie of Duntreath, to
" be publiſhed at the Kirk of Strablane."

It is to be obſerved, that the inhabitants of the country
were obliged to enter into ſuch engagements with him, to ſe-

cure them againſt the depredations of a banditti employed by himſelf to plunder. And as he poſſeſſed power enough to overawe even juſtice itſelf, it is not to be wondered at, that he obtained ſuch an order in his own behalf. Such an incident ſhould teach us to ſet a high value upon the happy privileges which we enjoy under a mild and ſafe government.

About 3 years ago, a number of old coins were found in this pariſh, incloſed in a log of wood. . They conſiſted of crowns, half crowns, and ſhillings of Elizabeth, James I. of England, and Charles I. A few gold coins were alſo found amongſt them, and ſome Dutch ducatoons; the value of the whole might amount to L. 40 ſterling. The log was about a foot and a half ſquare. A ſmall triangular opening was cut into the ſurface of one of the ſides; by this aperture, the log had been excavated, and the treaſure depoſited. It was then cloſed up with a piece of wood, neatly fitted to the place, and faſtened with wooden pegs. As none of the coins bear a later date than the reign of Charles I. they muſt have been concealed during the troubles which preceded or ſucceeded the death of that monarch.

The hiſtory of the log itſelf is ſomewhat ſingular. It can be traced back for 40 years. At that time, it is remembered to have ſerved as a prop to the end of a bench in a ſchoolhouſe, near the church. Afterwards, it was uſed as a play thing by children, who amuſed themſelves with carrying it to the top of a declivity, whence it rolled to the bottom. It then lay many years on the wall of the church-yard. At laſt, it was appropriated by a crazy old woman, a pauper, who lived in a hut by herſelf. She uſed it as a ſeat for above a dozen of years. She dying, a neighbour was employed to waſh the clothes that were found in her houſe. As fuel was ſcarce, the log was laid on the fire to heat water for that purpoſe; it not burning quickly, the waſher woman took it off,

and

and proceeded to cleave it with a hatchet. At the first stroke, the treasure came out and was secured by the woman, who perceiving the value, wished to conceal it. In a few days however, it was divulged. But the woman's husband, who was a worthless fellow, got hold of it, and decamped with the whole amount; a few pieces excepted, which he had previously sold. He has not since been seen in the country, and has left his wife to support 5 children by her own industry.

CLACKMANNANSHIRE

CLACKMANNANSHIRE

KINROSS-SHIRE

PERTHSHIRE

STIRLINGSHIRE

FIFE

FIRTH OF FORTH

KEY TO PARISHES

1. Logie (part: mostly in Stirlingshire in 1790's)
2. Alva (in Stirlingshire in 1790's)
3. Tillicoultry
4. Dollar
5. Clackmannan
6. Alloa

PARISH OF ALLOA.

(County of Clackmannan—Presbytery of Stirling—Synod of Perth and Stirling.

Drawn up from the Communications of the Rev. Mr. JAMES
FRAME, *and of* JOHN FRANCIS ERSKINE, *Esq. of* ALLOA,
Representative of the MARR *Family.*

Origin of the Name.

THE name, like most other places, has been variously
spelt. In the charter granted by King Robert, in the
9th year of his reign, (anno 1315), to *Thomas de Erskyne*,
it is spelt *Alway*; and, in some subsequent ones, *Aulway*,
Auleway, and sometimes *Alloway*. Camden, in his *Britannia*,
seems to think it the *Alauna* of the Romans [*]. He says,
" Ptolemy

[*] When the Romans crossed the Forth, it seems probable, that it was either
by the ford of Manor, a small creek, about 6 miles higher up the water than
Alloa, or at the ford of the Frosk, which is only a mile and a half from it.
There are vestiges of a Roman causeway, running into the river at Manor;
and it is only within these 13 or 14 years, that the remains of a small *castellum*,
for protecting the passage, have been been totally defaced. In 1774, a sword,
or dagger, of a composition resembling brass, was taken up in a salmon net,
between the ford of Frosk and Manor. It had on its point a piece of a human
scull. It appeared to be of Roman workmanship; and seems to confirm the
opinion, that this part of the river had been frequented by the Romans, as a
passage from the south to the north. This dagger was presented by Mr.
ALEXANDER COLDSTREAM, schoolmaster at Crieff, (into whose hands it fell,
when schoolmaster at Alloa), to the Society of Antiquarians in Perth.

" Ptolemy places Alauna fomewhere about Sterling ; and it
" was either upon *Alon*, a little river, that runs here into the
" Forth, or at *Alway*, a feat of the Erfkines ‡"

Situation.—Alloa is a port in the county of Clackmannan,
fituated on the north fide of the river Forth, weft long. 3° 45"
lat. 56° 10'. It is about 27¼ miles higher up the frith than
Leith, and 17 lower down the river than Stirling. The windings of the Forth, between Stirling and Alloa, are very remarkable ; the diftance, from the quay of Alloa, to the quay
of Stirling, meafured in the centre of the river, is 17 miles,
and to the bridge of Stirling it is 19½ miles ; whereas the
diftance, by land, from Alloa to the bridge of Stirling, does
not exceed 7 miles, though the turnings in the road are numerous. It is the moft confiderable port in the river ; for
the upper part of the Frith of Forth begins at Kennet Pans
and Higgins Neuk.—There are 3½ feet greater depth of water, in the harbour of Alloa, than on the bar of Leith.

Extent, and Soil.—The parifh is, on an average, about
4 miles from E. to W. and about 2 miles from N. to S.
It confifts of about 3,900 acres. It is bounded on the
fouth by the Forth ; and the bend of the river is fo great,
that the banks meafure about 5½ miles. The grounds,
on the banks of the Forth, are flat, and of a very
rich

‡ It might feem whimfical to derive the name of Alloa from the Greek, and
yet there are feveral circumftances, which might tend to juftify that conjecture.
Αλωα was a rural feaft of the Athenians, which was adopted by the Romans, and
anfwered to our *harveft home*. It was alfo ufed to fignify a grove, or fruitful
plain, well adapted to the celebration of fuch a feaft. If we fuppofe, that the
Romans made good their paffage acrofs the Forth, about the time of harveft,
we may eafily conjecture that they fhould conceive the idea of celebrating their
harveft feaft, at a time which they thought propitious to their wifhes, efpecially
in a fituation peculiarly fitted for that purpofe ; and hence they might very naturally affix to that place the name of Αλωα.

rich *carse*, or kerse foil. Those on the banks of the Devon, are a good carse or clay, though not quite fo fertile. The
grounds rife pretty fuddenly from the carfes, and are of a light
kind, but fertile. Towards the centre of the parifh, the
grounds are pretty high. They are moft agreeably diverfified ;
but the land is much inferior in quality.

Town and Tower, &c.—The fituation of the town is pleafant. There are ftrata of rock, that run a confiderable way
between the kerfe and the high grounds, and break off about
the Ferry, a little above the harbour. On part of this rock
is built the Tower, and the ancient part of the town of
Alloa.—The Tower is the refidence of the reprefentatives
of the family of MARR, and is now poffeffed by a grandfon
of the late Earl ; who has repaired the houfe, and made great
improvements on the land. It was built prior to the year
1300. The higheft turret is 89 feet from the ground, and
the thicknefs of the walls is 11 feet. Notwithftanding its being
fituated on a flat, there is a moft uncommonly fine rich profpect, from the top of the Tower ; and 9 counties can be difcerned from it. The gardens, which were laid out by the late
Earl, in the old tafte, of long avenues, and clipt hedges, are
confiderably modernized ; and the large lawn is now dreffing
up ; fo that the many fine trees in it will be fhewn to advantage. There was originally a natural wood to the eaftward,
and the greateft part of it ftill remains. All kinds of trees,
thrive remarkably well ; and there are oaks, beeches, elms,
planes or fycamores, limes, and afhes of confiderable circumference. There is an uncommon fine black poplar, that meafures 13½ feet round, at the height of 3 or 4 feet from the
ground. The town formerly almoft furrounded the tower,
as in the rude ages they afforded mutual benefits to each other.
Within thefe 30 years, many old houfes, fituated near the tower,

have

have been purchased by the family. Most of the streets are narrow and irregular*.

Harbour, Dock, and Ferry.—At the end of this walk, is the harbour of Alloa, where, at neap tides, the water rises from 12 to 15 feet, and at spring tides from 17 to 22. The quay is built of rough hewn stone, in a substantial manner; and runs within the land, and forms a *pow*, or small creek, where the rivulet, that runs through the N. E. end of the town, falls into the river. There is an act of parliament, that lays a small duty on the anchorage, for support and improvement of the harbour; and this last year, the trustees of this fund have considerably widened the pow.—A little above the harbour, there is an excellent dry dock, capable of receiving vessels of great burthen; both from the depth of the water, which is 16 feet at spring tides, and the width of the gates, which is 34½, free of all obstructions. Opposite to the dock, there is a great depth of water, with excellent anchorage, and full room to swing the largest vessel. As the dock has no connection with the harbour, nor is situated near any buildings, the crews of the vessels that are repairing can cook on board.—Above the dry dock there is a ferry, which is sometimes called the *Craig Ward*, and sometimes the *King's Ferry*, where two very complete piers have been built, one on each side of the river; which renders it an easy, safe, and

commodious

---

* The late Earl seems to have been particularly attentive to the healthiness of the town, and to have endeavoured to make the streets broader, and as straight as the irregularity of the former ones would admit of, so as to unite them. He built one street on a regular plan. It runs in a line parallel to the gardens. It is called *John's Street*, and leads to the harbour. It is between 76 and 80 feet broad, and terminates in a beautiful gravel walk. A row of lime trees, on every side, affords an agreeable shade in summer, and a comfortable shelter in winter.

commodious paſſage, at all times of the tide, The breadth of the water here, at high tide, is above half a mile [*].

Glaſs-Houſe, Tile and Tan-work.—To the weſt of the ferry ſtands a glaſs-houſe, for making bottles, which is thought to be the moſt conveniently ſituated of any in Britain. It can have whatever quantity of coals it requires, at a very eaſy rate, as they are conveyed from the pits, to the very door of the glaſs-houſe, by a waggon way. There is a pier adjoining to the houſe, by which all materials wanted are loaded and unloaded. It is ſaid, that there are propoſals making for building another houſe. The extent, to which the manufactory of glaſs has been carried, is amazing. It is not half a century, ſince one glaſs houſe at Leith, and one at Glaſgow, ſupplied all Scotland, while the Company wrought the one half year at the one place, and the next at the other. Similar obſervations might be made on other manufactures, and lead to very enlarged ſpeculations.—A little to the N. W. of the glaſs-houſe, there is a tile and brick work, upon a pretty large ſcale, and well employed. Above that, there is a good tan-work.

Fiſhing, Iſlands, Water Fowls, &c.—Before we leave the river, upon whoſe banks all theſe different works are ſituated, we muſt take notice of the fiſhing. It is certain, that, for many years, numbers of people took to the fiſhing of ſalmon, during the ſummer months, but in a bad ſtile, with what is called *pock nets.* They were not very ſucceſsful, as might

have

[*] If the ſcheme of making turnpike roads, on both ſides, takes place, this will be one of the ſhorteſt, and moſt agreeable communications, opened between the north and the ſouth, with ſcarcely any interruption from wind or tide. Mr. ERSKINE has lately begun to feu out ground for a NEW TOWN, between John Street and the Ferry, on a beautiful field, and regular plan. It promiſes to be an airy healthy place, and excellently calculated for thoſe who are carrying on buſineſs at the harbour.

have been forefeen; however, they continued, though with fmall advantage, till a law-fuit was carried on againft them by the town of Stirling; and the mode of pock nets being condemned, on an old act of parliament, they were reftrained within certain limits, from fifhing in that manner; and the fifhing, fince that time, has been moftly abandoned §.—After paffing the ferry of *Craig Ward*, the river becomes narrower; and there are fome beautiful iflands, which are called *Inches*. Thefe furnifh excellent pafture for cattle during the fummer, and are efteemed medicinal for fuch as are weakly or fick. They are a gentle kind of falt marfh, as they are entirely covered with water in fpring tides. Thefe Inches are fre-quented by great quantities of water fowl, viz. wild ducks, teals, widgeons, gulls, &c. &c. Here they find fhelter, and a variety of food fuited to their nature. Sometimes fcarts, or cormorants, goofeanders, &c. appear here. The ftormy pet-terels, or what the failors call *Mother Cary's chickens*, were feen about the Ferry laft winter; and one of them was killed by Mr. Erfkine, junior. It was thought fingular to fee thefe birds, who feldom appear near the land, fo far up the country. Upon the point of thefe inches, they erect what are called *yares*, a fort of fcaffold projecting into the water; upon which they build little huts to protect them from the weather; from thefe fcaffolds they let down, at certain times of the tide, their nets, and are often very fuccefsful in taking the fmaller fifh, fuch as herrings, *garvies*, or fprats, *fparlings*, or fmelts, fmall whitings, haddocks, fea trouts, and eels. In this manner fal-

mon

§ Had this reftraint operated as it ought to have done, and obliged them to have exchanged their method, and employed the long nets, the beft effects would probably have followed. The excufe generally given for not trying it, is the depth of water, and foulnefs of the bottom. The laft, it is thought might be partly remedied; and the fuccefs which attends this method, a little farther weft, and in the fame parifh, gives great encouragement to make the experiment.

mon are ſometimes caught; as well as Congo eels, ſturgeon, foals, turbots, cod, gurnet, or piper, and ſkate.*—Sometimes, about the end of September, there comes a vaſt ſhoal of fiſh, called *gandanooks*, or *Egyptian herrings*. They have a faint reſemblance of the mackarel, but with a long ſharp bill, like a ſnipe. This becomes fatal to them on our muddy banks, as the bill is fixed in the mud; and in this way they are entangled, and caught in great quantities, on the ebbing of the tide. They are not an unpleaſant fiſh, but rather dry; they are however a great relief to many poor people. Porpoiſes now and then appear here, and ſometimes ſmall whales have been ſeen and taken †.

Tullibody.—In proceeding up the river, we come to the barony of Tullibody. The houſe is ſet down in the Carſe, almoſt cloſe to the water ſide. Behind it, on the north, there is a beautiful bank, well furniſhed with a variety of fine trees; and on each hand of this bank, almoſt at equal diſtances from the houſe, there are two prominences, jutting out into the Carſe, which ſeem to protect and ſhelter the lower grounds. The one on the eaſt is covered with trees, and the one on the weſt with ſome farm houſes.

Rivers, Fiſh, &c.—In the front of the houſe is the river, with two of the Inches formerly mentioned. From this, up

to

* In September 1777, a ſkate, of the ſpecies of the ſharp noſed ray, was caught here, which was of a very large ſize. The length, from the tip of the noſe to the end of the tail, was 7 feet 3 inches; the breadth, from the extremity of one fin to that of the other, 5 feet 3 inches; and it weighed 13½ ſtones Dutch weight, which is about 2⅕ cwt. avoirdupoiſe.

† About 2 years ago, an *angler*, or *fiſhing frog*, was thrown aſhore at the Ferry. It is a fiſh of a very uncommon appearance, reſembling a frog in its tadpole ſtate. They ſometimes grow to a large ſize, and are thought to be a great enemy to the dog fiſh.

to the *Cambus*, they continue to fish with tolerable success. General Abercromby now lets the fishing for 40l. per annum, which formerly only gave 5l. Upon the west, and not a mile from the house of Tullibody, the river Devon discharges itself into the Forth; and vessels of tolerable burden can load and unload, at a pier, built at the mouth of the Devon. Sloops and large boats, loaded with grain, come up near to the village of Cambus, to supply the mills, and a brewery, and to carry off the manufactures of both. A high dam-head, erected for driving the corn and barley mills on each side of the river, forms a great obstruction to the salmon getting up the Devon. They are seen often attempting this, but they seldom succeed, except in high tides. An oil mill has lately been erected on this river, which is said to perform a great deal of work. On the other side of the Devon, there is a rich flat piece of ground, called *West Cambus*, belonging to Lord Alva. It consists of 160 acres of ground, which is let in two farms, one of which has the corn mill. The tenants pay kain, cess and schoolmaster's salary, over and above their rent. The lands of Bandeath, Kersie, and part of the Frosk, which all lie on the other side of the Forth, are bound and thirled to the mill of West Cambus*.—West Cambus is bounded by the parish of Logie,

both

---

* Some years ago, between the Cambus and the Frosk ford, there was dragged up a brass collar, with this inscription on it: " ALEXANDER STEUART, " *found guilty of death for theft, at Perth, 5th December* 1701, *and gifted by the* " *Justiciars, as a perpetual servant to Sir* JOHN ARESKEN *of* ALVA." This collar is now in the possession of the Antiquarian Society of Scotland, with the following copy of the justiciar's gift, which is taken from the original in the Duke of Atholl's charter house:

" At Perth, the 5th day of December 1701. The commissioners of Justi- " ciary of the south district, for securing the peace in the Highlands, considering " that Donald Robertson, Alexander Stewart, John Robertson, and Donald " M'Donald, prisoners within the tolbooth, and indicted and tried at this Court,

" and,

both on the north and weft. The lands of Eaft Cambus run
along the banks of the Devon, until they meet with the upper
barony of Tullibody †. The Upper and Lower baronies of
Tullibody,

‹‘ and, by virtue of the inqueft, returned guilty of death ; and the commiffion-
“ ers have changed their punifhment of death to perpetual fervitude, and that
“ the faid pannels are at the court's difpofal : Therefore, the faid commiffioners
“ have given and gifted, and hereby give and gift the faid Donald M'Donald,
“ one of the faid prifoners, as a perpetual fervant to the Right Honourable
“ John Earl of Tullibardine ; recommending to his Lordfhip to caufe provide
‹‘ an collar of brafs, iron, or copper, which, by his fentence or doom, whereof
‹‘ an extract is delivered to the magiftrates of the faid burgh of Perth, is to be
“ upon his neck, with this infcription, ‘ Donald M'Donald, found guilty of
“ death for theft, at Perth, December 5. 1701, and gifted, as a perpetual fervant,
“ to John Earl of Tullibardine :’ And recommending alfo to his Lordfhip, to
“ tranfport him from the faid prifon once the next week. And the faid com-
‹‘ miffioners have ordained, and hereby ordain the magiftrates of Perth, and
“ keeper of their tolbooth, to deliver the faid Donald M'Donald to the faid
“ Earl of Tullibardine, having the faid collar and infcription, conform to the
“ fentence and doom aforefaid. Extracted from the books of adjournal of the
“ faid diftrict by me James Taylor, writer to his Majefty's fignet, clerk of court
“ *Sic fubfcribitur James Taylor, Clk.*”

Since this account was wrote, it has been found to be a miftake, that this
collar was taken up near the Cambus; for it was dragged by a net out of the
Forth, oppofite to *Chamberlain' Lands*, in the parifh of Logie, whereof Sir John
Arfkin is fuperior. But as the hiftory of this collar was probably unknown
to Mr. WRIGHT, when he wrote the account of the parifh of LOGIE, it is inferted here as a curious fact, well worthy of being generally known.

† Here there are fome fine crofts, which are fuppofed to have given the name
of *Tullibothy*, or *Tullibody*, (i. e. *the croft of the oath*), to the barony and village,
which ftands at the head of it. Many new houfes have been built of late.
There are the remains of an old church in Tullibody ; the lands of which, with
the inches and fifhings, are narrated in a charter by DAVID I., who founded the
abbey of Cambufkenneth, in the year 1147 ; and are made over to that abbacy,
together with the church of Tullibody, and its chapel of Alloa. There are no
records of the union of thefe two churches of Alloa and Tullibody. It feems
probable, that it was about the beginning of the Reformation. It appears from
JOHN KNOX, that, in the year 1759, when *Monfieur d'Oyfel* commanded the French
troops

Tullibody†, or what are called the *Carſe* and *Dryfield*, contain about 1,100 acres. The tenants pay *kains* and ceſs, and are obliged to carry their farm barley 6 miles, if required ; but

troops on the coaſt of Fife, they were alarmed with the arrival of the Engliſh fleet, and thought of nothing but a haſty retreat. It was in the month of January, and at the breaking up of a great ſtorm. William Kirkcaldy of Grange, attentive to the circumſtances in which the French were caught, took advantage of this ſituation, and marched with great expedition towards Stirling, and cut the bridge of Tullibody, which is over the Devon, to prevent their retreat. The French, finding no other means of eſcape, took the roof off the church, and laid it along the bridge where it was cut, and got ſafe to Stirling. It is generally believed, that this church remained in the ſame diſmantled ſtate till ſome years ago, that George Abercromby, Eſq. of Tullibody, covered it with a new roof, and erected within it a tomb for his family. There is ſtill a large burying ground round this church ; and on the north ſide of it, where there had been formerly an entry, there is a ſtone coffin, with a niche for the head, and two for the arms, covered with a thick hollowed lid, like a tureen. The lid is a good deal broken ; but a curious tradition is preſerved of the coffin, viz. " That a certain young lady of the neighbourhood had declared her af-
" fection for the miniſter, who, either from his ſtation, or want of inclination,
" made no returns ; that the lady ſickened and died ; but gave orders not to
" bury her in the ground, but to put her body in the ſtone coffin, and place it
" at the entry to the church." Thus was the poor vicar puniſhed ; and the ſtone retains the name of the *Maiden Stone.*

　† On the eaſt end of the village and crofts, there was a large rugged piece of ground, upwards of 140 acres, formerly let at 40l. Scotch, or 3l. 6s. 8d. Sterling. Between 60 and 70 years ago, it was incloſed, and planted with firs. When they were between 40 and 50 years of age, they were cut, and ſold at from 50l. to 60l. per acre ; and the ground is now planted with oaks, which are in a very thriving condition.—Immediately on the eaſt of this wood, there is a riſing ground, in the upper barony of Alloa, called *Lorn's Hill,* probably from its being the ſpot where the Marquis of Lorn encamped, when in purſuit of the Marquis of Montroſe in the civil wars. Mr. Erſkine, about 14 years ago, built a farm houſe and good offices on it. It was formerly a dreary and uncultivated waſte, though the grounds were beautifully varied. Mr. Erſkine has humoured the lying of the ground, in forming his incloſures and clumps, and belts or ſtrips of planting ; ſo that it is at preſent a pleaſant ſpot, and will, in a few years, become a very agreeable farm ſtcad.

but this feldom or never happens. They are fubjeâ alfo to a *darg* (or day's work), for every acre, or 10d. per annum. All multures are aboliſhed.

Shaw Park.—On the N. E. extremity of the pariſh, ſtands SHAW PARK, the feat of LORD CATHCART. The houfe and offices take up a pretty large fpace. The grounds about it are delightfully varied, and fet off the large plantations to great advantage. The late Lord beſtowed a very large fum of money, on it and the houfe ; which ſtands high, as the ground rifes to it gradually from the Forth, which is about 2 miles diſtant. It commands an extenfive profpeâ. From the drawing room windows, you have in view a fine reach of the river, with the towers of Alloa and Clackmannan, and the caſtle of Stirling; and even the hills of Tinto, in Clydefdale, and Ben Lomond, are diſtinâly feen.

Artificial Lake, Mills, &c.—Upon the eaſtern extremity of the pariſh, there is a large artificial piece of water, that looks like a lake. It was made about the beginning of the century, at a very confiderable expence, for the ufe of the Alloa coal works. It is called *Gartmorn Dam.* The head, which was heightened and repaired a few years ago, is faced with rough hewn ſtone, and meafures upwards of 320 yards. When the dam is full, it covers 128 Scotch acres of ground, nearly equal to 162 Engliſh ſtatute acres. There is a fluice, which regulates the quantity of water to be conveyed into a lade, which firſt drives a mill, originally ereâed for grinding fnuff, but now better employed in chipping and grinding wood and dye ſtuffs. A lint mill has, within thefe few years, been built, juſt before the water is conveyed into pipes for forcing it up to the engine, for raifing the water out of the coal pits, and to another for drawing up the coals. Having performed thefe

important

important purpofes, for which the large refervoir was originally made, the fame water is again collected into a fmaller dam, and from thence conveyed in a lade, to a fine fet of mills in the town of Alloa, for grinding wheat, oats, and malt, and making pearl barley. There are two large wheels, of 19 feet diameter, in the centre of the houfe, which drive the whole machinery in both ends of the mills. Though all the mills are feldom employed at the fame time, they can be wrought, on a great exertion, and are capable of grinding 400 bolls, about equal to 250 quarters, in a day *.—From thefe mills the water falls into a rivulet, that runs through the town, and drives a fnuff and fulling mill ; it then paffes through Mr. Erfkine's pleafure grounds, till it comes near the harbour; where it is again confined by a ftrong dam of earth ; and a large fluice is built in it, of hewn ftone, with a long trough of ftone, which gives the water a prodigious velocity, for clearing the harbour of the mud : fo that this little water, originally a fmall branch of the Black Devon, (fed only by a few fprings, and the furface water), is made to ferve the moft important purpofes, by driving 7 mills, within this parifh, befides cleaning the harbour.

Agriculture.—About 20 years ago, the hufbandry of this parifh was uncommonly bad, particularly in the barony of Alloa†. On the expiration of the *tacks* (leafes), a great change

* Thefe mills have been erected within thefe 10 years. The building is 93 feet long, over walls, 31 feet broad, and 32 high. The machinery alone coft 500l. and is uncommonly well executed. From the time the foundation ftone was laid, it was not quite 12 months before the mills began to work ; and, notwithftanding the great ftrefs upon fuch new walls, they were fo well built, that there is not the fmalleft crack to be obferved.

† The farms were fmall, and the miferable *fteadings* (the old phrafe for a farm houfe and offices), denoted the poverty of the tenants, who relied folely on the driving

change took place. The ſizes of the farms were enlarged; the tenants were no longer obliged to drive coals; all ſervices and thirlages were aboliſhed; incloſing went briſkly on, and the fences are now remarkable, both for ſtrength and beauty. A wall of 2¼ feet high, built with ſtone and lime, is placed within a foot of the thorns, according to Sir *George Suttie's* method, thus mixing the ſecurity of the fence with the beauty and warmth of the hedge. There are many clumps and ſtrips of planting interſperſed through the farms; ſo that, in a few years, what was a moſt uncomfortable dreary waſte, will become one of the beſt cultivated, and moſt beautiful ſpots in Scotland. The improvement of agriculture has, indeed, been moſt uncommonly rapid in this little corner, perhaps more ſo than in almoſt any other*. There are ſix threſhing machines

in

driving of the coals for the payment of their pittance of rent; and contented themſelves with ſcratching a ſmall part of their grounds, the produce of which was ſcarcely ſufficient to maintain themſelves and their cattle. There were no incloſures, and the ground was over-run with *whins* (furze), broom, and all kinds of weeds, which but too plainly marked the poverty, ſloth and ignorance of the poſſeſſors.

* Juſt as the ſpirit of improvement was beginning to ſhew itſelf, an intelligent Eaſt Lothian farmer took a farm in this pariſh, (conſiſting of upwards of 200 Scotch acres, or 254 Engliſh ſtatute acres), who was remarkable for his good plowing, draining, and dreſſing of his grounds. His example quickened the diligence of his neighbours. A few years after he was ſettled here, he propoſed to his landlord and brother farmers, to have trials of ſkill among the ploughmen; which ſcheme was eagerly adopted, and PLOWING MATCHES were firſt eſtabliſhed in 1784. Laſt ſpring, (1791), 40 ploughs appeared, in an oblong field of 12 Scotch, or 15 Engliſh acres, all with two horſes, and no drivers. The improved chain plough, on Small's conſtruction, was the only one uſed; and it was computed that 1,600l. never placed the horſes and ploughs on the field. The ſituation, being ſhort ridges on a gentle declivity, ſet off the ſhew to the greateſt advantage; ſo that, to any one fond of huſbandry, the ſight was moſt uncommonly delightful and pleaſing. In ſhort, the good effects of this inſtitution have ſurpaſſed the warmeſt expectations of its promoters. From this period

in this parish. The last erected was by a farmer, who has only 60 Scotch, or 76 English acres of ground; and as improvements are daily making in them, and the price is reduced, it is probable that, in a very short time, they will be held to be as indifpenfibly neceffary to a farm as the fanners *.

There is no particular rotation or courfe of crops univerfally followed here. The turnip husbandry cannot be well adopted, as the low grounds are carfe, or rich clay, and moft of the higher grounds have a fubfoil, of a cold ftiff till (or barren clay); fo that the damage done, by poaching the ground, in taking off the crop, overbalances any advantage, that could poffibly accrue from the cultivation of that ufeful root, fo beneficial to farmers, in a more favourable foil †.—The following rotation is practifed by fome of the farmers, on carfe lands: The 1ft year, fallow; the 2d, wheat; the 3d, beans; the 4th, barley and grafs feeds; the 5th, hay; the fecond crop cut for foiling horfes and cattle in the houfe; then broke up in the 6th year for oats. Sometimes a crop of hay is taken in the 6th, foiling, &c. and then it is broke up in the 7th year

for

riod may be dated the excellent plowing that appears in this fmall county; and as many places, in diftant parts of the country, have followed the example, it is to be hoped, that they have reaped equal benefit from it. The name, therefore, of HUGH REOCH, *of the Hiltown of Alloa*, deferves to be gratefully remembered by every lover of agriculture.

* The threfhing machines, or mills, were firft introduced into common ufe in this fmall county, Mr. GEORGE MEIKLE having erected one that went by water, at Kilbagie, in the neighbouring parifh of Clackmannan, in 1787. It was Mr. Meikle, who erected the machinery of the mills of Alloa.

† Thofe who attempted turnips have been obliged to give them up, as well as the fowing of wheat on a clover lay; for whether it got 1, 2, or 3 plowings, a light brown grub worm deftroyed the root of the wheat. This misfortune might poffibly be overcome, if a large quantity of hot lime were laid on the clover juft before it is plowed up. This, however, is only *conjecture*, as no fuf-ficient trial has yet been made of it.

for oats. Some farmers sow clover alone; others mix a little rye-grafs with it.

In the higher grounds, or, as they are sometimes improperly called, *Dryfield*, some farmers have, the 1ft year fallow, or potatoes; the 2d, wheat; the 3d, beans and peafe; the 4th, barley and grafs feeds; the 5th hay, the fecond crop being cut for foiling, or fometimes paftured. Some take, in the 6th year, hay, and then it is paftured for 1, 2, 3 or 4 years, and afterwards broke up for oats.—When the ground is defigned to be paftured, white clover, (and fometimes a little yellow), with a fmall quantity of narrow-leaved plantain, or rib grafs is mixed with the red clover and rye grafs. The produce varies confiderably.

PRODUCE on CARSE LANDS.

Per Scotch acre. WHEAT. *Bolls**.		*Per Eng. acre.* *Quar. Bufb.*		*Per Scotch acre.* OATS. *Bolls.*		*Per Eng. acre.* *Quar. Bufb.*	
14,	great crop, *equal to*	5	5	14,	great crop, *equal to*	8	6
12,	———— =	4	6½	13,	———— =	8	1
10,	good crop, =	4	0	10,	good crop, =	6	2
9,	medium, =	3	5	9,	medium, =	5	5
8½,	———— =	3	3	8½,	———— =	5	2
	BARLEY.				BEANS.		
10,	good crop, *equal to*	6	2	10,	good crop, *equal to*	4	2¾
9,	———— =	5	5	9,	———— =	3	7¼
8,	medium, =	5	0	5,	medium, =	2	1¼
7½,	———— =	4	5½				

SOWN GRASS HAY †.

Stones, Tron Weight.			*Avoirdupoife Weight.*		
320,	great crop,	*equal to*	2 tons,	8 cwt.	
240,	medium,	=	1 —	17 —	

PRODUCE

* *The bolls of wheat, per* SCOTCH *acre, are* LINLITHGOW *meafure; and thofe of barley, oats, beans, &c.* STIRLINGSHIRE *meafure. The proportion, above ftated, of the produce per* ENGLISH *acre, is* STANDARD *meafure.*

† *There is little or almoft no hay made from old grafs, or, what is called in Scotland, natural grafs.*

PRODUCE *on the* INFERIOR SOILS, *commonly called* DRYFIELD.

Per Scotch acre.	WHEAT.	*Per Eng. acre.*		*Per Scotch acre.*	PEASE.	*Per Eng. acre.*	
Bolls.		*Quar.*	*Bush.*	*Bolls.*		*Quar.*	*Bush.*
8, medium crop,	=	3	1¼	5, medium crop,	=	2	1¼
	BARLEY.				HAY.		
6½, ————	=	4	2	*Stones, tron weight.*		*Avoird. weight.*	
	OATS.			200 medium crop =		1 ton 12 cwt.	
6¾, ————	=	4	3				

The QUANTITY *of* SEED.

Per Scotch acre.		WHEAT.	*Per Eng. acre.*		*Per Scotch acre.*		OATS.	*Per Eng. acre.*	
Firlots.	*Pecks.*		*Bush.*	*Pecks.*	*Firlots.*	*Pecks.*		*Bush.*	*Pecks.*
4	0	*about equal to*	3	1	4	0	*nearly equal to*	4	3
3	0	=	2	0½	3	2	=	4	1½
		BARLEY.							
3	0	*nearly equal to*	3	2½					
2	3	=	3	1½					

EXTENT *of* FARMS FORMERLY.

Scotch acres.		*Eng. acres.*
From 30 or 40,	*equal to*	38 or 51
To 60 or 70,	=	76 or 89

FORMER RENT *of* CARSE LANDS.

From 20s. to 24s. *equal to* from 15s. 8¾d. to 18s. 10½d.

FORMER RENT *of* INFERIOR LAND, *or* DRYFIELD.

From 3s. to 4s. or 5s. *equal to* from 2s. 4¼ to 3s. 1¾d. or 3s. 11¼d.

EXTENT *of* FARMS *at* PRESENT.

Scotch acres.		*Eng. acres.*
From 60 to 90,	*equal to*	from 76 to 114
——— 120 to 160,	=	——— 152 to 203
——— 200 to 360,	=	——— 254 to 457

PRESENT RENT *of* CARSE LANDS.

From 30s. to 40s. *equal to* from 23s. 7d. to 31s. 6d.

PRESENT RENT *of* INFERIOR LAND, *or* DRYFIELD.

From 10s. to 21s. *equal to* from 7s. 10½d to 16s. 6¼d.

Formerly

Formerly the rents of the parish were partly paid in *kind* *。 Those of the barony of Alloa are now wholly paid in *money*, except a few kain, which are paid over and above the stipu‑ lated rent. The tenants likewife pay half of the cefs, or land tax. Although the rents throughout the parish are con‑ fiderably raifed, they are not thought to be over-rated ; and the profperity of the induftrious and intelligent tenants plainly demonftrate it †.

Implements

* When the tenants are poor, *paying their rent in kind* may be detrimental to them ; for, in bad years, they find it difficult, if not impoffible, to pay the fti‑ pulated quantity of grain ; and as the price of it, in thofe years, muft of courfe be high, the tenant incurs a heavy debt, which many abundant crops will not enable him to get the better of. There are, however, various opinions on this point ; many infifting, that, in long leafes, it is the only equitable method ; and, in fome parts of the country, the payment in kind is indifpenfible.

† On letting the new tacks (or leafes), there was a fmall farm, in the upper barony of Alloa, poffeffed by a man, named DONALDSON, of whofe anceftors the following traditional tale is told :—" That King James V., when out a hunting, being once benighted, and thrown out from his attendants, took fhelter in this poor cottage, where he was hofpitably received and entertained ; the *goodman* (*i. e.* the farmer or landlord), calling to his wife to bring the hen that fat neareft the cock, (which is always reckoned the beft one), and make a fup‑ per. The King, delighted with the frank, hofpitable manner of his landlord, defired, that the next time he was at Stirling, he would call at the caftle, for *the Goodman of Ballinguiack* *. Donaldfon did as he was defired, and was aftonifhed to find that the King had been his gueft. He was on this dignifi d with the name of *King of the Muirs ;* and this title has defcended from father to fon ever fince." This tradition made the proprietor loth to turn out the tenant, efpecially as he was defirous of trying the experiment, whether thefe kind of tenants could be taught any thing of improved hufbandry ; but, to his great mortification, he has found that the man, though only about 40 years of age, could not conquer his bad habits, or profit in the leaft from the example of his diligent neigh‑ bours. There certainly muft have been fomething peculiarly depreffing in the

bondage

* BALLINGUIACK *is a narrow path, leading down the north weft fide of the rock at Stirling ; and the King is faid to have taken this title, when in difguife.*

Implements of Hufbandry.—There is now fcarce one of the old awkward carts to be met with †. The farmers, at prefent, ufe large carts, with iron axles, drawn by two horfes; and, in hay or harveft time, they have large open bodies to fit the fame wheels, in which they carry great loads, frequently from 90 to 100 ftone tron weight, (which is nearly from 18 cwt. to a ton avoirdupoife), of well made hay. However, what was afferted by the late Lord Kames, in his *Gentleman Farmer*, that " a well conftructed one-horfe cart, is the moft profitable carriage," feems now to be almoft generally acknowledged; and the farmers here will probably adopt them very foon. Since the two-horfe ploughs have become general, the breed of horfes ufed by the farmers is confiderably improved. Formerly, they had miferable *garrans*, not worth more than 5l. or 6l. a piece; now, it is no uncommon fight to fee, in a farmer's plough, horfes which are worth from 36l. to 48l. the pair. The ploughs now ufed are chiefly of *Small's* conftruction, with an iron head and caft iron mould board. They coft from 2l. to 2l. 10s. according to the weight of the iron.

Servants.—All the principal farmers here prefer *married* fervants,

---

bondage of fervices, fo univerfally impofed on the old tenants of Scotland, as it feems to have rendered them almoft incapable of becoming farmers. They feem to have been only fitted for fervants; and, did not their pride prevent them, they would enjoy more comfort and happinefs as day labourers. This obfervation is at leaft juft with regard to this parifh.

† Formerly, all the implements of hufbandry ufed here were ill conftructed. Some years ago, it was a rarity to find a farmer with *fpoke and nave wheels* to his cart. The carts in common ufe, confifted of a few boards ill put together, and of a fize not larger than a good wheel barrow, placed upon a thick wooden axle, which was fixed to fome low wheels, compofed of 3 pieces of wood, joined together by two or three large wooden pins. The axle turned round with the tumbril wheels.

ſervants, as being more ſteady, orderly and tractable. The farmer provides him a houſe as near to his own as poſſible. It is much to be wiſhed that this cuſtom was more univerſal, as it is a moſt beneficial one to the country. It is, in fact, having cottagers on the very beſt eſtabliſhment ; for the ancient kind of cottars were but too often miſerably oppreſſed by the tenants, on whoſe farms they were eſtabliſhed; as they often exacted their ſervices more rigorouſly, than the landlords did from the tenants. But as the ploughmen, in this diſtrict, receive their ſtated fee (or wages), kitchen money and meal, and pay only 10s. or 12s. for their cottages, (though indeed they generally have them *gratis*), beſides their maſters' horſes drawing home their coals for them, no oppreſſion can well take place. They have alſo the advantage of having their wives, and ſuch of their children as can work in the fields, always at hand, who receive the common wages during hay-making and harveſt ; and are likewiſe often employed in picking ſtones off the land, and pulling or cutting down weeds. All this is of conſiderable benefit, both to maſters and ſervants, and tends to rear up an uſeful, healthy generation of labourers.

Sale of Grain.—There is not the ſmalleſt reſemblance of a public market for grain, within the pariſh or county ; but the farmers find no difficulty in diſpoſing of their crops by private bargain. The moſt ſubſtantial ſell their grain, by the higheſt price of the Mid Lothian, or the Haddington fiars ; that is, they give two or three months credit to the purchaſer, at the price which is the average of the year. Smaller tenants ſell their grain, for the current price at the time of their delivering it.

Hay,

Hay.—The collieries in the neighbourhood use a consider-able quantity of hay : Their usual price is 4d. per stone ; and the hay is weighed, at the place where it is stacked to be used. Some of the farmers have found out their mistake, in deferring the cutting of their hay till late in the season, thinking, by so doing, to increase the quantity. It does so indeed to the eye ; but in reality it is quite the reverse : For hay, cut at the proper time, retains all the seed in it, and therefore it weighs considerably heavier, and has more nourishment in it ; and the second crop of grass is earlier, and more plentiful. Besides, it does less damage to the ground ; so that the greedy farmer cheats himself in every respect. Few, or almost no farmers, consume any quantity of hay themselves ; but this will probably come in course, as their knowledge improves ; for though much has been done, and that rapidly too, there are yet many *arcana*, in this pleasant art, that the farmers have still to learn.

Sheep, Cattle and Manure.—There are few or no sheep kept in the parish ; nor is there much anxiety about the breed of cattle. There is little or almost no attention paid to the Dairy, although milk, in all its shapes, would find a good and steady sale in the town of Alloa. Some, who have kept an exact account of the sale of this article, are of opinion, that 6l. or 7l. might be easily made of a cow in the year. —The farmers are diligent in procuring manure from the town of Alloa ; but the quantity would be considerably en-larged if the streets were properly cleaned. Few farmers have limed to any extent, though the practice is creeping in. There is no limestone in the parish ; but it is brought, both burnt and unburnt, from Lord Elgin's limeworks at Charles-town, near Limekilns. The price of the slacked lime, deli-vered at the shore of Alloa, is about 7d. the wheat boll (Linlithgow

lithgow meafure), which is rather more than four Winchefter bufhels. The farmers generally bring up the raw lime ftones, and burn them on their lands.

Inclofures.—The glebe of Alloa was one of the firft inclo-fures of the parifh, which was executed by the prefent incum-bent in 1761. It is a light, but fertile foil. It had been fo much neglected, that it then produced nothing but wild mu-ftard *, and innumerable weeds. After inclofing and laying it down in clover, the crop was fold green for upwards of 8l. per acre. Some few people near the town followed the mini-fter's example, and with good fuccefs. Upwards of 7 guineas per acre were got for the clover crop of 4 acres of the glebe, in 1791.

Farms.—There are various opinions concerning the fize of farms. In general, fmall farms are reckoned moft advantage-ous for the country ; but it is feldom that any definition of a large or fmall farm is given. They are commonly ftated by the rents ; whereas the number of acres, capable of being cul-tivated to advantage, fhould be fpecified †. People, in gene-ral,

* It is a curious fact, that, in fome of Mr. ERSKINE's old rentals, among the different grains paid by the tenants, a fmall quantity of *muftard feed* is men-tioned, though the cultivation of it here is now totally unknown.

† Some years ago, the late Mr. WEDDERBURN of St. Germains, in Eaft Lo-thian, publifhed an ingenious and fenfible pamphlet, on this moft important que-ftion, " What *proportion* of the produce of arable land ought to be paid as *rent* " to the landlord ?" A book deferving the attention of every landholder and tenant in the kingdom, as the knowledge of it would greatly tend to their mutual benefit. Mr. Wedderburn ftates, that a farm of 120 Scotch = 152 Englifh acres of good land, is fuch an one as will enable a man to bring up a ufeful family with credit and comfort. Double that quantity of ground, he calls a *middle fized* farm ; and three times the fize, (360 Scotch = 457 Englifh acres)

ral, are apt to form opinions from local circumſtances, and to apply them indiſcriminately to all ſituations. What appears a large farm, in ſome parts of the country, would be called a moderate one, nay perhaps a ſmall one, in others. It is an undoubted fact, that in this pariſh, until the farms were enlarged, huſbandry was at a very low ebb. Any one, who remembers the grounds in their former ſtate, and who ſees them now, cannot but acknowledge the different appearance that the country makes. Formerly, the miſerable tenants had wretched accommodation for their families, or produce of their fields or cattle ; ragged children, with ſcanty education ; and wretched complaints of poverty at every term. There are now ſubſtantial houſes, and convenient offices ; a double, and often a triple produce ; fields beautifully dreſſed and incloſed ; a wealthy tenantry, and growing improvements*.

Coal.

aeres), a *large* one ; and thinks that few or none ſhould exceed it. Large farms, ſome people maintain, depopulate the country, and occaſion the riſe of all kinds of proviſion, &c. &c.; but there are others who hold a very different opinion; and, if we may be allowed to judge by analogy, with ſome appearance of reaſon. It is allowed, that no trade can be carried on to advantage without a ſufficient ſtock ; that the diviſion of labour, and large dealings, enable people to ſell at a leſs profit, as the quantity ſufficiently recompences for the lowneſs of the price. Why ſhould the farming trade totally differ from all others? A certain ſize of a farm is abſolutely neceſſary to carry on the buſineſs with any proſpect of ſucceſs. In thoſe parts of Britain, where improvements have been carried on to the greateſt extent, were they brought about by large or ſmall farms ? Examine them minutely, and ſee where the greateſt ſkill is diſplayed, or the largeſt produce brought to market.

* The leaſes are commonly given for 19 years ; but where the ground was ſo wild, that it required a tedious and expenſive proceſs for the melioration of it, 2 nineteen years were given, with a ſmall riſe of rent at the commencement of the ſecond period. This is thought to be no more than equitable. Many gentlemen, who have tried improving ground themſelves, are thoroughly ſenſible, that the beſt part of a 19 years tack paſſes away before any adequate profit can be received for the expence laid out ; and the farmer, who, from his knowledge and ſkill, adds to the ſtock of the community, is certainly entitled to ample retribution.

Coal.—The colliery of Alloa having been long eſtabliſhed *, there are ſtill many ancient cuſtoms in it. The colliers could not leave their work ; of courſe ſome recompence † was neceſſary from the maſter. As the colliers in this work generally bind themſelves for a certain term of years, little alteration has taken place in this old cuſtom, notwithſtanding the new collier law, which paſſed in 1775 ‡. The colliers, in all countries, are generally an unruly ſet of labourers ; and thoſe of this work were like their neighbours. About 30 years ago, they were perſuaded to give ſome little education to their children ; and a few years after (when in ſearch of a new ſchoolmaſter for them), the proprietor of the colliery was lucky

* This pariſh has been long famous for the fine coal mines in it. How long they have been wrought is uncertain. There are accounts of the expence of working them in 1623. The price was then 6s. 8d. per chalder. The ſame meaſure has been ſold at a conſiderably lower price within theſe 35 years.

† The allowance given to the old collier, when paſt labour, was two pecks of meal per week, each weighing 8 lb. Dutch, or 8 lb. 11 oz. avoirdupoiſe ; and he had his free houſe and garden, and likewiſe his firing, continued to him, the ſame as when working. Every widow had one peck of meal per week, a free houſe, &c. &c. ; and if ſhe had any ſons grown up, who were able to carry on their father's work at the coal wall, they continued at it, for behoof of the family, as they did in their father's lifetime, until they were married.

‡ There were ſome parts of the old law which were barbarous, and which undoubtedly required to be aboliſhed ; but it is queſtioned, whether the total repeal of it has made the collier happier, or if it has had the effect of inducing common labourers to commence colliers, or to train up their children to the buſineſs, as was ſaid to be the expectations of the promoters of it ; nor is the price of working coal reduced. It is well known to all coalmaſters, that a collier can never earn ſo much in any work, as in that in which he was brought up. The preſent law has unhappily encouraged vagrancy amongſt the colliers ; and, whenever they begin to wander, they generally bid farewel to induſtry. On going to a new place, they conſtantly, on ſome pretence or other, get money, And as the collier has broken all ties of relationſhip and habits, his head is continually on the rack to contrive ſome method to ſhift his place, in hopes of getting more money from a new maſter, without working for it.

lucky enough to find an old ferjeant of the Royals, a diligent
virtuous man, who not only brought the children, but even
their parents, into fome kind of order and difcipline. This
has greatly affifted the prefent proprietor, who, during the
refidence of 21 years, has paid particular attention to the colliers, and has now the pleafure of feeing a very great reformation among them. They were formerly remarkable for their
ignorance and diffolutenefs of manners. They are now rather
above the ordinary rate of the common people*. Each collier
has a free houfe and garden, a quantity of meal proportioned
to the number of the family, at the rate of 10½d. per peck,
and their firing: Each family, upon an average, confumes
rather more than 7 cwt. per week. The colliers are paid by
the piece; their earnings, therefore, depend on their own
diligence and fkill. The price of working varies according to
the quality of the different feams of coal. A good collier can
clear from 25l. to 35l. per annum; an extraordinary clever
one may perhaps exceed this by 10l. or 12l. The depth of
a bearing pit cannot well exceed 18 fathom, or 108 feet.
There are traps, or flairs, down to thefe pits, with a hand
rail to affift the women and children, who carry up the coals
on their backs. The price given by the colliers is 4d. per
chalder, of 30 cwt. A diligent bearer often brings up, from
the bottom of the pit, 6 chalders, or 9 tons of coal in the
week †. When the pits exceed the depth that bearers can

carry

---

* They have a fund, like other friendly focieties, for burying their dead,
paying their fchoolmafters, affifting thofe that are ill, and giving a fmall trifle
annually to the widows. There are 4 *bailies* intrufted with the management
of this fund. The principal one is appointed by the proprietor of the work,
for 7 years; the 3 others are annually chofen by him, from a lift of 9 given into
him by the colliers. They hold courts, to take cognizance of any difpute or
mifbehaviour in the colliery, and exact fines from the offenders, which are
thrown into the general fund.

† The weight which a good bearer can carry, is very great. Some years
ago,

carry up the coal, the collier's price is reduced, as the maſter is obliged to draw them up by gins, which is either wrought by horſes, or driven by water. The water gin, which has been in uſe here for theſe 70 or 80 years, is a moſt ingenious ſimple machine *. There are two collieries in the barony of Alloa, the oldeſt of them, called the *Alloa Pits*, is about 1½ mile diſtant from the ſhore; the other is the *Colly-land*, and is about double that diſtance. There are various ſeams in each colliery; ſome of 3, 4, 5 and 9 feet in thick-neſs. They dip to the N. E. about 1 in 6 or 7.

The pits are free of all noxious damps, and have in general a good roof and pavement, although there are iron ſtones over ſome of the ſeams. The engine pit of the Alloa coal is about 48 fathom deep; and the coal is drained by a water engine, there having been a large reſervoir of water collected (as has been already mentioned), for that purpoſe, about the beginning of the century, as the ſteam engine was then but lately invented,

---

ago, the proprietor weighed a piece of coal, that a *lame* woman had brought out of a pit, 12 fathoms deep, and was aſtoniſhed to find it full 2 cwt. Another woman carried an uncommon large piece of coal, from the mouth of the pit to the overſeer's houſe, a diſtance of 400 yards; and, by the meaſure of this piece of coal, it muſt have weighed 3 cwt.

* It is a wheel of 18 feet diameter, and appears as if two wheels were joined together, with the buckets of the one reverſed from thoſe of the other. The axle is 39 inches diameter, to which the rope that draws up the tubs, or corve, is fixed. There is a ciſtern placed over the wheel, divided in the middle. Each diviſion has a valve, exactly over the centre of the different buckets, which valve is opened by a ſlider moved from the bottom; ſo that when the wheel turns round, it draws up the tub, or corve, of coals, weighing 6 cwt. and lets down the empty one, on ſhutting the valve of thoſe buckets, and opening the other, the corve that has juſt been emptied is let down, while a freſh corve full of coals is brought up.—The late Mr. Brown, the famous engineer and operative coal-maſter at Newcaſtle, was ſo ſtruck with it, when he was at Alloa in 1774, that he took a drawing of it; and, on his return to Newcaſtle, contrived one on the ſame principles, to anſwer for their deep pits.

invented, and not well known in Scotland. The engine pit of the Collyland is about 46 fathom deep; and the coal is drained by a steam engine, supposed to be one of the best of the old construction. This was erected in 1764*.

The

* It has often been asserted, that there have been more estates lost than made, (especially in Scotland) by working coal mines. There probably has been some foundation for such an assertion. The expences of winning and keeping up a colliery are considerable, and the commodity will not bear a great price; so that it is only a large quantity, that can produce a profit adequate to the expence. While the coals of the barony of Alloa were brought to the shore in small carts by the tenants, the quantity was uncertain, and often not very considerable. In 1768, a waggon way was made to the Alloa pits, which proved to be so great an advantage, that it induced the proprietor to extend it to the Collyland, in 1771. The sales were by these means increased, from 10,000 or 11,000 chalders, to 15,000 or 16,000. In 1785, the Alloa waggon way was worn out, and required to be renewed. This was done on a new plan; and it is now acknowledged to be the most complete in Britain. A description of it may therefore be thought useful.

The sleepers are very broad, and only 18 inches from centre to centre. A rail of foreign fir, 4 inches square, is pinned down to them; and another rail, of the same dimensions, is laid over it, and the whole well beat up in good clay; on the top of the upper rail is laid a bar of malleable iron, of $1\frac{3}{4}$ inches breadth, and nearly six-8ths thick. The waggons have cast iron wheels, $27\frac{1}{2}$ inches diameter, and are supposed to weigh altogether about a ton. A waggon carries 30 cwt. of coals, and 3 waggons are linked together by chains; so that 1 horse draws $4\frac{1}{2}$ tons of coal at once; and the declivity of the way is so gentle, that the same horse draws with ease the 3 empty waggons back to the coal-hill. The advantage of putting the weight into 3 waggons, in place of 1, is very considerable: They are easier to fill and empty; and the throwing the weight over a greater surface, does less damage to the waggon way, and is likewise easier for the horse as it is well known, that almost the only stress a horse has, on a good waggon way, is in the first starting of the waggon; therefore, if the whole $4\frac{1}{2}$ tons were put into one waggon, the difficulty would be great; but as the waggons,

The large coal ſent to ſea is ſold at the ſhore, from 8s. 6d, to 9s. per chalder, of 30 cwt. The ſmaller coals, which are called *chaws*, are ſold on the coal-hill, for 13d. per cart † of 6 cwt.—The coal of the barony of Alloa is thought to be the fartheſt weſt of any coal north of the Forth.—The colliers prefer working in the night time ; ſome go into the pits between 8 and 9, and others again later. Thoſe who are anxious, on any particular occaſion, to draw a large ſum on the Saturday, continue a very long time at their work : The uſual time is from 10 to 12 hours. The men are, in general, rather of a low ſtature, though there are ſome of them 6 feet. Many of the young women are pretty. On Sundays and holidays, both men and women are clean and neatly dreſſed. They eat conſiderably

gons, when ſtanding ſtill, are cloſe to one another, and the chains that link them together are 2 feet long, the horſe has only 30 cwt. of coals to put in motion ; for, when he ſtarts the firſt waggon, the impetus of it, if it does not actually move, at leaſt greatly aſſiſts in moving the ſecond and third The firſt expence of making this kind of waggon way, is undoubtedly great, being at leaſt 10s. per running yard ; yet the proprietor has been long ago reimburſed, and is a conſiderable gainer ; for although this road has been made theſe 6 years, it has required no repair worth mentioning, and it is now near as good as when firſt laid.

† About 35 years ago, this kind of coal was ſold for 6d. The price has riſen gradually as the demand has increaſed. The conſumption of coal in Scotland is conſiderably greater than formerly; which is probably owing, in ſome meaſure, to the improvements of agriculture, &c. the country people having learnt to eſtimate the value of their time; and, by calculating how much is conſumed in making peats, they find, that coals, though brought from a great diſtance, is a cheaper, as well as a pleaſanter fuel.—The effect that any *extraordinary diſtreſs* in the country has, on the ſale of coal, is very evident. On the ſhock that credit received, by the great failures in 1772, the ſale of coals, at this port, diminiſhed one third; and it was 4 years before the uſual demand took place : And the conſequences of the miſerable crop in 1782, were felt, pretty nearly in the ſame manner, in 1783.

confiderably more meat than other labourers, and are, on the whole, a happy race of people. They are generally healthy; few of them, however, work at the coal wall after 63 years of age; but they are able to do fome eafy work below ground, for many years after that time of life. The women live longer than the men.

The following tables may be depended on as particularly exact. The account of the births and burials are taken from the books of the collier's fund.

TABLE I.

Shewing the Number of MALES and FEMALES in the COLLIERY of ALLOA, at all Ages, in 1780.

Years of age.	Males.	Females.	Years of age.	Males.	Females.	Years of age.	Males.	Females.	Years of age.	Males.	Females.
At 1	5	6	At 22	5	2	At 43	1	1	At 64	1	2
2	14	16	23	2	6	44	1	2	65	0	1
3	8	4	24	6	6	45	1	3	66	1	0
4	9	7	25	2	1	46	2	1	67	1	1
5	2	4	26	5	9	47	3	4	68	0	1
6	9	10	27	0	3	48	4	9	69	0	0
7	6	16	28	4	5	49	2	2	70	3	1
8	2	6	29	2	1	50	1	2	71	1	0
9	7	9	30	1	4	51	0	1	72	0	0
10	6	5	31	2	2	52	2	2	73	1	0
11	6	6	32	0	0	53	1	2	74	0	2
12	7	8	33	3	1	54	0	0	75	0	1
13	6	4	34	3	2	55	2	1	76	0	0
14	5	7	35	1	4	56	0	2	77	0	1
15	6	5	36	5	5	57	1	2	78	2	1
16	5	6	37	3	4	58	3	1	79	0	0
17	5	4	38	2	3	59	2	1	80	1	1
18	7	3	36	2	1	60	2	1	84	0	1
19	6	6	40	3	4	61	0	2			
20	5	3	41	2	1	62	1	1		227	248
21	1	1	42	1	1	63	2	4			

TABLE II.

Shewing the Number of MALES *and* FEMALES *in the* COLLIERY *of* ALLOA, *at all Ages, in* 1791.

Years of age.	Males.	Females.	Years of age.	Males.	Females.	Years of age.	Males.	Females.	Years of age.	Males.	Females.
Under 1	3	7	At 21	7	8	At 42	2	1	At 63	0	2
At 1	5	15	22	8	4	43	1	3	64	1	2
2	4	6	23	5	6	44	4	1	65	2	3
3	8	11	24	3	7	45	0	1	66	0	0
4	6	9	25	4	6	46	2	3	67	1	0
5	4	6	26	5	4	47	0	3	68	1	0
6	5	3	27	2	2	48	3	3	69	1	2
7	7	5	28	4	6	49	2	1	70	0	3
8	6	8	29	0	4	50	1	3	71	1	0
9	2	4	30	6	3	51	0	1	72	0	0
10	7	10	31	5	2	52	1	4	73	0	1
11	6	5	32	4	4	53	1	1	74	0	0
12	6	3	33	0	2	54	2	2	75	0	1
13	8	6	34	3	5	55	2	3	76	0	2
14	5	6	35	0	2	56	0	0	77	1	1
15	7	4	36	6	2	57	3	5	78	0	1
16	7	6	37	5	2	58	2	2	79	0	0
17	5	5	38	3	3	59	4	3	80	0	1
18	8	9	39	0	3	60	2	4	92	0	1
19	3	4	40	5	7	61	1	2			
20	3	6	41	0	3	62	0	1		231	289

TABLE III.

SUMMARY VIEW of the two preceding TABLES.

Total number in 1780.	Ma.	Fem.	Tot.	Total number in 1791.	Ma.	Fem.	Tot.
Under 7 years of age	57	53	110	Under 7 years of age,	42	62	104
From 7 to 14 ——	39	45	84	From 7 to 14 ——	40	42	82
—— 14 to 20 ——	34	27	61	—— 14 to 20 ——	33	34	67
—— 20 to 27 ——	21	28	49	—— 20 to 27 ——	34	37	71
—— 27 to 34 ——	15	15	30	—— 27 to 34 ——	22	26	48
—— 34 to 41 ——	18	22	40	—— 34 to 41 ——	19	22	41
—— 41 to 48 ——	13	21	34	—— 41 to 48 ——	12	15	27
—— 48 to 55 ——	8	10	18	—— 48 to 55 ——	9	15	24
—— 55 to 62 ——	9	10	19	—— 55 to 62 ——	12	15	27
—— 62 to 69 ——	5	9	14	—— 62 to 69 ——	6	10	16
—— 69 to 76 ——	5	4	9	—— 69 to 76 ——	1	7	8
—— 76 to 80 ——	3	3	6	—— 76 to 80 ——	1	3	4
Aged, 84 ——	0	1	1	Aged, 92 ——	0	1	1
	227	248	475		231	289	520

TABLE

TABLE IV.

Shewing the Numbers of BIRTHS *and* BURIALS, *in the* COLLIERY *of* ALLOA, *during the following Years*.*

Years.	BIRTHS.	BURIALS.			Total.
		Children.	Youths.	Aged.	
1782	18	7	1	2	10
1783	16	6	0	5	11
1784	15	8	3	4	15
1785	13	5	1	3	9
1786	13	4	0	6	10
1787	22	25	4	9	38
1788	22	7	2	5	14
1789	26	11	1	3	15
1790	26	12	0	2	14
1791	14	9	1	3	13
Totals,	185	94	13	42	149
Avera.	18 5-10ths	9 4-10ths	1 3-10ths	4 2-10ths	14 9-10ths

Some of the colliers have left the work between the years 1780 and 1791, and perhaps a few have come into it ; but the variations are certainly not greater, than what happens in moſt pariſhes, which have the ſame number of ſouls. The increaſe, by the above tables, is 3 and 6-10ths per annum ;

Which, in 11 years, amounts to 39.6-10ths. Number by numeration 514.6-10ths
Number in 1780, - - 475 ——— in 1791, - 520
Difference, - 5.4-10ths.

Manufaƈures.—Formerly this pariſh was famous for manufaƈuring tobacco ; but it is long ſince it loſt its reputation for that article ; although there is ſtill a little ſnuff made here. For a long time the camblet branch took the lead, and was conſidered as the ſtaple manufaƈure. It is in the neighbourhood of the wool of the Ochils ; and the young people were

* *N. B. Within this period there was one ſtill birth, which is not taken notice of, either in the births or burials.*

were bred to thefe woollen employments. An early education in this branch gave them a great fuperiority ; and this pre-eminence opened up a variety of markets, both at home and abroad. Great quantities were fent to England ; which, after being dreffed up, and finished off with a peculiar neatnefs, were returned and fold in our markets, at a very advanced price. The late Lord CATHCART, when prefiding at the Board of Police, was attentive to this circumftance, and pro-pofed to bring people from England, who fhould inftruct them in dreffing their camblets. At that time the demand was great, and the patriotic propofal was not accepted. Till within thefe few years 100 looms have been employed in this branch. Whether the demand for camblets has diminished, or that the young people have figured to themfelves an eafier, or more fpeedy way of getting wealth, by the fea, or the occupations connected with the diftillery, or to whatever caufe it is owing, there is undoubtedly a great decreafe in this manufacture. At prefent, there are not above 40 camblet looms, and per-haps as many employed in ferges, and inferior forts of woollen ftuffs. The manufacture of narrow and broad cloths has been lately introduced, and promifes well. Scotch, Englifh, and Spanifh wool have all been made ufe of in this trade ; and fome very beautiful cloth has been produced. The coarfeft kinds are moftly fold in the Fife markets ; the fineft in the neighbourhood to perfons of the firft rank. About 19 or 20 hands are employed in this cloth manufacture, each of whom make good wages[*]. There are 30 or 40 people employed in

the

[*] Though it is fuppofed, that there can be no great difference in the rate of wages, between this and other places, yet it may anfwer fome purpofes to thofe who pay attention to this fubject, to ftate them exactly. A broad cloth wea-ver can make from 20d. to 2s. per day ; a man fpinning by the jenny, 4 fpinel a day, 1s. 6d. ; a woman, fcribling, per day, 10d. ; a man, fcribling upon difh cards, per day, 2s. ; ditto, hand cards, per day, 1s. 4d. ; women, fpinning fine yarn by the hand, 8d. ; a man, dreffing cloth, per day, 1s. 6d. ; a man, dying wool, per day, 2s.

the woollen branches, in the village of Tullibody. The inhabitants of all the villages, at the foot of the Ochils, are difpofed to the like employments; and, from their long and early habits, thefe ftations feem proper for feconding the efforts of the woollen manufacturers.

The *linen* manufactures, of every denomination, carried on here, are moftly for home confumption, and generally according to the tafte and fancy of private families.—Of late, *muflin* looms, with fly fhuttles, have been fet up, and do a great deal of bufinefs. The webs are fent, ready warped, from Glafgow, and the cloth is returned. Eight or 10 looms are already employed, and there is a demand for 20 more; as there feems to be here, as well as in other places, a growing fpirit for thefe cotton branches.

A *Foundery*, upon a fmall fcale, has been for fome time eftablifhed here. The metal was generally brought from Carron, and employment given in cafting waggon wheels, pots of different fizes, and other fmall articles in that way. —There are a few *nailers* here, and manufacturers of other branches of *iron* work, * for the fhipping.—There is a very ingenious man, who makes large portable *fill-yards* for weighing cattle, carts, &c. He has been employed at Dundee and Greenock, for erecting public ones, which have given great fatisfaction; and the demand for them feems to be increafing. —There are a few *rope-makers* here. There are likewife fome good wriglits † (carpenters), in all branches.—There is a *fhip-builder,*

* The late Earl of Marr was very affiduous in procuring the beft tradefmen to fettle at Alloa. There was a remarkable good fmith then fixed here. *Still-yards* and *beams* were particularly well executed. Ever fince his time, there has been a fucceffion of good hands in that branch.

† There is a native, a cabinet-maker, who returned here, (where he has a fmall property), about 24 years ago, after having been long in London. He was

builder, who bears a very good character, and has a very ingenious young man, a ſon, breeding under him.

Markets, Prices of Proviſions, &c.—There are 4 ſtated
annual fairs in Alloa, viz. on the ſecond Wedneſdays of February, May, Auguſt and November; and 2 weekly markets,
on Wedneſday and Saturday. The manner of living, of all
ranks of people in Scotland, is conſiderably changed within
theſe 30 years. In 1763, there were but 4 bakers in Alloa,
2 of whom had but little employment : There are now 14.
Some of them carry on a pretty extenſive trade. The mode of
living, probably, has more affected the wages of labourers,
&c. than the price of grain, though that muſt have ſome influence on them. In order to judge of this, the following
prices of the fiars are given. It is much to be regretted, that
there is not ſome ſuch method fallen on, to record the prices
of meat, &c. at 4 different times of the year :

MID-LOTHIAN

was reckoned one of the beſt journeymen there. And it deſerves to be mentioned, that in one of the firſt ſhops in London, where 80 hands were employed,
3 of the very beſt were born in this pariſh. And a young man, who ſerved his
apprenticeſhip with the above mentioned cabinet-maker here, is now foreman in
a very principal cabinet warehouſe in London.

perfectly exact, yet there is no appearance, that the omissions of any one period differ greatly from those of another; and it must be observed, that the number of boys and girls are nearly equal. The progressive average more readily points out the rise and fall, than could be seen from a comparison of 25 years, from 1668 to 1692, with the same number of years, from 1693 to 1717.

An Account of the Number of Baptisms of Males and Females, in the Parish of Alloa extracted from the public Register, from the Year 1668 to 1790; with a Progressive Average of 25 Years.

Years.	Boys.	Average.	Girls.	Average.	Total.	Average.	Years.	Boys.	Average.	Girls.	Average.	Total.	Average.
1668	41		45		86		1694	55	52	64	46	119	99
69	35		26		61		95	62	53	69	47	131	100
1670	52		41		93		96	65	54	50	48	115	102
71	46		33		79		97	47	53	51	48	98	102
72	59		35		94		98	54	53	53	49	107	102
73	51		43		94		99	40	53	44	49	84	103
74	51		29		80		1700	43	53	33	49	76	102
75	49		51		100		1	48	53	45	49	93	103
76	30		36		66		2	63	54	59	49	122	103
77	51		50		101		3	56	54	56	50	112	104
78	40		50		90		4	54	54	58	50	112	105
79	52		45		97		5	47	54	50	50	97	104
1680	52		54		106		6	58	54	52	51	110	105
81	56		37		93		7	48	54	51	51	99	105
82	52		48		100		8	55	54	54	51	109	106
83	58		36		94		9	53	54	48	51	101	106
84	51		46		97		1710	51	54	55	52	106	106
85	54		46		100		11	62	54	57	52	119	106
86	58		48		106		12	59	54	65	53	124	107
87	59		44		103		13	63	54	60	53	123	103
88	51		51		102		14	57	55	58	53	115	108
89	43		62		105		15	52	55	74	54	126	109
1690	42		57		99		16	52	55	62	54	114	109
91	59		64		123		17	81	56	71	55	152	111
92	65	65	31	44	96	95	18	66	55	73	56	139	112
93	75	75	56	44	131	96	19	63	56	75	56	138	113

Years.	Boys.	Average.	Girls.	Average.	Total.	Average.	Years.	Boys.	Average.	Girls.	Average.	Total.	Average.
1720	76	56	71	56	147	113	1756	63	57	56	55	119	113
21	73	56	62	57	135	114	57	53	57	55	55	108	113
22	64	57	78	58	142	116	58	52	56	55	55	107	112
23	67	58	69	58	136	117	59	57	56	54	55	111	112
24	61	59	55	59	116	118	1760	47	56	55	56	102	112
25	61	59	42	60	103	119	61	77	57	62	56	139	114
26	51	59	46	60	97	119	62	71	58	70	56	141	115
27	64	59	58	60	122	119	63	67	58	59	57	126	116
28	56	59	55	60	111	119	64	82	59	74	58	156	119
29	59	60	48	59	107	119	65	57	59	71	59	128	120
1730	57	60	40	59	97	119	66	70	61	68	60	138	122
31	70	60	57	59	127	120	67	67	62	65	61	132	124
32	54	61	58	59	112	120	68	84	63	79	62	163	126
33	67	61	54	59	121	121	69	58	63	76	63	134	126
34	62	61	52	59	114	121	1770	74	64	78	63	152	128
35	53	62	51	59	104	121	71	82	65	63	63	145	129
36	54	61	62	59	116	121	72	70	65	75	64	145	130
37	41	61	55	59	96	120	73	88	66	66	64	154	131
38	70	61	47	59	117	120	74	63	60	77	65	140	131
39*	51	61	35	58	86	119	75	88	66	74	65	152	132
1740	50	61	49	57	99	118	76	84	67	65	65	149	133
41	37	60	36	56	73	116	77	72	68	57	66	129	134
42	49	59	53	56	102	114	78	77	69	84	67	161	135
43	56	58	50	54	106	113	79	74	69	69	67	143	136
44*	55	58	65	54	120	112	1780	80	70	79	67	159	137
45	56	57	65	53	121	111	81	100	71	75	68	175	140
46	56	57	53	53	109	110	82	93	73	68	68	161	142
47	57	56	58	52	115	109	83	70	74	65	69	135	143
48	69	56	63	52	132	109	84	65	74	73	70	138	144
49	73	57	62	52	135	109	85	103	76	75	70	178	147
1750	69	57	61	53	130	111	86	81	76	68	71	149	147
51	53	57	58	53	111	111	87	72	77	68	71	140	147
52	54	57	56	53	110	111	88	91	78	86	72	177	149
53	65	57	62	54	127	111	89	92	78	74	72	166	150
54	61	57	62	54	123	112	1790	74	79	90	72	164	151
55	61	57	72	55	133	131							

The

** The decrease that appears, from 1739 to 1744, was probably owing to the Seceders neglecting to register their children's names. We are now enabled, from the *Parliamentary Register* (which is kept here with care), to furnish a pretty correct list for 8 years (preceding 1792), of marriages and births. As the lists of marriages were always esteemed pretty exact, 20 years have been taken, and compared with the 8 years preceding 1792, which we call the *Parliamentary Register*, from its being kept in consequence of the act of parliament in 1784.

The amount of these 20 years is 876; average, 43, and 4 fifths.

The amount of the last 8 years is 349; average, 43, and 5 eighths. This wonderful coincidence makes it evident, that there can be little error.

The births, in 8 years, 1,226; average, 153, and 1 fourth.

The deaths, in ditto, 1,170; average, 146, and 1 eighth.

The deaths in 1787 are remarkable; no less than 249; about 100 of which were children, carried off by the small pox. Fevers and fluxes proved very fatal that year.

The following tables of enumeration are thought to be particularly exact. They were all taken by the same man; who, in each of them, set down the names of every head of a family.

An Account of the Population of the Parish of Alloa, taken in 1784.

Divisions	Families	Souls	Divisions	Families	Souls
Alloa, Coal Bridge and Glass-House,	1042	3482	Village of Tullibody, -	71	290
Country, - - -	97	536	Ditto of Cambus, -	42	178
Colliery, - - -	126	539	The whole parish, -	1378	5025

An Account of the Population, taken in 1788.

Divisions	Houses	Famil.	Males	Femal.	Total	Burghers	Antibur.	Episcopals
Town of Alloa, - -	381	906	1531	1779	3310	308	425	29
Coal Bridge, - -	4	15	29	26	55	0	5	0
Glass-Work, - -	13	36	76	81	157	15	4	14
Total in the town of Alloa, &c.	398	957	1636	1886	3522	323	434	43
—— Country, - -	89	89	283	275	558	14	32	9
—— Village of Tullibody, -	70	87	140	198	338	40	20	0
—— Ditto of Cambus, -	18	38	74	97	171	13	26	0
—— The Colliery, -	134	143	258	319	577	2	0	0
—— The whole parish, -	509	1314	2391	2775	5166	392	512	52

An Account of the Population, taken in 1791.

Divisions	Houses	Families	Males						Females						Grand total	Burghers	Antiburghers	Episcopals
			Under 10 years	From 10 to 16	From 16 to 50	From 50 to 70	From 70 to 100	Total	Under 10 years	From 10 to 16	From 16 to 50	Frm 50 to 70	From 70 to 100	Total				
Town of Alloa,	391	833	374	170	620	181	35	1380	321	151	792	261	36	1561	2941	194	311	17
Coal Bridge,	5	13	11	4	8	4	0	27	11	5	10	4	0	30	57	0	6	0
Glass Work,	13	33	15	9	33	4	2	63	26	6	36	2	1	71	134	1	2	8
Alloa, Coal Bridge, and Glass Work,	409	879	400	183	661	189	37	1470	358	162	838	267	37	1662	3132	195	319	25
Country,	90	113	79	46	141	18	13	285	63	35	155	19	3	275	560	27	27	7
Village of Tullibody,	89	91	46	17	70	14	14	148	39	23	100	22	4	188	336	37	21	0
Ditto of Cambus,	35	35	15	4	28	8	0	55	11	11	32	13	0	67	122	2	9	0
The Colliery,	143	152	75	52	141	27	12	297	95	47	166	36	11	355	652		0	0
The whole parish,	766	1270	615	302	1041	256	41	2255	566	278	1291	357	55	2547	4802	263	376	32
The return to Dr. Webster, in 1755, is stated at	—	—	—	—	—	—	—	—	—	—	—	—	—	—	5816			
Decrease,	—	—	—	—	—	—	—	—	—	—	—	—	—	—	1014			

* Prior to the year 1788, there was every reason to believe, that the parish was increasing, as many new houses had been erected, and the glass-house and dry dock established, where many hands are employed, and the colliery considerably extended; all which must certainly more than

Cuſtom-houſe, &c.—The public revenue, and matters of trade, are managed by a cuſtom-houſe, which was eſtabliſhed here a ſhort time after the Union. It was at firſt only a creek, belonging to the port of Borrowſtownneſs. The port of Alloa not only comprehends the town of Alloa, but alſo the creeks of Clackmannan, Kennetpans, Kincardine, Cambus and Manor, on the north ſide of the river; Airth, Dunmore, or Elphinſtone, and Fallin, on the ſouth, together with the ſhore of Stirling.—The ſhips and veſſels belonging to the port, by the returns lately made, amount to 115; their tonnage to 7,241; for the navigation whereof 500 men are employed. The ſtaple trade for theſe ſhips is coal. The greateſt number of the veſſels are employed in the coaſt trade. About 50,000 tons of coal are annually ſent, from the port to places within the frith of Forth, and to parts in the eaſt and north of Scotland. The export and import trade is alſo conſiderable; it is carried to and from the ports of Denmark, Norway, Germany,

make up the deficiency, that might have happened, from the falling off of the camblet trade.

The enlargement of the farms would probably have been given, as a principal reaſon for the diminution, if the 3 enumerations had not proved, that the country part of the pariſh at leaſt was not decreaſed. The largeſt farm was let between the years 1784 and 1788; and the numbers in the country had increaſed in thoſe few years 22 ſouls. The diminution is principally in the town of Alloa, which has indeed been moſt rapid and aſtoniſhing; and can only be accounted for, by the failure of the great diſtilleries in the neighbourhood, who purchaſed large quantities of malt made in this town; which buſineſs employed a conſiderable number of hands in carrying it on, who were ſuddenly thrown out of employment; and much about the ſame time, a cotton work was ſet up at Down, which is not above 10 or 12 miles to the weſtward of this pariſh; and the report, of their giving great encouragement, to the young as well as the old, probably induced many to emigrate from this pariſh, and thereby has occaſioned a temporary decreaſe: But as the collieries, and other branches of trade, are in a very flouriſhing way, it is probable that a ſhort time will replace the deficiency.

many, Holland, Portugal, &c. Coals are the great article of exportation: 6,000 tons are annually exported, with valuable quantities of bottles from the glafs-houfe. The importation generally confifts of very confiderable quantities of flax, lint-feed, and other articles from Holland; of grain, and wood of all kinds, iron, &c. the produce of the northern countries *.— The Excife here is conducted by a fupervifor and 4 officers; and the revenue, though it is much diminifhed, fince the failure of the great diftilleries, is yet confiderable, being about 5,000l. Sterling. When the diftilleries were flourifhing, they fome-times paid 23,000l. of duty in 6 weeks time.

Poft Office.—The poft office has been eftablifhed for up-wards of 30 years. Formerly there was a runner between this and Stirling : now there is a regular poft office eftablifh-ed. The poftage of a fingle letter from Edinburgh is 3d.; from London 10d. A poft has lately been extended to Kin-cardine; and from thence to Culrofs, Dumfermline, and the Ferries. This is a great convenience. Upwards of 300l. of annual revenue arifes from the poft office.

Heritors and Rent.—The principal heritor of the parifh is Mr. ERSKINE of Marr. He refides almoft always at Alloa, and pays the greateft attention to every fcheme of improve-ment and police. Next to him, in valuation, is General ABERCROMBY of Tullibody. When in the country, he refides at his father's houfe of Brucefield, in the neighbouring parifh of Clackmannan, and contributes very cheerfully every affift-ance for the good of the parifh, that lies in his power. Lord
CATHCART'S

---

* From an abftract of the tonnage, taken from the anchorage duty at the fhore of Alloa, it appears, that in 1774, the number of fhips, which had been in the harbour, were 555; the tonnage 20,036. In 1791, the fhips were 772; the tonnage 48,524.

CATHCART's valuation is very fmall, his principal property lying in the parifh of Clackmannan ; but his houfe and pleafure grounds are in this parifh, and he frequently refides among us. We are always much indebted to his Lordfhip, for his advice and affiftance when in the country. Lord ALVA, refiding always out of the parifh, gives us only the benefit of a ready and cheerful concurrence, with every meafure propofed by the refiding heritors. All thefe gentlemen hold confiderable property in other parifhes. The valued rent is 7,492l. 19s. 2d. Scotch. The real rent is probably about 4,000l. Sterling.

Police.—The *good* of the place, and the adminiftration of *juftice*, are in the hands of his Majefty's juftices of the peace, and the fheriff-depute. There is only one fheriff-depute for this and the neighbouring county of Stirling. He appoints his fubftitutes; and one conftantly refides here, who keeps his courts in this town. The quarter feffions, and other meetings of form, either by the juftices of the peace, or fheriff, are held in the county town of Clackmannan, about 2 miles diftant. There is a baron bailie, named by the proprietor of the eftate of Marr. He decides on petty offences, and debts not exceeding 40s.; and regulates the ftents and ceffes, and other matters of police within the town and barony.—An *admiral court* was formerly kept here, in virtue of a commiffion from the Lord Vice Admiral of Scotland. The jurifdiction of this court extended from the bridge of Stirling to Pettycur, near Kinghorn, on the north fide of the Forth, and from Stirling Bridge to Higgin's Neuck on the fouth. For fome time paft, no deputation has been granted, and of courfe no court kept. The want of an admiral court has been complained of, as *a very material grievance*. For want of this, every little trifling difpute, which happens at the port, muft be carried before the

Admiralty

Admiralty Court at Edinburgh, at a very confiderable expence.
Befides, a moft ferious injury feems likely to arife, from the
fhipmafters cafting their ballaſt into the river, without any
court to check them ; which, in procefs of time, muft interrupt the navigation, and hurt the public as well as individals.
It is thought, that an admiral court would fpeedily put a ftop
to this complaint.

Services, &c.—All kinds of perfonal fervices from tenants
may be faid to be abolifhed, as thofe on the eftate of Tullibody are feldom or never exacted *. The feuers in the town
are obliged to turn out, in cafe of any accident at the dam-
head of Gartmorn, &c. This cannot well be looked on as a
great hardfhip, as moft of the property would be confiderably
affected by any inundation. The family of MARR were found
by the Court of Seffion, after a long litigation, to have a right
to draw cuftom for goods paffing through the town, as they
were obliged to keep up the ftreets, &c.

Roads.—The ftatute labour for the roads, is, as in other
places, under the direction of the juftices of the peace. The
cotter's labour is converted into money, and fometimes the
farmer's carriages. The country, for fome time paft, has been
amufed with fchemes for turnpike roads ; and perhaps this
has occafioned a remiffnefs in the exaction of the ftatute work.
Owing to this, and the many heavy carriages while the diftilleries were flourifhing, the roads are exceedingly bad. It
is

* When Mr. ERSKINE relieved his tenants of the thirlage, he inclined to have
done the fame with the multure of the malt, from the brewers in the barony of
Alloa; but as that was in fuch a number of hands, and thefe continually changing, he found it impracticable. The brewers ftrongly litigated the point about
20 years ago. It was at length decided in favour of the proprietor.

is not doubted but that some reform, in a matter so interesting to the public, will soon take place.

Church, &c.—The church of Alloa was repaired and enlarged in 1680, by virtue of a commission from the archbishop of St. Andrews. Its length is 65 feet, exclusive of Mr. Erskine's aisle ; and the breadth 30 feet, besides 12 feet of addition to the north. At the west end it has 2 rows of galleries. It is now too small and incommodious for the numerous inhabitants of this parish ; for it is extremely crowded when there are 900 hearers, which is often the case. There have been many deliberations about building a new one, for upwards of 30 years past. To this the heritors are strongly encouraged, by a donation lately made of 1,200l. by Lady CHARLOTTE ERSKINE* ; who also left 800l. Sterling, the interest of which is to be applied for an assistant minister, whose income altogether now exceeds 70l. per annum.—The present church has a good appearance to the south. The front is of hewn stone. There is a statue in a niche of St. MUNGO,

holding

---

* This sum her Ladyship, (who was a daughter of CHARLES Earl of HOPETON, and widow of THOMAS Lord ERSKINE, son of the last EARL of MARR), generously bequeathed for fears to the poor, and to such as had no legal rights to any The latter, however, were to pay a moderate rent for them; part of which sum was to go towards augmenting the salary of the assistant minister. Many years ago, an assistant minister was established here, by a donation from Mr. JOHNSTONE, a merchant in Alloa, who left some houses in the town, the rent of which, with the interest of 600l., that he had in the hands of a company of merchants in Glasgow, to be applied for the maintenance of an assistant minister. The company was dissolved many years ago ; and the 600l. was allowed to remain in the hands of one of the partners, who had a good land estate, but who unfortunately became bankrupt some years afterwards, and the whole was lost, and nothing left for the assistant minister, but the rents of the houses. This loss was replaced by the worthy Lady CHARLOTTE ERSKINE,

holding an open book * ; and another of MOSES, putting off his fhoes before the burning bufh, with the text from *Exodus* iii. 5. The church ftands on a gently rifing ground, on the weft fide of the gardens of Alloa, and is fet off by fome old trees near it †.

Stipend, &c.—The victual is converted, on an average of 25 years prior to 1760, and 25 years prior to 1790 ‡.

	1760.	1790.	1760.	1790.
Bolls.		Per Bolls.		
	s. d. 12ths	s. d. 12ths	l. s. d. 12ths	l. s. d. 12ths
3 chal.=32 barley, 10 10 10		16 4 1	17 8 10 8	26 2 10 8
2 do. =48 meal, 10 3 2		14 2 3	24 12 8	34 3 0
Money, 40 0 Scotch,	-	-	33 6 8	33 6 8
Vicarage, 71l. 3s. 2d. Scotch,	-	-	5 18 7 2	5 18 7 2
Feu rent of a houfe, 12l. Scotch,	-	-	0 0 0	1 0 0
Communion elements, 8ol. Scotch,	-	-	6 13 4	6 13 4
N. B. The feu was afcertained in 1760.				
Total, -			88 0 1 10	107 4 5 10

befides two carts of coals per week, *craig-leave, i. e.* paying for the collier's labour. Part of the vicarage is paid out of the

* St. MUNGO is reckoned the tutelary faint in this, as in many other parifhes of Scotland. He was a native of Culrofs, and is faid to have been educated by St. SERVANUS, commonly called St. *Serf.* This laft feems to have been an itirerary apoftle, who for fome time carried on his fpiritual functions at Tullibody, a part of this parifh, and moft probably devolved the charge upon St. Mungo.

† ALEXANDER Lord ERSKINE, in the 15th of King JAMES IV. (1503) founded a chaplaincy within the parifh kirk of Alloa, in honour of the holy and undivided Trinity, Father, Son, and Holy Ghoft, of the bleffed Virgin Mary, and St. Kentigern, for which he mortified a certain annuity, to maintain a fit and qualified perfon to celebrate divine fervice at St. Katherine's altar, &c. &c.

‡ By decree of the court of tiends, 13th February 1793, the ftipend is augmented to 11 chalders, half meal, and half bear, to be paid at the rate of the fiar prices of Clackmannan. The mode of augmentation is new : The 400l. Scotch, which made part of the ftipend, is now converted into 4 chalders ; 2 chalders are added, which, with the 5 formerly paid, make 11 in all : 8ol. Scotch,

the neighbouring parishes, and by such a number of hands, as makes the collection of it both very disagreeable and difficult. Mr. Erskine has relieved both the minister and tenants of the greatest part of the vicarage on his estate. The glebe is about 11 Scotch acres, (very nearly equal to 14 English), of fertile ground. Formerly it was over-run with weeds; but, by laying it down in grass, and pasturing, it now yields fine crops. The greatest part of the glebe lies close to the town, and the remainder very near it. The manse, which was repaired in 1776, is beautifully situated at the head of John's Street, and has a garden adjoining of about half an acre.—By the Earl of Marr's forfeiture in 1715, the Crown is patron.— There is an Antiburgher and a Burgher meeting-house in the town, both well attended, and the people are much improved in the civilities of life. There is likewise a chapel of the Scotch Episcopal church. Their number is small; but they have been joined by several of the glass-house work people, whose education

Scotch, for communion elements, is continued : and 71l. 3s. 2d. Scotch, vicarage, paid as *use and wont*. The additional 2 chalders may seem a small augmentation for so large a parish; but the conversion of the money into grain makes it considerable, and gives a security for the stipend's rising with the other necessaries of life.

At the Reformation, the stipends of the Protestant clergy were fixed, to be paid at the rate of so many chalders of victual, (the general term in Scotland for all kinds of grain), part of which was paid in kind, and part in money, converting the chalder, in the rich counties, at 100l. Scotch the chalder, and at 80l. Scotch in the less fertile ones. It is greatly to be regretted, that the whole stipend was not paid in victual; as by that means the value of them would have kept pretty nearly an equal pace with the value of estates. This method should now be absolutely fixed ; or if, from local situations, it should be very inconvenient to the clergy, to receive the whole in victual, one third might be converted into money ; and the value of the bolls should be estimated by an average g 25 years; and at the end of the 25 years, a new conversion might be taken; but no alteration should be made, unless the price of victual (*i.e.* th medium price of barley and malt), differed from the former one 6d. pence per boll.

education leads them to prefer that form of worſhip. The five clergymen, who are in town, live in the greateſt harmony and good intercourſe with one another †.

Schools and Donations.—There is a numerous and flouriſh- ing ſchool, conducted by a *rector* and *doctor*, (i. e. a maſter and uſher), both of whom have very good apartments. The rector takes boarders, and gives them every private aſſiſtance. The pious Lady CHARLOTTE ERSKINE left 300l. Sterling for educating poor children, and having them cathechiſed on Sun- day evenings ; which, according to the direction of Mr. ERS- KINE, to whoſe care it was committed, has been begun, and promiſes great ſuccefs, under the direction of the doctor, who aſſembles them, with all who chooſe to attend on the Sunday evenings. This meeting the miniſters occaſionally attend, and mark the progreſs of the young, when the moſt diligent are rewarded with little books. Her Ladyſhip likewiſe bequeath- ed 300l. towards aſſiſting the ſchools of the colliery. The charitable donations of this lady ought not to be omitted in this place, though they are deeply engraven in the hearts of many. Children of all ſects have acceſs to the benefit of theſe ſchools. There are likewiſe ſeveral private ſchools, where ſome of the younger and poorer ſcholars are educated. In the village of Tullibody, there is a numerous ſchool, patronized by Gene- ral ABERCROMBY. In the colliery there are two ſchools, to accommodate what are called *the Upper* and *Lower Works,* i. e. the *Collyland* and *Alloa.* All theſe ſchools are well attended, and promiſe much public benefit.

Mineral

---

† Dr. JAMES FORDYCE, author of the *Sermons to Young Women,* was laſt mini- ſter of this pariſh. He was admitted in October 1753, and went to London in 1760, when he was ſucceeded by the preſent incumbent.

Mineral Waters and Foffils.—There are many fprings, ftrongly impregnated with fteel. One of them is within the houfe of Alloa; but it is not known that any of them have been fufficiently analyfed, to fpeak of their effects. There are various quarries in the parifh; fome very indifferent, a few very good. One of them has been wrought upwards of 100 years. It is a remarkably good ftone in every particular, excepting the colour, which is a faint red; but it endures all kinds of fatigue. A very great quantity has been made ufe of, although it lies very deep in the earth, and of courfe is expenfive to work. There is another quarry on the eaſt fide of the parifh, of a good quality, and uncommonly white. There are feams of coal underneath each of thefe quarries. There is a field of yellow clay, or ochre, excellently adapted for fine bricks. It fometimes fupplies the place of lime on the outfides of houfes; but its various qualities have not yet been afcertained.

Wild Animals.—The wild animals are the fame as are common to all the Low Country: hares, rabbits, foxes, badgers, otters, *foumarts*, or polecats, and *floats*, or ermines. Thefe laſt are very rare. There are no wild cats. The birds moſt numerous are partridges. Some few quails and land rails are fometimes feen in autumn; but they are abundant in the breeding feafon. The whiftling or grey plovers alight fometimes on the high grounds in fpring, and likewife the dotterels, both on their way to the Ochils. The bittern is become very fcarce. Curlews frequent the fide of the Forth. There are few herons that breed here. There are thrufhes, blackbirds, woodlarks, bull finches, and all the finch tribe; fky larks, buntings, yellow hammers, and waterwagtails, white and yellow; in fummer, ftone-chatterers, and various kinds of fwallows; in winter, the feveral kinds of fieldfares, woodcocks and fnipes, and fome-

times

times ſnow birds. The lapwing, or green plover, breeds on the
high grounds; but as cutlivation advances, their numbers vi-
ſibly decreaſe. The hoody, or Royſton crow, breeds here. Jackdaws, crows, magpies and ravens are often ſeen, but do not
breed. There are alſo hawks, kings-fihers, ſandlarks, water
crows, and ſome few of the long eared bats, owls and ſcreech
owls.

Antiquities.—About a mile eaſt of the town, there is a
large upright ſtone, 7 feet 4 inches above the ſurface of the
ground. It is three feet broad, and thought to be very deep
in the earth. The old people uſe to ſpeak of the figure of a
man on horſeback, which they had ſeen on it. If any thing
of that kind, or letters (as it is ſaid), have been formerly obſerved, they are now totally effaced *.

Ancient Families and Eminent Perſons.—There are no families of any conſequence now exiſting, which were originally
of this pariſh. The branch of the ABERCROMBIES, which ſettled at Tullibody towards the end of laſt century, are deſcend-
ed from the family of Birkenboig in Banff-ſhire, where it has
been long eſtabliſhed.

The Lords CATHCART only made this the ſeat of their reſidence, upon parting with the great eſtate and beautiful place
of Auchincruive, which they poſſeſſed for ages in Ayr-ſhire.
Their

* When the adjacent farm was encloſing, upwards of 20 years ago, a ditch
was made cloſe to the ſtone, when many human bones were diſcovered; which
proves, that a battle or ſkirmiſh had ſome time or other taken place near that
ſpot; and probably ſome man of eminence was buried hard by, as it was a
common practice of the Picts on ſuch occaſions. There are two ſtones reſembling this one, in the neighbouring pariſh of Alva, at no great diſtance from the
church, but not cloſe to one another. They are both near the foot of the
Ochils.

Their poffeffions in this, and the adjoining parifhes, defcended to the late Lord Cathcart from his grandmother Lady SHAW; whofe hufband had purchafed them, in the beginning of this century, at a judicial fale, from the Bruces of Clackmannan.

Neither can the ERSKINES be faid to be originally of this parifh, although they got the lands, which they are now poffeffed of, in the reign of King Robert Bruce. They were originally fettled in Renfrewfhire. They fucceeded by a female, in 1461, to the earldom of Marr; but it was not until the year 1561 that they got poffeffion of it. It was at that time declared in parliament, that, in juftice, the earldom of Marr belonged to JOHN LORD ERSKINE, who, in the year 1571, was elected regent of Scotland, on the death of the Earl of Lennox. How honourably he filled that troublefome ftation, is recorded by all our hiftorians[*]. Unfortunately he was cut off by a fudden death. The famous GEORGE BUCHANAN has celebrated his virtues in an elegant epitaph.

Thefe matters, however, belong rather to *hiftory* than to a *ftatiftical account*; but it would be improper to omit mentioning the laft EARL OF MARR, who had a great turn for embellifhing the country. LORD HADINGTON, in his *Treatife*

on

---

[*] The family of ERSKINE have often been honoured with having their infant fovereigns intrufted to their care, (particularly King JAMES V. the unfortunate Queen MARY, JAMES VI. and his fon Prince HENRY), which facred truft they moft faithfully difcharged. They have fome curious papers relative to thofe tranfactions.—The regent's fon was brought up with King James VI. He was appointed ambaffador to England a fhort time before Elizabeth's death. The ambaffador's prefent is ftill preferved in the family: It is a bafon and ewer, remarkable for its workmanfhip, and the elegance of its fhape. Lord Marr, in his embaffy, is fuppofed to have contributed towards the peaceable acceffion of King James to the throne of England. The Duke of SULLY mentions him in his memoirs, and calls him his friend. On the Duke's return to France, the famous HENRY IV. wrote a letter to Lord Marr, which is ftill preferved in the archives of the family.

on Foreft Trees, fays, " It was the late EARL of MARR, that
" firft introduced the *wildernefs way of planting* among us,
" and very much improved the tafte of our gentlemen, who
" foon followed his example." And the gardens at Alloa,
which were laid out according to the fafhion of the times,
were long vifited and admired. The Earl, unhappily for his
country, himfelf and family, was principally concerned in
the rebellion 1715. But whatever errors he may have fallen
into, it cannot be denied, by any one who reads the papers
he has left behind him, that he had the general improvement
of his country greatly at heart. His only amufement, during
the long exile in which he died, was to draw plans and de-
figns, for the good of that much loved country from which
he was banifhed; and there is one paper*, dated in 1728,
which

* Speaking of the public works neceffary for the improvement of Scotland,
Lord Marr fays, " All ways of improving Edinburgh fhould be thought on :
" as, in particular, making a large bridge, of three arches, over the grounds be-
" twixt the North Loch and Phyfic Garden, from the High Street at Halker-
" ftone's Wynd to the Multurfey Hill, where many fine ftreets might be built,
" as the inhabitants increafed. The accefs to them would be eafy on all hands,
" and the fituation would be agreeable and convenient, having a noble profpect
" of all the fine ground towards the fea, the frith of Forth, and ccaft of Fife.
" One large and long ftreet, in a ftraight line, where the Long Gate is now;
" on one fide of it would be a fine opportunity for gardens down to the North
" Loch; and one on the other fide, towards Broughton. No houfes to be on
" the bridge, the breadth of the North Loch; but, felling the places in the
" ends of the bridge for houfes, and the vaults and arches below for warehoufes
" and cellars, the charge of the bridge might be near defrayed.

" Another bridge might alfo be made on the other fide of the town, and al-
" moft as ufeful and commodious as that on the north. The place where it
" could be moft eafily made is St. Mary's Wynd and the Pleafants. The hollow
" there is not fo deep as where the other bridge is propofed; fo that it is thought
" two ftories of arches might raife it near upon a level with the ftreet at the
" head of St. Mary's Wynd. Betwixt the fouth end of the Pleafants and the

Potter-

which takes notice of the improvements of the metropolis, that have been since carried into execution, and which deserves to be more generally known.

The

" Potter-Row, and from thence to Bristo Street, and by the back of the wall
" at Herriot's Hospital, there are fine situations for houses and gardens. There
" would be fine avenues to the town, and outlets from it for airing, walking,
" &c. &c. by these bridges; and Edinburgh, from being a bad incommodious
" situation, would become a very beneficial and convenient one: And, to make
" it still more so, a branch of that river, called the Water of Leith, might, it is
" thought, be brought from somewhere about the Colt Bridge, to fill and run
" through the North Loch, which would be of great advantage to the conveni-
" ence, beauty, cleanliness and healthfulness of the town.

" The making a canal betwixt the rivers of Forth and Clyde would be a
" great improvement to Scotland, as well as of great service to the trade of the
" whole island, especially the India trade, by saving a dangerous long passage
" round Britain, since, by that canal the west and east sea would be joined.
" The way for leading of this canal is from near Glasgow, by Kilsyth, to the
" mouth of the river Carron below Falkirk. It is practicable, as Mr. Adair,
" Mr. Smith, Mr. M'Gill, and Mr. Soracold judged, who travelled twice over
" the ground, with a view to this work. From the hills of Campsie, and the
" river Carron they thought there would be water sufficient got for filling the
" canal; and that, by the assistance of several sluices near to Glasgow and some
" in other parts, the canal would be made practicable for flat bottomed boats of
" a very considerable burden. They computed that 30,000l. Sterling might do
" the work; but, should it cost the double, it would be well bestowed, and be
" soon repaid by the profit arising from the canal."

Having said so much of this unfortunate nobleman, it is no more than justice to the inhabitants of this and the neighbouring parishes, to mention their behaviour to him during his exile, while the estate continued under the direction of the commissioners of the forfeited estates. They contributed considerably towards assisting him under his misfortunes. Nor should an instance of gratitude pass unnoticed: The Earl, whose taste for architecture was generally known, introduced the celebrated Mr. GIBBS into business, the beginning of this century. Mr. Gibbs dying without children, left the greatest part of the fortune he had acquired to LORD ERSKINE, the son of his first patron.

The following is a copy of the complimentary poem (above mentioned), wrote by George Buchanan upon JOHN EARL of MARR, who was regent of Scotland, during the minority of King JAMES VI.

JOANNI ARESKINO, Comiti MARRIÆ, SCOTORUM PROREGI.

Si quis ARESKINUM memoret per bella ferocem,
  Pace gravem nulli, tempore utroque pium ;
Si quis opes ſine faſtu, animum ſine fraude, carentem
  Rebus in ambiguis ſuſpicione fidem ;
Si quod ob has dotes, ſævis jactata procellis
  Fug⁺ in illius patria feſſa ſinum;
Vera quidem memoret, ſed non & propria : laudes
  Qui pariter petet has unus & alter erit.
Illud ei proprium eſt, longo quod iu ordine vitæ
  Nil odium aut livor quod reprehendat habet.

PARISH OF CLACKMANNAN.

(County of Clackmannan, Synod of Perth and Stirling, Presbytery of Stirling.)

By the Rev. Mr. Robert Moodie.

Name, Extent, and Surface.

CLACKMANNAN, fignifies the Kirk Town, or village of Annan; from a well known Gaelic word, and Annand, the original name of the family of Annandale. In the beginning of the 12th century, one of the firft of the Bruces who fettled in Scotland married Agnes Annand, heir to the Lordfhip of Annandale; and foon after that period, the Bruces were in poffeffion of Clackmannan: fo that there is little doubt of this being the origin of the name.—This parifh is of a very irregular form. It extends from S. W. to N. E. nearly 6 miles, and about 5 miles from S. E. to N. W. At one place, however, it is not above 2 miles in breadth: and a diftrict of about 1300 acres of it, on the N. W. fide, is disjoined from the reft of the parifh by a part of the parifh of Alloa, of about 2 furlongs in breadth, which joins
the

the pariſh of Tillicoultry.—There are no hills in the pariſh : the ground, however, is very much varied ; but none
of it ſo ſteep as to interrupt the purpoſes of agriculture.

Villages.—Clackmannan is the head town of the county.
It is beautifully ſituated on an eminence, gently riſing
out of a plain, from E. to W., to the height of 190
feet, above the level of the river Forth. On each ſide
of the village, the ground has a gradual deſcent ; but is
more bold and rapid from the W. end, where the old
tower of Clackmannan is placed.—The ſcenery, beheld
from this tower, is uncommonly picturefque and beautiful.; and has been veiwed with admiration by every traveller of taſte. The whole country around forms, as it
were, one grand amphitheatre, where all the objects are
diſtinctly ſeen, yet not ſo near, as to difguſt the eye.
They are, at the ſame time, infinitely varied. Beyond
the town of Stirling, 9 miles to the W., the high mountains of Ben-More, Ben-Lady, and Ben-Lomond, are ſeen
at the diſtance of 20 miles, raiſing their romantick tops
above the clouds. From the bold ſcenery of the town and
caſtle of Stirling, and the high jutting, rugged rocks a-
round it, the river Forth defcends through a valley of ſeveral 1000 acres of the richeſt carſe land ; ſometimes fplit-
ting afunder, and forming, here and there, ſmall beautiful iſlands, which are always green. The fields, on every ſide of it, exhibit, in time of harveſt, the moſt luxuriant, variegated, profpect, which the eye can behold.
The various windings of the river are, at the ſame time,
diverfified in every poffibility of ferpentine form, that can
add the moſt exquiſite beauty to the furrounding ſcenery.
It paſſes by the village of Clackmannan, at the diſtance of
an Engliſh mile to the S., where it is a mile in breadth.

Thre

Three miles below, it fpreads out, and forms the appearance of an extenfive inland lake, about 30 miles in circumference; having, on its different fides, the villages, harbours, and numerous fhipping of Kincardine, Borrof-tounnefs, and Grangemouth. Ships of various burdens are perpetually paffing in full fail up and down the river; while its banks are adorned by the feats and wooded pleafure-grounds of the feveral noblemen and gentlemen; fome of which are laid out with much elegance and tafte.

On the N. fide of the village of Clackmannan, a fmall beautiful river iffues from a deep glen, or hollow, fhaded with large trees overhanging its banks; and, bending for a fhort fpace through a verdant plain, it enters again a thick wood, which reaches within 200 yards of the tower, and which the river disjoins from the wood of Alloa, and the extenfive pleafure-grounds laid out by the late Earl of Mar: at the W. end of which, at the diftance of 2 miles from Clackmannan, is fituated the village and tower of Alloa, with the harbour and fhipping.

The view towards the N. is bounded, at the diftance of 4 miles, by the extenfive range of the high Ochil mountains, interfected here and there by deep hollow glens; in one of which, on a kind of promontory, with a deep ravine on every fide, ftands the ruins of Caftle Campbell, famous for being the original feat of the family of Argyll. Thefe monntains are covered with perpetual verdure, and form a fecure barrier againft the violence of the northern blaft. They not only add a high degree of beauty and grandeur to the furrounding fcenery; they alfo fuggeft to the mind the idea of fomething more ufeful and more valuable, from the rich filver mines lately difcovered in that part of them, commonly known by the name of the Alva Hills. From the W. to the S. E., the view from

Clackmannan.

Clackmannan is terminated by the Campſie Hills, and the high grounds in the neighbourhood of Falkirk and Linlithgow. The intermediate country is all rich and diverſified : a great part of it alſo is claſſick ground. Not far from the extenſive Carron iron works, the Tor-wood, famous for the retreat of Sir William Wallace, appears in full view ; at a ſmall diſtance from which is ſeen the well known field of Bannockburn, the pride of the Scotch warrior.—The bleak and barren track of land, bounded by the Saline hills, to the E. and N. E., interſperſed here and there with freſh water lakes, and ſome very thriving plantations, forms a ſtriking contraſt to the whole ſcene.

The village of Clackmannan itſelf, however, does by no means correſpond with a ſituation ſo uncommonly beautiful. Its ſtreet is broad and regular enough ; but many of the houſes are wretched and mean. In the middle of the ſtreet, ſtands the tolbooth and court-houſe ; a heap of ruins ! and a nuiſance to the publick. Here, however, the ſheriff ſometimes holds his courts * ; the county fiars are annually ſtruck here ; and here the members of parliament for the county have been always elected.

---

* The counties of Clackmannan and Stirling have one ſheriff-depute between them ; and the moſt part of the buſineſs is tranſacted by two ſubſtitutes, who have only very ſmall ſalaries allowed for their trouble. Moſt of the ſheriff-ſubſtitutes in Scotland are in the ſame ſituation. Would it not be an object worthy of the attention of the legiſlature, to have this uſeful claſs of men placed on a more independent footing, by allowing them ſalaries more adequate to the importance of the truſt committed to them ? This could be done, either by a ſmall tax on the fees of court, or in any other way that might be leaſt oppreſſive to the country. The independence of our judges is one of the greateſt bleſſings of the Britiſh conſtitution. Before the heritable juriſdictions were aboliſhed, the proprietors of the eſtate of Clackmannan were heritable ſheriffs of this county.

ed. The village is upon the eftate of Clackmannan, and pays feu-duty to the proprietor of that eftate. It contains 117 houfes, 194 heads of families, and 639 fouls; 281 of whom are male, and 358 female. It cannot be faid to have any trade: the artificers which live in it are chiefly employed for the ufe of the furrounding country *.

There is alfo one other village in the parifh, called New-town Shaw, upon the eftate of Lord Cathcart. It is in-creafing very rapidly; and, from the extenfive iron works lately begun by the Devon Company in its immediate neighbourhood, we may naturally expect, that, in a fhort time, it will be in a very flourifhing ftate. With fuch a certain profpect of fuccefs, however, it is aftonifhing to fee, how little attention is paid to the form and regularity of its buildings.

Climate and Difeafes.—The climate is, upon the whole, rather healthy than otherwife. Though, from its vicinity to the furrounding hills, it is expofed to frequent and heavy rains, and the air thereby rendered lefs falubrious; yet frequent inftances of longevity are found among the inhabit-

---

* There are three bakers in the village, and eight grocers, or fhop-keepers. It has always had a pretty good inn; but feldom has been without a dozen of tippling-houfes: a circumftance not very favourable to the morals of the people. It has two fairs in the year; one in June, and the other in September, called Bartholomew's Fair; where horfes, black cattle, coarfe linen and woollen cloth, and all kinds of hardware and haberdafhery goods are expofed. Formerly, this laft was a great market for wool brought from the fouth country: of late years, however, very fmall quantities of that article have been brought to it.

There is a tambouring fchool lately begun in the village, by fome Glafgow manufacturers, in which about forty young girls are taught; but it is difficult as yet to fay, whether it may have a good or a bad effect. The fame company have likewife begun to teach a few boys to weave with the fly fhuttle.

inhabitants. In 1791, one perfon died at the age of 95 ; at prefent, there is one man in the parifh above 90, another 89, and feveral others near to that period. The fmall pox is the moft frequent, and moft fatal epidemical diforder. The young are fubjected to its ravages every two or three years. In fome years, it is more fatal than in others. In 1790, almoft one half of the children, that were feized with it in the village of Clackmannan, died. This is not to be wondered at : Confidering the bad treatment, it is rather aftonifhing how any efcape. As foon as the infection has feized the child, he is put to bed ; a large fire is kindled ; he is fmothered up with blankets, that he may not catch cold ; while, to haften the eruption, a mixture of warm milk and whifky is, from time to time, poured down his throat. Among many of the farmers, however, and better fort of the inhabitants, inoculation is become frequent, and is practifed with great fuccefs. Only two inftances have occurred in the parifh, during the laft 14 years, of children dying, where this mode has been ufed ; and even thefe two inftances, it is faid, were owing to the parents not attending to the directions of the furgeon. Yet, notwithftanding all this, the prejudice againft inoculation is deeply rivetted in the minds of the great body of the people. They look upon it as a tempting of Providence ; and would confider themfelves as guilty of a fpecies of murder, if the event fhould prove fatal. There have been fome inftances of children dying by the meafles and hooping-cough ; but thefe are not numerous *.

Lakes,

* In 1785, after a very hot fummer, and a fudden fall of rain in the month of Auguft, a dyfentery made its appearance, and raged with fuch uncommon violence, that even in the fmall village of Clackmannan alone, upwards of twenty perfons, almoft all of them heads of families, fell victims

Lakes, Rivers, Tides, &c.—The river Forth forms the S. boundary of this parish. It is a mile in breadth, and of a depth fufficient for very large veffels. It has two pows or creeks in the parish; Clackmannan pow on the W. boundary, and that of Kennetpans towards the E., about a mile and a half diftant from the other: both of which are in the diftrict of the port of Alloa. The pow of Clackmannan is formed by the mouth of the river Black Devon. The mean depth of water at the ufual fhipping place, is 10 feet, and 20 feet at the mouth of the harbour. It was formerly crooked, and ran out a confiderable way to the W.; but was made ftreight, and deepened in 1772, by the proprietor, Sir Lawrence Dundas. The pow at Kennetpans, belonging to Mr. Bruce of Kennet, is much fmaller than the other, but capable of being greatly enlarged. It has 17 feet of water at fpring tides[*].

The

tims to its direful influence. It was more fatal in the village than in the neighbourhood. This, perhaps, may have been owing to the little care that is taken to keep the ftreets clean. Before every door is a dunghill, on which every fpecies of nuifance is thrown, without the leaft regard to decency and cleanlinefs; fo that the infection fpreads with rapid progrefs.

In 1789, a nervous fever, with very ardent fymptoms, proved fatal to feveral ftout young men in the lower part of the parifh. Since that time, it has appeared in other parts, but with much lefs violence; though, in fome inftances, protracted to a great length.

[*] From many circumftances, it is highly probable, that the river was much broader at this place in former times, than it is at prefent. A village, called Ferrytown, at the diftance of five furlongs from the river, feems to have once ftood on its banks. The intervening ground ftill goes by the name of Saltgrafs, and is under the level of high fpring tides, which ftrong fea walls, or banks, prevent from overflowing it. One of thefe walls feems to have been built at a very early period: too flight and fuperficial, however, to refift the violence of the tides, which frequently broke it down, and overflowed the land, till at length a reduction

The tides in the river Forth, for ſeveral miles, both a-
bove and below Clackmannan, exhibit a phenomenon not
to be found (it is ſaid) in any other part of the globe.
This is what the ſailors call a *leaky tide*, which happens
always in good weather during the neap tides; and ſometimes alſo during the ſpring tides, if the weather be uncommonly

tion of the rent became abſolutely neceſſary. By this time, the ſediment
of the river, which is a blue mud or ſoft clay, had again accumulated,
and formed a conſiderable track of fine rich land. In order, therefore, to
ſecure the old ſaltgraſs, as well as to make a new acquiſition of 50 acres,
Mr. Erſkine of Mar, the proprietor (who has been ſo good as to furniſh
an account of ſeveral of theſe facts), in 1776, began a new bank or
wall, much ſtronger than the former, and finiſhed it in little more than
ſix months. The length of the wall is 1380 yards; the height, 8 feet. It
has a ſlope to the river of 2½ feet for every foot of perpendicular height;
and the ſide next the water was covered with ſods, or turf, of one foot
in thickneſs. The ſide next the land was ſown with graſs ſeeds, and has
one foot of a ſlope for every foot of perpendicular height. There were
35,916 cubical yards of earth moved to form this wall, beſides 915 yards
for turf; making in whole 36,831 cubical yards, at 5 d. the yard. The
whole expence amounted to about 786l. Sterling. This, however, has
not only effectually ſecured the old ſaltgraſs land; it has alſo gained 50
acres of new land; which (deducting the repairs the old wall muſt have
received) yielded, during the firſt ſeven years of a leaſe, an intereſt of 4
per cent. for the money laid out; and the remaining twelve years, an
intereſt of 7 per cent. It will probably amount to 12 per cent. when the
preſent leaſe expires, as the land is of the richeſt quality. A great error
was committed by the tenant who got the leaſe of this new land. Inſtead of allowing it to remain in graſs for ſome years, it was immediately ploughed, and thereby prevented from conſolidating in a proper
manner. The conſequence was, it remained much longer in a wet ſtate
than arable land ought to do.

This error was avoided, when, ſeveral years afterwards, another
track of land, adjoining to the above, was in the ſame manner gained
from the river, to the eſtate of Lord Dundas. It was paſtured upwards
of ſeven years; and the good effects now appear: it produces the moſt
luxuriant crops. The expence attending this acquiſition did not exceed
one-third part of the former. Beſides, a part of the wall encloſing it is

fo

commonly fine. When the water has flowed for 3 hours, it then runs back for about an hour and a half, nearly as far as when it began to flow; it returns immediately, and flows during another hour and a half to the same height it was at before: and this change takes place both in the flood and ebb tides. So that there are actually double the number of tides in this river that are to be found any where else. In very boisterous weather, however, these leaky tides are by no means regular; the water only swells and gorges, without any perceptible current, as if the two tides were acting against each other. The cause of this singular phenomenon in the tides of the river Forth may be a subject of inquiry to the philosopher; for it has not as yet been discovered.

The river Devon forms the N. boundary of the parish. It takes its rise in the Ochil Hills, and, running 10 miles directly eastward, it makes a turn to the W., at a place called the Crook of Devon. It passes the Rumbling Bridge and Cauldron Lin, where it forms a scenery, wild and beautiful, and romantick beyond all description. It then

---

so constructed, that a waggon road is formed on the top of it, for the purpose of carrying coals to such vessels as are too large for going up the pow of Clackmannan to the usual shipping place. There is another track of land formed by the river in the same manner as the above, to the E. of the harbour of Kennetpans, belonging to Mr. Bruce of Kennet, and which that gentleman also proposes to embank.

Such undertakings, when properly conducted, are attended with many advantages: They not only add to the extent and value of estates, but they also contribute very much to the safety of the navigation, by contracting the river, and thereby clearing and deepening its channel.

There was formerly a salmon fishing on the river Forth at this place; but it has been discontinued for fifteen years. Previous to that period, the salmon was commonly sold here at 1 d. the pound. There are always a few cruives placed in the river, in which a variety of small fish are now and then caught; but these seldom turn to much account.

then winds through a deep rich valley, till it falls into the
river Forth, 4 miles to the W. of Clackmannan, and a
very few miles only from the place where it takes its riſe.
In time of floods, owing to the high hills through which
it paſſes, it comes down with a dreadful and irreſiſtible
rapidity ; very frequently ſweeping along with it fields of
corn, and ricks of hay, and, at times, even bridges, and
every thing that is in its way.

> " All that the winds had ſpar'd
> " In one wild moment ruin'd ; the big hopes
> " And well-earn'd treaſures of the painful year
> " Roll mingled down."   THOMSON.

In general, however, it is only a ſmall river ; large e-
nough, at the ſame time, to become navigable, if its channel were properly cut. In 1776, a ſurvey and eſtimate,
made by Mr. James Watt engineer, under the direction
of the late Lord Cathcart, was given in to the Board of
Police in Scotland, for the purpoſe of improving the in-
ternal commerce of this country, by cutting ſeveral navigable canals. Among other plans given in by Mr. Watt,
that of making the Devon navigable for ſeveral miles was
one. The eſtimate of the expence amounted only to a-
bout 2000l. pounds Sterling. Had this plan been carried
into execution, a track of more than 10,000 acres of coal,
at preſent entirely locked up from the ſea ſale, would
have been expoſed to the publick market ; beſides many
other advantages of trade, that muſt have accrued to the
neighbouring country. The extenſive iron works now begun by the Devon Company, on the banks of this river,
renders it highly probable, that the plan will ſtill be executed ; the advantage of water carriage being ſo much
ſuperior to that of land. The Devon abounds in trout,

and

and falmon are fometimes caught in it, which come up from the river Forth, in time of fpawning : a practice, however, very deftructive to the fifhery.

There is another river called Black Devon, which takes its rife in the Saline Hills ; and, running W. through the middle of this parifh, falls into the Forth at Clackmannan pow. In its courfe, it fupplies with water two corn mills and a lint mill. Two water lades, or aqueducts, are alfo taken off from it ; one of which drives an engine on the Clackmannan coal, and the other fupplies a great refervoir which drives the engine on the Alloa coal. This refervoir goes by the name of Gartmorn Dam ; but it is in fact a fmall beautiful lake, of 130 acres in extent, having a little ifland in the middle of it, and abounds with perch, fome pike, and various kinds of trout. Part of it is in the parifh of Alloa ; but by far the greateft part is in the parifh of Clackmannan. There is another fmall lake in the parifh, called Tullygarth Dam, confifting of 45 acres in extent, where a few fifh are fometimes to be found. In time of great drought alfo, the river Black Devon, at one place, forms the appearance of a fmall lake, by having its water collected together, for the fupply of the mills and coal machinery.

Heritors and State of Property.—The principal heritors, according to their valued rent, are, Lord Dundas, Mr. Erikine of Mar, Mr. Bruce of Kennet, Lord Cathcart, Mr. Abercromby of Bruccfield *, and Lord Alva, one of the Judges of the Court of Seffion ; befides a confiderable number of fmaller heritors and feuars. It is a fingular circum- ftance,

---

* The fee of this eftate belongs to Mr. Abercromby's fecond furviving fon, Major-General Sir Robert Abercromby, late Governor of Bombay, and at prefent Commander in Chief of his Majefty's forces in India.

ſtance, that the eſtates, in this pariſh, of all theſe gentlemen juſt mentioned (one only excepted), form but a ſmall part of their landed property. They all poſſeſs eſtates in other pariſhes; and the conſequence is, only two of them have their reſidence here. The eſtate of Clackmannan, belonging to Lord Dundas, is ſtrictly entailed, as well as the eſtate belonging to Mr. Erſkine of Mar. The houſe upon the eſtate of Clackmannan is almoſt a ruin, and not fit to be inhabited; the proprietor, however, it is ſaid, intends to take the advantage of ſo delightful a ſituation, and to build a houſe ſuited to it, near to the ſite of the old tower. From the ſeat of the family of Mar being at Alloa, in the immediate neighbourhood, there never was a houſe upon their eſtate in this pariſh. The houſe upon the eſtate of Sauchy is placed at the diſtance of about 60 yards within the pariſh of Alloa; but the greateſt part of the pleaſure-grounds, and even part of the garden, are in the pariſh of Clackmannan. The pleaſure-grounds are laid out and beautified with much taſte and judgment. A great part of theſe grounds, when in the poſſeſſion of Sir John Shaw, once formed a deer park, conſiſting of 100 acres, and ſurrounded by a very high wall. The only houſe in the pariſh, that deſerves the name of elegant, is juſt now finiſhed by Mr. Bruce of Kennet, from a beautiful deſign of Mr. Harriſon of Lancaſter. Placed in one of the fineſt ſituations the country affords, it is alſo built in a ſtyle of ſuperior elegance to moſt of the houſes to be met with in Scotland; and exhibits in all its parts an equal attention to convenience and utility, as it does to elegance and taſte.

Soil, Acres, Rent, &c.—The pariſh of Clackmannan conſiſts of 7132 acres; 166 of which are natural wood,
and

and 538 new plantations, all in a thriving ftate, and fome
of them nearly ready for cutting. There are upwards of
20 acres of mofs in the parifh, and 70 acres of land from
which the mofs has been removed, now under pafture and
hay. A cold clay foil, with a wet bottom, predominates
over a very great part of the parifh ; fome of it fo poor
indeed as not to be worth the labouring. A few fpots
however of a light dry foil, and even of a rich black loam,
with a fine bottom, are to be found here and there. Part
of the land in the neighbourhood of the villiage is of this
quality ; and accordingly the rent of it is proportionably
high. But the richeft and largeft track of land lies on the
banks of the river Forth, confifting of 1000 acres of excellent carfe foil, all very fertile. From this, it will eafily
appear, that the rent of the land muft be very much varied, according to its quality ; rifing from almoft nothing,
to 43 s. the acre. The real rent of the parifh is 4700l.
Sterling, and is approaching towards 5000l., as the prefent leafes expire. The valued rent is 9155l. 17l. 4d.
Scotch ; which probably was the real rent at the time of
the valuation.

State of Agriculture, &c.—The agriculture of this parifh
has undergone a very great change during thefe laft 15
years. Many of the farms have been greatly enlarged *,
which has enabled the tenant to adopt every new improvement. The fuccefs of one has induced others to follow the example : and at this time, almoft all the farmers
in

* At prefent, there are about forty farms fewer in the parifh than
were about twenty years ago. Some of the farmers now poffefs farms to
the extent of 700 acres ; befides having what are called led farms, in the
adjoining parifhes, to a very great extent. From this, it may be the opinion of fome perfons, that feveral of the farms in this parifh are too
large, while others are undoubtedly too fmall.

in the pariſh, ſmall as well as great, practiſe the moſt improved mode. They have laid aſide thoſe reſtraints, by
which deep-rooted prejudice, in favour of uſe and wont,
had ſo long fettered their forefathers. Inſtead of the mode
formerly followed, of a continued rotation of beans, barley, and oats, on the beſt lands, that of ſummer fallow,
wheat, beans, barley, graſs, and oats, is now univerſally
adopted ; while the lands of inferior quality have crops
ſuited to their ſoil. The ſoil in general is not favourable
for turnips ; yet where it is favourable, theſe have been
ſown, and with ſucceſs. The moſt part of the wet lands
have been drained, and the ridges made ſtreight *, and
thrown into a proper ſize. Two horſe ploughs, of Small's
conſtruction, are uſed over all the pariſh.

But the moſt material circumſtance, in favour of the
agriculture of this pariſh, is a ſpirit of emulation that was,
with much propriety, raiſed amongſt the ploughmen themſelves. About 10 years ago, a number of gentlemen in
this neighbourhood formed themſelves into a ſociety, under the name of the Clackmannanſhire Farmer Club, for
promoting the purpoſes of agriculture. One of their firſt
ſteps was to inſtitute ploughing matches among the ſervants, in which honours and rewards were beſtowed upon
the beſt workmen. From 40 to 50 candidates have often
ſtarted upon theſe occaſions †. The firſt prize has been
always a ſilver medal ‡ ; and three or four ſmaller pecuni-

ary

---

* The carſe lands excepted : The ridges there are, in general, crooked, and, when made ſtreight, take a long time (ſay the farmers, though
with very little juſtice), to be formed into a proper ſoil.

† In 1790, the miniſter of Clackmannan had his glebe and farm ploughed in one day by forty-nine two horſe ploughs : The greateſt number
ever known to ſtart at once in this country.

‡ Alexander Vertue, at that time a ſervant to a farmer in the pariſh

of

ary rewards are given to the next beft, according to their merit. Nothing of this kind had been hitherto known in Scotland; but the example has been followed in many parts of the country, and with much fuccefs.

Beans are fown here as foon in the month of February as the weather permits; oats immediately after, and barley from the 20th of April to the 20th of May: wheat is fown from the 15th of September to the end of October, and fometimes during the two following months; though it feldom turns out well after the middle of November. Harveft commences about the middle of Auguft, and fometimes continues to the end of October. The average produce on the beft lands, when the mode above mentioned is followed, may be computed at 10 bolls of wheat from the acre, 7 of beans, 7 of barley, and 8 of oats *, and 300 ftone of hay, Dutch weight. There have been inftances, however, of much greater increafe, particularly of wheat and oats, even to the extent of 15 bolls the acre.

---

of Clackmannan, gained the firft prize at the firft of thefe ploughing matches. In fummer 1793, he was fent for to his Majefty's farm at Windfor, where it was expected he was to continue. He carried a plough with him from Scotland, and began his work in prefence of his Majefty, and a number of noblemen and gentlemen. It was acknowledged, that land fo well ploughed had never before been feen in that country. Next morning, however, inftead of going to his work, as he was defired the preceding evening, he was told, "Not to go near the King's farm at " Windfor, *on any account whatever,* nor to have the fmalleft inter- " courfe with any of his Majefty's farm fervants." After receiving a reward for his trouble, he left his plough, by fpecial defire, and returned to Scotland. It is difficult to conceive, how, in this inftance, the jea- loufy of the Englifh ploughmen prevented the falutary effects intended by this inftructor.

* Stirlingfhire firlot is ufed here for oats and barley; Linlithgow for wheat; and a firlot for beans and peafe, about a peck in the boll larger than the Linlithgow wheat firlot.

acre. But theſe are very rare : for when at any time the crop is uncommonly luxuriant, it is generally lodged by the heavy rains, which are frequent here in the month of Auguſt, and thereby rendered of little value. The average produce of the whole of crop 1792, even from the beſt lands, did not exceed 4 bolls the acre. The conſequence was, that hardly any of the tenants were able to pay, from this crop, above a third part of their rent; while ſome had not as much as defrayed the expences of ſeed and labour. In this ſtate of real diſtreſs to the ſmall tenants, ſome of the proprietors, with much humanity, made a reduction of the rent, for that year, to ſome of their tenants, and lengthened out the term of payment to others *.

Price

---

* The farmers here have ſome advantages, and ſome diſadvantages, which perhaps are not peculiar to them. Thirlage is fortunately aboliſhed over the greateſt part of the pariſh ; but where it is not, it is ſtill a cauſe of much complaint, and of real loſs to the farmer. It is, indeed, a curſe of an unknown magnitude ; and it is aſtoniſhing how proprietors of land, who have it in their power, do not ſee their own intereſt in putting an end to it altogether. Where it does exiſt, nearly a tenth boll is paid for grinding the corn. Yet, notwithſtanding this, there is not a farmer who would not willingly make a reaſonable allowance for the mill rent. What loſs then can proprietors ſuſtain ? Let them think for a moment; let them conſider the hardſhips to which they expoſe the very perſons, whom it is their intereſt as well as duty to encourage and protect. A ſmall farmer (we ſhall ſuppoſe), who pays the higheſt demand for his little ſpot (and muſt pay it), toils and labours, with unremitting attention, to make it produce what is ſufficient to ſupport his family, and to anſwer the term day of his landlord. He is ſurely entitled to bring the produce of his labour to the beſt market. Inſtead of this, however, he dare not ſell one boll of oats, without being ſubjected to a penalty. He muſt take them all to the mill, and intruſt them, for days and nights, to the care of perſons, in whom he very often can place no confidence : while at the ſame time, he expoſes them to be deſtroyed by the numerous ſwarms of vermin which uſually frequent theſe places. His family ſuffers: his

Price of Labour.—The beſt men ſervants get 8l. Sterling yearly, 6¼ bolls of oat meal, and 1l. 6s. Sterling, for what is called *kitchen-money*, beſides a houſe and yard, if they are married : women ſervants get 3l. yearly : day labourers get 1s. a-day, and 1s. 2d. in harveſt : women reapers get 1s. in harveſt, and a glaſs of whiſky in the morning ; a very bad practice, and which frequently leads them on to habits of drinking whiſky during all their lives. Maſons get 1s. 8d. a-day, and wrights 1s. 6d.

Collieries.—There are 3 collieries in the pariſh, Clackmannan, Sauchy, and Kennet. Clackmannan coal conſiſts of 4 ſeams, known by the names of main coal, 9 feet thick ; cherry coal, 2 feet 10 inches ; ſplint coal, 2 feet 8 inches ; and coal Mozey, 2 feet 3 inches. The main coal was wrought in the laſt century, and terminated about

his landlord muſt alſo ſuffer. This is a real grievance, and ought to be redreſſed. There is a mill in this pariſh, which goes by the name of the *Thieves Mill.*

The invention of threſhing mills will, in all probability, ſoon prove uſeful to agriculture. The firſt of theſe was erected at Kilbagie, in this pariſh, by Mr. George Meikle engineer. It is driven by water, and threſhes eight or ten bolls in an hour. It is undoubtedly one of the greateſt improvements in huſbandry, and promiſes to be of general utility. Threſhing mills are now uſed in many parts, both of Scotland and England ; and commiſſions for them, it is ſaid, have arrived from ſome of the northern kingdoms of Europe. They are now made of various ſizes ; ſo that farmers in this place, who poſſeſs no more than thirty acres of land, find it their intereſt to uſe them. There are already nine of them in this pariſh ; two of which are driven by water ; and ſome of them by two, and ſome by four horſes, according to their ſize. Their price is from 25l. to 60l. Sterling.

The great advantage to be derived from threſhing mills is, that, beſides threſhing much cleaner than by the uſual mode, they give the farmer a command of the market, to which he can bring, upon any emergency, a great part of his crop, at the ſhorteſt notice.

bout the year 1763. The cherry and ſplint ſeams begaṅ
to be wrought about 30 years ago, and are working at the
preſent time. The coal Mozey ſeam is alſo working at
preſent : it was begun in 1792 ; previous to that period,
it could not be wrought to any advantage. In this coal
work, the method called the *long way*, is now introduced ;
that is, no part of the coal is left for pillars, but the whole
taken out, which ſaves a great part of the coal. In ſome
of the pits, the coal is brought to the top by women
and boys ; and in others, by means of machinery. The
coal is kept dry by means of an engine driven by water ;
which is much leſs expenſive than a fire engine. The
price of coal varies according to the demand. In general,
the price of great coal upon the hill is 5 s. the ton ; of
chows, 4 s. About 7000 tons are annually exported to
Leith, Dunbar, Perth, Dundee, Montroſe, and other places.
Theſe are taken to the harbour in waggons of a ton and
a half : the mean diſtance from the pits being about three
quarters of a mile *.

The working of the Sauchy coal is of a very old date.
It is kept dry by a very powerful fire engine. It conſiſts
of 4 ſeams : the firſt, or uppermoſt, is 3 feet thick ; the
ſecond is 5 feet ; but this one has no roof, ſo that it has
never been wrought : the third is 5 feet, and is an excel‧
lent coal : the fourth is 9 feet : This laſt, however, is 16
fathoms below the bottom of the preſent engine pit, which
is 47 fathoms deep. Previous to this period, a great part
of the Sauchy coal has been exported ; but as it is now in
the poſſeſſion of the Devon Company, it is highly probable,

---

* A collier, with his wife and daughter, earns 12 s. in five days, which
is all the time he works in the week. Beſides this, he has his meal from
the proprietor at 8½ d. the peck ; a free houſe and yard, and other bounties, to the amount of 30 s. yearly.

bable, that the moſt of it will be uſed for their iron work.

The Kennet coal conſiſts of two ſeams; one of 30 inches thick, and another of 36. It was given up in 1726, and began again to be wrought in 1759. It has at preſent a ſmall fire engine; but it is probable, it was once level free, as there is no trace remaining of any engine being upon it when it was firſt wrought. The diſtilleries in the pariſh conſume a great part of this coal. It produces yearly about 6000 tons of great coal, beſides a conſiderable quantity of chows. After the year 1788, when the diſtilleries were ſtopped, about 2000 tons were yearly ſhipped for Leith. It has alſo a very extenſive land ſale *.

Diſtilleries.—The two great diſtilleries of Kilbagie and Kennetpans are both in the pariſh of Clackmannan; and, previous to the year 1788, the manufacture of Scotch ſpirits was carried on at them to an extent hitherto unknown in this part of the iſland of Great Britain. The diſtillery laws have undergone various changes in Scotland. Before the year 1784, the duty was levied by a preſumptive charge upon the waſh (that is, fermented worts), taking it for granted, that the waſh would produce one-fourth part in low wines, and that theſe low wines would produce three-fifth parts in ſpirits: hence, 100 gallons of waſh

was

---

* During Cromwell's uſurpation, when the Engliſh ports were ſhut up by the Dutch, one of the above coal works was let to a Mr. Marjoribanks, a merchant in Edinburgh, at the yearly ſum of 1666l. 13s. 4d. Sterling.

Formerly there were ſalt pans in this pariſh, both at Kennetpans and at Clackmannan pow, owing perhaps to the coal being ſo readily procured; but theſe have been diſcontinued for a number of years. The water at this place, indeed, does not appear to be ſalt enough for that purpoſe.

was ſuppoſed to yield 15 gallons of ſpirits, and duty was charged accordingly; but inſtead of 15, 20 gallons of ſpirits were often drawn from the 100 of waſh. In Scotland, the ſurplus above 15 gallons was uniformly ſeized, as ſpirits preſumed to be fraudulently obtained ; while in England the diſtiller was allowed the full exerciſe of his genius, and got permits for the removal of his actual produce. At this period, the quantum of duty on a gallon of ſpirits was more than double of what it has ever been ſince. But the high rate of duty afforded ſuch temptation to ſmuggling, that the conſumption of ſpirits in Scotland was chiefly ſupplied by the manufacture of illegal ſtills, and by ſmuggling from abroad. Great diſtillers could not ſmuggle ; and being continually ſubjected to the ſurveys of the exciſe, the two diſtilleries of Kilbagie and Kennetpans depended entirely on the London market for the ſale of their produce ; where, previous to the year 1784, they carried on an advantageous trade : though the duty on a gallon of ſpirits in England was 13⅔ pence higher than in Scotland ; and though they had, at ſhipping their ſpirits for England, to pay down this difference on every gallon ſhipped. In 1784, a law was paſſed, rendering the duties, and mode of levying them, the ſame both in Scotland as in England ; and at the ſame time reducing the rate of duty each gallon about one half of what it had been formerly ; while it allowed the manufacturer a credit for 20 gallons of ſpirits from the 100 gallons of waſh, and granted permits accordingly. The London diſtillers expected, that by this equalization plan, the Scotch could not continue their trade to London, and pay the duties in the ſame manner with themſelves. But in this they were miſtaken ; for the trade increaſed. And it is the opinion of the beſt informed diſtillers, that the London diſtillers are not a

match

match for the Scotch under an equal law. This mode was continued till July 1786, when the licenfe act took place, impofing 30s. a gallon yearly on the contents of every ftill ufed for diftillation in Scotland; continuing the laft plan with refpect to England (where the duty amounted to 2s. 6d. for the gallon of fpirits), and impofing an additional duty of 2s. on the gallon of fpirits fent from Scotland to England : which additional duty was to be paid in London, on the arrival of the fpirits in the river Thames.

This act was paffed as an experiment, and was to continue for two years. Under it, the London diftillers expected, that the Scotch could not continue the trade to London. This trade, however, ftill continued to increafe; which increafed alfo the aftonifhment of the London traders, who gave in a reprefentation to the Treafury upon the fubject. In confequence of which, and upwards of fix months previous to the natural expiration of the law, another law was paffed, impofing a duty of 6d. a gallon on all Scotch fpirits fent to England, in addition to the former 2s.; while the duty on fpirits manufactured in England was allowed to remain at the 2s. 6d. When this act was paffed, the Scotch diftilleries ftopped payment. The law continued in this way till July 1788, when the licenfe duty in Scotland was doubled, and made 3l. a gallon, on the contents of the ftill; and at the fame time laying the trader under fuch reftrictions, when he worked for England, as to amount to a prohibition againft his entering that market. And in July 1793, the licenfe has been raifed to 9l. Sterling a gallon yearly. Previous to the year 1788, the quantity of corn ufed annually at the diftillery of Kilbagie alone, amounted to above 60,000 bolls, and the annual quantity of fpirits made, to above 3000 tons. The black cattle fed annually were about 7000; fwine 2000.

The

The cattle were fold to butchers, who drove them to the Edinburgh and Glafgow markets : the fwine were killed and cured into bacon and pork for England. The work people employed were nearly 300. The diftillery and utenfils coft upwards of 40,000l. Sterling ; and when fold by the truftee for the creditors of the former proprietor, yielded about 7000l. Sterling.

No fituation could have been more eligible for a diftillery than Kilbagie ; and it was erected in the moft fubftantial manner. The buildings occupy a fpace of above 4 acres of ground ; all furrounded by a high wall. The barns for malting are of a prodigious fize, and are 4 ftories in height. A fmall rivulet runs through the middle of the works, and drives a threfhing mill, and all the grinding mills neceffary for the diftillery ; befides fupplying with water a canal, which communicates with the river Forth, of about a mile in length, cut for the purpofe of conveying both the imports and exports of the diftillery.

The diftillery at Kennetpans, which is advantageoufly fituated on the very banks of the river Forth, was in proportion to that of Kilbagie, as three to five. And before thefe two diftilleries were ftopped, they paid to government an excife duty confiderably greater than the whole land tax of Scotland. At prefent, the duty paid by both is about 8000l. Sterling yearly. There is an engine, of Bolton and Watt's conftruction, at the diftillery of Kennetpans, being the firft of the kind that was erected in Scotland.

Iron Works.—The extenfive and valuable feams of coal and lime-ftone on the eftate of Sauchy, belonging to Lord Cathcart, induced fome gentlemen, under the firm of Devon

von Company, to eftablifh iron works of confiderable extent. Thefe confift at prefent of two blaft furnaces, and
are fituated on the banks of the river Devon, near to the
old tower of Sauchy. The fituation, and fingular conftruction of the Devon iron works, begun in July 1792,
merit the attention of the curious in mechanicks and architecture. A fteep bank rifes more than 50 feet above
the level of the river, and is compofed of a mock, or very
thick ftratum of free-ftone, very dry and uniform in its
texture, and almoft free from cracks and fiffures. Inftead
of the ufual method of building with ftone and lime, the
feveral parts of the works have been formed in this bank,
by excavations made in the rock. Two furnaces, which
are each above 40 feet high, and 14 feet diameter, and alfo
the fpacious arches which give accefs to the workmen, at
the bottom of the furnace, to draw off the liquid metal
and flag, are cut out of the rock. The roof which covers
the cafting houfe, a room 70 feet long, 50 feet wide, and
23 feet high, is fupported by the fides of the quarry, and
the folid pillars of the rock that were left for this purpofe
in making the excavation. In like manner, is formed the
engine houfe, and its apparatus, which is intended to fupply
the two furnaces with wind, by throwing at each vibra-
tion of the engine a fufficient quantity of air, out of a
large cylinder, into a long gallery or clofe mine, formed
in the rock. This magazine of wind will contain above
10,000 cubic feet of air, much condenfed by the power of
the engine, as the gallery is very clofely fhut up, and made
air-tight; having only two apertures, one to receive the
fupply of air from the air pump, and the other to admit a
pipe that conducts the condenfed air to blow the two
furnaces.

The

The Devon iron works are within 3 Englifh miles of the port and harbour of Alloa, where the produce and manufactures of thefe works are intended to be fhipped ; and from which, by a retour carriage, the proprietors can eafily bring any fupplies of iron-ftone, iron-ores, lime-ftone, timber, or any other materials that may be ne-ceffary *.

POPULATION TABLE FOR 1791.

Number of fouls †,	2528	From 10 to 20,	484
Males,	1205	From 20 to 50,	1000
Females,	1323	From 50 to 70,	360
Souls under 10,	633	From 70 to 100,	51
			Heads

* This undertaking muft already have coft a large fum of money, although as yet only in its infant ftate : but the advantages that muft refult from it to every clafs of people, and to the landholders of this county in particular, give great caufe to wifh for its extenfion and profperity. The fituation has many peculiar advantages. The whole country around it abounds in coal, as well as in ftrata of iron-ftone ; and a vein of rich kidney iron ore, 18 inches thick, has been found in one of the neighbouring hills. There is alfo a very fine lime-ftone rock, within a few miles of it, lately difcovered in the Menftry hills, belonging to Major General Abercromby of Tullibody. So that when we add to all thefe advantages, the practicability of cutting a navigable canal to join the river Forth, we may reafonably expect that this undertaking will prove fuccefsful.

† In the year 1755, the number of fouls in the parifh of Clackmannan was, according to Dr. Webfter's report, 1913 : fo that there is an increafe fince that period of 615. This may eafily be accounted for, from the number of people who, for many years, crowded to this place, in order to be employed at the diftilleries. It is probable, that the number of colliers has alfo increafed ; of thefe, there are in the prefent lift 605 fouls. Previous to the year 1788, the numbers in the parifh were much greater than in 1791; for when the diftilleries gave over working, a

great

Heads of families,	681	Weavers,	-	23
Of whom are		Butchers,	-	7
Married, -	460	Millers,	-	2
Bachelors, -	39	Day labourers,		114
Widowers, -	33	Glazier,	-	1
Widows, .	100	Diftillers,	-	2
Eftablifhed Church,	391	Ale and whifky fellers,		23
Antiburghers,	51	Carters,	-	10
Burghers, -	59	Gardeners,	-	10
Relief, -	180	Coopers,	-	2
Houfes, -	511	Cadgers,	-	2
Men fervants in their own		Coal grieves,	-	3
houfes, -	49	Miners,	-	6
Ditto in families,	121	Sailors,	-	7
Women fervants,	79	Tide waiter,	-	1
Farmers, -	51	Grocers or fhopkeepers,		12
Colliers, who are heads of		Horfes,	-	412
families, -	116	Black cattle,	-	394
Bakers, -	4	Ploughs,	-	100
Tailors, -	11	Carts,	-	192
Shoemakers, -	12	Four wheeled carriages, viz.		
Wrights, -	23	A coach and two chaifes,		3
Mafons, -	10	Pigeon houfes,		6
Smiths, -	15			

TABLE

great many families left the parifh. Thefe are now (1794) returning, and many more may be expected; both on account of the diftilleries, which are again reviving, and the Devon iron work. So that in a few years, it is highly probable, that the population of this parifh will be much greater than it is at prefent.

TABLE *of* MARRIAGES, BIRTHS, *and* BURIALS *for* 21 *years.*

Years.	Proclama-tions.	Marriages in the parish.	Inter-marriages with other parishes *.	Births.	Burials.
1773,	16	12	4	67	33
1774,	10	8	2	69	57
1775,	20	16	4	60	45
1776,	21	16	5	81	47
1777,	24	17	7	68	81
1778,	29	17	12	94	40
1779,	23	15	8	77	26
1780,	35	25	10	90	81
1781,	27	21	6	92	64
1782,	33	19	14	78	62
1783,	21	15	6	90	90
1784,	28	21	7	86	55
1785,	29	22	7	94	66
1786,	43	34	9	76	54
1787,	47	39	8	81	89
1788,	34	29	5	82	39
1789,	26	17	9	77	31
1790,	25	22	3	69	76
1791,	20	20	—	73	82
1792,	27	18	9	73	53
1793,	19	13	6	65	65
Total,	557	416	141	1642	1236
Average,	27	20	7	78	59

Poor.—The funds for the support of the poor arise from the interest of 250l. Sterling, from the weekly collections at the church door, from fines on account of misdemeanours,

* Where the women only have left the parish.

demeanours, and from a general voluntary fubfcription by
the heritors, whether refident or non-refident, and all the
inhabitants in the parifh. The heritors and kirk-feffion,
about 20 years ago, formed themfelves into a committee,
which meets monthly, for the management of thefe funds.
Into this committee are chofen, from time to time, fuch
of the other inhabitants of the parifh as are beft acquainted with the ftate of the poor in their immediate neighbourhood *.

Subjoined is a table, fhowing the number of monthly
penfioners in the parifh of Clackmannan for 17 years prior
to 1794, together with an exact account of the money
received for the maintenance of the poor. But befides
the regular penfioners, needy perfons, from time to time,
receive extraordinary fupplies. Thefe are not marked in
the following table; but the furplus will fhow the fum
allotted to them.

TABLE

---

* A clerk and treafurer receives a proper allowance yearly out of the
funds for keeping the books, and paying the money to the poor. Thefe
receive charity in proportion to their wants; in general, from 2 s. to 6 s.
monthly, according as they are able to work lefs or more. If, at any
time, they are in diftrefs, without having any perfon to attend them, a
keeper is appointed to this office, and is paid out of the funds. None of
the poor are allowed to beg; which feems to be a fevere reftraint upon
fome of the idle ones.

Before they are admitted upon the monthly roll, they are alfo obliged
to give to the treafurer an inventory of their effects, which, at their
death, are difpofed of for the benefit of the fund, provided they have no
children in need of them.

TABLE.

Years.	Number of Penſioners.		Yearly Income.		
1777,	—	13	—	L. 100	1	1¾
1778,	—	40	—	89	7	6¾
1779,	—	43	—	102	14	7½
1780,	—	42	—	113	16	6
1781,	—	44	—	137	18	6¾
1782,	—	48	—	108	10	0½
1783,	—	57	—	118	11	7¼
1784,	—	57	—	140	11	11¼
1785,	—	51	—	166	14	2
1786,	—	43	—	143	5	10¼
1787,	—	46	—	155	7	5
1788,	—	42	—	178	18	7½
1789,	—	43	—	118	18	1½
1790,	—	42	—	110	16	9¼
1791,	—	43	—	109	1	11¼
1792,	—	38	—	126	0	8¾
1793,	—	41	—	134	7	8¼
Total,		733		L. 2155	3	3¾
Average,		43		L. 126	15	0

School.—The pariſh ſchoolmaſter's ſalary is 200 merks. About 2 years ago, the heritors voluntarily agreed to double this ſum during the life of the preſent incumbent : ſo that this doubled ſalary, together with the other emoluments, make his income about 40l. Sterling a-year, excluſive of the ſchool wages and a good houſe and garden. Beſides the parochial ſchool, there are 5 other ſchools eſtabliſhed in different parts of the pariſh, which are remote from the village of Clackmannan *. Each of the

3 col-

* Michael Bruce taught one of theſe ſchools—Michael Bruce, the ingenious poet of Kinroſsſhire, whoſe premature death is ſo pathetically,

and

3 collieries has one of thefe. Sometimes, indeed, there are even fchoolmafters, paid by fubfcription, according to the diftance which fuch inhabitants are from the parifh fchool, who are able to bear this expenfe. At prefent, one of thefe fubfcription fchoolmafters receives upwards of 50l. a-year ; fo that the whole yearly income of the different fchoolmafters in this parifh muft amount to more than 170l. Sterling.

Church,

and fo juftly lamented, by the elegant Author of the Mirror (No. 36). A very fhort time before his death, he taught the fmall fchool of For- reft Mill, worth only about 12l. Sterling a-year ; and it was the higheft preferment to which he attained. Yet, in this obfcure retreat, in the bleakeft corner of the parifh, living in a wretched hovel, and ftruggling under all the hardfhips of poverty, he wrote LOCHLEVEN, one of the fineft defcriptive poems in the Englifh language.

The following are extracts taken from his holograph letters ftill ex- tant, and in the poffeffion of the Reverend Dr. Baird, Principal of the Univerfity of Edinburgh ; and they put this fact beyond a doubt.

———— " I have wrote a few lines of a defcriptive poem, *Cui titu-* " *lus eft Lochleven.* You may remember you hinted fuch a thing to me ; " fo I have fet about it, and you may expect a dedication. I hope it will " foon be finifhed, as I, every week, add two lines, blot out fix, and " alter eight. You fhall hear the plan when I know it myfelf. Fare- " well. I am, your's, &c. MICHAEL BRUCE."
Forreft Mill, July 28. 1766.

To Mr. David Arnot of Portmoag.

And, in another letter to the fame perfon, he gives an account of a vi- fit to the Ifland of Lochleven, and exclaims bitterly againft the men who conveyed him thither, for not allowing him more time to examine its antiquities.—" They," fays he, " who confider it in no other view than " as capable of feeding a dozen or fourteen cattle, when their work was " over, would not ftay a minute longer, had it been to difcover the " great toe of St. Moag, who is buried there. My defcription of it, in " the poem Lochleven (which, by the bye, is now finifhed) runs thus " ———— I am, &c. MICHAEL BRUCE."
Forreft Mill, December 1. 1766.

A fecond edition of Michael Bruce's Poems is now in the prefs.

Church, &c.—The church is an old mean structure, in the form of a crofs, evidently built at different periods, and now in a very ruinous state. The manfe was built about the year 1740. It is beautifully situated on the S. fide of the ridge on which the village stands, and commands a moft delightful view of the whole country along the banks of the river Forth. Lord Dundas is patron. —The ftipend confifts of 24 bolls of barley, 24 bolls of meal, 16 bolls of oats, and 50l. Sterling in money, exclufive of 40l. Scotch for communion elements, and 20l. Scotch for grafs mail ; with a glebe of about 4 acres of good land, and what is called *craig leave* coal, that is, free coal, except paying the collier, which is about one-third part of the value *.

The records of the kirk-feffion commence in the year 1593, and are almoft entire from that period.

Though there are a variety of fectaries in the parifh, only one of them (the Relief) has a meeting-houfe in it ; the reft go to meeting-houfes in the adjoining parifhes.

Antiquities.—Clackmannan has, for many generations, been the feat of the chief of the Bruces in Scotland. It is not certain, however, at what precife period John de Bruce, third fon of Robert, one of the Earls of Annandale, became proprietor of it. King David II. gave it to his kinfman, Robert Bruce, the firft laird of Clackmannan. (*Dilecto confanguineo,* faith the charter, dated at Perth the 9th of December, a. regni 39), which muft have been a very fhort time only before his death. It is probable, indeed,

---

* Since this account was written, the Court of Teinds (of this date, November 19. 1794.) have granted an augmentation of four chalders of victual, one half in meal, and the other in barley ; befides an addition of 5l. Sterling to the communion element money.

deed, that King David refided at Clackmannan, at leaft, during the firft part of his reign; fince we find, that, in the year 1330, his chamberlain, Reginald More, fettled his publick accounts there *.

The old tower, which ftill remains, is faid to have been built by King Robert Bruce. From the ftyle of the building, indeed (for there is no date upon it), it appears to have been erected about his time; and, from feveral names of places, we may conclude, that it actually was the refidence of fome of the kings; as the following names feem to indicate; *King's Seat Hill*, *King's Meadow Park*, and others of a fimilar nature, in the vicinity of the tower. The greateft height of this tower is 79 feet. It contains a variety of apartments, and has been furrounded by a moat, with a draw-bridge, part of which ftill remains. Adjoining the tower, ftands the old manfion, the refidence of the family, till the direct line became extinct. Both the tower and houfe, however, are faft crumbling into ruins, and exhibit a fad fpectacle of human grandeur. Though faid to have been once the abode of kings, and, for many ages, the chief refidence of one of the moft ancient families in the kingdom, yet they now afford only a very comfortlefs dwelling to a common ploughman.

Henry Bruce, Efq., the laft laird of Clackmannan, died in 1772; and in him ended the direct line of that ancient family. His widow, Katharine Bruce, furvived him till November 1791, when fhe died, by means of an accidental fall, at the great age of 95 †. She had in her poffeffion

an

---

* See " Accounts of the Chamberlain of Scotland, in the years 1329, 1330, and 1331, from the originals in the Exchequer," publifhed by Mr. John Davidfon in 1771.

† The memory of this lady will ever be revered by all who knew her.

She

an immenſely large ſword, with a helmet, ſaid to have been uſed by King Robert Bruce at the battle of Bannockburn ; both of which ſhe bequeathed as a legacy to the preſent Earl of Elgin. The direct male line of the family of Bruce of Clackmannan being extinct, a diſpute is now keenly agitated by two claimants for the chiefſhip, the Earl of Elgin and Alexander Bruce, Eſq. of Kennet ; but unleſs ſome farther evidence be adduced, than what has yet appeared, it is not probable, that it will ſoon be terminated in favour of either of the parties. It is aſtoniſhing, therefore, how Mr. Aſtle, in his late publication, " On the Seals of the Kings of Scotland," &c. ſhould, without heſitation, and without ſhowing any good evidence, have aſſigned the chiefſhip to the Earl of Elgin.

A tree of the family of the Bruces, from their firſt arrival in Britain, is in the poſſeſſion of that nobleman, left to him as a legacy by the late lady of Clackmannan ; a copy of which alſo is in the poſſeſſion of Lord Dundas. It is dated 1686 ; but upon what grounds its authenticity depends, it has not as yet been ſhown. This, however, muſt be judged of, in a great meaſure, according as the facts related in it agree or diſagree with the general tenor of hiſtory. If this tree ſhall be pronounced authentick,

She was one of thoſe rare characters, which at times appear on earth as the ornaments of their nature. To all the high ſentiments of a dignified and enlightened mind, ſhe added thoſe amiable virtues of the heart, which render their influence irreſiſtible. As long as ſhe lived, therefore, the Tower of Clackmannan was frequented by her numerous friends and acquaintances, of various ranks, and of all ages ; for her extreme weight of years had not made the leaſt impreſſion upon that happy vivacity and cheerfulneſs of temper, which had always made her company ſo much the admiration and the delight of her friends. She was formed to ſupport to the laſt, with undiminiſhed dignity, the character of the race from which ſhe was ſprung.

rick, it evidently makes Mr. Bruce of Kennet the chief of the Bruces; fince, according to it, he is defcended from Sir Robert Bruce, the eighth laird of Clackmannan, being three generations later than the Earl of Elgin, who is defcended from Sir David Bruce, the fifth laird of Clackmannan, according to this tree. On the margin of the tree is a narrative, giving an account of the family of the Bruces *.

Mr. Bruce of Kennet has alfo a claim to the attainted title of Lord Burleigh. His grandmother, by the father's fide, was Mary Balfour, the youngeft daughter of the fourth Lord Burleigh; whofe only fon Robert killed a man in 1707, and was condemned to die, but efcaped from prifon

previous

---

*Copy of the Narrative on the Margin of the Family Tree of the Bruces of Clackmannan.

READER,

Since we are to fpeak of the genealogie of that heroick Prince King Robert Bruce, take notice, in the firft place, that this firname (whither corruptly pronounced for Le Preux (the valiant), as in the old records it is oftentimes written Le Breufe, or a Topicall firname De Bruis, from a town and caftle of that name in the Grifons country, hath originally from France; where, about the year 1145, lived Peter Brucie, famous for writing againft the Romifh errors of tranfubftantiation, whofe followers, by the Popifh writers, are ftiled Petro Brufiani. About the year 1050, divers noblemen of Normandy, coming over with Q. Emma, fettled themfelves in England; after her death (being hated of the Englifh) were forced to retire for Scotland, which was then nearly allied to the Duke of Normandy, by reafon that King Kenneth the III. and King Malcolm the II. married two daughters of that houfe amongft the reft.

I. Adelme le Bruis, Preus or Breos (for fo diverfly is he named), obtained in Scotland the lands of Bouilden. This Adelme joined, in the year 1066, with William the Baftard, Duke of Normandy, in the conqueft of England; and, for his valiant fervice, was highly rewarded with great lands there, namely, the caftle and barony of Skelton, and lordfhip of Cleveland, the lands of Hert, Hertneffe, Hertlepool, Danby, Levington, Yarum, Guifburgh, Shorp, Sibthrop, Carleton, Weftly Brofton, and

previous to the day of his execution. He was concealed for fome years, and after his father's death, joined in the Rebellion in 1715; in confequence of which, the title was attainted.—The queftion, therefore, is, whether this Robert was to be confidered as dead in law, upon his being condemned (which was before his father died), fo that no after deed of his could affect the title as to the next heir? If this be the cafe, as the title is faid to be to heirs whatfoever, Mr. Bruce of Kennet muft have a juft claim to the title of Burleigh, by virtue of his grandmother's right, as the other fifter was never married.

There

and Uplythan. He had two fones, 1. Robert, his fucceffor; 2. William, prior of Guifburgh. He carried, in his coat of arms A a lyon rampant P: He had a younger brother, named William le Brees, Lord of Bremner, in Suffex.

II. Robert Bruce, elder fone to Adelme, affifted Edgar (fone to K. Malcom Cranmore) in recovery of the Crown of Scotland, ufurped by Duncan, his baftard brother, and Donald Bane his uncle; he married Agnefs Annand, heir of the Lordfhip of Annandale, who bare him two fones; 1ft. Adam, Lord of Skelton; 2d. Robert, Lord of Annandale. He founded the priory of Guifburgh, anno 1120, and endowed it richly with lands and tythes. He affifted St. David, then Earle Huntingtone, in founding the abbey of Selkirk, which afterwards, when he came to the Crown, tranfported to Kelfo. This Lord Robert, as witnefs in the charter of mortification, has contributed his lands of Bouilden for increafing the patrimony thereof. He died anno 1141, and was buried in the monaftery of Guifburgh: fo that they are miftaken who account this Robert to be the man who affifted William the Conqueror anno 1068, being fome 75 years before his death. His brother William, prior of Guifburgh, died A. D; 1155.

III. Robert, fecond of that name, was fecond Lord of Annandale, in right of his mother, and Lord of Cleaveland, Hert, Hertnefs, and Hertpool, by his father's gift. He conformed to the cuftoms of thofe times, appointing his father's bearing, affumed the coat of Annandale O, a chief and faltier G, and having no fons by his firft wife Alifa, or Avifa, he gave fundry mortifications to the canons of Guifburgh; he gave alfo many lands

There is another old tower fituated on the banks of the Devon, belonging to Lord Cathcart. It has been for many years in the poffeffion of his family, and is ftill more entire than the tower of Clackmannan. There was alfo one

---

lands in marriage with his daughters, whofe pofterity carry his arms, with alterations, namely, Johnfton, Kilpatrick, Moffet, Tweedy, Tait, Litle, Corry, Hert, Greir, Jardin, Boys. By his fecond wife, Juditha, daughter to William of Langcafter, Lord of Kendell, he had,

IV. William, third Lord of Annandale and Cleveland, a vialant religious nobleman, who lived in the days of K. Alexander II. in the 19th year of his reigne. He is witnefs in a charter granted by him to Abbey of Kelfo; he confirmed his predeceffor's donation to the monaftery of Kelfo and Guifburgh, adding moreover a new gift of certain lands in Hertlepool to the canons of Guifburgh. He married Ifabel, daughter to William the Lyon, begotten upon the daughter de Avenell.

V. Robert his fon, third of that name, and fourth Lord Annandale and Cleaveland, married Ifabella, daughter to Gilbert of Clare, Earl of Clare, Glocefter, and Hertfoord; had three fons, 1. Robert, his fucceffor; 2. John, of whom many of the furname of Bruce in Scotland are defcended; 3. Sir Bernard, of Conington, in England.

VI. Robert, fourth of that name, and fifth Lord of Annandale, married Ifabell, fecond daughter to Prince David Earl of Huntington and Chefter, and got with her the lordfhip of Garioch. He was, for his exceeding valour, firnamed the Noble. In the year 1264, he, with John Balioll, Lord of Galloway, was fent with an army to the affiftance of K. Henry the III. of England againft the Barons.

VII. Robert, his fon, fifth of that name, Lord of Annandale and Garioch, married Martha Countefs of Carrick.

The clandeftine marriage, fpoken of by our hiftorians, was not betwixt her and the Lord Robert Bruce, but with Thomas Mackintzgart, her firft hufband; who (being Earl of Carrick in her right), in the year 1270, was fent with other noblemen to the wars of the Holy Land with 1000 foldiers; and, dying there without iffue, left his lady a widow, whofe marriage the King procured to his coufin Lord Robert Bruce, whereby he became Earl of Carrick. She bare many children to him; 1. Robert, fixth of that name, thereafter King of Scotland; 2. Edward Earl of Carrick and King of Ireland; 3. Sir Neil Bruce, taken in Kildrimmie;

one of the fame kind at a place called Hart-fhaw, which belonged originally to the Stewarts of Rofyth; from which family Oliver Cromwell, by the female line, is faid to have been defcended. It was probably the hunting feat of that family, as the name denotes. Very few veftiges, however,

---

drimmie; 4. and 5. Thomas and Alexander, taken in Galloway: Thefe three were bafely murdered by King Edward Long Shanks. His firft daughter Chriftian was married firft to Sir Andrew Murray, Lord Both-well. After his death (he being killed at Stirling 1297), fhe was married to Donald Earl of Mar. Second daughter Eufeme, married to Sir Thomas Randolph, fheriff of Roxbrugh, and great Chamberlain of Scotland. Third, Marjory, married Sir Neill Campell of Loch. The fourth married to Sir Chriftopher Seaton of Seaton. This Robert is he who contended with Baliol, for the crown, and being perfidioufly ufed by King Edward Long Shanks (who made ufe of his power and friends to conquer Scotland, under pretence of maintaining his title), at length perceaveing the treachery, and labouring in vain to get his fon, the Lord Robert Bruce, in his own power, whom King Edward caufed to be keept in Cailis as a pledge to bind his father to his fervice, and fo to withdraw himfelf into Scotland, brocken with grief and in-dignation. As he returned from Hert to Annandale, he deceafed in the way, about Pafche 1304, and was buried in the monaftery of Holm Coultran. Obferve, here the reader is admonifhed of fome miftakes in writers of hiftory; fome placing another Robert betwixt this Earl of Carrick and Robert the Noble, who married one of the heirs of Hunt-ingtoun; fome afferting that Robert the Noble himfelf was Baliol's com-petitor; fome writing that Robert Earl of Carrick, who contended with Baliol, was the fame which afterwards fo happily came to the crown; whereas indeed Robert the Noble was father to the Earl of Carrick, and dyed before Alexander the III. King Robert alfo was but a child of ten or twelve years in the time of contention, his father being ftill alive, who (as faid is) dyed anno 1304.

VIII. King Robert Bruce married, firft Ifabell, daughter to Gratney Earl of Mar, by whom he had one daughter Mariorie, whoe bare to her hufband, the Lord Walter Stewart of Renfrew, Robert King of Scotland; and fecondly, he married Ifabell de Bourk, daughter to Haymer Earl of Ulfter in Ireland, who was mother to King David and to Mar-

garet

however, of this tower, except the coat of arms, are now remaining. The proprietor, it feems, in the beginning of this

garet Countefs of Sutherland. King David had no iffue, whereby the crown fell to the houfe of Stewart.

IX. Edward Earl of Carrick and King of Ireland (younger brother to King Robert), married Ifabell, daughter of John Earl of Athol, fifter daughter to the Lord Cumine Stair at Dumfries. She bare to him three fons, fucceffively one after another Earls of Carrick ; Robert, killed at Duplin ; 2. Earl Alexander, killed at Haledon-hill, both without iffue ; 3. Earl Thomas married Dornagilla Cumine, daughter to Red John Cumine, widow of Archibald Douglafs Lord of Galoway (in her right), by whom he had one daughter Eleonor, who married Sir James Sandelands, to whom her uterine brother William Earl of Douglafs gave in portion with her the barony of Weft Calder ; of which mariage, the Barons of Weft Calder and Lords of Torphichen are defcended. In this Thomas ended the male iffue of Robert Bruce firft Earl of Carrick, whereupon that Earldom was beftowed on John Stewart, Lord of Kyle, eldeft fone to King Robert Stewart, who thereafter was King, called Robert the III. : and the Earldom of Carrick was annexed to the principality.

X. King David Bruce, in the 39th year of his reign, 1369, gave the barony and caftle of Clackmannin, which of old belonged to the crown, to his kinfman. " Delecto confanguineo," faith the charter, dated at Perth the 9th of December, a regni 39.

Robert Bruce defcended of William Adelmes' brother, whofe fucceffor (after the houfe of Annandale were extinct). did fucceed as chief, and fo affumed the armes, to wit, a chief and faltier, fo carried by the lairds of Clackmannin. The houfe of Airth giving for difference a ftar in chief, and Earlfhall defcended from Airth for a farther difference, adeth a flower de lis, in memory of his advancement by King Charles the VIII. of France (for his great fervices) to the barony of Concrefault, which he excambed with the Lord Monneypenney for the lands of Earlfhall in Fyffe.

XI. Sir Bernard Bruce, third fon to the forefaid Robert fourth Lord of Annandale, by the favour of elder brother, Robert the Noble, who married David Earle of Huntingtoun's daughter, obtained the marriage of the heir of Cunnington, in Huntingtonnfhire, and Exton in Rutland-fhire, in England, holding in fee of the Earls of Huntingtoun. To him

fucceeded

this century, pulled it down, for the purpofe of building a mill, and fome farm houfes.

Character

fucceeded his fon Barnard II. his fon Barnard III. his fon Barnard IV. who had no iffue. His younger brother John Br. had two daughters, 1. Jean, who got the lands of Exton, of whom defcended the Hunting-touns of Exton ; 2. Agnes Bruce got the lands of Connington, whofe fucceffor is Sir Robert Cotton of Connington, the famous antiquary.

We come now to fpeak of Adam Lord of Skelton, eldeft fon to Robert firft Lord of Annandale, whofe fucceffors carried in their coat of arms, A; a lyon rampant, P. His fon, Adam Bruce (fecond of that name), had for his fucceffor Peter, I, a mighty baron, who married the daughter of Stephen of Campeigne (fifter's fon to the Conqueror), Earle Albemarle and Holdernefs. His fon Peter II. married Havifa, grandchild and heir to William of Lancafter, Lord of Kendall, in whofe right he and his heirs poffeffed that barony : He died at Merfilles in France (as he returned from the Holy Land) 1219. His fon Peter III. had no children ; and he was laft of the male fucceffion of Adam Lord of Skelton. His great inheretance was divided amongft his four fifters; 1. Agnes brought to her hufband Sir Walter Faulconbridge the barony of Skelton ; 2. Lufie and her hufband, Sir Marmaduke Thueng, had the barony of Danby ; 3. Margaret Bruce and her hufband, Robert Rofs, Lord of Warkcaftle, got the Lordfhip of Kendall. Laderina, with her hufband John de Bella Aqua, had the lands of Carleton.

XII. William le Breos, for fo he and his pofterity is cald, brother to Adelme, for his fervice in the conqueft, got from William of Normandy the caftle and barony of Bremwer in Suffex.

XIII. Peter le Breos, his fon, fecond Lord of Bremwer, married Havifa, daughter of William de Momara Earl of Lincoln, in her right; fhe dyed in the Holly Land, 1128.

XIV Phillip le Breos, his fon, third Lord of Bremwer, a valiant nobleman, was one of the firft adventurers in the conqueft of Ireland. He married Bertha, fecond daughter to Millo Fitz-Walter, Earle of Herefoord. She had three brethren, Rodger, Walter, and Henry, one after another Earls of Hereford, who leaveing no iffue, Bertha augmented her hufband Philip with the Lordfhip of Brecknock, in Brecknockfhire, and Abergaveny, in Munmuthfhire in England.

XV. William, his fon, fourth Lord Bremwer, and alfo Lord of Brecknock and Abergaveny, married Eva, one of the five daughters and co-

heirs

Character of the People.—The great diverfity of ranks and employments in this parifh, renders the character of the people equally diverfified. In general, however, they are a fober, induftrious, and religious people; though inftances of great profligacy now and then occur. Many of the lower ranks are much addicted to the drinking of whifky; which is often the caufe of much mifery to their families. The great body of the farmers are a moft intelligent and refpectable clafs of men; many of them poffeffing

heirs (after the death of their five brethren) of William Marfhall, the great Earl of Pembroke. She had two fons.

XVI. William, who dying without iffue, left his fucceffion to his brother.

XVII. Robert, who married Helen, daughter to Allan de Vitro Pont, &c. This Robert did quit his own arms, and affumed thofe òf Annandale, they being the only male-heirs of the family defcended from Adelme. King Robert, his brother Edward, and his fons, all earls of Annandale, being extinct without iffue, fo that this Robert remained chief, affuming the primitive terms which his fucceffors carry unto this day from him, many bearing the name of Bruce, are defcended: whofe fon,

XVIII. Robert I. Laird of Clackmannan, married —— Stuart, daughter to the Laird of Rofenyth, who bare to him three fons; 1. Robert; 2. Edward; 3 Thomas; and a daughter, who married the Laird of Balnagoun: but his fon,

XIX. Robert, fecond Laird of Clackmannan, married —— Scrymgeure of Didop, by whom he had 1ft. David, 2d. Bruce of Munies.

XX. David, third Laird of Clackmannan, married the daughter to the Lord of Lorn.

XXI. David, fourth Laird of Clackmannan, married 1ft. —— Stirling, daughter to their Laird of Keir: 2. He married Herris, daughter to the Laird Taregles, on both of whom he had iffue, as in the tree to be feen.

XXII. Sir David, fifth Laird of Clackmannan, married Jennet Blacketer, daughter to the Laird of Tullialan, &c.

XXIII. John, fixth Laird of Clackmannan, married —— Murray, daughter to the Laird of Polmaee.

XXIV.

feffing fentiments and manners fuperior to their rank in life. The higher ranks in this parifh have been, from time immemorial, uniformly diftinguifhed by their exemplary conduct, and their regular attendance upon all the ordinances of religion * ; and it is but juftice to fay, that they ftill

XXIV. Robert, feventh Laird of Clackmannan, fucceeded John, and married —— Murray, daughter to the Laird of Tullibara, by whom he had iffue.

XXV. Sir Robert, eighth Lord of Clackmannan, had to his firft wife Jennet Wardlaw, daughter to the Laird of Tory. After her death, he married Helena Durie of the houfe of Durie. What numerous iffue he had by them, it is needlefs here to repeat, fince the tree clearly points them out.

XXVI. Robert, ninth Laird of Clackmannan, married Elifabeth Halliburton, daughter to the Laird of Pitcur, and had by her Sir Henry ; 2. George Bruce of Comery. He had alfo three daughters ; 1. Catherin, married Robert Watfon, brother's fon of Cafters ; 2. Jean married Weemys of Pitney ; 5. Helena married Alexander Bruce of Kinnaird.

XXVII. Sir Henry, tenth Laird of Clackmannan, hade to his firft wife Lady Mary Shan, daughter of Sir Alexander Shan of Sauchy, by whom he had Sir David, his fucceffor ; 2. Captain John Bruce, who married —— Robertfon of Bedlay ; 3. Henry Bruce. He had alfo a daughter, Jeanie, who married James Bruce of Powfoules. His fecond lady was the Countefs of Dundie.

XXVIII. Sir David Bruce, prefent Laird of Clackmannan, married Margarett M'Kenzie, eldeft daughter to the Vifcount of Tarbert, and has by her Elizabeth Bruce, &c. who God long continue.

Amen, Amen

Prænobilis illuftriffimæ & antiquitate haud ulli fecundæ Brufiorum familæ genealogiam in hac tabula delineatam, honoratiffimo viro D. Davidi Brufio, Eq. A & Baron Gentis fuæ principi fubmiffe dicavit.

M Joh. Sz·mbatinus Hungarus. A. Do. 1686.

* The late Lord Kennet, one of the Members of the Court of Seffion, and of the High Court of Jufticiary, had his refidence in this parifh. His publick virtues, and his character as a judge, are too well known to need any encomium. His private life was no lefs amiable and refpectable He was a bleffing to all ranks in this corner of the country, in which he lived.

ftill continue to deferve this character, which certainly has a happy influence upon the manners of the inferior orders of the people.

Mifcellaneous Obfervations.—Many dreadful accidents have happened in this parifh. Several perfons have been drowned; feveral hurt and killed, and burnt to death, at the public works. Two children had their brains dafhed out, by coal waggons going over their heads. Two young men belonging to the parifh had their lives wonderfully preferved, after falling from heights, almoft incredible to be told. One fell 75½ feet from a high tower, and was little hurt; the very fame perfon, fometime after, fell 30 feet from the roof of a houfe, and was not hurt. Another perfon fell into an old coal-pit, 70 feet deep, and was got out fafe, having only his thigh bone bro en. Thefe old open coal-pits, without the leaft fence around them, are frequent in all the collieries of this parifh. They are a publick nuifance, by which the lives of men are often expofed to real danger.

At the colliery of Sauchy, there is at prefent a woman who has twins; fhe herfelf was a twin, and her mother was one of three at a birth. Two fifters in the parifh were lately the mothers of three dumb children.

A young cow, fome years ago, produced a calf when fhe was exactly 3 months old.

About 20 years ago, a very large fpreading afh tree was ftruck by lightning, and has fince exhibited a fingular phenomenon. The lightning had ftruck one half, only,

of

lived. When he died, the tears of the widow and the fatherlefs were fhed upon his grave: For " the caufe which he knew not, he literally " fearched out."

Multis ille bonis flebilis occidit.

of its branches, and, penetrating all the way down one ſide of the trunk, tore up and laid open the roots of the ſame ſide. Since that time, one half of the tree has decayed, while the other remained healthy. The bark was entire all round the trunk; but the healthy branches continued yearly to decreaſe a little. No farther obſervations, however, can now be made upon it: for though it appeared to be a great natural curioſity, yet the proprietor, it ſeems, has not conſidered it in this point of view, and, not thinking of the philoſophical purpoſes to which it might have been ſubſervient, has lately cut it down.

This pariſh ſtill opens a wide field for improvements of various kinds. There was formerly a ferry boat on the river Forth, oppoſite the village of Clackmannan. This would ſtill be of great uſe and convenience to the country, both to the north and ſouth. The harbour at Clackmannan Pow, by a ſmall expenſe, may be rendered a ſafe and convenient landing place. And a village alſo might be built at that place, ſo as to have many advantages of ſituation.

The whole county of Clackmannan, and this pariſh in particular, has long laboured under the greateſt inconvenience, from the uncommonly bad ſtate of the public roads. Fortunately, however, the gentlemen of the county have at laſt got their eyes opened to their true intereſt. A turnpike road bill for this county is juſt now depending in Parliament, and with every proſpect of ſuccefs.

PARISH of DOLLAR,

(County of Clackmannan, Presbytery of Stirling, Synod of Perth and Stirling.)

By the Rev. Mr John Watson, *Minister.*

Origin of the Name.

THE word Dollar is faid to be Gaelic. According to fome it was formerly fpelt *Dollard,* from *doll,* a plain, or vale, and *ard,* a hill, or high land. This is perfectly applicable to its real fituation, the principal part of the parifh being a beautiful plain or valley, of about an Englifh mile in breadth, lying along the foot of a high range of hills, known by the name of *the Ochil-Hills.* According to others, it may be expreffed *Doil-lar,* fignifying a hidden or concealed place. This alfo is expreffive of its real fituation; which is low and not feen at any great diftance, when one approaches it in any direction.

Situation, Extent, Form, and Appearance.—It is fuppofed to be equally diftant from Stirling, Kinrofs, and Dumfermline; and is reckoned about 12 Englifh miles from each. The

middle

middle and principal part of the pariſh, in which both the church and the town ſtand, is an extenſive and gently ſloping plain, beautifully interſperſed with ſmall villages, farm houſes, and incloſures; and, taking in with it a ſmall part of Muckart on the Eaſt, and Tillicoultry on the Weſt, it forms a kind of amphitheatre, of an oval figure, of about 3 miles in length, and one in breadth; bounded by the Ochil-hills on the North, and a riſing ground on the South. This beautiful plain would ſeem to have been laid down, and ſmoothed by the great hand of nature, to be the ſcene of ſports and exerciſes, ſuch as thoſe of the ancient Olympic games. It is of a ſouthern expoſure; and, when viewed from the riſing grounds, particularly on the South, the pleaſed and admiring beholder would be ready to pronounce it the moſt delightful ſpot in the world.

River and Fiſh.—The water of *Dovan*, which runs from E. to W. nearly divides the pariſh. The Dovan is not navigable, being a ſmall but beautiful ſtream of pure limpid water. Its channel, at a medium, may be about 100 feet in breadth. Here it gently glides over a bed of pebbles, where, finding itſelf at eaſe (as it were,) after having been daſhed and broken in its narrow and rugged channel, through the pariſhes of Glendovan and Muckart, it ſeems to ſport itſelf in many beautiful meanders; winding from ſide to ſide of the valley, as if loth to leave the delightful haughs of Dollar. But at times, when ſwelled by heavy rains, which come down in torrents from the hills, it ſuddenly overflows its banks to a conſiderable extent, to the no ſmall damage of the farmer, whoſe lands are ſituated by the ſide of it. The river, being ſmall, does not admit of many kinds of fiſh; yet there are very fine freſh-water trouts, of a conſiderable ſize, taken in it, as well as ſparrs, in great numbers. In harveſt,

ſea

fea trouts are likewife killed in it, from 2 lib. to 4 lib. weight. And, in the feafon, falmon are caught from 5 lib. to 20 lib. About 20 or 30 years ago, falmon were found in Dovan in great plenty ; but, from the illegal and murderous manner of killing them with fpears, at an improper feafon, their numbers of late have greately decreafed. As there are but few or none killed now, but by gentlemen in the way of fport, or by fome of the poorer fort of the people, for the ufe of their families, the prices cannot well be afcertained.

Bridges.—There was a very good ftone bridge over the Dovan nearly oppofite to the church ; but fome years ago it was carried down by a flood. At prefent, a wooden bridge is about to be put over it, near the fame place, by the voluntary fubfcriptions of a few public-fpirited perfons in the neighbourhood ; which will be of very great convenience to the people in this place, particularly upon the fabbath ; as many of the parifhioners have to crofs the Dovan in their way to church. The want of a bridge would not have been felt fo much here 20 or 30 years ago, as the people in this place were very expert at croffing the river on *flilts.* † And there are ftill fome who crofs it in this way. But fince the time that the bridge was built, this practice has been generally laid afide.

Climate and Difeafes.—The air in this place is remarkably pure and healthy ; the country being free and open, neither
                                                     cumberd

---

‡ Thefe ftilts were two branches of a tree, of a proper ftrength, with a cleft or fmall branch preferved in each, of a fufficient widenefs to receive a perfon's foot, about 18 or 20 inches from the root end. Upon which the perfon being mounted, with a foot on each cleft or projecting branch, and the top or fmall end of the ftilt in each hand, they ftalked through the river at the fords. This they called *ftilting.*

cumbered with woods, nor infected with marſhes The purity and ſweetneſs alſo of the water, (which, perhaps, is exceeded by none,) coming through rock or ſand, and free of metallic ſubſtances, muſt alſo contribute greatly to the health of the inhabitants ; and this bleſſing they uſually en-joy in an uncommon degree. As a remarkable inſtance of this, the miniſter, in the whole courſe of his parochial viſita-tion from houſe to houſe, did not find one ſingle ſick perſon in the pariſh ; and ſcarcely any complaining of ailmentts, ſuch as coughs, ſhortneſs of breath, &c. ; though it was in the month of December, when complaints of this nature are more frequent; eſpecially among ſuch as are advanced in life. Some few were indeed labouring under the natural in-firmities incident to old age ; there being ſeveral who were arrived at the advanced age of 80 and upwards. The ſalu-brity of the air is alſo much owing to the dryneſs of the ſoil, which readily imbibes the rains that fall upon it; while the many ſmall rivulets, which come down from the higher grounds, carry off the ſuperfluous waters, without allowing them to ſtagnate on the ſurface, and to breed noxious vapours to be exhaled into the air. Epidemical diſeaſes are therefore unknown here ; except thoſe which are of a common and general nature. Such as the ſmall-pox, chin-cough, &c. The ſmall-pox, at times, carries off many of the children ; inoculation not having yet got much into practice.

Soil and Surface, Sheep, Wool, and Cultivation.—The ſoil in this pariſh is of various kinds. That of the Ochil-hills, which lie towards the North, is partly rocky, partly moſſy, and partly gravel. The hills are covered with a beauti-ful green ; but part of the ſoil being now waſhed off by the ſtorms, in the courſe of time, the rocks in ſome places begin to appear. They afford excellent paſture for ſheep ; of

which

which about 1640 are fed upon that part of them belonging
to this parish. The mutton, and especially the wool, produced upon the Ochils, (as they are sometimes called,) is confidered as of a superior quality ; particularly that upon the farm
called *Craiginnan*, which is the property of the Duke of Argyll. Towards the foot of the hills, the soil, in general, is
light and gravelly, causing a quick vegetation. In dry seasons, it is indeed apt to be parched ; but in wet seasons, the
crops are moderately good. The greater part of the flat-ly-
ing ground in the bottom is likewise of a light gravely na-
nature, and usually yields rather an early harvest. Along
the banks of the Dovan, the soil is mostly of the haugh
kind ; and some of it a deep clay. Upon the south side of
the Dovan, the ground is rather wettish and clayey, but, with
proper attention and culture, it is capable of very considerable improvement. And some of the farms, which are under
proper management, make very good returns.

Produce, Seasons, &c.—The ordinary crops raised in this
parish, are barley, oats, pease, beans, and potatoes. There
is also some wheat and hay ; but not much. The usual time
of sowing oats, pease, and beans, in this parish, in ordinary
seasons, is the months of March and April, and the barley
in May. It is usually over by the 20th of the month.—The
harvest commonly begins towards the end of August, or beginning of September ; and, excepting some late spots, is
over by the tenth of October. As soon as the barley, oats,
and pease are got in, the potatoes are taken up and housed,
which concludes the harvest work.

Improvements.—Agriculture, in this parish, until within
these few years, has continued much in the same state that
it was about 150 years ago ; the feuers, who possess the
greatest

greateſt part of the pariſh, following the ſame ſyſtem of
farming, that had been handed down to them by their fathers. What indeed proved an inſurmountable bar to improvement, was, the lands of different proprietors lying
interſperſed with one another, commonly called *run-rig*,
which wss a caſe that very much prevailed through many
parts of Scotland ; but it is now hardly known in this part of
the country. About 16 years ago, a very conſiderable part of
the beſt lands in the pariſh, which lay in that ſtate, were divided ; when the different proprietors got their reſpective
proportions of ground laid together, each by itſelf. This has
been productive of ſeveral very deſirable conſequences ;
ſuch as, cutting off endleſs quarrels and diſputes, that were
continually taking place between the different proprietors, or
their tenants, about their encroaching or treſpaſſing upon
one another ; and ſo eſtabliſhing peace and harmony amongſt
neighbours, inſtead of ſtrife and variance. It has alſo opened up a door to improvements of every kind. For, immediately upon the ground being divided, the different proprietors incloſed and ſub-divided, with ditch and hedge, their reſpective proportions of land. And the ſeveral incloſures are
now alternately under oats, barley, hay, paſture, &c. to the
no ſmall benefit of the proprietors, and the pleaſure of the
traveller. Some late purchaſers are carrying on very conſiderable improvements in the modern ſtyle ; the agreeable and
beneficial effects of which are daily appearing.

Minerals.—This part of the country abounds in coal, of
different qualities. Three coal-works are going on at preſent in this pariſh ; two upon the South ſide of the Dovan ;
the one at Mellack, the property of the Duke of ARGYLL ; the
other cloſely adjoining to it, but belonging to Lord ALVA.
Upon the North ſide of the Dovan, and near to the town
of

of Dollar, there is another coal-work, belonging also to the
Duke of Argyll. Thefe works employ in whole about 18
working people ; befides a horfe gin for drawing the coals.
From thefe coal-works, and thofe of Blarngone, (in the parifh of Foffoway, but immediately upon the border of this
parifh on the S. E.) very great quantities of coals are annually carried many miles into Strathern, on the North fide
of the Ochil hills.—Iron-ftone is alfo found in different parts
of the parifh, and faid to be of very excellent quality. It is
working at prefent by the Dovan Company, who are now e-
recting a public work at Sauchie, fome miles to the weftward, in the parifh of Clackmannan. * The Ochil hills confift chiefly of whin-ftone ; but free-ftone alfo is found in different places of the parifh.

Hills, Rivulets, &c.—The only hills in this parifh, are
the Ochils. They begin in the parifh of Dumblane, immediately Eaft from the Sherriff-muir, and ftretch in an eaftern
direction many miles into Fife. In this parifh they are of
confiderable height ; perhaps fome thoufand feet. They are,
as already obferved, of a beautiful green ; afford excellent
pafture for fheep, and produce mutton of the fineft flavour.
From

* Some time ago, a vein of LEAD was difcovered in the Ochil hills, a little
above the town of Dollar; and wrought by a Company for feveral years.
From this work, a confiderable quantity, both of Lead and of Copper Ore,
is faid to have been fhipped off for Holland. But it is faid that the Company,
fomehow difagreeing among themfelves, gave it up. Neverthelefs, it is believed, that if a Company of fpirit were to make a thorough trial, it might
turn to good account. SILVER ORE, in confiderable quantities, is likewife
faid to have been found in the Glen of *Care*, or rather of *Cairn*, on the Weft
of Caftle-Campbell; but that it did not anfwer the expence of working it.
PEBBLES, of confiderable value, have alfo been found upon the top of a hill
above Caftle-Campbell, called the *W'Lile W'ife*.

From their verdant fides, many beautiful rivulets of the fineft water are daily gliding down, for the health and refrefhment of the inhabitants who dwell below.

Roads.—There are two high-ways paffing through this parifh, leading from Stirling to Kinrofs. The one is upon the fouth fide of the Dovan ; and the other upon the north fide. That upon the fouth fide of the Dovan is only in part formed, but not gravelled ; and as it paffes through clay grounds, it is fcarcely paffable in winter. But that upon the north fide of the Dovan, as it paffes along the foot of the Ochil hills, where the bottom is a hard channel, is equally firm and paffable at all feafons ; and therefore is moft frequented. The proper ftage upon that road, between Stirling and Kinrofs, is Dollar. The greateft fault of it is, that it is too narrow ; for, in fome places, two carriages meeting can do no more than pafs. Were it only widened a little, nature has fufficiently gravelled it. They who have marked it out at firft, humouring the nature of the ground along the foot of the hills, have formed it much after the manner of a ferpentine walk. It is very much frequented, not only by thofe who travel from Stirling to Kinrofs, but alfo by thofe who go to Perth, Dundee, &c.

Population.—The population of this parifh has decreafed very little within thefe 40 years.

POPULATION TABLE OF THE PARISH OF DOLLAR.

No. of fouls in 1755, as returned to Dr Webfter, - 517
Ditto in 1792, - - 510

Decreafe 7

FAMILIES, &c.		No. of Mechanics,	24
No. of families in the town,	51	(viz.) —— Smiths, -	3
—— Ditto in the country,	71	—— Mafons, -	2
—— Seceders of all denomina-		—— Wrights, or joiners,	2
tions, -	17	—— Weavers, .	5

AGES, and SEXES. *Mal. Fem. Tot.* —— Tailors, . 4

	Mal.	Fem.	Tot.		
Children under 5	27	25	52	—— Shoe-makers, .	2
—— Between 5 and 10	30	38	68	—— Dyers, .	2
Between 10 and 20	31	37	68	—— Coopers, .	1
Persons aged 20 and				—— Bakers, .	1
upwards,	-		322	—— Butchers, .	2
					— 24

Total 510

CONDITIONS, PROFESSIONS, &c. —— Carters, . 1

No. of proprietors,	-	19	—— Excife officers, .	1
—— Minifters,	-	1	—— Keepers of public houfes,	2
—— School-mafters,	-	1	—— Male fervants, .	30
—— Merchants,	-	2	—— Female ditto, .	29
—— Miners,	-	18	—— Servants, chiefly men, em-	
—— Muficians,	.	4	ployed at the bleach-field,	
—— Corn millers,	-	2	in the heat of the feafon,	30
			—— Poor on the roll, yearly,	9

EXTRACT from the REGISTER of BIRTHS, MARRIAGES, and DEATHS, *for the laſt ten years, viz. from the firſt of Ja-nuary* 1783, *to the firſt of January* 1793.

YEARS.	BIRTHS.	MARRIAGES.	DEATHS.
1783	13	3	14
1784	14	4	
1785	16	4	16
1786	9	2	14
1787	12	2	14
1788	16	4	10
1789	19	6	6
1790	12	6	11
1791	11	4	17
1792	21	0	9
Total	143	35	119
Annual average	$14\frac{3}{10}$	$3\frac{5}{10}$	$11\frac{9}{10}$

Proviſions

Provisions and Labour.—The price of barley, oats, meal,
&c. are regulated by the fiars of Clackmannan, the head
town in the county. The price of butcher meat is usually
from 3d. to 4½d. *per* lib. Dutch weight; a good hen sells at 1s;
chickens from 4d. to 6d. each, according to their age and
fize; eggs from 3d. to 4d. *per* dozen. † The ordinary price
of butter at present is 6d. *per* lib; cheese 3½. The wages
of men labourers are from 10d. to 1s. *per* day; in harvest, they receive 13d. or 14d. *per* day; and for cutting
hay, 1s. 6d. The wages of women who work without
doors, at hay-making, weeding potatoes, &c. are 6d. *per*
day; except in harvest, when they receive 10d. *per* day: out of
which wages, both men and women furnish their own provisions. The average annual wages of farm servants, of
men that are able to hold the plough, thresh the barn, &c.
when they eat in the house, are 6 l; and 2 l. 10 s. for women. A mason's wages are from 1 s. 8d. to 2 s. *per* day;
a wright's, or joiner's wages, from 1 s. 6d. to 1 s. 8d; a tail-
or's wages, 8d; and a flater's, 2 s. *per* day.

Bleachfields and Mills.—There is a very fine bleachfield in
this parish beautifully situated on the banks of the Dovan. It
was erected by Mr WILLIAM HAIG, the present proprietor, in
the year 1787. The machinery, which is excellent, is driven
by water from the Dovan, while the canals, boilers, &c. are
plentifully supplied, at all seasons, with the finest filtrated
water from the hills. The trade of this field has much increased since its first commencement. For the first and
second years, there were scarcely 6 acres of ground under
cloth. Whereas, in the present year, 1793, there are 20 acres
covered with it. The greatest part of the cloth, bleached at
this field, is the diaper, or table linen of Dunfermline, the
first

† Till within these two or three years, a hen might have been bought for
9d; chickens for 4d. per pair; and eggs for 3d. per dozen.

firſt town in *Britain,* (we may even ſay in the *World,*) for
this manufacture ; the table linen made there being, both in
point of quality and variety of patterns, incomparably ſuperior to what is to be found any where elſe. Nor can any
place ſupply the demands to London, and other places for
that article, upon the ſame terms. Beſides, the author is
well informed, that improvements are daily making in ſeveral branches of that buſineſs, which promiſe to be of great
ſervice with regard to the elegance of the patterns *. The
new chemical method of bleaching, by the *oxygenated muriatic
acid,* has been tried at this field with much ſucceſs. In the
year 1790, Mr Haig gained a premium from the Honourable
Board of Truſtees for that method of bleaching. Since that
time, he hath made ſeveral valuable diſcoveries, both as to
the preparation and application of this acid, and finds it very
uſeful ; particularly at the end of the ſeaſon, when the ſun
ſo greatly loſes its influence. He then finiſhes off goods by
this method of bleaching, which otherwiſe could not be
done until the next year. By this method, he bleaches cotton
goods through the whole ſeaſon ; and finds it much better
adapted for cotton than for linen. In this pariſh there are
two mills for grain, one of them has machinery for making
barley, and rollers for grinding malt. There are alſo two
waulk mills for ſcouring cloth, &c.

Church, School, and Poor—The Duke of Argyll is ſuperior
and patron * as well as titular of the tithes. The value of
the

* Some light cotton goods have, for ſome years paſt, been ſent here from
Glaſgow ; and, by reaſon of the exceeding fineneſs of the water, have been
returned with a moſt excellent colour ; very much to the ſatisfaction of the
employers.

* The greateſt part of the pariſh was formerly the property of that family.
But in the year 1605, it was feued out by ARCHIBALD Earl of ARGYLL,
and

the living, exclufive of the manfe and glebe, has, for fome
years paſt been confidered, at an average, to be about 80 l.
The church was rebuilt in the year 1775, and is confidered
as very neat for a country church. The manfe, at prefent,
is out of repair.—Mr John M'Arbrea, the parifh fchool-maſ-
ter, teaches Englifh, Latin, writing, arithmetic, &c. and is
much refpeéted. His fixed falary is only 100l. Scotch, but
he draws the intereſt of 560 merks Scotch, of funk money,
befides perquifites, as precentor and feffion clerk, ‡ &c.—The
poor upon the roll, are fupported by the public colleétions
on fabbath, and the intereſt of feveral fums of money,
funk by different perfons † for that purpofe. They receive their ſtated allowance monthly, which amounts to about
17l. Sterling *per annum*; befides occafional fupplies perfons
or families in diſtrefs, which amount to about 4 l. or 5 l.
Sterling more. There have been no beggars in this parifh
in the memory of man.

Antiquities.

and Dame Agnes Douglas, Counteſs of Argyll, referving only Caſtle-
Campbell, and two farms in the neighbourhood.

‡ The fchoolmaſters, eſtablifhed in this parifh, have, from time immemorial, been men of a liberal education, and feveral men of eminence have been
taught at this fchool. Many of Mr M'Arbrea's fcholars fill refpeétable
places in the church, both in the eſtablifhment and the feceffion. The fchool
was ereéted in the reign of King Charles I. as appears from the decreet of
locality, dated 1640, for 100 merks Scotch. In 1766, the heritors added 50
merks. The above 500 merks were funk by one Archibald Paterson,
merchant in Edinburgh July 18, 1652; and the other 60 by one Kirk, in
Dollar.

† Mr John Gray was ordained in the year 1709. He was the firſt that was
fettled in this parifh after the Revolution. He was commonly ſtiled *the Baron*;
from his having, while miniſter here, purchafed two baronies of land : Firſt,
that of Teaffes in Fyfe, for which he paid upwards of 3,333 l. Sterling. Afterwards he purchafed the barony of Foſſoway, in Perthfhire, for which he
paid

Antiquities.—In the neighbourhood of the town of Dollar, there are two little round mounds *, about a quarter of a mile diſtant from each other. But the principal antiquity in this pariſh, is the venerable remains of Castle Campbell † : anciently

paid upwards of 1,611 l. Sterling. At his death, he left for the uſe of the poor in this pariſh, 300 merks Scotch money.—Miſs Jean Gray, his only child, of reſpeᶜtable memory, ſome few years before her death, which happened in the year 1792, ſold both of theſe baronies of land; that of Teaſſes for 13,500 l. Sterling, and that of Foſſaway for 6,500 l. Sterling; amounting in whole to 20,000 l. Sterling. At her death ſhe left many conſiderable legacies : among theſe there was 50l. Sterling to the poor of this pariſh, and a very elegant folio bible to the kirk-ſeſſion, for the uſe of the miniſter.

* In the one of theſe, ſome years ago, were found two urns, filled with human bones; but upon what occaſion, or by whom they were depoſited there, is not known. The other mound remains in the ſame ſtate it hath been time immemorial.—Towards the end of the laſt century, a man was burnt for a wizard, at the foot of the Gloom Hill, not many yards from the town of Dollar.

† It would ſeem not to be now known, *when* or *by whom* this venerable pile of building was firſt erected. But the ruins plainly ſhew, that it had been deſigned for a place of ſtrength; and therefore was probably built in the turbulent days of old, when family feuds ſo unhappily prevailed among the Scotch barons. Nor can we diſcover the preciſe period when it came into the poſſeſſion of the family of Argyll : But, from the inventory of their titles, that family appears to have poſſeſſed that barony, and the lands belonging to it, called the Lordship of Campbell, ſo far back as the year 1465. The lands were then held of the biſhop of Dunkeld. Formerly, it went by the name of the Castle of Gloom : but for what reaſon, we are not certain. Tradition, indeed, which wiſhes to inform us of every thing, reports, that it was ſo called from the following circumſtance : A daughter of one of our Scotch Kings, who then reſided at Dunfermline, happening to fall into diſgrace for ſome improper behaviour, was, by way of puniſhment, ſent and confined in this caſtle; and ſhe, (not reliſhing her ſituation, which probably might be in ſome vault or other) ſaid, that it was a *gloomy priſon* to her. Hence, ſays tradition, it came to be called the Caſtle of Gloom. Very near to

it

anciently the occasional residence of the Noble Family of Argyll : a family which, for ages, has been eminently distinguished

it on the Coast, there is a green hill, which still goes by the name of *Gloom-Hill*, the property of Mr John Moir, writer to the signet.

And now that we have mentioned tradition, we shall present the reader with an anecdote concerning this place, from the same source, which, perhaps, 'may be more curious than true. In going down from the castle, towards the point of the rock which overhangs the glens, there is a passage cut down through the rock to the side of the burn, in the bottom of the glen. This passage is said to be from top to bottom more than 100 feet deep, and six feet wide. The design of it was to get water conveyed, or brought up from the burn or rivulet below, in the time of a siege. This seems the more likely, as it appears to have been cut out with steps, which are now mostly filled up with earth. This passage, partly from the trees, and partly from the frightful rocks overhanging it, is now become so dark and gloomy, that a person can see but a very little way down into it : and indeed, to look into it, would be sufficient to make a person of weak nerves shudder. It is called KEMP's SCORE or CUTT, from its having been made by one of that name; who is said to have been a man of gigantic stature and strength, and at the same time of a very bold and resolute temper. It is reported, that he had committed many depredations, and at last was so daring as to enter the palace at Dunfermline, and carry off the King's dinner; but that a young nobleman, who happened to be in disgrace for improper behaviour towards the King's daughter, hearing of it, pursued the said Kemp, and having cut off his head, threw the body into the water of Dovan, a little above the back mill, and, as his name was WILLIAM, so the place where this happened, is called WILLIE's POOL, to this day. But on his carrying the head with him to Court, he obained his pardon, and was received into favour again.

But to return to the castle, that ancient seat of the Argyll Family : The name was, by an act of the Scotch Parliament, in, or before the year 1493, changed to that of the *Castle of Campbell*, by which name it has ever since been denominated. It is reported, that this was amongst the first of those places in Scotland, where the sacrament of the Lord's Supper was dispensed, after the Reformation. And it is certain, from his own history, that the famous JOHN KNOX, the Scotch reformer, did preach here. For he tells us, that, upon his being called over by the English Congregation at Geneva, who had chosen him for their pastor; he sent over his family before him, but he him-

self

guifhed for their attachment to religion, liberty, and patriotifm. And the prefent worthy head, and reprefentative of
that noble Family, treading in the fteps of his illuftrious anceftors, dignifies and adorns the exalted ftation which he fills.
By the lapfe of time, and the violence of ftorms, a very confiderable part of Caftle-Campbell is now fallen down ; and
other parts of it are nodding over their foundations. The
tower is yet nearly entire. The afcent is by a fpiral ftair,
which is continued to the top. It is vifited by moft ftrangers who come here ; and though it is a pretty fatiguing walk
up to it, yet when they reach the top of the tower, which is of
confiderable height, they are much pleafed, not only with the

view,

felf remained behind in Scotland, for fome time ; during which, he paffed to
ARCHIBALD, whom he ftiles " the Old Earl of ARGYLL," then refiding at
the Caftle of Campbell, and there he taught, or preached, certain days. It is
not improbable, therefore, that he difpenfed the Sacrament of the Lord's Supper there, at the fame time. One of the company, who was then ftaying
with the Earl at Caftle Campbell, was the laird of Glenorchy, one of the anceftors of the prefent family of BREADALBANE ; who importuned the Earl to
defire Mr KNOX to ftay fome time with them ; but Mr Knox could not confent to it. This ARCHIBALD was the 4th Earl of ARGYLL ; and is faid to have
been the firft man of quality who embraced the Proteftant Religion in Scotland, and contributed all in his power to bring about the Reformation.

The Caftle of Campbell continued to be the occafional refidence of the
family of Argyll, as appears from the fervices which the vaffals were obliged,
by their charters, to perform to the family, when refiding there ; until that
magnificent building was burnt down by the Marquis of MONTROSE, about
the year 1644 ; and ever fince it has been in ruins. And not only the Caftle of Campbell, but the whole of the parifhes, both of Dollar and Muckart,
were burnt , the inhabitants being vaffals of the family of Argyll, excepting
one houfe in Dollar, which they imagined to belong to the Abbey of Dunfermline. There was likewife only one houfe faved from the flames, in
Muckart ; which they imagined to be in the parifh of Foffoway ; being nearly adjoining to it. Befides that, there was a fheep-houfe that efcaped the
general conflagration. Every other houfe in both parifhes was, by the
Grahams, burnt to the ground.

view, but more particularly with the furrounding fcene, which is truly enchanting.

Romantic Scenery around the Caftle.—The fituation of thefe venerable ruins is fomewhat retired backwards amongft the hills, with a beautiful opening before it, as it were a kind of vifta, through which to view the plains below : And being pretty high, it commands a confiderably extenfive profpect towards the Forth, and the adjacent country. It is fituated upon the top of a round mound, which would feem to have been partly formed by the hand of nature, and partly finifh- ed by art. It ftands a little back from the point of a high rock ; having a deep ravine or glen upon each hand ; with very fteep banks, whofe declivity commences from the very foot of the walls on both fides, and is almoft wholly inacceffible. In the bottom of the glens, run murmuring rivulets of the pureft water, which come down from the mountains behind, and unite their ftreams immediately below the caftle. Each of the rivulets furnifhes a beautiful cafcade, to entertain the eye of their vifitants, and fomewhat reward them for the fa- tigue they have had in climbing the hill. The mound on which the caftle ftands, was formerly disjoined from the mountains behind, with a fofse, or ditch, fhelving down to the bottom of the glen on both fides, which renders it almoft inacceffible on every fide ; the entry, then, being by a draw- bridge, which was let down or taken up as occafion requir- ed. The banks of the glens, on both fides, are beautifully a- dorned with natural woods, which nearly cover the faces of the rugged rocks with which this romantic fcene is inter- fperfed. It is almoft furrounded with hills. Immediately behind it, is the hill called the *White Wifp ;* which fo much overtops all its fellows, that it furnifhes a rich and extenfive profpect. From this elevated fituation, looking towards the

South,

South, may be feen the Frith of Forth, with the adjacent country, as far as the hill of Tintoc in Clydefdale. Then turning to the North, one fees the moft part of the fhires of Perth and Fife, as far Eaft as Dundee, and the German O-cean; with the Lothians on the oppofite fide of the Forth. A little to the South-Weft of the White Wifp, is the place called the *King's Seat;* where, according to tradition, the kings of Scotland, then refiding at Dunfermline, fat, and viewed the hunting of the wild bears, which then haunted a-mongft thefe hills; whence feveral places, particularly in the farm of Craiginnan, immediately above the Caftle, are named, fome of them, *the Bear's den,* and others, *the Bear's Know,* to this day. Thus, the fcene around this ancient feat of Campbell, confifting of rocks, and woods, and glens, and mountains, contains a pleafing mixture of the beautiful, the picturefque, and the awfully romantic.

Literary Shepherd.—There is living at prefent in this pa-rifh, in a very advanced age, a man who was bred up, and lived merely as a fhepherd, and who received only a common education; and yet poffeffes a valuable library of books, con-taining upwards of 370 volumes; confifting of folios, quar-tos, octavos, duodecimos, and decimo-quartos. They are u-pon many different fubjects, as divinity, hiftory, travels, voy-ages, &c. befides magazines of various kinds, fuch as the Scots, the Univerfal, and the Chriftian magazines; a complete fet of the Spectator, Guardian, Tatler, Rambler, &c. They are all of them his own chufing and purchafing. They are neatly bound, and lettered on the back. His name is upon a printed ticket, and pafted on the infide of the board of each volume; with a mark, generally of blue paper, cut on purpofe, and placed in each volume, to prevent folding in the leaves. The books are all clean, and in excellent order. Be-

fides

fides theſe, he has feveral volumes of pamphlets, &c. lying
in numbers unbound. His name is JOHN CHRISTIE : he
was born in this parifh, and baptized on the 12th of October
1712, and has lived in it from his infancy. His brother William, and his fifter Margaret, who are a few years younger,
live in the fame houſe with him, and all the three remain
unmarried.

General Character, &c.—The people are fober, regular, and
induſtrious in their different profeſſions and employments ;
and live in peace and harmony with one another. The common employment of the women, except fuch as are engaged
with farmers for hufbandry work, is that of fpining wool for
the manufacturers in Stirling, Bannockburn, &c. They all
enjoy, in their refpective ftations, a reafonable fhare of the conveniences and comforts of life ; and fome feem well contented
with the condition in which Providence has placed them.
They are much of the ordinary fize, and fpeak the Englifh
language tolerably well, without any remarkable provincial
dialect.

PARISH of TILLICOULTRY.

(County of Clackmannan, Presbytery of Dumblane, Synod of Perth and Stirling.)

By the Rev. Mr. William Osburn, *Minister.*

Etymology of the Name.

THE origin of the name is generally fuppofed to be Gaelic, and Tillicoultry compounded of the three words, *Tullich,* *cut* and *tir.* Thefe words fignify literally, the *mount* or *hill* *at the back of the country,* and feem to refer to the Kirk-hill, and the Cuninghar ; a rifing ground, which begins near the houfe of Tillicoultry and the old kirk, and runs in a S. E. direction till it reaches the Dovan. This rifing ground has a ftrikingly romantic appearance, as one approaches it, either from the Eaft or the Weft. And as it interfects a beautiful plain, which begins at the Abbey-Craig near Stirling, and extends to Vicar's Bridge, it has juftly been diftinguifhed as the termination of the plain, or ftrath. But the author of this account hopes he will not be accufed of affectation, if he ventures to give a Latin derivation, and confiders Tillicoultry as compounded either of *Tellus culta,* or *Tellus cultorum* *Dei.*

Dei. If the firſt be adopted, we may ſuppoſe the name took
its riſe, from the place having been once in a high ſtate of
cultivation, probably from the introduction of the Italian agriculture. But if the ſecond, it may denote the reſidence of
ſome of the *Culdees,* or a place appropriated to the worſhip
of God, either by the Culdees or the Druids. For on the
ſouth end of the Cuninghar, the rude remains of a Druidical
circle are ſtill to be ſeen, and on the north-eaſt extremity of
the riſing ground, the old church was ſituated. The writer
hereof is no admirer of the Gaelic ; but as Gaelic derivations are at preſent faſhionable, and as every place in this
country is ſuppoſed, by our learned antiquarians, to have an
old Gaelic name, he is afraid little attention will be paid to
theſe *Latin* etymologies. It muſt, however, be allowed, that
Tillicoultry is no great corruption of *Tellus culta,* or of *Tellus cultorum Dei.*

Situatizn.—Tillicoultry is an inland country pariſh, and
preſents little uncommon or ſplendid for deſcription. It
comprehends a conſiderable part of the Ochils, where theſe
hills are higheſt ; but the principal part of the pariſh lies at
the foot of the hills, verging towards the ſouth. The river
Dovan waſhes its banks on the north.

Appearance, Form, &c.—The appearance of the pariſh,
whether we view the hills or the plain, is beautiful and pleaſant. A great part of the low ground is encloſed, and affords a variety of agreeable landſcapes, and the beauty of the
ſcene is much encreaſed by the windings of the Dovan,
which in miniature reſemble thoſe of the Forth. The ſhape
of the whole pariſh is a rhomboid or an oblong, which has
the two longeſt ſides on the E. and W. each meaſuring almoſt 6 Engliſh miles. The S. ſide of the oblong meaſures
neal

near 2½ miles, and the N. fide one mile. The low grounds taken alone form alfo an oblong, the length of the fides from E. to W. being rather more than 2¼ miles, and the breadth from S. to N. about 1¼ mile.

Extent and Elevation.—Tillicoultry confifts of more than 6000 Scotch acres, of which quantity, 4000 are in the Ochils, and the remaining 2000 acres form the low arable ground at the foot of the hills, and to the fouth of the bank dykes. About 1100 or 1200 acres of arable land, by far the beft and moft valuable in the parifh, lie between the bank dykes, at the foot of the hills, and the loweft part of the banks of Balharty and Coalfnaughton, fouth of the Dovan, and about 800 or 900 acres lie fouth of the river, from the foot of the banks. The hills, according to an actual furvey, exclufive of the Mill-Glen farm, contain 2902 acres. The elevation of the ground, on the north banks of the Dovan; at the bridge, is not more than 20 feet, or at moft 30 feet above the level of the Forth, at fpring tides; and the S. W. corner of Tillicoultry, which approaches neareft to that river, is diftant from it about 3 miles. The ground at Coalfnaughton is near 300 feet above the Dovan; and at Balharty it is about 300 feet.

Soil and Surface.—The foil is in general *dry-field*, rich in quality. When properly taken care of, it bears excellent crops, both of corn and hay, and gratefully repays the labour of the husbandman. At the foot of the hills, the foil is a fine quick loam, but not very deep. The crofts are, in many places, covered with ftones almoft innumerable, fmooth in their furface, and in general twice as large as a man's fift. They appear to be natural to the foil, and not brought thither by any inundation; but many entertain a different opi-

nion

nion. Some farmers think them an advantage to the crops, as in hot dry ſummers they keep the ground moiſt and cool, and in winter warm. Vaſt quantities have been gathered, which, in labouring, proves a great eaſe both to the plough and the ploughman. The haughs, near the Dovan, preſent a deep loam mixed with ſand, and the ſoil is very different from that of the crofts. The farm of Gutters is in part clay, and bears fine crops of wheat as well as other grains. The lands ſouth of the Dovan are much inferior to thoſe on the north ſide. In ſome places, the ſoil is a clay, of a cold na-ture ; in others it is a light loam, mixed with ſand and gra-vel, on a till bottom, and in others it is a deep rich loam. A conſiderable part of the ground is covered with heath, and would not be eaſily improved, either for tillage or paſture. Perhaps the beſt improvement would be, to encloſe the moors, and to plant them with Scotch firs, larches, and o-ther foreſt trees.

Agriculture.—In the county of Clackmanan, agricultural improvements are much attended to, and have been brought to great perfection. Richer crops of wheat, barley, or hay, are ſeldom to be met with ; and the ploughs uſed, and the mode of ploughing, are no where ſurpaſſed. A plough and ploughman were ſent this ſummer from Clackmannanſhire to Windſor, to give a proper ſpecimen of plowing on his Ma-jeſty's farm.

Crops and Multures, &c.—The farmers in Tillicoultry do not pretend to take any lead in agricultural improvement. They profit, however, by the obſervations and the practice of others. Two horſe ploughs are getting into general uſe, which are a great improvement in huſbandry. The crops

principally

principally attended to, are oats and barley. Wheat is too much neglected, except by Mr Johnston, and even peafe and beans. Crops of turnips are feldom to be met with, and cabbages are never raifed in our fields. It is difficult to afcertain the rent and produce of the land *per* acre. The farms are commonly let at a certain rent *in cumulo*, and the farmers, not knowing the meafure of their fields, feldom pay attention to the produce of particular acres. The refult of many enquiries is, that an acre of the beft land, well manured, will produce from 7 to 10 bolls of oats, each boll weighing 14 or 15 ftone, yielding about a boll of meal. The oats generally produce 14 pecks of meal, befides paying the multure, and all other mill-dues. The multure is no lefs than the 13th peck. An acre of the fame land will yield from 7 to 11 bolls of barley, each weighing about 18 or 20 ftone. At an average, however, an acre will not yield above 6 or 7 bolls, whether of barley or oats. Our dry-field barley is remarkably good, being very thin in the rind ; and is reckoned, by maltmen and diftillers, equal to any raifed in the Carfe. A good deal of wheat has of late been fown in the farm of Gutters, and an acre commonly produces from 8 to 10 bolls. Forty bolls of potatoes have been raifed on an acre, and one farmer in particular had 18 bolls on the 4th of an acre. The writer of this account had accefs to fee a remarkable crop of potatoes, raifed in Mr Barclay's garden, the produce being no lefs than 105 pecks, or 6 bolls and 9 pecks, raifed from one peck planted.

Farms, Rents, Pafture, Stock, &c.—The farms are in general fmall, and there are only 5 tenants whofe rent exceeds 50 l. Sterling *per annum.* A great part of the parifh is inclofed, and laid down in grafs, and is let annually for fummer graz-
zing;

zing. The rent of farms fluctuates, but graſs parks commonly let well. * The groſs rental of the pariſh is above 1700l. Sterling, and the valuation is rated, in the old ceſs books of the county, at 3389 l. 5 s. 10d. Scotch. There are in Tillicoultry employed in plowing, carting, and other country work:

Horſes,	-	116	Milk Cows,	-	132
Ploughs	-	36	Cottagers ditto	-	63
Carts	-	89			

Hill Farms, Sheep and Wool.—The hills have a verdant and beautiful appearance. They afford excellent paſture for ſheep, and are divided into 5 farms. They will maintain about 3500 ſheep; and, at an average, an acre will not only maintain, but fodder one ſheep. The paſture is graſs, interſperſed with heath, bent and ling. The heath is ſhort and wearing out. The Mill-Glen and Fore-hill farms are inferior

rior

* For 15 years paſt, almoſt all the farms, which have been let, have been taken by ſtrangers from other pariſhes in the neighbourhood, and who are Seceders. If the preſent ſyſtem prevail for other 15 years, the greateſt part, if not the whole of the pariſh, will be poſſeſſed by perſons not belonging to the eſtabliſhed church. It is but doing juſtice to a worthy man, (whoſe ſweetneſs of temper, benevolence of heart, and gentlemany behaviour, will be remembered with pleaſure, at leaſt while the preſent generation laſts,) to mention, that Mr Barclay Maitland improved and beautified the pariſh in a high degree, by his numerous incloſures and plantations. His taſte and attention every where appear. Mr Tait alſo merits praiſe for his improvements on the lands of Harvieſton, which he has wholly encloſed. He has carried on his improvements, for many years, with much ſpirit and judgment, and, it is preſumed, with great advantage to himſelf. His uniform practice has been to fallow his fields, and, after manuring them well with dung and lime, to ſow them with barley and graſs ſeeds. One of his incloſures, which contains 5 and a half Scotch acres, has been let this ſeaſon for grazing, at 4 guineas per acre, the rent being 23 l. 2 s. Sterling.

rior to none in the Ochils, for producing excellent mutton and fine wool. The wood of thefe farms is much fuperior to that of Bruich and the back hills, as the pafture is naturally much finer. The farms are commonly fupplied from Tweeddale with young fheep of the black-faced kind : the farmers fometimes breed young fheep, which, on the whole, they find better, ftronger and more profitable, than thofe from Tweeddale. But as the hills are ftormy, they cannot keep the lambs in winter. All the Mill Glen farm is good pafture, but in the reft of the hills, there are near 400 acres of little or no value, as they are covered with channel and mofs. The very beft white fleeces yield about 4 lib. of wool, valued at 10d. *per* pound ; and the beft fmeared fleeces 6 lib. at 5d. or 6d. The average weight of a white fleece is about $2\frac{1}{2}$ lib. and of a fmeared one, 4 lib. The whole of what was formerly a common‡ is now the property of Mr Bruce, except *Bruich*, which belongs to Mr Tait, and as much as will maintain 48 fheep.

Hills and Minerals.—Bencleugh, the property of Mr Johnfton, is the higheft in the Ochils, and is 2300 feet above the level of the Forth at Alloa. The Ochils prefent a confiderable variety of ftrata. The fummits of the central parts, particularly Bencleugh, are compofed of granites, both red and gray. Many varieties of thefe are extremely beautiful,

‡ When Lord Colvil feued the eftate, he gave his vaffals a right of pafturing fheep and other cattle on the hills. Some of them had a limited number of fheep affigned them, and others an unlimited number. In the year 1769, Mr Barclay Maitland commenced a procefs againft the feuers, for a divifion of the common hill, which contained about 300 acres. The procefs was withdrawn from the Court of Seffion in 1774, and referred to arbiters, and all the feuers difpofed of their property for low ground, or a diminution of their feu-duty. The *Mill-Glen* was no part of the common hill.

tiful, and contain large diſtinct chryſtals of black *Schort.* The next chain, of which the *King's Seat* is the higheſt, and belongs to that claſs called ſecondary mountains, conſiſts of ſtrata of *Argillaceous Schiſtus.* Below this, in various parts, are found craigs or rocks of *Bafaltes,* or whinſtone. The Caſtle Craig is of this fort, and is peculiarly intereſting to the naturaliſt, as it is in part compoſed of nodules of whin-ſtone, exhibiting concentric cruſts of decompoſed bafaltes, like the coats of an onion, furrounding a harder nucleus. Garnets are not uncommon in the micaceous Schiſtus, which forms the ſhade between the granitical and argillaceous Schiſtus. There are many veins of copper in the hills. * Iron-ſtone, of an exceeding good quality, has been found in many different places. Some veins in *Watty-Glen* are as rich as any diſcovered in Scotland. The Dovan Company have a leaſe of the iron-ſtone belonging to Mr Bruce, and have employed, during the greateſt part of this year, 64 miners and 10 women bearers. At an average, each miner gains 1 s. 6d. *per* day, and a bearer 8d. A great many *ſtrings,* or veins of rich iron ore of the kidney kind, have been diſcovered in the hills, equal in quality to any diſcovered in this country, and by no means inferior to what is brought from England. Some ſmall trials have been made with one of the veins, and it is to be regretetd that they are diſcontinued. Befides copper, there is a great appearance, in the hills, of different

* Some of theſe were wrought near 50 years ago, to a very conſiderable extent in the Mill-Glen. Four different kinds of copper ore were diſcovered, the thickeſt vein of which was about 18 inches. The ore, when waſhed and dreſſed, was valued at 50 l. Sterling *per ton.* A Company of gentlemen at London were the tackſmen, and for ſeveral years employed about 50 men. After a very great ſum of money was expended, the works were abandoned, as unable to defray the expence.

ferent minerals, fuch as filver, lead, cobalt, antimony, fulphur, and arfenic, but no proper trials have yet been made. A fmall edge ftratum of dark blue clay, $2\frac{1}{2}$ feet thick, was lately found, which, it is thought, will prove exceeding good for building furnaces, and making fire bricks. There is plenty of free-ftone of a good quality for building; and ftones have been cut in the quarries from 8 to 10 feet in length.

Coal.—The whole parifh, fouth of the hills, abounds with coal, which is the property of Mr Bruce, except in Mr Johnfton's eftate. The coal has not been wrought to any great extent, unlefs where it is drained by the prefent level. There are 4 different feems of coal which the level drains. The firft is a mixed cherry coal, 3 feet thick, and 12 fathoms from the furface. The 2d is a rough foft coal of an excellent quality, 6 feet thick, and 15 fathoms deep. The 3d is a remarkably good clean fplint, $2\frac{1}{2}$ feet thick, and 20 fathoms deep. And the 4th, which is reckoned the principal feam, is about 5 feet thick, and lies at the depth of 30 fathoms. It is a hard durable fplint well adapted for exportation and the foreign market, particularly Holland. Only the 2d and fourth feams have been wrought; † the roofs are all good, except that on the 2d feam, where it runs towards the crop. But it is very valuable, as it contains balls of ironftone in the roof, of an exceeding good quality. Eighty acres of the 2d feam, and 20 of the fourth, may ftill be wrought by the level; but by erecting a fteam engine, an immenfe quantity may be gained. The Devon company have been
tackfmen

---

† Twenty pickmen ufed to be employed in the coal-work; and about 3000 chalders of great coal were exported annually from the harbour of Alloa; but for 4 years paft, the working of the coal has been difcontinued. There is no doubt, however, but that, in procefs of time, the coal will be a moft profitable concern, as there are inexhauftible fields of it to be found.

tackſmen of the coal for more than a year, and a half, but have wrought none, except a very ſmall quantity for land ſale. The deſign of taking a coal, without working it, is *incomprehenſible*. While coals remain under ground, they are of no value, either to the proprietor or the tackſmen.

Gate Mail.—The great coal, when led to the ſhore of Alloa for exportation, pays a tax of fourpence Sterling per chalder to the family of Mar, called *Gate Mail*. It was originally demanded, for the liberty of exporting the coal from the *Pow of Alloa*, and becauſe the road leading through the eſtate to the harbour was a private one, though uſed by the public. This road is repaired by Mr Erſkine at a conſiderable annual expence ; at the ſame time it ſeems extraordinary, that there is not a public road leading from Tillicoultry to a public harbour, and to a market town, in which a cuſtom-houſe is eſtabliſhed by authority.

River, Floods, Fiſh, Pearls, Swans, &c.—The Devon is a beautiful river, but not navigable. After running in the Ochils about 8 miles in an eaſterly direction from its ſource, it makes a wide circuit. round Muckart. Then taking a weſterly courſe at the Crook, and forming the romantic fall at the Caldron Lin, it divides the arable land of Tillicoultry, into two almoſt equal parts. The valley, through which it paſſes, is diſtinguiſhed by *Newte* in his Tour, as being one of the moſt pleaſant places, or, as he expreſſes it, the *Tempe* of Scotland. The Devon frequently ſwells with rain, and overflows its banks ‡.   It abounds with excellent trout

and

‡ A very remarkable and uncommon flood happened in September 1785, which carried away a prodigious quantity of corn, broke down a ſtone bridge at the Rack mill in Dollar, and occaſioned other very extraordinary damage.

The

and parr, which afford much amusement to the angler. In the deep pools, pikes and eels are found. Salmon come from the Forth in great numbers to spawn; and we have plenty of delicious sea trouts, both white and grey, in the harvest and spring. In some places, the banks of the Devon present singular concretions of hardened clay, in a great variety of fantastic shapes. Pearls of a small size have been found in the bed of the river; and, in very severe winters, swans have been known to resort to its banks.

Rivulets and Burn Trouts, &c.—The hill burns, or rivulets, abound with trouts of a very delicious quality and flavour, and are taken in great numbers after rain. None were ever discovered in the *Glooming-side Burn,* though it has plenty of water, and remarkably fine streams and pools. Trouts have even been put into it, but without the desired effect. This is supposed to arise from some bed of sulphur, or other mineral hurtful to fish, over which the burn passes.

Birds and Quadrupeds.—The birds are the same as in the neighbourhood, and it is needless to specify them, as they are enumerated in the statistical account of Alloa. Till of late, the bulfinch was a stranger here, but he is now frequently to be met with. The woodlark ought to be particularly mentioned, as one of our sweetest warblers. He begins to sing early in the spring, and continues till late in harvest. Like the nightingale, he is frequently heard singing in
the

The river rose in 4 or 5 hours more than 13 feet above its usual height, at Tillicoultry bridge. A woman, who was assisting a farmer in removing his corns, on the south side, was forced away by the rapidity and violence of the stream, and brought in safety to the opposite bank. Her clothes had made her float on the surface of the water, though she was carried down about a quarter of a mile.

the moſt melodious, enchanting manner, in the clear, ſtill ſummer evenings. On theſe occaſions, he commonly prolongs his ſong till midnight, and ſometimes till the morning. For two or three years we were viſited with a *magpie*, which was not variegated with black and white plumage, but was *entirely white*,—" *Rara avis in terris*". The other magpies aſſociated with him, and did not conſider him in any degree as ſtrange. In the hills there are muir-fowls, plovers and dotterels. The muir-fowls are not ſo frequent as formerly, as the heath is wearing out, and in conſequence of this the ſhelter is not ſo good. The birds of paſſage are ſwallows, cuckoos, fieldfares and woodcocks ; and we are alſo viſited at times with herons, ducks, and ſea gulls. Eagles are ſometimes ſeen on the hills. The wild quadrupeds are, hares, rabbits, foxes, hedge-hogs, weaſels, polecats, badgers and otters. The ſkin of the otter is valuable as a fur, and fetches a good price.

Orchards and Plantations.—There are two ſmall orchards, planted chiefly with apple trees, which contain about ſix acres, and, ſome years, bear conſiderable quantities of fruit. Above 100 acres are planted with foreſt trees, and many of the incloſures are ſurrounded with ſingle rows of planting. All kinds of foreſt trees thrive well, particularly oaks, elms, aſhes, beeches, planes, and Scotch firs *.

Climate.—The air is healthy, dry, and warm, ſubject neither to fogs nor damps. Snow does not lie long on the low ground, particularly between the Devon and the hills, which is probably owing to the natural warmth of the air or ſoil. The healthineſs of the two villages, at the foot of the hills, is undoubtedly

* About 60 years ago, the common broom grew ſo tall and luxuriant near the manſe, that the crows and magpies built their neſts in the branches.

doubtedly much encreafe, by their being well fupplied with plenty of excellent water.

Difeafes.—There are no difeafes any way peculiar to Tillicoultry, § or that can be faid to be prevalent. Epidemic difeafes, fuch as fevers, fluxes, the fmall-pox, the meafles, and the chincough attack us at times, but not more frequently than they do others. Rheumatifms are not uncommon, as the people are much expofed to rain and cold, in following their employments in the fields. ¶ Within thefe 25 years, a great many young perfons have died of confumptions, but the author is not able, either to afcertain the number, or point out the caufes. Slow fevers fome times are prevalent. And people have been known to recover, after remaining in them 30, or even 40 days. The ague ufed to be frequent, but it is now almoft unknown. This happy change is perhaps owing to the lands being better drained than formerly, or to the houfes being kept more cleanly, warm,

§ The laft time the plague was in Scotland, it did not reach Tillicoultry, though a good many perfons died of it at Alva. One man however having died fuddenly in the Wefter town, the people were afraid to touch the corpfe, or even to enter the houfe. It was pulled down, and the fmall eminence, which this occafioned, was called Botchy Cairn.

¶ It is worth mentiouing that one WILLIAM HUNTER, a collier, was cured in the year 1758, of an inveterate rheumatifm or gout, by drinking freely of new ale, full of barm or yeft. The poor man had been confined to his bed for a year and a half, having almoft entirely loft the ufe of his limbs. On the evening of *Handfel Monday*, as it is called, (*i e.* the firft Monday of the New Year, O. S.) fome of his neighbours came to make merry with him. Though he could not rife, yet he always took his fhare of the ale, as it paffed round the company, and, in the end, became much intoxicated. The confequence was, that he had the ufe of his limbs the next morning, and was able to walk about. He lived more than 20 years after this, and never had the fmalleft return of his old complaint.

warm, and dry. The dyſentery was unknown here for many years. It has, however, appeared of late three different times, and carried off a good many perſons, chiefly women. As this alarming malady always broke out in the end of harveſt, ſome have been apt to imagine, that, if it was not caught by infection, it aroſe from the colds and damps to which the people were expoſed in reaping, or to a frequent uſe of potatoes not brought to a proper ſtate of maturity. The people have in general an averſion to inoculation for the ſmall-pox, yet this prejudice is beginning to wear away ‡.

Population.—Tillicoultry is a ſmall pariſh, yet pretty populous for its ſize.

Population Table of the Parish of Tillicoultry.

For theſe 18 years paſt, the annual average number of fouls has been	874
The higheſt real number of any year during that period, was	919
And the loweſt,	829
Difference,	90
In the year 178 , the number of fouls was	903
Of theſe there belonged to the Eſtabliſhed Church,	742
And to the Seceſſion,	161

The following *Liſts* were taken in January 1792, and ſhew the *Numbers, Ages, Conditions*, and *Employments* of the inhabitants at that time.

NUMBERS

‡ Many children took the ſmall pox, laſt year, in the natural way, only one of whom died, being a ſickly child. Were the ſmall-pox to be always equally favourable, inoculation would fall into diſuſe. The author has ſometimes remarked, that when the ſame diſeaſes, ſuch as dyſenteries, fevers, and the ſmall-pox, have prevailed in Alva and Tillicoultry, more in proportion have died in Alva than here. This was probably occaſioned by the houſes being more crouded together in the one place than the other, and the air being more confined, and the infection more liable to ſpread.

Numbers, Sexes, and Ages,

Total number of fouls, 853

—— Families, - 212

Males, - 373

Females, - 480

—————

Majority of females, 107

No. of perfons under 10 years of

age, - - 238

———— Between 10 and 20, 163

—————————— 20 and 50, 301

—————————— 50 and 70, 124

—————————— 70 and 85, 27

Conditions, Country, Reli-

gion, &c.

No. of married perfons, 278

———— Widowers, - 9

———— Widows, - 54

———— Bachelors who keep houfe, 11

———— Perfons refiding but not

born in Tillicoultry, 200

———— Born abroad, 5

———— Heritors, 10

———— Clergymen, 1

———— School-mafters, 1

———— Communicants of the

Eftablifhment, - 359

———— Ditto of the Secefiion, 97

———— Epifcopalians, 2

———— Cameronians, 1

Occupations.

No. of Farmers, - 34

———— Weavers, - 21

———— Wrights, - 6

———— Mafons, - 7

———— Smiths, - 3

No. of Shoe-makers, 3

—— Tailors, - 8

—— Miners, - 4

—— Labourers, - 51

—— Gardeners, - 1

—— Millers, - 1

—— Dancing mafters, - 1

—— Male houfe fervants, 1

—— Female ditto, - 12

—— Male labouring fervants, 25

—— Female ditto, - 12

Annual Averages, for 21 years.

No. of Marriages ¶, - 7

—— Baptifms for ditto, 30

—— Burials for ditto ¶, 18

—— Males born for ditto, 15¾

—— Females born for ditto, 14

—— Perfons in each family, 4

—— Ditto in each farmer's

family, - 5

Proportions.

Of males to females, nearly *as* 3 *to* 4

Of married men and widow-

ers, to Bachelors who keep

houfes, about 13 1

Of widowers to widows, 1 6

Of males born to females, 20½ 19

Or about, 13 12

Total number of males born

during the laft 21 years, 329

Ditto of females within that

period, - 304

————

Majority of males born, 25

Annual average of more males

than females, 1 *to* 1 *and* a-fifth

Increase

¶ For 12 months preceding November 1789, there were only two grown
up perfons buried in the church yards of Tillicoultry ; and for 12 months preceding June of the prefent year 1793, there have been neither marriages nor
proclamations.

INCREASE.

No. of ſouls in 1755,	-	787			
——— Ditto in 1782, (as above,)		853	Increaſe,	-	96
——— Ditto in 1793	-	909	Ditto	-	56

Total increaſe in 38 years, 152

Cauſes of the Increaſe.—By comparing Dr Webſter's liſt with the number of inhabitants during the two laſt years, there is an evident increaſe. It is perhaps owing to the eſtabliſhment of the Devon company in the neighbourhood of, and the working of iron-ſtone in Tillicoultry, that the number of the inhabitants has ſo greatly encreaſed ſince the beginning of the year 1792. It is ſomewhat remarkable, that when the liſts were taken in January 1792, all the maſons, miners, and labourers were employed, but there were ſcarcely any of the labourers employed in the pariſh.

Prolific Mothers.—There are at preſent living in Tillicoultry eleven married women, who have been delivered of twin children. One of them has had twins two different times, and another, in the year 1765, about three years before the birth of her twins, brought forth THREE children at one birth, all boys and of a good ſize. Two of the children died in the firſt month, and the third, a healthy child, died of the ſmall pox when two years old. But what is ſtill more uncommon, in the year 1752, Katherine Hunter, the wife of George Sharp a labourer, brought forth FOUR CHILDREN at one birth,—two males and two females. They were all baptized, but being ſmall and weakly, none of them lived above three weeks.

Villages and Houſes.—Tillicoultry contains three villages, *Weſtertown*, *Earlſtown* and *Coalſnaughton*, and all the inhabitants

tants live in thefe except 36 families. Of thefe families on‧ ly three refide in the Ochils. The houfes confift of nothing but the ground floor, except 8, of which, 5 houfes have on‧ ly one ftory raifed above the ground floor, two have 2 ftories, and one has three ftories, and there are only three houfes, the manfe included, which are fubject to the duty on win‧ dow lights.

Manufactures.—Tillicoultry has been long famous for weaving a courfe woolen cloth, called *Tillicoultry Serge.* It is a fpecies of fhaloon, having *worfted* warp and *yarn* waft, and is reported to have been wrought here, as early as the reign of MARY Queen of Scots. The average price is 1s. Sterling per yard. Though the manufacture has now, in a great meafure, left us, and gone to Alva, *(like the arts and fciences, from Eaft to Weft,)* yet all the cloth of this kind is fold in the markets, under the name of *Tillicoutry Serge.* It is much to be regretted, that more attention is not paid to this manufacture in the place where is was invented, or at leaft brought to the greateft perfection. About 50 years a‧ go, a ferge web from Alva would not fell in the market, while one from Tillicoultry remained unfold. But this is by no means the cafe at prefent. The author of this account can give no precife ftatement of the quantity of ferge wrought here, as the ftamp mafter keeps no lift. He fup‧ pofes, however, that he ftamps annually 7000 ells of ferge, and an equal quantity of plaiding. Some of the weavers are now employed in making muflins, but as this branch is ftill in its infancy, it is impoffible to fay with what advantage it may be attended.

Prices of Labour and Provifions.—The prices of labour, and of many of the neceffaries of life, have rifen much, and

are

are still rising. It may be said to be nearly double of what it was 50 years ago. For example, the wages of a taylor per day, besides his diet, was 4d. Sterling, now they are 8d; of a day labourer, 5d. or 6d. now 10d. or 1s; of a mason, 1s. now 1s. 6d. and 1s. 8d. or 2s; of a labouring servant per annum, 3l. now from 6l to 10l. The price of a fowl was 5d. now it is 1s. and sometimes more; of a pound of butter, 5d., now 9d. or 10d. and of a pound of cheese, 2d. now 4d.

Roads.—The roads along the hill foot have a gravel bottom, and are tolerably good, and likewise the road which leads from the hill foot to Coalfnaughton by the bridge. But the south road, which comprehends a space of more than 2 English miles, is in a wretched state, having been much neglected of late years, and the greatest part of it never having been properly made, at least to the eastward Coalfnaughton.

Church.—The patron and superior of Tillicoultry, is JAMES BRUCE, Efq; at present a minor, and an enfign in the army. He is also titular of the teinds, and all the heritors and feuers hold of him. * The present minister † is a bachelor ‡. The manse

---

* His immediate ancestors were the late proprietors of Kinrofs. He is a descendent of the celebrated Architect, Sir WILLIAM BRUCE. It is supposed by PINKERTON, with a great degree of probability, in his collection of ancient Scottish poems, that Sir JOHN BRUCE of Kinrofs was the author of the well-known, and much esteemed poem, HARDYKNUTE, which has been commonly ascribed to Mrs WARDLAW. It is probable, also, that Sir John was the author of the VISION, and some other excellent Scottish poems.

† The names of his predecessors in office, as far as they are known, and the dates of their ordinations, are subjoined.

MINISTERS

‡ It may be accounted a singular fact, that none of the ministers of Tillicoultry have been married, since the Revolution 1688, except Mr Taylor.

manfe was built in 1766, and is the fecond in the fame place, fince the year 1730. The new church is fituated near the manfe, almoft equi-diftant from the 3 villages, and was built in 1773. It is a fmall neat building, well lighted, but not very commodioufly feated. There are two church-yards, one where the old church was fituated, ‖ and the other at the new church. The old manfe has long been converted into

a

MINISTERS *of Tillicoultry for the laſt* 146 *years.*

	Date of admiſſion.		Time of Incumbency.		
	Months.	Years.	Years.	Months.	Days.
Mr Andrew Rhynd, (the precife date of his admiſſion, uncertain), -		1648 about	21	0	0
Mr John Foreſt, ordained -	30 Oct.	1669	6	4	0
Mr Robert Keith, -	27 Feb.	1676	16	1	15
Mr Robert Gourlay, -	13 Apr.	1692	22	2	22
Mr John Taylor, -	7 July	1714	13	6	15
Mr Robert Duncan ¶, -	25 Jan.	1728	2	4	0
Mr Alexander Steedman, -	27 May	1731	34	4	0
Mr James Gourlay, -	25 Sep.	1765	8	5	0
Mr William Ofborn, -	24 Feb.	1774	20	0	8
			145	4	0

¶ *Mr* DUNCAN's *Lectures on the Epiſtle to the Hebrews were publiſhed after his death, and are much eſteemed for their piety, orthodoxy, and learning.*

‖ The old church and manfe were fituated near the houfe of Tillicoultry. The church belonged to the Abbey of Cambufkenneth, having been granted to it by King MALCOLM, together with the tythes and pertinents. But after the Reformation, the family of MARR became heritable proprietors of the church, parfonage, vicarage, and 10 acres of gebe. And as the abbot and convent of Cambufkenneth had fet the teinds in tack to the COLVILLS of Culrofs, the proprietors of Tillicoultry, JOHN Earl of MARR, May 30th 1622, ratified the tacks, and alfo the feu charters, and infeftment of the glebe; and granted procuratory for refigning the fame into the hands of his Majefty, in favour of JAMES Lord COLVIL, and his fon.

a ſtable, and the old glebe is an orchard. The ſtipend conſiſts of 120l. Scotch, including communion-element money,
34 bolls of oats, 24 bolls of barley, and 6 bolls of meal. It
commenced in the year 1648, and ſince that time there has
been no augmentation. The miniſter has the privilege of
getting his coals for paying the collier the price of working,
and he has alſo property in the hills, for maintaining 7 or 8
ſheep. The glebe was exchanged in the year 1730, when
the manſe was removed to its preſent ſituation. It lies in 4
different pieces, and ought to conſiſt of 13 acres.

School.—There is a parochial ſchoolmaſter, whoſe ſalary is
100l. Scotch. He has alſo a dwelling houſe and garden.
His annual income, including ſalary, and all emoluments,
both as ſchool maſter and ſeſſion clerk, is extremely ſmall,
and ſeldom exceeds 20l. Sterling. The ſchool is kept in the
Weſtertown, which is by no means centrical or convenient
for the reſt of the pariſh. The ſchool wages are low, and
Engliſh, writing, and arithmetick are taught for 2s. per
quarter, Engliſh alone being only 1s. 3d.

Poor.—The poor are maintained without any aſſeſſment,
and there are no beggars. The capital of the poor's money
is 212l. Sterling, and the annual average collection at the
church door, has been about 12 guineas, for 18 years paſt.
The intereſt of the capital, together with the collections,
and the profits ariſing from the mortcloths, proclamations of
marriages, and incidental fines, conſtitute the funds by which
the poor are maintained. The number of perſons at preſent
ſtatedly ſupplied from the public charity is 7. But, beſides
theſe, the kirk ſeſſion occaſionally aſſiſts a great many more, ‡
by

‡ It is ſaid that about 40 or 50 years ago, people were very ſhy in receiving money from the poor's funds, but this delicacy ſeems now to have entirely vaniſhed.

by giving them money, buying cloths, paying their houfe rents
and fchool fees for their children. Till within thefe 4 years,
intereft at 5 *per cent.* has been received for the poor's money,
but the rate at prefent is only 4 *per cent.* The annual average of the mortcloth money is 2l. 4 s. Sterling ; of the proclamations, 14s. 10d ; of incidental fines, 13s. 6d ; of perfons
occafionally affifted, 11s ; and of children whofe fchool wages
are paid, 5 s or 6s. The loweft ftated weekly allowance is
6d, and the higheft is from 1 s. to 15d.

Proprietors.—Befides Mr Bruce, there are other 9 heritors,
namely, Lord Cathcart, John Johnfton, Efq; of Alva, John
Tait, Efq; of Harviefton, John Harrower, John Paton, Hugh
Hamilton, Marion Dryfdale, James Ure, and Robert May.
All the heritors have houfes in Tillicoultry, and refide in
them, except Lord Cathcart and Mr Johnfton, who have
fplendid feats in the neighbourhood.

State of Property.—The eftate of Tillicoultry has been in the
poffeffion of 7 different families fince the commencement of
the laft century, and has been 6 times fold §. The advance
of the price, at the two laft fales, deferves to be noticed ; the

price

§ It came into the poffeffion of the anceftors of Lord Colvil of Cul-
ross, in the reign of James III. *anno* 1483, and continued in that family till
the year 1634, when it was fold to William Alexander of Menftry, a
Poet of great genius, and afterwards created Earl of Stirling. Several
of his poems are printed in Drummond of Hawthornden's Collection, and
his *Parænefis*, or exhortation on government, which is dedicated to Prince
Henry, the fon of King James VI. does great honour, both to the prince
and the peer. The eftate was next purchafed by Sir Alexander Rollo of
Duncrub, in the year 1644; by Mr John Nicolson of Carnock in Stirling-fhire, in 1659 ; by Lord Tillicoultry, one of the fenators of the College of Juftice, and a Baronet, in 1701 ; by the Hon. Charles Barclay
Maitland, of the family of Lauderdale, in 1756; and by James Bruce,
Efq; of Kinrofs, in 1780.

price paid by Lord TILLICOULTRY being 3,494 l. Sterling ; by Mr BARCLAY MAITLAND 15,000 l. and by Mr BRUCE 24,000. Before the laſt ſale, a part of the eſtate was ſold to Mr JOHNSTON of Alva ; but the feus, † which Mr Barclay purchaſed at different times, were fully equivalent to this part. This eſtate, which, for a century and a half, has been always floating in the market, and has ſo frequently changed its proprietors, is now ſtrictly entailed, and will remain in Mr Bruce's family, the entail of the eſtate of Kinroſs having been transferred by act of Parliament to Tillicoultry. The number of the old feus, or parts, was 40, but they are now moſtly bought up, and again united with the eſtate, or in the poſſeſſion of Mr TAIT. The lands of Killtown, where Tillicoultry houſe is ſituated, and the lands of *Colerſtown* or *Collintown*, belonging to Mr JOHNSTON, were not fued. It is difficult to afcertain the quantity of land belonging to each of the feus, as more or leſs ſeems to have been given, according to the quality and value of the ſoil. One original 40th part at Drimmy contains at preſent, nearly as much arable land as a 40th part and a half at Ellertown, and near as much as two 40th parts at Cairnſtown. ¶ Tillicoultry pays an annual feu-duty of 7 l. 6s. Sterling, and 166 bolls of ſalt, called *King's malt*. This is a part of the Lordſhip of Stirling, having been originally paid at the caſtle of Stirling, for the uſe of the King's family, but was transferred, at an early period, to the Earl of MARR, as a ſecurity for ſome money lent to the Crown.

Ancient

† Lord COLVIL feued the greateſt part of his eſtate to his tenants, whom he diſtinguiſhes in his charters, as *auld, kindly, native tenants*, and referved to himſelf a certain annual feu-duty, which appears to have been the old rent.

¶ It appears from the meal paid as feu duty by the feuars of Cairnſtown, and the money paid by the other feuars, that a boll of meal, and 3s. 4d. Sterling, were confidered as being of equal value, in the concluſion of the 16th, and beginning of the 17th centuries.

Ancient Charter.—Between 5co and 6oo years ago, Tillicoultry belonged to the family of MARR ; and an original
charter, granted by King ALEXANDER III. of Scotlano, in
the 14th year of his reign, is ftill in the poffeflion of Mr ER-
SKINE of MARR, who has obligingly favoured the author
with a copy. This charter is twice referred to by Bifhop
KIETH, in his hiftory of the Bifhops. It is elegantly written
on parchment, with a very fair hand, and fine ink, and is in
every refpect a remarkable curiofity. The whole parchment
is near a fquare of $9\frac{1}{2}$ inches, and the writing only meafures
6 inches by 8 §.

Eminent

§ As this charter is no lefs a curiofity than many of thofe contained in
ANDERSON's *Diplomata Scotiæ*, the fubjoined copy will be an acceptable prefent to antiquarians : " ALEXANDER, Dei gratia, Rex Scotorum, omnibus
probis hominibus totius terre fue—Salutem. Sciant prefentes et futuri quod
ALEUMUS de MESER, filius et heres quondam ALEUMI de MESER, totam
terram fuam de TULLICOULTRY, cum pertinentiis, in feodo de Clackmanan,
quam de nobis tenuit hereditarie, per defectum feruitii de dicta terra nobis de-
biti, coram pluribus noftri Regni magnatibus, fcilicet, ALEXANDRO CUMYN,
Comite de Bouchan, tunc Jufticiario Scotie, HUGONE de ABYRNITH, Magif-
tio, W. WISCHARD tunc Cancellario, FERGUSIO CUMYN, WALTERO de A-
BERNYTH, WILLIELMO de LYSURSER, et NICHOLAO de RUTYRFORD, ac
multis aliis, die Sancte Trinitatis, anno gratie millefimo ducentefimo fexa-
gefimo primo, apud Cadrum Puellarum, per fuftum et baculum nobis reddi-
diffet, et totum jus fuum quod habuit in dicta terra cum pertinentiis, vel ha-
bere potuit pro fe et heredibus fuis in perpetuum quietum clamaffet, nos totam dictam terram de TULLICOULTRY, cum pertinentibus, WILLIELMO Comiti de MARR, dilecto noftro et fideli pro homagio et feruitio fuo, dedimus
conceflimus, et hac prefenti carta noftra confirmavimus, fine aliquo retinemen-
to, tenendam et habendam eidem WILLIELMO, et heredibus fuis, de nobis
et heredibus noftris in feode et hereditate per eafdem divifas per quas
WALTERUS, filius ALANI Senefcalli, tunc Jufticiarius Scotie, et Ro-
GERUS AUENEL, tunc vicecomes de STRIUELYN, predicto ALEUMO, patri
dicti Aleumi, ex precepto inclito recordationis domini ALEXANDRI Regis,
patris noftri cariffimi, affignauerunt et tradiderunt, cum incremento quod per
eafdem WALTERUM filium ALANI, et ROGERUM AUENEL factum fuit, MA-
THEO

Eminent men.—Lord COLVIL, who was raised to the peer-age by James VI. in 1609, was a man of a military genius, and served with much reputation, in the wars under HENRY the IV. of France. Returning to Scotland, loaded with ho-nours, he resided at Tillicoultry, and in his old age, revisited the French court. As he appeared in the old fashioned mi-litary drefs, which he had formerly worn in the wars, the courtiers were all amazed when he entered the royal prefence. But no fooner did HENRY obferve the old warrior, than he clafped him in his arms, and embraced him with the great-eft affection, to the utter aftonifhment of all prefent. After his return, Lord COLVIL fpent much of his time at Tillicoul-try, and was particularly fond of walking on a beautiful ter-race, at the north end of the Kirk-hill, and of repofing him-felf under a thorn tree, the venerable trunk of which ftill re-mains

THEO CLERICO de Tullicoultry, in nemore, in faltibus, in planis et afperis, in terris, et aquis, in pratis et pafcuis, in moris et marefiis, in ftagnis et malendi-nis, cum focco et facca, cum furca et foffa, cum *Tol et Them et infundethef*, et cum omnibus aliis juftis pertinentiis fuis, et cum omnibus natiuis ejufdem terre, qui die collationis facte predicto Aleumo patri dicti Aleumi, in dicta ter-ra manentes fuerunt, libere, quiete, plenarie et honorifice, per feruitium u-nius militis, faluis noftris eleemofinis. Conceffimus etiam eidem WILLIELMO, ut ipfe et heredes fui, habeant et teneant dictam terram in liberum foreftum. Quare firmiter prohibemus, ne quis fine eorum licentia in predicta terra fe-cet, aut venetur fuper noftram plenariam forisfacturam decem librarum. Teftibus, venerabili patre GAMELINO, epifcopo Sancti Andree, ALEXANDRIO CUMYN, Comite de Bouchan Jufticiario Scotie, WALTERO Comite de MON-TETH, JOHANNE CUMYN, WILLIELMO de BREECHYN, EUSTACHIO de Tur-ribus, REGINALDO LE CHEN, apud Forfar, viceffimo primo die Decembris, anno regni noftri quarto decimo.''

After the granting of this charter, Tillicoultry remained for a confidera-ble period in the poffeffion of the family of MARR ; but on account of a pre-tended fucceffion to Lady ISABELLA DOUGLAS, Countefs of MARR, was feiz-ed by the Crown, notwithftanding an exprefs declaration and promife, by ROBERT III. under the Great Seal, that he would accept of no lands belong-to that lady.

mains. It unfortunately happened, that ſtanding one day on a ſtone, and looking up to the thorn tree, deſcribing his battles, he fell down the ſloping bank of the terrace, and, it is ſaid, was killed on the ſpot, in the year 1620. It may not be improper to add, under this article, that in the popiſh legends, Tillicoultry is mentioned as having been viſited by St. Serf or Servanus, and the ſcene of ſome of his pretended miracles. St. Serf lived in the end of the 6th century, and there is a particular account of him in *Winton's Chronicle* ‖, a manuſcript in the Cottonian library †. Notwithſtanding the very remote antiquity of St Serf, his memory is ſtill, in ſome degree, preſerved, though his name is almoſt entirely forgot; but he is repreſented, by tradition, as a holy man, who travelled about the country, with a *Scape Goat* ‡, which was unfortunately killed. There is a heap of ſtones, called *Cairn Cur* or *Gur*, which ſeems to have been intended to perpetuate the ſtory of the goat. The name has an evident affinity to the Latin word *Caper*, and to the Gaelic, *Gobhur*, which ſignifies a goat.

Antiquities.

‖ Winton, the author of the chronicle, was canon regular of St Andrews, and prior of the monaſtery of Loch Leven, and lived in the end of the 14 century.

† An excerpt from this chronicle was lately publiſhed by Pinkerton, in the Appendix to his collection of Old Scottiſh poems. One of the miracles reported to have been performed by St Serf, was, the raiſing two young men to life, who appear to have been brothers. The account given of this in the chronicle, if not very elegant, has at leaſt the merit of being abundantly brief:

" In Tullycultry, til a wif
" Two ſonys he raiſit frae ded to lyf."

‡ In Winton's chronicle, in place of a ſcape goat, mention is made of a *ram*. The killing of the ram occaſioned another miracle. The ſtory is abundantly ludicrous, and as ludicrouſly related by the poetical biographer:

This

Antiquities.—There are few curiosities, or remains of antiquity*. The rude Druidical circle, on the south end of the Cuninghar, deserves some small notice. It is composed of granites about 5½ feet long, and its diameter is near 60 feet. The spot was covered by the late proprietor, with a circular thicket of Scotch firs, and is marked by Stobie, in his splendid map of Perth and Clackmannan shires. On the castle Craig, the foundations § of a round circular building are still visible.

Character,

This holy man had a ram,
That he had fed up of a lam :
And oysit hym til folow ay,
Quherevir he passit in his way.
A theyf this scheppe in Ackien stal,
And et hym up in pecis smalle.
Quhen Sanct Serf his ram had myst,
Quha that it stal was few that wist :
On presumption nevirthelesi,
He that it stal arestyt was ;
And til Sanct Serf syne was he broucht.
That scheipe he said that he stal noucht ;
And tharfor, for to swer an athe,
He said that he walde nocht be laythe.
But sone he worthit rede for schayme,
The scheype that bletyt in his wayme.
Swa was he taynetyt schamfully ;
And at Sanct Serf askyt mercy.

* It is reported, there was a Roman station on the north end of the Cuninghar. About 50 years ago, the place was dug by order of Sir Robert Stuart, and several urns, containing human bones, were found.

§ Between these and the hills, there has been a ditch by way of defence. The vulgar tradition is, that the *Peychts* had a strong fortification in this place, and that the stones of the edifice were carried away, when the castle of Stirling was built. A large stone coffin, neatly cemented with whitish clay, was discovered about 8 years ago, in the midst of a great cairn or heap of stones in Wertertown, anciently called Cairntown. It was filled with fine earth, and contained two small bones.

Character, &c.—We have our good qualities as well as our bad. Publicly to expofe the one might give offence, and could do no good. To praife the other might appear oftentation and flattery. It is, however, but juftice to mention, that the people are fober and induftrious, and attached to the King and Conftitution, and to the Prefbyterian form of worfhip and Church Government. The men moftly betake themfelves to country work, or to employments connected with hufbandry. Few of them enlift in the army, and not many of them engage in the feafaring line. The women are thrifty and laborious, attentive to their families, and are much employed in fpinning worfted and woolen yarn ; particularly the latter. All ranks drefs better and finer than they formerly did. And as an inftance of refinement in the furniture of the houfes, it may be mentioned, that in the year 1764, there were only 9 or 10 clocks in the parifh, whereas, at prefent, there are above 60.

Difadvantages.—It is apprehended, that Tillicoultry will decreafe in the number of its inhabitants, from the following caufes :—1ft The divifion of the common in the hills.—2d The fale of many of the feus, each of which maintained families ;—3d The neglect of the coal ; and, 4th, The fmall attention and encouragement which is given to the weaving of Tillicoultry ferge. It muft be acknowledged, however, that the eftablifhment of the Devon Company, in the immediate neighbourhood, will, perhaps, overbalance all thefe apparent difadvantages, though the writer of this account is by no means fanguine in his expectation of that effect.

Sources of Melioration.—The following particulars are humbly fubjoined, as probable fources of improvement, and melioration :—1ft, If the public fchool were fituated more in the centre

centre of the parifh, or if a fchool were eftablifhed at Coals-
naughton. 2dly, If a bridge were built over the Dovan, below the Weftertown. 3dly, If the farmers were to fallow
more of their land, and to pay more attention to fowing
wheat. 4thly, If fome encouragement were given to the weaving of Tillicoultry ferge. 5thly, If the coal were to be wrought
as extenfively as formerly, for fupplying the country and the
foreign markets. 6thly, If a waggon-way were made for
carrying the coals to Alloa harbour. 7thly, If a navigable
canal were made by means of the Devon to join the Forth.
8thly, If fome public works, fuch as an woolen manufactory,
or a cotton mill, or a printing field, were erected at the Weftertown, as the fituation is thought highly convenient and
advantageous for fuch ufeful works. But the great fources
of improvement and melioration are, honefty, induftry, fobriety, and a regard to religion, without which, and the bleffing of God, all human fchemes will be nugatory and vain.

INDEX

Index

Index

Index

Index